THE OFFICIAL®
IDENTIFICATION
AND PRICE GUIDE TO

Antiques and Collectibles

THE OFFICIAL®
IDENTIFICATION
AND PRICE GUIDE TO

Antiques and Collectibles

DAVID P. LINDQUIST

Caroline C. Warren
Assistant Editor

TWELFTH EDITION

HOUSE OF COLLECTIBLES • NEW YORK

Important Notice. All of the information, including valuations, in this book has been compiled from the most reliable sources, and every effort has been made to eliminate errors and questionable data. Nevertheless, the possibility of error, in a work of such immense scope, always exists. The publisher will not be held responsible for losses which may occur in the purchase, sale, or other transaction of items because of information contained herein. Readers who feel they have discovered errors are invited to *write* and inform us, so they may be corrected in subsequent editions. Those seeking further information on the topics covered in this book are advised to refer to the complete line of *Official Price Guides* published by the House of Collectibles.

Published by: House of Collectibles
201 East 50th Street
New York, New York 10022

Distributed by Ballantine Books, a division of Random House, Inc., New York, and simultaneously in Canada by Random House of Canada Limited, Toronto.

Cover photo by George Kerrigan

Text design by Holly Johnson

Manufactured in the United States of America

Library of Congress Catalog Card Number: 90-648332

ISBN: 0-876-37845-9

Twelfth Edition: September 1992

10 9 8 7 6 5 4 3 2 1

For Bea,
a loving mother
and grandmother

Contents

Acknowledgments

No book exists without the enormous help of many people. A guide such as this involves more people than I could possibly list and still keep your attention in this section. You will find all of the contributors listed both at the back of the book in a special addendum, and with each section. So let me just say to them, thank you!

Special acknowledgment must go to my business partner, Maggie Lindquist, who has worked to develop the computer format for this book, and whose unflagging efforts made it initially possible. Secondly, I must thank my assistant editor, Caroline Warren, for her incredible efforts that go into each and every volume. She worked on an average of 30 hours a week on this book alone. It is through her efforts of coordination and data gathering that it is possible for me to produce this book. It's not easy to coordinate a stable of contributors and see that each contributor understands the same goals and approaches the problem with the same concept of terminology. Caroline has worked ceaselessly to make this happen. A great measure of assistance with the preparation of this volume was provided by two of my staff at Whitehall at the Villa: John Bloedorn, assisting with data entry, and Keith Wenger, who provided so much of the photographic work. I would also like to thank Alda Leake Horner, who helped get this book going, and continues to support our efforts.

Finally I would like to thank the former editor-in-chief of House of Collectibles, Dorothy Harris, who roped me into this task a few years ago, and who gave me her total and unflagging support in every effort. And I would like to thank the new editor-in-chief, Owen Lock, and his assistant, Stephen Sterns, for their faith and effort in behalf of this new and completely revised edition. I hope you enjoy this book as much as those of us who have worked on it have enjoyed preparing it for you.

REFERENCE KEY

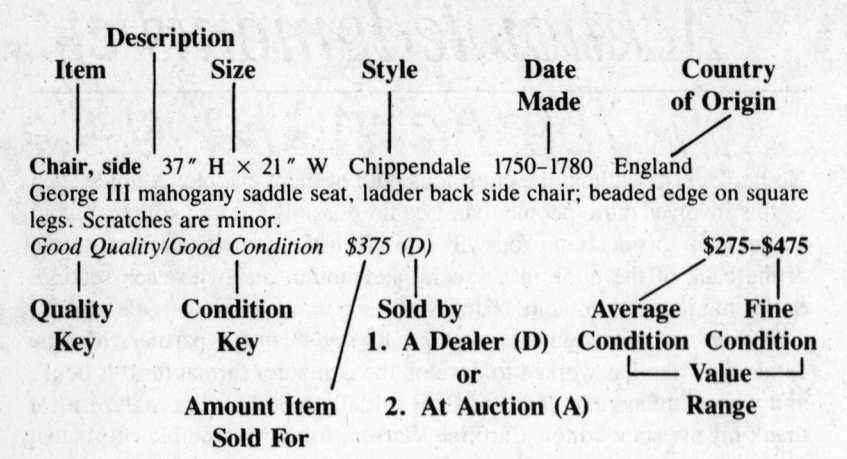

Description

Item | **Size** | **Style** | **Date Made** | **Country of Origin**

Chair, side 37″ H × 21″ W Chippendale 1750–1780 England
George III mahogany saddle seat, ladder back side chair; beaded edge on square legs. Scratches are minor.
Good Quality/Good Condition $375 (D) $275–$475

Quality Key | **Condition Key** | **Sold by** | **Average Condition** | **Fine Condition**

1. A Dealer (D) **Value Range**

or

Amount Item Sold For | **2. At Auction (A)**

The Antiques Market in the Early 1990s

While 1991 proved to be an incredibly tumultuous time for the antiques market, it was also a time that validated many of the long-term fundamentals of this market. For those who know antiques, there were few surprises. Certainly we saw a major decline in activity in the first three to six months of 1991. The antiques auction and show markets were weak, and shop business throughout the country was slack. And yet, through all of that the perennial value of buying antiques remained constant. Fine things continued to sell well, and people who had disposable income continued to invest in their life-style by purchasing art and antiques. People who should not have been investing in antiques did not do so, as expected. Antiques are, after all, not a good investment when one speaks of liquidity. They are a good value in terms of life-style. Antiques are a good investment for the long term, and that is what the first half of 1991 proved, when other investment opportunities seemed less attractive. The second half of 1991 saw even greater strength in the solid middle and upper end of the antiques market, an incredible resurgence at the antiques shows, both in attendence and in sales, and led, I think, quite solidly into 1992.

UNDERSTANDING THE MARKET

The key to understanding the antiques market is really twofold—collecting, and the impact of real estate. It is the collector and his insatiable need to acquire ever-finer objects (and more of them), and his need to learn more about his field, that drives an important, though limited, sector of the antiques market. It is this person, the true collector, who keeps the market alive and well, through thick and thin. The collector will invest every spare nickel in his passion. It is this person who kept the 1991 market afloat. He is not buying to decorate the living room. He is not buying a painting because he needs something with a splash of orange to go with the new sofa, nor is he buying a beautiful piece of Tiffany art glass because he needs purple on the third shelf on the right-hand side of the breakfront. He is simply buying because he has a passion to own those objects. Because of the collector, there is always that part of the market surviving through the worst of all economic conditions. In fact, many of the great collections in this country were built during the Depression. They were built because collectors took advantage of depressed times and plentiful goods to acquire more and finer objects for their personal collections. Collectors have shaped and maintained the market, not only through 1991, but at all times.

What has hurt the antiques market has not been disinterested collectors then, but the decline of the real estate market. I've written time and again that if one wants to understand where the antiques fads of tomorrow are going to appear, the types of antiques that are going to be acquired by the masses—in short, where the antiques market is headed—one needs to look to the real estate market, specifically to what is being restored, and what is being built new. The types of houses being built and sold will determine the kinds of antiques that will sell. For example, the trend in new housing (what little there is at the moment) continues to be large homes in the Tudor, Regency, or modified chateau styles, with large dining rooms and high ceilings, on well-landscaped pieces of property. The kinds of antiques that people have been buying for these houses include large dining room tables, sets of dining chairs, sideboards, breakfronts, and the like. These new houses feature formal living areas needing formal English, French, and American furniture. In the less formal areas of the house, such as the kitchen/great room area, Country American, French, and English furniture works well and has been selling well. One popular style of home that is currently being restored is the 1920s Tudor style. Again, formal furniture is in demand for these homes.

However, new house construction and house restoration has dropped drastically over the last year and a half, and the impact of that has been severe in all sectors of the market in early 1991. So, for the time being, the demand for suitable antiques to furnish fashionable homes has also been greatly curtailed.

WHERE ARE THE DECORATORS?

Slow real estate has had a second related impact on our business that is equally important: the decline of the role of the decorators in the antiques market. I've always found it amusing that antiques dealers love to stand around at an antiques show and complain about the decorators. "Oh," says one, "I just don't understand how a person can possibly come into my booth and need a decorator to assist him in making a decision." Or another says, "I wish those decorators would just go away. They make life so difficult." Now one goes to an antiques show and hears new complaints from the same dealers. This time, it's "I just don't understand where the decorators are. They've always been so important to the business at the show. I just can't understand why that decorator that bought so much for that client's house last year isn't here this year." It's really funny to hear the carryings on over the lack of decorators today. Well, whether you loved them or hated them before, whether you love them or hate them now, the fact is that the decorators are an enormous part of the antiques business, and they don't have work.

Nobody is renovating or building new houses, and that means nobody is decorating houses. Decorators today are lucky if they are helping people put up new wallpaper, new curtains, new draperies, or redoing upholstery—in the old house, in the old room. They are not going out the way they were and doing whole houses, room therapies, and all the things that helped make our market so incredibly strong.

A GLIMMER OF HOPE

Nineteen ninety-two has seen both a major increase in new home starts and a major boom in the sale of older properties. It is fairly easy to extrapolate from this that by late 1992 and early 1993 the decorators should once again be busy and hopefully back in the shops and shows, and back in the auction houses with their clients in tow, buying to decorate homes. This decorator impact is the greatest aspect of the antiques market in America today. Most people are not collectors, and so while the collectors support the bottom line of the market, and they keep us afloat, they alone do not keep us in the good times we were once rolling in as antiques and art dealers. It is people furnishing their homes who provide the real gravy, the real excitement, the real bulk of buying in the antiques business. And that will have to build itself slowly through 1992 and into 1993 as a resurgence in the real estate market takes place.

LOWER INTEREST RATES

Lower interest rates are, of course, the reason for the resurgence in the real estate market. In addition to their impact on real estate, they also have two major impacts on the antiques business. The first is that dealer costs are down—the costs of operating an antiques business has declined with the decline in interest rates. The second is there is little incentive for individuals to keep their money in low-interest–bearing accounts. People who can afford it are deciding that they would rather spend their money on things they want, be that a house, a painting, a secretary, a new chest of drawers, or a fine silver tea service. They are deciding that the value in tangible goods far surpasses the value of money in the bank in today's low-interest economy.

All indications from what one reads, as well as from consulting local and regional financiers, suggest that while there may be some minor fluctuations in interest rates, the general trend will continue in the levels that we are seeing now or even lower through perhaps as late as 1996. These low costs for financing of inventory for dealers, and for financing shops and real estate, will greatly enhance the liquidity of antiques dealers who do not own their entire inventory, but have to borrow to build their stocks. These continued low-interest rates will, I believe, equally stimulate collectors and individuals to put their money into objects rather than into cash.

Assuming that the economy begins the gradual improvement that most prognosticators predict (and by gradual, one certainly means that it will be this year or later before we see a real improvement in the economy), we should be in for a good year in 1992 and perhaps a banner year in 1993. While many dealers are saying we will never return to the boom years of the 1980s, I feel that is very short sighted. The fact is that a vast number of people want antiques, and the availability of goods is limited. With demand exceeding supply, combining with a steadily improving economy, we should be headed back to very good financial times in the antiques business. It may not lead to inflation, but it should lead to steady, good business.

New for the Twelfth Edition

Since the eleventh edition, we have almost completely redone the twelfth edition—90 percent of the entries are completely new! We continue to provide strong coverage in the broad basic categories of antiques, such as silver and furniture (you'll find my latest articles on furniture included). Our chapter on ceramics has been totally reorganized according to early, middle, and late time periods. Within these periods, you will find makers and manufacturers in alphabetical order. The chapter on garden accessories has been greatly expanded, as has the chapter on textiles, reflecting the current interest in those areas.

I am including some exciting new areas of coverage in the twelfth edition. The chapter on metalwares covers copper, iron, tin, pewter, and brass and is full of authoritative information. We also feature excellent new chapters on movie memorabilia, postcards, *Peanuts*® collectibles, American stoneware, antique and modern teddy bears, Wallace Nutting photographs, and candy containers—all by experts in those areas. I hope you will find the new twelfth edition even better than the eleventh!

Using This Guide

This is a price guide to *retail* values of antiques and collectibles commonly found for sale in the United States. Antiques and collectibles may be found in antiques shops or junque emporiums, at fine antiques shows or gargantuan flea markets, at major auction galleries or country estate sales, at well-managed tag sales or family-run garage sales. Whatever the situation, the purpose of *The Official Identification and Price Guide to Antiques and Collectibles* is to acquaint you with what those items typically sell for in retail shop and show situations, thus providing a benchmark against which other values may be assessed.

Several features make this guide completely unique among the plethora of guides now available. All prices are actual sale results—the item was actually sold by a dealer (D) or auctioneer (A) for the listed price. Judgments of both quality and condition are included in the description of each item in the book.

For example:

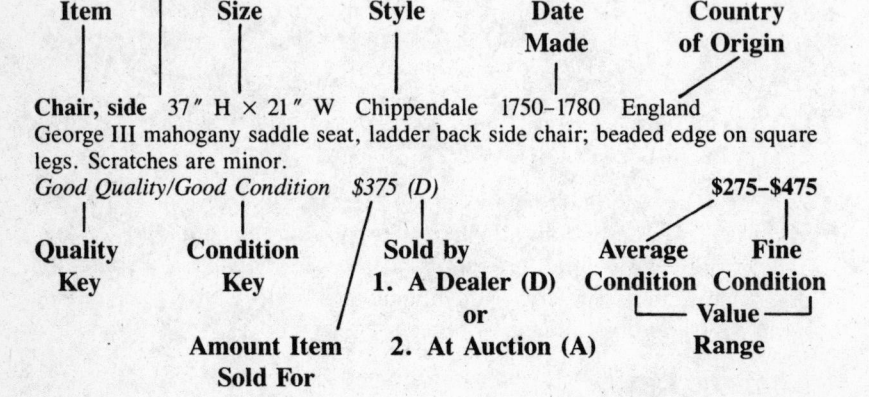

REFERENCE KEY

Descriptions are as complete as possible. However, occasionally some information simply was not available, such as size and actual selling price. The items listed without a selling price are included because of

6

their importance in understanding the category. Most likely, the item is still available and will sell within the given value range.

Additionally, and of enormous value to you, a price range (value range) is given. This range indicates what the same-quality item would sell for in a different condition.

Often a photograph is provided. What is so unique is the attempt to fully portray an item, its condition, and the quality in the written description. A photo may be worth a thousand words, *but* cracks, chips, repairs, new feet, new veneers, reduced sizes, etc., do not show up in a photograph! Without our very careful descriptions, the photos would be meaningless.

Each section is arranged alphabetically by item name, country, date, and style. Changes from this order are noted in the text. At the end of each section there is a listing of resource materials for continued research, fakes alerts as needed, and collector club information when appropriate. If there are subsections within a chapter, you will be notified on the first page of that chapter, with a list of subsections.

Throughout this guide look for my analysis boxes $\boxed{-DL}$ (appearing directly below a description)—short statements giving pertinent information about a particular antique and its value. These bits of information will guide you in understanding why a particular item may have a sale price far different from the price range quotation. Or they may note an aspect of *regionalism* important to the price information given. I will occasionally provide boxed reminders as to the structure of the presentation—just in case you read the data sections *before* you read this section!

In addition to editorial work throughout the book, any section that does not have a contributor or advisor listed was researched and compiled by my staff and me.

QUALITY AND CONDITION KEYS

Quality and condition are the essential elements in determining the collectibility (i.e., desirability) of an object. Whether the item is an Austrian transfer-printed plate or a Newport, RI, secretary, quality and condition determine value. Such terms—quality and condition—have meaning only as they relate within a range of objects.

QUALITY KEY

The Quality Key terms used in the guide are: *good quality*, *very good quality*, and *superior quality*. The use of these terms by each contributor is defined at the start of the major categories. When terms are not defined, the following definitions apply:

Good Quality: a collectible example exhibiting the standard characteristics of the object.

Very Good Quality: a more desirable example because of above-average workmanship and design.

Superior Quality: the object exhibits nearly every known feature found on such items, and the workmanship and design are of the highest quality.

You will find that in some sections quality has nothing to do with condition. In other categories condition will impinge on quality. In general, throughout the guide quality is totally distinct from condition. After all, it is certainly possible to have a magnificent example of a piece yet find it in shabby (and, one hopes, restorable) condition.

CONDITION KEY

Condition also has been ranked for each category by the contributors. In many sections specific definitions with examples are provided. When not specific, the following definitions prevail:

Poor: although salable at some price because of some other merit, the piece is in obviously bad condition—i.e., missing parts, breaks, very bad restoration, etc.

Average: this is the condition, before restoration, in which objects are most frequently found; cleaning may be necessary.

Good: the condition is above average; no parts missing, no major cleaning needed—the price is ready to use or display.

Fine: the piece is in near original condition or has been restored to near original condition. (While excessive restoration would lower value, that would be obvious in the description of the object. All objects are fully described as to condition and originality.)

Each object has been ranked by quality and condition. Furthermore, a price range has been provided that notes what the object might have sold for, in the expert opinion of the data provider, had it been in *average* or *fine* condition. Any item in *poor condition* has, in general, a value of 50 percent (or less) of that of the same item in average condition. Remember that condition is to antique value what location is to real estate value. Check each section for any variation in these rules of thumb.

Antiques and Collectibles

Advertising

*(See also Ephemera, Movie Posters and Lobby
Cards, Postcards)*

Advertising items continue to be purchased for decorative purposes or collected in categories. The two types of acquirers make for some rather wild price fluctuations. The person who can't live without a Busch Brownie tray from around 1915 showing steamboats at the St. Louis levee will pay far more for it than a collector of advertising trays. Thus, the collector might say: "I wouldn't pay a penny over $100 for it. The steamboat nut might pay $450! After all, that's cheap compared to a Currier & Ives print at $4,000 to $6,000."

The prices listed in this section are collector purchases, *not* decorator purchases or whim purchases. You may indeed see similar items for far more. If so, wait, unless you can't live without it. You will find the items within the listed ranges!

Although advertising dates from the 18th century, the preponderance of collected items are from 1880 to 1940, with more modern things coming on strong at flea markets and similar "low end" markets.

Fakes are quite common in the advertising field, especially Coca-Cola trays. In fact, the Coca-Cola area is rife with fakes and reproductions. And of course, it's important to remember that advertising toys, such as tractors, have been made continuously. Look for natural wear. Be aware of the antiques field so that an unknown item will yell "fake" when you run across it. When buying at a large flea market, look at a lot of booths before buying. If a fake is on the loose, it will probably be in several dealers' booths!

CURRENT TRENDS

The market trend for advertising memorabilia is straight up. Several world auction records were set this year at Oliver's Auction Gallery in Maine. Part of the fabulous pioneering collection of Harry Burstein sold at auction during the summer of 1991. A Campbell's Soup sign from Burstein's collection brought $93,500, a world record for a tin sign. The same sign not in the same condition sold for $44,000 in April 1989. The world-record price for a paper sign was also set this year at Oliver's: a Kickapoo Indian patent medicine paper sign from 1892 brought $55,000.

For the world-record setter and the average collector alike, here are some areas to watch. Coca-Cola memorabilia is the hottest area of advertising. It is collected at all levels in all categories. Tobacco, beer, and whiskey signs are popular, as are food signs—especially Grape-Nuts—for the kitchen. Early advertising featuring women is very collectible. Sporting advertisements, especially baseball, are strong. Tin containers are also good sellers, with tobacco, gun powder, and coffee containers being especially popular.

CONDITION KEY

Fine: no damage; possibly in original container or other protective device.

Good: all original aspects are clear; no damage.

Average: minor wear, minor surface abrasions, nothing disfiguring.

Poor: disfigured by fading, cracking, folding, marring, etc.

QUALITY KEY

Good Quality: worth collecting but quite common.

Very Good Quality: a less common item with good color (when appropriate), interesting content (i.e., features a special person, an unusual event, etc.).

Superior Quality: a rare item of fine color (when appropriate) and incorporating many special features.

Calendar　23″ H × 2″ W　1914　United States
One of the rarest known ammunition calendars; Selby Loads; pristine; framed.
Superior Quality/Fine Condition　$1165 (A)　　　　　　　**$800–$1200**

Calendar　1927　United States
U.S. Cartridge calendar; full pad; mallards flying toward viewer.
Very Good Quality/Fine Condition　$900 (A)　　　　　　　**$600–$900**

Calendar　1930　United States
Winchester calendar; hole at top; minor edge damage; band at top.
Good Quality/Average Condition　$445 (A)　　　　　　　**$400–$600**

Clock　1951　United States
Painted face; wooden frame with Coca-Cola logo in smaller concentric inner circle.
Good Quality/Good Condition　$85 (A)　　　　　　　**$60–$90**

Coffee bin　c. 1900　United States
Pittsburgh Wholesale Grocery, Pittsburgh, KS, coffee bin; good stenciling.
Good Quality/Good Condition　$400 (A)　　　　　　　**$300–$500**

Coffee bin   c. 1900   United States
Old Glory Mocha and Java Flavored coffee bin; outstanding graphics.
Superior Quality/Fine Condition $4500 (A)   **$2400–$4500**

Coffee bin   c. 1910   United States
Blanke's coffee bin; lady on horse; great graphics; some dents and minor paint chips.
Superior Quality/Good Condition $2100 (A)   **$1200–$2400**

Poster   27.5″ H × 21.5″ W   1883   United States
Thoroughmade Plug poster; Mensing & Steecher Litho., Rochester, NY; "Save the Tags" written on all sides.
Superior Quality/Good Condition $1880 (A)   **$1500–$2000**

Poster   15″ H × 2″ W   1885–1900   United States
California breakfast food poster; Hopcraft & Co., NY, lithographer; colors are dark blue, light blue, and white; minor foxing along edges.
Good Quality/Good Condition $100 (A)   **$75–$150**

Poster   14.5″ H × 11.25″ W   1885–1900   United States
Poster for Austen's Forest Flower Cologne, W. J. Austen & Co., Oswego, NY, copyright 1888; bands have rusted; some tearing where bands are attached.
Good Quality/Average Condition $55 (A)   **$45–$90**

Poster   31.5″ H × 45″ W   c. 1898–1900   United States
Great Pabst Brewing Company factory scene; backed with Japanese mulberry paper; graphics are superb; great color; Wilman Bros. Litho.
Superior Quality/Fine Condition $2300 (A)   **$1500–$2500**

Poster   26″ H × 20″ W   c. 1910   United States
Prince Albert poster; wonderful design, bold color; super frame with arrows inlaid in border.
Superior Quality/Fine Condition $1800 (A)   **$1200–$1800**

> Allow $400 on framing this one!—*DL*

Poster   30″ H × 21″ W   c. 1915   United States
Worcester Salt poster; factory in background; train zigzags into foreground; good detail; beautiful frame.
Very Good Quality/Fine Condition $500 (A)   **$300–$500**

> Note that framing has impacted value. Often prints and posters are worth far less unframed than well-presented and ready to display.—*DL*

Poster   25″ H × 17″ W   c. 1925   United States
Wells Richardson & Co.; Butter color poster; overall staining; matted and framed.
Very Good Quality/Average Condition $280 (A)   **$150–$325**

> Value was increased by framing.—*DL*

Sign   28″ H × 12″ W   c. 1895   United States
Scotts Emulsion of Pure Cod Liver Oil; linen poster; metal bands; Donaldson Bros. Litho; fine color. *(See photo 1, center)*
Superior Quality/Fine Condition $3200 (A)   **$2000–$3500**

Sign   28″ H × 12″ W   c. 1895   United States
Tarrants Selzer Aperient; little girl on swing; linen with metal bands; outstanding lithography; good condition and color. *(See photo 1, right)*
Superior Quality/Fine Condition $2525 (A)   **$2000–$3500**

Photo 1. Signs. CREDIT: OLIVER
AUCTION GALLERY, KENNEBUNK, ME
(See pp. 13, 15)

Photo 2. Sign. CREDIT: OLIVER
AUCTION GALLERY, KENNEBUNK, ME
(See p. 15)

Sign 19.5″ H × 13.5″ W c. 1899 United States
Lipton's cardboard; great color; framed.
Superior Quality/Fine Condition $2000 (A) **$1200–$1800**

Sign 25″ H × 14″ W c. 1905 United States
Grape-Nuts tin sign showing girl and St. Bernard walking to school; "To school well fed on Grape-Nuts. 'There's a Reason.' ''; outstanding condition; very bright; self-framed.
Superior Quality/Fine Condition $1900 (A) **$1200–$2000**

Sign 39″ H × 27″ W c. 1908 United States
Diplomat Whiskey tin sign; great gold frame; group of wonderful gentlemen sitting around large table; Charles Litho, Chicago; large and dramatic.
Superior Quality/Fine Condition $3900 (A) **$2500–$4000**

Sign 16.5″ H × 2″ W 1910 United States
Tin self-framed sign; Springfield Brewer; American Art Works, Coshocton, OH; minor touch up.
Very Good Quality/Good Condition $500 (A) **$400–$600**

Sign c. 1915 United States
Reverse glass eglomisé sign; original frame; G. W. Schmidt Whiskey; inset with picture of lovely lady sipping whiskey; scattered flakes in glass; small piece missing on left side; very rare.
Superior Quality/Average Condition $1650 (A) **$1500–$2500**

Sign 28″ H × 12″ W c. 1920 United States
Quaker Bitters, Donaldson Bros., Five Points, NY; great graphics. *(See photo 1, left)*
Superior Quality/Fine Condition $3300 (A) **$2000–$3500**

Sign c. 1920 United States
F. W. Woolworth reverse-glass sign; some damage in upper left-hand corner.
Very Good Quality/Average Condition $475 (A) **$400–$600**

Sign c. 1925 United States
Hy-Quality Coffee lady in a swing; very nice condition. *(See photo 2)*
Very Good Quality/Fine Condition $1875 (A) **$1500–$2000**

Sign 1935–1940 United States
Coca-Cola sign; 1 dent on "C" in "Cola"; good color.
Good Quality/Average Condition $55 (A) **$50–$90**

Thermometer c. 1923 United States
Coca-Cola themometer in shape of bottle; some dirt and minor rust.
Good Quality/Good Condition $50 (A) **$50–$75**

Thermometer 1939 United States
Coca-Cola thermometer; lady drinking from a bottle.
Good Quality/Good Condition $70 (A) **$50–$75**

Thermometer 1941 United States
Double Coke bottle thermometer; couple of rust spots on area near thermometer numbers; unusual.
Very Good Quality/Good Condition $175 (A) **$150–$225**

Thermometers 17″ H, 30″ H c. 1920 United States
Two tin Coke thermometers; smaller one has broken glass.
Good Quality/Average Condition $65 (A) **$75–$125**

Tin c. 1920   United States
Buster Brown allspice tin; some flaking to paper on one side but not on either image of Buster Brown; rare.
Very Good Quality/Good Condition $135 (A)   **$125–$225**

Tray 13″ L × 10.5″ W   1905   United States
Coca-Cola serving tray; woman with bottle; some fading, edge damage.
Superior Quality/Good Condition $2500 (A)   **$2500–$2750**

Tray 16.5″ Dia.   1909   United States
Coca-Cola serving tray; very nice condition; minor paint loss.
Superior Quality/Fine Condition $1550 (A)   **$1200–$1800**

Tray c. 1930   United States
Miller High Life beer tray with lovely lady sitting on moon holding a glass of beer; common but charming.
Good Quality/Good Condition $100 (A)   **$75–$125**

Tray 1932   United States
Coca-Cola serving tray; some scratches and edge damage.
Good Quality/Average Condition $275 (A)   **$250–$400**

BIBLIOGRAPHY

Klug, Ray. *Antique Advertising Encyclopedia*. Exton, PA: Schiffer Publishing Ltd, Vol. 1, 1978 (price guide updated in 1988 and 1989); Vol. 2, 1985.

Kovel, Ralph and Terry. *Kovel's Advertising Collectibles Price List*. New York: Crown Publishers, 1986.

COLLECTORS' CLUBS

The Ephemera Society of America, 124 Elm St., Bennington, VT 05021.

National Association of Paper and Advertising Collectibles, PO Box 471, Columbia, PA 17512.

Tin Container Collectors Association, 11650 Riverside Drive, North Hollywood, CA 91620.

American Indian Art

This chapter is arranged by the following subcategories:
ART, BASKETS, CLOTHING, DOLLS, POTTERY, RUGS.

Advisor: **DAWN E. RENO**

Dawn E. Reno, an antiques dealer and collector for over a decade, is considered a national expert on antiques and has written such books on the subject as The Official Identification and Price Guide to American Indian Collectibles, The Official Identification and Price Guide to American Country Collectibles, *and* Collecting Black Americana, *as well as hundreds of articles for such periodicals as* The Antique Trader, Antiques and Collectibles, Hobbies, MassBay Antiques, *and many others. She is currently working on a book about advertising collectibles, as well as completing a novel.*

INTRODUCTION

The American public has had a wavelike love affair with items made by native Americans, with interest in collecting Indian pieces coming in rolling tides. It began when Columbus first came to our shores, rose again when easterners first started exploring the "Wild West," and gained momentum once again during the Roaring Twenties and again during the 1950s, when Roy Rogers and the Lone Ranger filled the television screen. Now, interest appears to be stemming from the American public's need to keep our land healthy, as well as the current decorating trends associated with the "country" look.

Collectors realize that the value of historical items native to the United States is also rising with the passing of the years. Buyers are taking advantage of the current upswing to purchase baskets, totems, clothing, pottery, jewelry, and art created by native Americans. Because of the influx of new collectors in an already tight market, prices keep rising, and the veteran collector is finding it more and more difficult to add new pieces to his or her collection. In late 1989, Sotheby's November 28 auction set a record for pottery prices with the sale of a Mimbres black-on-white picture bowl for $82,500, as well as a record for an American

Indian item—a magnificent First Phase Navajo blanket—which was purchased by a New York collector for $522,500. There have been few sales
since that time that have reached such high prices, but several have come
close. In addition, other records have been set and will continue to be
set. In fact, the summer issue of *American Indian Art* magazine reported
in their "Auction Block" column that "the market is still alive and
well," with sales in that column totaling $5 million, "certainly the high-
est aggregate ever."

OVERVIEW OF THE FIELD

When the United States was still forming its borders, well over one
hundred American Indian tribes inhabited the lakes, mountains, plains,
and deserts of this country. They left behind a heritage far richer than
what the white man brought with him from distant shores. Much of that
history, those cultures, were destroyed in the first century of our nation's
existence. Whole tribes died of flu or other viruses brought to them by
fair-haired strangers. Some moved to other parts of the continent, pushed
from their homes, their hunting grounds, their sacred burial grounds, by
easterners moving west. The balance of those original tribes, forced to
live on reservations, struggle to keep their society alive and, to this day,
battle for the rights that were theirs.

Even during their struggles, these native peoples created some of the
most artistic, yet useful, objects this world has known. The tribes of the
Southwest use the local clay out of which they construct magnificent
pottery urns, bowls, and jars. Northwest Coast groups use grasses and
hemps found in their region to weave baskets strong enough to hold
water. The northernmost tribes carve giant trees into totems that tell of
their origin, their family history, and their reverence for nature.

Each item that native Americans made for their own use, whether as
simple as a spoon or as elaborate as a piece of clothing, was lovingly
decorated and made with pride and with true artistic license. Such work
should not only be appreciated and highly valued but also should be
protected for future generations.

REPRODUCTIONS AND FAKES

Both old and modern items are avidly collected. Modern items are often
bought by collectors directly from the responsible artisans. If one buys
only from trusted dealers or from auctioneers willing to back up their
statements with a provenance, one will have few worries about fakes.
However, it never hurts to educate yourself because no one is infallible,
and dealers make mistakes as easily as do the rest of the population.

Reproductions are usually fairly easy to spot. First of all, they are usually factory-made. Once you are able to pick up a piece of pottery or a Kachina doll and see the marks in the piece that tell you human hands have touched it, it will not be difficult for you to spot a machine-made piece. Be aware of the styles followed by certain tribal members, as well as what the new pieces look like versus the old ones (i.e., new Kachinas are far more detailed and highly carved than the older ones).

Factories, like those in Hong Kong or Taiwan, are required to mark their pieces. Artists and artisans do not usually use a stamp but rather will sign their pieces or weave in some indication of their signature. Thus, be wary of pieces that are stamped with someone's name; incised signatures, on the other hand, are usually made by the artist.

The easiest way to avoid repros/fakes is to buy directly from the artist/ artisan. In this manner, you may build a relationship with that person and find out a little of his/her background and family history (important to those collecting pottery or jewelry because the art is passed down within the family), and you can get the artist/artisan to sign and date the pieces for you. If you believe you may want to sell your collection one day or are thinking of leaving it to your own family members, it will ultimately be worth more if the artist has indicated his/her name and a date on his/her work.

CONDITION KEY

Fine Condition: the piece may look as though it was never used; there will be no cracks, lines, or missing pieces; leather will still be stiff, all beadwork will be intact, and there will be no rips or tears in blankets/ rugs or clothing.

Good Condition: slight wear marks may be visible; on extremely old pottery, age lines may be seen; some small beads may be missing on moccasins or other pieces decorated with beadwork; rugs/blankets will be slightly faded, and some fringe may be worn.

Average Condition: the age and wear will be apparent; fading rugs/blankets will be included in this category, as well as pottery that has wear chips around its rim, baskets with slight imperfections, and clothing with worn spots.

Poor Condition: pottery that has large cracks or chunks missing, blankets/rugs that are ripped and need repair, and jewelry with stones missing will be in this category; it is not suggested that you buy an object in poor condition unless you are sure you will not find another like it at any price.

For Quality Key, use the key shown in the "Using This Guide" section at the front of the book.

> Price ranges in this section are taken from auctions, sales, and dealers. It is important to remember that prices realized will vary, depending on whether the sale was in a high-demand area of the country or in a generalist shop, where the price will be lower.—*DL*

ART

Acrylic Navajo 1983
"Gathering of the Medicine Men," by Jackie Tobaahe Gene (Navajo); framed, dated 1983, and signed.
Good Quality/Fine Condition   **$130–$190**

Bronze 11″ × 11″ Contemporary
"Piegan Brave," #34/35, by Bob Scriver, CAA (1914–); mounted on a walnut base; depicts an Indian warrior from the "Horn Society" mounted on a war pony; sculpture is titled, dated, numbered, and signed.
Very Good Quality/Fine Condition   **$1500–$2100**

Bronze 32″ × 18″ Contemporary
Bronze shield with turquoise bear paw, by Charles Pratt, who was born on an Indian reservation in Concho, OK, and began his career in art when his grandfather taught him how to make figures out of clay. He creates large-scale and miniature works in cast bronze, metal sculpture, and stone carvings. Talents also include being an accomplished silversmith. He is listed in the 14th edition of *Who's Who in American Art* and has won more than 250 awards. His works are held in the Heard Museum, the Philbrook Art Center, and many others.
Superior Quality/Fine Condition   **$2600–$3000**

Drawing 15″ × 10″ c. 1880–1920
"Warrior"; colored "warrior" drawing showing several Indians on horses.
Good Quality/Good Condition   **$45–$75**

Drawing c. 1880
Kiowa ledger drawing.
Superior Quality/Good Condition   **$5000–$6000**

Drawings c. 1885
Two colored ledger drawings showing Indians riding horseback.
Good Quality/Average Condition   **$100–$200**

Etching c. 1910
Matted and framed etching by Edward Borien depicting 2 mounted riders; from Borien estate.
Good Quality/Good Condition   **$75–$100**

Oil and watercolor 18″ × 13″ Mid-20th century
"Chief," by Carl Sweezy (1879–1953), Arapaho; depicts chief in a ¾ left head and torso view; matted, titled, and signed.
Good Quality/Good Condition   **$500–$675**

Painted boxes Contemporary
Group of 3 award-winning carved cedar boxes, by Jamie Tawodi Reason (1847–). Reason is a self-taught artist who began carving in 1976. He is keeping alive

the Cherokee art of carving cedar boxes, which were used to hold sacred items such as gourd rattles and fans. He focuses on nature, using the eagle feather as a recurring theme in his work. Reason's work can be found in galleries throughout the United States and Great Britain. He has won many awards for his work.

Superior Quality/Fine Condition **$200–$2000 each**

Painting 14″ × 20″ Early–mid-20th century
"Deer Dancers," by Tonita Pena.
Very Good Quality/Fine Condition **$2000–$2300**

Painting 5.5″ × 7″ Contemporary
"Turtle," by Tony Da.
Very Good Quality/Fine Condition **$1000–$1500**

Painting 7″ × 16″ Contemporary
"Yeibechai Dance," by Harrison Begay (1917–).
Very Good Quality/Fine Condition **$1100–$1600**

Paintings 8″ × 13″ 1880s–1920
Kiowa sketchbook of 53 paintings, Haungooah (Silverhorn).
Superior Quality/Good Condition **$110,000–$115,000**

Painting 9″ × 7″ c. 1940
Signed, matted, and framed watercolor of an Indian on a horse, by Ralph Tillman.
Good Quality/Good Condition **$50–$70**

Painting c. 1975
Subject is an Indian man, by Robert Redbird.
Good Quality/Good Condition **$120–$195**

Painting c. 1975
Winter tepee scene in oak frame, by Robert Redbird.
Good Quality/Good Condition **$250–$300**

Sand painting 12″ × 16″ Navajo c. 1950–1980s
"Lonewolf Pottery," framed; signed by Redgoat (Chenya Redgoat).
Good Quality/Good Condition **$95–$125**

Sand painting Navajo Contemporary
"House of Many Paints," by Francis Miller.
Good Quality/Good Condition **$50–$100**

Sand painting Navajo Contemporary
Original sand painting done by Judy Lewis from Window Rock, AZ; means "good luck."
Good Quality/Good Condition **$100–$150**

Tempera painting Mid-20th century
Depicting 5 male dancers and 2 female drummers under a stylized sky, by Justino Herrera (1920–?); Southwestern; Cochiti Pueblo.
Good Quality/Good Condition **$300–$500**

Tempera painting 1975
Depicts a single Kachina dancer; by Robert Montoya (San Juan Pueblo), signed "Soe-Kuwa-Pin '75."
Good Quality/Good Condition **$100–$200**

Watercolor Mid-20th century
Beatien Yazz–Jimmy Toddy (1928–); Navajo; entitled "Yeibichai Dancers."
Good Quality/Good Condition **$195–$265**

Watercolor 4″ × 3″ 1973
"Cheyenne Girl," by Bert D. Seabourn (1931–); left profile of subject, matted and framed on reverse, signed LC and dated '73.
Good Quality/Good Condition   **$50–$75**

Watercolor 19″ × 14″ Contemporary
"Yesterday," by Mirac Creepingbear (1947–) (Kiowa-Pawnee-Arapaho); depicts face of male Indian with eyes closed superimposed over another of the same, only a left profile view with 2 riderless horses above; matted, framed, and signed.
Good Quality/Good Condition   **$75–$125**

> Examples in the following categories are presented in chronological order by tribe: unknown date, late 19th century, early 20th century.—*DL*

BASKETS

Aleut 10″ × 25″ c. 1880
Carrying basket; large, finely twined with native cord and with rim loops; red and blue geometric designs.
Good Quality/Good Condition   **$175–$200**

Aleut c. 1890
Classic fine twined basket with lid and with red wool floral designs.
Good Quality/Good Condition   **$300–$375**

Apache 9″ Dia. Early 20th century
Dark arrowpoint designs woven into sides.
Good Quality/Good Condition   **$350–$400**

Apache 14″ H c. 1900
Burden; woven with the "Ti" band; upright warps with 3 bands of dark brown designs, the bottom with rawhide support skin and hide bands stretched at the top rim, with rawhide fringe at sides, the top with rawhide binding rubbed with "sacred" yellow pigment. Originally purchased at San Carlos Reservation.
Very Good Quality/Good Condition   **$900–$1100**

Photo 3. Creek work baskets. CREDIT: DONALD VOGT *(See p. 23)*

Apache 19″ Dia. Late 19th century
Coiled basketry tray, woven in willow and devil's claw with concentric geometric bands.
Very Good Quality/Good Condition **$800–$1000**

Apache 10″ × 7″ c. 1935
Tall coiled basket with striking dogs, birds, swastikas, and arrowheads.
Very Good Quality/Good Condition **$800–$1000**

Cherokee 16″ H × 12.5″ Dia. Late 19th century
Storage; North Carolina Cherokee museum-quality splint basket.
Superior Quality/Good Condition **$400–$600**

Chippewa 3.5″ × 6″ Early 20th century
Coiled grass and birch bark, green and white porcupine-quill-decorated lid in a leaf design.
Good Quality/Good Condition **$75–$175**

Creek c. 1920
Work baskets, used for chafing and winnowing. *(See photo 3)*
Good Quality/Good Condition **$100–$200**

Haida 8″ × 3″ c. 1920
Oval plaited basket with 2 bands of line designs.
Good Quality/Good Condition **$75–$100**

Haida 6″ × 4″ c. 1920
Rare round, twined bowl with openwork and with a shoulder.
Good Quality/Good Condition **$125–$250**

Hopi 16″ Dia. Mid-20th century
Coiled basketry storage bowl, decorated overall with "smiling" dark red and brown deer on a natural ground, coiled loop handles; minor stitch damage.
Good Quality/Good Condition **$250–$350**

Klamath 5″ × 8.5″ 1900–1930
Twined, polychrome with red, yellow, and natural colors in banded designs.
Good Quality/Good Condition **$110–$160**

Klamath 11″ × 7.5″ c. 1910
Twined; unusual large, round twined basket with lid and carrying handle.
Good Quality/Good Condition **$175–$225**

Klickitat 16″ × 10″ c. 1890
Large rectangular embricated storage basket with rim loops (some damage) and with geometric designs.
Good Quality/Average Condition **$300–$400**

Klickitat 6″ × 5.5″ c. 1890
Rare, small embricated Klickitat basket with rim loops.
Good Quality/Good Condition **$150–$200**

Maidu 16″ Dia. Late 19th century
Coiled basketry tray, decorated with plumed triangular motifs in reddish brown on a golden ground; rim damage. Provenance: collected by a teacher in the service of the Department of the Interior, Office of Indian Affairs, stationed at Carson, NV, Indian School, 1895–1910.
Good Quality/Average Condition **$375–$450**

Maidu 24″ × 18″ Late 19th century
Basket; a superior-quality basket by fine basket makers.
Superior Quality/Fine Condition **$8500–$9000**

Mission 6.5″ H × 15″ D Probably late 19th century
Coiled storage basket, the banded flaring body woven in dark brown triangular motif, with faded yellowish-brown designs near rim.
Good Quality/Good Condition   **$375–$435**

Navajo 11″ × 3″ c. 1935
Classic coiled Navajo wedding basket with spirit-release line.
Good Quality/Good Condition   **$200–$275**

Navajo-Ute 3.25″ × 17″ Dia. Early 20th century
Coiled basketry tray; polychrome ''wedding'' style; excellent condition.
Good Quality/Fine Condition   **$250–$300**

Paiute 12″ × 10″ c. 1900
Rare, openwork, twined, conical burden basket with red line design.
Very Good Quality/Good Condition   **$200–$300**

Panamint 6.25″ Dia. Early 20th century
Figurative basket.
Very Good Quality/Fine Condition   **$1760–$2000**

Papago 2.5″ × 11.5″ Early 20th century
Coiled, polychrome with black, green, and natural colors in a 5-pointed star/flower design.
Good Quality/Good Condition   **$65–$105**

Papago 5″ × 6″ × 8″ Early 20th century
Coiled oval with black terraced designs; handle.
Good Quality/Good Condition   **$30–$60**

Salish c. 1890
Rectangular embricated basket with geometric designs.
Good Quality/Good Condition   **$110–$175**

Salish 21″ × 2″ c. 1910
Rectangular embricated tray with handles and geometric designs.
Good Quality/Good Condition   **$160–$225**

Tlingit 5.5″ Dia. Early 20th century
Rattle-top.
Superior Quality/Good Condition   **$1100–$1500**

CLOTHING

Apache Late 19th century
Woman's hide cape, fringed and scalloped around the bottom with a row of coiled red, white, and blue beads around the edges. The neck opening is surrounded by a large circle of tin cones in a double row; also, a smaller circle of brass medallions and blue and white seed beads in rope pattern; across the bottom is a row of tin cones and a row of large metal medallions.
Good Quality/Good Condition   **$950–$1100**

Apache 32″ × 6.5″ c. 1890
Moccasins with hide soles and toe guard, tall yellow muslin tops.
Good Quality/Good Condition   **$60–$100**

Arapaho 11″ × 4″ c. 1880
Classic full-beaded moccasins with buffalo hide soles and sinew sewn.
Good Quality/Good Condition   **$600–$800**

Blackfoot Mid-19th century
Beaded hide shirt.
Very Good Quality/Good Condition — $4125–$4400

Comanche 10″ L Mid-19th century
Beaded hide moccasins.
Good Quality/Good Condition — $1540–$1750

Hopi Late 19th century
Costume for Snake Dance.
Very Good Quality/Good Condition — $2200–$2600

Kiowa 51.75″ L Mid-19th century
Dress of beaded hide.
Superior Quality/Fine Condition — $18,700–$19,400

Navajo 43″ × 26.5″ Mid-19th century
Classic dress half.
Very Good Quality/Good Condition — $2475–$2600

Navajo 41″ × 31″ Mid-19th century
Dress panel.
Very Good Quality/Good Condition — $3080–$3500

Northern Plains 36″ L Mid-19th century
Man's shirt; quilled hide.
Superior Quality/Fine Condition — $12,100–$12,500

Santee Sioux 9″ L Early 20th century
Moccasins; quilled and beaded hide.
Very Good Quality/Good Condition — $3300–$3600

Sioux 1860s–1970s
Beaded shirt; from the Ghost Dance period.
Good Quality/Good Condition — $2200–$2500

Sioux Early 20th century
Beaded vest.
Good Quality/Good Condition — $1760–$2000

Southern Plains 10″ Mid-19th century
Beaded hide moccasins; sinew-sewn, decorated with cobalt blue, lavender, waxy yellow, pony trader blue, green, black, white, and clear red beads; excellent to near mint condition.
Very Good Quality/Fine Condition — $400–$600

Zuni Probably 20th century
Belt with concha inlay.
Good Quality/Good Condition — $2585–$3000

DOLLS

Acoma 11.75″ H and 13.5″ H Early 20th century
Kachina, 2 wooden dolls; exceptionally fine condition.
Superior Quality/Fine Condition — $18,700–$19,500

Cheyenne 2″ × 1″ c. 1920
Tiny, full-beaded, hide toy moccasins.
Good Quality/Good Condition — $65–$85

Cree 11.5″ H Early 20th century
Fine buckskin costume with beading around yoke and fur trim; felt face; papoose on back.
Good Quality/Good Condition **$155–$175**

Hopi 7.5″ H c. 1930s–1940s
Kachina, older Sipikne (Zuni Warrior God).
Good Quality/Good Condition **$90–$150**

Hopi 8″ H Mid-20th century
Kachina, wood. Kachinas made from around the 1940s to the present are more artistically rendered and more detailed than earlier Kachinas from the 19th century. Older dolls were basic block figures made with trade cloth clothes. New dolls use good cotton for the clothes, beautiful colors—some even have muscles!
Superior Quality/Fine Condition **$10,450–$11,500**

Hopi Contemporary
Two Kachinas done by Henry and Mary Sheldon (husband and wife carvers); Mary does miniatures and Henry does large Kachinas; Mary's work averages $400–$600. The Cumulus Cloud Kachina by Henry goes for $2000–$2500.
Superior Quality/Fine Condition **$2000–$2500**

Navajo 12.5″ H Contemporary
Carved and painted Yeibichai (Navajo deity); signed Tom W. Yazzie. His dolls usually fetch higher prices.
Good Quality/Good Condition **$150–$200**

Navajo 17″ × 15″ Contemporary
Figure of a woman working at a loom.
Good Quality/Good Condition **$30–$50**

> Cheapo tourist item!—*DL*

Osage 2.5″ H to 6″ H Mid-19th century
Three cloth dolls. These are no longer being made, so a collector is lucky to find one of these.
Very Good Quality/Good Condition **$2970–$3000**

Zuni 16″ H Early part 20th century
Kachina; wood.
Superior Quality/Fine Condition **$7150–$7775**

POTTERY

Acoma Contemporary
Animal; black-on-white turtle, signed Hailstorm.
Good Quality/Good Condition **$95–$125**

Acoma 3.25″ × 4″ Contemporary
Bowl; black on white with serrated and fineline designs; signed Lucy M. Lewis, Acoma, NM.
Good Quality/Good Condition **$95–$125**

Acoma 6″ Dia. c.1930s
Canteen. *(See photo 4, left rear)*
Good Quality/Good Condition **$195–$250**

Acoma 4.25″ Dia. c. 1930s
Canteen. *(See photo 4, left front)*.
Good Quality/Good Condition **$150–$200**

Photo 4. Acoma, Hopi, and Navajo canteens. CREDIT: DONALD VOGT
(See pp. 26, 28)

Anasazi 9″ × 5″ Prehistoric
Rare Rugas-area pottery bowl in excellent condition.
Superior Quality/Fine Condition   **$200–$300**

Apache 1″ × 1.5″ 1986
Very small painted bowl, signed C. Bogulas.
Good Quality/Good Condition   **$30–$50**

Casas Grande 7″ × 7″ 1200–1300 AD
Prehistoric pottery jar; Ramos polychrome with black and dark red on buff colors; repaired, with minor restoration.
Good Quality/Good Condition   **$65–$110**

> Prehistoric pieces, if broken, do not get the high prices this author feels they deserve. Generally, early-20th-century pottery gets higher prices.—*DL*

Casas Grande 7″ × 7″ Contemporary
Jar; 4 polychrome with black, white, and sienna on buff colors in an encircling snake design; signed Felix Ortiz.
Good Quality/Good Condition   **$75–$100**

Hopi 3.6″ × 7″ Contemporary
Bowl; 4-color, polychrome, stylized modern parrot; feather, geometric, and linear designs; signed Fawn.
Good Quality/Good Condition   **$150–$200**

Hopi 5″ × 6.5″ Early 20th century
Jar; polychrome with dark brown and sienna on yellow colors in concentric circle; curvilinear, geometric, and linear designs.
Very Good Quality/Good Condition   **$400–$550**

Hopi 7″ Dia. Contemporary
Canteen by G. Kahe. *(See photo 4, right front)*
Good Quality/Good Condition $250–$300

Hopi 5.5″ × 5.5″ Contemporary
Jar; black on red with sworl, terraced, featherlike, and concentric circle designs;
signed S. (Sunbeam) Davis.
Good Quality/Good Condition $95–$125

Isletta 3.5″ to 4.5″ Contemporary
Four Kachina figures, including a Cholawitze (Fire God), flower/laguna corn-
type, and others; signed Zuni (Fred and Maggie).
Good Quality/Good Condition $140–$170

Jemez 1.5″ × 2.25″ Contemporary
Bowl; 5-color polychrome; signed Rebecca T. Gachupin.
Good Quality/Good Condition $20–$30

Mimbres 10.5″ Dia. Prehistoric
Black-on-white picture bowl. These were the top-notch prehistoric pottery mak-
ers. Their designs differed from most of their contemporaries by using symbol-
ism and nature figures—like butterflies, rather than using abstract designs.
Mimbres pieces get exceptionally high prices for prehistoric pottery.
Superior Quality/Fine Condition $25,300–$29,500

Mimbres 9″ Dia. Prehistoric
Black-on-white picture bowl.
Superior Quality/Fine Condition $82,500–$85,000

Navajo 7″ × 4″ c. 1935
Classic black Navajo pottery with rope-design rim.
Good Quality/Good Condition $50–$100

Navajo 5.5″ Dia. Contemporary
Canteen by Marie Naschitty. *(See photo 4, right rear)*
Good Quality/Good Condition $50–$85

Niadi 1.75″ × .75″ c. 1970
Rare, miniature, painted pottery bowl by the famous potter Niadi.
Superior Quality/Fine Condition $50–$100

San Ildefonso 6.75″ Dia. Contemporary
Blackware bowl, by Marie and Santana.
Superior Quality/Fine Condition $1045–$1150

San Ildefonso 8.75″ Dia. Contemporary
Blackware jar, by Marie.
Superior Quality/Fine Condition $2200–$2500

San Ildefonso 4.75″ H Contemporary
Blackware jar, by Marie and Julian.
Superior Quality/Fine Condition $1980–$2100

Santa Clara 11″ H Contemporary
Redware vase made by Margaret Tafoya.
Superior Quality/Fine Condition $2750–$3000

Santa Clara 13″ H Contemporary
Blackware olla, made by Margaret Tafoya.
Superior Quality/Fine Condition $5250–$5750

Santo Domingo 17″ Dia. Contemporary
Dough bowl.
Superior Quality/Fine Condition $4125–$4425

Zia 18″ Dia. Contemporary
Polychrome olla, made by Sofia Medina.
Very Good Quality/Fine Condition $1375–$1500

Zia 19″ H Late 19th century
Polychrome olla.
Superior Quality/Fine Condition $6050–$6500

Zuni 16.25″ H Late 19th century
Polychrome canteen.
Very Good Quality/Good Condition $3575–$4000

Zuni 11.5″ H Late 19th century
Polychrome olla.
Very Good Quality/Good Condition $1210–$1500

RUGS/BLANKETS

Chimayo 14″ × 17″ Contemporary
Woven fringed wool in blue, red, green, and white.
Good Quality/Good Condition $30–$50

Chimayo 14.5″ × 15″ 1960–1990
Sampler, in red, gray, aqua, and white; large Thunderbird and banded designs.
Good Quality/Good Condition $15–$20

Navajo 18″ × 18.5″ Mid-20th century
Mat, with white and red geometrics on black ground.
Good Quality/Good Condition $55–$75

Navajo 16.5″ × 36″ 1960–1990
Throw, in mottled gray, yellow, brown, white, and orange; banded and serrated designs.
Good Quality/Good Condition $25–$40

Navajo 16″ × 34″ 1960–1990
Throw, in dark brown, gray, red, white, orange, and blue; serrated diamond designs.
Good Quality/Good Condition $25–$50

Navajo 18.5″ × 35″ Contemporary
Throw, in black, red, white, and mottled green; serrated designs.
Good Quality/Good Condition $25–$50

Navajo 18″ × 20.5″ 1925–1950
Sampler, in dark brown, white, and orange; serrated diamond and hold-cross designs.
Good Quality/Good Condition $25–$45

Navajo 21.5″ × 42″ Mid-20th century
Throw, in black, white, gold, and gray colors in serrated diamond designs.
Good Quality/Good Condition $45–$75

Navajo Age unknown
Third Phase blanket. One of the most collectible of Indian blankets.
Superior Quality/Fine Condition $25,000–$26,500

Navajo 34.5″ × 46″ Contemporary
Pictorial weaving, Linda Nez.
Very Good Quality/Good Condition $1650–$1800

The QUALITY KEY measures the stylishness and collectibility of an antique.

Good Quality: Exhibits standard characteristics of the object.

Very Good Quality: A more desirable example because of above-average workmanship and design.

Superior Quality: Exhibits nearly every known feature found on such items, with workmanship and design of the highest quality.

Navajo 72″ × 46″   Age unknown
Two Grey Hills, weaving.
Very Good Quality/Good Condition   **$2970–$3100**

Navajo 52″ × 72″   1840–1880
Late Classic wearing blanket. All Late Classic (1840–1880) pieces are very collectible.
Superior Quality/Good Condition   **$9900–$10,200**

Navajo 30″ × 50″   Mid-20th century
Red, gray, black, and white in 3 vertical rows of serrated diamonds.
Good Quality/Good Condition   **$55–$75**

Navajo 38″ × 53″   c. 1930s
Klagetoh area rug in red, gray, black, and white.
Good Quality/Good Condition   **$200–$300**

Navajo 42″ × 50″   Mid-20th century
Teec-Nos-Pos outline in black, dark gray, white, green, light gray, cocoa, medium brown, and gold.
Good Quality/Good Condition   **$300–$400**

Navajo 60″ × 105″   c. 1950s
Crystal area; vegetable dye with dark brown, gold, light gray-brown, white, and medium brown; narrow- and wide-banded arrowhead and hourglass designs.
Very Good Quality/Good Condition   **$850–$1350**

Navajo 77″ × 120″   1930–1950
Dark brown, red, gray-brown, and white.
Very Good Quality/Good Condition   **$2250–$3250**

Navajo 58″ × 38″   c. 1950
Classic natural wool; Two Grey Hills weaving.
Good Quality/Good Condition   **$525–$700**

Navajo 24.5″ × 34″   Mid-20th century
Fancy older "American flag" in red, white, and purple; has 50 stars.
Good Quality/Good Condition   **$225–$325**

Navajo 51.5″ × 65″   c. 1925
Fancy old Teec-Nos-Pos/Red Mesa outline in red, maroon, orange, green, yellow, blue, black, gray, tan, and white; excellent condition.
Very Good Quality/Fine Condition   **$1800–$2500**

Yevishai 20″ × 29″   Contemporary
Different-color skirts on the women is unusual.
Good Quality/Good Condition   **$300–$400**

BIBLIOGRAPHY

Appleton, LeRoy H. *American Indian Design and Decoration*. New York: Dover Publications, 1971.

Bataille, Gretchen M., and Sands, Kathleen Mullen. *American Indian Women: Telling Their Lives*. Omaha: University of Nebraska Press, 1984.

Bennett, Edna Mae, and John F. *Turquoise Jewelry of the Indians of the Southwest*. CO: Turquoise Books, 1973.

Brown, Dee. *Bury My Heart at Wounded Knee*. New York: Bantam Books, 1961.

Brownell, Charles De Wolf. *The Indian Races of North and South America*. Philadelphia: Hurlbut, Scranton and Co., 1865.

Bunzel, Ruth L. *The Pueblo Potter: A Study in Primitive Art*. Dover Publications: Philadelphia, 1865; New York, 1972.

Catlin, George. *Letters and Notes on the Manners, Customs and Conditions of the North American Indians*. New York: Dover Publications, 1973.

James, George Wharton. *Indian Blankets and Their Makers*. New York: Dover Publications, 1974.

Sides, Dorothy Smith. *Decorative Art of the Southwest Indians*. New York: Dover Publications, 1961.

Tanner, Clara Lee. *Indian Baskets of the Southwest*. Tucson: University of Arizona Press, 1983.

Yenne, Bill. *The Encyclopedia of North American Tribes*. Bison Books, 1986.

MUSEUMS

Some museums that own collections of American Indian art and artifacts include the Arizona State Museum, Tucson, AZ; Daybreak Star Arts Center, Seattle, WA; Museum of the Plains Indian and Crafts Center, Browning, MT; Sioux Indian Museum and Crafts Center, Rapid City, SD; Southern Plains Indian Museum and Crafts Center, Anadarko, OK; Museum of American Indian Art, New York; Heard Museum, Phoenix, AZ; Smithsonian Museum, Washington, DC; Alaska State Museum, Juneau, AK; Cherokee National Historical Society, Inc., Tahlequah, OK; Institute of American Indian Arts Museum, Santa Fe, NM; and Society for American Indian Studies and Research, Hurst, TX.

Arts and Crafts Movement

(See also Silver)

This chapter is arranged by the following subcategories:
FURNITURE, METALWARE, POTTERY, TEXTILES.

Advisor: **BRUCE JOHNSON**

Bruce Johnson is a widely published columnist and author of several books on the Arts and Crafts movement, including the Official Identification and Price Guide to Arts and Crafts *(New York: House of Collectibles) and* Gustav Stickley's 1912 Craftsman Furniture *(Asheville: Knock On Wood Publications). Johnson lives in a 1914 Arts and Crafts home in Asheville, NC, where he writes and directs the annual Grove Park Inn Arts and Crafts Conference. His mailing address is Bruce Johnson, PO Box 8773, Asheville, NC 28814.*

SURVEY OF THE FIELD

The Arts and Crafts movement originally blossomed in America between 1895 and 1924, as designers such as Gustav Stickley and Harvey Ellis, architects such as Frank Lloyd Wright and George Grant Elmslie, and potters such as William Grueby and George Ohr rebelled against the mass-produced vulgarities of the late Victorian industrialized society.

In place of ornamental but flimsy furniture, homes, and decorative arts, they proclaimed a need to return to simple, pure forms, handcrafted by men and women deemed as important as artists though they worked with wood, metal, and clay rather than oil and canvas. Highly ornate walnut, rosewood, and mahogany gave way to strong, masculine oak; imported porcelain was replaced with vases and bowls made in nearly every region of the country and using native clays; highly polished silver was supplanted by hand-hammered copper and brass that was chemically treated to achieve an immediate dark patina. "Hand Craftsmanship" became the slogan of the Arts and Crafts Movement.

World War I brought an end to the Arts and Crafts movement, as troubles abroad made concerns over decorative arts pale in comparison. After the Treaty of Versailles was signed, Americans found themselves moving in two directions: some sought a return to Colonial American furniture in their homes; others were enamored of the newly discovered Art Deco designs brought back from Europe. Simple and strong but definitely outdated, the Mission oak furniture, art pottery, and hand-hammered metalware of the Arts and Crafts Movement was pushed aside in the rush toward yet another new style in decorative arts.

Evidence of the glory of the Arts and Crafts movement remained in attics, barns, and basements until the early 1970s, when historians, authors, and designers began to place it in perspective. Once the glitter of the Art Deco, Danish Modern, and chrome furniture began to tarnish, Americans slowly began to realize that what had formerly been dismissed as a failed experiment was actually at the root of the much larger modernism movement. No longer footnotes in history, Gustav Stickley, Frank Lloyd Wright, Charles Limbert, Elbert Hubbard, and other early-20th-century designers have become household names to those who study the history of the decorative arts. As a result, the furniture, art pottery, and metalware that survived over seven decades of neglect and abuse have become highly sought after by a new generation of antiques collectors. Uninspired by Chippendale chests and Eastlake dressers, this new crowd has proved that they are unafraid to spend as much on a Gustav Stickley box settle as on a new car.

TRENDS IN ARTS AND CRAFTS COLLECTING

The new breed of Arts and Crafts collectors has brought a seemingly absent element to antiques collecting: independence. Gone are the days when a serious collector would never consider making an important purchase without the guidance of an Israel Sack or a John Walton. Arts and Crafts collectors have been called closet intellectuals, quietly reading all they can lay their hands on in order to learn more about the designs and the designers of the movement. Semiannual auctions at the major East and West Coast auction houses are no longer reunions for veteran dealers. Instead, the dealers bemoan the fact that they cannot compete with the "new money" in the hands of the young collectors who have come to inspect, ponder, and bid for themselves as they scramble to improve their collections.

Along the way they have quickly learned their lessons and soon play a role in the establishment of trends among their peers. Rocking chairs and ordinary library tables are now considered commonplace; unsigned armless rockers in less than mint condition often remain homeless for months in a dealer's showroom. While smaller servers have always been popular, larger sideboards were considered "white elephants" until early 1988, when collectors desiring a complete Arts and Crafts dining room, rather than just an example or two, suddenly began competing for them. In a similar instance, single dining chairs are uninspiring, but a matched set of four or six can send a collector into ecstasy.

Whereas in recent years collectors have rushed to grab any example of certain forms, most notably the rarer box settles, china cabinets, and double beds, the decade of the 1990s will demonstrate that condition is every bit as important as form. During the 1980s many overrefinished, overrestored, or overrepaired examples of rare forms soared to astronomical prices. As a result, more examples of Stickley, Limbert, Grueby, and Roycroft came onto the market, as major periodicals displayed banner headlines announcing the latest record-breaking sale. Nearly every antiques dealer in the country began looking for Arts and Crafts furniture, pottery, and metalware, and many were successful. What they discovered, however, is that the supply began to balance the demand, and prices for many forms began to slip in 1990.

Arts and Crafts collectors have learned that the antiques they collect are not as rare as many once believed. What remains a rarity, however, is an Arts and Crafts antique that is well designed and well documented and retains its original, unblemished finish, regardless of whether that is a Stickley shellac, a Grueby mat glaze, or a Dirk Van Erp copper lamp patina. After Arts and Crafts fell out of style in the 1920s, many examples of furniture were refinished, many vases and bowls were chipped through careless handling, and many hand-hammered lamps and chandeliers were polished.

National publicity has led to the discovery and the sale of many such pieces through any of the scores of shops, galleries, and auction houses now selling Arts and Crafts antiques. Astute collectors have come to realize that while a Gustav Stickley box settle is still a rare find, rarer still is a Gustav Stickley box settle with an original finish in excellent condition. Prices for refinished examples, even of rare forms, have now settled down to a more predictable range. Mint condition antiques, even such common forms as library tables, bookcases, and rocking chairs, continue to increase in value, though not at the breakneck pace of the 1980s.

Collectors and dealers who invest heavily in refinished, damaged, or repaired examples of Arts and Crafts antiques will be leaving themselves open to financial risk this year, for Arts and Crafts collectors have already proved that they will not pay 1988 and 1989 record-breaking prices for anything but the very best—in terms of condition, as well as form.

Advanced collectors have distinguished themselves from the horde of novices by being able to identify an unsigned or refinished example that no one else had noticed. The secret of their success is simple: they study books and catalog reprints. They know how to distinguish between the hardware used by Gustav Stickley and that of firms producing similar furniture. They can recognize a Mathew Daly painting on a Rookwood vase without needing to find his initials on the bottom. And they can identify a Dirk Van Erp lamp without having to draw attention to themselves by dismantling the shade and base.

FAKES

Fakes and forgeries have been a part of every popular American antique genre for decades, and now the fledgling Arts and Crafts movement must confess to having been burned. At a recent New York auction a standard Gustav Stickley dropfront desk worth approximately $3,000 was transformed into a $21,000 desk by a craftsman with a talent for adding inlaid decorations. Only one dealer in a crowd of five hundred people recognized the fraud, and that was because he had seen the same desk sell a few months earlier—but without any inlay.

Collectors have to be aware of the financial incentives that tempt craftsmen into transforming an authentic Gustav Stickley antique (or that of any popular maker whose furniture is worth tampering with) into one that is considered more valuable. The simple addition of slats under each arm can change an $800 Morris chair into a $3,500 chair. The sudden appearance of cutouts in a standard Limbert table can add several hundred dollars in value—enough to buy several hundred saber saws. The addition of a scrap of a paper label or a partial or faint decal—barely distinguishable and conveniently illegible but considered "proof" by a novice collector anxious to find a piece of signed Stickley—can turn a generic piece into an apparent rarity.

The solution is again simple: study the books and catalog reprints. If the piece in question does not match the dimensions and design in the catalog, be suspicious. Ask for a second opinion from an unbiased but experienced collector. Demand a written receipt from the seller guaranteeing a complete refund if you later discover and prove (a bit tricky, though) that it is a fake or has been altered. It is easier to say no, however, than to prove later that a crime has been committed. And it is less expensive.

The problem that is going to emerge in a few years concerns reproductions. Right now several craftsmen are pursuing legitimate businesses making accurate reproductions of rare Arts and Crafts furniture and lighting fixtures. Most craftsmen are attempting to mark their reproductions clearly and permanently (and often date them), but collectors must be aware that an unscrupulous dealer might remove the mark and the date, strip the piece of its finish, add evidence of wear normally associated with an eighty-year-old antique, and apply a finish that looks appropriately old. The result might be a spindle Morris chair that appears to have been made in 1907 in the Craftsman Workshops of Gustav Stickley but in reality is less than ten years old.

In this instance a catalog reprint may seem to confirm the authenticity of the piece, for most modern craftsmen have copied the identical dimensions and designs from those same catalogs. Distinguishing a reproduction that has been "antiqued" from a true antique requires a trained eye, for the differences are often too subtle to describe in print. Collectors can best prepare themselves by studying legitimate examples at galleries and Arts and Crafts auctions, where each piece has previously been subject to a careful examination. Most frauds can be expected to surface at country auctions and flea markets, where receipts are a rarity and bargain prices are not unexpected. Nevertheless, be suspicious of a piece that is being sold as "rare Gustav Stickley" at an unusually low price. Although you don't want to pass by a bargain, you also don't want to spend several hundreds or thousands of dollars on a fake.

CONDITION KEY

As Arts and Crafts antiques become more valuable, condition becomes more important. Since most of the furniture of this era was mass-produced, collectors will often pass on a refinished or badly damaged example, knowing the possibility exists that a better example will surface in the future. Only those pieces known to be experimental or extremely rare (such as Gustav Stickley inlaid and spindle furniture) will draw record-breaking prices despite some obvious flaws.

For the vast majority, however, this condition key will apply.

FURNITURE

Fine: original finish; original hardware unpolished; original leather upholstery still flexible; minimal wear; no water stains; no previous repairs.

Good: original finish showing signs of wear; original hardware showing signs of wear; original leather brittle but usable; signs of wear; any previous repairs done properly.

Average: original finish nearly gone or refinished professionally; original hardware polished; original leather torn and/or unusable; water spots apparent; minor repair or regluing required; reupholstered appropriately.

Poor: badly refinished; original hardware missing; reupholstered in inappropriate fabric; excessive wear; evidence of poorly executed repairs; additional major repairs required.

POTTERY

Fine: no chips or cracks; no glaze imperfections.

Good: one hairline crack or glaze imperfection; no chips.

Average: small chip needing repair or previously professionally repaired.

Poor: noticeable chip or crack on rim; clear evidence of earlier repairs.

METALWARE

Fine: never polished; only faint evidence of any wear.

Good: never polished; evidence of expected wear.

Average: never polished; obvious wear has reduced original patina in places; may have been cleaned; minor dent.

Poor: polished or repaired; major dent.

QUALITY KEY

To an Arts and Crafts collector, "quality" is an abstract term that often has to be wrestled into submission. The term more frequently used and just as difficult to define is "design." In the field of art pottery, every firm has its own elements that go into the determination of its quality. It is impossible to compare, for instance, a Grueby vase with a Rookwood vase. Each has a different set of criteria against which each example must be compared.

Arts and Crafts furniture, though, shares many of the same elements; thus, it is possible to work toward a general clarification of Good—Very Good—Superior regardless of whether the example at hand is a signed Gustav Stickley or an unsigned generic piece. The following guide may be used for furniture.

Superior: Height, width, and depth are in ideal proportion to one another. One does not dominate or detract from the others. Slats appear under the arms of chairs and settles but are not spread so far apart that the spaces between them become more obvious than the slats themselves. Corbels, either decorative or functional, support chair arms. Key joints feature exposed tenons; keyed tenons add yet another feature to the design. False tenons (nailed or glued on) are a negative. Joints will be pegged as both a functional and a decorative effect. Arched cross-stretchers on chairs and tables are a plus, as are arched toeboards on china cabinets, bookcases, and settles.

Box settles are considered more purely Arts and Crafts than drop-arm settles. Slant-arm Morris chairs are more desirable than flat-arm Morris chairs. Several small panes of glass in a bookcase or china cupboard door are more pleasing than one large pane or one with false mullions placed across the front of it. Heavy, hammered hardware is a sign of quality; lightweight, stamped hardware is not.

Very Good: fewer of the above.

Good: very few of the above.

FURNITURE

Armchair 40″ H × 30″ W Barrel back 1914 United States
Curved vertical slats under arms and back; spring seat reupholstered.
Very Good Quality/Good Condition $1000 (D)   **$700–$1100**

Bookcase 56.5″ H × 42.5″ W × 13″ D Stickley, Gustav 1905 United States
Two doors with 8 panes each, gallery top, through tenons on sides, #716.
Very Good Quality/Fine Condition $2500 (A)   **$1500–$2500**

Bookcase 49″ H × 61″ W × 13″ D Lifetime 1912 United States
Oak, 3 doors with 8 panels each, arched toeboard.
Very Good Quality/Fine Condition $2500 (A)   **$2000–$2500**

Box settle 32″ H × 76″ W × 32″ D 1910 United States
Oak, 8 slats, 3 under each arm; arms and back same height; reupholstered spring seat.
Good Quality/Good Condition $2000 (D)   **$1000–$2000**

Cabinet, china 62″ H × 46″ W × 14″ D Stickley Bros. 1912 United States
Oak; 2 doors, each with 1 small window over larger retangular pane of glass; adjustable shelves; overhanging top.
Very Good Quality/Good Condition $500 (A)   **$400–$600**

Cellarette 26″ H × 16″ W × 16″ D Imperial Furniture 1910 United States
Drop-down door under simple drawer and overhanging top; original finish.
Very Good Quality/Fine Condition $650 (A)   **$400–$600**

> Note that the original finish contributed to a top-dollar price even at auction (so often a wholesale market).—*DL*

Chair/table 30″ H × 42″ Dia. 1920 United States
Oak, lift-up round table that converts to a chair with drawer beneath seat.
Good Quality/Fine Condition $250 (A)   **$200–$300**

Chair, child's 23″ H × 14″ W Stickley, Gustav 1910 United States
Oak, 2 horizontal slats, leather seat, refinished.
Very Good Quality/Fine Condition $300 (A)   **$200–$300**

Chair, dining 37″ H × 18″ W × 17″ D Stickley, Gustav 1912 United States
Three horizontal back slats; wrap-around new leather seat.
Very Good Quality/Good Condition $250 (D) **$200–$300**

Chair, dining 38″ H × 22″ W Roycrofters 1913 United States
Oak; inscribed GPI for Grove Park Inn; leather seat; arms added in 1919; refinished.
Very Good Quality/Good Condition $250 (D) **$200–$300**

Chair, Morris 38″ H × 36″ W 1906 United States
Oak; flat arms over 4 slats; through tenons; original upholstery. *(See photo 5)*
Very Good Quality/Good Condition $1200 (A) **$800–$1400**

Chair, Morris 39″ H × 30″ W × 36″ D Stickley, Gustav 1906 United States
Oak, flat arm over 16 square spindles; adjustable back; new upholstery.
Superior Quality/Good Condition $5000 (A) **$4000–$6000**

Chair, Morris 41″ H × 27.5″ W Stickley, L & J G 1909 United States
Oak, flat arms supported by long corbels; no slats under arms; spring cushion seat (new upholstery).
Good Quality/Good Condition $650 (A) **$500–$800**

Chair, Morris 41″ H × 27″ W 1910 United States
Oak, flat arm, adjustable back, refinished, new upholstery.
Good Quality/Good Condition $300 (A) **$250–$400**

Chair, side 34″ H × 17″ W Stickley, L & J G 1912 United States
Oak, 3 horizontal back slats; drop-in leather seat (new upholstery); refinished.
Good Quality/Good Condition $150 (D) **$100–$200**

Desk 46″ H × 42″ W × 11.5″ D Stickley & Ellis 1903 United States
Drop-front with 3 inlaid panels above 3 drawers and open compartment; Gustav Stickley and Harvey Ellis.
Superior Quality/Fine Condition $93,000 (A) **$60,000–$100,000**

Desk 30″ H × 35″ W × 19″ D Lifetime 1915 United States
Four square legs under 2 drawers and overhanging top; splashboard; refinished.
Very Good Quality/Good Condition $350 (A) **$200–$400**

Footstool 5″ H × 12″ W Stickley, Gustav 1905 United States
Oak, with leather-covered frame on short, flared legs; #302.
Good Quality/Good Condition $250 (D) **$200–$400**

Footstool 15″ H × 20″ W × 16″ D Stickley, Gustav 1907 United States
Oak, #300, with straight stretcher and replaced wrap-around leather seat; refinished.
Very Good Quality/Good Condition $750 (D) **$650–$950**

Lamp, table 20″ H × 17″ W × 17″ D 1910 United States
Four slag glass panels in wood frame above square wooden base; original finish.
Very Good Quality/Fine Condition $250 (D) **$150–$250**

Magazine stand 42″ H × 19″ W × 12″ D Stickley, Gustav 1914 United States
Oak; open back; ends with 3 slats; arched apron.
Superior Quality/Fine Condition $1100 (D) **$800–$1200**

Photo 5. Morris chair.
CREDIT: BRUCE
JOHNSON *(See p. 39)*

Photo 6. Table. CREDIT: BRUCE JOHNSON *(See p. 41)*

Plant stand 18″ H × 15″ W × 15″ D 1915 United States
Oak, #5873; 4 posts with double stretchers; arches under top shelf; original finish.
Good Quality/Fine Condition $550 (A)   **$450–$550**

Rocker 35″ H × 18″ W Stickley, Gustav 1912 United States
Oak; 5 vertical slats across back; open arms; reupholstered spring seat; refinished.
Good Quality/Average Condition $200 (D)   **$150–$350**

Rocking chair 38″ H × 25″ W Morris 1912 United States
L. & J. G. Stickley #831 with open arms supported by long corbels; adjustable back; no cushion.
Good Quality/Average Condition $1000 (A)   **$800–$1400**

Server 33″ H × 32″ W × 16″ D Stickley, L & J G 1912 United States
Oak, #751, blind drawer with backsplash on overhanging top; original finish.
Very Good Quality/Fine Condition $650 (A)   **$500–$700**

Settle 37″ H × 40″ W × 20″ D Limbert 1910 United States
Oak, #807, arms lower than back; slats across back; open arms; spring seat.
Very Good Quality/Good Condition $350 (A)   **$300–$400**

Settle, box 29″ H × 69″ W × 25″ D Limbert 1909 United States
Oak, with 4 slats under each arm, 12 across back; #561; refinished; new upholstery.
Superior Quality/Good Condition $1900 (A)   **$1500–$2500**

Sideboard 60″ H × 56″ W × 18″ D Lifetime 1915 United States
Oak; mirrored splashboard with through tenons; 3 short and 1 long drawer over 2 doors.
Good Quality/Fine Condition $1200 (A)   **$1000–$1500**

Table 30″ H × 48″ W × 30″ D Greene & Greene 1907 United States
Inlaid mahogany table with single drawer; ebony inlay and decorations. *(See photo 6)*
Superior Quality/Fine Condition $80,000 (D)   **$60,000–$100,000**

Table 30″ H × 42″ W × 28″ D Limbert 1912 United States
Oak oval table with trapezoidal cutouts at either end; footrest shelves.
Superior Quality/Fine Condition $1200 (A)   **$1000–$1500**

Table, dining 30″ H × 54″ Dia. 1915 United States
Oak; round top with 3 leaves; square pedestal and feet.
Very Good Quality/Good Condition $850 (A)   **$850–$900**

Table, lamp 30″ H × 42″ Dia. Young, J. M. 1908 United States
Oak; circular overhanging top; arched cross-stretcher; refinished.
Very Good Quality/Good Condition $500 (A)   **$400–$700**

Table, library 30″ H × 48″ W × 30″ D Stickley, Gustav 1906 United States
Oak, #615, with 2 drawers with hammered pulls, long corbels on legs and through tenon; refinished.
Superior Quality/Good Condition $900 (A)   **$750–$1100**

Table, library 29″ H × 48″ W × 32″ D Stickley, L & J G 1912 United States
Oak; single drawer with hammered pulls: through tenons; overhanging top; refinished.
Very Good Quality/Good Condition $650 (A)   **$600–$800**

Tabouret   16″ H × 14″ Dia.   Stickley, Gustav   1914   United States
Oak, #601; circular top over 4 legs and arched stretchers.
Very Good Quality/Fine Condition $600 (A)   **$400–$600**

Umbrella stand   33″ H × 11″ W × 11″ D   Stickley, Gustav   1912   United
States
Oak, with 4 tapering posts with copper drip pan.
Very Good Quality/Fine Condition $350 (D)   **$300–$400**

Walking stick   35″ H   Roycroft   1903   United States
Tapering form of oak, with leather thong.
Very Good Quality/Fine Condition $200 (A)   **$100–$200**

Wardrobe   60″ H × 60″ W   1915   United States
Oak; 3 sections; middle door with mirror over drawer; side sections paneled.
Very Good Quality/Fine Condition $1500 (A)   **$1200–$1800**

Window seat   24″ H × 24″ W × 18″ D   Limbert, Charles   1907   United
States
Oak, canted sides with 4 square cutouts; original leather cushion; refinished.
Superior Quality/Good Condition $3800 (A)   **$1500–$4500**

METALWARE

Bookends   4″ H × 6″ W   Roycroft   1910   United States
Pair, copper, rectangular form with design of impressed owl.
Very Good Quality/Fine Condition $200 (A)   **$100–$200**

Bookends, brass   6″ H × 3″ W   Roycroft   1915   United States
Pair, rectangular form with tooled flowers.
Good Quality/Fine Condition $150 (A)   **$100–$150**

Bowl   3″ H × 10″ Dia.   Heinrich, Joseph   1910   United States
Hammered nickel-silver open bowl with rolled rim.
Very Good Quality/Fine Condition $100 (A)   **$75–$125**

Bowl   5.5″ H × 8″ Dia.   Stone, Arthur   1915   United States
Wide-mouth form with chased band and flared foot. *(See photo 7)*
Superior Quality/Fine Condition $2000 (D)   **$1500–$2000**

Candle sconces   10″ H × 3″ W   Roycroft   1912   United States
Pair, hammered copper with tooled edge.
Very Good Quality/Fine Condition $175 (D)   **$100–$200**

Candlesticks   12″ H × 6″ Dia.   Brass   1900–1910   United States
Pair, tapering cylindrical stem rising from circular foot.
Very Good Quality/Fine Condition $500 (D)   **$200–$500**

Candlesticks   11″ H × 4″ Dia.   Jarvie   1905   United States
Pair; egg-shaped socket atop slender stem on circular base.
Very Good Quality/Fine Condition $1200 (A)   **$800–$1200**

Lamp, table   32″ H × 20″ Dia.   Benedict Studios   1906   United States
Tapering copper base and flared font; mica shade.
Very Good Quality/Fine Condition $2500 (A)   **$2000–$3000**

Letter opener   6″ L   Roycroft   1920   United States
Acid-etched finish on knife form; copper.
Good Quality/Good Condition $25 (D)   **$20–$30**

Photo 7. Bowl.
CREDIT: BRUCE
JOHNSON
(See p. 42)

Photo 8. Pitcher. CREDIT: BRUCE
JOHNSON *(See p. 44)*

Photo 9. Vase. CREDIT: BRUCE
JOHNSON *(See p. 45)*

Pin 1″ H × 2″ W　Jensen, Georg　1920　United States
Sterling silver overlapping figure-8 form with central bead.
Superior Quality/Fine Condition　$150 (A)　　**$100–$150**

Tray 23″ W × 11″ D　Stickley, Gustav　1909　United States
Hand-hammered copper; oval form with handles at either end; polished years ago.
Superior Quality/Good Condition　$500 (A)　　**$450–$650**

Vase 9″ H × 5″ Dia.　Dirk Van Erp　1910　United States
Cylinder form with swollen top, hand-hammered copper.
Very Good Quality/Fine Condition　$500 (A)　　**$300–$500**

POTTERY

Bowl 2.5″ H × 8″ Dia.　Fulper　1911　United States
Open bowl with notched outer rim; blue interior glaze; yellow outer glaze.
Very Good Quality/Fine Condition　$200 (A)　　**$100–$200**

Bowl 3″ H × 6″ Dia.　1915　United States
Chased bowl with painted flowers on blue ground; clear high glaze; by North Dakota School of Mines.
Very Good Quality/Fine Condition　$500 (A)　　**$400–$500**

Bowl 4″ H × 7″ Dia.　Dedham　1930　United States
Decorated with rabbits on blue band around lip.
Superior Quality/Fine Condition　$300 (A)　　**$200–$300**

Candlesticks 9″ H × 3.5″ Dia.　Clewell　1910　United States
Pair bronze-clad candlesticks of tapering form.
Superior Quality/Fine Condition　$450 (A)　　**$350–$450**

Humidor 8.5″ H × 4″ Dia.　Dedham　1917　United States
Brass screw-handle top holding lid in place; elephant decoration.
Superior Quality/Fine Condition　$2000 (D)　　**$1500–$2500**

Pitcher 11″ H × 6.5″ Dia.　Newcomb　1905　United States
High glaze over decorated scene of trees. *(See photo 8)*
Superior Quality/Fine Condition　$1500 (A)　　**$1000–$1500**

Plate 10″ Dia.　Dedham　1915–1930　United States
10″ plate with 2 scottie dogs painted on center.
Very Good Quality/Good Condition　$800 (D)　　**$500–$900**

Teapot 7.5″ H × 3.5″ Dia.　Ohr, George　1905　United States
Lidded teapot with snakelike spout under metallic black glaze.
Superior Quality/Fine Condition　$1500 (A)　　**$1200–$1500**

Tile 6″ H × 6″ W　Grueby　1905　United States
Undecorated green tile.
Good Quality/Good Condition　$100 (A)　　**$50–$150**

Tile 6″ H × 7″ W　Grueby　1905　United States
White polar bear on blue background.
Superior Quality/Fine Condition　$450 (A)　　**$400–$500**

Vase 4″ H × 4″ Dia.　Van Briggle　1902　United States
Swollen shoulder decorated with stylized poppy buds under green matte glaze.
Superior Quality/Fine Condition　$1400 (A)　　**$1000–$1400**

Vase 7″ H × 4.5″ Dia. Ohr, George 1903 United States
Bulbous bottom with wide cylinder neck and 2 curving handles; blue and pink glaze.
Superior Quality/Fine Condition $1700 (D)   **$1500–$2000**

Vase 12″ H × 5.75″ Dia. Grueby 1904 United States
Tall vase with rolled rim, decorated with applied leaves under green glaze. *(See photo 9)*
Superior Quality/Fine Condition $2800 (A)   **$2500–$3500**

Vase 7″ H × 4″ Dia. Marblehead 1908 United States
Wide mouth and swollen shoulder on tapering base; decorated with stylized flowers in brown and yellow.
Superior Quality/Fine Condition $1500 (D)   **$1000–$1500**

Vase 12″ H × 4″ Dia. Clewell 1910 United States
Long flared neck on bulbous shoulders; coated with patinated bronze.
Very Good Quality/Fine Condition $500 (A)   **$300–$500**

Vase 7″ H × 4.5″ Dia. Hampshire 1910 United States
Swollen shoulder on tapering form, decorated with spiked leaves and green glaze.
Very Good Quality/Fine Condition $250 (A)   **$150–$250**

Vase 7″ H × 5″ Dia. Newcomb 1910 United States
Bulbous form tapering to footed base; decorated with white and yellow flowers on blue background.
Superior Quality/Fine Condition $400 (A)   **$200–$400**

Vase 10″ H × 4″ Dia. Saturday Evening Girls 1910 United States
Wide mouth on swollen cylinder form; blue glaze.
Very Good Quality/Fine Condition $300 (A)   **$200–$300**

Vase 13″ H × 5″ D Teco 1911 United States
Tall vase with flared base and corset-shaped body, green rust glaze.
Very Good Quality/Fine Condition $850 (A)   **$800–$1000**

Vase 13.5″ H × 5″ Dia. Rookwood 1913 United States
Wide mouth on cylinder form, decorated with blue landscape; artist Edward Hurley.
Very Good Quality/Fine Condition $1200 (A)   **$800–$1200**

Vase 12″ H × 4.5″ D Fulper 1914 United States
Wide mouth and short neck on swollen shoulder and tapering form; green glaze.
Very Good Quality/Fine Condition $325 (D)   **$250–$350**

Vase 4.2″ H × 2.5″ Dia. Overbrook 1915 United States
Rolled up, short neck on square, bulbous borm; decorated with Oriental geometric design.
Very Good Quality/Fine Condition $250 (A)   **$200–$250**

Vase 7.5″ H × 3.5″ Dia. Rookwood 1917 United States
Incised by Charles Todd with green and blue flowers on yellow ground.
Superior Quality/Fine Condition $400 (A)   **$300–$400**

Vase 9″ H × 4″ Dia. Rookwood 1918 United States
Wide mouth on swollen cylinder form with floral design.
Very Good Quality/Fine Condition $500 (D)   **$400–$500**

Vase 8″ H × 4″ Dia. Pewabic 1919 United States
Carved vase with cut-back squares under royal blue glaze.
Superior Quality/Fine Condition $450 (A)   **$400–$500**

Vase 8″ H × 4″ Dia.   Weller Pottery   1925   United States.
Bulbous form with flared rim.
Very Good Quality/Fine Condition $175 (D)   **$100–$200**
Vase, floor   18″ H × 8.5″ Dia.   Teco   1909   United States
Swollen cylinder form with rolled rim under green matte glaze.
Superior Quality/Fine Condition $2000 (A)   **$1500–$2000**

TEXTILES

Curtains   72″ H × 31″ W each   1910   United States
Pair of linen curtains decorated with stylized red roses.
Superior Quality/Good Condition $250 (D)   **$200–$300**
Pillow, linen   17″ W × 13″ D   1910   United States
Decorated with stylized red roses and green leaves.
Very Good Quality/Fine Condition $150 (A)   **$100–$150**
Rug   10′ W × 13′ D   1910   Unknown
Geometric pattern of "U" in black and gray background.
Very Good Quality/Fine Condition $1000 (A)   **$800–$1000**
Table runner   60″ L × 12″ W   1910   United States
Machine-woven cotton fabric decorated with red and yellow stylized flowers.
Very Good Quality/Fine Condition $50 (D)   **$25–$50**

BIBLIOGRAPHY

Anderson, Timothy; Moore, Eudorah; and Winter, Robert. *California Design 1910.* Pasadena, CA: California Design Publications, 1974; Santa Barbara, CA: Peregrine Smith, 1980.

Anscombe, Isabelle, and Gere, Charlotte. *Arts and Crafts in Britain and America.* New York: Rizzoli International Publications, 1978.

The Arts and Crafts Quarterly (periodical). David Rago, ed. and publ. Trenton: Arts and Crafts Quarterly, 1987–present.

The Artsman (periodical). Philadelphia: Rose Valley Press, 1903–1907.

Bavaro, Joseph, and Mossmann, Thomas. *The Furniture of Gustav Stickley: History, Techniques, Projects.* New York: Van Nostrand Reinhold, 1982.

The Book of the Roycrofters. Roycroft Shop catalog: 1919 and 1926 (catalog reprint). East Aurora, NY: House of Hubbard, 1977.

Brandt, Frederick. *Late 19th and Early 20th Century Decorative Arts.* Richmond: Virginia Museum of Fine Arts, 1985.

Brooks, H. Allen. *Frank Lloyd Wright and the Prairie School.* New York: George Braziller, 1984.

Callen, Anthea. *Women Artists of the Arts and Crafts Movement 1870–1914.* New York: Pantheon Books, 1979.

Cathers, David. *Furniture of the American Arts and Crafts Movement*. New York: New American Library, 1981.

———. *Genius in the Shadows: The Furniture Designs of Harvey Ellis*. New York: Jordan Volpe Gallery, 1981.

Champney, Freeman. *Art and Glory: The Story of Elbert Hubbard*. Kent, OH: Kent State University Press, 1983.

Clark, Garth, and Hughto, Margie. *A Century of Ceramics in the United States 1878–1978*. New York: E. P. Dutton, 1979.

Clark, Robert Judson, ed. *The Arts and Crafts Movement in America 1876–1916*. Princeton, NJ: Princeton University Press, 1972.

Cole, G. D. H., ed. *William Morris: Selected Writings*. Centenary edition. London: Nonesuch Press, 1948.

The Craftsman (periodical). Gustav Stickley, ed. Eastwood and New York: Craftsman Publishing, 1901–1916.

Cummins, Virginia. *Rookwood Pottery Potpourri*. Silver Spring, MD: Leonard and Coleman, 1980.

Danforth Museum of Art. *On the Threshold of Modern Design: The Arts and Crafts Movement in America*. Danforth, MA: Danforth Museum of Art, 1984.

Darling, Sharon. *Chicago Furniture: Art, Craft & Industry 1833–1933*. Chicago: Chicago Historical Society, 1984.

———. *Chicago Metalsmiths*. Chicago: Chicago Historical Society, 1977.

Davey, Peter. *Architecture of the Arts and Crafts Movement*. New York: Rizzoli International Publications, 1980.

Doros, Paul. *The Tiffany Collection of the Chrysler Museum at Norfolk*. Norfolk, VA: The Chrysler Museum, 1978.

Edwards, Robert, ed. *The Arts and Crafts Furniture of Charles Limbert* (catalog reprint). Watkins Glen, NY: American Life Foundation, 1982.

———. *The Byrdcliffe Arts and Crafts Colony*. Wilmington, DE: Delaware Art Museum, 1985.

Eidelberg, Martin, ed. *From Our Native Clay*. New York: American Ceramic Arts Society and Turn of the Century Editions, 1987.

Evans, Paul, *Art Pottery of the United States* (2nd ed.). New York: Feingold & Lewis Publishing, 1987.

Freeman, John Crosby. *The Forgotten Rebel, Gustav Stickley and His Craftsman Mission Furniture*. Watkins Glen, NY: Century House, 1965.

Garner, Philippe. *Twentieth-Century Furniture*. New York: Van Nostrand Reinhold, 1980.

Gray, Stephen, and Edwards, Robert, eds. *The Collected Works of Gustav Stickley* (catalog reprint). New York: Turn of the Century Editions, 1981.

Gray, Stephen, ed. *The Mission Furniture of L. and J. G. Stickley* (catalog reprint). New York: Turn of the Century Editions, 1983.

———. *The Early Work of Gustav Stickley* (catalog reprint). New York: Turn of the Century Editions, 1987.

———. *Lifetime Furniture* (catalog reprint). New York: Turn of the Century Editions, 1981.

———. *Limbert's Holland Dutch Arts and Crafts Furniture* (catalog reprint). New York: Turn of the Century Editions, 1981.

———. *Roycroft Furniture* (catalog reprint). New York: Turn of the Century Editions, 1981.

———. *Quaint Furniture: Arts and Crafts* (reprint of Stickley Brothers catalog). New York: Turn of the Century Editions, 1981.

———. *Arts and Crafts Furniture: Shop of the Crafters at Cincinnati* (catalog reprint). New York: Turn of the Century Editions, 1983.

Hamilton, Charles. *Roycroft Collectibles*. New York: A. S. Barnes and Co., 1980.

Hamilton, Charles; Turgeon, Kitty; and Rust, Robert. *History and Renaissance of the Roycroft Movement*. Buffalo, NY: Buffalo & Erie County Historical Society, 1984.

Hanks, David. *The Decorative Designs of Frank Lloyd Wright*. New York: E. P. Dutton, 1979.

Henderson, Philip. *William Morris: His Life, Works and Friends*. New York: McGraw-Hill, 1967.

Hunter, Dard. *My Life with Paper*. New York: Alfred A. Knopf, 1958.

Huxford, Sharon and Bob. *The Collectors' Encyclopedia of Weller Pottery*. Paducah, KY: Collector Books, 1979.

Johnson, Bruce. *The Official Identification and Price Guide to the Arts and Crafts*. New York: House of Collectibles, 1988.

Kaplan, Wendy, ed. *The Art That Is Life: The Arts and Crafts Movement in America 1875–1920*. Boston: Museum of Fine Arts, 1987.

Keen, Kirsten Hoving. *American Art Pottery 1875–1930*. Philadelphia: Falcon Press, 1978.

Keramic Studio, a Monthly Magazine for the China Painter and Potter (periodical). Syracuse, NY: Keramic Studio Publishing, 1899–1930.

Koch, Robert. *Louis C. Tiffany's Glass, Bronzes, Lamps*. New York: Crown Publishers, 1971.

Kornwolf, James M. H. *Baillie Scott and the Arts and Crafts Movement*. Baltimore: John Hopkins Press, 1972.

Kovel, Ralph and Terry. *The Kovels' Collectors Guide to American Art Pottery*. New York: Crown Publishers, 1974.

Lambourne, Lionel. *Utopian Craftsmen: The Arts and Crafts Movement from the Cotswolds to Chicago*. Salt Lake City, UT: Peregrine Smith, 1980.

Ludwig, Coy. *The Arts and Crafts Movement in New York State 1890s–1920s*. Layton, UT: Peregrine Smith, 1983.

Makinson, Randell. *Greene and Greene: Architecture as a Fine Art*. Salt Lake City, UT: Peregrine Smith, 1977.

———. *Greene and Greene: Furniture and Related Designs*. Salt Lake City, UT: Peregrine Smith, 1979.

Manson, Grant Carpenter. *Frank Lloyd Wright to 1910: The First Golden Age*. New York: Van Nostrand Reinhold, 1958.

Marek, Don. *Arts and Crafts Furniture Design: The Grand Rapids Contribution 1895–1915*. Grand Rapids, MI: Grand Rapids Art Museum, 1987.

Nelson, Scott; Crouch, Lois; Demmin, Euphemia; and Newton, Robert. *A Collectors' Guide to Van Briggle Pottery*. Indiana, PA: Halldin Publishing, 1986.

The Newark Museum Collection of American Art Pottery. Newark, NJ: Newark Museum, 1984.

Page, Marion, *Furniture Designed by Architects*. London: The Architectural Press, 1983.

Poesch, Jessie. *Newcomb Pottery*. Exton, PA: Schiffer Publishing, 1984.

Roycroft Handmade Furniture (1912 catalog reprint). East Aurora, NY: House of Hubbard, 1973.

Rubin, Jerome and Cynthia. *Mission Furniture*. San Francisco: Chronicle Books, 1980.

Smith, Mary Ann. *Gustav Stickley: The Craftsman*. Syracuse, NY: Syracuse University Press, 1983.

Stickley Craftsman Furniture Catalogs (Gustav Stickley 1910 catalog and L. & J. G. Stickley 1912 catalog reprint). New York: Dover Publications, 1979.

Stickley, Gustav, ed. *Craftsman Homes*. New York: The Craftsman Publishing Co., 1909; Dover Publications, 1979.

———. *More Craftsman Homes*. New York: The Craftsman Publishing Co., 1912; Dover Publications, 1912.

Stott, Mary Roelofs. *Elbert Hubbard: Rebel with Reverence*. Watkins Glen, NY: American Life Foundation, 1984.

Tiller, A Bimonthly Devoted to the Arts and Crafts Movement (periodical), Bryn Mawr, PA: The Artsman, 1982–1983.

Twombly, Robert. *Louis Sullivan: His Life and Work*. Chicago: The University of Chicago Press, 1986.

William Morris and Kelmscott. London: The Design Council, 1981.

Wright, Frank Lloyd. *An Autobiography*. New York: Duell, Sloan and Pierce, 1943.

Barometers

Advisors: **CHARLES E. and JILL PROBST**

Charles E. and Jill Probst are noted show dealers and owners of Charles Edwin Inc., Fine Antique Clocks and Barometers, PO Box 1340, Louisa, VA 23093; (703) 967-0416; by appointment.

SURVEY OF THE FIELD

HISTORY

Some of the foremost thinkers of the 17th century, intent upon discovering the natural laws of the universe, provided the groundwork for the development of the mercury barometer as we know it today. During the period from 1640 to 1660 Galileo set the stage for serious research into the existence of atmospheric pressure through his attempts to create a vacuum. In 1644 his colleague, Evangelista Torricelli, documented an experiment that tied the fundamental principles together through use of a tube and a jar of mercury. Shortly after this discovery, René Descartes and Blaise Pascal, working in France, studied the differences in air pressure at various elevations. In 1648 Descartes added a paper scale for measurement to the top of Torricelli's mercury tube and effectively created the mercury barometer.

In England, around 1660, the correlation between variations in atmospheric pressure and changes in the weather was observed. Experiments by Robert Boyle and Robert Hooke were well documented by 1670, and the leading clock and instrument makers of the time began to construct barometers intended for domestic use. The English had the lead in the manufacture of barometers well in hand by the time William III ascended to the throne, and they dominated world production for the next two centuries.

To this day the largest quantity and the widest range in styles of mercury barometers available to collectors are of English origin. Most other European countries and America have produced examples of mercury barometers since the mid-17th century but none so prolifically as the English.

TRENDS DURING THE PAST YEAR

In recent business years, pricing of the standard forms (English Victorian banjos with convex mirrors, late sticks with ivory plates, etc.) has become confused. Wide ranges in prices for barometers of similar forms occur throughout the antiques trade. The main reason is that dealers who still depend on England as their primary source are paying premium prices, largely due to adverse exchange rates, while dealers who can find barometers in the United States are often able to pay less. Ranges in price can easily be 100 percent or more.

Very rare barometers, made prior to 1800, continue to escalate at over 25 percent per year regardless of source.

Well-informed buyers and collectors with thorough knowledge of the field can find well-priced barometers by shopping in the United States. Barometers purchased in Europe are clearly no longer the bargains they used to be.

COLLECTING INFORMATION

As in any specialist field, the most informed buyer of barometers gets the best and purest examples for his or her collection. Because of the fragile nature of barometers and their operating mechanisms, restoration is a very large presence and one that can have a major effect on value if overdone or improperly done. Additionally, replacement parts, aside from the often-replaced glass mercury tube itself, are rife in barometers. Condition and degree of replacement and restoration aside, the most desirable era in the development of the barometer has to be the late-17th and early- to mid-18th centuries, from about 1680 to about 1770. This is the period of the "name" makers in England: Quare, Tompion, Patrick, Whitehurst, Orme, Martin, Ramsden, and so on. All of these men contributed in some way to the field of barometers, unlike later makers, who just turned out pedestrian examples like cookies from a cutter. The early clientele was wealthy, and the makers were eager to please with fine cabinetry and metalwork.

Beginning in the last quarter of the 18th century, England saw a great influx of immigrants from all over Europe, and the instrument makers of Italian origin began to produce mercury barometers in England in great variety and quantity, marked with their own names. Although the "stick" form, in which the atmospheric pressure reading is taken directly from the top of the exposed tube, continued to be produced, the dial or "banjo" form saw its first popularity and soon outnumbered the sticks. Barometers intended for use at sea began to appear in quantity in the last days of George III's reign and by the 1820s were being made for both the Royal Navy and merchants. Many marine barometers are marked with Liverpool origins, where the major ships' outfitters practiced. With the advent of the Victorian period, about 1840, barometers began to be made with engraved ivory register plates. The final significant development in English barometers, then, at around 1870, has to be the glorious "Admiral Fitzroy" type, produced with paper plates bearing the copious advice of England's first meteorologist (but never made by Fitzroy himself).

American barometers were first produced in large numbers after about 1850. Most are of stick form and tend to be machine-made, similar to the mantel and shelf clocks of the era. These can often be found for a few hundred dollars. Restoration costs, however, frequently exceed purchase prices due to economies in the original production, such as grain painting, thin veneers, machine-made moldings, and crude assembly methods.

French barometers of any period are rarely seen in the United States. The French produced very decorative dial barometers from the mid-18th century onward, but the fragile construction of the elaborately carved, often gilded or painted soft-wood cases can push restoration costs to astronomical levels. French stick barometers, while more robustly made, are found in very small numbers. French barometers that have been recently imported by a dealer (probably restored in France or England) are costly but usually in the best overall condition.

FAKES ALERT

"Faking" in barometers can take many forms, but the practice of outright manufacturing of "antique" barometers is largely limited to early and highly desirable forms. Since the wood case is the dominant element of any barometer, a good working knowledge of furniture construction, coupled with some awareness of common faking methods—such as overall staining to simulate age—will usually reveal bogus goods. A barometer is, after all, small enough to hold in two hands and examine closely.

Outright faking of barometers is not so widely encountered as is the practice of misrepresenting the instruments as being much older and more original than they really are. The problems of cross-replacement of parts and wrong restoration get worse with time, as the delicate nature of the instruments causes them to pass through some "restoration" process, qualified or otherwise, every few years of their lives.

Misrepresentation has also had a boost in the last few decades as mid-20th-century reproductions, made in England and Portugal, have begun to age and pass through the salesrooms and dealers' shops. To the uninformed buyer, one pretty stick barometer looks much like another, and many modern products are being passed off as much older and more valuable than they really are. The modern reproductions of banjo barometers, with aneroid movements, don't really fool anyone, but the mahogany sticks and brass marine barometers on gimbals are doing a good job.

There are several good reference books on the subject of mercury barometers, but there are virtually no large public collections to study in this country and few places where a would-be collector can examine several examples at once.

CONDITION KEY

FINE CONDITION

There should be no replacement in cabinet work and no major deterioration in veneer or other wood decoration; no visible splits in veneers on the front of banjo cases, a sign of excessive drying of secondary wood and costly structural problems. All brass or ivory register plates should be uncorroded and unmodified. Stick barometers with silvered brass register plates should not have the plate cut upward to accommodate a longer replacement tube, a common practice. Original engraving should be crisp and easily readable on brass register plates. Old silvering on register plates is a plus but is seldom encountered; careful and sympathetic re-silvering by traditional methods is to be expected.

All moving parts should operate correctly and easily. Replaced gimbal assemblies on marine barometers are acceptable if the proper form is used and the case is not modified. There should be no missing parts (a common problem on the banjo form). Original or very old glass mercury tubes are a plus but have virtually no effect on market value; "working condition" is a dominant factor and usually means a replaced tube. When present, glass should be original or at least old. Brass fittings and furniture on the case should not be excessively corroded.

GOOD CONDITION

There should be minimal replacement/repair in cabinet work: e.g., minor molding replacements in cornices, no repairs to swan-neck cornices on banjos, minor repairs to loose or missing decorative stringing, no visible veneer patches anywhere on the case, old finishes renewed but not stripped first. Engraved brass register plates should be as in Fine Condition, above. Ivory register plates on stick barometers may be discolored but not warped or visibly broken.

Proper replacement of missing small parts is allowable—e.g., set knobs on banjo barometers, brass finials on all types, small brass fittings on post-1840 banjos; proper replacement of thermometers, never with white-stemmed medical thermometers. Glass mercury tube should be clean and in working order. Boxwood cistern on stick barometers should be in good order; a proper replacement is acceptable.

AVERAGE CONDITION

This means repaired or replaced cornices on both stick and banjo forms; replaced cistern covers on stick barometers; some corrosion in engraved brass register plates and brass fittings on cases; some veneer separations around outer edges of banjo cases, probably accompanied by loose or missing sections of stringing.

There may be proper replacement of ancillary instruments (hygrometer assembly, thermometer box and backplate, various brass bezels) on later banjo barometers; dirty and "alligatored" finishes (unless proved to be original); probably some missing elements of small fittings, such as set knobs on banjo barometers, brass finials, etc.

POOR CONDITION

This includes damaged or dried-out wood cases, the single largest cost element in restoration; broken cornices or cornices with missing moldings on any case style; damage to cases and register plates of stick barometers caused by improper replacement of tubes and cisterns; missing major components on any barometer (e.g., any engraved register plate, any major subassembly such as hygrometers or thermometer boxes on banjos).

QUALITY KEY

Note: This is not a condition statement but strictly a measure of the stylishness of the piece.

Foreword on quality: The best divisions for quality are not so much in the forms but more in the times they were produced. The earliest barometers, from about 1680 to 1770, were evolving from scientific curiosities to the household toys of the very wealthy. Much experimentation was under way by the makers, and the interest level of collectors in these instruments is high. The cases were beautifully made, and the components were the best the times could produce. Everything was either decorated in the highest fashion of the time or couched in the leading scientific thought.

From about 1775 to about 1830, the decorative element took the fore. Scientific interest dropped off, and the makers got on with the business of selling to the best market of all: the growing and affluent middle class.

The barometers made in the very early 19th century through about 1830 are still the most sought after today.

The Industrial Age saw a surge in the volume of barometers produced worldwide but with an attendant drop in quality. The instruments produced after 1840, with some exceptions, are still relatively affordable but are increasing in price at a rate of about 20 percent a year.

SUPERIOR QUALITY

In barometers, early is better, and any instrument made before 1800 should be considered "early."

Complexity in the manufacturing process denotes quality in an instrument as fundamentally simple as a barometer: e.g., decorative and/or highly figured veneers, complex stringing and/or cross-banding on cases, the use of decorative inlay work, highly decorative flourishes in engraving, unique brass castings or fittings on the case.

Decorative carving is an element that is found on early stick barometers (usually 1700 to 1760) and, conversely, on very late Victorian barometers. The forms produced between 1760 and about 1860 carried almost no carving at all, so the presence of carving in general is not a major deciding factor in the overall quality of a barometer.

Japanned or chinoiserie-decorated cases in barometers were produced from the very earliest stick-form instruments all the way through to mid-19th-century banjo forms. Japanned cases of any age are quite rare and are a major quality factor.

Any complex mechanism in a barometer is a plus factor in quality. Some examples are 18th-century stick barometers with catgut hygrometer mechanisms; 19th-century large banjo barometers with clocks integrated into their cases; mid-19th-century marine barometers with sympiesometers.

Any unusual case form in a barometer will generally be of both higher quality as a decorative piece and higher desirability to a collector. Some forms encountered are the angle or "signpost" barometer, sometimes incorporated in the outer frame of a mirror or perpetual calendar; the "bayonet tube" stick barometer, with the midsection of its tube hidden inside the front of the wood case; the inverted banjo form, with the dial at the top of the case instead of in the midsection; the very early and rare Georgian clock-form case in veneered walnut, usually by a famous maker.

The size of the dial is a great factor in determining quality in a banjo barometer. The eight-inch-diameter dial was produced in overpowering quantities from its inception in about 1785, so any variation is a good one. The ten-inch dial is more desirable, but the twelve-inch and larger dials are quite rare and often in cases of superb quality. Conversely, the very small dials have an appeal to collectors also, and examples can be found in six-, five-, five-and-one-half-, and even four-inch diameters. These small-dial banjo barometers were usually made between 1825 and about 1855.

VERY GOOD QUALITY

The conventional forms of barometers made between about 1775 and 1830, such as simple mahogany sticks and nicely inlaid eight-inch banjos, fill the middle ground between the rare early instruments and the mass-produced Victorians. As such, they are the overwhelming choice of those furnishing with the Georgian look and period. The cases are strong and well made, the brass register plates are nicely engraved, and the decorative value is high. So also is the price. Some forms, such as the Regency period sticks with glazed doors over the register plates, may command higher selling prices than plain mahogany examples by noted makers from half a century earlier.

During this period some very fine ten-inch-dial banjo barometers were made by prominent makers, and they are of higher decorative value than their eight-inch counterparts. A very few twelve-inch-dial banjos were also made and are of good quality.

The first marine barometers to be produced in quantity began to appear about 1810. They are very slim sticks, hanging from simple brass gimbals, and they have mahogany cases with turned-wood cistern covers. Their register plates are very small and are protected by a door that closes, with a thermometer mounted on its inner side. In about 1825 the cistern cover was made of brass, and around 1830 the closing screw for the cistern went inside, out of sight. Around 1835 or 1840 ivory register plates began to be used, and the top of the barometer changed to a simple dome with glass over the register plates.

GOOD QUALITY

Good quality after 1840 is a function of separating the most mass-produced barometers from the more unusual examples. The names shown on the register plates are rarely makers but more usually the sellers, so makers' names are of no impact on the value or quality of the product.

The good-quality Victorian barometers are usually veneered with highly figured wood, sometimes with inlays of brass or mother-of-pearl, and the stick barometers commonly have engraved ivory register plates. Cases of all forms are veneered in rosewood, mahogany, sometimes oak, and rarely walnut. Banjo barometers usually have swan-neck cornices, later evolving (about 1860) to the pointed ''tulip'' top. The decorative stringing around the edges of the banjo cases disappears by about 1865, and in about 1880 the white porcelain dial with silkscreened red and black lettering appears. About 1860 stick barometers became very slim, with simple flat faces and exposed ivory register plates. In the closing years of the century the ivory is replaced with "ivorine," a synthetic substitute.

The bright spot at the end of the era is the Admiral Fitzroy barometer, named after the captain of Darwin's ship, *Beagle*, and England's first real weatherman. Fitzroy didn't make barometers, but he did publish his forecasts of the weather in the London newspapers, and his voluminous instructions for predicting the weather by use of the mercury barometer were reproduced onto decorative paper plates that graced the fronts of Fitzroy barometers forever more. The barometers made between about 1875 and 1900 are the most desirable and often are found in elaborately carved oak or mahogany cases, complete with chemical-filled "storm bottles" and full-color plates.

AMERICAN BAROMETERS

Stick barometer   40.5″ L   Federal   1845–1865   United States
Rosewood; rectangular with floral abalone inlay; mercury pressure dial with ivory face inscribed "E. & G.W. Blunt, New York"; mercury thermometer; interesting exposed "works."
Superior Quality/Fine Condition $2640 (A)   **$2000–$3500**

Stick barometer   38″ H × 2.5″ W × 2″ D   Victorian   1865–1885   United States
Pine-cased with paper register plate behind glass and thermometer with silvered brass plate, signed H. A. Simmons, Fulton, NY; grain-painted case with original finish, replaced tube, original valve.
Good Quality/Fine Condition $1300 (D)   **$700–$1300**

ENGLISH BAROMETERS

Banjo barometer   40″ H × 10″ W × 2″ D   Regency   1810–1815   England
Very clean and original; shell-inlaid mahogany; 8″ dial, signed "John Pochaine, Newcastle"; mellow brown color, good quality engraving on register plates; finish repolished, plates resilvered, tube replaced.
Very Good Quality/Fine Condition $2350 (D)   **$1600–$2400**

Banjo barometer   45″ H × 12″ W × 3″ D   Victorian   1840–1845   England
Original; mahogany; 10″ dial, by Cetti of Reading; superb mahogany veneers with ebonized trim, fine-quality engraving on backplates; old finish, plates resilvered, tube replaced.
Superior Quality/Fine Condition $2600 (D)   **$1800–$3000**

Banjo barometer   39″ H × 10″ W × 2.5″ D   Victorian   1855–1860   England
Very original and clean; rosewood, with 8″ dial, no maker's name shown; high-quality brass fittings on case, overall very good color; finish repolished, register plates resilvered, tube replaced. *(See photo 10)*
Very Good Quality/Fine Condition $1550 (D)   **$750–$1500**

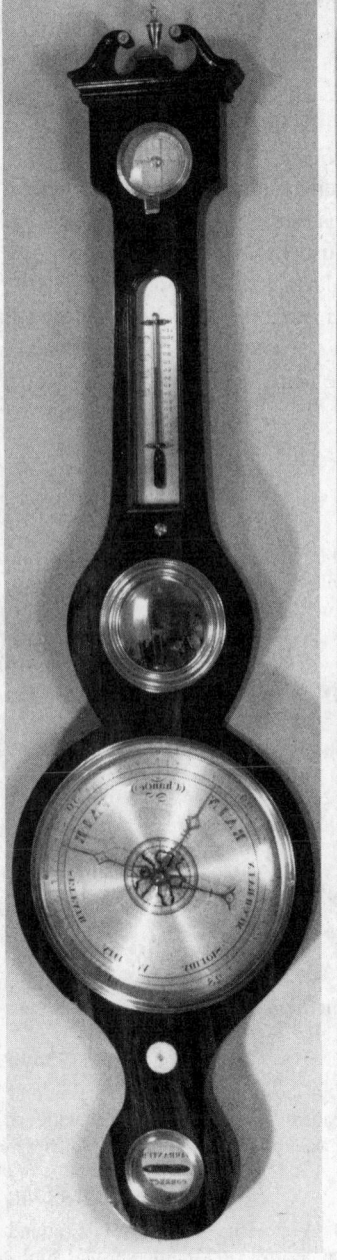
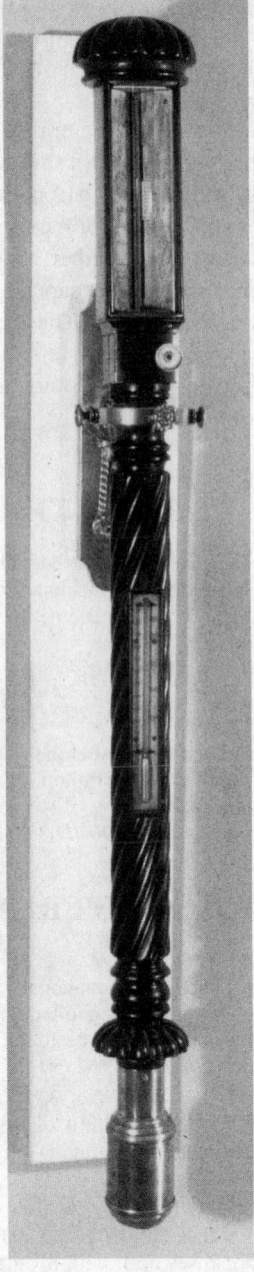
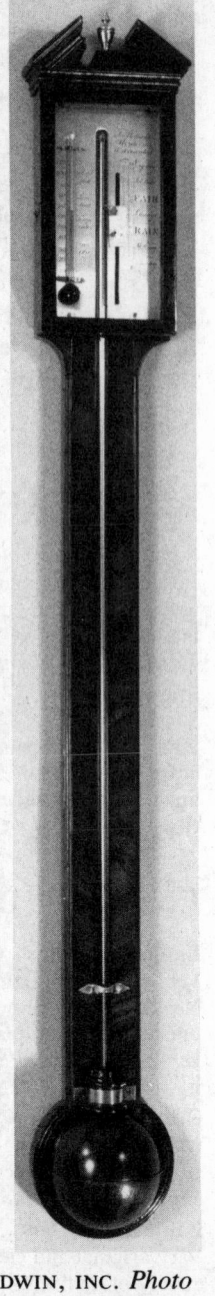

Photo 10 (left). Banjo barometer. CREDIT: CHARLES EDWIN, INC. *Photo 11 (center). Marine barometer.* CREDIT: PRIVATE COLLECTION. *Photo 12 (right). Stick barometer.* CREDIT: CHARLES EDWIN, INC. *(See pp. 57, 59)*

Fitzroy barometer 49″ H × 10.5″ W × 3.5″ D Victorian 1885–1900 England
Spectacular, carved oak, in superb original condition, with very good paper backplates, storm bottles, and thermometer; no significant replacements.
Superior Quality/Fine Condition $2450 (D) **$1750–$2450**

Fitzroy barometer 35.5″ H × 6.5″ W × 2.5″ D Victorian 1885–1900 England
Unusually small, mahogany-cased, unsigned; profusely worded paper backplate with Fitzroy's rules for predicting weather; all original, tube cleaned and refilled.
Very Good Quality/Fine Condition $1500 (D) **$900–$1500**

Marine barometer 38″ H × 2.5″ W × 2.5″ D George III 1815–1820 England
Early English, mahogany with ebonized boxwood cistern, by Thomas Blunt, London; very clean and original example by noted maker; tube replaced, scales resilvered, gimbal replaced.
Superior Quality/Fine Condition $6500 (D) **$4500–$7500**

Marine barometer 36.5″ H × 3″ W × 3″ D Victorian 1830–1845 England
Very clean and original, solid rosewood with ivory scales, by S. A. Cail, Newcastle; fine old gimbal, possibly original; tube and cistern replaced.
Very Good Quality/Fine Condition $5500 (D) **$4500–$6000**

Marine barometer 40″ H × 4.5″ W × 4.5″ D Victorian 1850–1860 England
Mahogany in a rope-twist-carved case with ivory scales, by J. Foster, Liverpool; fine original condition and old finish; tube and cistern replaced, modern custom wall mount. *(See photo 11)*
Superior Quality/Fine Condition $6000 (D) **$4500–$6500**

Stick barometer 36″ H × 6″ W × 3.5″ Dia. George II 1740–1750 England
Very original and fine, walnut-veneered, with engraved, silvered register plates by James Mann, London; outstanding for its fine state of preservation and finish.
Superior Quality/Fine Condition $10,000 (D) **$6000–$12,000**

Stick barometer 40″ H × 4.5″ W × 2″ D George III 1750–1780 Scotland
Mahogany with winter and summer indications on nicely engraved silvered backplate, by MacFarlane, Perth; uniquely Scottish form of stick, probably originated by Knie of Edinburgh; plate resilvered; tube replaced.
Superior Quality/Fine Condition $3600 (D) **$2750–$4000**

Stick barometer 38″ H × 5″ W × 3″ D Regency 1830 Scotland
Mahogany, with glazed door over silvered scales, by John Stopani, Aberdeen; very clean condition; replaced cistern cover, tube, thermometer. *(See photo 12)*
Very Good Quality/Fine Condition $2800 (D) **$2000–$3000**

FRENCH BAROMETERS

Dial barometer 41″ H × 24″ W × 2″ D Louis XVI 1780–1800 France
In 6-sided, carved, gilded case with paper scale over wood plate; thermometer in carved crest at top, graduated in old French inches; case in very good condition, mercury tube replaced.
Superior Quality/Fine Condition $5500 (D) **$3000–$6500**

The CONDITION KEY measures the degree of repair-restoration.

Poor Condition: Missing parts, breaks, and/or very bad restoration (possibly collectible because of some other merit).

Average Condition: Small parts may be missing, and cleaning may be necessary (the condition in which most objects are found).

Good Condition: No parts missing, no major cleaning needed—ready to use or display.

Fine Condition: Near original condition or restored to near original condition.

Stick barometer   42″ H × 5.5″ W × 3″ D   Regency   1810–1820   France
Mahogany-veneered with silvered brass backplates, 2 thermometers with Reaumur scales, a glass cistern, ormulu mounts; signed Ferari Opticien, Lille; tube and thermometers replaced, finish repolished, scales resilvered.
Superior Quality/Fine Condition *$4250 (D)*   **$3500–$4500**

BIBLIOGRAPHY

Banfield, Edwin. *Barometers: Stick or Cistern Tube*. Trowbridge, Wiltshire, England: Baros Books, 1985.

———. *Barometers: Wheel or Banjo*. Trowbridge, Wiltshire, England: Baros Books, 1985.

Bolle, Bert. *Barometers*. Suffolk, England: Antique Collectors' Club, 1984.

Goodison, Nicholas. *English Barometers 1680–1860*. Suffolk, England: Nicholas Goodison, 1977.

Baskets

(See also American Indian Art)

SURVEY OF THE FIELD

The art of basketry is indeed a reflection of America's cultural past. Long before this nation's first colonization, the American Indian had achieved artistic excellence as a basket weaver. Indian baskets are said to be the world's finest. Each basket was woven for a specific purpose and with the utmost care. These baskets were not only used to hold food and water and for ceremonial purposes, but some were also used for cooking. The work is unique because only materials from nature—pine needles, straw, leaves, willow, porcupine quills, vines, reeds, and grass—were used. Dyes were made from bark, roots, or berries. Their distinctive designs have made them sought after by most basket enthusiasts.

TYPES

There are several types of basket construction. Wickerwork, the most common and widely used technique, is nothing more than an over-and-under pattern. Twining is similar except that two strands are twisted as they are woven over and under, producing a finer weave. Plaiting gives a checkerboard effect and can be either a tight weave or left with some open spaces. Twillwork is much the same except that a diagonal effect is achieved by changing the number of strands over which the weaver passes. Coiling is the most desirable weave for the collector. This technique has been carefully refined since its conception around 7000 B.C. Fibers are wrapped around and stitched together to form the basket's shape. Most of these pieces were used either for ceremonial purposes or for holding liquids, since the containers made in this fashion were tightly woven and leakproof.

TRENDS IN BASKET COLLECTING

Baskets are available in a wide range of prices and types. Because of their decorative appeal they are now avidly sought by collectors. They may be collected by general category, such as Indian, Appalachian, Nantucket, etc., or simply acquired in a wide variety of types and styles.

CARE OF BASKETS

Baskets are easy to care for, but a few basic rules must be followed.

1. Never wash an Indian basket. Dust it gently, using a very soft sable artist's brush.

2. Do not subject Indian baskets to the sun as it will fade the patterns.

3. Do not wash any basket made of pine needles, straw, grass, or leaves.

4. Willow, oak, hickory, and rattan baskets may be washed in a mild solution of Murphy's Oil Soap and dried in a sunny location.

QUALITY AND CONDITION KEYS

Please refer to the chapter "Using This Guide" to determine the Quality and Condition Keys for this section.

> Values for Nantucket baskets are driven upward by three factors: they are an interesting form of Americana, they are exquisitely woven, and a large number of people with more money than sense have invaded the island—and they all want an "old" Nantucket basket to establish their legitimacy on the island.—*DL*

Nantucket   8″ H × 14.5″ W × 7.5″ D   United States
Oval, with a turned wood base and bentwood handle; noticeable reed damage on sides.
Good Quality/Average Condition $990 (A)   **$900–$1500**

Nantucket   6.5″ H × 12.5″ Dia.   United States
Oval swing-handle basket by Jose Formosa Reyes; signed on bottom; noticeable reed repairs and new rim. *(See photo 13, upper right)*
Superior Quality/Average Condition $1550 (A)   **$1500–$3000**

> The work of Reyes is the most desired of all Nantucket-signed work.—*DL*

Nantucket   6.75″ H × 9″ Dia.   1865–1885   United States
Swing-handle basket of rattan staves into a hardwood base having 2 deep rings and 4 scribe lines; carved oak handle attached to an oak ear tapering into base; handle carved "C. Morslander."
Superior Quality/Fine Condition $1975 (A)   **$1200–$2400**

Nantucket   3.5″ H   1865–1885   United States
Round; swing handle; nice patina; possibly by Sandsbury; slight reed damage. *(See photo 13, upper left)*
Superior Quality/Good Condition $600 (A)   **$500–$900**

Nantucket   3.5″ H × 9″ Dia.   1865–1885   United States
Round; double-handle sewing basket; early basket with nice patina; turned bottom plate; double heart handles in excellent condition. *(See photo 13, upper right center)*
Superior Quality/Fine Condition $775 (A)   **$600–$1000**

Photo 13. Nantucket baskets. CREDIT: RAFAEL OSONA *(See p. 62 and below)*

Nantucket 9″ H × 17.5″ Dia. 1885–1900 United States
Double-handle bushel basket; woven rattan; repairs and cracked bottom plate.
(See photo 13, bottom left)
Very Good Quality/Average Condition $2090 (A) **$1500–$2500**

Nantucket 4.5″ H × 9.5″ Dia. 1900–1910 United States
Shallow swing handle; circular basket of oak staves into a maple base with 3
scribe lines; shaped handle attached to brass ears; single wrap rim; dark patina;
some damage.
Very Good Quality/Good Condition $775 (A) **$700–$1200**

Nantucket 7.75″ H × 12″ Dia. 1900–1910 United States
Shaped swing handle, incised turned base bearing printed paper label "Lightship
basket made by William D. Appleton, Nantucket, Mass."
Very Good Quality/Fine Condition $1700 (A) **$1500–$2200**

Nantucket 7″ H × 9.5″ W 1975 United States
Pocketbook basket with carved-bone whale on lid, plaque; ivory buttons on han-
dle pins and ivory peg fastener; maker's name incised at base.
Good Quality/Fine Condition $450 (A) **$400–$600**

Splint 5.5″ H × 9″ Dia. 1865–1885 United States
Painted splint basket of circular, straight-sided form with bound rim and foot;
carved wooden handles; exterior painted red (breaks); Northeast.
Good Quality/Average Condition $300 (A) **$200–$325**

Splint   15.5″ H × 17.25″ Dia.   Indian   1865–1885   United States
Painted covered splint basket, with domed cover above bulbous body, decorated
with red stripes, Northeast.
Good Quality/Fine Condition $100 (A)   **$100–$175**

Splint   9.5″ H × 7″ W   1885–1900   United States
Painted, splint double-melon basket; with a single splint handle; painted green
(damaged); Northeast.
Very Good Quality/Average Condition $350 (A)   **$225–$400**

Splint   7″ H × 12″ W   Indian   1885–1900   United States
Painted and decorated 2-handled North American Indian basket; swabbed in
yellow, blue, and salmon.
Good Quality/Fine Condition $650 (A)   **$450–$650**

Wall basket   30″ H   Indian   1865–1885   United States
Three-pocket wall basket; wooden hanging loop above 4 graduated pockets,
traces of red stain (minor breaks); Northeast.
Very Good Quality/Good Condition $2100 (A)   **$1500–$2400**

BIBLIOGRAPHY

Ketchum, William. *American Basketry and Wooden Ware*. New York:
    Macmillan, 1974.

Boxes

(See also Arts and Crafts Movement, Silver)

Boxes have been used "forever" to store things. From the Egyptian period we have surviving boxes of the most extraordinary quality—veneered and inlaid—from several thousand years B.C. Jeweled boxes, boxes of precious metals, strong boxes, and ordinary containers were first made for use and later collected. Boxes are one of the most important areas of collecting and decorating.

Boxes are generally available in quantity, at affordable prices, from the 18th, 19th, and early 20th centuries. Except for solid-gold snuff boxes, the vast range of metal, porcelain, and wood boxes are affordable and collectible within a variety of budgets.

FAKES ALERT

Except for rare silver and gold items or Sèvres and other rare porcelain boxes, fakery is generally not a problem. Repairs and replacement of parts is a problem, and you must carefully inspect all parts. Boxes with repairs or restorations (replaced parts) are certainly collectible, but the price should be commensurate with condition and originality.

CONDITION KEY

Fine: fine finish or patina as appropriate; no rubbing of gilding or decoration on porcelain objects; minor repairs of the highest quality.

Good: nice finish or patina, perhaps a little overcleaned; minor repairs can be spotted by close inspection.

Average: finish or patina acceptable; repairs needed or old repairs are too obvious.

Poor: finish poor or patina ruined; missing parts; breaks; poor-quality old repairs.

Originality is *not* considered in condition statement, but is *specified* in each individual description.

QUALITY KEY

Good: a nice piece worthy of collecting but having no distinguishing characteristics.

Very good: an example that reflects several of the most desired characteristics of the type.

Superior: a superlative example that has nearly all of the desired characteristics of the type.

This is not a condition statement but strictly a measure of the stylishness of the piece.

Apothecary chest   16″ H × 12″ L   Victorian   1845–1865   England
Mahogany; fully fitted, hinged top revealing compartments; hinged front revealing drawers and compartments for bottles; brass carrying handles. *(See photo 14)*
Superior Quality/Fine Condition $4800 (D)   **$3500–$5000**

Book box   4″ H × 8″ W × 10″ D   1865–1885   England
Spine of book pulls out to reveal interior; geometric parquetry design all over.
Very Good Quality/Good Condition $1200 (D)   **$800–$1300**

Chest   7.5″ H × 12″ L   Queen Anne   1700–1750   England
Walnut oyster veneer and brass-bound rectangular chest with fleur-de-lys scroll-cut mounts; lift top and fall front exposing compartment and 2 drawers; minor damage.
Superior Quality/Good Condition $1200 (A)   **$1000–$1800**

Chest   10.5″ H × 18.5″ L   Queen Anne   1700–1750   England
Walnut oyster veneer, brass-bound rectangular chest with scroll-cut brass mounts; interior fitted with baize trays.
Superior Quality/Fine Condition $2000 (A)   **$1200–$2400**

Cribbage box   3.5″ H × 13″ W × 5″ D   Victorian   1865–1885   England
Mahogany with rosewood and exotic wood inlaid top; fitted interior.
Good Quality/Good Condition $165 (D)   **$150–$250**

Decanter box   10.5″ H × 8.5″ W × 11″ D   Georgian   1780–1800   England
Mahogany decanter box with marquetry inlaid cartouche, satinwood banded and inlaid exterior and lid interior; brass feet; no decanters.
Superior Quality/Good Condition $1850 (D)   **$1750–$2500**

Decanter box   11.5″ H × 9″ W × 5″ D   1850–1865   England
Walnut box with original faceted decanters (2); brass carrying handle; large cut-glass decanters with minor chips.
Very Good Quality/Good Condition $1450 (D)   **$1200–$1800**

Desk, writing   11″ H × 23″ W × 11.75″ D   Campaign   1800–1830   England
Brass-bound mahogany field writing desk with printing press, originally invented by James Watt; press for duplicating charts, maps, and battle plans.
Superior Quality/Fine Condition $2000 (D)   **$1500–$2500**

Games box   2″ H × 20″ W × 20″ D   Faux books   1865–1885   England
Pair of "History of England" dark green leather volumes; opens to checkerboard or backgammon board; ornately tooled; apparently original faux-tortoise papier-mâché dice cups, original pieces; wear to gilding.
Superior Quality/Good Condition $575 (D)   **$450–$675**

Games box   8″ H × 13″ L × 6.5″ D   Victorian   1865–1885   United States
Parquetry-inlaid; a "sailor's return" piece. *(See photo 15)*
Very Good Quality/Good Condition $625 (D)   **$550–$650**

Gun box   27.5″ H × 33″ W × 9″ D   Georgian style   1845–1865   England
Mahogany with brass fittings on custom-made stand; central inset ring handle.
Very Good Quality/Fine Condition $1450 (D)   **$1200–$2200**

Humidor   6″ H × 11.5″ W × 9.5″ D   Victorian   1850–1865   England
Bird's-eye maple humidor; refitted interior.
Good Quality/Good Condition $675 (D)   **$600–$900**

Jewelry casket   5″ H × 13″ W × 10″ D   Victorian   1845–1865   England
Gentleman's jewelry casket with diamond-shaped parquetry top within line inlay
and crossbanding; yewwood veneered interior.
Good Quality/Good Condition $675 (D)   **$500–$750**

Knife box   14″ H   George III   1780–1800   England
Serpentine front and sloping lid, cover inlaid with small oval satinwood stylized
conch shell, checkered inlay, lozenge keyhole, fitted interior; restorations.
Superior Quality/Average Condition $715 (A)   **$700–$1500**

Knife box   15″ H × 9.5″ W × 11″ D   George III   1800–1830   England
Mahogany with serpentine case and slanting, hinged lid with feather and star
satinwood inlay, opening to refitted interior; raised on ogee bracket feet; some
veneer damage and losses.
Very Good Quality/Average Condition $165 (A)   **$375–$675**

> Note the description: a *refitted* interior! With original openings for cutlery,
> the price range would be $900–$1500.—*DL*

Knife boxes   13.5″ H × 9″ W × 9″ D   George III   1800–1830   England
Pair; mahogany with satinwood and olivewood inlaid oval pattern medallion on
slanted, hinged lid; opens to fitted interior; inside lid inlaid with star; serpentine-
fronted case, brass side handles.
Very Good Quality/Fine Condition $3300 (A)   **$3500–$5500**

> *Vast* numbers of fakes are arriving from England. Smell the box for fresh
> lacquer! Look for wear and repair. Look for artificial finish blemishes.
> —*DL*

Lap desk   15.75″ L   Victorian   1865–1885   England
Rosewood; rectangular form with corners inset with brass banding, lid centered
by brass escutcheon, opening to green tooled-leather writing surface and various
compartments.
Good Quality/Good Condition $300 (A)   **$250–$400**

Letter box   7.36″ H × 9.25″ W × 6.25″ D   George IV   1800–
1830   England
Rosewood with gilt-bronze finial; rectangular form with open turned-spindle
sides, button feet, removable interior partition; some veneer cracks; "in" and
"out" sides.
Superior Quality/Fine Condition $1200 (A)   **$900–$1500**

Naval architect's box   8″ H × 38″ W × 11″ D   Victorian   1845–
1865   England
Mahogany; fully fitted interior containing original drafting instruments and detailed records of commissions.
Very Good Quality/Fine Condition $1700 (D)   **$1500–$2000**

Photo 14.
Apothecary
chest. CREDIT:
WHITEHALL
AT THE
VILLA,
CHAPEL HILL,
NC *(See*
p. 66)

Photo 15. Games box. CREDIT:
WHITEHALL AT THE VILLA, CHAPEL
HILL, NC *(See p. 67)*

Photo 16. Stationery box. CREDIT:
WESCHLER'S, WASHINGTON, DC
(See p. 69)

Sewing box 12″ L George III 1800–1830 England
Satinwood and walnut inlaid; almond-shaped hinged lid inlaid with alternating
bands of satinwood within cross-banded borders; conforming base with divided
interior.
Superior Quality/Fine Condition $935 (A) **$800–$1200**

Sewing box 7.5″ H × 12″ W × 12″ D 1845–1865 England
Amboyna and rosewood parquetry; satinwood interior fitted for sewing notions;
splendid interior decoration.
Very Good Quality/Good Condition $1250 (D) **$850–$1250**

Sewing box 3.5″ H × 8.5″ W × 5″ D Victorian 1865–1885 England
Burl and mahogany with shield-shaped mother-of-pearl insets.
Good Quality/Good Condition $115 (D) **$100–$200**

Snuff box 3.5″ H × 1.5″ Dia. Victorian 1865–1885 England
Barrel shaped, with ivory "taps."
Good Quality/Good Condition $135 (D) **$100–$200**

Stationery box 11.5″ H × 12.25″ W × 9.5″ D Victorian 1865–
1885 England
Mahogany tambour box with sloping case and tambour door, opening to fitted
interior, above a long drawer with brass flush handle. *(See photo 16)*
Good Quality/Fine Condition $475 (A) **$375–$600**

Tea box 7″ H × 11.5″ W × 6.5″ D George III 1780–1800 England
Traveling tea box, probably for military use; rich mahogany with campaign hard-
ware.
Very Good Quality/Good Condition $850 (D) **$800–$1100**

Tea caddy 9.5″ W 1800–1830 Anglo-Indian
Silver-mounted; ivory and rosewood; hinged rectangular top banded with foliate-
engraved ivory, enclosing a fitted interior on ball-and-claw foot.
Superior Quality/Good Condition $1430 (A) **$1200–$1800**

Tea caddy 6.25″ H × 11″ L Lacquer 1830–1845 China
Chinese export; rectangular shape with canted corner; gilt-decorated panels of
Chinese scenes; fitted with 2 pewter canisters; 4 giltwood dragon's-claw feet;
cracks and chips.
Very Good Quality/Average Condition $550 (A) **$500–$750**

Tea caddy 6″ H Neoclassical 1800–1830 Contintental
Urn-form tea caddy.
Very Good Quality/Fine Condition $725 (A) **$600–$900**

Tea caddy George III 1750–1780 England
Ivory and tortoise shell; inlaid with silver and mother-of-pearl; perfect Adam
period piece.
Superior Quality/Fine Condition $1650 (A) **$1800–$3500**

Tea caddy 6″ H 1780–1800 England
Fruitwood, pear-shaped; hinge needs resetting to eliminate "gaping smile."
Superior Quality/Good Condition $2200 (A) **$2500–$4500**

> There seems to be no end to the price escalation of fruit-shaped caddies.
> Beware of fakes now appearing.—*DL*

Tea caddy 6.75″ H × 10.5″ W George III 1780–1800 England
Inlaid satinwood; slightly domed lid with silvered handle; opens to pair of lidded
tin containers; on ogee bracket feet.
Superior Quality/Good Condition $1650 (A) **$1200–$1800**

Tea caddy 9″ W George III 1780–1800 England
Satinwood and mahogany; hinged lid centered by an oval enclosing 2 lidded canisters.
Very Good Quality/Good Condition $2750 (A)   **$1500–$2400**

Tea caddy 5.25″ H George III 1780–1800 England
Paper-roll decorated inlaid fruitwood; hexagonal body with hinged lid and brass handle; conforming case with paneled sides; decorated all over with gold paper in floral designs; losses.
Very Good Quality/Good Condition $715 (A)   **$650–$1200**

Tea caddy 6″ H George III 1800–1830 England
Fruitwood, pear-form; stem lacking, lock plate missing.
Good Quality/Poor Condition $715 (A)   **$1250–$2500**

Tea caddy 5.5″ H George III 1800–1830 England
Fruitwood, apple-form; of typical form and fitted with a stem; color mottled.
Very Good Quality/Good Condition $1650 (A)   **$1500–$2500**

Tea caddy 6″ H George III 1800–1830 England
Fruitwood, pear-form; restored (patch in front near lock).
Very Good Quality/Good Condition $1430 (A)   **$1500–$2500**

Tea caddy 9.25″ H Georgian 1800–1830 England
Mahogany with satinwood and ebony inlay; 3 lidded compartments and brass ball feet.
Good Quality/Good Condition $385 (A)   **$350–$500**

Tea caddy 6″ H Georgian 1800–1830 England
Fruitwood, pear-form.
Superior Quality/Fine Condition $1550 (A)   **$1500–$2500**

Tea caddy 6″ H Georgian 1800–1830 England
Fruitwood, pear-form.
Superior Quality/Fine Condition $1650 (A)   **$1500–$2500**

Tea caddy 7.5″ H × 11.75″ W × 6.5″ Late Georgian 1800–1830 England
Mahogany; fully fitted; exceptional carving.
Superior Quality/Fine Condition $1000 (D)   **$1000–$1500**

Tea caddy 6.5″ H × 9.5″ W × 7″ D Regency 1800–1830 England
Mahogany; kingwood interior; cut-glass bowl inside.
Good Quality/Good Condition $400 (D)   **$400–$700**

Tea caddy 5.5″ H × 7″ W Regency 1800–1830 England
Ivory-inlaid tortoise shell, with oxbow-fronted hinged lid with stepped center section opening to 2 covered wells; conforming body with shaped lower rim; fruitwood bun feet.
Very Good Quality/Fine Condition $1540 (A)   **$1250–$2200**

Tea caddy Regency style 1825–1835 England
Tortoise shell with mother-of-pearl marquetry; Oriental shape on ivory ball feet.
Superior Quality/Good Condition $2650 (A)   **$1850–$3000**

Tea caddy 7.5″ H × 11.5″ W × 6″ D 1830–1845 England
Canted top, mahogany with satinwood and ebony inlay; missing bowl.
Good Quality/Good Condition $675 (D)   **$600–$800**

Tea caddy 11″ L Regency 1830–1845 England
Rosewood; coffer form with shaped top and bun feet.
Very Good Quality/Good Condition $360 (A)   **$350–$500**

Tea caddy   9.5″ H × 6.25″ Dia.   William IV   1830–1845   England
Rosewood; octagonal stepped lid with knopped finial opening to a well; underside of top inlaid with rosewood and burl elm; octagonal body raised on stepped plinth.
Superior Quality/Fine Condition $660 (A)   **$600–$1200**

Tea caddy   3.75″ H × 6.5″ W   Victorian   1865–1885   England
Decorated with penwork; rectangular lid reserved with an abbey; conforming body and lid decorated with stylized oak leaves.
Very Good Quality/Fine Condition $550 (A)   **$400–$650**

Tea caddy   5.5″ H × 8″ W × 5″ D   George III style   1885–1900   England
Walnut, tulipwood, mahogany, and fruitwood inlaid; stepped lid with brass handle; top and sides inlaid with paterae within crossbanded borders; interior altered.
Superior Quality/Average Condition $1650 (A)   **$1000–$1800**

Tortoiseshell box   12″ L   Asprey   1885–1900   England
Tortoise shell and ivory; rectangular form, slightly domed lid edged with ivory-molded borders; applied ivory key plate; labeled "Asprey, London."
Very Good Quality/Fine Condition $1100 (A)   **$900–$1200**

Candy Containers

Advisor: **CAMILLE T. ZAGAROLI**

Camille T. Zagaroli lives with her husband, Robert, and their three cats in Yardley, Pennsylvania. She is a dealer and appraiser of dolls and a passionate collector in several other areas, such as candy containers. Mrs. Zagaroli can be reached at (215) 493-8734.

Just imagine the excitement of a young child upon coming downstairs on Christmas morning and finding a Santa Claus or Belsnickel dressed in fur and finery, wearing a full beard, and best of all, each filled with candies and sweets. In times past, this same scene was repeated at each holiday throughout the year, with Easter sharing equal importance with Christmas. Easter morning brought the thrill of furry bunnies, chickens, ducks, lambs, and goats.

These colorful toys originated in Germany in the second half of the 19th century, and manufacture continued into the early 20th century. They were usually made of papier-mâché and pressed into many different forms. Some were gaily painted, while others were covered with fur, silks, velvets, and other fabrics. You will find various animals and figures pulling sleighs or wagons, holding skates, standing on drums or tree stumps—each opening to a surprise of goodies.

The child in all of us, remembering the excitement and mystery of various holidays past, has made these containers highly desirable and an important collectible in the market today. Values are constantly soaring to such heights that it makes us marvel at the original prices of 2 cents to 50 cents each. Prices now range from under $100 to well above $1000, depending on rarity, age, and condition.

Many collectors will search for just one type of container or holiday. Christmas is considered the most popular season, and Easter comes in a close second.

There are new and reproduced examples on the market at present, but they are easily identified by their shiny appearance and lack of wear. Candy containers are usually found at doll and toy shows, shops specializing in dolls and toys, and occasionally in antiques auctions featuring dolls and toys.

Bear 5.5″ H Bisque c. 1910 Germany
Rare Dressel and Kister porcelain candy container made for Tobler chocolates in Switzerland; bear is sitting on a tree stump and holding a ball; incised with mark and 2363.
Superior Quality/Fine Condition $400 (D)   **$375–$425**

Bird on a stump 5″ H c. 1910 Germany
Wood, composition, and chalk; polychrome.
Good Quality/Average Condition $28 (A)   **$25–$75**

Dog 5.5″ H Bisque c. 1910 Germany
Rare all-porcelain dog thought to have been made by Dressel and Kister; dog's face has gently painted eyes, nose, whiskers, open mouth with tongue and teeth; all white.
Superior Quality/Fine Condition $400 (D)   **$375–$450**

Dog 8″ H × 8″ W Rabbit fur c. 1920 Germany
Standing dog covered in rabbit fur; amber glass eyes; head comes off to reveal papier-mâché candy container inside; fur covers entire body, including long tail. *(See photo 17)*
Superior Quality/Fine Condition $550 (D)   **$400–$600**

Dutch maiden 8″ H Bisque and papier-mâché c. 1900 Germany
Incised "GH" on back of bisque head; on bottom marked "D.R.G.M. 408292"; original brown mohair wig done in 2 long braids; bisque head and glass eyes; open mouth; wooden legs and shoes on bottom of container.
Superior Quality/Fine Condition $500 (D)   **$450–$600**

Easter egg 7.5″ H × 6″ W Papier-mâché c. 1920 Germany
Half doll on top of egg is painted in pastel colors; hat with yellow and orange feather and a green bow; orange bow on bosom; papier-mâché egg is covered with faded green silk.
Good Quality/Average Condition $95 (D)   **$85–$125**

Photo 17 (left). Dog candy container.
CREDIT: ALDA LEAKE HORNER *(See above)*

Photo 18 (right). Rabbit candy container.
CREDIT: ALDA LEAKE HORNER *(See p. 74)*

Puppy 2.5″ H c. 1910 Germany
Papier-mâché with white paint, black muzzle and glass eyes; minor edge damage.
Good Quality/Average Condition *$35 (A)* **$30–$50**

Rabbit 8″ H c. 1920 Germany
Brown and white, glass-eyed rabbit made of papier-mâché; suit is beige cotton flannel with a boa around the neck; black leather shoes are original.
Very Good Quality/Fine Condition *$400 (D)* **$350–$500**

Rabbit 12″ Fur c. 1920 Germany
Rabbit fur covers papier-mâché body and head; head comes off to reveal candy container; pink glass eyes, intaglio nose and mouth; eating a carrot; squeaker in his back is still working. *(See photo 18)*
Superior Quality/Fine Condition *$500 (D)* **$400–$600**

Rabbit 7.5″ H Papier-mâché c. 1926 Germany
Glass-eyed, seated rabbit; head comes off to reveal candy container; tips of ears are missing.
Very Good Quality/Average Condition *$45 (D)* **$35–$45**

BIBLIOGRAPHY

Albertson, Karla Klein. "Christmas Collections, Old and New." *Early American Life*, December 1990, p. 27.
This article features the Christmas season but has useful material in general, giving sources and Christmas Collectors' organizations.

Schiffer, Margaret. *Holidays: Toys and Decorations*. Exton, PA: Schiffer Publishing, 1985. Paper.
This colorful book shows examples from all of the major holidays, beginning with New Year's Day through to Christmas Day.

AUCTION HOUSES

The following auction houses have several sales a year that include candy containers. Write to receive information and catalogs.

Richard Opfer Auctioneering, Inc.
1919 Greenspring Drive
Timonium, MD 21093
(301) 252-5035

Thieraults, Inc.
PO Box 151
Annapolis, MD 21404

Skinner, Inc.
357 Main Street
Bolton, MA 01740
(508) 252-5035

Ceramics

(See also Stoneware—American)

Advisors: SUSAN and AL BAGDADE

Susan and Al Bagdade, authors of Warman's English and Continental Pottery and Porcelain: An Illustrated Price Guide *(2nd edition, 1991), have for some years written "Answers on Antiques," a column in* The Antique Trader Weekly. *Their other columns also appear regularly in* Antique Week, Antiques and Collecting Hobbies, *and* Yesteryear. *Their business—The Country Peasants—specializes in Quimper.*

Al and Susan Bagdade are located at 3136 Elder Court, Northbrook, IL 60062; (708)498-1468.

The ceramics section has an entirely new organization this year. We have divided the field of ceramics into three periods—early, middle, and late. The next several pages contain introductory material on each of these broad periods. Within each period, listings are arranged as follows (with each type of ceramics having its own brief introduction).

Early period: Chelsea-Derby, Creamware, Delft, Meissen, Salt-glazed stoneware, Sèvres, Wedgwood, Worcester.

Middle period: Flow Blue, Irish Belleek, Ironstone, Lusterware, Majolica, Mocha ware, Staffordshire.

Late period: Amphora—Turn-Teplitz, Austria, Bavaria, Clarice Cliff, Doulton and Royal Doulton, Moorcroft, Quimper, Royal Bayreuth, Schlegelmilch.

STATE OF THE MARKET

The cooled economy is reflected in the antique ceramic market place. Many dealers are reporting that their inventories are moving quite slowly, if at all, and it is not unusual to find choice pieces redisplayed after a year's time. The auction houses are listing more "N.S." or "No Sale" on the prices—realized sheets than in previous years. Those items crossing the block are often struggling to reach the preauction estimates.

The glamour porcelains, including Meissen, Sèvres, Worcester, and Vienna, have their legion of followers, and the top pieces are still attracting interest. Significant collections coming up for consideration are also strong islands in this dull sea. An example is the Brunner collection of

Gaudy Dutch and spatterware sold at Wolf's, which recorded many record prices for select items. However, this is the exception rather than the norm.

The collector with available cash should do very well in today's market, as dealers must move merchandise to survive. Prices should be negotiable, and the collector will often find that dealers are adding select items from their own collections in order to stimulate interest.

Middle- and low-range ceramics are also in the doldrums, with a few exceptions. Select examples of such popular categories as Quimper and Historic Staffordshire are still recording strong prices. The art pottery of De Morgan, Ruskin, Clarice Cliff, and Moorcroft appear to be holding their own.

EARLY PERIOD

The search for a true white, hard-paste porcelain in Europe to rival the porcelain from the Far East ended with the development of a satisfactory body at Meissen about 1707–1710. Prior to this date, earthenware and stoneware were the basic ceramic bodies, but the porous surface of this material necessitated the use of glazes to render the piece useful.

Lead glazes, salt glaze, and ferrous dips were the most common types of surface treatments. The heavy weight and relative fragility were also a detriment. The use of lead and tin glazes reached their peak in the many Dutch centers located around Delft.

Major centers for both hard and soft paste were developed at Meissen, Sèvres, and Vienna under royal protection and patronage. Many of the best artisans were drawn to these centers. Some of the finest porcelains were designed and executed during the 18th century. Other continental centers included Ludwigsburg, Furstenberg, and the KPM, or King's Porcelain Factory, to mention a few.

Across the channel, ceramicists dabbled with hard paste at Plymouth and Bristol, but soft paste and its many hybrids were to set the tone for the future of the English ceramics industry. The finer-grained earthenware known as creamware was an acceptable alternative to hard paste, though it was never meant to challenge porcelain.

Josiah Wedgwood is generally acknowledged as the genius of the period, and certainly his experimentation with bodies and glazes would justify this claim. Although the potteries of Chelsea, Worcester, Bow, Astbury, and Liverpool are often overlooked, their craftsmanship rivaled any on the Continent.

The earliest style of decoration emulated oriental porcelain. Blue-painted or printed underglazed designs of Europeanized oriental themes, called chinoiserie, were the most prevalent at Worcester, Liverpool, and many other English potteries. Low-temperature overglaze decoration came into vogue, and the expanded palette of colors became the norm as the century drew to a close.

MIDDLE PERIOD

The 19th century is often characterized as the golden age of ceramics. The increased wealth of the middle class and the opening of new markets abroad, most notably in the United States, resulted in the formation of large centers for ceramic production to meet the increased demand. The Staffordshire district became a major center in England, and Dresden, Prussia, Limoges, Carlsbad, and Thuringia were hard-paste centers on the Continent.

Earthenware and soft-paste porcelain were the staple bodies in England, but hybrids such as Spode's New Stone, Mason's ironstone, and bone china were introduced, with an important impact on the industry. Experimentation continued to find a more perfect vehicle for decoration.

The reign of Victoria strongly influenced the type of decoration found on ceramics of the period. Over- and underglazed decorations ranged from the finely executed pieces of the Flight and Barr combinations to the exuberant applied florals that covered the body of Coalbrookdale pieces.

Several old techniques were resurrected and adapted to the 19th century. Copper, silver, and pink lusters had roots back to the Hispano-Moresque of the 14th and 15th centuries. The tin- and lead-glazed earthenware of the early Italian period found new form at Minton and George Jones in the fabulous shapes and colors known as majolica. The groundwork was laid for the next century and its dramatic changes.

LATE PERIOD

The Art Nouveau, Art Deco, and Arts and Crafts movements had a significant impact on styles throughout the 20th century. Experimentation with colors, glazes, and shapes were the hallmark of the Massier studios in France, Boch Freres in Belgium, the potters at Turn-Teplitz, and Zsolnay in Hungary. Better examples from these potteries are highly collectible today.

Solid houses such as Meissen, Doulton, Royal Worcester, and the potters around Delft, to name a few, augmented their lines with examples from these movements.

The Austrian and Bavarian potteries produced large quantities of dinnerware for American consumption. The same can be said for the many potters in the Limoges district of France. The desire for European porcelain often outstripped the supply. Many of these potteries manufactured wares for the large department stores across the U.S. Newly emerged countries, such as Czechoslovakia, were quick to fire up their furnaces to feed the hungry consumer.

The Art Deco designs found form in the hands of Susie Cooper and Clarice Cliff. Bright colors and zigzag lines characterized these ceramics. The Modern movement at Quimper was a departure from the traditional peasant pottery to the sharp angles and bright colors of Art Deco.

American potteries are most frequently associated with the Arts and Crafts movement, but outstanding examples of this art form can be found in the works of William De Morgan, Pilkington, and the bizarre stoneware of the Martin brothers.

QUALITY KEY

Quality refers to importance in a specific category.

Good Quality: items that are fairly common, not exhibiting any outstanding characteristics of design or execution.

Very Good Quality: items that are less frequently seen and have artistic value.

Superior Quality: items that are considered top of the line in design, execution, and rarity. These tend to be quite expensive.

CONDITION KEY

Condition refers to physical status of each example.

Fine: piece is in mint condition, with crisp colors.

Good: piece shows signs of wear, slight rubbing, or wear to glaze and gilding.

Average: piece may have minor or repaired chips, small hairlines, small losses of design or color.

Poor: piece has been repaired or restored, with loss of body material. Decorations are often faded, stained, or lost; hairlines are significant. Such a piece is considered a "filler" in a collection (until a better example becomes available) or a "cabinet" piece for decorative purposes.

The more modern (Middle and Late Period) pieces will be far less valuable in a condition less than fine. As years pass, that situation will gradually change—especially for Middle Period pieces after the year 2000.—*DL*

EARLY PERIOD

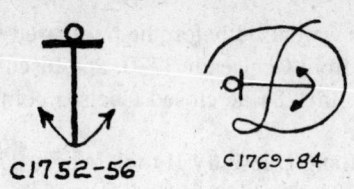

CHELSEA
LONDON, ENGLAND
c. 1745–1769

C1752-56   C1769-84

Soft-paste porcelains were made at Chelsea by 1745. Nicholas Sprimont was in charge. Pieces were ornate and made for the upscale market. The mark used was an incised triangle and a painted mark of a trident piercing a crown.

A "raised anchor" mark was used from 1749 to 1752. Pieces from this period have oriental motifs or simple floral designs.

1752–1756 was the "red anchor" period. Small "moons" are seen on these porcelains when held to the light.

1756–1769 was the "gold anchor" period. Pieces were richly decorated and ornately gilded. Many Chelsea pieces had no mark at all.

In 1770, William Duesbury of the Derby factory purchased the Chelsea factory; 1770–1784 wares are called Chelsea-Derby. With the interchange of molds, clay, and workmen, it is difficult to distinguish between Chelsea and Derby porcelains of this period. Duesbury used the Chelsea gold anchor on some Derby pieces. In 1784 the molds and workers were transferred to Derby.

References

John Bedford, *Chelsea and Derby China*, Walker and Company, 1967.

Museums

Colonial Williamsburg Foundation, Williamsburg, VA; Fitzwilliam Museum, Cambridge, England; Gardiner Museum of Ceramic Art, Toronto, Canada; Museum of Fine Arts, Boston, MA; Victoria and Albert Museum, London, England.

Reproduction Alert

Samson made copies of Chelsea pieces. Other forgeries include pieces with red or gold anchor marks.

DERBY
DERBY, ENGLAND
1755–PRESENT

C1782-1825

William Duesbury I opened the Derby works in 1755. He used chinoiserie designs, exotic bird paintings, and blue-and-white motifs. No marks were used before he purchased the Chelsea factory. Some workers came from Chelsea in 1770, and biscuit porcelain and figure groups were made. In 1784 he closed Chelsea completely, and the craftsmen went to Derby.

William Duesbury II took over in 1786, and made great advances until 1797. They added landscapes, maritime subjects, and hunting scenes. Workmanship was excellent.

Kean became a partner in 1795, but work declined. Robert Bloor leased the factory in 1811. Imari patterns and rich gilding typified this period. Many figures were also made. The factory was sold in 1848.

References

F. A. Barrett and A. L. Thorpe, *Derby Porcelain, 1750–1848*, Faber and Faber, 1971; John Twitchett, *Derby Porcelain*, Barrie and Jenkins, 1980.

Museums

Derby Museum and Art Gallery, The Strand, Derby, England; Gardiner Museum of Ceramic Art, Toronto, Canada.

Collectors' Club

Derby Porcelain International Society, The Honorary Secretary, c/o 31 Beaumont, Oxford OX1 2NZ, England; £25; quarterly newsletter, journal, occasional essays.

Cachepot and stand   10″ L   Chelsea-Derby   1750–1780   England
Lozenge shape, pierced lid with crabstock handle, applied flowerheads and foliage; red anchor mark.
Very Good Quality/Fine Condition $2750 (A)   **$2000–$3500**

Dish   8.25″ Dia.   Chelsea-Derby   1750–1780   England
Leaf shape molded as overlapping green leaves edged in turquoise or dark green, purple veins; double stalk handle; Derby, c. 1765.
Very Good Quality/Fine Condition $500 (D)   **$400–$600**

Dish   10″ Dia.   Chelsea-Derby   1750–1780   England
Fluted circular shape, painted scattered floral sprays and insects; lobed brown line rim; stress crack on rim; red anchor mark.
Very Good Quality/Average Condition $1050 (A)   **$750–$1250**

Figure   5.5″ H   Chelsea-Derby   1750–1780   England
Standing gardener in pink jacket and turquoise breeches, leaning on flowered tree stump; dog at feet; gold anchor mark; repairs.
Very Good Quality/Average Condition $650(D)   **$650–$800**

> Note that time and again, early pieces have repairs, yet sell readily. Ceramics are very delicate and rarely survive 200 years unscathed. Forget the old hogwash about only collecting perfect porcelains!—*DL*

Pitcher 6″ H   Chelsea-Derby   1830–1845   England
White, raised tulips on pebble ground, salt glaze finish; Bloor Derby. *(See photo 19)*
Good Quality/Fine Condition   *$75 (A)*   **$75–$150**

Plates, set of 6 8.5″ Dia.   Chelsea-Derby   1770–1775   England
Painted festoons of pink roses hung from *bleu celeste* borders edged with gilt scrollwork; rim chips; gold anchor and D marks.
Very Good Quality/Average Condition   *$2500 (A)*   **$2000–$3000**

Teabowl and saucer   Chelsea-Derby   1750–1780   England
Fluted body, multicolored painted flower sprays and scattered sprigs, brown line rim; red anchor mark.
Very Good Quality/Fine Condition   *$1150 (A)*   **$750–$1250**

Teabowl and saucer   Chelsea-Derby   1750–1780   England
Fluted body; painted vignettes of figures and buildings in rustic landscapes; red and puce borders; scattered flowers and insects.
Superior Quality/Fine Condition   *$2100 (A)*   **$1500–$2500**

CREAMWARE
ENGLISH/CONTINENTAL
c. 1740–PRESENT

Creamware is cream-colored earthenware that presents a thin body plus a clean and brilliant glaze. It did not attempt to imitate porcelain but was readily accepted. The materials are the same for salt glaze, but creamware is fired at a lower temperature and glazed with lead.

Enoch Booth of Tunstall invented the glaze that provided the cream color. Both Whieldon and Wedgwood used this glaze. Enameled decorations were added about twenty years later. Other areas also produced creamware products.

China clay and china stone from Cornwall were introduced into the body and glaze to improve creamware in 1868. This made the ware paler, lighter, and more brilliant in the glaze. Most creamware was unmarked before pieces made by Wedgwood.

Between 1760 and 1820 creamware was the main product in England. Its prominence provided the death blow to tin-glazed earthenware in England and the Continent since many Staffordshire potters established factories in France and directly threatened the faience factories and sale of porcelains.

References

Donald Towner, *Creamware*, Faber and Faber, 1978.

Museums

Castle Museum, Norwich, England; Cincinnati Art Museum, Cincinnati, OH; Victoria and Albert Museum, London, England.

Figure 7″ H × 10″ W × 4.12″ D Creamware 1920–1930 England
Polar bear seated on haunches; rectangular base; signed "J. Skeaping"; Wedgwood.
Very Good Quality/Fine Condition $395 (D)   **$300–$450**

Hot water jug, covered 7.88″ H Creamware 1750–1780 England
Painted large open flower in orange-red, yellow, and green outlined in black; orange-red dentil border, entwined strap handle with flower terminals; domed cover with flower finial; spout chips; Leeds.
Superior Quality/Good Condition $1250 (A)   **$1000–$1800**

Jug, cream 3″ H Creamware 1780–1800 England
Blue, black, and iron-red enameled, vertical-banded chintz pattern; grooved strap handle; mask spout.
Very Good Quality/Fine Condition $480 (A)   **$350–$550**

Plates, set of 6 10″ Dia. Creamware 1780–1800 England
Blue figure in chinoiserie landscape in center; feathered leaf border; Liverpool.
(See photo 20)
Superior Quality/Fine Condition $700 (D)   **$500–$700**

Puzzle jug 7.5″ H Creamware 1770–1780 England
Baluster body, waisted circular foot, tubular loop handle, pierced band of circles under tubular rim with 3 short nozzles; Leeds.
Superior Quality/Fine Condition $1225 (A)   **$800–$1500**

Teabowl and saucer Creamware 1800–1830 England
Iron-red "King's Rose" pattern; pink diamond border.
Very Good Quality/Fine Condition $155 (D)   **$100–$175**

Teapot 5.5″ H Creamware 1780–1800 England
Globular shape; reeded, interlaced handle, painted formal rose spray in iron-red, green, and yellow; flower finial.
Very Good Quality/Fine Condition $275 (A)   **$225–$375**

Toby jug 9.6″ H Creamware 1780–1800 England
Seated man in gray tricorner hat, mottled blue coat, yellow waistcoat, gray breeches, barrel between legs, ale mug on knee; canted square base.
Superior Quality/Fine Condition $850 (D)   **$600–$900**

Wall pocket 11.75″ H Creamware 1780–1800 England
Cornucopia-shaped, shell-molded with a panel enclosing relief portrait of Plenty, pierced and molded with flowers; rust, blue, pink, yellow, and gilt.
Very Good Quality/Fine Condition $350 (D)   **$250–$400**

DELFT, DUTCH AND ENGLISH

The Porcelain Claw
C1764

DELFT, HOLLAND, c. 1613–PRESENT
BRISTOL, LAMBETH, AND LIVERPOOL, ENGLAND, 1690–1790

Italian potters brought the tin enamel techniques to Delft. By the mid-1600s, over thirty manufacturers were making imitations of Japanese and Chinese porcelains in blue-and-white tin-glazed wares. Other blue-and-

Photo 19. Pitcher.
CREDIT: AL BAGDADE *(See p. 81)*

Photo 20. Plate.
CREDIT: AL BAGDADE *(See p. 82)*

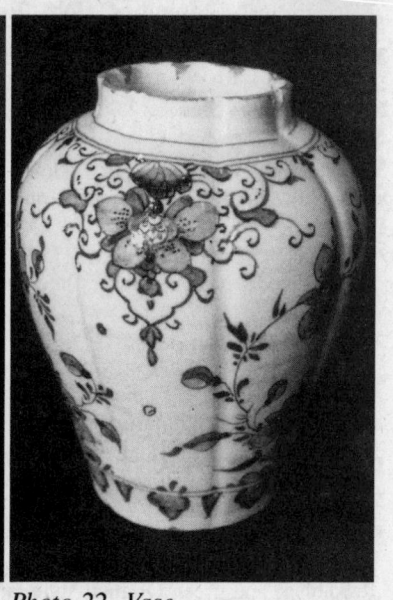

Photo 21. Tobacco jar.
CREDIT: AL BAGDADE *(See p. 84)*

Photo 22. Vase.
CREDIT: AL BAGDADE *(See p. 85)*

white wares included Dutch subjects (such as windmills), ships, portraits, landscape views, and Bible stories. They were made mainly
between 1640 and 1740, and few pieces were marked.

After 1700, polychromes inspired by Japanese Imari wares were introduced. Plates, tiles, and vases were made, along with novelties such as
cow jugs, violins, figures, and shoes.

The introduction of Wedgwood's creamware in the second half of the
18th century and works by Meissen and Sèvres resulted in Delft's decline. By the 19th century only three pottery factories remained.

De Porcelyne Fles is still in business today after starting in 1653.

English Delft centers were Bristol, Lambeth, and Liverpool after starting in London in the mid-17th century. Apothecary wares, barber bowls,
and puzzle jugs were popular at Lambeth. Plates, bowls, and flower
holders with naive treatments and bluish tones were predominant at Bristol. Liverpool Delft resembled Chinese porcelains. All of these areas fell
into decline by 1790 due to the popularity of Wedgwood's creamware.

References

Frank Britton, *London Delftware*, Jonathan Horne, 1987; Diana Im-
ber, *Collecting European Delft and Faience*, Praeger, 1968.

Museums

Ashmolean Museum, Oxford, England; Gardiner Museum of Ceramic
Art, Toronto, Canada; Gemeente Museum, Arnhem, The Netherlands;
Henry Ford Museum, Dearborn, MI; Rijksmuseum, Amsterdam, The
Netherlands.

Charger 13.75″ Dia. Delft 1690–1700 England
Adam and Eve in polychromes, London type, blue dash border.
Superior Quality/Fine Condition $3900 (A)   **$2500–$4500**
Charger 15.5″ Dia. Delft 1750–1780 Holland
Blue painted basket of flowers in center, stylized floral border; rim chips, hair-
line.
Very Good Quality/Average Condition $930 (D)   **$1000–$1800**
Flower brick 4.88″ L Delft 1750–1780 England
Rectangular shape with pierced top, blue painted flower sprays.
Very Good Quality/Fine Condition $475 (A)   **$400–$600**
Jar, tobacco 10.5″ H Delft 1750–1780 Holland
Blue and white Indian seated by tobacco jar; "De Drie Klockken" mark. *(See
photo 21)*
Very Good Quality/Good Condition $750 (D)   **$600–$1000**
Plate 13.12″ Dia. Delft 1700–1750 England
Red, blue, and green Oriental-style landscape, leafy border.
Very Good Quality/Fine Condition $445 (A)   **$300–$500**

Plate 9″ Dia. Delft 1800–1830 Holland
Blue and white bird motif amid flowers.
Good Quality/Fine Condition $11 (A)   **$60–$90**

> What a bargain—but that's why people spend hours and hours at an auction to make one purchase.—*DL*

Posset pot, covered 9.88″ H Delft 1780–1800 England
Red, green, and blue birds, rocks and flowers with leaves, double-scroll handles with blue dashes.
Very Good Quality/Fine Condition $2890 (A)   **$2500–$4500**

Punch bowl 13.36″ Dia. Delft 1750–1780 Holland
Blue painted formal flowers and scrollwork, lappet borders.
Very Good Quality/Fine Condition $680 (A)   **$750–$1200**

Vase 11.36″ H Delft 1700–1750 England
Baluster shape, blue painted butterfly and plants, stiff leaf border on spreading foot.
Superior Quality/Fine Condition $820 (A)   **$800–$1200**

Vase 8.5″ H Delft 1750–1780 England
Lobed ovoid form; blue foral design; unmarked. *(See photo 22)*
Very Good Quality/Good Condition $250 (D)   **$200–$325**

Vase 9.6″ H Delft 1700–1750 Holland
Ribbed ovoid shape; blue painted Oriental-style garden landscape with birds under paneled border.
Very Good Quality/Fine Condition $350 (A)   **$300–$450**

$$\mathcal{K.P.M.}$$

MEISSEN
1710–PRESENT
NEAR DRESDEN, GERMANY

The Meissen factory was the first hard-paste porcelain factory in Europe. Johann Böttger, along with several collaborators, was responsible for this discovery, and the factory received a royal patent in 1710.

Various periods at Meissen were named for the artists who worked there: 1710–1719, the Böttger period, was characterized by the Kakiemon palette and pieces in Chinese and Japanese styles. The Horoldt period, 1720–1731, saw much expansion of the factory, designs from Japanese Imari porcelains, and the introduction of the "Blue Onion" pattern. Horoldt continued at Meissen when Kaendler, the most famous sculptor, came to Meissen in 1731. Kaendler modeled the famous swan set of 1,400 pieces, but he is best known for his figurines from the Italian Comedy, mythological and allegorical pieces, and his Crinoline groups.

Meissen reached its peak about 1750. After the Seven Years' War, a disaster for Meissen, the factory was slow to recover. In the meantime, competitors such as Sèvres came to the forefront.

During later periods at Meissen many Kaendler models were revived. Today the factory operates as the State's Porcelain Manufactory.

The crossed-swords mark started about 1720 in blue. Slashes across the mark denote pieces of lesser quality, factory seconds. The AR mark was used on porcelains for the court, c. 1730.

Fakes Alert

Helena Wolfsohn's decorating workshop in Dresden copied the AR monogram on her many thousands of reproductions. Samson made numerous Meissen copies, especially of the Crinoline groups. Other German factories, such as Hutschenreuther and the Thieme factory, copied Meissen examples.

The Meissen "Onion" pattern is the most copied pattern. More than 60 European and Oriental factories copied this theme, with varying names, since it was not protected by a copyright.

References

Robert Röntgen, *The Book of Meissen*, Schiffer Publishing, 1984. A beautifully illustrated and thoroughly researched text. The emphasis is on the 19th- and 20th-century products. At $95 it is the best work on this major factory. Robert Röntgen, *Marks on German, Bohemian, and Austrian Porcelain*, Schiffer Publishing, 1981. This book includes all of the fake Meissen marks attributed to the minor factories that produced them. It provides the same data on KPM and Vienna. It is a bible for identifying any and all Germanic pieces made to date. Ingelore Menzhausen, *Early Meissen Porcelain in Dresden*, Thames & Hudson, 1990.

Museums

Gardiner Museum of Ceramic Art, Toronto, Canada; Schlossmuseum, Berlin, Germany; Art Institute of Chicago, Chicago, IL; Meissen Porcelain Museum, Meissen, Germany; Wadsworth Atheneum, Hartford, CT; Stadtmuseum, Cologne, Germany.

Bowl 6″ Dia. Meissen 1780–1800 Germany
Rust, green, and orange port scenes in matte gilt cartouches; rust, purple, and yellow flowers with green leaves, purple scene on interior; repaired; blue crossed swords mark. *(See photo 23)*
Very Good Quality/Average Condition $250 *(A)*   **$250–$400**
Bowl, covered 9.88″ Dia. Meissen 1780–1800 Germany
Underglaze blue Oriental flowering branches and scattered butterflies; artichoke finial; blue crossed swords and star mark.
Very Good Quality/Fine Condition $600 *(D)*   **$400–$600**
Coffeepot 8.88″ H Meissen 1700–1750 Germany
Fluted pear-shaped body, puce-painted wheat sheaf, chrysanthemum and flowers accented with gilt, cell border on cover; blue crossed swords and dot mark.
Very Good Quality/Fine Condition $275 *(A)*   **$250–$450**

Figure 7.36″ H Meissen 1780–1800 Germany
Harlequin as sailor against tree trunk, oar over shoulder, puce waistcoat, yellow jacket and striped trousers; flower-encrusted, scroll-border base; blue crossed swords mark.
Superior Quality/Fine Condition $1760 (A)   **$1500–$2500**

Figure 1.12″ H Meissen 1800–1830 Germany
Nesting hen in violet, brown, manganese, and orange-accented feathers; green-accented nest; blue crossed swords mark.
Very Good Quality/Fine Condition $500 (A)   **$350–$500**

Figure 3.5″ H Meissen 1885–1900 Germany
Figural slipper; cobalt, orange, and gold florals; bird on instep; blue crossed swords mark.
Good Quality/Fine Condition $125 (D)   **$75–$125**

Plates, set of 5 9.88″ Dia. Meissen 1780–1800 Germany
Painted sprays of German flowers and scattered sprigs; ozier molded border; gilt rim; blue crossed swords mark.
Very Good Quality/Fine Condition $880 (A)   **$600–$900**

> These plates will bring much more offered retail as two pairs ($450–$600 per pair) and a single ($150–$225). Only in sets of eight or more does porcelain increase in value.

Tea and coffee set Coffeepot 10.5″ H Meissen 1845–1865 Germany
Coffeepot, teapot, creamer, covered sugar bowl; gilt swags on white ground; blue crossed swords mark.
Very Good Quality/Fine Condition $1700 (D)·   **$1500–$2500**

Teabowl and saucer Meissen 1780–1800 Germany
Painted banded hedges and sprigs in Kakiemon pallette; molded bands of hatched chevrons; blue crossed swords mark.
Very Good Quality/Fine Condition $600 (A)   **$500–$1000**

SALT-GLAZED STONEWARE
STAFFORDSHIRE, ENGLAND
1671 THROUGH 19TH CENTURY
RHINELAND, GERMANY
1500s–PRESENT

John Dwight discovered the salt-glaze technique in England and received a patent in 1671. Early salt-glazed pieces from the Staffordshire area were thin, lightweight, and made as competition for porcelain. Later a brown salt-glazed stoneware was developed in the second half of the 18th century for beer jugs, flasks, tankards, and industrial wares.

Wedgwood and Wood made salt-glaze stoneware in the late 17th century. Enameled stoneware pieces started about 1750. These required a second firing at a lower temperature than the salt-glaze oven to "fix" the color to the object. Porcelain decorative motifs were enameled on salt-glaze pieces.

Animal figures were popular salt-glaze examples. Most were made in a two-piece mold and united with slip.

By the early 16th century, brown salt-glaze wares were made in Germany as drinking vessels for taverns. These were exported to England for over two hundred years.

References

J. F. Blacker, *The ABC of English Salt-Glaze Stoneware from Dwight to Doulton*, Stanley Paul and Co., 1922; Arnold Mountford, *The Illustrated Guide to Staffordshire Salt-Glazed Stoneware*, Barrie and Jenkins, 1971.

Museums

British Museum, London, England; City Museum and Art Gallery, Stoke-on-Trent, England; Fitzwilliam Museum, Cambridge, England; Kunstgewerbe Museum, Cologne, Germany; Metropolitan Museum of Art, New York, NY; William Rockhill Nelson Gallery of Art, Kansas City, MO.

Figure 4.75″ H Salt glaze 1700–1730 England
High heeled; tooled upper surface and sole; dark brown iron dip glaze.
Superior Quality/Fine Condition $1670 (A)   **$1200–$1800**
Jug 5.12″ H Salt glaze 1780–1800 England
Baluster shape, flared lip, strap handle.
Good Quality/Fine Condition $150 (D)   **$75–$150**
Plate 7.5″ Dia. Salt glaze 1780–1800 England
Painted flowering peony and prunus blossom in famille rose colors; molded green diaper border.
Good Quality/Fine Condition $235 (A)   **$125–$250**
Plate 9″ Dia. Salt glaze 1780–1800 England
Basketweave and diapered border.
Very Good Quality/Fine Condition $145 (A)   **$150–$275**
Plate 9.25″ Dia. Salt glaze England 1750–1780
Latticework cartouche surrounded by C-scrolls on molded diamond and diaper ground, out-turned rim. *(See photo 24)*
Very Good Quality/Fine Condition $400 (D)   **$300–$450**
Soup plate 9.25″ Dia. Salt glaze 1780–1800 England
Center enameled with shepherd and flock; basketweave and diapered border.
Very Good Quality/Fine Condition $192 (A)   **$150–$275**
Teapot 3.75″ H Salt glaze 1750–1780 England
Globular shape; painted with man in pink coat with house in background; reverse with shepherd holding crock beside classical ruins; green spotted crabstock handle, spout, and finial.
Superior Quality/Fine Condition $960 (A)   **$800–$1200**
Tureen, covered 10.25″ H-H Salt glaze 1700–1750 England
Press-molded overall seed pattern relief; 3 lion mask feet; rim chips.
Very Good Quality/Good Condition $2500 (D)   **$1500–$3000**

SÈVRES
1756–PRESENT
PARIS   *1753*

After the Sèvres factory moved from Vincennes in 1756, Louis XV became involved in the factory's production. The right to do gilding and the use of colored grounds was granted exclusively to Sèvres. This gave them a virtual monopoly on fine porcelain making in France. The first products were all soft-paste porcelain, from 1756 to 1770.

Various background colors included gros bleu, bleu celeste, rose pompadour, and bleu roi, plus various shades of yellow, green, and claret. All sorts of decorative porcelains were made in addition to figures.

Hard-paste porcelain was started at Sèvres about 1770. During the factory's long history various directors influenced the decorations and products made.

Letter dates were used from 1753 to 1793. The mark usually was blue but could be brown or purple. Initials below the mark indicated the artist. "R" was the first letter date on hard paste.

Fakes Alert

Many Sèvres examples have been faked. There is a tremendous amount of fake Sèvres around, especially pieces in soft paste said to be made before 1770. Samson made numerous copies of Sèvres pieces—all in hard paste.

References

Carl C. Dauterman, *Sèvres Porcelain: Makers and Marks of the 18th Century*, Metropolitan Museum of Art, 1986; Egan Mew, *Royal Sèvres China*, Dodd, Mead & Co.

Museums

Gardiner Museum of Ceramic Art, Toronto, Canada; Musée National de Ceramique, Sèvres, France; Art Institute of Chicago, Chicago, IL; British Museum, London, England; Frick Collection, New York, NY; Musée des Arts Decoratifs, Paris, France; Musée du Louvre, Paris, France.

Bourdaloue 10″ L Sèvres 1700–1750 France
Blue lapis ground; each side painted with mixed garden spray of flowers in narrow gilt kidney-shaped ribbon panels, flanked by gilded festoons and scrolls; gilt rim; blue interlaced L's and date mark.
Very Good Quality/Fine Condition $1400 (A) **$1200–$2500**

Coffee can and saucer Sèvres 1785 France
Gilt star decoration on blue lapis ground; gilt line borders; blue interlaced L's and date mark.
Good Quality/Fine Condition $1000 (D) **$750–$1200**

Cup and saucer Sèvres 1750–1760 France
Gilded shield enclosing 3 lions and chevron below a coronet in elaborate wreath with chain and badge; scroll and diaper border; blue interlaced L's and date mark.
Superior Quality/Fine Condition $3500 (A) **$2000–$3500**

Egg cup 1.5″ H Sèvres 1763 France
Blue and gilt continuous band of chevrons interlaced with coral red and gilt foliage; purple ground of gilt designs; blue interlaced L's and date mark.
Good Quality/Fine Condition $475 (A)   **$400–$600**

> Egg cups are quite rare and are highly collectible.—*DL*

Plates, set of 5 9.5″ Dia. Sèvres 1780–1800 France
Center painted with spray of roses in wavy gilt and blue circular line panel, sprigged band of summer flowers between narrow wavy blue ground band and blue scrolling; chips; blue interlaced L's, date mark.
Very Good Quality/Good Condition $1750 (A)   **$1200–$2000**

Plates, set of 7 9.25″ Dia. Sèvres 1811–1812 France
Center painted with bouquet of garden flowers; border of gilt flowerheads on green ground between chevron bands; red "de Sèvres," 1811, 1812, and painter's marks.
Very Good Quality/Fine Condition $4900 (A)   **$2800–$4200**

Sauceboat 10″ L Sèvres 1780–1800 France
Fabric-draped finial, bird handles, reserves of scientific instruments, gilt dot pattern ground; repaired. *(See photo 25)*
Good Quality/Average Condition $100 (A)   **$250–$450**

Sauce dishes, pair 7″ Dia. Sèvres 1845–1855 France
Border of painted animals in elaborate scrollwork alternating with trophies and Louis Philippe monogram; gilt medallion in center; "Chateau de Fontainbleu" and date marks.
Good Quality/Fine Condition $250 (A)   **$500–$900**

WEDGWOOD

WEDGWOOD
1759–PRESENT
NEAR STOKE-ON-TRENT, ENGLAND   1929–PRESENT

After a partnership with Thomas Whieldon, Josiah Wedgwood went into business for himself in 1759 at Burslem, near Stoke-on-Trent in England. He experimented with a variety of glazes on earthenwares. In 1764 he perfected creamware, which became Queen's Ware after he presented a set to Queen Charlotte.

Black basalt was the first ornamental ware developed by Wedgwood. It was a finely grained unglazed black stoneware made between 1767 and 1796 and was used for utilitarian wares and large relief plaques, vases, busts, medallions, seals, and small intaglios, mostly with classical subjects.

Jasper is probably Wedgwood's best-known product. Started in 1774, it was known as a "dry body" because it was nonporous and unglazed. It was made in several shades: blue, green, lilac, yellow, maroon, black, and white. Multicolor jasperware is the rarest and most highly prized (read "most expensive") of all jasperware products. "Solid" jasper had the body colored throughout, while white jasper "dip" was a white jasper body with the color laid on the surface. Classical motifs

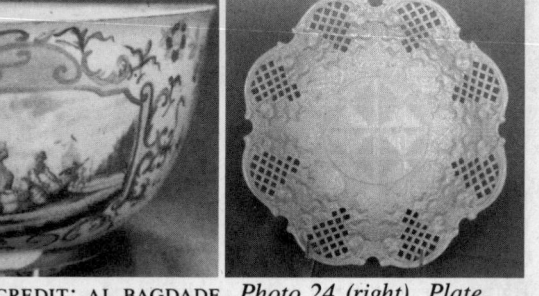

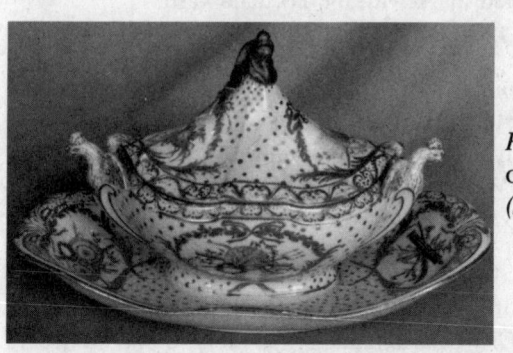

Photo 23 (left). Bowl. CREDIT: AL BAGDADE. *Photo 24 (right). Plate.*
CREDIT: AL BAGDADE *(See pp. 86, 88)*

Photo 25. Sauceboat.
CREDIT: AL BAGDADE
(See p. 90)

Photo 26 (left). Plate. CREDIT: AL BAGDADE. *Photo 27 (right). Vase.*
CREDIT: AL BAGDADE *(See pp. 93, 94)*

were prominent on all of the jasper examples. Wedgwood's replica of the Portland vase in 1790 was a high point in production.

Lusters were formed by applying iridescent or metallic films to the surface of ceramic wares. The effect was obtained by using metallic oxides of gold, silver, copper, and so on. Lusters were decorated by the resist method. Moonlight luster is a type of splashed or marbled pink or purple gold luster with tinges of yellow and green; it was developed between 1805 and 1815. Fairyland luster was produced from the designs of Daisy Makeig-Jones from 1915 to 1931. Often fantastic and grotesque figures were utilized in the designs.

The Wedgwood factory has manufactured bone china of high quality since 1878, using the printed mark with the Portland vase.

References

David Buten, *18th Century Wedgwood*, Methuen, 1980; a well-illustrated guide that aids in identifying and dating wares in seven ceramic bodies; Alison Kelly, *The Story of Wedgwood*, Viking, 1975; a good overall view of the Wedgwood factory. Robin Reilly, *Wedgwood* 2 vols., Stockton Press, 1989; a definitive work on Wedgwood.

Museums

Birmingham Museum of Art, Birmingham, AL; Buten Museum of Wedgwood, Merion, PA; City Museum and Art Gallery, Stoke-on-Trent, England; R. W. Norton Art Gallery, Shreveport, LA; Wedgwood Museum, Barlaston, England.

Collectors' Clubs

The Wedgwood Society, The Buten Museum of Wedgwood, 246 N. Bowman Avenue, Merion, PA; membership: $10.

The Wedgwood Society of New York, 5 Dogwood Court, Glen Head, NY 11545; membership: $22.50.

Bowl 8.5″ H Wedgwood jasper 1845–1865 England
Crater type; square base, 2 loop handles, white cameos of classical figures; dark blue ground; "WEDGWOOD" mark.
Very Good Quality/Fine Condition $750 (D)   **$500–$750**
Bowl 4.5″ Dia. Wedgwood luster 1910–1930 England
Butterfly luster; pearlized interior with butterfly; blue exterior with butterflies, gold rim.
Good Quality/Fine Condition $195 (D)   **$125–$195**
Bowl 8″ Dia. Wedgwood luster 1910–1930 England
Fairyland luster; octagonal shape; exterior decorated with "Moorish" pattern; interior with "Smoke Ribbons" pattern; gilt Portland Vase and 25125 marks.
Superior Quality/Fine Condition $3465 (A)   **$2000–$3500**

Covered butter dish 7″ Dia. Wedgwood 1865–1885 England
Majolica; shell pattern; white and brown shells, yellow trim, turquoise ground, waves, and seaweed; impressed "WEDGWOOD" mark.
Superior Quality/Fine Condition $650 (D) **$400–$650**

Figure 17″ H × 10.25″ Dia. Wedgwood basalt 1865–1885 England
Bust of Mercury with winged helmet; circular base.
Superior Quality/Fine Condition $1100 (D) **$800–$1200**

Jug 6.12″ H Wedgwood jasper 1919 England
Pear shape, loop handle, applied white band of classical figures and Cupid; geometric floral borders, crimson ground; impressed "WEDGWOOD" mark.
Very Good Quality/Fine Condition $175 (D) **$125–$175**

Mug, handleless 2.75″ H Wedgwood 1910–1930 England
Brownies, green leaves, and berries on white ground, titled "Bacon Fat," brown and orange rim; Daisey Makig Jones; marked "WEDGWOOD ETRURIA."
Very Good Quality/Fine Condition $180 (D) **$125–$200**

Pitcher 7.5″ H Wedgwood 1885–1900 England
Terra cotta; raised pink, blue, green, and yellow enamel florals; impressed "WEDGWOOD" mark.
Superior Quality/Fine Condition $925 (D) **$600–$1000**

Plate 10″ Dia. Wedgwood 1865–1885 England
Mottoes from Chaucer series, First of English Poets mark, "But what art thou that floates and doune"; polychrome, yellow birds, green flowers, green and brown rim.
Very Good Quality/Fine Condition $250 (D) **$150–$250**

Plate 8.75″ Dia. Wedgwood 1865–1885 England
Majolica; shaped green leaf; tan edge, turquoise ground, brown leaves, purple grapes; impressed "WEDGWOOD" mark.
Superior Quality/Fine Condition $295 (D) **$150–$300**

Plate 10″ Dia. Wedgwood 1900–1910 England
Man on horseback with lady in center, houses and trees in ground, rust and gold border, floral inner border, pink and yellow flowers; marked.
Very Good Quality/Fine Condition $75 (D) **$50–$75**

Plates, set of 10 8.75″ Dia. Wedgwood 1885–1900 England
Raised gold design, plum and blue-green basketweave ground; impressed "WEDGWOOD" mark. *(See photo 26)*
Very Good Quality/Fine Condition $1210 (A) **$800–$1200**

Sugar bowl 4.25″ H Wedgwood jasper 1891–1910 England
White cameos of classical figures, blue ground; impressed "WEDGWOOD" mark.
Good Quality/Fine Condition $125 (D) **$75–$125**

Teapot 7″ H Wedgwood jasper 1865–1885 England
White cameo panels of classic figures separated by vertical stripes; dark blue ground, widow finial on lid; "Wedgwood" mark.
Very Good Quality/Fine Condition $600 (D) **$300–$600**

Tile 6″ × 6″ Wedgwood 1900–1910 England
Blue transfer of Priscilla and John Alden on white ground.
Good Quality/Fine Condition $85 (D) **$40–$85**

Vase 10″ H Wedgwood basalt 1830–1845 England
Raised design of cupids in panther-drawn chariot on 1 side, ram-drawn on reverse; grape-decorated handles; "Wedgwood" mark.
Very Good Quality/Fine Condition $750 (D)   **$400–$750**

Vase 9″ H Wedgwood luster 1910–1930 England
Baluster shape; Fairyland luster; "Boys on a Bridge" pattern in blue, green, and orange; pattern #Z5360; Portland Vase mark.
Very Good Quality/Fine Condition $525 (A)   **$300–$600**

Vases, pair 9.88″ H Wedgwood jasper 1865–1885 England
White cameos of hanging swags, stiff leaf design form base; dark blue ground; "Wedgwood" mark.
Very Good Quality/Fine Condition $900 (D)   **$700–$1200**

Vases, pair 8″ H Wedgwood luster 1910–1930 England
Butterfly and luster, gold and multicolored butterflies on pearlized cream ground; #Z4832. *(See photo 27)*
Very Good Quality/Fine Condition $800 (A)   **$600–$1200**

WORCESTER AND ROYAL WORCESTER
1751–PRESENT
WORCESTER, ENGLAND

 1750–1790

 F B B 1813–1840

 1862 – 1875

The first period at Worcester was known as the Dr. Wall period, named after one of the original founders (1751–1776). Mostly table and small decorative wares were made, especially tea and dessert services. After 1755 they used transfer printing extensively.

The Davis-Flight period (1776–1793) emphasized neoclassical styles. Many whiteware blanks were purchased from France because there was a shortage of clay in the region. The company received a Royal Warrant from George III in 1789.

During the Flight and Barr period (1793–1807) patterns were rather plain. The Barr, Flight, and Barr period (1807–1813) was a very decorative era, with careful attention to details. The period from 1813 to 1840 is known as Flight, Barr, and Barr. Porcelains from this period were very high quality and richly painted. Gilt trim frequently was used.

In 1840, Flight, Barr, and Barr merged with the Chamberlain factory, and quality declined. Kerr and Binns took control from 1852 to 1862, and the factory had an artistic recovery. R. W. Binns formed the Worcester Royal Porcelain Company Ltd. in 1862, and their products carried the "Royal Worcester" name.

During the 1870s, James Hadley was one of the best artists at Royal Worcester. The factory continued to make bone china patterns into the 20th century. Dorothy Doughty gained international fame for modeling birds. The founding of the Dyson Perrins Museum at Worcester in 1951 marked the bicentenary of the Worcester Porcelain Company. The listings below cover only 18th-century Worcester porcelain.

Fakes Alert

Samson and other Continental artists copied 18th-century Worcester examples. Booths of Tunstall reproduced many Worcester designs using the transfer-printing technique. Both Austria and Rudolstadt made copies of Royal Worcester wares. The vast majority of these now antique fakes were made in hard-paste porcelain rather than the soft paste of the originals.

Market Trends

Period Worcester porcelain is one of the most saleable products in the American ceramics market. It is widely recognized, understood, and collected. Respectable prices are paid by collectors throughout the country.

Museums

Dyson Perrins Museum, Worcester, England; Gardiner Museum of Ceramic Art, Toronto, Canada; Seattle Art Museum, Seattle, WA; Art Institute of Chicago, Chicago, IL; British Museum, London, England; Henry Ford Museum, Dearborn, MI; Robertson Center for the Arts and Sciences, Binghamton, NY.

References

Dinah Reynolds, *Worcester Porcelain 1751–1783: An Ashmolean-Christie's Handbook*, Phaidon-Christie's, 1989; John Sandon, *Worcester Blue and White Porcelain 1751–1790*, Barrie and Jenkins, 1981; Henry Sandon, *The Illustrated Guide to Worcester Porcelain*, Herbert Jenkins, 1969; Henry Sandon, *Royal Worcester Porcelain*, Barrie and Jenkins, 1973.

Basket 6.6″ Dia. Worcester 1750–1780 England
Painted open spray of flowers and leaves in center; flared border pierced with linked circles; applied yellow and green flowerheads on exterior, painted flowerheads on interior.
Very Good Quality/Fine Condition $2470 (A) **$2000–$3500**

> With an original underplate, add a grand!—*DL*

Basket 5.36″ W Worcester 1820–1830 England
Rectangular; painted branches of fruit entwined with blue flowers on light green ground; gilt gadrooned rim; gilt overhead handles; Flight, Barr and Barr.
Very Good Quality/Fine Condition $950 (A) **$800–$1600**

Bottle 10″ H Worcester 1750–1780 England
Blue transfer of chinoiserie scene; blue crescent mark.
Very Good Quality/Fine Condition $550 (D) **$300–$600**

Butter tub, covered   4.75″ Dia.   Worcester   1750–1780   England
Cylinder shape; blue floral decoration; molded floral finial on domed cover.
Very Good Quality/Fine Condition $350 (A)   **$300–$500**

Milk jug   4.5″ H   1750–1780   England
Blue printed florals and butterfly, blue crescent mark. *(See photo 28)*
Very Good Quality/Fine Condition $250 (A)   **$200–$450**

Sweetmeat dish   5.88″ H   Worcester   1750–1780   England
"Blind Earl"; molded rosebud and leaves, blue painted scattered insects, twig
handle; blue crescent mark; c. 1760.
Superior Quality/Fine Condition $2550 (A)   **$2000–$3500**

Tankard   4.75″ H   Worcester   1750–1780   England
Bell shaped; grooved handle; black printed bust of King of Prussia; Fame blow-
ing trumpet, martial trophies; RH Worcester and anchor mark; firing crack in
handle.
Very Good Quality/Good Condition $595 (D)   **$400–$650**

Tankard   6.12″ H   Worcester   1750–1780   England
Cylinder shape; grooved strap handle; blue printed "Parrot Pecking Fruit" pat-
tern; blue crescent mark.
Very Good Quality/Fine Condition $250 (D)   **$200–$350**

Tankard   4.5″ H   Worcester   1800–1830   England
Cylinder shape; black bat-printed view of Worcester in gilt rectangular frame;
yellow ground, gilt line rims.
Very Good Quality/Fine Condition $1600 (A)   **$800–$1600**

Teabowl and saucer   Worcester   1750–1780   England
Blue painted "Prunus root" pattern; blue crescent mark.
Very Good Quality/Fine Condition $375 (A)   **$250–$450**

Vase   7.5″ H   Worcester   1750–1780   England
Pair of painted exotic birds in gilt shield and scalloped cartouches reserved on
blue scale ground; 2 small birds in panels and gilt bands on neck; worn gilt; blue
fretted square mark.
Very Good Quality/Good Condition $1400 (A)   **$1200–$1800**

MIDDLE PERIOD

FLOW BLUE
STAFFORDSHIRE, ENGLAND
EARLY VICTORIAN, 1835–1850s
MID-VICTORIAN, 1860s–1870s
LATE VICTORIAN, 1880s–1890s, EARLY 1900s

   Josiah Wedgwood was the first maker of "Flow" or "Flowing Blue"
china, starting about 1820, and it was marketed in many countries. The

mid-1800s until the early 1900s were the peak years of Flow Blue production.

To achieve the Flow Blue process, a transfer-printed design, originally in cobalt oxide, receives volatizing agents such as lime of chloride or ammonia, which cause the pattern to "bleed" during the glaze-firing stage. The cobalt changes to a deep blue color during the firing. The degree of flowing varies considerably from piece to piece.

At first the Flow Blue patterns were Oriental in style, with the name of the pattern incorporated with the maker's mark. During the Victorian period, scenics and florals were popular patterns, and some Art Nouveau designs were used. Although most designs were applied by transfers, some hand-painted designs were made.

More than 1,500 patterns were manufactured during the peak years of Flow Blue production. Sometimes the same pattern name was used by one or more manufacturers.

Early Flow Blue is characterized by a dense coloration; the later pieces had a softer look. In the mid-Victorian period other colors were used, and some gold was added to enhance the designs.

To identify the pattern and maker, one needs to study the backstamp. Sometimes the location of the factory is also included in the marks.

Fakes Alert

Blakeney Pottery Limited of Stoke-on-Trent has been producing new Flow Blue since 1968. Examples are called "Victorian Reproductions" and have large blue roses.

References

Mary Gaston, *The Collector's Encyclopedia of Flow Blue China*, Collector Books, 1983; Petra Williams, *Flow Blue China: An Aid to Identifications*, Fountain House East, 1971; Petra Williams, *Flow Blue China II*, Fountain House East, 1973; Petra Williams, *Flow Blue China and Mulberry Ware* (rev. ed.), Fountain House East, 1981; Veneita Mason, *Popular Patterns of Flow Blue China with Prices*, Wallace-Homestead, 1982.

Museums

Margaret Woodbury Strong Museum, Rochester, NY.

Collectors' Club

Flow Blue International Collectors' Club, David Seal, Membership Chairman, PO Box 203, Rockford, IL 61105; newsletter, *Blueberry Notes*.

Photo 28. Milk jug.
CREDIT: AL BAGDADE *(See p. 96)*

Photo 29 (left). Plate. CREDIT: AL BAGDADE. *Photo 30 (right). Plate.*
CREDIT: AL BAGDADE *(See pp. 99, 100)*

Photo 31. Cream and sugar. CREDIT: AL BAGDADE *(See p. 102)*

Berry bowl 5″ Dia. Flow Blue 1885–1900 England
"Touraine" pattern; "Stanley" mark.
Good Quality/Fine Condition $45 (D) **$20–$45**

Bone dish 6″ L Flow Blue 1885–1900 England
"Marguerite" pattern; "W. H. Grindley" mark.
Good Quality/Fine Condition $40 (D) **$20–$40**

Creamer 6″ H Flow Blue 1830–1845 England
"Indian Jar" pattern; rim repair; "T. and J. Fulnival"; c. 1843.
Superior Quality/Average Condition $180 (D) **$180–$275**

Cup and saucer Flow Blue 1830–1845 England
Handleless; "Pelew" pattern.
Very Good Quality/Fine Condition $75 (D) **$40–$75**

Cup and saucer Flow Blue 1885–1900 England
"Canton" pattern; hairline on handle; "James Edwards" mark.
Very Good Quality/Average Condition $140 (D) **$140–$250**

Cup and saucer Flow Blue 1885–1900 England
"Gironde" pattern; "W. H. Grindley" mark.
Very Good Quality/Fine Condition $110 (D) **$60–$110**

Cup and saucer Flow Blue 1900–1910 England
"Temple" pattern.
Very Good Quality/Fine Condition $125 (D) **$70–$125**

Cup and saucer Flow Blue 1900–1910 England
"Candia" pattern; "Cauldon" mark.
Very Good Quality/Fine Condition $100 (D) **$65–$100**

Pitcher 5.5″ H Flow Blue 1885–1900 England
"Non pareil" pattern; crazing; "Burgess and Leigh" mark.
Very Good Quality/Average Condition $150 (D) **$150–$300**

Pitcher 6″ H Flow Blue 1885–1900 England
"Tyne" pattern; "Ford and Sons" mark.
Superior Quality/Fine Condition $175 (D) **$90–$175**

Pitcher 9.5″ H Flow Blue 1885–1990 England
"Gironde" pattern; "W. H. Grindley" mark.
Superior Quality/Fine Condition $325 (D) **$150–$325**

Plate 9.75″ Dia. Flow Blue 1830–1845 England
"Pelew" pattern; "E. Challinor" mark. *(See photo 29)*
Very Good Quality/Fine Condition $95 (D) **$50–$95**

Plate 9.5″ Dia. Flow Blue 1830–1845 England
"Scinde" pattern.
Very Good Quality/Fine Condition $95 (D) **$45–$95**

Plate 10″ Dia. Flow Blue 1830–1845 England
"Pelew" pattern; "E. Challiner mark"; c. 1840.
Superior Quality/Fine Condition $150 (D) **$60–$150**

Plate 9″ Dia. Flow Blue 1845–1865 England
"Japan" pattern; "J. Tell" mark.
Very Good Quality/Fine Condition $75 (D) **$35–$75**

Plate 9.25″ Dia. Flow Blue 1845–1865 England
"Chusan" pattern; "Ashworth" mark; c. 1845.
Superior Quality/Fine Condition $140 (D) **$70–$140**

Plate 10″ Dia. Flow Blue 1845–1865 England
"Formosa" pattern; "T. J. & J. Mayer" mark.
Superior Quality/Fine Condition $150 (D)   **$70–$150**

Plate 10″ Dia. Flow Blue 1885–1900 England
"Fairy Villas II" pattern; "W. Adams" mark; rim chip.
Very Good Quality/Average Condition $50 (D)   **$50–$100**

Plate 7″ Dia. Flow Blue 1885–1900 England
"Kyeer" pattern; "W. Adams" mark.
Very Good Quality/Fine Condition $58 (D)   **$25–$65**

Plate 9.88″ Dia. Flow Blue 1885–1900 England
"Alton" pattern; "W. H. Grindley" mark; crazing.
Very Good Quality/Good Condition $90 (D)   **$50–$110**

Plate 10″ Dia. Flow Blue 1900–1910 England
"Yeddo" pattern; "Royal Staffordshire Pottery, Burslem, England" mark. *(See
photo 30)*
Good Quality/Fine Condition $35 (A)   **$20–$35**

Plate 9″ Dia. Flow Blue 1900–1910 England
"Florida" pattern; "Johnson Bros." mark.
Good Quality/Fine Condition $80 (D)   **$50–$80**

Platter 13″ L Flow Blue 1830–1845 England
"Amoy" pattern; "Davenport" mark; c. 1844.
Superior Quality/Fine Condition $400 (D)   **$200–$400**

Platter 12.36″ L Flow Blue 1900–1910 England
"Peach" pattern; "Johnson Bros." mark.
Very Good Quality/Fine Condition $100 (D)   **$50–$100**

Platter 11″ L × 8.5″ W Flow Blue 1900–1910 England
"Yeddo" pattern; "Ashworth" mark.
Very Good Quality/Fine Condition $135 (D)   **$65–$135**

Soup plate 10.25″ Dia. Flow Blue 1885–1900 England
"Hamilton" pattern; "J. Maddock & Son" mark.
Good Quality/Fine Condition $35 (D)   **$20–$35**

Soup plate 10″ Dia. Flow Blue 1900–1910 England
"Yeddo" pattern; "Ashworth" mark.
Very Good Quality/Fine Condition $110 (D)   **$50–$110**

Soup plate 9.75″ Dia. Flow Blue 1885–1900 England
"Alaska" pattern; "W. H. Grindley" mark.
Very Good Quality/Fine Condition $85 (D)   **$35–$85**

Soup tureen Flow Blue 1845–1865 England
"Indian Fest" pattern; stand and ladle.
Superior Quality/Fine Condition $1675 (D)   **$900–$1800**

Teabowl and saucer Flow Blue 1845–1865 England
"Tonquin" pattern; "Heath" mark.
Very Good Quality/Fine Condition $90 (D)   **$45–$90**

Vase 4.5″ H Flow Blue 1900–1910 England
"Dorothy" pattern; "Johnson Bros." mark.
Good Quality/Fine Condition $70 (D)   **$30–$70**

Vegetable bowl Flow Blue 1885–1900 England
Open; "Waldorf" pattern; "New Wharf Pottery" mark.
Very Good Quality/Fine Condition $115 (D)   **$60–$115**

Vegetable bowl   Flow Blue   1900–1910   England
Covered; "Florence" pattern; "Wood & Son" mark.
Very Good Quality/Fine Condition $195 (D)   **$95–$195**

IRISH BELLEEK
COUNTY FERMANAGH, IRELAND
1860–PRESENT

1863–1890

Located in County Fermanagh, the Belleek manufactory was founded by David McBirney and Robert Armstrong about 1860. Early Belleek wares made extensive use of native and nearby marine motifs: seashells, coral, marine plants and animals, dolphins, and sea horses, as well as the Irish shamrock. Many of these themes continue to the present day. The factory produced both utilitarian and decorative wares.

Belleek porcelain is extremely light and thin and has a creamy ivory surface and iridescent luster. The Belleek glaze is its most distinctive feature. Openwork baskets are the most recognized item produced at Belleek; they were introduced by William Henshall in 1865. These baskets have the mark impressed on a bar of clay attached to the bottom. All of the work was done by hand. These are intricate and highly decorated works that were not duplicated by any other factory.

Belleek is usually glazed parian, but some vases and figurines are unglazed. Dinner and tea services are popular, with the shell motif and shamrock predominating in the decorations. Every piece is still hand-crafted.

Collecting Information

The symbols usually incorporated into the marks are the shamrock, Irish wolfhound, Irish harp, and round tower. From 1863 to 1890 the marks were printed or impressed into the clay. Usually they were black but could be red, green, or blue. From 1891 to 1916 "Co. Fermanagh, Ireland" was added to the mark. In 1927 the registration circle was added to the mark. In 1956 the letter *R*, for "registry," was added as a trademark. Various green marks were used from 1946 to 1980, and then a yellow mark was introduced. A brown/gold mark has been used to stamp pieces made from 1980 to the present.

References

Richard K. Degenhardt, *Belleek*, Portfolio Press, 1978; good all-around book on Belleek and very well illustrated; Walter Rigdon, *Illustrated*

Collectors' Handbook, Wilkins Creative Printing, 1978; illustrates the various patterns and marks utilized.

Museums

National Museum, Dublin, Ireland; Ulster Museum, Belfast, Northern Ireland; Victoria and Albert Museum, London, England; Visitor's Center, The Belleek Pottery, Belleek County, Fermanagh, Northern Ireland.

Collectors' Club

The Belleek Collectors' Society, 144 W. Britannia St., Taunton, MA 02780; quarterly newsletter, *The Belleek Collector*.

Basket 8.25″ L Irish Belleek 1863–1891 Ireland
Body formed from cream-glazed criss-cross strands; rectangular wicker-work base; rim with applied flowers; branch handles; applied ribbon impressed with Belleek Co. Fermanagh mark; minor rim chips.
Very Good Quality/Good Condition $1345 (A)   **$800–$1600**

Cream and sugar Creamer 3.5″ H Irish Belleek 1926–1946 Ireland
"Ribbon" design; 3rd black mark. *(See photo 31)*
Good Quality/Fine Condition $135 (D)   **$65–$135**

Creamer Irish Belleek 1891–1926 Ireland
Shamrock design with brown twig handle; 2nd black mark.
Good Quality/Fine Condition $175 (D)   **$90–$175**

Dejeuner set Tray 16.25″ L Irish Belleek 1891–1926 Ireland
Tray, teapot, sugar bowl, creamer, 2 cups and saucers, "Neptune" design; pink trim, shell feet; 2nd black mark.
Superior Quality/Fine Condition $3600 (D)   **$2000–$4000**

Honey pot 6.5″ H Irish Belleek 1891–1926 Ireland
White and green flowers, applied stand, black arts cane handle, stump feet; 2nd black mark.
Very Good Quality/Fine Condition $395 (D)   **$225–$400**

Milk jug 6.5″ H Irish Belleek 1926–1946 Ireland
"Shamrock" design; 3rd black mark.
Good Quality/Fine Condition $195 (D)   **$95–$195**

Mug 3.25″ H Irish Belleek 1950–1970 Ireland
Paneled body; "horn" design; 3rd black mark.
Good Quality/Fine Condition $75 (D)   **$35–$75**

Salt 3″ L × 2″ W Irish Belleek 1891–1926 Ireland
Oval; "New Shell" design; green and coral trim; 2nd black mark.
Good Quality/Fine Condition $65 (D)   **$25–$65**

Sandwich tray 8″ L Irish Belleek 1950–1970 Ireland
"Limpet" pattern; shell-shaped dish; with cup.
Superior Quality/Fine Condition $125 (D)   **$50–$125**

Vase 10″ H Irish Belleek 1891–1926 Ireland
"Aberdeen" design; overall applied flowers; 2nd black mark.
Very Good Quality/Fine Condition $495 (D)   **$275–$495**

Vase 5.5″ H Irish Belleek 1891–1926 Ireland
Mirror image, shell design, pink trim; 2nd black mark.
Superior Quality/Fine Condition $450 (D) **$200–$450**

Vase 9.25″ H Irish Belleek 1925–1946 Ireland
Applied florals, 2 cutout handles; "Princess"; 3rd black mark.
Superior Quality/Fine Condition $650 (D) **$250–$650**

Vase 13″ H Irish Belleek 1926–1946 Ireland
"Vine" design; pearlized leaves; 3rd black mark.
Very Good Quality/Fine Condition $600 (D) **$250–$600**

Vase, tulip 6″ H Irish Belleek 1891–1926 Ireland
White with green trim; 2nd black mark.
Superior Quality/Fine Condition $495 (D) **$200–$495**

Vases, pair 9.25″ H Irish Belleek 1930–1950 Ireland
"Aberdeen" design; ewer shape with ribbed body and raised floral reliefs; chips
to florals; 3rd black mark.
Very Good Quality/Good Condition $660 (A) **$400–$1200**

C 1845

IRONSTONE—
WHITE AND PATTERNED, 1840s–1891
MASON'S IRONSTONE, 1813–1848
GAUDY IRONSTONE, 1850–1865
ENGLAND

Gothic-shaped white ironstone china was first produced in Staffordshire
about the 1840s. Numerous firms made white ironstone, including James
Edwards, T. J. & J. Mayer, J. Wedgwood, William Adams, and C.
Meigh and Sons, to name a few. After 1891, ironstone diminished in
popularity as the demand for porcelains increased.

In 1813, Charles and George Mason patented the ironstone formula
and manufacturing technique. Though they were not the first to make
this earthenware, they were certainly the most successful. Mason's Patent
Ironstone became dominant in the field. The first designs were transfer-
printed Orientals. A tremendous variety of items was made, from complete dinnerware sets to ornamental pieces.

Gaudy Ironstone was produced in the Staffordshire district of England
from 1850 to 1865. Designs were similar to Gaudy Welsh patterns. Some
pieces featured copper lustering, and some utilized the flow-blue technique.

References

Jean Wetherbee, *A Look at White Ironstone*, Wallace-Homestead, 1980;
Jean Wetherbee, *A Second Look at White Ironstone*, Wallace-Homestead,
1984; these books feature many designs and patterns by white-ironstone

manufacturers; Geoffrey A. Godden, *The Illustrated Guide to Mason's Patent Ironstone China*, Barrie & Jenkins, 1971.

Museums

City Museum and Art Gallery, Stoke-on-Trent, England; Potsdam Public Museum, Potsdam, NY; Victoria and Albert Museum, London.

Collectors' Club

Mason Collectors' Club, Elizabeth Jenkins, Home Farm Cottage, Glenthorne, Countisbury, Lynton, North Devon EX356NQ, England; membership: £30; four newsletters per year.

Cream and sugar Creamer 7″ H Ironstone 1845–1865 England
White; impressed "Sydenham" shape and "T. & R. Boote" marks. *(See photo 32)*
Very Good Quality/Fine Condition $240 (D)   **$100–$250**

Milk jug 4.75″ H Ironstone 1800–1805 England
Painted elaborate floral decoration in famille rose colors; border of gilt whorl panels and key fret rim; red Turner Patent Ironstone mark.
Very Good Quality/Fine Condition $500 (D)   **$350–$500**

Mug 4.75″ H Ironstone 1885–1900 England
White ground; large blue border band; 4 small blue bands below; unmarked.
Very Good Quality/Fine Condition $145 (D)   **$75–$145**

Pitcher 8.12″ H Gaudy ironstone 1845–1865 England
Yellow tulip-type flowers, cobalt stems with copper luster accents, pebble-textured ground.
Very Good Quality/Fine Condition $250 (D)   **$150–$250**

Plate 8.5″ Dia. Gaudy ironstone 1845–1865 England
Shaped rim; cobalt and copper luster vase with mauve open flower in center; scattered green leaves and tendrils; border of open iron-red flowerheads, cobalt leaves and tendrils; unmarked.
Very Good Quality/Fine Condition $175 (D)   **$100–$175**

Plate 8.5″ Dia. Gaudy ironstone 1845–1865 England
Gaudy pattern in iron-red, blue, and copper luster; unmarked. *(See photo 33)*
Very Good Quality/Fine Condition $135 (D)   **$90–$135**

Plate 9.75″ Dia. Ironstone 1845–1865 England
"Scalloped" pattern; impressed "Adams" mark. *(See photo 34)*
Good Quality/Fine Condition $18 (D)   **$10–$25**

Platter 11″ L × 8″ W Ironstone 1865–1885 England
Tea leaf pattern; "Alfred Meakin" mark.
Very Good Quality/Fine Condition $45 (D)   **$20–$45**

Platter 16″ L × 13″ W Ironstone 1885–1900 England
"Tea leaf" pattern; "Mellor, Taylor & Co." mark.
Very Good Quality/Fine Condition $165 (D)   **$95–$165**

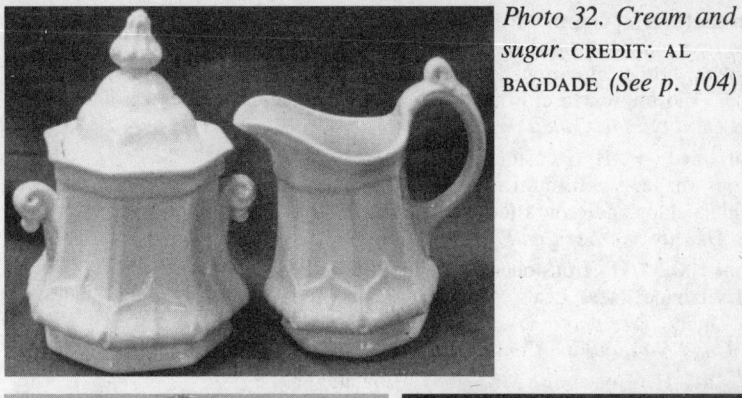

Photo 32. Cream and sugar. CREDIT: AL BAGDADE *(See p. 104)*

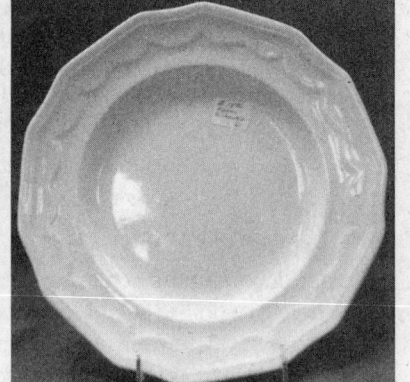

Photo 33 (left). Plate. CREDIT: AL BAGDADE. *Photo 34 (right). Plate.* CREDIT: AL BAGDADE *(See p. 104)*

Photo 35 (left). Teapot. CREDIT: AL BAGDADE. *Photo 36 (right). Vase.* CREDIT: AL BAGDADE *(See p. 106)*

Soup plate 9.88″ Dia. Ironstone 1845–1865 England
Large iron-red flowerhead in center and cobalt leaves and small yellow flowers; gold trim; border of cartouches with small red flower in each; blue cobalt "late Spode" and impressed crown mark.
Good Quality/Fine Condition $45 (D)   **$35–$85**

Sugar bowl 4″ H Ironstone 1845–1865 England
Bulbous shape; small multicolored flower on each side; red and blue band on shoulder; chips and crow's foot.
Good Quality/Average Condition $10 (A)   **$10–$45**

Teapot 10.5″ H Ironstone 1845–1865 England
Chinese shape, "Tea Leaf" pattern, "Stone China" and "Anthony Shaw Burslem" mark. *(See photo 35)*
Very Good Quality/Fine Condition $325 (D)   **$225–$325**

Vase 10″ H Ironstone 1865–1885 England
Twelve sides, "Imari" pattern in iron-red, blue, and gilt. *(See photo 36)*
Very Good Quality/Fine Condition $300 (D)   **$225–$400**

Vegetable dish 9.5″ H Ironstone 1845–1865 England
Covered and footed; Sydenham shape; British Registry mark.
Very Good Quality/Fine Condition $195 (D)   **$125–$195**

LUSTERWARE
ENGLAND
19TH CENTURY–PRESENT

Luster decoration is achieved by applying thin metallic films to china or earthenware bodies. Gold luster comes from gold oxide, copper luster from copper oxide, silver luster from platinum, and pink or purple luster from "purple of cassuis." Accurate dating for the start of luster decoration in England is not available.

"Resisting" involved keeping parts of an object white with wax or paper cutouts so that when the luster solution was applied, it would not affect the resisted parts. Overglaze enamels could be added to lustered ground. Reserved panels could also be transfer-printed, painted, or left plain.

"Splash," or Sunderland luster, was a mottled type of pink luster used on a white body.

Objects receiving the luster treatments included jugs, mugs, tea and tablewares, and plaques. Many manufacturers made lustered objects.

References
John Bedford, *Old English Lustre Ware*, Walker and Co., 1965; J. T. Shaw, *The Potteries of Sunderland and District*, Sunderland Library, 1961.

Museums
Art Institute of Chicago, Chicago, IL; Cincinnati Museum of Art,

Cincinnati, OH; City Museum and Art Gallery, Stoke-on-Trent, England; Sunderland Museum, Sunderland, England.

Bowl 4″ H × 11.25″ Dia. Lusterware 1830–1845 England
Dark green transfer of ship, "The Sailor's Farewell"; Masonic design and nautical verses; hairlines, yellowed rim repair; Sunderland style.
Very Good Quality/Average Condition $150 (A) **$350–$650**
Cake plate 10″ H-H Lusterware 1885–1900 England
Two small handles; overall luster.
Good Quality/Fine Condition $16 (D) **$10–$20**
Chocolate set Lusterware 1845–1865 England
Tankard pot; 6 tall mugs; ornate embossed designs with gold decorations and pink luster trim.
Good Quality/Fine Condition $150 (D) **$75–$150**
Creamer 3″ H Lusterware 1845–1865 England
Blue marbleized band, copper luster band.
Good Quality/Fine Condition $22 (D) **$15–$30**
Creamer 4″ H Lusterware 1845–1865 England
Bulbous shape; ornate grapevine design.
Good Quality/Fine Condition $28 (D) **$20–$35**
Creamer 2.25″ H Lusterware 1865–1885 England
Tan sanded center band, copper luster body.
Very Good Quality/Fine Condition $15 (A) **$20–$35**
Cup and saucer Lusterware 1830–1845 England
Handleless, gold rims, Sunderland style. *(See photo 37)*
Good Quality/Fine Condition $15 (D) **$20–$35**

> Sunderland-style pieces vary greatly throughout the country. Prices *appear* to be on the verge of a major jump—*DL*

Goblet 4.12″ H Lusterware 1845–1865 England
White band with purple luster, green, and dark red enameled floral designs.
Good Quality/Fine Condition $65 (D) **$35–$65**
Jug 5.88″ H Lusterware 1830–1845 England
Printed and colored cartoon of scenes of Napoleon and Marat; silver luster rim.
Very Good Quality/Fine Condition $650 (A) **$350–$650**
Jug 9.88″ H Lusterware 1830–1845 England
Printed and colored view of iron bridge at Sunderland, flanked by verse and "Sailor's Fairwell"; pink luster trim.
Very Good Quality/Fine Condition $725 (A) **$600–$1200**
Jug 6″ H Lusterware 1830–1845 England
Black printed fight between Tom Cribb and Tom Molinaux; cream ground, silver luster rim, spout, and borders.
Very Good Quality/Fine Condition $495 (A) **$350–$600**
Jug 5.25″ H Lusterware 1845–1865 England
Bird hunting scene; pink luster banding; hairline crack.
Good Quality/Average Condition $90 (D) **$90–$225**
Pitcher 8.75″ H Lusterware 1830–1845 England
Polychromed black transfers of Garibaldi, The Agamemnon in a Storm, and Ancient Order of Foresters; repair to handle.
Very Good Quality/Average Condition $150 (A) **$150–$375**

Pitcher 4.75″ H Lusterware 1830–1845 England
Iron-red transfer of piper in woodland scene, iron-red and pink luster accents, copper luster body. *(See photo 38)*
Very Good Quality/Fine Condition $95 (D)   **$45–$95**

Pitcher 4″ H Lusterware 1830–1845 England
Quilted body, silver luster leaves and neck wreath, orange florals. *(See photo 39)*
Very Good Quality/Fine Condition $285 (D)   **$150–$285**

Pitcher 5.75″ H Lusterware 1845–1865 England
Center cocoa brown band with luster flowers, cocoa brown band on neck with luster flowers, fancy handle; rim roughness.
Good Quality/Good Condition $95 (D)   **$50–$115**

Pitcher 2.5″ H Lusterware 1885–1900 England
Center yellow band with luster florals and leaves, copper and luster body.
Good Quality/Fine Condition $58 (D)   **$25–$65**

Soup plate 9.6″ Dia. Lusterware 1845–1865 England
Pink luster open flower in center; border of pink luster grape clusters, leaves and tendrils.
Good Quality/Fine Condition $58 (D)   **$35–$65**

Teapot 7″ H × 10″ L Lusterware 1830–1845 England
Rust, mauve, and green florals, pink luster bands. *(See photo 40)*
Very Good Quality/Fine Condition $295 (D)   **$150–$295**

Teapot 6.25″ H Lusterware 1845–1865 England
Squat, rectangular shape; small blue enamel flowerheads, scattered yellow enamel stylized flowerheads; copper luster body.
Very Good Quality/Fine Condition $85 (D)   **$60–$135**

Teapot 6.5″ H Lusterware 1845–1865 England
Squat, rectangular shape; pink luster leaves and rim bands, bunches of green grapes; unmarked.
Very Good Quality/Fine Condition $145 (D)   **$80–$165**

1865 - 1906

MAJOLICA
1850–PRESENT
ENGLISH AND CONTINENTAL

Leon Arnoux introduced majolica at Minton in 1850. It was a stone-type earthenware body with good sharp form, vibrant colors, and a thick tin glaze. There was a heavy reliance on natural themes such as florals and animals. Typical Victorian majolica examples include large garden ornaments plus all sorts of plates and dishes that were utilitarian and decorative.

Other English manufacturers of note were George Jones and Sons, Holdcroft, and Wedgwood. After George Jones left Minton, he established his own Trent Pottery and manufactured ornamental bowls, wall plaques, and lidded vases, as well as ordinary majolica wares.

On the Continent, majolica was made by Sarregamines in France, by

Photo 37 (left). Cup and saucer. CREDIT: AL BAGDADE. *Photo 38 (right). Pitcher.* CREDIT: AL BAGDADE *(See pp. 107, 108)*

Photo 39 (left). Pitcher. CREDIT: AL BAGDADE. *Photo 40 (right). Teapot.* CREDIT: AL BAGDADE *(See p. 108)*

Photo 41 (left). Plate. CREDIT: AL BAGDADE. *Photo 42 (right). Pitcher.* CREDIT: AL BAGDADE *(See pp. 111–112)*

Villeroy and Boch and Zell in Germany, and by companies in Austria, Bavaria, and Italy.

Fakes Alert

Gurgling pitchers, especially fish, are being brilliantly reproduced today. They are unmarked. Look for a flat matte finish on the bottom edge as the major clue. Also look for a lack of wear and discoloration on the unglazed base rim.

Museums

Cleveland Museum of Art, Cleveland, OH; City Museum and Art Gallery, Stoke-on-Trent, England; Victoria and Albert Museum, London; British Museum, London, England; Cooper-Hewitt Museum, New York, NY; Henry Ford Museum, Dearborn, MI; Minton Museum, Stoke-on-Trent, England; Wadsworth Atheneum, Hartford, CT; Wedgwood Museum, Barlaston, England.

Collectors' Club

Majolica International Society, 1275 First Avenue, Suite 103, New York, NY 10021; membership, $35; quarterly magazine.

Centerpiece 11.36" H Majolica 1865–1885 England
Modeled as 2 putti carrying shell, draped in ivy and barley; oval seaweed base; turquoise, green, yellow, and puce; impressed "Minton" and date (1867) mark.
Very Good Quality/Fine Condition $1400 (A)			**$1200–$2400**
Cigarette holder 8.5" H Majolica 1865–1885 Germany
Standing brown figural monkey with mauve shorts, yellow basket with pink interior on back; cobalt basket with pink interior on brown base; unmarked.
Very Good Quality/Fine Condition $325 (D)			**$225–$350**
Covered cheese dish 10" Dia. Majolica 1865–1885 England
Dogwood design; large series of dogwood pieces by George Jones; double-branch handle; turquoise ground, pink interior, pink and white flower, green leaves; British Registry mark, 1873.
Superior Quality/Fine Condition $995 (D)			**$500–$1000**
Dish 7.88" H Majolica 1865–1885 England
Green leaf resting on brown branch with acorns; blue titbird with yellow breast seated on end; impressed Minton mark; 1867.
Very Good Quality/Fine Condition $610 (A)			**$400–$900**
Jug 10" H Majolica 1865–1885 England
Multicolored relief of tavern scene; geometric bands; mottled blue ground; impressed Minton mark.
Very Good Quality/Fine Condition $595 (D)			**$300–$600**
Plate 8.5" Dia. Majolica 1845–1865 England
Raised florals; scalloped rim; overall green glaze; impressed "Minton" mark.
Very Good Quality/Fine Condition $60 (D)			**$45–$90**

Plate 9″ H Majolica 1885–1900 France
Turquoise and white ground with purple and olive-green asparagus with green stems; marked "Depose KG Luneville."
Very Good Quality/Fine Condition $155 (D)   **$100–$175**

Plate 7.5″ Dia. Majolica 1930–1950 France
Two grape clusters, large grape leaves and tendrils, shaded olive-green to tan ground; "PV Made in France" mark.
Good Quality/Fine Condition $15 (D)   **$10–$25**

Plate 9″ Dia. Majolica 1900–1910 Germany
Dark gray bird, gray ground, orange trim. *(See photo 41)*
Good Quality/Fine Condition $100 (D)   **$50–$100**

Plate, oyster 9.12″ Dia. Majolica 1845–1865 England
Green center well with ring of white shells; 3 white and 3 mauve oyster wells with yellow conch shells and coral between; impressed Minton mark.
Very Good Quality/Fine Condition $265 (D)   **$125–$275**

MOCHA WARE
STAFFORDSHIRE, ENGLAND
1760–1939

Mocha ware was made as utilitarian pottery for the ordinary man. It originated in the Staffordshire region of England in the late 1700s.

William Adams made mocha examples at his Cobridge factory for public houses, so wares were mostly jugs, coffeepots, porringers, butter dishes, and tankards.

Pieces usually were decorated with broad bands of colored slip that were blue, gray, or coffee-colored. Potters put a mixture called "tea" into the slip, which caused the color to spread out in treelike fronds that contrasted with the pale earthenware tones underneath. Some also had black rings added.

Patterns included Tree, Shrub, Fern, Seaweed, and Landscape. Others were Cat's Eye and Worm. Mocha examples rarely had a maker's mark.

Museums

City Museum and Art Gallery, Stoke-on-Trent, England.

Bowl 4″ H × 8.5″ Dia. Mocha ware 1845–1865 England
Light blue and black earthworm design, tooled rim with orange-tan band, black and green stripes; hairlines on base, stains.
Superior Quality/Average Condition $660 (A)   **$450–$750**

Chamber pot 2.5″ H Mocha ware 1865–1885 England
Yellowware body, white band with bluish seaweed; minor crazing.
Very Good Quality/Good Condition $150 (A)   **$100–$175**

Jug 6.75″ H Mocha ware 1830–1845 England
Bulbous shape; bands of brown and dark orange with earthworm between, white ground.
Superior Quality/Fine Condition $880 (A)   **$600–$1200**

Mug 3.5″ H   Mocha ware   1845–1865   England
Blue, white, and brown earthworm center band with black stripes; yellow ochre and brown border stripes; leaf handle; edge flakes.
Very Good Quality/Good Condition $383 (A)   **$300–$475**

Mug 4.36″ H   Mocha ware   1845–1865   England
Blue, brown, and white marbleized center band; blue, black, and white border stripes, leaf handle; hairline.
Superior Quality/Average Condition $740 (A)   **$500–$900**

Pitcher 7″ H   Mocha ware   1845–1865   England
Center band of brown and white double-earthworm pattern on blue band with green and black border stripes; rim hairline; stains.
Superior Quality/Average Condition $1015 (A)   **$1000–$1800**

Pitcher 8″ H   Mocha ware   1845–1865   England
Green seaweed design, brown bands. *(See photo 42)*
Superior Quality/Fine Condition $975 (D)   **$1000–$1800**

Salt 3.25″ Dia.   Mocha ware   1845–1865   England
Seaweed decoration, gray band with black stripes; rim chips.
Very Good Quality/Good Condition $220 (A)   **$150–$325**

Tea caddy 4.88″ H   Mocha ware   1845–1865   England
Black, tan, and blue geometrics; lip repaired.
Superior Quality/Average Condition $575 (A)   **$500–$1000**

STAFFORDSHIRE

The word "Staffordshire" immediately conjures up different things to different people. For some collectors, the great pottery and porcelain factories are thought of—Wedgwood, Ridgway, Minton, etc. For others, only the makers of Historical Blue are brought to mind—Clews, Thomas Major, or perhaps the Wood family. Others would think only of the fantastic array of figures made (and not even marked) by hundreds of small to large potteries throughout this great potting area.

While Historical Blue remains at a high level for American scenes, the other pieces of this genre bring quite affordable prices. Many people amass table and dessert services of the various colors and patterns, mulberry continuing to be particularly popular (read "very expensive"). The most interesting areas of price escalation have been in figural pieces.

Eighteenth- and early 19th-century pieces have long brought hundreds of dollars—pairs of sheep, cows, deer, etc. Dormant for many years, the last three years have seen astonishing rises for Victorian period Staffordshire District animal figures. Rabbits, zebras, elephants, fine dog pairs—all have skyrocketed. Only inkwells and cottages have suffered, due to prolific modern pieces flooding the market. New dogs are generally so hideously obvious that as yet they have not depressed that market—and probably won't.

Interestingly, the human figural prices are suddenly moving upward in the market. Whether sold as decorative pieces or mounted as lamps, figures of Scottish hunters, frolicsome lassies, and famous highwaymen are being snapped up at shows and shops—for steadily higher and higher prices. Staffordshire pieces, with their quaintness and exciting colors, seem to have displaced Oriental items as the favored decorative accents throughout the country. Look for continued price increases for several more years.

References

Arthur Coysh, *Blue and White Transfer Ware 1780–1840*, David and Charles, 1970; A. W. Coysh and R. K. Henrywood, *The Dictionary of Blue and White Printed Pottery 1780–1880, Vol. 2*, Antique Collectors' Club, 1989; P. D. Gordon Pugh, *Staffordshire Portrait Figures and Allied Subjects of the Victorian Era*, rev. ed., Antique Collectors' Club, Ltd., 1987.

Museums

City Museum and Art Gallery, Stoke-on-Trent, England; Fitzwilliam Museum, Cambridge, England; The Henry Francis DuPont Winterthur Museum, Winterthur, DE; Victoria and Albert Museum, London, England; Wellcome Museum, London, England.

Basket and stand, pair 11″ L Staffordshire 1845–1865 England
Blue transfer of chinoiserie pattern; unmarked.
Very Good Quality/Fine Condition $880 (A) **$800–$1500**

Children's mug 2.25″ H Staffordshire 1845–1865 England
Green transfer of "The Seasons—Month of May"; young man and woman in garden and "cheered by the balmy breath of May—the trees are decked with blossoms gay."
Good Quality/Fine Condition $145 (D) **$75–$145**

Creamer, cow 6″ H Staffordshire 1845–1865 England
Red-brown spots; green base. *(See photo 43)*
Very Good Quality/Fine Condition $350 (D) **$250–$450**

Figure 8.5″ H Staffordshire 1800–1830 England
Standing cockerel; cream body with brown and yellow sponging; domed green circular base; minor restoration.
Very Good Quality/Good Condition $2250 (A) **$1500–$2500**

Figure 8.25″ H Staffordshire 1845–1865 England
Standing hurdy-gurdy player wearing lilac-lined white coat, flowered breeches, turquoise waistcoat and black hat; green and brown washed base.
Good Quality/Fine Condition $265 (A) **$275–$475**

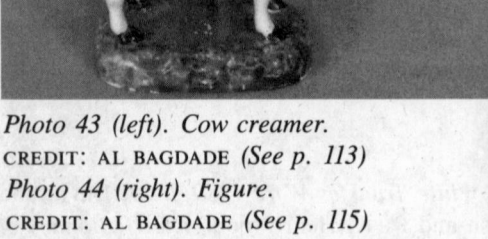

Photo 43 (left). Cow creamer.
CREDIT: AL BAGDADE *(See p. 113)*
Photo 44 (right). Figure.
CREDIT: AL BAGDADE *(See p. 115)*

Photo 45 (left). Plate. CREDIT: AL BAGDADE. *Photo 46 (right). Platter.*
CREDIT: AL BAGDADE *(See p. 115)*

Photo 47. Teapot.
CREDIT: AL BAGDADE
(See p. 115)

Figure 7.5″ H Staffordshire 1845–1865 England
Seated figure with feathered gray surface with white; blue collar and gold bow.
Very Good Quality/Fine Condition $500 (D) **$300–$500**

Figure 14″ H Staffordshire 1845–1865 England
Prince Albert and Victoria, faux clock, multicolored. *(See photo 44)*
Very Good Quality/Fine Condition $285 (D) **$175–$375**

Figures, pair 3.75″ H Staffordshire 1800–1830 England
Gray-brown standing elephants on oval bases with green accents.
Good Quality/Fine Condition $400 (A) **$400–$600**

Jug 6.25″ H Staffordshire 1800–1830 England
Relief busts of Wellington and General Hill.
Good Quality/Fine Condition $200 (A) **$125–$200**

Pitcher 4.25″ H Staffordshire 1800–1830 England
Pottery; bulbous shape; blue transfer of Oriental courtyard scene on each side; spout chip.
Good Quality/Good Condition $110 (A) **$75–$135**

Plate 8″ Dia. Staffordshire 1822–1841 England
"Sheltered Peasants" design; dark blue transfer; impressed R. Hall mark.
Very Good Quality/Fine Condition $105 (A) **$50–$125**

Plate 9″ Dia. Staffordshire 1845–1865 England
"Corean" pattern; mulberry transfer.
Good Quality/Fine Condition $35 (D) **$25–$60**

Plate, ABC 7″ Dia. Staffordshire 1800–1830 England
"Highland Dance"; green, rose, yellow, gold and black transfer. *(See photo 45)*
Good Quality/Fine Condition $75 (D) **$50–$115**

Plates, set of 8 8.75″ Dia. Staffordshire 1830–1845 England
"Blue Willow" pattern.
Good Quality/Fine Condition $100 (D) **$200–$300**

Platter 18″ L × 14″ W Staffordshire 1830–1845 England
Brown transfer of "Oriental" pattern.
Very Good Quality/Fine Condition $110 (D) **$60–$175**

Platter 15″ L Staffordshire 1830–1845 England
"Picturesque views of Hudson River" gray transfer; Clews. *(See photo 46)*
Very Good Quality/Fine Condition $400 (D) **$300–$500**

Spaniels, pair 10″ H Staffordshire 1865–1885 England
Orange and black on white ground; unmarked.
Good Quality/Fine Condition $220 (A) **$600–$900**

> A bargain or a major misrepresentation by the auction house. The color combination is unknown to me before 1980 reproductions!—*DL*

Sugar bowl 6.25″ H Gaudy Staffordshire 1845–1865 England
Orange, green, and red-brown flowers; stains, small hairlines.
Good Quality/Average Condition $125 (A) **$125–$200**

Teapot 5.88″ H Staffordshire 1750–1780 England
Solid agate, globular shape, curved spout, loop handle, recumbant lion finial, 3 paw feet, repair to spout.
Superior Quality/Average Condition $425 (D) **$400–$750**

Teapot 8.5″ H Staffordshire 1845–1865 England
"Rebecca at the Well" design, flowers, domed cover, medium blue transfers. *(See photo 47)*
Very Good Quality/Fine Condition $300 (D) **$250–$450**

LATE PERIOD

C 1892

AMPHORA
TURN-TEPLITZ BOHEMIA (NOW CZECHOSLOVAKIA)
1892–PRESENT

In 1892, Riessner and Kessel started the Amphora Porzellan Fabrik to make earthenware and porcelain at Turn-Teplitz in Bohemia. Mostly porcelain figures and Art Nouveau stylized vases were made for export. Marks included a variety of stamps. Many firms were located in the Teplitz area at the turn of the century.

Basket 7.75″ H Turn-Teplitz 1910–1930 Austria-Bohemia
Four crossing handles with cobalt jewels, green blown-out leaves; body with bunches of burnished gold grapes; cobalt base; iridescent colors.
Good Quality/Fine Condition $475 (D) **$200–$475**

Bowl 6″ Dia. Turn-Teplitz 1900–1910 Austria-Bohemia
Stylized floral decor in colors.
Good Quality/Fine Condition $95 (D) **$25–$95**

Bowl 12″ H × 15″ L Turn-Teplitz 1910–1930 Austria-Bohemia
Footed; reticulated body with applied leaves and chestnuts; 2 double-twist gold handles; Art Nouveau style; "Amphora" mark.
Very Good Quality/Fine Condition $625 (D) **$275–$625**

Ewer 12.5″ H Turn-Teplitz 1910–1930 Austria-Bohemia
Handpainted enameled flowers; "Stellmacher" mark.
Good Quality/Fine Condition $125 (D) **$50–$125**

Figure 16″ H Turn-Teplitz 1900–1910 Austria
Standing woman holding 2 baskets; tan and soft pastel colors; "Amphora Teplitz" mark.
Very Good Quality/Fine Condition $375 (D) **$150–$375**

Pitcher 14″ H Turn-Teplitz 1900–1910 Austria-Bohemia
Blown-out green iridescent flowers on cream ground, flower-form opening, applied stems; Art Nouveau style; "Amphora" mark.
Very Good Quality/Fine Condition $325 (D) **$150–$325**

Vase 7.25″ H Turn-Teplitz 1900–1910 Austria-Bohemia
Three scenes of men in various pursuits; blue shades with tan and brown matte and gloss finish; 3 small handles; Art Nouveau style; "Amphora" mark.
Very Good Quality/Fine Condition $350 (D) **$175–$350**

Vase 6″ H Turn-Teplitz 1900–1910 Austria-Bohemia
Glazed fireplace on neck, gold trim, cream ground, green handles; "Paul Dachsel" mark. *(See photo 48)*
Superior Quality/Fine Condition $2500 (D) **$1000–$2500**

Vase 9.5″ H Turn-Teplitz 1910–1930 Austria-Bohemia
Blown-out, etched shell decoration in earthtones; large blue, cobalt, pink, and green jewels on body; cobalt rim with pink and green jewels; "Amphora" mark.
Very Good Quality/Fine Condition *$285 (D)* **$125–$285**
Vase 11″ H Turn-Teplitz 1910–1930 Austria-Bohemia
Bronze ground with applied frog and wolfhound; "Imperial Amphora" mark.
Very Good Quality/Fine Condition *$650 (D)* **$350–$650**

AUSTRIA

1718–PRESENT

M Z

c-1900

The Vienna factory was the second factory in Europe to make hard-paste porcelain. Du Paquier founded the factory in 1718 with assistance from Meissen workers. The factory was sold to the state in 1744. The shield mark was introduced at this time. The factory closed in 1864.

Many of the 19th- and 20th-century porcelain factories are classified with Bohemia porcelain because of their location.

Some additional factories making decorative and utilitarian porcelains included Brux, Frauenthal, Turn, Augarten, Wienerberger, Spitz, and Neumann.

Michael Powolny and Berthold Loffler founded the Wiener Keramik Studio in 1905 and made tablewares and figures in earthenware and porcelain. Many utilized Art Nouveau and Art Deco designs.

References

George Ware, *German and Austrian Porcelain*, Lothar Woeller Press, 1951. This is a good general reference, and it seems to be the only one available on this subject.

Museums

Österreichisches Museum für Angewandtekunst, Vienna, Austria; Vienna Kunsthistorisches Museum, Vienna, Austria.

Bowl 10″ L × 8″ W Austria 1900–1910 Austria
Rectangular; center portrait of "Constance" in colors; hunter-green border with red medallions, gold trim; blue beehive mark.
Superior Quality/ Fine Condition *$795 (D)* **$350–$795**
Box 5.5″ H × 7.75″ W Austria 1910–1930 Austria
Green and gray figural turtle bottom with gold trim; cover with kneeling children in natural colors; satin finish; Ernst Wahliss.
Very Good Quality/Fine Condition *$365 (D)* **$150–$365**

Dish 7.5″ W Austria 1900–1910 Austria
Multicolored scene of herdsman and woman; ornate rim; imperial crown china, "Austria" mark.
Very Good Quality/Fine Condition $135 (D)   **$50–$135**

Ewer 7″ H Austria 1910–1930 Austria
Portrait of lady in period clothes; raised decor, green ground, recticulated handles; "Victoria Austria" mark.
Very Good Quality/Fine Condition $150 (D)   **$60–$150**

Milk pitcher 4.5″ H Austria 1910–1930 Austria
Figural elk herd in natural colors.
Good Quality/Fine Condition $90 (D)   **$40–$90**

Plate 10″ Dia. Austria 1900–1910 Austria
Center scene of "The Gleaners" in colors, dark brown border with gold tracery.
Superior Quality/Fine Condition $495 (D)   **$200–$495**

Plate 8.25″ Dia. Austria 1910–1930 Austria
Center scene of maiden and angel by stream, blue border; signed "Kauffmann"; "Victoria Austria" mark.
Very Good Quality/Fine Condition $115 (D)   **$50–$115**

Plates, set of 8 9″ Dia. Austria 1900–1910 Austria
Each with different fish in natural habitat in colors; dark green borders with gold trim; "Imperial Psalma Austria" mark.
Very Good Quality/Fine Condition $180 (D)   **$180–$325**

Vase 8″ H Austria 1900–1910 Austria
Portrait of Madam LeBrum in colors, signed "Wagner"; blue beehive mark.
Superior Quality/Fine Condition $895 (D)   **$350–$895**

Vase 4.5″ H Austria 1900–1910 Austria
Rust, green, and apricot pods, green jewels on rim, tan ground, gold rim and handles; red "Ernst Walhiss Alexandra Porcelain Works" mark. *(See photo 49)*
Superior Quality/Fine Condition $1600 (D)   **$700–$1600**

Vase 10″ H Austria 1910–1930 Austria
Multicolored Kauffman-type scene; green ground; gold handles; ruffled rim; "Victoria, Austria" mark.
Good Quality/Fine Condition $65 (D)   **$35–$65**

Vase 7″ H Austria 1910–1930 Austria
Green basketweave ground, applied leaves with gold berries, 2 handles.
Very Good Quality/Fine Condition $195 (D)   **$90–$195**

Bavaria
1917

BAVARIA
c. 1713–PRESENT
(NOW GERMANY)

Many factories were making porcelains in Bavaria by the 18th century. Some of these included Bauscher, J. N. Muller, Schumann, Thomas, and Seh, Scherzer and Company. At first the Bayreuth factory made faience and brown glazed wares; porcelains were started in 1745 when Frankel and Schrook took over.

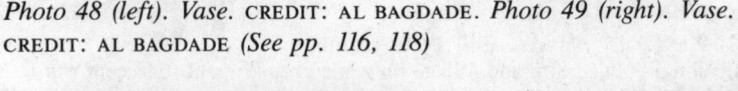

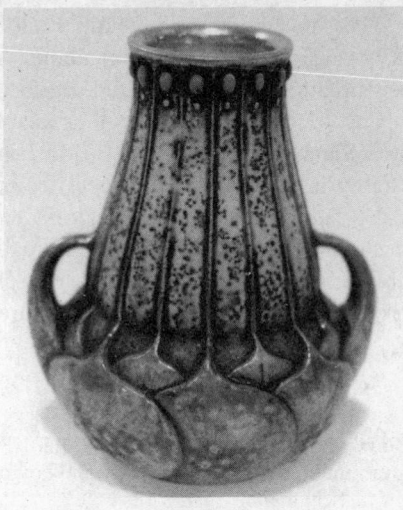

Photo 48 (left). Vase. CREDIT: AL BAGDADE. *Photo 49 (right). Vase.*
CREDIT: AL BAGDADE *(See pp. 116, 118)*

Photo 50. Cookie dish.
CREDIT: AL BAGDADE *(See p. 120)*
Photo 51. Vase.
CREDIT: AL BAGDADE *(See p. 122)*

The Tirschenreuth Porcelain Factory was founded in 1838 and made utilitarian and decorative porcelains. The Porcelain Factory Lorenz Hutschenreuther in Selb acquired the factory in 1927.

Carl Magnus Hutschenreuther established a factory to make porcelains at Hohenberg, Bavaria, in 1814. His son Lorenz established his own factory in Selb. These two factories coexisted even though they were the same family. The Lorenz factory acquired many additional firms and made fine-quality porcelains. Eventually both branches of the family were united in 1969 under the name Hutschenreuther AG. The company still produces limited-edition plates, figures, dinnerware, and other china.

Museums

Sèvres Museum, Sèvres, France.

Bowl   11.5″ L × 6.75″ W   Bavaria   1885–1900   Germany
Oval; multicolored scene of lady and boy picking wheat; blue sides, white pierced rim; ''Schumann'' mark.
Good Quality/Fine Condition $36 (D)   **$20–$36**

Bowl   9.5″ Dia.   Bavaria   1910–1930   Germany
Multicolored plumed bird and foliage on white ground; gold iridescent rim.
Good Quality/Fine Condition $25 (D)   **$10–$25**

Chocolate pot   10.75″ H   Bavaria   1900–1910   Germany
Small pink and blue flowering vines on white ground; fancy handle and thumbrest.
Good Quality/Fine Condition $60 (D)   **$35–$60**

Chocolate pot   9.5″ H   Bavaria   1900–1930   Germany
Wide gold bands, pink flowers, gold handle; ''Bavaria'' and crown mark.
Good Quality/Fine Condition $75 (D)   **$40–$75**

Cookie dish   11″ H-H   Bavaria   1910–1930   Germany
Multicolored flowers in center; cobalt border with gold trim; white handles with gold trim; ''PM Bavaria'' mark. *(See photo 50)*
Good Quality/Fine Condition $40 (A)   **$25–$40**

Dinner service, part   Bavaria   1925–1930   Germany
Ten dinner plates, 10 luncheon plates, 12 bread and butter, 11 cups, 12 saucers, 2 salt and peppers, 2 small serving bowls; cream ground, 3 rectangular green designs on borders, gilt rims; Art Deco.
Very Good Quality/Good Condition $425 (D)   **$275–$500**

Hair receiver   4.5″ Dia.   Bavaria   1910–1930   Germany
White, yellow, and green florals; pale yellow ground; ''Z.S. Bavaria'' mark.
Good Quality/Fine Condition $39 (D)   **$20–$45**

Hatpin holder   4.75″ H   Bavaria   1910–1930   Germany
Closed bottom, attached base; cream ground with rust-colored flowers; unmarked.
Good Quality/Fine Condition $85 (D)   **$45–$85**

Pitcher   5.25″ H   Bavaria   1885–1900   Germany
Paneled body; green and purple grapes on light green ground; gold rim, foot and handle trim.
Good Quality/Fine Condition $65 (D)   **$30–$65**

Pitcher and 6 mugs Pitcher 15″, mugs 6″ Bavaria 1885–1900 Germany
Gooseberry design; whitened gilt raised ovals on rims; orange shading to rust;
gilt rims; artist signed Jaegar and Company.
Superior Quality/Fine Condition $625 (D) **$225–$625**

Plate 9.12″ Dia. Bavaria 1910–1930 Germany
Center romantic classical scene of 2 figures and Cupid in rust, green, brown,
and yellow on white ground; shaped black and gold inner border and rim; pierced
outer border.
Very Good Quality/Fine Condition $75 (D) **$25–$75**

Plates, set of 8 10.75″ Dia. Bavaria 1910–1930 Germany
Gold florals, embossed center with geometrics, deep cream ground; signed
"Koy" and "Royal Bavaria" marks.
Good Quality/Fine Condition $300 (D) **$150–$300**

Tea service Bavaria 1910–1930 Germany
Teapot, creamer, sugar bowl, 5 cups and saucers, 5 dessert plates; yellow luster
with black and white checkerboard rims.
Good Quality/Fine Condition $78 (D) **$50–$85**

Vase 10″ H Bavaria 1900–1910 Germany
Green and purple grapes, gold double handles; Marktschwaben mark.
Good Quality/Fine Condition $75 (D) **$35–$75**

Clarice Cliff
WILKINSON LTD
ENGLAND

CLARICE CLIFF
BURSLEM, ENGLAND
1925–1963

C1930

Clarice Cliff apprenticed at A. J. Wilkinson Ltd's Royal Staffordshire
Pottery in Burslem. Soon she was decorating bowls and vases from the
Newport factory they acquired. She utilized vivid colors and eccentric
Art Deco designs with chunky angular shapes. Every piece was hand-
painted with designs that were quite innovative.

In addition to her successful Bizarre ware, Clarice Cliff introduced
patterns called Applique, Fantasque, Gay Day, Latonia, Lodere, Ravel,
and the most popular, Crocus. Shapes also had special names. Customers could order a specific shape with the pattern of their choice. Designs
had circles, squares, bands, diamonds, conical shapes, and simple landscapes with flowers. All sorts of shapes were made. Many unusual color
combinations were utilized.

Wilkinson, after several mergers, is now owned by the Wedgwood
group.

References

Leonard Giffin and L. & S. Meisel, *Clarice Cliff: The Bizarre Affair*,
Adams, 1988; Peter Wentworth-Shields and Kay Johnson, *Clarice Cliff*,

L'Odeum, 1976; Howard Watson, *Collecting Clarice Cliff*, Kevin Francis, 1988.

Museums

Brighton Museum, Brighton, England

Collectors' Club

Clarice Cliff Collectors' Club, Leonard R. Griffin, Fantasque House, Tennis Drive, The Park, Nottingham NG7 1AE England.

Bowl 8.75″ Dia. Clarice Cliff 1930–1950 England
"Honeyglaze," orange-red, blue and purple crocus pattern, brown band, green rim.
Very Good Quality/Fine Condition $195 (D)   **$125–$195**
Bowl 5.5″ Dia. Clarice Cliff 1930–1950 England
Freeform; striated brown and green glaze.
Good Quality/Fine Condition $200 (A)   **$100–$200**
Cake stand 11″ H Clarice Cliff 1930–1950 England
"Subway Sadie"; baluster-turned figural finial above dish with stylized floral design; turned base; "Fantasque by Clarice Cliff Wilkinson Ltd England" mark.
Superior Quality/Fine Condition $1600 (A)   **$900–$1600**
Pitcher 5.12″ H Clarice Cliff 1930–1950 England
"Bizarre"; blue crocus design; yellow band on neck, light blue band on base; "Bizarre by Clarice Cliff, Wilkinson Ltd England" mark.
Very Good Quality/Fine Condition $500 (D)   **$325–$500**
Pitcher 8.5″ H Clarice Cliff 1930–1950 England
Molded parrot on side in colors, ribbed body, branch handle.
Good Quality/Fine Condition $450 (A)   **$250–$450**
Plate 10″ Dia. Clarice Cliff 1900–1910 England
"Tonquin" pattern; blue transfer.
Good Quality/Fine Condition $10 (D)   **$5–$10**
Plate 10″ Dia. Clarice Cliff 1930–1950 England
"Rural scenes"; center transfer of man chopping tree in colors; brown border of farm implements.
Good Quality/Fine Condition $20 (D)   **$5–$20**
Tea and coffee set Clarice Cliff 1930–1950 England
Teapot, coffeepot, milk pitcher, creamer, open sugar bowl; "Stamford" shape, "Viscaria" design; yellow and mauve open flowers, mauve bases, cream-tan ground.
Superior Quality/Fine Condition $2200 (D)   **$1200–$2200**
Toast rack 6.5″ L Clarice Cliff 1910–1930 England
"Bizarre"; orange sun, blue water, yellow and green trees; "Handpainted Bizarre by Clarice Cliff, Newport Pottery England" mark.
Very Good Quality/Fine Condition $395 (D)   **$250–$450**
Vase 8.12″ H Clarice Cliff c. 1930 England
"Crocus" pattern; blue, orange, and purple flowers; cream ground, yellow top band, wide rust and green band; "Crocus Bizarre by Clarice Cliff, Newport Pottery England." *(See photo 51)*
Superior Quality/Fine Condition $650 (A)   **$500–$900**

DOULTON AND ROYAL DOULTON
DOULTON OF LAMBETH
LAMBETH, NEAR LONDON
1815–1956

1880-1902

John Doulton founded the Lambeth Pottery in 1815 in Lambeth, near London. The firm was known for its production of utilitarian stonewares, including bottles, barrels, flasks, and jugs. In 1835, the addition of the steam-powered potter's wheel greatly increased the firm's production. Architectural terra cotta, garden ornaments, drain pipes, and the like were popular items.

During the last quarter of the 19th century, Doulton joined forces with the Lambert School of Art, employing great numbers of artists at the factory. By the early 20th century, production by artists decreased. However, at that time, Leslie Harradine was renown for his stoneware figures of Dickens' characters and flasks featuring politicians. In the 1920s and 1930s the factory produced many commemorative wares. Production ceased in 1956.

DOULTON OF BURSLEM
STAFFORDSHIRE, ENGLAND
1877–PRESENT

1882 1902   1882 - 1902

Henry Doulton acquired the Nile Street Pottery of Burslem in 1877. The firm produced very high-quality porcelain as well as inexpensive earthenware tablewares. Charles Noke joined the firm in 1889. When Doulton exhibited at the Chicago Columbian Exposition, Noke's vases were displayed. His pieces featured contemporary figures portrayed as historical personages.

The Burslem factory produced earthenware tableware and also fine bone china with elaborate designs and decorated in gold. Doulton was granted the Royal Warrant of Appointment by King Edward VII in 1901. From then on, the name "Royal Doulton" was used.

Biscuit jar 7.25″ H Doulton 1885–1900 England
Impressed ferns and plants, leaves in brown accented in gold, blue, and beige ground, silicon glaze; "Doulton Lambeth" mark.
Very Good Quality/Fine Condition $280 (A) **$200–$350**
Biscuit jar 7.75″ H × 6″ Dia. Doulton 1930–1950 England
Bunches of multicolored flowers on cream ground, embossed green and cobalt rim and base; silverplated cover and handle.
Good Quality/Fine Condition $175 (D) **$90–$175**

Bowl 5.5″ H × 9.25″ Dia. Doulton 1885–1900 England
Footed; gold and silver flowers in relief, tapestry finish; "Doulton Burslem."
Very Good Quality/Fine Condition *$395 (D)*   **$200–$395**

Bowl 7.5″ H Doulton 1930–1950 England
"Chinese Jade"; squat, globular shape, molded with trailing and scrolling fruiting vines and veined in tones of green on white ground; printed crowned lion
and script "Chinese Jade", "Noke" and "HN" marks.
Superior Quality/Fine Condition *$2400 (A)*   **$1200–$2400**

Bowl and stand 5.5″ H × 9.25″ Dia. Doulton 1900–1910 England
Gold and silver flowers in relief, tapestry finish; "Doulton Burslem."
Very Good Quality/Fine Condition *$395 (D)*   **$200–$450**

Figure 17″ L Doulton 1910–1930 England
Rouge flambé, half-seated rhinoceros; mottled hide and feet.
Superior Quality/Fine Condition *$1250 (D)*   **$500–$1250**

Figure 7.5″ H Doulton 1930–1950 England
"Janice"; "HN2022"; 1949.
Very Good Quality/Fine Condition *$450 (D)*   **$250–$450**

Figure Doulton 1948–1953 England
Henrietta Maria; "HN 2005." *(See photo 52)*
Very Good Quality/Fine Condition *$300 (A)*   **$150–$300**

Jardinière 9″ H × 10″ Dia. Doulton 1910–1930 England
Shakespeare series; multicolored scene of Hamlet and Ophelia.
Very Good Quality/Fine Condition *$325 (D)*   **$175–$325**

Jug, character Doulton 1940–1950 England
Auld Mac; small size; "D5824," "A" mark. *(See photo 53)*
Good Quality/Fine Condition *$245 (D)*   **$125–$245**

Loving cup 9.5″ H Doulton 1906–1928 England
"Bayeaux tapestry" design.
Very Good Quality/Fine Condition *$325 (D)*   **$150–$325**

Mug 5″ H Doulton 1900–1910 England
Stoneware; relief busts of Edward VII and Queen. *(See photo 54)*
Very Good Quality/Fine Condition *$225 (D)*   **$125–$225**

Pitcher 6.5″ H Doulton 1920–1930 England
"English cottages" series ware. *(See photo 55)*
Very Good Quality/Fine Condition *$215 (A)*   **$175–$275**

Pitcher 5.5″ H Doulton 1930–1950 England
"Dickensware"; tan ground. *(See photo 56)*
Very Good Quality/Fine Condition *$160 (A)*   **$125–$250**

Plate 7.25″ × 7.25″ Doulton 1910–1930 England
Dickensware; Tony Weller; signed "Noke."
Very Good Quality/Fine Condition *$125 (D)*   **$70–$125**

Toby jug 9.5″ H Doulton 1950–1970 England
Seated Cliff Cornell in brown suit.
Superior Quality/Fine Condition *$435 (D)*   **$300–$475**

Vase 7.5″ H Doulton 1880–1928 England
Blue "Babes in Woods" series, children with umbrella.
Very Good Quality/Fine Condition *$535 (D)*   **$300–$575**

Photo 52 (left). Figure. CREDIT: AL BAGDADE. *Photo 53 (right, top).*
Character jug. CREDIT: AL BAGDADE. *Photo 54 (right, bottom). Mug.*
CREDIT: AL BAGDADE *(See p. 124)*

Photo 55 (left). Pitcher. CREDIT: AL BAGDADE. *Photo 56 (right).*
Pitcher. CREDIT: AL BAGDADE *(See p. 124)*

Vase 11.5″ H Doulton 1885–1900 England
Multicolored flowers outlined in gold on bottom, gold pattern on neck, double gold handles; "Doulton Burslem" mark.
Good Quality/Fine Condition $235 (D)   **$175–$275**
Vases, pair 9.5″ H Doulton 1885–1900 England
Cylindrical body incised with band of donkeys in landscape; incised floral borders; brown, blue, and gray tones; Hannah Barlow.
Very Good Quality/Fine Condition $1195 (A)   **$900–$1800**

MOORCROFT
BURSLEM, STAFFORDSHIRE
1897–PRESENT

William Moorcroft first worked as a potter at James Macintyre and Company Ltd. of Burslem. He made vases, bowls, and biscuit jars called Aurelian ware in blue, red, and gold plant forms.

Florian ware featured poppies, violets, or cornflowers applied in relief or slip-trail outlines in patterns such as Claremont, Hazeldene, Honesty, Pansy, Pomegranate, and Flamminium lusterwares.

Moorcroft built his own pottery in 1913, concentrating on flambé or transmutation glazes. He was appointed potter to Queen Mary in 1928. When he died in 1945, his son continued the company.

Walter's works included Caribbean and marine life designs, and he continued the flambé colors and experiments.

References

Paul Atterbury, *Moorcroft Pottery*, Richard Dennis and Hugh Edwards, 1987; A. W. Coysh, *British Art Pottery, 1870–1940*, Charles E. Tuttle, 1976.

Museums

Everson Museum of Art, Syracuse, NY

Candlesticks, pair 10″ H Moorcroft 1900–1910 England
"Carnation"; slip-trailed flowerheads and foliage highlighted in light and dark blue; screw threads on interior of sconce; printed "Florian" and incised "WM" marks; Art Nouveau style.
Very Good Quality/Fine Condition $1185 (A)   **$900–$1800**
Pitcher 6.5″ H Moorcroft 1900–1910 England
"MacIntyre Dura Ware"; raised slip floral design in green and blue in pink ground; brown mark.
Very Good Quality/Fine Condition $895 (D)   **$600–$1200**
Plate 9.25″ Dia. Moorcroft 1910–1930 England
Yellow shades with pink and green florals, cobalt ground, signature mark. *(See photo 57)*
Very Good Quality/Fine Condition $450 (D)   **$250–$450**

Vase 9" H Moorcroft 1900–1910 England
Florian, green and blue poppy design on cream ground; #40173; green "W. Moorcroft" script mark.
Very Good Quality/Fine Condition *$995 (D)* **$600–$1000**

Vase 11.75" H Moorcroft 1900–1910 England
Florian, "Iris" design; tube-lined stylized irises in light and dark green on mottled blue and green ground; green signed "W. Moorcroft des."
Superior Quality/Fine Condition *$2100 (A)* **$1200–$2100**

Vase 9" H Moorcroft 1904–1913 England
Ovoid shape; waisted foot; green and white tube-lined flowerheads and foliage; shaded blue ground; printed "MacIntyre" and script "WM" marks.
Very Good Quality/Fine Condition *$1590 (A)* **$900–$1600**

Vase 6.75" H Moorcroft 1910–1930 England
"African Lily" pattern; pink, yellow, and green florals, light green ground, teal blue interior; signature mark. *(See photo 58)*
Superior Quality/Fine Condition *$675 (D)* **$400–$675**

Vase 8.75" H Moorcroft 1916–1918 England
"Black trees" design; tube-lined with olive-green and white trees set among rolling hills with flying seagulls, reserved on black ground; impressed "Moorcroft Burslem, England" and blue marks.
Superior Quality/Fine Condition *$6730 (A)* **$3500–$7000**

Vase 7.25" H Moorcroft 1920–1930 England
Multicolored orchid decoration on mottled green ground; red "Moorcroft" and "Potter to HM the Queen, England" mark.
Very Good Quality/Fine Condition *$350 (D)* **$200–$350**

Vase 10.5" H Moorcroft 1930–1940 England
Tapered cylinder form; tube-lined with 3 sprays of blue tulips and light green foliage, blue and yellow chevron borders; chip on foot rim; impressed "Moorcroft, made in England" and blue "W. Moorcroft" marks.
Very Good Quality/Good Condition *$3275 (A)* **$2000–$3350**

Vase 4" H Moorcroft 1930–1950 England
Rose and purple flowers on blue-green ground.
Good Quality/Fine Condition *$150 (D)* **$75–$150**

Vase 6.25" H Moorcroft 1930–1950 England
Blue, lavender, and pink clematis design, medium blue shading to cobalt ground.
Very Good Quality/Fine Condition *$225 (D)* **$125–$225**

QUIMPER
1685–PRESENT
BRITTANY, FRANCE

Quimper 1890 – 1922

1898 – 1904

In 1685 Jean Baptiste Bousquet founded the first factory in Quimper in the province of Brittany, using patterns inspired by Moustiers, Nevers, and Rouen. There was good clay there and abundant wood for the firing ovens. In 1731, Pierre Bellevaux introduced the Chinese-inspired blue-and-white color scheme, Oriental subject matter, and the intertwining

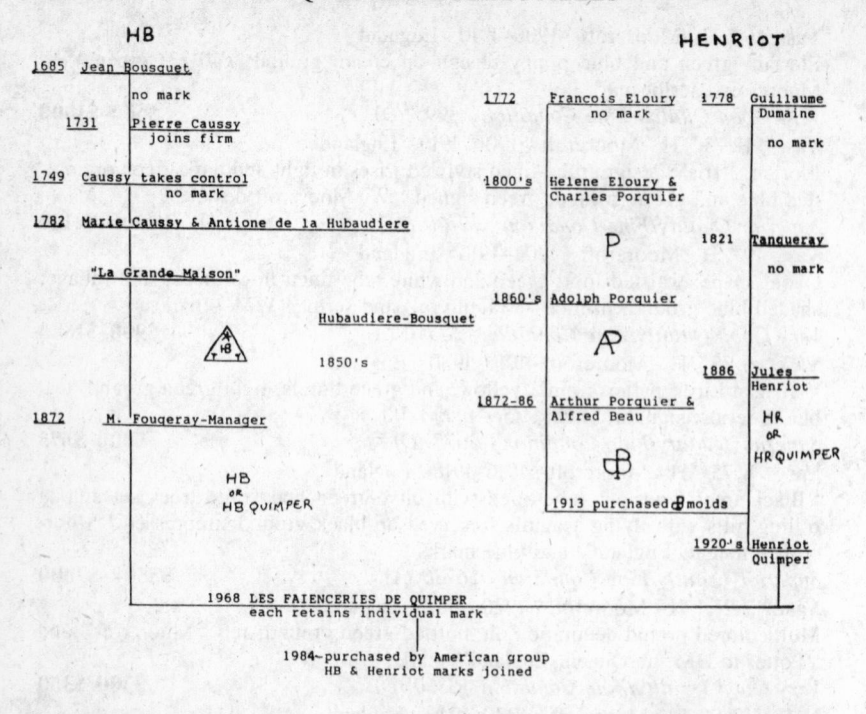

```
        HB                                              HENRIOT

1685  Jean Bousquet
            no mark                    1772   Francois Eloury   1778   Guillaume
   1731      Pierre Caussy                       no mark               Dumaine
             joins firm
                                                                      no mark
1749  Caussy takes control           1800's  Helene Eloury &
            no mark                           Charles Porquier
1782  Marie Caussy & Antione de la Hubaudiere
                                                P            1821   Tanqueray
      "La Grande Maison"
                                                                  no mark
                         Hubaudiere-Bousquet   1860's  Adolph Porquier
                               1850's
                                                AP
                                                             1886   Jules
                                                                   Henriot
1872       M. Fougeray-Manager      1872-86  Arthur Porquier &       HR
                                             Alfred Beau              or
                                                                  HR QUIMPER
                HB                              ⊕
                or
             HB QUIMPER                1913 purchased ⊕ molds
                                                             1920's  Henriot
                                                                    Quimper

          1968 LES FAIENCERIES DE QUIMPER
            each retains individual mark

              1984—purchased by American group
              HB & Henriot marks joined
```

border pattern of leaves and flowers. Pierre Clement Caussy expanded
the works and brought "decor rayonnant." Francois Eloury opened a
rival factory in 1776, and Guillaume Dumaine opened a third factory
several years later. By 1780 there were three rival factories in Quimper.

The Grand Maison HB developed through marriage. During the 19th
century essential Breton characteristics began to appear: the primary colors, the concentric banding in blue and yellow for border trim, and the
single brush stroke creating a flower or leaf. Scenes of Breton peasants
predominated. The Eloury factory went to Charles Porquier and then to
Adolphe Porquier. In 1872 the master artist Alfred Beau produced Breton
scenes and figurals.

Jules Henriot took over the Dumaine factory in 1884 and added the
Porquier factory in 1904. Meheut introduced Art Deco and Art Nouveau
to the Henriot factory in 1925. Prominent artists included Sevellec, Mail-
lard, and Nicot.

During the 1920s, HB introduced the Odetta stoneware line with earth
colors and shadowed figures. In 1968, HB and Henriot merged. The
factory was purchased by an American couple in 1984.

Quimper has become a very collectible item, and prices have risen
accordingly in the past few years.

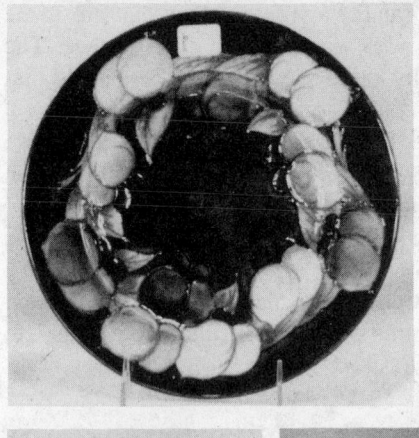

Photo 57. Plate.
CREDIT: AL BAGDADE *(See p. 126)*

Photo 58 (left). Vase. CREDIT: AL BAGDADE. *Photo 59 (right). Bowl.*
CREDIT: AL BAGDADE *(See pp. 127, 130)*

Photo 60. Pitcher.
CREDIT: AL BAGDADE *(See p. 131)*

Fakes Alert

There is a line called "Musée Qualité" reproductions that are made from old molds that have a brown wash over a crazed glaze surface. The marks are in brown, and originally these pieces had paper labels that identified them as reproductions.

The Blue Ridge Pottery in the United States and several Japanese firms make pottery utilizing a peasant motif similar to Quimper. The Malicorne area near Paris produced peasant pottery with a "PBx" mark. Examples have been found with the "x" removed and sold as Quimper.

The Quimper factory itself is reproducing many of the older pieces, such as figural candlesticks and figural bookends in addition to complete sets of the dinnerwares.

References

Sandra V. Bondhus, *Quimper Pottery: A French Folk Art Faience*, published privately, 1981; this is the definitive work on Quimper; photos are outstanding, including pages from the original catalogs in color and black and white; Millicent S. Mali, *French Faience, Fantaisie et Populaire of the 19th and 20th Centuries*, United Printing, 1986; a small section on Quimper but good backgrounds on all other French faience that influenced Quimper.

Museums

Musée de Faiences de Quimper, Quimper, France; Victoria and Albert Museum, London; Villa Viscaya, Miami, FL.

Newsletter

Quimper Faience, Inc., 141 Water Street, Stonington, CT 06378; subscription: 3 years for $10.

Bowl 12.25″ Quimper 1880–1890 France
Interior vertical ribbing; peasant man in green top, yellow pantaloons, peasant woman in green dress, rust apron, blue blouse; blue chain border with 4 blue dots and florals; scalloped rim; "HB" mark.
Very Good Quality/Fine Condition $450 (D)   **$275–$450**

Bowl 12″ H-H Quimper 1920–1930 France
Multicolored male musicians in center, blue *decor riche* border, green sponged rim, foot, and handles; blue "Henriot Quimper" mark. *(See photo 59)*
Very Good Quality/Fine Condition $595 (D)   **$350–$600**

Candlestick 7″ H Quimper 1920–1930 France
Two cartouches of peasant man and woman, blue and white designs with orange-yellow trim; base with blue and white lines, "HQ Quimper" mark.
Very Good Quality/Fine Condition $215 (D)   **$125–$225**

Chamberstick 5.5″ Dia. Quimper 1920–1930 France
Peasant woman and scattered flowers in typical colors; ring handle with blue
dashes; "Henriot Quimper, France" mark.
Very Good Quality/Fine Condition *$230 (D)*   **$125–$250**

Cheese dish, covered 9″ Dia. Quimper 1930–1950 France
Octagonal shape; peasant woman on cover, olive-green twisted handle, multi-
colored flowers; blue scalloped rim; "Henriot Quimper France" mark.
Very Good Quality/Fine Condition *$275 (D)*   **$150–$275**

Figure 8.75″ H Quimper 1920–1930 France
St. Vierge in colors; "Henriot Quimper" mark.
Very Good Quality/Fine Condition *$265 (D)*   **$175–$275**

Figure 8″ H Quimper 1920–1930 France
"Three Godmothers"; 2 seated, 1 standing; old women in blue and green shades;
white faces and coifs; raised "L.H. Nicot" on front, "Henriot Quimper" mark;
modern movement.
Superior Quality/Fine Condition *$450 (D)*   **$275–$450**

Figure 8.75″ H Quimper 1930–1950 France
Seated peasant man in tan pantaloons, royal blue jacket, purple hat, playing
bagpipes, seated on rust barrel; green base; "Henriot Quimper" mark.
Very Good Quality/Fine Condition *$225 (D)*   **$125–$225**

Figure 10.25″ H Quimper 1930–1950 France
Standing figure of "St. Anne" in yellow dress, blue stripes and dots, holding
child; square base; "Henriot Quimper" mark.
Very Good Quality/Fine Condition *$275 (D)*   **$150–$275**

Holy water font 9.5″ H Quimper 1910–1930 France
Figural cross; peasant man on knees; "Henriot Quimper" mark.
Very Good Quality/Fine Condition *$225 (D)*   **$125–$225**

Pitcher 5.75″ H Quimper 1930–1950 France
Peasant in green coat, blue pantaloons, yellow gaiters; rust, blue, yellow, and
green florals, blue and yellow banding; "Henriot Quimper France" mark. *(See
photo 60)*
Very Good Quality/Fine Condition *$125 (D)*   **$75–$125**

Pitcher, syrup 5″ H Quimper 1900–1910 France
Covered; blue and white starflower pattern; "H.B." mark.
Very Good Quality/Fine Condition *$175 (D)*   **$100–$175**

Planter 7″ H Quimper 1910–1930 France
Figural swan; cartouche on breast of seated peasant woman with egg basket;
blue and mustard body sponging; "Henriot Quimper" mark on interior.
Very Good Quality/Fine Condition *$495 (D)*   **$300–$500**

Plate 9.6″ Dia. Quimper 1930–1950 France
Cobalt flower with green and pink leaves, dark red and blue sponged chains
outlined in gold, ivory ground, blue sponged rim; "Henriot Quimper" mark.
(See photo 61)
Good Quality/Fine Condition *$105 (D)*   **$60–$110**

Plate, oyster 8.75″ Dia. Quimper 1930–1950 France
Yellow center rim with rust floral, blue sponged border, oyster-holders outlined
in blue sponging with florals; "Henriot Quimper 114" mark.
Good Quality/Fine Condition *$140 (D)*   **$75–$140**

Tray 12.5″ L Quimper 1910–1930 France
Oval; scalloped edge; peasant woman in blue skirt, green top, rust apron; floral rim and on each side of peasant; "Henriot Quimper France" mark.
Very Good Quality/Fine Condition $300 (D)   **$175–$300**

Vase 4.12″ H Quimper 1910–1930 France
Peasant woman in blue blouse, purple dress, yellow apron, yellow umbrella with blue and gold dots; 2 large blue and red flowers on reverse, typical red and blue floral and 4-dot design; "HR Quimper" mark. *(See photo 62)*
Very Good Quality/Fine Condition $150 (D)   **$75–$150**

Wall pocket 8″ L Quimper 1900–1910 France
Figural bagpipe; multicolored male peasant facing forward, yellow bow figural trim, floral at each end; "HR Quimper" mark.
Very Good Quality/Fine Condition $310 (D)   **$175–$325**

AFTER 1902

ROYAL BAYREUTH
1794–PRESENT
TETTAU, BAVARIA

Wilheim Greiner and Johann Schmidt founded a porcelain factory in 1794 in Tettau and survived many difficulties and changes in ownership. The name was Porcelain Factory Tettau from 1902 to 1957; then it became Royally Privileged Porcelain Factory Tettau GMBH. The name "Royal Bayreuth" is used in the United States to identify its products.

Floral and animal forms were made, including fruits, vegetables, lobsters, tomatoes, and people. Many were inexpensive novelty and souvenir items. Today the factory produces limited-edition collectibles and dinnerware.

Rose Tapestry was made in the late 19th century. Its texture was similar to needlepoint tapestry and was called "matte finish" china. Sunbonnet Babies were created in the early 1900s. Beach Babies and Snow Babies also were made.

References

Joan and Marvin Raines, *A Guide to Royal Bayreuth Figurals*, privately printed, 1973; Joan and Marvin Raines, *A Guide to Royal Bayreuth Figurals: Book 2*, privately printed, 1977; Virginia and George Salley, *Royal Bayreuth China*, privately printed, 1969.

Basket 3.75″ H × 4.25″ W Royal Bayreuth 1900–1910 Germany
Yellow roses on front and back, pink roses on rim.
Very Good Quality/Fine Condition $335 (D)   **$150–$350**

Basket 5″ H × 5.5″ Dia. Royal Bayreuth 1900–1910 Germany
Tapestry, courting couple in colors; blue mark.
Superior Quality/Fine Condition $350 (D) **$175–$350**

Bowl 11.5″ Dia. Royal Bayreuth 1900–1910 Germany
Two game birds in meadow setting in colors, gold rococo border.
Very Good Quality/Fine Condition $170 (D) **$100–$200**

Box 5.75″ L Royal Bayreuth 1900–1910 Germany
Tapestry, multicolored scene of lovers in woodland setting; unmarked.
Superior Quality/Fine Condition $595 (D) **$300–$600**

Celery tray 11.5″ L × 5″ W Royal Bayreuth 1910–1930 Germany
Figural tomato design in red and green; blue mark.
Very Good Quality/Fine Condition $185 (D) **$100–$200**

Cream and sugar Royal Bayreuth 1900–1910 Germany
Rose tapestry; one-color roses.
Superior Quality/Fine Condition $337 (D) **$175–$375**

Creamer 3.5″ H Royal Bayreuth 1900–1910 Germany
Figural murex shell; mother-of-pearl finish; blue mark.
Good Quality/Fine Condition $65 (D) **$40–$65**

Creamer 4.5″ H Royal Bayreuth 1900–1910 Germany
Black figural crow; blue mark.
Very Good Quality/Fine Condition $120 (D) **$70–$120**

Dresser set Royal Bayreuth 1900–1910 Germany
Rose tapestry, 2-color roses; hair receiver, powder box, hatpin holder, tray.
Superior Quality/Fine Condition $1400 (D) **$700–$1400**

Dresser tray 11.5″ L Royal Bayreuth 1910–1930 Germany
Multicolored scene of man with horses.
Very Good Quality/Fine Condition $325 (D) **$175–$325**

Match holder 3″ H × 2.5″ Dia. Royal Bayreuth 1900–1910 Germany
Multicolored sunset sailboat scene; blue mark.
Good Quality/Fine Condition $55 (D) **$25–$55**

Milk pitcher 6″ H Royal Bayreuth 1900–1910 Germany
Devil and cards design; blue mark.
Superior Quality/Fine Condition $269 (D) **$175–$300**

Milk pitcher 5″ H Royal Bayreuth 1910–1930 Germany
Tankard shape; sunbonnet babies, babies cleaning; blue mark.
Very Good Quality/Fine Condition $295 (D) **$200–$295**

Mug 8″ H Royal Bayreuth 1900–1910 Germany
Multicolored scene of Arabs mounted on horses, with mosque.
Very Good Quality/Fine Condition $325 (D) **$175–$325**

Nappy 5″ L Royal Bayreuth 1900–1910 Germany
Leaf shape; Brittany girl scene.
Very Good Quality/Fine Condition $150 (D) **$75–$150**

Pitcher 4″ H Tapestry 1900–1910 Germany
Three-color roses, gold handle, blue mark. *(See photo 63)*
Very Good Quality/Fine Condition $192 (A) **$125–$200**

Pitcher 7″ H Royal Bayreuth 1900–1910 Germany
Tankard shape; sunbonnet babies ironing; gold trim and handles.
Superior Quality/Fine Condition $525 (D) **$300–$525**

Photo 61 (left). Plate. CREDIT: AL BAGDADE. *Photo 62 (right). Vase.*
CREDIT: AL BAGDADE *(See pp. 131, 132)*

Photo 63 (left). Pitcher. CREDIT: AL BAGDADE. *Photo 64 (right).*
Pitcher. CREDIT: AL BAGDADE *(See pp. 133, 135)*

Photo 65. Plate. CREDIT: AL BAGDADE
(See p. 135)

Pitcher 4.75″ H Royal Bayreuth 1910–1930 Germany
Rose tapestry, blue mark.
Very Good Quality/Fine Condition $255 (D)   **$175–$275**

Pitcher 7.5″ H Royal Bayreuth 1910–1930 Germany
Black, red, and white "Devil and Cards"; green mark. *(See photo 64)*
Superior Quality/Fine Condition $302 (A)   **$225–$375**

Plate 6″ Dia. Royal Bayreuth 1900–1910 Germany
Rose tapestry, 3-color roses, fancy gold rim.
Very Good Quality/Fine Condition $145 (D)   **$75–$145**

Plate 7.5″ Dia. Royal Bayreuth 1900–1910 Germany
Sunbonnet babies washing in colors; blue mark. *(See photo 65)*
Superior Quality/Fine Condition $250 (D)   **$150–$250**

Plate 6.5″ Dia. Royal Bayreuth 1910–1930 Germany
"Jack and the Beanstalk" nursery rhyme in colors.
Good Quality/Fine Condition $90 (D)   **$45–$90**

Plate, serving 12″ Dia. Royal Bayreuth 1900–1910 Germany
Garland of leaves and berries in center; dark green border with sheep in forest
and mountain scenes; blue mark.
Very Good Quality/Fine Condition $110 (D)   **$50–$110**

Vase 6″ H Royal Bayreuth 1900–1910 Germany
Scene of cavaliers in colors on top; green shaded base; blue mark.
Good Quality/Fine Condition $95 (D)   **$45–$95**

Vase 7″ H Royal Bayreuth 1900–1910 Germany
Multicolored cow scene with orange body.
Very Good Quality/Fine Condition $150 (D)   **$75–$150**

Vase 6″ H Royal Bayreuth 1900–1910 Germany
Multicolored scene of elk and 3 hounds in river; tapestry finish.
Very Good Quality/Fine Condition $375 (D)   **$200–$375**

Vase 5.25″ H Royal Bayreuth 1910–1930 Germany
Rose tapestry, apricot roses; blue mark.
Superior Quality/Fine Condition $385 (D)   **$250–$450**

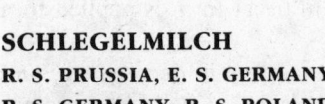

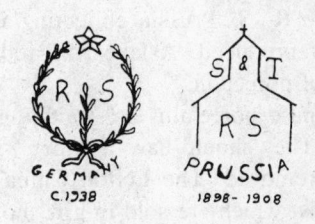

SCHLEGELMILCH
**R. S. PRUSSIA, E. S. GERMANY,
R. S. GERMANY, R. S. POLAND
1861–1950s**

R. S. Prussia

Erdmann Schlegelmilch started to manufacture hard-paste porcelains at Suhl, Thuringia, in 1861. His brother Reinhold established his factory at Tillowitz, Upper Silesia, in 1869. These factories were the first privately owned porcelain factories in the region. Their peak years were from the mid-1870s until the early 1900s. Both brothers used the "RSP" (R. S. Prussia) mark. A tremendous variety of porcelains were made, including complete dinner sets. There seems to be an endless number of "RSP" molds. Floral themes were the most common.

The Suhl factory stopped producing RSP-marked porcelains in 1920. The Tillowitz factory finally came under the Polish Socialist government in 1956 after being affected by various boundary changes.

E. S. Germany

Erdmann's factory at Suhl was associated with the E. S. marks. These porcelains were different in shape and decor from the RSP examples. Many designs reflected the influence of the Art Nouveau period.

R. S. Germany

The R. S. Germany forms and decorations reflected the Art Deco period. Here Reinhold concentrated on tablewares. "Germany" was used in a mark similar to the "RSP" mark, except "Prussia" was replaced. Many patterns were created for large department stores in America.

R. S. Poland

R. S. Poland examples have mostly classical decorations and are simpler than the RSP examples. Art objects were favored over tablewares. R. S. Poland examples are quite rare because few pieces were exported after World War II. The factory came under the control of the Socialist government in Poland in 1956.

Collecting Hints

Not all RSP examples are marked. One must study the mold and decor of an unmarked piece to see if it matches a known design or mold.

Fakes Alert

Since R. S. Prussia collecting is so popular, there are now pieces being reproduced. A fake RSP red mark in decal form is applied to a piece of porcelain.

Japanese porcelains are imitating RSP examples in decor, type, and mold. They should have a paper "Made in Japan" label, but these are easily removed. The Lefton China Company also manufactures reproductions, which are sold in gift shops and flea markets.

References

Mary Frank Gaston, *The Collectors Encyclopedia of R.S. Prussia and Other R.S. and E.S. Porcelains*, Collector Books, 1982; George W. Terrell, Jr., *Collecting R.S. Prussia, Identification and Values*, Books America, 1982.

Collectors' Club

International Association of R.S. Prussia Collectors, Inc., Mary McCaslin, 22 Canterbury Drive, Danville, IN 46122; membership: $20.

Basket 6.36″ L Schlegelmilch 1910–1930 Germany
Multicolored scene of lady and child in center, luster finish with gold gilt handle and decoration; "Royal Saxe, Germany" mark.
Very Good Quality/Fine Condition $125 (D)   **$70–$125**

Berry set 10.5″, 5.5″ Dia. Schlegelmilch 1885–1900 Germany
Bowl, 6 matching bowls; blown-out acorn mold with floral centers.
Very Good Quality/Fine Condition $525 (D)   **$250–$525**

Berry set Bowl 10.25″ Dia. 3″ H Schlegelmilch 1910–1930 Germany
Master bowl, 4 small bowls, white and pink roses, green leaves, gold trim, scalloped borders. *(See photo 66)*
Very Good Quality/Fine Condition $350 (A)   **$150–$350**

Berry set Bowl 10″, plate 5″ Dia. Schlegelmilch 1930–1950 Germany
Bowl, 6 plates; overall floral design in colors.
Very Good Quality/Fine Condition $295 (D)   **$150–$295**

Bowl 11″ Dia. Schlegelmilch 1885–1900 Germany
"Sitting Basket" design; high-gloss finish; medallion mold.
Very Good Quality/Fine Condition $225 (D)   **$125–$225**

Bowl 9.25″ Dia. Schlegelmilch 1885–1900 Germany
Large Easter lilies; plume mold; red mark.
Very Good Quality/Fine Condition $250 (D)   **$125–$250**

Bowl 10.25″ Dia. Schlegelmilch 1885–1900 Germany
Pink poppies in center, cobalt, green, and brown florals on sides; mold #95, unmarked.
Very Good Quality/Fine Condition $865 (D)   **$500–$900**

Bowl 10″ Dia. Schlegelmilch 1900–1910 Germany
"Snowbird" scene; icicle mold.
Superior Quality/Fine Condition $2050 (D)   **$1000–$2200**

Bowl 10″ Dia. Schlegelmilch 1930–1950 Germany
Multicolored scene of woman with cows near cottage; 2 small handles.
Very Good Quality/Fine Condition $235 (D)   **$125–$250**

Cake plate 10.5″ Handle to handle Schlegelmilch 1900–1910 Germany
Two white lilies with green leaves; mold #205; red mark. *(See photo 67)*
Good Quality/Fine Condition $195 (D)   **$125–$225**

Cake plate 11″ Handle to handle Schlegelmilch 1910–1930 Germany
Large peach and yellow roses, gold trim.
Good Quality/Fine Condition $55 (D)   **$25–$55**

Cheese and cracker plate 8.5″ Dia. Schlegelmilch 1910–1930 Germany
Two-tier; pink orchid decoration.
Very Good Quality/Fine Condition $125 (D)   **$70–$125**

Chocolate cups/saucers 3.5″ H Schlegelmilch 1900–1910 Germany
Light yellow and green pearl luster; gold medallion; sprays of white flowers and green leaves; medallion mold; set of 4.
Very Good Quality/Fine Condition $350 (D)   **$200–$350**

Cream and sugar   Schlegelmilch   1885–1900   Germany
Pink bands on foot and lip; small roses; gold trim; mold #603; red mark.
Very Good Quality/Fine Condition $225 (D)   **$125–$225**

Dresser set   Tray 12″ Handle to handle   Schlegelmilch   1910–1930   Germany
Tray, large hair receiver, covered powder jar; green and rust floral and leaf
pattern on cream ground; handpainted "R. S. Germany" mark.
Very Good Quality/Fine Condition $245 (D)   **$125–$250**

Hatpin holder   4.75″ H   Schlegelmilch   1900–1910   Germany
Closed bottom; pink and yellow roses on white and green ground; red mark.
Very Good Quality/Fine Condition $140 (D)   **$80–$140**

Marmalade jar   4″ H   Schlegelmilch   1930–1950   Germany
With underplate; white flowers on matte green and beige shaped ground; blue
mark.
Very Good Quality/Fine Condition $125 (D)   **$70–$125**

Photo 66 (left). Berry set. CREDIT: AL BAGDADE. *Photo 67 (right). Cake plate.* CREDIT: AL BAGDADE *(See p. 137)*

Photo 68.
Teapot
CREDIT:
AL BAGDADE
(See p. 139)

Pitcher 6″ H Schlegelmilch 1885–1900 Germany
"Hidden Image" design; maroon florals and shaded blue to white ground.
Very Good Quality/Fine Condition $325 (D) **$200–$325**

Plate 9″ Dia. Schlegelmilch 1885–1900 Germany
Center scene of "Dice Players" in colors, cream and dark green paneled border,
maroon rim with gold beading; red "R. S. Prussia" and blue beehive mark.
Very Good Quality/Fine Condition $395 (D) **$200–$400**

Plate 11.5″ Dia. Schlegelmilch 1900–1910 Germany
"Victorian Vignette"; center courting scene, 4 smaller panels with courting
scenes; mold #182; red mark.
Superior Quality/Fine Condition $725 (D) **$400–$725**

Plate 11″ Dia. Schlegelmilch 1900–1910 Germany
Four swans with red beaks and black heads on blue water with gold drippings,
satin finish, icicle mold; red mark.
Superior Quality/Fine Condition $625 (D) **$300–$625**

Plate 9.5″ H-H Schlegelmilch 1910–1925 Germany
Portrait of young woman in center; 6 flowered wells; scalloped border; open
handles; "E.S. Germany Royal Saxe" mark.
Very Good Quality/Fine Condition $169 (D) **$125–$200**

Plate 11.5″ Dia. Schlegelmilch 1910–1930 Germany
White, green, and pink lilacs; gold and green trim, gold border.
Very Good Quality/Fine Condition $110 (D) **$50–$110**

Shaving mug 3.5″ H Schlegelmilch 1885–1900 Germany
Molded flowers on rim and base; body with pink roses on medium blue ground;
carnation mold.
Superior Quality/Fine Condition $350 (D) **$150–$350**

Teapot 6.25″ H × 8.6″ L Schlegelmilch 1900–1910 Germany
Light mint green, white flower with red centers, gold dentil rim, gold trim, satin
finish, mold #507; red mark. *(See photo 68)*
Very Good Quality/Fine Condition $600 (D) **$400–$600**

Teapot 8.5″ H Schlegelmilch 1910–1930 Germany
Cabbage rose design; burnished gold trim; steeple finial.
Very Good Quality/Fine Condition $125 (D) **$70–$125**

Toothpick holder Schlegelmilch 1885–1900 Germany
Blue floral decoration, ruffled rim; mold #502; unmarked.
Good Quality/Fine Condition $95 (D) **$45–$95**

Tray 11.5″ Dia. Schlegelmilch 1885–1900 Germany
Painted roses in center; red mark.
Good Quality/Fine Condition $165 (D) **$125–$165**

Tray 10″ Dia. Schlegelmilch 1900–1910 Germany
Applied figural peacock in center; pearlized finish; Art Nouveau style; "E.S.
Germany Prov. Saxe" mark.
Very Good Quality/Fine Condition $245 (D) **$175–$245**

Urns, covered 11.75″ H Schlegelmilch 1885–1900 Germany
Pair; mill scene on one, castle scene on other; small curved handles.
Superior Quality/Fine Condition $3475 (D) **$2000–$3500**

Vase 9″ H Schlegelmilch 1900–1910 Germany
Gold ground with overall pink roses; red "Royal Vienna" and "R.S. Prussia" marks.
Very Good Quality/Fine Condition $350 (D) **$175–$350**

BIBLIOGRAPHY

Atterbury, Paul. *The History of Porcelain*. London: Orbis Publishing, 1982. A good general overview of porcelain production in England and the Continent. The appendix has a good section on fake marks.

Bagdade, Susan and Al. *Warman's English and Continental Pottery and Porcelain: An Illustrated Price Guide*. Willow Grove, PA: Warman's Publishing Co., 1987. An all-around reference and price guide, featuring over 200 of the most collected categories, along with marks, factory histories, collectors' clubs, and museums. A glossary of terms and a list of reference books on each subject is included.

Cushion, J. P., and Honey, W. B. *Handbook of Pottery and Porcelain Marks*. Boston: Faber and Faber, 1986. A complete marks book that covers most countries, including some of the more modern marks. Maps of each area illustrate the sites of ceramics production.

Feild, Rachael. *Macdonald Guide to Buying Antique Pottery and Porcelain*. London: Macdonald & Co., 1987. A handy reference book that illustrates what to look for in determining the age and authenticity of a piece of pottery or porcelain.

Godden, Geoffrey. *Godden's Guide to English Porcelain*. London: Granada Publishing, 1978. Godden is the dean of English ceramics. This book discusses many of the smaller companies and explains the types of pastes used for production.

Jewitt, Liewellynn. *The Ceramic Art of Great Britain*. Poole, Dorset: New Orchards, 1985. The classic work on the development of the ceramics industry in England, it contains many line drawings and marks to help illustrate each section.

Meister, Peter Wilhelm, and Reber, Horst. *European Porcelain of the 18th Century*. Oxford, England: Phaidon Press. This is a beautifully illustrated general text that examines shapes, styles, and decorative techniques.

Mundt, Barbara, and Fay-Halle, Antionette. *Porcelain of the Nineteenth Century*. New York: Rizzoli, 1983. This handsome book covers the most productive period of porcelain manufacture. It aids in establishing style as reflected by the changes in that century.

Savage, George. *English Ceramics*. New York: Alpine Fine Arts, 1981. This book briefly covers some of the more important English companies. The illustrations are lavish, with emphasis on 18th-century factories.

Character Collectibles

(See also Comic Books, Peanuts)

Advisor: **HARRY L. RINKER**

Harry L. Rinker is a nationally recognized authority on collectibles and antiques. Editor, author, educator, and former museum director, Mr. Rinker is co-founder, with David Lindquist, of The Antiques and Collectibles Information Service, which sponsors major educational seminars each year. Write A.C.I.S., 5093 Vera Cruz Rd., Emmaus, PA 18049; (215) 965-1122.

Character collectibles divide into two basic groups: advertising characters and characters from cartoons, comics, and film. Both groups had their origin in the final decades of the 19th century. The use of a comic or cartoon character in the advertising sphere did occur, but this was the exception, not the rule.

The first comic character was the Yellow Kid, but he did not appear in strip form on a daily basis. That honor was achieved by Bud Fisher's Mutt and Jeff in 1907. Walt Disney and others pioneered the art of the movie cartoon in the mid-1930s. At the end of the 1930s the paperback comic book with original art, rather than a reprinting of newspaper comic strips, arrived on the scene.

Character collectibles should not be confused with collectibles that are characterizations of real people. The character collectibles found in this category relate only to fictitious characters. Ownership of the rights to a character may rest with the creator or his heirs or have passed through several hands, as have the rights to both the Lone Ranger and Hopalong Cassidy.

Character images appeared in almost every known form, from pinback buttons to toys. They could be found in the kitchen (Aunt Jemima plastic salt and pepper set), washroom (Gold Dust Twins powdered soap box), bathroom (Hopalong Cassidy dental kit), living room (Little Orphan Annie and Sandy planter), bedroom (Dennis the Menace bedspread), and even outdoors (Lone Ranger flashlight). Their "golden age" covers the 1930s through the early 1960s.

A key to collecting character items is their original packaging or box. If the box or package contained an image of the character, the object is not complete without it. Often the box is worth more than the object that came in it.

The character collectibles market expands on an annual basis as television, film, comics, and advertising introduce new characters into our lives. Objects dealing with characters that are less than thirty years old should be viewed primarily as speculative. Not enough time has passed for a clear perception to be had of the long-term ability of these characters to evoke a high level of nostalgia. There are always exceptions, none more dramatic than the continued growth in value of "Star Trek" material.

CONDITION AND QUALITY KEYS

A character collectible in *Fine Condition* has almost no signs of wear or use. All parts are present, including the original packaging, although it may show some signs of wear due to storage. An object in *Good Condition* has minor wear and a few minor nicks and scratches. Its paint or lithography is all original. A professional restoration of an average object can raise it to this level. The packaging is missing. A character collectible in *Average Condition* shows signs of heavy use, but the object is still functional, may have minor parts missing, and often has some retouching of paint or the lithography. An average object has the potential for restoration. An object in *Poor Condition* has no potential for restoration. It has key pieces missing, especially in the central design areas. In many instances, its only value is for replacement parts.

The *Superior Quality* character collectible has strong design and aesthetic elements, along with the ability to evoke a high level of nostalgia. It should be of sufficient size to be an accent piece on display. A *Very Good Quality* object still contains a universally recognizable character, but it will be a lesser form. A *Good Quality* object contains a character that does not have a strong identity and is ordinary in design and form. It also has limited display possibilities.

In the area of character collectibles, country of origin has little bearing on price. In general, from the late 19th century on, most toys were designed in the United States and manufactured abroad. By 1990, over three-quarters of all toys were designed in the United States, but 90 percent were manufactured abroad. Assume the item was designed in the United States unless otherwise indicated in the listings below.—*DL*

Amos an' Andy 8 ″ H Ashtray 1940
Plaster; figures standing on either side of barrel; "I'se Regusted" on front of base.
Very Good Quality/Fine Condition $75 (D)   **$60–$85**

Barney Google 8″ L Pull toy 1924
Tin litho; Spark Plug with jockey on green base, Barney Google on yellow base, interconnected to 4-wheel superstructure, when pulled figures bob up and down alternately as if dashing into the lead.
Superior Quality/Fine Condition $8,250 (A) **$5000–$8500**

Batman 8″ × 12.5″ × 1″ Colorforms 1976
Full-color box; thin vinyl characters of Batman, Robin, Joker, and Penguin; background; reissue set; copyright DC Comics Inc.
Good Quality/Fine Condition $45 (A) **$25–$50**

Betty Boop 10″ String holder 1920–1930
Paint over plaster; full head, string draws through mouth.
Very Good Quality/Good Condition $110 (D) **$65–$135**

Blondie 10.5″ × 14.5″ Paper doll book 1941
"Blondie in the Movies"; Whitman #979; dolls based on Blondie movie version; Dagwood doll is 11.75″ H; 6 pages of clothing for each character.
Very Good Quality/Fine Condition $250 (A) **$100–$300**

B.O. Plenty 8″ H Windup 1950s
Marx; tin litho; depicts B.O. Plenty holding Baby Sparkle and present marked "For Baby Sparkle"; back marked "B.O. Plenty"; hat moves up and down; figure rocks back and forth.
Very Good Quality/Fine Condition $225 (A) **$100–$300**

Brownies 7.5″ × 10.5″ Song folio c. 1904
"Libretto of Palmer Cox's Brownies"; soft cover, 16 pages; music by Malcolm Douglas; front cover has depiction in red on white background of various Brownie characters by Cox; stiff paper pages; rare.
Good Quality/Average Condition $30 (D) **$25–$50**

Bugs Bunny 10.5″ Tie 1940s
Preknotted, clip-on; plum color; picture of Bugs in yellow and white with red accents.
Good Quality/Fine Condition $55 (A) **$40–$60**

Buster Brown 5.25″ Mechanical pencil 1950s
Red and white hard plastic; ¾″ red plastic bust of Buster on top; "Ritepoint" on silvered clip.
Very Good Quality/Fine Condition $45 (D) **$25–$50**

Buster Brown 2.75″ oval Pocket mirror 1900s
Oval cello pocket mirror; inscription in gold lettering; young lady wearing red shawl against a background of fused dark green colors; mirror on reverse.
Very Good Quality/Fine Condition $65 (D) **$50–$75**

Captain Midnight 4″ L Mailing tube 1947
Spy-scope mailing tube; cardboard cylinder; 2 leaflets from Ovaltine premium offer; spy-scope not included.
Good Quality/Fine Condition $40 (D) **$25–$50**

Captain Midnight 5″ H Shake-up mug 1957
Red plastic mug; blue lid; color Captain Midnight decal on side; issued by Ovaltine; 15th anniversary sponsorship premium.
Good Quality/Fine Condition $75 (D) **$50–$75**

Charlie Chan Better Little Book 1942
"Villainy on the High Seas"; Whitman #1424.
Good Quality/Fine Condition $30 (A) **$20–$40**

Dick Tracy   Target game   1961
Battery-operated; "Silent Ray Gun" shoots beam of light at revolving cardboard
drum; drum has 6 sides and targets; "Electronic Photocell Bullseye" and auto-
matic scorer; American Doll & Toy Corp.; original 12″ × 10″ × 11″ H red,
white, blue, and yellow box; 11″ L solid black plastic pistol; instruction sheet
included.
Very Good Quality/Fine Condition $100 (D)   **$75–$100**

Dick Tracy   6.15″ H   Glass   1970s
Clear; weighted bottom; dual depiction of Tracy in flesh, dark blue, red, and
dark red; holding a pair of revolvers; Chester Gould signature; red, white, and
blue logo of Domino's Pizza around bottom; produced by Brockway Glass; never
distributed; 1 of 3 examples.
Good Quality/Fine Condition $700 (D)   **$400–$700**

Donald Duck   6″ × 7″ scoop   Shovel   1939
Ohio Art Co.; long handle; Donald Duck dipping foot in ocean, nephews in
background; dated "copyright 1939 W.D.P."
Good Quality/Good Condition $90 (D)   **$75–$110**

Felix the Cat   3″ H   Glass figure   1930s
Clear, hollow; 1″ diameter base; name on chest in small raised letters; indistinct
inscription on reverse.
Very Good Quality/Fine Condition $175 (D)   **$75–$200**

Felix the Cat   .8″ Dia.   Pep pin   1945–1947
Litho; Kellogg's; from a set of 86.
Good Quality/Fine Condition $45 (D)   **$25–$50**

Flash Gordon   4.5″ × 8″   Pencil case   1951
Manufactured by Eagle Pencil Co.; copyright 1951 by King Features Syndicate;
comic strip illustrations.
Good Quality/Fine Condition $25 (D)   **$15–$35**

Flying Nun   7″ × 9″ × 4″ D   Lunch box   1968
Embossed metal; Aladdin; copyright Screen Gems Inc.
Very Good Quality/Fine Condition $85   **$75–$100**

Fred Flintstone   12″ H   Squeak toy   1960
Vinyl; orange suit, green tie; marked "Hanna Barberra Productions."
Good Quality/Good Condition $15 (D)   **$10–$18**

GI Joe   5″ × 6.5″ × 13.5″   Foot locker   1960s
Hinged wooden chest; dark olive green; olive green cord handle on each end;
GI Joe sticker and stencil area for name, rank, and serial number on lid; paper
insert showing placement of military equipment on inside lid; plastic tray;
Hasbro.
Good Quality/Fine Condition $60 (A)   **$40–$75**

Howdy Doody   1″ Dia.   Watch   1940–1960
Girl's size; metal; bright silver case; dial face has full-color portrait of Howdy;
eyes are tiny die-cut holes, eyeballs move slowly back and forth; Patent Watch
Co., NY; blue vinyl straps.
Good Quality/Fine Condition $400 (D)   **$200–$400**

Howdy Doody   Ring   1950s
"Poll-Parrot" premium; white plastic; raised image of Howdy accented in red
and blue.
Good Quality/Fine Condition $60 (D)   **$25–$75**

Little Orphan Annie 3″ H Annie/Sandy shakers 1940s
Painted plaster; Annie has red hair, red dress with white trim, and she holds a blue cap in her lap; Sandy is brown with tan muzzle and eyes, blue name inscription on chest; cork stopper in bottom.
Good Quality/Fine Condition $45 (D)   **$25–$50**

Little Orphan Annie 6.25″ × 9″ × 2″ Puzzle 1960s
Jigsaw of Annie, Sandy, Warbucks, and Punjab at restaurant table; unopened box; Jaymar.
Good Quality/Fine Condition $15 (A)   **$10–$15**

Lone Ranger 2.5″ × 2″ Dia. Egg cup 1950s England
Glossy white ceramic; raised portrait on side; "Lone Ranger Inc" on bottom.
Good Quality/Good Condition $30 (A)   **$20–$50**

Mama Katzenjammer 2.5″ × 3″ × 2.5″ Bank Early 1900s Austria
Glazed pottery; figural; light brown; coin slot in top of head; stamped "Austria" on bottom side.
Very Good Quality/Fine Condition $125 (A)   **$75–$100**

Mortimer Snerd 3″ × 8″ × 6.5″ H Car 1930s
Tin litho; windup crazy car; Marx; car spins around and rears up on hind wheels.
Very Good Quality/Fine Condition $500 (A)   **$300–$600**

Popeye 3.5″ Dia., 3.25″ H Cream pitcher 1930s Japan
Porcelain; aged white, blue trim line around upper edge and handle, depiction of Popeye and Olive taking a stroll; "Made in Japan" stamped on bottom.
Very Good Quality/Fine Condition $85 (D)   **$75–$100**

Popeye 5″ H Jointed wooden doll 1930s
Wood; segmented; elastic stringing; flesh head and arms with black anchor tattoos; black knob pipe; painted white sailor cap, red collar, black shirt, blue legs, orange shoes; "Popeye" and King Features copyright in small letters on chest.
Good Quality/Good Condition $150 (D)   **$100–$200**

Superman 7″ × 10″ × 5″ D Lunch box 1980
Red, hard-plastic, blue handle; 6.5″ tall hard-plastic thermos; pictures of characters on 2 stickers on front; Aladdin Industries, Inc.; copyright DC Comics, issued for Superman II movie.
Good Quality/Fine Condition $35 (A)   **$20–$50**

Tarzan 41″ × 80″ Poster 1932
"King of the Jungle"; 3-sheet, full-color; poster reads "With the Lion Man (Buster Crabbe) and Francis Dee From Story By Charles Thurley Stonham."
Superior Quality/Good Condition $800 (A)   **$700–$1000**

Three Stooges 19.5″ × 19.5″ Board game 1959
"Fun House"; Lowell Toy Corp, 3-D card pieces, Flying Saucer spinner board, small plastic pawns.
Very Good Quality/Fine Condition $300 (A)   **$200–$400**

Remember, the price range shows what the same item would sell for in average condition (left column) and fine condition (right column). Any item in poor condition has, in general, a value of 50% (or less) of that of the same item in average condition.

Uncle Fester 11″ H Hand puppet 1964
Soft vinyl head, cloth body; head is bright white with purple eyebrows and red lips; outfit is black, green, and purple on pink background; green "Uncle Fester" on bottom; Ideal; 1964 copyright Filmways TV Productions Inc on neck.
Good Quality/Fine Condition $90 (A)   **$75–$100**

Uncle Wiggily Book 1939
"Uncle Wiggily and the Red Spots"; published by Platt & Munk Co., Inc; illustrations by George Carlson.
Good Quality/Fine Condition $18 (D)   **$10–$22**

BIBLIOGRAPHY

Longest, David. *Character Toys and Collectibles*. Paducah, KY: Collector Books, 1984.

———. *Character Toys and Collectibles, Second Series*. Paducah, KY: Collector Books, 1987. Both volumes are primarily priced picture books. The first book contains chapters on Disney comic and film, radio, comic, puppet, space and superhero, and Western hero characters. A catchall chapter contains material that does not fit anywhere else. The second volume follows much the same format as the first, with added material on Hollywood personalities and Kewpie dolls.

Robison, Joleen, and Sellers, Kay. *Advertising Dolls: Identification and Value Guide*. Paducah, KY: Collector Books, 1980. Although primarily a priced picture book, the captions contain a wealth of information about the characters. The book deals with both contemporary and collectible dolls.

MUSEUMS

Margaret Woodbury Strong Museum, Rochester, NY.
The Museum of Cartoon Art, Port Chester, NY.
Smithsonian Institution, Washington, DC.

Clocks

(See also Watches)

Advisor: **ROBERT O. STUART**

Robert O. Stuart is the owner of Robert O. Stuart, Inc., an antiques concern that specializes in period American formal and high-style Country furniture and decorative accessories. One of America's premier shop and show dealers and a nationally recognized lecturer-educator, Mr. Stuart resides with his family in Limington, Maine, where he also pursues other interests. In addition to an open showroom in Limington, he participates in major antiques shows in the United States. Robert O. Stuart Antiques, Box 104, Jo Joy Road, Limington, ME 04049; (207) 793-4522. Special thanks to Jonathan Snellenberg, head of the Clocks Department at Christie's.

The section below deals with the more commonly collected clocks of the 18th, 19th, and early 20th centuries. Clocks such as these are of interest both to collectors and to people seeking attractive timepieces for their homes.

The past year has seen a resurgence of interest in clocks, especially tall-case clocks. Prices have marched steadily upward, but demand has remained strong. The sinking dollar has, of course, contributed to price escalation in the English and European fields.

Although fakes can be a problem, butchery is a greater problem. Most reproductions are easy to spot—they show no wear and tear, no accumulation of dirt and grime, no tarnish, no oxidation, no signs of refinishing or restoration. Don't buy them—they are truly a poor investment at any price.

Harder to identify are the clocks that have been altered or embellished. Look for faces that don't fit snugly within their hoods. Does the hood of the tall-case clock match the style of the case? Are the woods compatible? Are the wooden works of a pillar and scroll clock replaced with brass works? Know what to expect, then spot what is inconsistent.

SURVEY OF THE FIELD— AMERICAN CLOCKS, C. 1750–1830

Pre-Revolutionary War clocks are far less common than the Federal-style clocks that came later. True William and Mary and Queen Anne clocks are rare. The evolution of Chippendale forms was significantly hampered by the Revolution, which had more impact on clock manufacture than on the production of other furniture forms. Brass was scarce, and the economy was crippled by the disruption in foreign trade and the impact of war. And after formal hostilities ceased, the beleaguered economy nearly succeeded in stopping the process of nation building where the entire British military establishment had failed. Not until the end of the first decade of the new century did the economy recover, and the changing fashions in no way lessened the colonial love affair with clocks. The Federal forms, principal among which was the Roxbury case, flourished and proliferated in every region.

Traditionally described under the headings tall, wall, and shelf clocks, a number of distinct forms emerged by 1820. Because clocks were both so expensive and so desired, some of the earliest efforts at mass production were directed to building equipment to manufacture clock movements. And great creative energy went into designing and building attractive cases to house them.

The most successful wall clock form, extremely popular in the early 19th century, was the banjo clock. By comparison, all other forms before 1820 are quite scarce. In contrast, shelf clocks appeared in great variety, although some, like the pillar and scroll, became more highly prized.

By midcentury, clocks and watches were made in such numbers by so many makers that whole books are now required to cover only small sections of the 19th-century clock industry. Thus, we are confining our energies to the more individual range of examples produced before 1820.

It is important to note that the maker of the movement and the maker of the case were not the same person. It is possible, therefore, to find movements by the same clockmaker in a wide variety of cases. The quality of the case is a major determinant of value. In the instance of production movements, such as those by Silas Hoadley and Riley Whiting, clock works were transported all over the country and put in cases made by cabinetmakers of varying skills.

During the past year the price of most clock forms has risen sharply, and the availability of better examples has obviously declined.

Collectors generally insist on the following rules: (1) that the movement and case be original to each other, and (2) that the dial not be repainted. A maker's name on a dial significantly affects the price, generally by at least a multiple of two and not rarely by three times. Of less consideration today than a few years ago is the originality of finials, fret, and feet. Restoration of any one of these influences price but far less dramatically than ten years ago.

In tall-case clocks the most important rule is to determine the originality of the name on the dial. Clocks with a "Willard" name are particularly to be examined, for there are perhaps as many improperly "signed" as there are genuine. Even Willard labels are known to be faked.

Names on wall and shelf clocks also require close inspection. Banjo clocks are subject to replaced glasses, which dramatically reduce their value. Early shelf clocks are subject to new feet and new pediments, which hurt their value more than the restoration of feet or fret on tall clocks. Wall and shelf clocks are also susceptible to replaced movements of a later date.

Please refer to the chapter "Using This Guide" to determine the Quality and Condition Keys for this section.

CURRENT TRENDS

Trends and patterns are discernible in the antiques market as in all others. In relation to clocks, two patterns in particular are worthy of note: Tallcase clocks, relative to other forms of furniture, are generally underpriced. Dramatic escalations have occurred in the last two years in other areas. Highboys and slant-front desks have tripled in price; chests, lowboys, and card tables have more than doubled. Clocks have only begun to move up.

A second pattern is the widening discrepancy in the price of collectorquality clocks relative to more common examples and to clocks in less than fine condition. Rare and unusual and fine clocks, in all categories, are bringing premium prices. The indications are that this trend will continue.

Astronomical regulator 87″ H Victorian 1858 United States
Walnut; signed "E. Howard & Co., Boston, patented May 11, 1858"; Graham dead beat escapement with jeweled pallets; 4-jar mercury pendulum numbered 3145/5 (lacking 2 jars); long duration.
Superior Quality/Good Condition $24,200 (A)   **$12,000–$18,000**

Banjo clock 35″ H Federal 1800–1830 United States
Mahogany; eagle brass finial; painted iron dial and 8-day weight-driven "t-bridge" movement; tapering throat and pendulum box framed by crossbanding and stringing; eglomise tablets; brass side arms; minor imperfections.
Very Good Quality/Good Condition $13,000 (A)   **$10,000–$15,000**

Bracket clock 18.75″ H George I 1700–1750 England
Ebony; quarter repeating; signed on dial and backplate "James Tunn, London"; profusely engraved; fine movement; on Tompson's system.
Superior Quality/Fine Condition $41,800 (A)   **$25,000–$50,000**

Where the value range clearly exceeds the amount sold for, this reflects price increases during the last year.

Bracket clock   18″ H   George I   1700–1750   England
Quarter repeating, lunar calendar; some revisions to movement; distress to case.
Very Good Quality/Average Condition $12,100 (A)   **$8000–$12,000**

Bracket clock   30.5″ H   George II   1700–1750   England
Signed on dial "Godfrie Poy, London"; gilt figure of Minerva surmounts inverted bell top above pierced gilt frieze with acorn finials; engraved dial; triple fusee movement; 12 tunes; ebonized.
Superior Quality/Fine Condition $27,500 (A)   **$20,000–$25,000**

Calendar clock   13.5″ H   1780–1800   France
Unusual small white marble and ormolu clock, signed on dial "Martinet, London"; inscribed "Let time fly & make use of it"; 2-train movement with anchor escapement; clock flanked by twin silvered thermometers.
Superior Quality/Good Condition $19,800 (A)   **$18,000–$22,000**

Carriage clock   8.25″ H   1780–1800   France
A very rare gilt *grande sonnerie* carriage clock with alarm, minute repeating and perpetual calendar; 4-train movement.
Superior Quality/Fine Condition $55,000 (A)   **$50,000–$75,000**

Desk clock   4.5″ H   Art Deco   1920–1930   France
Arched silver case *guilloché* with translucent blue enamel within white border, on molded lapis lazuli base; perpetual lever escapement; repeating. *(See photo 69)*
Superior Quality/Fine Condition $22,000 (A)   **$20,000–$25,000**

Globe timepiece   27″ H × 15″ W   Victorian   1830–1865   United States
Walnut; T.R. Timby, Saratoga Springs and Baldwinsville, NY; arched case housing a lithographed globe by Gilman Joslin and minute aperture below.
Very Good Quality/Average Condition $500 (A)   **$4000–$6000**

Grande sonnerie   44″ H   Laterndluhr   1820–1830   Germany
Inlaid mahogany; signed "Ludwig Helbig/ in Wien"; architectural pediment; round enamel dial, gilt bezel; glass door on trunk; glass panel on base; Graham dead beat escapement and Harrison maintaining power; spring suspension; beat adjustment.
Very Good Quality/Good Condition $22,000 (A)   **$10,000–$15,000**

Longcase clock   80.25″ H   William III   1690–1700   England
Inlaid panels of floral marquetry; ebonized twist columns; square dial with spandrels; silvered chapter ring; 5-pillar movement with anchor escapement; shown in *The Longcase Clock*, Robinson; restorations.
Very Good Quality/Good Condition $22,000 (A)   **$25,000–$30,000**

Longcase clock   103.5″ H   Queen Anne   1700–1720   England
Arabesque marquetry case; caddy-top hood with gilt urn finials; 12″ square dial silvered chapter ring; crown spandrels; 5-pillar movement, anchor escapement; count wheel. *(See photo 70)*
Superior Quality/Good Condition $27,500 (A)   **$22,000–$26,000**

Longcase clock   103″ H   George II   1700–1750   England
Inscribed "Isaac Nichals/Wells"; highly developed, carved and gilt; 8-day brass movement.
Superior Quality/Fine Condition $29,700 (A)   **$20,000–$30,000**

Longcase clock   8′ H   George III   1750–1780   England
Mahogany; by Henry Watson, Blackburn; 8-day brass movement with hour strike, lunar dial, center calendar; Lancaster case with blind fret decoration and flame veneers.
Superior Quality/Fine Condition $25,000 (D)   **$22,000–$27,500**

Photo 69. Desk clock.
CREDIT: CHRISTIE'S, NEW YORK *(See p. 150)*

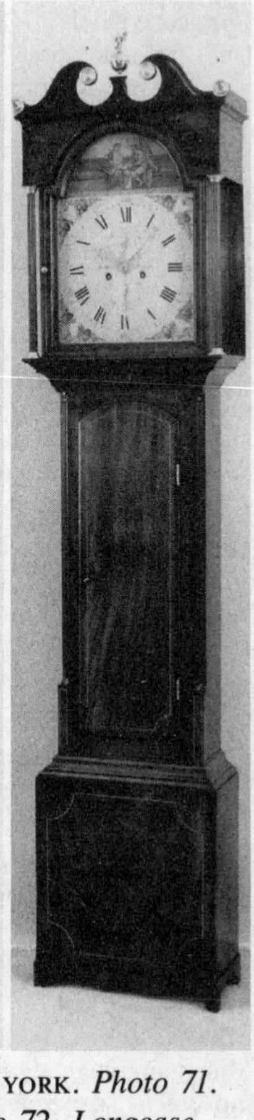

Photo 70. Longcase clock. CREDIT: CHRISTIE'S, NEW YORK. *Photo 71. Longcase clock.* CREDIT: CHARLES EDWIN, INC. *Photo 72. Longcase clock.* CREDIT: CHRISTIE'S, NEW YORK. *Photo 73. Longcase clock.* CREDIT: CHARLES EDWIN, INC. *(See pp. 150, 152)*

Longcase clock 7'8" H   George III   1800–1810   England
Mahogany; by Robert Bunyan, Lincoln; 8-day brass movement with hour strike; honey-colored case with kingwood banding and many inlays; dial with gilded corner painting. *(See photo 71)*
Superior Quality/Fine Condition $13,500 (D)   **$12,500–$15,000**

Longcase clock 116" H   1750–1780   Holland
Rare; burl walnut, with planisphere; price is the result of auction fever. *(See photo 72)*
Superior Quality/Fine Condition $63,800 (A)   **$20,000–$30,000**

Longcase clock 7'7" H   Regency   1830–1845   Scotland
Mahogany; by Robert Sharp, Edinburgh; 8-day movement with hour strike; string inlay on case; quarter columns on trunk; theatrical scene in dial arch. *(See photo 73)*
Good Quality/Good Condition $9500 (D)   **$8500–$10,000**

Longcase clock 7'3" H   Victorian   1830–1865   Scotland
Oak; by James Boyd, Cupar-Fyfe; 8-day brass movement with hour strike, case with quarter columns on trunk; flower-painted dial; very nice small size.
Good Quality/Good Condition $6500 (D)   **$6000–$7500**

Longcase regulator 78.5" H   1830–1865   United States
Very important—1 of first used to standardize railroad timekeeping in U.S.; 5 pillars, dead beat escapement with jeweled pallets, 4-wheel train; Harrison maintaining power, mercury pendulum.
Superior Quality/Fine Condition $35,200 (A)   **$30,000–$35,000**

Lyre clock 21.75" H   Louis XVI   1780–1800   France
Signed on dial "Hardi A Paris"; ormolu-mounted white marble; swinging movement suspended from knife-edge by gridiron; unusual pinwheel escapement—anchor with radial pallets; crutch with micrometer beat adjustment.
Superior Quality/Fine Condition $24,200 (A)   **$12,000–$18,000**

Mantel clock 16.5" H   Empire   1800–1825   France
Ormolu; Callisto seduced by Jupiter masquerading as Diana; movement with anchor escapement, thread-suspended pendulum, striking hour and half-hour on bell by means of count wheel.
Very Good Quality/Fine Condition $6600 (A)   **$3000–$5000**

Mantel clock 20" H   Victorian   1830–1865   United States
Cast-iron front; polychrome, mother-of-pearl and gilt decorated case; paper dial; unsigned 8-day time and strike brass movement; labeled Bradley & Hubbard, West Meriden, Conn.
Very Good Quality/Good Condition $150 (A)   **$200–$300**

Mantel regulator 15.25" H   Louis XVI   1780–1800   France
Signed on dial and movement "Robin A Paris"; case attributed to Pierre-Philippe Thomire; 2-train movement; dead beat escapement; pendulum suspended from inverted knife-edge in gimbal bracket.
Superior Quality/Fine Condition $27,500 (A)   **$30,000–$35,000**

Mantel regulator 22.75" H   1800–1830   France
Mahogany; signed on dial and calendar wheel "Champion A Paris"; cylindrical movement suspended from portico; pinwheel escapement with adjustable anchor; knife-edge suspension; gridiron pendulum. *(See photo 74)*
Superior Quality/Fine Condition $55,000 (A)   **$55,000–$60,000**

Mantel regulator   23″ H   Charles X   1800–1830   France
Dial signed "Ferrenbach A Chalons Sur Marne"; cylindrical case suspended within a portico; circular movement with pinwheel escapement; minor imperfections.
Very Good Quality/Good Condition $4400 (A)   **$4000–$6000**

Mantel regulator   18.5″ H   Charles X   1800–1830   France
Mahogany; dial signed "Collumb-Clerc Eleve de Robin"; cylindrical case suspended within portico; circular movement with dead beat escapement; knife-edge suspension to fine gridiron pendulum; count wheel.
Very Good Quality/Fine Condition $4180 (A)   **$4000–$5000**

Mantel regulator   21″ H   Skeletonized   1810–1820   France
Signed on dial "Bosset A Paris"; 2-train movement with pinwheel escapement; gridiron pendulum suspended from spring; crutch with micrometer beat adjustment; striking hour and half-hour by count wheel.
Superior Quality/Fine Condition $44,000 (A)   **$30,000–$35,000**

Portico clock   26″ H   Louis XVI   1780–1800   France
Signed on dial "Beliard A Paris"; 4 fluted columns forming Temple of Minerva with trophy of arms flanked by 2 figures of Minerva; movement with pinwheel escapement; sunburst and Apollo mask pendulum.
Superior Quality/Fine Condition $12,100 (A)   **$12,000–$18,000**

Shelf clock   22″ H   Victorian   1830–1865   England
Gilt brass; month tripod timepiece; signed on backplate "Thos. Cole, London, No. 1889."
Superior Quality/Fine Condition $16,500 (A)   **$12,000–$18,000**

Shelf clock   36″ H × 12.5″ W × 7″ D   Chippendale   1800–1810   United States
Mahogany; kidney dial inscribed "John Bailey, Lynn" within gilt oval; 8-day weight-driven drop-vitrine movement; base with recessed panel and flaring French feet; old finish, cornice replaced; MA. *(See photo 75)*
Very Good Quality/Good Condition $4300 (A)   **$6000–$10,000**

Shelf clock   34.5″ H   Federal   1800–1830   United States
Mahogany; hood with scrolled crest and brass urn finial above eglomise tablet framed by half-round molding; 8-day weight-driven movement; projecting base, mahogany panel, on molded base (restoration); MA.
Good Quality/Poor Condition $1800 (A)   **$2000–$3000**

Shelf clock   Federal   1800–1830   United States
John Taber, Alfred, ME; mahogany; painted dial; weight-driven, 8-day movement.
Very Good Quality/Good Condition $4000 (D)   **$4000–$6000**

Shelf clock   Federal   1800–1830   United States
Inlaid mahogany case with French feet; pierced fret; kidney-shaped dial signed "Adam Willard/Boston."
Very Good Quality/Good Condition $35,000 (D)   **$30,000–$50,000**

Shelf clock   36″ H   Empire   1830–1865   United States
Joseph Ives, Bristol, CT, labeled; good stenciling.
Good Quality/Good Condition $250 (D)   **$250–$500**

Tall case   76″ H   Late Stuart   1680–1700   England
Olivewood, parquetry case in good condition; movement retained; London.
Superior Quality/Average Condition $18,700 (A)   **$12,000–$18,000**

Photo 74 (left). Mantel regulator. CREDIT: CHRISTIE'S, NEW YORK. *Photo 75 (right). Shelf clock.* CREDIT: SKINNER, INC., BOLTON, MA *(See pp. 152, 153)*

Photo 76. Tall case. CREDIT: JOHN DELANEY, WEST TOWNSEND, MA
Photo 77. Tall case. CREDIT: R. O. STUART. *Photo 78. Tall case.*
CREDIT: SKINNER, INC., BOLTON, MA. *Photo 79. Wall clock.* CREDIT:
CHRISTIE'S, NEW YORK *(See pp. 155, 156)*

Tall case Chippendale 1780–1800 United States
Cherry case; painted dial signed "Simeon Jocelin/ New Haven" (CT); simple case.
Good Quality/Good Condition $15,000 (D)   **$15,000–$20,000**

Tall case Chippendale 1780–1800 United States
Cherry; signed "Ezra Bethelder/Danvers, Mass."; broken arch with inlaid terminals; fluted columns and quarter columns; ogee feet.
Very Good Quality/Good Condition $15,000 (D)   **$15,000–$20,000**

Tall case Chippendale 1780–1800 United States
Cherry; signed "John Bailey" (Hanover, MA); pierced fret; ogee feet; painted dial.
Very Good Quality/Average Condition $15,000 (D)   **$15,000–$20,000**

Tall case 7′5″ H Chippendale 1780–1800 United States
Rare; cherry; block front; exceptional wood and color; 1 finial replaced; old touch-up to dial paint; moonphase; 8-day brass movement; unsigned.
Superior Quality/Good Condition $35,000 (D)   **$30,000–$60,000**

Tall case 7′11″ H Chippendale 1780–1800 United States
Tiger maple; rocking ship movement; signed "James Corliss/Weare" (NH).
Superior Quality/Fine Condition $45,000 (D)   **$40,000–$60,000**

Tall case Federal 1780–1800 United States
Inlaid mahogany; signed "Simon Willard" (Roxbury, MA); scrolled and pierced-fret brass stop-fluted columns and corner columns; French feet; painted dial. *(See photo 76)*
Superior Quality/Fine Condition $100,000 (D)   **$80,000–$150,000**

Tall case 7′8″ H Federal 1780–1800 United States
Painted dial signed "Abel Hutchins, Concord" (NH); maple case; French feet; moonphase, 8-day brass movement. *(See photo 77)*
Very Good Quality/Good Condition $12,500 (D)   **$14,000–$18,000**

Tall case 87″ H Federal 1800–1810 United States
Mahogany; polychrome "Prince of Wales" crested, painted iron dial with second hand, calendar aperture; 8-day weight-driven brass movement; case with inlay and brass stop-fluting; old finish; very minor imperfections. *(See photo 78)*
Superior Quality/Good Condition $14,000 (A)   **$15,000–$20,000**

Tall case 93.5″ H Federal 1800–1810 United States
Mahogany; molded swan's-neck cresting; shortened urn finial; 8-day weight-driven movement and painted moon-phase iron dial with gilt fan spandrels; brass mounted columns; reeded quarter columns; RI.
Superior Quality/Average Condition $9500 (A)   **$12,000–$15,000**

Tall case 9.5″ H Federal 1800–1810 United States
Mahogany; pierced fretwork hood with 3 reeded plinths on arched cornice molding and glazed door enclosing painted iron dial and 8-day brass weight-driven movement; flanked by fluted columns; molded and inlaid waist door; inlaid base; loss of height; signed Simon Roxbury.
Superior Quality/Poor Condition $20,000 (A)   **$20,000–$30,000**

Tall case 91.5″ H Federal 1800–1810 United States
Cherry; painted iron moon-phase dial with second hand and calendar aperture; inscribed "Tim Chandler, Concord"; 8-day weight-driven brass movement; replaced feet; other minor imperfections; NH.
Very Good Quality/Average Condition $12,000 (A)   **$15,000–$20,000**

Tall case   7'7" H   Federal   1800–1830   United States
Signed "F. Wingate, Augusta, Me./ No. 186"; flame birch and bird's-eye maple; pierced fret; fluted and quarter columns.
Good Quality/Good Condition $11,000 (D)   **$12,500–$15,000**

Tall case   Federal   1800–1830   United States
Cherry, inlaid case; unsigned, painted dial; scrolled feet; fluted columns and quarter columns; ME.
Good Quality/Average Condition $8500 (D)   **$8000–$12,000**

Tall case   Federal   1800–1830   United States
Mahogany; pierced fret over arched molding; polychrome dial with rocking ship; 8-day weight-driven brass movement; mounted reeded columns on bonnet and waist; label with provenance; Roxbury, MA.
Superior Quality/Good Condition $25,000 (A)   **$25,000–$35,000**

Tall case   85" H   Federal   1830–1845   United States
Case putty-painted red-orange and mustard on ivory; painted wood dial with patriotic motif inscribed "S. Hoadley, Connecticut"; 30-hour wood weight-driven movement; lacks finial and key; dial left corner damaged.
Superior Quality/Good Condition $9000 (A)   **$10,000–$15,000**

Tall clock   8'1" H   Federal   1780–1800   United States
Painted dial signed "John Bailey/Hanover" (MA); pierced fret; fine figured mahogany; tall French feet; fluted columns and quarter columns; best proportions; moon-phase, 8-day brass movement.
Superior Quality/Fine Condition $20,000 (D)   **$20,000–$30,000**

Tall clock   7'7" H   Federal   1800–1830   United States
Fine cherry and figural maple inlaid case; 8-day wood and brass movement; 1 hand missing; finial replaced; unsigned, painted dial; NJ.
Very Good Quality/Average Condition $5500 (D)   **$6000–$10,000**

Urn clock   16" H   Louis XV   1765–1770   France
Ormolu; signed on dial and movement "Tavernier A Paris"; case signed "Osmond"; bell and pendulum lacking; auction fever caused this price.
Superior Quality/Fine Condition $38,500 (A)   **$8000–$12,000**

Wall clock   54" H   Victorian   1830–1865   England
Mahogany "Act of Parliament" clock; painted dial marked "Dwerri House & Carter—Berkeley Square"; brass 8-day weight-driven movement; no pendulum or weight. *(See photo 79)*
Good Quality/Average Condition $2300 (A)   **$1000–$1500**

BIBLIOGRAPHY

No quality comprehensive book exists, but a few standard general references are listed here. The best books are regional and specialized, but to list one would be to list twenty.

Distin, William H., and Bishop, Robert. *The American Clock*. New York: E. P. Dutton, 1976.

Dworetsky, Lester, and Dickstein, Robert. *Horology Americana*. New York: Authors, 1972.

Palmer, Brooks. *The Book of American Clocks*. New York: Macmillan, 1950.

――――. *A Treasury of American Clocks*. New York: Macmillan. 1963.

MUSEUMS

Even lesser clocks are always interesting in a way that lesser furniture frequently is not, and small museums with only a few clocks are worth looking at. Larger collections may be found in the following:

The Willard Clock Museum, Grafton, MA.
The American Clock and Watch Museum, Bristol, CT.
The Time Museum, Rockford, IL.
Winterthur, Winterthur, DE.
J. Cheney Wells Collection, Sturbridge Village, MA.
Henry Ford Museum, Dearborn, MI.
The Metropolitan Museum of Art, NY.

COLLECTORS' CLUBS

Many specialized clock and watch collector societies and clubs are active. The most important is the National Association of Watch and Clock Collectors, Inc., Columbia, Pennsylvania.

Comic Books

Advisor: **ROBERT M. OVERSTREET**

Robert M. Overstreet is the author of The Overstreet Comic Book Price Guide *(New York: Avon, 1992). He can be reached at 780 Hunt Cliff Drive, N.W., Cleveland, TN 37311; (615) 472-4135.*

HISTORY

The first comic books were published at the turn of the century and had cardboard covers. All of them contained strip reprints that were adapted from the newspapers into this format. Some of the early titles were *Buster Brown*, *Mutt and Jeff*, and *Bringing Up Father*. These were very popular into the early 1930s.

In 1933 the first "official" comic book, *Funnies on Parade*, was given away as a test for public demand. In 1934 the first newsstand book, *Famous Funnies*, was published. The success of this title paved the way for many other tities. Comic books did not explode into the mainstream of American life until the appearance of Superman in *Action Comics*, No. 1 (dated 6/38) in April 1938. This single book changed the fabric of comic book publishing forever. The superhero was "in," and superheroes became one of the main subjects for comic books.

One important exception would be the early Disney characters, which were instantly popular. Because of the success of the animated shorts of Mickey Mouse, he began to appear in children's books as early as 1930. He received his own series, *Mickey Mouse Magazine*, in 1933; this eventually changed into a comic book, *Walt Disney's Comics & Stories*, in 1940. This collectible title is still being published, along with a host of other Disney character books. Donald Duck had his first "official" appearance in 1934 in a cartoon, *The Wise Little Hen*, although Donald had appeared in 1931 in *The Adventures of Mickey Mouse*, #1. Donald's career in comic books began in 1938, and by 1940 he had become a cover star on Disney's main title *Walt Disney's Comics & Stories*.

As mentioned, the superhero dominated the comic book stands in the 1940s, with hundreds of titles published. After the war sales began to slump, and the comics industry responded with Western, crime, love, and a host of funny animal, humorous, and other subjects in their titles. With horror, science fiction, and war (Korean) added a few years later, these genres dominated the 1950s stands. Most superhero books died in the early 1950s.

Also in the early 1950s, comic books were under attack by various educators. Senate hearings were held, and the comics industry was forced to set up an authority that would police and approve (with their seal) all newsstand comic books. As a result of the bad publicity and stricter standards, many publishers perished. The late 1950s is known as "the Dark Ages of Comics."

However, some of the superheroes survived this bleak period. Batman, Superman, and Wonder Woman never missed an issue and are still going strong today. It should also be noted that while most comic books published in the 1950s were in trouble, many of the Disney and Warner Brothers characters comics were selling in high volume—some over 1 million per issue!

In 1956, *Showcase* #4 was published, bringing back The Flash from the 1940s. In 1959 he began his own series, and one year later *The Green Lantern* and *Justice League of America* were published. In 1961, Marvel Comics came out with *The Fantastic Four*, followed by *The Incredible Hulk* in 1962 and *The Amazing Spider-Man* in 1963. The superhero was returning to the stands. In fact, an explosion of superhero comics began to occur, bringing in "The Silver Age of Comics."

In 1949 the first television tie-in comic book, *Howdy Doody*, was published. This began a new genre and a long list of comic book titles based on television shows that lasted through the 1960s. All of these titles are currently collected in the market. A few of the hottest titles are *Jackie Gleason, I Love Lucy, Rawhide, Rocky and His Fiendish Friends, Space Ghost, The Munsters, Leave It to Beaver, Flintstones*, and *Dark Shadows*. All of these books are relatively inexpensive and represent the early establishment and development of television. They all have the potential for increased demand in the future.

Comic books are collected and become valuable for many reasons. Usually the books that made the strongest impression on us as kids will be the ones sought after today. Yes, nostalgia plays an important role in what gets on our want lists. First issues are important. The first appearances of major characters are important. The issues that explain their origins are also collected. Many of the best artists have large fan followings. Some collectors collect only a certain company, a particular character, or a genre of comic (such as science fiction). There are collectors for every type of comic book, so whatever your collecting interest, there is much from which to choose.

Currently, there are dozens of publishers who are producing hundreds of comic book titles. The market is wide open, with new publishers and titles appearing and disappearing at a rapid pace. Determining what current titles are or are not likely to be collectible in the future is difficult and chaotic.

MARKET REPORT

The comic book market has enjoyed unprecedented growth during the past several years, more than doubling in size. The current comic book market is very volatile, with Silver Age books (1950s–'60s) such as *Amazing Spider-Man*, *Captain America*, *Showcase*, *Brave and the Bold*, *Iron Man*, *Justice League*, *Batman*, *Green Lantern*, *Fantastic Four*, *X-Men*, *The Atom*, etc., at the top of the list. The high demand for these and other titles is forcing prices up at a fast pace.

The backbone of the comics market has always been the 1940s comics. The superheroes, such as *Batman*, *Superman*, *Captain America*, *Captain Marvel*, *Green Lantern*, *The Flash*, and *Wonder Woman* are the most collected. The most collected companies are DC, Marvel, Dell, Centaur, and Fawcett. *Dick Tracy* is hot, and *Classic Comics* have been coming on strong. Early rare issues of *Mickey Mouse* and *Donald Duck* have been setting record prices. Almost all comics from this period enjoy a large collector base and continue to be good investment material.

The latest sensation on HBO—"Tales from the Crypt"—has brought much attention to the original 1950s comic books of the same title, upon which the series is based. Even demand for the sister titles, *Haunt of Fear* and *Vault of Horror*, is up. All Atlas horror and science-fiction titles are hot, especially those titles that launched the Marvel superheroes of the 1960s, such as *Tales of Suspense*, *Strange Tales*, *Journey into Mystery*, and *Tales to Astonish*. TV comics of the 1950s and 1960s continue to be popular. *I Love Lucy*, *Gunsmoke*, *Rawhide*, *Dark Shadows*, *Star Trek*, *Rocky and Bullwinkle*, and *Jackie Gleason* are just a few of the top titles.

Recently, 1970s comics have been enjoying increased interest. Most titles that have recently become very hot from the 1960s are now being collected from the 1970s and 1980s. A few titles to watch are *Iron Man*, *Captain America*, *Challengers*, *Batman*, *Superman*, *Action*, *Detective*, *Conan*, *Doom Patrol*, and *Spider-Man*.

The 1980s produced many winners, with *Teenage Mutant Ninja Turtles* currently very hot. *Warning*: Issues #1 and #2 have recently been counterfeited. A few recent popular titles are *Aliens*, *Batman*, *Spider-Man*, *Dick Tracy*, *Longshot*, and *Punisher*. Unfortunately, thousands of titles filled the market during this period, and the failures have far outnumbered the winners. We have always recommended that beginners just buy reading copies of what they personally like. If some of these turn into a good investment, then they are ahead of the game.

CONDITION AND QUALITY KEYS

Comic books are a special case for grading and valuing. Age, popularity of the heroes, quality of design and color, the artist-creator, and a host of other factors have an impact on price. A standard of grading exists within the industry, and that system is used in this chapter instead of the systems of condition and quality used throughout most of this guide. A full listing of gradations may be found in Mr. Overstreet's comic guide. In this section, three grades and their respective prices are provided. To provide a broad perspective we have chosen to list #1's from a myriad of types and periods.

GRADING DEFINITIONS

The hardest part of evaluating a comic is being honest and objective with yourself, and knowing what characteristics to look for in making your decision. The following characteristics should be checked in evaluating books, especially those in higher grades: degree of cover luster, degree of color fading, staples, staple areas, spine condition, top and bottom of spine, edges of cover, centering, brittleness, browning/yellowing, flatness, tightness, interior damage, tape, tears, folds, water marks, color flaking, and general cleanliness.

Warning about restoration: Many rare and expensive key books are being upgraded from lower grades to fine or very fine condition through restoration. It has been brought to our attention that some dealers have been selling these books to unsuspecting collectors/investors and not telling them of the restoration. In some cases these restored books are being priced the same as unrestored books. *Very important:* Examine books very closely for repairing or restoration before purchase. The more expensive the book, the greater the likelihood of restoration. Major things to look for are bleaching, whitening, trimming, interior spine and tear reinforcement, gluing, restapling, missing pieces replaced, wrinkles pressed out of covers, recoloring, and reglossing covers. Dealers should state that a book has been restored and not expect to get as much as an unrestored book would bring. *Note:* Cleaning, stain removal, rolled spine removal, staple replacement, etc., if professionally done, would not be considered restoration as long as the printed condition of the comic has not been changed.

Very important: A book must be graded in its entirety, not by just the cover alone. A book in any of the grades listed must be in its *original unrestored* condition. *Restored books* must be graded as such; i.e., a restored grading fine might be worth only the same as a very good or even a good copy in its unrestored state. The value of an extensively restored book may improve a half-grade from its original unrestored state. After these characteristics have been examined, a comic book may be assigned to one of the following grades:

Near Mint: like new or newsstand condition but with very slight loss of luster, a slightly off-center cover, or a minor printing error. Could have penciled arrival dates, slight color fading, and white to extra-white cover and pages. Any noticeable defects would be very minor and attributable to the cutting, folding, and stapling process.

Fine: tight cover with some wear but still relatively flat, clean, and shiny, with no subscription crease, writing on cover, yellowed margins, or tape repairs. Stress lines around staples and along spine beginning to show; minor color flaking possible at spine, staples, edges, or corners. Slight yellowing acceptable.

Good: an average used copy complete with both covers and no panels missing; slightly soiled or marked with possible creases, minor tears or splits, rolled spine, and small color flaking but perfectly sound and legible. A well-read copy but perfectly acceptable, with no chunks missing. Minor tape repairs usually occur and slight browning (no brittleness) acceptable, although tape repairs should be considered a defect and priced accordingly.

	Good	Fine	N-Mint
Abbott & Costello #1, Feb. 1948	$22	$65	$135
Action Comics #1, June 1938 (Origin & 1st appearance of Superman)	$6000	$15,000	$32,500
Adventure Comics #32, Nov. 1938	$93	$235	$560
Adventures of the Fly #1, Aug. 1959	$26	$80	$185
Amazing Spider-man, The #1, Mar. 1963	$275	$1100	$2750
Animal Man #1, Sept. 1988	$3.15	$5.50	$12
Aquaman #1, Jan.–Feb. 1962	$28	$64	$135
Avengers, The #1, Sept. 1963	$180	$390	$800
Batman #1, Spring 1940	$2420	$6050	$14,500

	Good	Fine	N-Mint
Blue Beetle, The #1, Winter 1939–40	$142	$355	$850
Boris Karloff Tales of Mystery #3, Apr. 1963	$1.15	$3.50	$8
Brave and the Bold, The #1, Aug.–Sept. 1955	$82	$245	$575
Brother Power the Geek #1, Sept.–Oct. 1968	$3.70	$7	$14
Captain America #100, Apr. 1968	$21	$60	$145
Captain America Comics #1, Mar. 1941	$1500	$3750	$9000
Classic Comics #1, Oct. 1941 (The Three Musketeers)	$257	$770	$1800
Conan the Barbarian #1, Oct. 1970	$15.50	$45	$100
Creepy #1, 1964	$3.35	$6	$12
Crime Does Not Pay #22, June 1942	$82	$245	$575
Crow, The #1, Feb. 1989	$1.35	$3	$6
Daredevil #1, Apr. 1964	$90	$260	$600
Dark Horse Presents #1, July 1986	$3	$8	$15
Detective Comics #27, May 1939 (1st appearance The Batman)	$6000	$15,000	$32,500
Dick Tracy Large Feature Comic #1, 1939	$86	$257	$600
Doctor Strange #169 (#1), June 1968	$7	$21	$40
Donald Duck Adventures #1, Nov. 1987	$.50	$1.50	$3
Eerie #1, Jan. 1947	$38	$115	$265
80-Page Giant #1, Aug. 1964	$10.15	$27.50	$70
Elementals, The #1, June 1984	$1.35	$4	$8
Elfquest #1, Aug. 1985	$.85	$2.50	$5
Excalibur #1, Apr. 1988	$3.15	$5.50	$10
Fantastic Four #1, Nov. 1964	$285	$1100	$3000
Faust #1, 1989	$2.85	$7.50	$15

	Good	Fine	N-Mint
Fight Against Crime #1, May 1951	$9.30	$28	$65
Flash, The #105, Feb.-Mar. 1959	$122	$354	$880
Gabby Hayes Western #1, Nov. 1948	$23	$70	$165
Ghost Rider #1, Sept. 1973	$3	$9	$18
Green Lantern #1, Feb. 1941	$583	$1460	$3500
Grimjack #1, Aug. 1984	$.40	$1.20	$2.40
Groo the Wanderer #1, Mar. 1985	$2	$6	$12
Hawkman #1, Apr.-May 1964	$19	$53	$150
Heart Throbs #1, Aug. 1949	$18.50	$56	$130
Hellblazer #1, Jan. 1988	$.45	$1.25	$2.50
Heroic Comics #1, Aug. 1940	$50	$150	$350
House of Mystery, The #1, Dec.-Jan. 1951-52	$46	$137	$320
Ibis, The Invincible #1, 1943	$75	$225	$525
Incredible Hulk, The #1, May 1962	$135	$405	$950
Infinity, Inc. #1, Mar. 1984	$.60	$1.75	$3.50
Iron Man (See photo 80) #1, May 1968	$28	$85	$200
John Wayne Adventure Comics #1, Winter 1949	$41	$122	$285
Joker, The #1, May 1975	$2.85	$8.50	$20
Journey Into Mystery #1, June 1952	$69	$235	$800
Jumbo Comics #1, Sept. 1938	$550	$1375	$3300
Justice League of America #1, Oct.-Nov. 1960	$130	$390	$900
Katy Keene #1, 1949	$65	$195	$455
KA-ZAR #1, Aug. 1970	$.60	$1.75	$3.50
Kid Colt Outlaw #1, Aug. 1948	$32	$95	$225
Kitty Pryde and Wolverine #1, Nov. 1984	$.75	$2.25	$4.50

	Good	Fine	N-Mint
Lash Larue Western	$55	$165	$385
#1, Summer 1949			
Little Dot	$45	$135	$320
#1, Sept. 1953			
Longshot	$3.35	$10	$20
#1, Sept. 1985			
Looney Tunes and Merry Melodies	$121	$365	$850
Comics			
#1, 1941			
Love and Rockets	$11.70	$35	$70
#1, July 1982			
Magic Comics	$108	$270	$650
#1, Aug. 1939			
Man-Bat	$1	$3	$6
#1, Dec.-Jan. 1975–76			
Man-Thing	$1	$3	$6
#1, Jan. 1974			
Marvel Comics Super Special	$3.50	$10.50	$24
#1, Sept. 1977			
Metal Men	$14	$42	$100
#1, Apr.-May 1963			
My Greatest Adventure	$43	$130	$300
#1, Jan.-Feb. 1955			
New Mutants, The	$1.25	$3.75	$7.50
#1, Mar. 1983			
Nick Fury, Agent of Shield	$3.60	$11	$25
#1, June 1968			
Not Brand Echh	$2.15	$6.50	$15
#1, Aug. 1967			

Photo 80 (left). Iron Man. CREDIT: COPYRIGHT © MARVEL
ENTERTAINMENT GROUP. *Photo 81 (center). The Question.* CREDIT:
COPYRIGHT © DC COMICS. *Photo 82 (right). The Vault of Horror.*
CREDIT: COPYRIGHT © WILLIAM M. GAINES *(See pp. 164, 166, 167)*

	Good	Fine	N-Mint
Nyoka, The Jungle Girl #2, Winter 1945	$34	$103	$240
Omaha the Cat Dancer #1, 1984	$1.70	$5	$10
Oswald the Rabbit Four-Color #21, 1943	$22	$65	$154
Our Army at War #1, Aug. 1952	$40	$120	$280
Outlaw Kid, The #1, Sept. 1954	$8.50	$25.50	$60
Pacific Presents #1, Oct. 1982	$.70	$2.10	$4.20
Pep Comics #1, Jan. 1940 (Introd. The Shield)	$200	$500	$1200
Phantom, The #1, Nov. 1962	$5	$15	$35
Phoenix #1, Apr. 1984	$1.35	$4	$8
Plastic Man #1, Nov. 1966	$1.70	$5	$12
Police Comics #1, Aug. 1941	$308	$770	$1850
Punisher, The V2 #1, July 1987	$1.85	$5.50	$11
Question, The (See photo 81) #1, Feb. 1987	$.75	$2.25	$4.50
Rawhide Kid #1, Mar. 1955	$21.50	$64	$150
Real Fact Comics #1, Mar.–Apr. 1946	$21.50	$64	$150
Rip Hunter Time Master #1, Mar.–Apr. 1961	$18	$54	$125
Rock and Roll Comics #1, June 1989 (Guns 'N Roses)	$1.50	$4.50	$10
Rocky Lane Western #1, May 1949	$44	$133	$310
Rusty Comics #12, Apr. 1947	$6.50	$19.50	$45
Saga of Swamp Thing, The #1, May 1982	$.25	$.75	$1.50
Sandman, The #1, Jan. 1989	$.70	$2	$4
Sea Devils #1, Sept.–Oct. 1961	$14	$42	$100
Showcase #1, Mar.–Apr. 1956	$70	$210	$485
Silver Surfer #1, Aug. 1968	$13.50	$40	$95

	Good	Fine	N-Mint
Spectacular Spider-man, The #1, Dec. 1976	$1.70	$5	$10
Strange Tales #1, June 1951	$80	$240	$560
Superman #1, Summer 1939	$4000	$11,000	$26,000
Tales From the Crypt #20, Oct.–Nov. 1950	$55	$165	$385
Tales of Suspense #1, Jan. 1959	$47	$140	$325
Tales to Astonish #1, Jan. 1959	$46	$138	$325
Teen-age Mutant Ninja Turtles #1, 1984	$31	$92.50	$185
Teen Titans #1, Jan.–Feb. 1966	$12	$36	$85
Thor #126, Mar. 1966	$5	$15	$35
Thunder Agents #1, Nov. 1965	$7	$21	$50
Two Gun Kid #1, Mar. 1948	$34	$100	$240
United Comics #1, Aug. 1940	$13	$40	$90
Untold Legends of the Batman, The #1, July 1980	$.70	$2	$4
Unusual Tales #1, Nov. 1955	$7	$21	$50
USA Comics #1, Aug. 1941	$350	$875	$2100
Vampirella #1, Sept. 1969	$10	$30	$70
Vault of Horror *(See photo 82)* #12, Apr.–May 1950	$116	$348	$810
Vietnam Journal #1, Nov. 1987	$.70	$2	$4
Voodoo #1, May 1952	$17	$51	$120
Walt Disney's Comics & Stories #1, Oct. 1940	$370	$1480	$3700
Web of Evil #1, Nov. 1952	$18	$54	$125
Web of Spiderman #1, Apr. 1985	$1.15	$3.50	$7
Weird Science #12, May 1950	$86	$257	$600
West Coast Avengers #1, Oct. 1985	$.85	$2.50	$5
What If . . . ? #1, Feb. 1977	$1.25	$3.75	$7.50

	Good	Fine	N-Mint
World's Finest Comics #2, Summer 1941	$196	$490	$1175
X-Factor #1, Feb. 1986	$1.35	$4	$8
X-Men #1, Sept. 1963	$110	$415	$990
Yellow Claw #1, Oct. 1956	$29	$86	$200
Young Allies Comics #1, Summer 1941	$250	$625	$1500
Young All-Stars #1, June 1987	$.70	$2	$4
Zip Comics #1, Feb. 1940	$117	$295	$700
Zoot #7, 1947 (Rulah, the Jungle Goddess begins)	$33	$100	$230
Zot! #1, Apr. 1984	$1.15	$3.50	$7

COMIC BOOK CONVENTIONS

Atlanta Fantasy Fair XV, August. Information: Atlanta Fantasy Fair, 691 Spring Forest Dr., Lawrenceville, GA 30243; (404) 961–2347.

Chicago Comicon. Information: Larry Charet, 1219-A West Devon Ave., Chicago, IL 60660; (312) 274–1832.

Childhood Treasures Show and Convention, July, Dallas, TX. Write Don Maris, PO Box 111266, Arlington, TX 76007; (817) 261–8745 before 10 P.M. Central Time.

Creation Con, 145 Jericho Turnpike, Mineola, NY 11501; (516) 746–9626. Contact about major events in Atlanta, Boston, Cincinnati, Cleveland, Detroit, London, Los Angeles, Philadelphia, Rochester, San Francisco, Washington, D.C.

Dallas Fantasy Fair. Contact Larry Lankford, (214) 349–3367.

Los Angeles Comic Book and Science-Fiction Convention. Contact Bruce Schwartz, 1802 W. Olive Ave., Burbank, CA 91506; (818) 954–8432. Monthly shows.

San Diego Comic Con, PO Box 17066, San Diego, CA 92117.

Dolls and Doll Accessories

***Advisor:* CAMILLE T. ZAGAROLI**

Camille T. Zagaroli lives with her husband, Robert, and their three cats in Yardley, Pennsylvania. She has had a lifelong interest in dolls but began to collect seriously in the mid-1950s. She is a dealer and appraiser of dolls and has been a judge at various doll functions. Mrs. Zagaroli is a member of United Federation of Doll Clubs and a charter member of Region 13, Delaware Valley Doll Club. She travels the United States and Europe in her quest for dolls and related materials. She can be reached at (215) 493-8734.

The primary purpose of a doll is as a plaything; hence, doll collecting is very personal. The first doll one buys, after childhood, is usually based on a childhood memory. "There's my doll!" is often heard at antiques shows and auctions. An absolute influence on doll collecting is nostalgia.

Nobody really knows when the first dolls were made as playthings, but surely some cave child held a smooth stone or piece of bone that had been carved into a human form, mimicking the mother with her baby. We know from treasures "rescued" from the tombs that Egyptians made linen dolls stuffed with flax.

Through the ages dolls have evolved from those primitive forms into the treasured objects we collect today, whether of cloth, wood, wax, bisque, china, composition, or hard plastic. Simply stated, doll collecting appeals to the child in all of us.

Dolls are one of the most sought after *collectibles* on the market today, not only because of their aesthetic quality but because they have proved to be a safe investment. During the last twenty years prices on antique and modern dolls have risen dramatically.

The Golden Age of Dollmaking (1875–1925) seems to appeal to the antique doll collector. There is also a broad base of interest in the modern doll, whose prices are generally more moderate. However, a rare modern doll can bring a higher price than some antique dolls. The No. 1 Barbie, for instance, c. 1959, mint, in the original box, can command a $2,000 price tag.

There is a wide price range, catering to every pocketbook. You may purchase a tiny antique doll for as little as $35 or an elegant French bébé for as high as $150,000. For the beginning collector there are still bargains in the doll world, and a very fine collection can be obtained on a moderate budget.

MARKET TRENDS

The market is an ever-changing affair. However, it appears that the early wooden doll (c. 1840) and the Schoenhut dolls and animals (Philadelphia-based firm, c. 1900) are escalating rapidly in interest and price.

Early 20th-century cloth dolls are showing major increases and are expected to continue. Steiff dolls and toys are becoming major collections in themselves, and one would be wise to focus on this trend. Kathe Kruse dolls of all eras are good investments, and the John Wright dolls of today are steadily appreciating.

The really big money will be in the exquisitely costumed French bisque dolls. The German characters, too, are becoming more sought after, and a steady increase is expected.

Barbie is still very much alive and is considered a good investment, along with the earlier Ginnys.

QUALITY KEY

Superior Quality: exquisitely detailed dolls of all media with few flaws.

Very Good Quality: workmanship is excellent; all elements stylistically correct for period.

Good Quality: a nice doll worthy of collecting but not necessarily for investment.

Poor Quality: be wary before you buy!

CONDITION KEY

Excellent Condition: mint, no hairline cracks on head or shoulderplate; original wig; original or appropriate clothing; good body.

Good Condition: perhaps a hairline crack that is not noticeable without a black light; minor repairs are allowed; original wig or good replacement; body in acceptable condition and may have minor cracks and some flaking; cloth dolls may show fading.

Average Condition: original wig in fair condition or fair replaced wig; may have minor cracks on face; body may have flaking of painted features; body may be replaced; chips in molded hair.

Poor Condition: cracked head and/or shoulderplate; fading of painted features; worn body.

PRICE ADJUSTMENTS FOR CONDITION

Repaired head: −60 to −80%
Repaired shoulderplate: −40 to −50%
Cracked head: −50 to −70%
Cracked shoulderplate: −30%
Chips on molded hair: −20 to −30%
Fading of painted features: −20 to −50%
Moderate kiln dirt (black specks): −30%
Worn body: −30%
Replaced body: −30 to −40%
Original good clothing in fine condition: +30 to +50%

Armand Marseille 26″ H 390 c. 1910 Germany
Composition ball-jointed body; spiral blue glass eyes, feathered eyebrows, accent dots on inner corners of eyes and on nostrils; lips with accent lines; exquisitely dressed in antique clothes and wig.
Superior Quality/Fine Condition $650 (D) **$400–$700**

Armand Marseille 11″ H 390 c. 1920 Germany
Child bisque head with original wig; composition ball-jointed body; appropriate clothes.
Good Quality/Good Condition $250 (D) **$95–$250**

C. M. Bergman 24″ H c. 1910 Germany
Marked bisque head, composition ball-jointed body; original human hair wig, sleep eyes, open mouth; exquisite costume.
Superior Quality/Good Condition $600 (D) **$650–$750**

Celluloid 16″ H Unmarked c. 1920 Germany
Character face with glass sleep eyes; original black wool wig and original clothes; black celluloid dolls of this size are extremely scarce.
Superior Quality/Fine Condition $475 (D) **$450–$575**

China head 15″ H c. 1860 Germany
Glazed shoulderhead with black, painted hair, center part, stippling around hair, molded ribbon and snood on hair; slender features, high-luster, blue, painted eyes; cloth body, china limbs; silk clothes. *(See photo 83, right)*
Superior Quality/Fine Condition $650 (D) **$250–$700**

China head 10″ H c. 1860 Germany
Biedermeier or bald head style with original wig (black spot under wig); rare size; beautiful pink luster and painting; original muslin body; wooden arms, hands, legs; appropriate clothes. *(See photo 83, left)*
Superior Quality/Fine Condition $400 (D) **$300–$500**

China head 18″ H c. 1865 Germany
China bonnet with applied flowers; blue china earrings; muslin body, kid arms; china legs and feet; original costume—all silk with silk chantilly lace (minor splitting); molded bonnet dolls are rare.
Superior Quality/Fine Condition $1600 (D) **$950–$2000**

China head   19″ H   Male   c. 1865   Germany
Perfect china head with center part; original black muslin suit, cotton vest and shirt; body stuffed with horsehair; china hands; shoulderhead marked "Made in Germany"; male china heads less common.
Superior Quality/Fine Condition $550 (D)   **$500–$700**

China head   19″ H   c. 1890   Germany
Common 1890s or low-brow style; original kid body and china hands; unmarked; appropriate clothes. *(See photo 84, right)*
Superior Quality/Fine Condition $150 (D)   **$85–$165**

China head   10″ H   c. 1890   Germany
Common or low-brow china; original muslin body; original china hands and legs; flat shoes; incised "3" on shoulder plate; appropriate clothes. *(See photo 84, left)*
Superior Quality/Fine Condition $85 (D)   **$65–$95**

China head   12″ H   c. 1890   Germany
Common low-brow style; original china arms and legs; original muslin body; dressed in black antique dress to resemble Mary Todd Lincoln.
Superior Quality/Fine Condition $185 (D)   **$100–$200**

Cloth character   17″ H   c. 1940   United States
Black folk-type doll with embroidered features, original clothes.
Superior Quality/Fine Condition $75 (D)   **$50–$75**

Composition   22″ H   c. 1924   United States
Unmarked girl-type mama doll (these were made by various American companies); composition head with molded hair, sleep eyes, open mouth with teeth; composition shoulder plate, arms and legs, cloth body.
Good Quality/Fine Condition $285 (D)   **$225–$285**

DOOR OF HOPE DOLLS

The Door of Hope home was founded by an American woman in China in 1910 and remained open until 1930. She rescued prostitutes who were too old to continue their vocation, drug addicts, widows, and anyone else needing help. To fund the home, the residents were taught to carve and dress dolls. The heads, and frequently the hands, were hand-carved in exquisite detail from pear or apple wood and touched with color. These character dolls were made to represent the good or wealthy life of all ages and stations of society. The clothes were all handmade of silks and fine fabrics befitting the character represented. The queues were made of human hair and inserted into the wooden heads. Just as with many collectibles, these beautiful dolls originally sold for a pittance. However, today they are highly prized dolls and avidly collected. Prices range in the hundreds of dollars.

Door of Hope Mission   8.5″ H   3 stages of man   c. 1915   China
Young male child with long human hair queue, silk-embroidered clothes of high-born child; pearwood head carved in Ning-Po Province; with young man and ancient, represents the 3 stages of man. *(See photo 85, left)*
Superior Quality/Fine Condition $450 (D)   **$350–$450**

Photo 83 (left). China head dolls. CREDIT: ALDA LEAKE HORNER. *Photo 84 (right). China head dolls.* CREDIT: ALDA LEAKE HORNER *(See pp. 171, 172)*

Photo 85. Door of Hope Mission dolls. CREDIT: ALDA LEAKE HORNER *(See pp. 172, 174)*

Photo 86. Ernst Heubach dolls. CREDIT: ALDA LEAKE HORNER *(See p. 174)*

Door of Hope Mission   12″ H   3 stages of man   c. 1915   China
Young man with pearwood head by carvers from Ning-Po; cloth body; carved hands; original handmade clothes; "Made in China" label. *(See photo 85, center)*
Superior Quality/Fine Condition $400 (D)   **$350–$500**

Door of Hope Mission   10″ H   3 stages of man   c. 1915   China
Ancient man with head and hands carved from pearwood by carvers from Ning-Po; original handmade clothes; deep wrinkles carved into face. *(See photo 85, right)*
Superior Quality/Fine Condition $400 (D)   **$300–$450**

Door of Hope Mission   He, 13″ H; she, 12″ H   Bride and groom   c. 1920   China
Pearwood heads by carvers from Ningo-Po region; cloth bodies; bride with elaborate hairdo and embroidered red outfit; groom with human hair queue; all clothes are handmade and original.
Superior Quality/Fine Condition $1200 (D)   **$1000–$1500**

Door of Hope Mission   11.5″ H   Mourning widow   c. 1920   China
Head and hands of pearwood, hand-carved in Ning-Po; headdress and jacket of hand-spun and hand-woven rice cloth; shirt and undergarments of unbleached muslin; rice cloth shoes.
Superior Quality/Fine Condition $600 (D)   **$450–$700**

Ernst Heubach   18″ H   Horseshoe mark   c. 1890   Germany
Child doll with beautifully painted face, feathered eyebrows and double row of lashes; kid body with rivet joints; original wig and chemise; fine antique costume; wistful expression. *(See photo 86, right)*
Superior Quality/Fine Condition $350 (D)   **$275–$350**

Ernst Heubach   14″ H   Horseshoe mark and WC   c. 1900   Germany
Bisque shoulderhead on kid body; composition arms and legs; replaced wig; beautiful antique costume. *(See photo 86, left)*
Superior Quality/Fine Condition $285 (D)   **$225–$285**

Ernst Heubach   27″ H   Koppelsdorf-Thur   1910   Germany
Character face; perfect bisque head, original mohair wig, sleep eyes, open mouth with 4 milk glass teeth; composition ball-jointed body; dressed in white antique costume.
Superior Quality/Fine Condition $900 (D)   **$750–$900**

Folk art cloth   18″ H   c. 1940   United States
All original and handmade black doll with dress, apron, kerchief; yarn hair.
Very Good Quality/Good Condition $250 (D)   **$150–$300**

Kämmer & Reinhardt   Head 12″ circ.   Simon & Halbig   c. 1914   Germany
Character baby; perfect bisque head on composition, bent-limb body; original wig, open mouth with spring tongue and milk-glass teeth; beautifully dressed in antique Christmas costume. *(See photo 87)*
Superior Quality/Fine Condition $450 (D)   **$375–$450**

Kestner   17″ H   "9"   c. 1880   Germany
Early child-doll, bisque shoulderhead on kid body; head is perfect oily bisque, plaster dome, good wig, sleep eyes, swivel neck, pouty face; bisque lower arms; cleft under nose; accented closed mouth.
Superior Quality/Fine Condition $750 (D)   **$750–$1000**

Kestner 26″ H 12 154 DEP c. 1892 Germany
Kid body with rivet joints, marked with Kestner crown and streamers—JDK Germany; beautifully painted bisque head with plaster dome and replaced wig; sleep eyes, open mouth; feathered eyebrows, double row of painted lashes; appropriate clothes.
Superior Quality/Fine Condition $900 (D)   **$800–$1000**

Kestner 19″ H G 129 11 1910 Germany
Child-doll; bisque socket head on ball-jointed body; plaster dome; original wig; well dressed; body marked "EXCELSIOR"; original sticker on body: "Made for F. A. Schwartz, Philadelphia."
Superior Quality/Fine Condition $750 (D)   **$750–$1000**

Papier-mâché 9.5″ H Black. c. 1890 Germany
Character face and sleep eyes; original wig and undergarments; appropriate old dress.
Superior Quality/Fine Condition $285 (D)   **$200–$285**

Parian 11″ H c. 1870 Germany
Early blonde, flat-top, covered-wagon hairdo; milk white complexion; original arms and legs; gold-colored taffeta dress over lace flounce; untinted bisque.
Very Good Quality/Fine Condition $150 (D)   **$125–$200**

Snow babies 3″ H c. 1910 Germany
Snow baby with brown bear.
Superior Quality/Fine Condition $95 (D)   **$85–$110**

Snow babies 3″ H c. 1910 Germany
Snow baby on back of a snow bear.
Superior Quality/Fine Condition $95 (D)   **$85–$100**

Snow babies 3″ H c. 1910 Germany
Snow bear on skis.
Superior Quality/Fine Condition $150 (D)   **$125–$175**

Snow babies 3″ H Santa c. 1910 Germany
Santa on snow bear.
Superior Quality/Fine Condition $175 (D)   **$165–$200**

Wax over papier-mâché 18″ H c. 1870 Germany
Rare modeled bonnet; original wig, cloth body, glass eyes; wooden arms and hands; wooden legs and flat wooden shoes; appropriate old clothes.
Very Good Quality/Good Condition $500 (D)   **$600–$800**

Wax over papier-mâché 21″ H c. 1870 Germany
Rare hairdo type, hair molded smooth over crown and held with red molded ribbon; delicately painted with feathered eyebrows and shaded lips; sleep eyes; original cloth body and limbs; nice old clothes.
Very Good Quality/Good Condition $500 (D)   **$600–$750**

The QUALITY KEY measures the stylishness and collectibility of an antique.

Good Quality: Exhibits standard characteristics of the object.

Very Good Quality: A more desirable example because of above-average workmanship and design.

Superior Quality: Exhibits nearly every known feature found on such items, with workmanship and design of the highest quality.

Wax over papier-mâché   18″ H   c. 1880   Germany
Bonnet head with molded derby bonnet and plume; unusual blue glass eyes; original cloth body; wooden extremities; nice old clothes; all in great condition.
Very Good Quality/Fine Condition $500 (D)   **$600–$800**

DOLL ACCESSORIES

Andirons   3.5″ H   c. 1905   United States
Miniature, wrought iron; handmade, good details; ball finials.
Very Good Quality/Fine Condition $94 (A)   **$50–$100**

Armoire   15″ H × 8″ W × 4″ D   1860–1880   France
Rosewood with white pine secondary; door with original mirror and ebony stringing over drawer; plinth base with piecrust trim; formed crest; original brass knobs; door and brass front with scribed decoration.
Superior Quality/Fine Condition $750 (D)   **$650–$1000**

Blocks   c. 1910   United States
Twenty-four wooden blocks with embossed and polychromed letters, scenes, etc.
Good Quality/Average Condition $66 (A)   **$60–$100**

Box   2.5″ Dia.   Bentwood   c. 1915   United States
Single-finger construction; old finish.
Good Quality/Good Condition $60 (A)   **$50–$75**

Buffet   25″ H × 18″ W   c. 1900   United States
Two over 2 full-length drawers; top has simple crest, original mirror over shelf; 2 small side shelves; oxbow-shaped top; shaped apron; brass pulls.
Superior Quality/Fine Condition $300 (D)   **$200–$350**

Carriage   30″ H × 24″ W   c. 1880   United States
Fancy tan wicker carriage with large wooden wheels and handle; strap springs; original mattress and pillow.
Superior Quality/Fine Condition $550 (D)   **$500–$750**

Carriage   23″ H × 29″ W   c. 1930   United States
Dark green wicker with adjustable back and hood; metal wire wheels; metal strap springs; wooden handle. *(See photo 88)*
Very Good Quality/Good Condition $350 (D)   **$250–$400**

Coffeepot   3.36″ H   c. 1910   United States
Miniature, tin.
Good Quality/Fine Condition $275 (A)   **$200–$300**

Covered sandbox   9.5″ H × 9.25″ W   c. 1925   United States
Wooden sandbox with adjustable canvas canopy; box is green with colorful decal of teddy bears and dolls; green awning with yellow and red stripes; all wooden trim is yellow.
Superior Quality/Good Condition $65 (D)   **$50–$75**

Fainting couch   10.5″ H × 19.5″ W   c. 1880   France
Rose silk upholstery with walnut trim.
Superior Quality/Fine Condition $300 (D)   **$225–$350**

Fainting couch   6.5″ H × 19.5″ W   c. 1880   United States
Walnut; fine legs and original cut-velvet upholstery and fringe.
Superior Quality/Fine Condition $250 (D)   **$225–$300**

Food mold   3.75″ Dia.   Turk's head   c. 1885   United States
Redware, with scalloped rim; greenish-brown mottled glaze; edge chips.
Good Quality/Average Condition $99 (A)   **$90–$125**

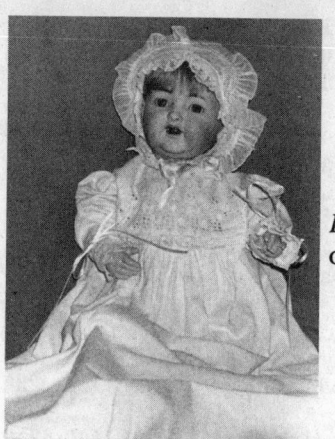

Photo 87. Kämmer and Reinhardt doll.
CREDIT: ALDA LEAKE HORNER *(See p. 174)*

Photo 88 (left). Doll carriage. CREDIT: ALDA LEAKE HORNER. *Photo 89 (right). Doll stroller.* CREDIT: ALDA LEAKE HORNER *(See pp. 176, 178)*

Photo 90. Tea set. CREDIT: ALDA LEAKE HORNER *(See p. 178)*

Laundry set Tub 7″ Dia. c. 1925 United States
Washing day necessities, including folding wash bench, blue metal washtub, tin "Sanitary" scrubboard, wooden barrel with clothespins, and wooden stocking stretcher.
Superior Quality/Fine Condition $95 (D)   **$85–$125**

Piano 20″ H × 17″ W × 10.5″ D Schoenhut c. 1920 United States
Fifteen white keys, 10 black keys, all working; with bench.
Superior Quality/Fine Condition $100 (D)   **$95–$150**

Sewing machine 6.5″ H Singer c. 1910 United States
Completely original and in working order; with "Singer" and Singer oval logo.
Superior Quality/Fine Condition $135 (D)   **$125–$175**

Stroller 28″ H × 36″ W Joel Ellis type c. 1880 United States
Wooden body, handle, wheels; metal strap hinges; adjustable canopy with leather top trimmed with ball fringe; blue cotton tufted upholstery; sides and back with original gold stenciling. *(See photo 89)*
Superior Quality/Fine Condition $750 (D)   **$600–$900**

Tea kettle 2″ H c. 1910 United States
Miniature, copper, 2″ swivel handle; beautifully handmade; dents and dark patina.
Good Quality/Average Condition $275 (A)   **$250–$300**

Tea kettle 3.6″ H c. 1910 United States
Miniature, cast iron, goose-neck spout, wire bail and tin lid; worn black paint.
Very Good Quality/Fine Condition $170 (A)   **$150–$200**

Tea set Teapot 5″ H c. 1892 England
Three pieces; Staffordshire; Punch & Judy, Allerton & Sons, England; decorated with red figures of Punch and Judy. *(See photo 90)*
Superior Quality/Fine Condition $165 (D)   **$150–$195**

Tea set Teapot 3.25″ H c. 1934 England
Little Princess tea set with picture of Elizabeth and Princess Margaret Rose in decal; blue luster trim; set is complete with 6 cups and saucers.
Superior Quality/Fine Condition $135 (D)   **$125–$150**

Tea set Teapot 7″ H c. 1892 Germany
Twenty-one-piece set, including teapot with lid, sugar with lid, creamer, 6 cake plates, 6 cups and saucers; polychrome decals of cats and dogs playing musical instruments.
Very Good Quality/Fine Condition $250 (D)   **$225–$300**

Toy monkey 7.5″ H Tin c. 1915 Anglo-American
Made to climb a string; worn polychrome paint and flocking.
Good Quality/Average Condition $60 (A)   **$60–$95**

Wagon 12.25″ L c. 1925 United States
Wood, wire, and sheet steel with worn original red paint; bed has faded stenciling "express"; twisted wire tongue.
Good Quality/Average Condition $600 (A)   **$600–$800**

BIBLIOGRAPHY

BOOKS

Coleman, Dorothy, Elizabeth, and Evelyn. *The Collector's Encyclopedia of Dolls*. New York: Crown Publishers, Inc., 1968.

Collier, Julie. *The Official Identification and Price Guide to Antique and Modern Dolls* (4th ed.). New York: House of Collectibles, 1989.

Foulke, Jan. *10th Blue Book of Dolls and Values*. Cumberland, MD: Hobby House Press.

Herron, R. Lane. *Price Guide to Dolls and Paper Dolls*. Des Moines, IA: Wallace-Homestead.

Mandeville, A. Glenn. *Ginny . . . An American Toddler Doll*. Cumberland, MD: Hobby House Press.

Smith, Patricia R. *Modern Collector's Dolls, Third Series*. New York: Distributed by Crown Publishers, Inc., 1976.

———. *Shirley Temple Dolls and Collectibles*. Paducah, KY: Collector Books, 1977.

———. *Madame Alexander Collector's Dolls* (Vol. 4). Paducah, KY: Collector Books, 1981.

Theriault, Florence, Editor, *Theriault's Doll Registry* (Vol. 3). Theriault's, Moreland Parkway, Annapolis, MD, 1981.

MAGAZINES

Dolls: The Collectors Magazine.
Doll News: Official Publication of the United Federation of Doll Clubs.

MUSEUMS

Fairfield Historical Society, 636 Old Post Road, Fairfield, CT 06430

The Mary Merrit Doll Museum, Route 422, Douglasville, PA 20015

The Museum of the City of New York, 1220 Fifth Avenue, New York, NY 10029

The Margaret Woodbury Strong Museum, 1 Manhattan Square, Rochester, NY 14607

House of a Thousand Dolls, PO Box 136, Loma, MT 59301

Hobby City Doll and Toy Museum, 1238 South Beach Boulevard, Anaheim, CA 92804

COLLECTORS' CLUBS

United Federation of Doll Clubs, Inc., PO Box 14146, Parkville, MO 64152 (contact to locate club in your area).

Ephemera—Paper

(See also Advertising, Movie Posters, Political Memorabilia, Postcards, Toys and Toy Trains, World's Fair Memorabilia.)

Advisor: **HARRY L. RINKER**

Harry L. Rinker is a nationally recognized author and lecturer. He is editor of Warman's Antiques and Their Prices *and* Warman's Americana and Collectibles. *His columns are published nationally. He is co-founder, with David Lindquist, of The Antiques and Collectibles Information Service, which sponsors major educational seminars each year. Write to A.C.I.S., 5093 Vera Cruz Rd., Emmaus, PA 18049; (215) 965-1122.*

Maurice Rickards, author of *Collecting Printed Ephemera*, defines ephemera as the "minor transient documents of everyday life," material destined for the wastebasket but never quite making it. The category is very broad, ranging from advertising material to valentines.

The vast majority of paper ephemera was mass-produced and printed. Items could be personalized by filling in blanks or attaching personal notes. A great deal of paper ephemera has no date or manufacturer identification. Since collectors collect primarily by category (e.g., calendars or tickets), the object and the decoration on the object are the critical elements.

Since paper ephemera was meant to be discarded, the quality of the paper varies considerably. Many magazines and newspapers are printed on wood pulp paper, now badly flaking and turning brown. Eighteenth-century publications often were printed on rag paper, so items from the 1700s may be in far better condition than those of the 1900s.

Some paper ephemera contain the highest-quality lithography done by American printers. Other examples are amateurish and homemade. In most cases an illustration, especially in color, makes a piece more valuable.

Paper ephemera has been collected since the 16th century. Early English collectors, who pioneered the collecting of paper ephemera, include John Seldon (1584–1654), Samuel Pepys (1633–1703), and John Bagford (1650–1716). The British have always led the way in collecting paper ephemera and continue to do so in the 1990s.

The major development in the paper ephemera field is the increasing number of specialized advertising and paper shows that are occurring across the country. There are specialized paper dealers whose activities are limited just to this show circuit. Since paper material can be shipped easily through the mail, many dealers are using mail auctions as a way of selling their merchandise. One area where this is especially strong is the postcard market.

Paper ephemera is often found framed. Potential collectors should carefully inspect any framed piece to make certain that the ephemera item is not glued or stuck in any fashion to the backing board or mat, that all frame material is acid-free, and that the piece is full size. The only safe way to do this is to ask that the piece be removed from the frame. Further, in any framed piece of printed ephemera, the key question to ask is how much value is in the frame itself. There is a strong tendency among dealers to destroy magazines to frame pages containing specialized advertisements. These sheets would normally sell for only a few dollars. In a frame the cost might well exceed $25.

CONDITION AND QUALITY KEYS

Because paper ephemera was mass-produced, a piece that is damaged (i.e., frayed edges, torn, soiled, foxed, or stained) rapidly decreases in value. Collectors know that they can afford to wait until a quality example can be found. Serious collectors rarely purchase an item below good condition.

A piece of paper ephemera in *fine condition* has the appearance of just coming off the press. *Good condition* allows for some very minor handling but absolutely no defects that affect the main display portion of the object. An *average condition* piece has some fraying around the edge, possibly a minor tear or two, crease marks from being folded, and some smudging and soil. A *poor condition* piece has signs of very heavy use, damage to the central display area, and possibly some portions missing.

The best pieces of paper ephemera *(superior quality)* have pizzazz. The surface gleams; it is almost glossy. The design component of the layout as well as the quality of the illustration is exceptionally strong. A *very good quality* piece is aesthetically pleasing but lacks the specialness of the best piece. A *good* piece has a rather ordinary and functional appearance. It certainly is not eye-catching. The layout may be plain or the design component forced.

In the listings below, country of origin has little bearing on price. Assume items were produced in the United States, unless otherwise indicated.

This is one of the great crossover categories in which many paper items might be thought of as ephemera or be collected as Art Deco items, pop culture memorabilia, world's fair memorabilia, etc. While specific examples are listed, you should view these items as generic. They represent similar programs, sheet music, postcards, etc.—*DL*

Advertisement   1884
"Duffy's Malt Whiskey"; the *Times*, Philadelphia; full-page ad; full-size engraving of embossed bottle, the factory, and the label listing cures and benefits.
Good Quality/Very Good Condition $50 (A)   **$40–$60**

Advertisement   6" × 7"   1907
Pepsi-Cola; newspaper ad; "The Dinner Drink PEPSI-Cola, The Original Pure Food Drink," picture of a bottle of Pepsi and full glass.
Good Quality/Fine Condition $35 (A)   **$25–$40**

Album page   6" × 4"   1907
Harry Houdini; signed in ink on pink page; "Love Laughs at Locksmiths/so does/Harry Handcuff Houdini/Jan 22 1907."
Very Good Quality/Excellent Condition $1200 (D)   **$1000–$1300**

Animation art   10" × 12"   1940
Fantasia; pencil on paper; Sorcerer with raised arms.
Very Good Quality/Excellent Condition $770 (A)   **$600–$800**

Autograph   3" × 3"   1945
Irving Berlin; Full thin black-ink signature on 3" × 3" Ten Sen military currency, with note stating "autographed by Irving Berlin 1945 Hickam Field, Hawaii"; unique item.
Good Quality/Excellent Condition $145 (D)   **$100–$150**

Book   11" × 11"
The Art of Hanna-Barberra, hardcover edition; dust jacket; published by Random House; ink signature on first endpaper.
Good Quality/Excellent Condition $350 (D)   **$250–$400**

Book
Music for Chameleons, Truman Capote; first edition; dust jacket; published by Random House; ink signature on first endpaper.
Good Quality/Excellent Condition $350 (D)   **$250–$400**

Box   10" × 13" × 2.5" D   1940
"Walt Disney's Pinocchio Candy Bar"; color; held 24 bars produced by Schutter Candy Co.; copyright 1940 WDP.
Very Good Quality/Excellent Condition $300 (A)   **$150–$350**

Calendar   10" × 14"   1959
Roy Rogers Ranch Calendar; Nestle Co. premium; copyright 1958; wall hanging; stiff paper; 6 months printed on each side; 7" × 8" color photo for each month; black/white illustrations; paper hinge seams at top; rare.
Very Good Quality/Fine Condition $175 (A)   **$100–$200**

Card   2.25" × 3.25"   1953–1955
Post cereal; #33, "Branding Time"; pop-out; color illustration; perforated; from set of 36 issued as box inserts.
Good Quality/Excellent Condition $45 (A)   **$25–$50**

Coloring book   8.5″ × 11″   1952
Roy Rogers and Dale Evans; color family photo on both covers; Whitman;
128 pgs.
Good Quality/Very Fine Condition $40 (A)   **$25–$50**

Coloring book   8.5″ × 11″   1964
"The Beatles" coloring book by Sallfield Publishing Co., copyright 1964 Nems
Enterprises, Ltd.; book has 124 pages—about 15 have been colored; aside from
the pages to color, there are 10 black/white photo pages; coloring book has a
very faint water stain that runs from front to back cover along the extreme bottom
right corner; cover has one light penciling at top and some other general wear;
overall clean.
Good Quality/Very Good Condition $50 (D)   **$25–$75**

Comic book
Gene Autry Comics; Vol. 1, no. 25, Mar. 1949; Dell; color photo on yellow
background on front cover; color photo of Autry, Champion, and female star on
back cover; black/white photos on inside covers.
Good Quality/Fine Condition $25 (A)   **$15–$50**

Fan   9.5″ H × 17″ W
"Bethany 1910"; early aviation scene of 10 aircraft hovering over airfield;
paper mounted on swiveled wood strips; closed size 1″ × 1.5″ × 9.5″; art
by George Blott; inscribed "Souvenir Cafe Martin/New York"; originally
perfumed.
Very Good Quality/Fine Condition $65 (A)   **$50–$75**

First-day cover
Jimmy Stewart and Frank Capra; Christmas; each signed name and added sketch;
Stewart drew Harvey, Capra drew small Christmas tree; black ink.
Good Quality/Fine Condition $175 (D)   **$125–$200**

First-day cover
Dr. Seuss; Christmas; silk toy bear cachet; added color original sketch of "Green
Eggs & Ham" and a signature on white blank area.
Very Good Quality/Fine Condition $125 (D)   **$75–$150**

Greeting card   7″ × 9″   1936
Christmas; single sheet, stiff card; Mickey Mouse, Minnie Mouse, and Donald
Duck stuffing a large envelope inscribed "Season's Greetings, Walt Disney" into
mailbox; envelope.
Good Quality/Fine Condition $265 (A)   **$200–$300**

Letter   6″ × 9″   Mar. 14, 1897
John Philip Sousa; hotel stationery; written in column style down center of page;
signed; "March 14, 1897 . . . When I return to New York . . . I will rehearse
the march . . . if effective will add it to my repertoire . . . Very Sincerely, John
Philip Sousa."
Very Good Quality/Very Fine Condition $425 (D)   **$375–$450**

Magazine   Mar. 2, 1942
Ginger Rogers; text and photos of Rogers's life, hometown, and ranch.
Good Quality/Very Good Condition $10 (D)   **$8–$15**

Magazine   Feb. 1955
Playboy; playmate is Jayne Mansfield.
Good Quality/Fine Condition $80 (D)   **$65–$100**

Music 1954
Harold Rome; 12 bars of music and words titled "Restless Heart," from *Fanny*, 1954; all black ink; fine large signature on lower blank area.
Good Quality/Mint Condition $95 (A)   **$50–$95**

Napkins 5″ × 5″   Late 1970s
Batman; package of 16; original cellophane bag; depicts Batman and Robin running; by Amacan; copyright 1966 DC Comics; sealed.
Good Quality/Mint Condition $20 (A)   **$10–$20**

Newspaper May 30, 1848
The *Democrat*, Bangor, ME; p. 1; early story about Siamese twins; article tells of their life in North Carolina.
Good Quality/Very Good Condition $50 (A)   **$40–$60**

Newspaper Aug. 23–35, 1787   England
The London Chronicle; news from Ireland, London, French Parliament, stock quotes; halfpenny tax stamp.
Good Quality/Fine Condition $25 (A)   **$15–$30**

Paper dolls 11″   1964
Patty and Cathy Duke; 31 outfits and miscellaneous accessories; 10″ × 13″ folder; Whitman; copyright 1964 United Artists Television Inc.
Very Good Quality/Fine Condition $60 (A)   **$50–$75**

Parasol 1939
Rice paper; balsa-like wood struts and ribs; 36″ open diameter; inscribed "1939 New York World's Fair" in black letters on large orange rings; exhibit buildings, Trylon, and Perisphere surround ring; bamboo support rod; blue wood hand grip; 26″ closed length.
Superior Quality/Fine Condition $150 (A)   **$100–$200**

Photograph 8″ × 10″
Ida Lupino; sepia; studio publicity pose; signed.
Good Quality/Fine Condition $45 (D)   **$40–$50**

Playbill
Richard Burton; *Hamlet* at Lunt-Fontanne Theatre; ink signature on chest; scarce.
Good Quality/Very Good Condition $95 (D)   **$75–$125**

Postcard 3.5″ × 5.5″   England
"Here's Good Hunting!" caption; Mickey and Minnie Mouse riding Horace, with Pluto racing alongside; black, white, red, and yellow.
Good Quality/Very Fine Condition $65 (A)   **$50–$75**

Poster 30″ × 40″   1964
Movie; lobby size; color; *Man's Favorite Sport*; Rock Hudson and Paula Prentice.
Good Quality/Very Good Condition $50 (A)   **$45–$60**

Poster 18″ × 24.5″   1968
"Nelson A. Rockefeller" 1968 campaign poster; nice colorful cartoon showing Rocky holding a cutout of the state of New York next to the Republican elephant and with money bags around his feet; light green background.
Good Quality/Excellent Condition $10 (D)   **$25–$50**

Program 5.5″ × 8.5″ Mar. 28–29, 1969
Fillmore East concert program; these dates featured Steppenwolfe, Julie Driscoll, Brian Auger, and the Trinity and John Hammond; each artist has a small photo and biography; also included is a ticket stub from the show; rest of magazine features music-related ads; cover has a bit of aging but is still bright.
Good Quality/Excellent Condition $25 (A) **$15–$25**

Puzzle 11.75″ × 19.75″ 1939
New York World's Fair; jigsaw; Parker Bros.; color aerial perspective illustration of exposition grounds; 8″ × 13″ × 1.5″ box; same illustration on lid; red, gray, and black "Puzzle Map" paper sticker on lid.
Good Quality/Excellent Condition $175 (A) **$100–$200**

Sheet music 10.5″ × 13.5″
"Get on the Raft with Taft"; 6 pages; cover is mostly black/white with some light pink tinting; inside margins have some small tape repairs; back cover has two strips where some surface paper was pulled off by tape; front is bright and clean.
Good Quality/Good Condition $12 (A) **$10–$25**

Sheet music 9″ × 12″ 1928
"The Sidewalks of New York"; 6 pages; brown/white cover with nice portrait of Al Smith; very small spine split but very clean.
Very Good Quality/Very Fine Condition $20 (A) **$10–$25**

Ticket 2″ × 4.5″ 1946
Los Angeles Coliseum Football; red numbers on blue and white background; UCLA Bruin conducting an orchestra of Disney characters; Southern Methodist opponent; souvenir stub; Sept. 27.
Good Quality/Excellent Condition $40 (A) **$25–$45**

Ticket (lot of 2) 2.5″ × 5″ 1937
Issued for Monday, May 31, 1937, Indianapolis Motor Speedway race; each ticket has facsimile signature of Eddie Rickenbacker, Speedway president; back of each has a stadium seating plan; one of the backs has an inked "Second Anniversary May 31, 1937"; each ticket is black, white, and blue/gray, and each has entry stub removed plus punched mark in center by ticket taker.
Good Quality/Very Fine Condition $20 (A) **$15–$25**

Toy 10″ × 14″ June 30, 1895
Presented by the New York *Herald*, 5th section; "The Battle of Flowers as Children's Toys"; girls in flowery carriage, flower girl; each picture has a front and back to be cut out and pasted on cardboard to complete toy.
Good Quality/Very Good Condition $10 (A) **$8–$12**

Trading card 3″ × 3.5″ 1951–1956
Howdy Doody "Royal" trading card; red, white, and blue card clipped from back of Royal Pudding box picturing Flub-A-Dub; no. 3 from set of 12; Kagran copyright, 1951–1956.
Good Quality/Excellent Condition $14 (A) **$10–$15**

Viewer 4″ × 7″ 1960
"13 Ghosts"; 3-D cardboard; red and blue transparent pieces; black/white illustrations of ghosts and skeletons; movie theater premium.
Good Quality/Mint Condition $25 (A) **$15–$25**

BIBLIOGRAPHY

House of Collectibles (eds.). *The Official Price Guide to Paper Collectibles* (5th ed.). New York: House of Collectibles, 1986. Covers advertising collectibles to world's fair materials, with sections on paper money and postage stamps not normally found in other paper price guides.

Rickards, Maurice. *Collecting Printed Ephemera*. New York: Abbeville Press, 1988. An excellent overview of the printed ephemera market with detailed sections on understanding the concept and its historical development; proper methods for displaying and storing paper materials, including the all-critical sources for supplies; using printing techniques to date pieces; and two major sections that explore the category and theme methods of collecting paper ephemera.

Rinker, Harry L. *Warman's Americana and Collectibles* (4th ed.). Radnor, PA: Wallace-Homestead Book Company, 1990. Provides detailed information about all of the major paper ephemera collectible categories ranging from advertising items to valentines.

Note: Almost every collectible category of paper ephemera has one or more specialized book and/or price guide.

MUSEUMS

American Antiquarian Society, Worcester, MA; New York Historical Society, New York, NY; Library of Congress, Washington, DC; Smithsonian Institution, Washington, DC.

COLLECTORS' CLUBS

Ephemera Society, 12 Fitzroy Square, London W1P 5HQ; Ephemera Society of America, PO Box 224, Ravena, NY 12143.

Folk Art—American

(See also Baskets, Glass—American Blown, Lighting Devices, Metalware, Silhouettes, Textiles, Walking Sticks and Canes)

American folk art includes categories that we have traditionally thought of as art—such as painting and sculpture—made by untrained people, but it also refers to objects made by untrained people for everyday use, the best of which are now being considered art. This year's selection will cover these everyday objects that combine utility with artistic design. Folk art continues to be made in the 20th century, but we will focus on 19th-century American folk art.

Folk art appeals to our democratic heritage. Rather than reflecting the culture of an elite few, it embodies the values of the ordinary Americans who made it. The naiveté, spontaneity, and untutored individuality are refreshing to many. Folk art also appeals to collectors because of its abstract qualities, which we find in the art of our own century and which works well in modern interiors.

American folk art was first collected in the 1920s, and by the end of the decade it was accepted by the New York art world as legitimate, if nonacademic, art. The first museum to feature American folk art was the Whitney Museum of American Art, based on Gertrude Whitney's collection. In recent years folk art has escalated in price. In 1987 and 1988 the National Gallery of Art in Washington held its first folk art exhibition, called *An American Sampler: Folk Art from the Shelburne Museum*. Prices for the finest pieces have risen astronomically during the past several years, but since folk art is such a broad area, there are still many categories that remain moderately priced—generally, the later pieces and ones that were more widely produced. Prices are basically the same throughout the country, without the regional variations found in other kinds of antiques.

Many of the objects collected today originally served important functions. Weather vanes were crucial for farmers whose crops depended on the weather, and they sometimes served to identify the owner's trade, such as cows for dairy farmers, nautical themes for shipbuilders and fishermen. Or a vane could simply use a commanding or majestic animal figure. Wooden vanes were made by hand in the early 1800s, and these are fairly rare. Later vanes were often constructed out of metal—either by hand or in a factory—and even when factory-made, they are highly valued if they show good design and are in sound condition. A good patina adds greatly to the value.

Weather vanes had an important purpose, but whirligigs were made just for fun, and their whimsical design reflects this. Whirligigs can have either three-dimensional or silhouette-style carving, or a combination of the two. The better examples often display a complex design and detailed carving. The older the better, but condition and original paint are also important for value. The degree of original paint remaining is as positive a factor as restoration is a negative one.

Boxes and shelves were used to store and carry things, and some—like document boxes—could be very important because they safeguarded the family Bible and other valuable papers. Painted boxes from the early 1800s are very popular with collectors. As with other painted objects, original paint that has not been disturbed by restoration greatly increases the value of a piece. True Shaker boxes, highly valued for their design and workmanship, must be documented or marked to be distinguished from the many period look-alikes and modern reproductions.

Kitchenware is very popular today with collectors who are cooking and entertaining at home. American kitchen utensils from the 19th century give any kitchen more individuality and warmth. Because of their mundane purpose, a great quantity of kitchen implements were made and still survive, so the collector should be discriminating. Buy only kitchenware made from the best-quality material and with the most appealing design.

All sorts of sculptures were made in the 19th century to serve a variety of purposes. Life-size cigar store figures of Indians or exotic Turkish characters made eye-catching advertisements. These figures, along with carousel and carnival figures, have universal appeal. This category can bring very high prices, especially when original paint, good carving, and an exciting design are present. More moderately priced are the sculptures of animals made for toys, although well-known carvers will bring top dollar prices.

CURRENT TRENDS

According to Tom Porter of Garth's Auctions in Delaware, OH, late-19th-century and early 20th-century folk art is still strong, particularly for pieces with great design. Weather vanes have shown a slight resurgence in the more common vanes, which sell strongly at $1000 or less. Treenware is strong if well decorated or if natural treen. Fire accessories are fairly rare, but recently they have been on the market. They have always sold well. Prices are soft in some areas. For instance, whirligigs are not selling well unless they are really fun. Likewise, carousel animals also have been somewhat overpromoted, and prices have not met expectations.

Roger Ricco of Ricco-Maresca Gallery in New York City notes an important trend in 20th-century folk art. The January 1991 sale at Sotheby's featuring 20th-century American folk art was very successful. Hirschl and Adler Folk had several shows that highlighted 20th-century material. Works by known artists like Howard Finster and William Hawkins are selling very well right now.

FAKES ALERT

Fakes are a problem in this field because prices are so enticing. Many of these objects are made from wood, and a faker can simply put a new piece out in the elements for a few years to produce an old, weathered look. So be on the lookout for appropriate wear—surfaces with more exposure or more use should show more wear. In wooden pieces, when age is difficult to determine, the careful collector will look for period colors and style of carving. If the wood seems old, but the piece has no unity of design, it may be a new piece made from old wood, and if so, it should be valued as a new piece. Old paint should be somewhat crazed, its surface covered with a network of tiny cracks. Since this effect also can be chemically produced, pay attention to style and design of the piece as a whole.

Metal weather vanes can also be faked, but again, the collector should expect to find appropriate wear, not uniform aging, which can be achieved with chemical treatments. Knowing the history of a piece, such as the family it belonged to, always helps ensure its authenticity.

The best insurance against being fooled by a fake is lots of hands-on experience with authentic pieces. Get to know reputable dealers and pump them for information. Go to museums and exhibits and see the best pieces for yourself. When you have a good feel for period pieces, you will be less likely to be fooled by modern fakes that have not captured the period style.

CONDITION

Expect signs of wear in appropriate areas. A piece that was meant to be used, as most of these were, is less valuable if it appears never to have been used. The most desirable pieces were used but well cared for. Many old painted pieces have lost much of their original paint or have been repainted to some degree. If they were repainted long ago and in a way that does not detract from the overall effect, this retouching is not too detrimental to value. Conservation—the normal upkeep for normal wear— is acceptable, but restoration—repair of a piece that has been broken or has been subject to excessive wear—is less acceptable.

Barber poles 35″ L   1885–1900   United States
Pair of turned and painted barber poles; painted red, white, and blue with traces of gilt at finials; Lowell, MA; wear; paint loss.
Good Quality/Average Condition $300 (A)   **$400–$600**

Bowl 7″ H × 19.5″ Dia.   1910–1930   United States
Unusual large red-painted wide pine bowl with molded lid.
Good Quality/Fine Condition $990 (A)   **$600–$900**

Box 33″ H × 21″ W   1830–1845   United States
Large oblong with fitted lid; covered in varnished wallpaper printed with a view of Harvard College; top labeled: "Joseph S. Tillinghast, Band Box Manufacturer . . . New Bedford"; some flaking.
Superior Quality/Good Condition $3025 (A)   **$2000–$3500**

Box 11.5″ H × 26″ W × 13″ D   1830–1845   United States
Vinegar-painted pine dome top with wrought-iron escutcheon and side handles; painted ochre with umber graining; minor wear.
Very Good Quality/Good Condition $750 (A)   **$600–$900**

Boxes Shaker style   1885–1900   United States
Six graduated oval boxes with natural varnish, ranging from 2.75″ H to 13.5″ H; imperfections.
Very Good Quality/Good Condition $2000 (A)   **$1500–$2400**

Figure 25″ H   1885–1900   United States
Carved-walnut, stylized, full-length figure of Abraham Lincoln wearing frock coat and stock tie; carrying rolled document in one hand; probably PA; Provenance: M. Finkel & Daughter, Philadelphia, PA.
Good Quality/Good Condition $1760 (A)   **$1500–$2500**

Fire hat 6.5″ H   1845–1865   United States
Fine black painted and gilded composition ceremonial parade fire hat; top with "J. G. C."; on front in ornamental gilt letters: "Philadelphia Hose Company"; fragments of paper label inside.
Superior Quality/Fine Condition $5775 (A)   **$3000–$6000**

Fireboard 22.75″ L × 36.25″ W   1885–1900   United States
Painted fireboard decorated in geometric pattern in blue, yellow, green, sienna, black, and white paint; some wear and paint loss.
Very Good Quality/Good Condition $2000 (A)   **$1500–$2500**

Firebucket 12.5″ H   Leather   1800–1830   United States
Painted dark green with polychrome full-length figure of George Washington holding a globe topped with an eagle; inscribed "Liberty," "Deo Et Patria," "S. Bourne," "1800"; New England; paint loss.
Superior Quality/Fine Condition $10,000 (A)   **$6000–$10,000**

It's got it all—George, history, and condition. Thus, a "barnburner" price! —DL

Firebucket 12.9″ H Leather 1830–1845 United States
Painted green and red; inscribed "F. Hooper" in black; paint loss; imperfections; New England.
Good Quality/Average Condition $250 (A)　　　　　　　**$250–$450**

Firebucket 12.75″ H Leather 1845–1865 United States
Painted green and red; inscribed "Waltham Fire Club 1824 N. Maynard" in gold; paint loss, wear, sagging shape; MA.
Good Quality/Average Condition $350 (A)　　　　　　　**$350–$700**

Firebucket 12.75″ H Leather 1885–1900 United States
Painted red and decorated with black medallion with eagle on American shield; inscription "Hose 2" in yellow, gold, red, and white; imperfections; shape sagging; New England.
Very Good Quality/Average Condition $400 (A)　　　　　**$400–$750**

Hat box 12″ H × 18.75″ W 1830–1845 United States
Wallpaper-covered; sides covered in "Walking Beam Side Wheeler" pattern; top with 2 cuddling dogs; by Joseph S. Tillinghast, New Bedford, MA; labeled; imperfections and old repairs.
Superior Quality/Good Condition $950 (A)　　　　　　**$750–$1200**

Hearth brush 27″ L 1830–1845 United States
Unusual grain-painted, baluster-turned brush with smoke-decorated paint along with painted leaves and flowers in gray on yellow ground.
Good Quality/Good Condition $440 (A)　　　　　　　**$225–$450**

Ship's figurehead 37″ H × 13.5″ W × 13″ D 1885–1900 United States
Painted and carved maiden figure with ringlet-carved hair held by 2 combs above torso with a carved blue dress and gold cameo on a scrolled base; repainted.
Very Good Quality/Good Condition $3300 (A)　　　　　**$3500–$6000**

Weather vane 8″ H × 29″ L 1845–1865 United States
Molded copper and cast-zinc, swell-bodied horse pulling a driver; fashioned in round from cast zinc; in small cart.
Superior Quality/Good Condition $3850 (A)　　　　　　**$3000–$5000**

Weather vane 39.5″ L 1865–1885 United States
Copper and zinc galloping horse with cast head, molded body, outstretched tail; similar to vane in *Ill. Cat. & Price List of Copper Weathervanes, Manufactured by J.W. Fiske.*
Superior Quality/Good Condition $13,200 (A)　　　　**$9000–$18,000**

Weather vane 34″ L 1885–1900 United States
Molded copper and zinc galloping horse; jockey with cast head; traces of original gilding; attributed to J. W. Fiske, NY; similar to one in *Ill. Cat . . . of Copper Weathervanes . . . by J. Fiske.*
Good Quality/Fine Condition $7700 (A)　　　　　　　**$5000–$8000**

Weather vane 16″ H × 28″ L 1885–1900 United States
Molded copper and zinc running horse; attributed to A. L. Jewell & Co., Waltham, MA; weathered surface.
Good Quality/Fine Condition $1800 (A)　　　　　　　**$1500–$2500**

Weather vane 20″ H × 43″ L 1885–1900 United States
Molded copper and zinc running horse with fine verdigris surface; "Colonel Patchen"; very natural and fluid movement; repair near rear foot. *(See photo 91)*
Superior Quality/Good Condition $4000 (A)　　　　　　**$3000–$5000**

Photo 91 (left). Weather vane.
CREDIT: SKINNER, INC., BOLTON,
MA. *Photo 92. Weather vane.*
CREDIT: SKINNER, INC., BOLTON,
MA *(See p. 191 and below)*

Weather vane   29″ L   1885–1900   United States
Molded copper cow with cast tail and horns; applied ears; fine verdigris surface.
Very Good Quality/Fine Condition $3000 (A)   **$2400–$3500**

Weather vane   38″ L   1885–1900   United States
Molded copper rooster with old gold paint; red paint at comb; attributed to L.
W. Cushing & Son, Waltham, MA; bullethole. *(See photo 92)*
Very Good Quality/Good Condition $1500 (A)   **$1200–$2500**

Weather vane   33″ L   1885–1900   United States
Fine molded copper cow with weathered gilt surface; attributed to Cushing &
White, Waltham, MA; bulletholes.
Very Good Quality/Good Condition $4600 (A)   **$3500–$6000**

Weather vane   28.5″ L   1865–1885   United States
Standing molded copper cow with horns above applied ears; pendant tail; traces
of original gilt; now mounted on black iron base; attributed to L. W. Cushing
& Sons, Waltham, MA.
Very Good Quality/Good Condition $3850 (A)   **$3000–$5000**

BIBLIOGRAPHY

Ames, Kenneth L. *Beyond Necessity: Art in the Folk Tradition*. New
    York: W. W. Norton, 1978.

Andrews, Ruth, Editor. *How to Know American Folk Art*. New York: E. P. Dutton, 1977.

Bishop, Robert, and Coblentz, Patricia. *A Gallery of American Weathervanes and Whirligigs*. New York: E. P. Dutton, 1981.

Christensen, Erwin O. *The Index of American Design*. New York: Macmillan, 1950.

Coffin, Margaret. *American Country Tin Ware, 1700–1900*. New York: Galahad Books, 1968.

Curry, David Park. *An American Sampler: Folk Art from the Shelburne Museum*. Washington, DC: National Gallery of Art, 1987.

Emmerling, Mary. *American Country South*. New York: Crown, 1989.

Fitzgerald, Ken. *Weathervanes and Whirligigs*. New York: Clarkson N. Potter, 1967.

Fried, Frederick. *Artists in Wood: American Carvers of Cigar-Store Indians, Show Figures, and Circus Wagons*. New York: Clarkson N. Potter, 1970.

Gould, Mary Earle. *Early American Wooden Ware and Other Kitchen Utensils*. Rutland, VT: C. E. Tuttle, 1962.

Jones, Michael Owen. *The Hand Made Object and Its Maker*. Berkeley: University of California Press, 1975.

Lipman, Jean, and Winchester, Alice. *The Flowering of American Folk Art, 1776–1876*. New York: Viking Press, 1974.

Little, Nina Fletcher. *Neat and Tidy: Boxes and Their Contents Used in Early American Households*. New York: E. P. Dutton, 1980.

MUSEUMS

Abby Aldrich Rockefeller Folk Art Center, Williamsburg, VA.

Hancock Shaker Village, Hancock, MA.

Henry Ford Museum and Greenfield Village, Dearborn, MI.

Historic Deerfield, Deerfield, MA.

Mercer Museum of the Bucks County Historical Association, Doylestown, PA.

Museum of American Folk Art, New York City.

Museum of Early Southern Decorative Arts, Winston-Salem, NC.

Mystic Seaport Museum, Inc., Mystic, CT.

National Gallery of Art, Washington, DC.

New York State Historical Association, Cooperstown, NY.

Old Sturbridge Village, Sturbridge, MA.

Pennsylvania Academy of Fine Arts, Philadelphia, PA.

Shelburne Museum, Shelburne, VT.

Smithsonian Institution, Washington, DC.

Furniture

(See also Arts and Crafts Movement, Boxes, Oriental Fine and Decorative Arts)

Throughout the world, furniture continues to be central to the antiques business. As interest intensifies and specialization by dealers increases, we felt it imperative to divide this category into four subsections: AMERICAN FURNITURE, AMERICAN FURNITURE—WICKER, CONTINENTAL FURNITURE, ENGLISH FURNITURE.

Be sure to read the articles on furniture before the listings begin.

AN INTRODUCTION TO FURNITURE ANALYSIS

© *David P. Lindquist*

With antique furniture, *awareness* is the supreme goal—fakery, restoration, repairs, and such abound in the marketplace. To be aware, one must *beware*. The key to awareness is looking for inconsistencies in the pieces of furniture: inconsistencies of style and inconsistencies in construction.

Fakery has been and is rampant in England and the United States, not to mention the Continent. *Marriages* of two pieces to create a more valuable piece are common: secretaries, chests-on-chests, linen presses, and corner cabinets are commonly created from two pieces. *Divorces* are equally abundant. Chests-on-chests were not popular for many years, so they were turned into two pieces, each singly more valuable than the whole! Highboys were frequently split apart by inheritance or damage to the legs, the top becoming a tall chest, the base becoming a lowboy. (*Photo 93* shows a highboy base converted to a lowboy. In this instance the job was poorly executed by insetting the top rather than having it overlap.) Nearly all antiques have *restoration*, but anything over 10 percent has a negative impact on value.

The *faker* has been busy in England since the early 1800s and in the United States since the late 1800s (especially in the early 1900s). Fakes are usually created out of authentic old pieces that were either out of style or badly damaged. *Reproductions* created in the 19th and early 20th centuries also cause a problem. After fifty to one hundred years they begin to look very authentic. It is vital to remember that all price ranges

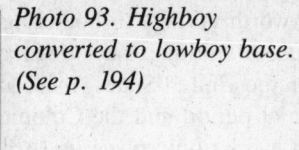

Photo 93. Highboy converted to lowboy base. (See p. 194)

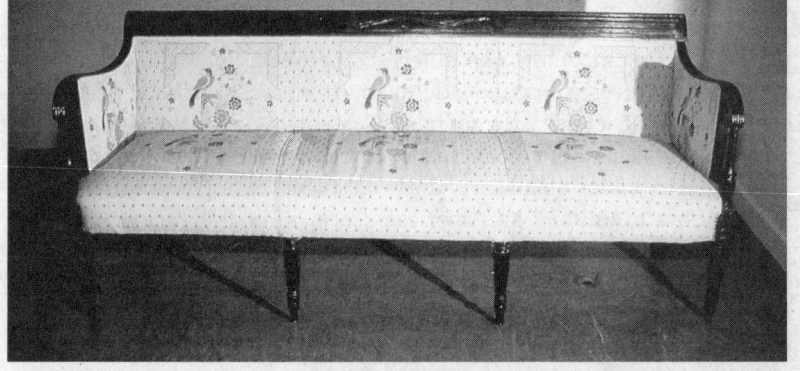

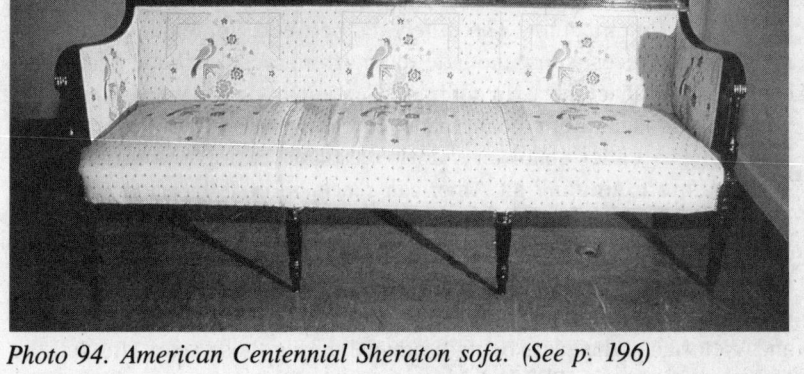

Photo 94. American Centennial Sheraton sofa. (See p. 196)

Photo 95. Nineteenth-century chairs. (See p. 196)

are worth faking. In both England and the United States, *all* types and values of antiques have been and are being faked.

In the United States, there are two major periods of interest—the Centennial period and the Colonial Revival period. No fakery or reproduction work took place in America until after 1885 (not 1876!). The Philadelphia Centennial exhibits had one area showing life-styles of earlier periods, using actual antiques. It was part of a revival of interest in the Pilgrim and Colonial periods, which led to the making of reproductions by about 1885. The highest period of reproductions by small shops and factories came about 1900 through 1940. *Photo 94* shows an American "Centennial Period" (1885–1900) Sheraton sofa, beautifully carved and perfectly detailed. Only an examination of tool marks and construction techniques reveals it as a late-19th-century copy worth $2,000 to $3,000 instead of an 1805 piece worth $30,000 to $50,000. Doweled construction and circular saw marks are the revealing characteristics on the interior frame of this piece.

Beginning in the teens and early 1920s, the Colonial Revival movement gained momentum. The difference between Centennial and Colonial Revival pieces is that the latter come from factories large and small, using modern machinery. In contrast, Centennial pieces were often made with early tools and often handmade, revealing modern tool uses only in hidden areas (under upholstery, doweled joints, etc).

If you are examining an American piece in an 18th-century style, it was either made in the general period (before 1820) or made after 1885 or so. There is no such animal as an antique-style piece of furniture made in the mid-19th century in America! We were enamored of only the latest style in this country between 1830 and 1885; only the Empire and Victorian styles were being produced during those years. In fact, the Colonial Exhibit in Philadelphia was a small, backwater exhibit. The major exhibits showed all of the latest designs made with the latest machinery.

In England, the situation was entirely different. No style once adopted ever completely lost popularity in England. They just kept on making those Queen Anne chairs, for example, year in and year out, generation after generation. See *photo 95* of various 19th-century Queen Anne Revival chairs. The key to understanding English furniture is the use of different construction techniques as the Industrial Revolution progressed. The English may have kept on in old styles, but they adopted new tools and machinery as they became available. Also, in England fakery has been a major problem since the early to mid-1800s. As soon as pieces made in the latest styles lost popularity, they were cut up and turned into 18th-century-style furniture—the English never waste anything! Victorian chests became Georgian chests, Victorian and Edwardian wardrobes became, and still become, Georgian breakfronts. Old oak and pine wardrobes became, and are becoming, pewter cupboards, bookcases, and so on. Thus, throughout the 19th century in England, many reproductions of 18th-century pieces were made; the construction and sometimes the form, however, were at variance with 18th-century construction and form. The same is true of the 20th century, with the interesting exception that English factories produced almost no reproductions of 18th-century furniture in mahogany. American factories in Grand Rapids, High Point, and elsewhere were turning out thousands and thousands of "suites" of Hepplewhite-, Chippendale-, and Sheraton-style furniture. Very little was produced in England. (As an aside, that situation has led to a major import-export market between the United States and England. American reproductions of the 20th century are now bought by English dealers, and daily container loads are shipped out of New York, Baltimore, and other ports headed for Southampton!)

GENERALITIES OF FURNITURE CONSTRUCTION

While virtually no statement can be made about furniture construction that does not have a few known exceptions, there are nevertheless some generalities that should always be kept in mind. These points can often quickly "clue you in" to a problem piece.

In examining chairs with stretchers and backsplats, immediately note several things. The side and rear stretchers should be flush against the sides and backs of the legs—never centered—in handmade chairs with straight stretchers (see photo 96), *not* turned stretchers. This is because a handmade joint will use mortise-and-tenon construction, and the accuracy necessary for the joint is most easily achieved by having the edge of the stretcher flush with the leg to which it attaches. If you see a centered stretcher, it almost always indicates doweled joints, and dowels indicate machine-made furniture.

Another easy clue in a chair with a backsplat is that in 95 percent of pre-1830 chairs the shoe for the splat is separate from the rear seat rail. If an 18th-century-*style* chair has a splat placed in the saddle that is one piece with the rear rail, the chair is quite probably an old reproduction or a fake. In *photo 96*, we see an integral shoe—on a rare 18th-century chair from the Anthony Hay Workshop, Williamsburg, VA, known for their *rare* use of the integral shoe.

Types of dovetailing are important. Machine-made dovetails are never found in antique furniture. In general, the larger the dovetail, the earlier the piece. Also, in general, the dovetails of the carcass will be considerably larger than those of the drawers. All dovetails of all carcass edges will be by the same hand, as will dovetails of the drawers.

Photo 96. Chair with stretchers. (See p. 197)

Photo 97. Shrinkage in a linen press. (See p. 199)

Photo 98. Shrinkage of inlay. (See p. 199)

Shrinkage will be present in *all* antiques. No shrinkage—no antique! Panels float in frames to allow for shrinkage, so you can see the finished-unfinished edges now exposed after generations of shrinkage. There will be splits at nails in the backs where the weakened board can easily split as it shrinks. Sides of chests, sideboards, cabinets, and the like will have old splits or show shrinkage away from the back or front of the piece. Drawer bottoms will show major shrinkage or gaps where the board pulled out of the groove at the front of the drawer. *Photo 97* shows shrinkage in an 18th-century linen press. *Photo 98* shows shrinkage of inlay. All round table tops will show measurable shrinkage across the grain—easily measured with a yardstick or tape. Remember, if it hasn't shrunk, it is not old!

Many antiques have pins or pegs, which either were used initially to hold a mortise-and-tenon joint or were added later to tighten a loose or repaired joint. In either case, the pegs are *never* round; they are squarish or multifaceted. Also, if the surface has not been recently sanded (severely sanded), the pegs will protrude slightly as they are pushed out by the wood shrinking around them.

Expect to find normal wear and softened edges. If it doesn't have wear, bangs, nicks, small repairs, and soft edges, it's almost certainly not over seventy-five years old! Let your fingers do the walking—feel all exposed edges, feet, base, back, molding, and so on. Any sharp edges should be carefully examined—the cause will almost always turn out to be recent repairs, replacements, or fakery. Normal wear should include worn drawer runners (with probable restoration of runner edges); scarred drawer bottoms; worn legs (chairs may lose several inches); stretchers showing where feet, mops, and such would normally rub; and many tables having sewing-bird scars on the underneath edges (round indentations about .25 inches in diameter). Always "test" a worn area by sitting in or at the piece and seeing if the wear is in a normal spot. If you have to be a contortionist to put your feet on the worn area, something is very, very wrong!

Hardware (if original) or holes from previous sets of hardware should be consistent with the period of the piece. Original hardware is seldom found (and adds a premium to value when present). However, there *must* be evidence of hardware having once been on the piece that is consistent with the purported age and style of the piece.

Patination and oxidation are basic to evaluating an antique. Undisturbed antique surfaces will be beautifully patinated on the finished surfaces and darkly oxidized on the raw exposed surfaces. Patination refers to the rich, dark, rather crusty finish created by the buildup of waxes, dirt, and constant rubbing of the surface by oily hands and cleaning. It cannot be duplicated mechanically. (That is why so many antiques shops now French-polish everything—it removes patination or hides new work and makes everything glow.) All wood oxidizes when exposed to air. It darkens, and the pores of the wood fill with dust particles and so forth. Again, this natural darkening (of backs, drawer bottoms, etc.) cannot be duplicated mechanically. Furthermore, any disturbance to oxidized surfaces leaves telltale light-colored areas that *never* again match the surrounding areas.

Finally, in general terms, always date a piece by the *latest original element*. For instance, if everything about a piece is stylistically Chippendale, but the *original* brasses are stamped ovals, the piece dates from the Hepplewhite period, not the Chippendale period. It doesn't matter how many elements are earlier in style, the *latest original* element in the history of style is the element by which the piece must be dated.

BEWARE, BEWARE, BEWARE

Ultimately, the key to analyzing a piece will be your ability to spot inconsistencies. You must constantly be aware of all of the tricks of the faker. You must be conscious of the history of antique furniture, revivals of styles, and so on. You must use your eyes and your fingers. And, finally, you must put it all together. Don't believe only your eyes, only your fingers, or only your knowledge of style and form. Put together all of your knowledge, and if the piece hangs together under that level of scrutiny, chances are very good that it is an honest antique.

RULES OF THUMB ARE MADE TO BE BROKEN

© *David P. Lindquist*

Scholarship in the antiques field—especially furniture—has advanced by quantum leaps in the past twenty years. The advances—mostly by American scholars, whose work has sought to delineate what is particularly American—have been eye-opening. There also has been far greater understanding of English and European cabinetmaking traditions through research into American cabinetmaking.

What was overlooked until recently was how the first American cabinetmakers were influenced by the respective European traditions in which they were originally trained. That is, a German-trained cabinetmaker continued to use the same construction techniques after he emigrated to America. The same is true of English, Scottish, or other immigrant workers. Add to this the eventual melding of traditions within various workshops, and you have a social history of American cabinetmaking traditions.

Here I wish to explore many of the "rules of thumb"—and myths—of furniture dating and identification. "Rules of thumb," those broad descriptive strokes, are indeed useful. It is helpful to say that "almost all chairs with integral shoes are 19th century or later." It is not helpful if you fail to recognize the importance of exceptions.

The key to understanding antiques and to uncovering fakes or reproductions is the uncovering of inconsistency. As I have written so often before, inconsistencies can be in either construction, style, or both. Obviously, rules of thumb that are broken are often signs of inconsistency—signs of trouble. So the value of this discussion is twofold: to alert you to what to expect and to alert you to the exceptions.

RULE 1

All furniture with oak secondary wood (the wood inside a piece) is English.

One should always consider this a sign that the piece is likely to be English and very likely the work of a city-trained cabinetmaker. In the British Isles, urban cabinetmakers used oak for drawer linings. It lasted longer, was neater to work with, and made a finer, cleaner drawer interior. However, country cabinetmakers often used oak as a secondary wood, and even as a primary wood, well beyond the Age of Oak.

Thanks in particular to the pioneering work of Wallace Gusler at Williamsburg, we now know that many American pieces have oak secondary wood. He realized and proved through wood analysis and excavation at cabinet shops what should have been obvious sociologically: British urban-trained cabinetmakers brought their wood preferences and construction techniques with them to the New World.

When you find oak secondary, think: "Likely English, possibly American." Then use the presence of other woods, styles, and construction to further your analysis of the piece.

RULES 2, 3, AND 4

Certain woods—black walnut, cherry, and tulip poplar—invariably indicate an American piece.

Again, this is quite a useful set of rules. Two are easily demonstrated as false, however. While you should think American (U.S. or Canadian) first when these woods are present, these are exceptions. "Virginia walnut" was imported into England extensively after the Continental walnut blight. It is found, however, only as a primary wood in Country (non-urban, especially non-London) pieces, and it may appear as a secondary wood in urban pieces. Cherry was used for some Country English furniture and used extensively in Country French furniture. Again, other criteria will help define the piece—wood can only serve as a "first notice."

Tulip poplar, so widely used in North America, is never found in English or European furniture. It is one very useful, totally safe rule of thumb. (Now, sure as I live and breathe, someone will find an exception.)

RULE 5

Chests with no drawer stops are pre-1730.

This means that the back of the chest stopped the drawers. It would also seem to suggest that all pieces with drawer stops are post-1730. Drawer stops are accomplished by lap-molded drawer edges (which often get broken) or more successfully by placing small stops at the back on the drawer runners or near the drawer front nailed to the drawer dividers.

Basically this rule is sound, but the exceptions are important.

Cabinetmakers learned as the years passed what Mother Nature did to their creations. She shrank them, she cracked them, and she eroded them through abrasion. To counter her work, cabinetmakers evolved new techniques.

By 1730 it was obvious that as chest sides shrank from front to back (paneled construction having been abandoned, as oak was abandoned as a primary wood, about 1680–1700), the nonpaneled sides were "pulling" the back forward. As this happened, drawers gapped open—they were literally being expelled from the chests. To counter the problem—which took twenty-five to thirty years to show itself—cabinetmakers began leaving a gap at the back behind the drawers and using "stops" placed on the runners or cross-pieces to stop the drawers.

Not everyone got the word quickly, however, and country-made pieces (English and American) often stop at the back as late as 1780–1800. Furthermore, the obverse of the rule is *not* true. Many pre-1730 pieces have been altered—by shortening the drawer sides and reattaching the drawer backs, then adding stops—to eliminate unsightly gaps.

Gapping drawers are a good sign of age (fakers never leave gapping drawers!), but you must rely on much more data to finalize the dating of a piece.

RULE 6

If it has dust covers or dust dividers between the drawers, it's English.

This rule relates to Rule 1 and is false (although useful as a signal) for the same reasons. British pieces, urban and rural, invariably have dust dividers. Continental pieces never have them. American pieces will or will not, depending on the training and heritage of the maker. Also, it seems certain that to cut costs of construction many English-trained cabinetmakers adopted the European tradition when they immigrated—dust covers are rather rare in American furniture.

Again, this rule is very useful for first impressions, but wood analysis, styles, and other aspects may very well prove the rule wrong.

RULES 7 AND 8

In drawer construction, quarter molding on the inside of the drawer sides is found only after 1830. Control supports to divide large drawer bottoms into two sections, reducing sag problems, are found only after 1830.

Neither of these rules is true. Superbly constructed pieces from as early as 1770 show these features. This is especially true of London pieces. The rules are valueless in studying American and European furniture because such fine techniques were used haphazardly at best.

Linen presses, chests-on-chests, secretary bases, and large chests all have centrally reinforced drawer bottoms after 1770 or 1780. Again, cabinetmakers were not stupid—they were not unresponsive to their clients' needs. When it was noticed that large, loaded drawer bottoms sagged after a few years, techniques were quickly developed to improve the situation. (It *is* true that by 1830 even the most backwater cabinetmakers in Britain were aware of these techniques.)

RULE 9

Table leaves, tabletops, and even round, tilt-top tea tables are always made of a single board.

This is most often the case—but not always. In the 18th and early 19th centuries, one expects tables of a formal nature to be made of wide, single boards. Thus, even large breakfast tables are frequently only one or two boards, depending on width. Certainly any leaf or tabletop under 25 inches will always be a single board.

For large pieces, however, and pieces made of woods such as maple, which are seldom found large enough for large, single boards, one may find multiple boards. Table leaves on a dropleaf table, for instance, may be made of a large board and a small board. When this happens, look for a balanced presentation. What was done to one drop leaf will have been done to the other drop leaf. On a round table, one will often find a large center board and two small flanking boards. And on very wide tables, expect two even-size boards.

RULE 10

All early-18th-century chairs have detached shoes, and all 19th- and 20th-century copies of 18th-century chairs have integral shoes.

The shoe is the horizontal piece at the base of the splat that either attaches to the rear seat rail (detached) or *is* the rear rail (integral). In 95 percent of all chairs, this rule holds true. But there are important documented exceptions in both England and the United States. One example is the chair production from 1760 onward at the Anthony Hay Workshop, Williamsburg, VA. One important defining characteristic of that shop's work is the use of the integral shoe.

FINAL THOUGHTS

The rules of thumb that have dominated thinking about antiques—most discussed here—are useful guides to quick analysis. These rules alert one. They shout, "Beware!" And we often need to be shouted at. We are all susceptible to being swept off our feet by a beautiful piece, failing to note the fakery that a rule of thumb would have announced.

However, we also are equally capable of missing a rarity, a bargain, a great find, because we reject it on the basis of one of these shorthand rules of analysis. Use all of your knowledge when you investigate a piece. Be alerted by rules of thumb, *not* blinded by them.

COUNTRY FRENCH FURNITURE

© *David P. Lindquist*

Despite the fact that 18th- and 19th-century furniture from the provinces of France is becoming ever more popular, there is a dearth of information about construction, repairs, hardware, and other key issues. In France, and here, some very good style books have been published, but there has been little on construction, on what makes Country French furniture unique and exciting, head and shoulders above the provincial furniture of any other country. Style and construction are the key factors—the pieces photographed in this article display well those characteristics. We will use them as the focus of our explanation.

AN ARMOIRE

The armoire is one of the most basic and useful of French pieces. Once used strictly to stock clothes, food, and so forth on shelves, its adaptive uses in the late 20th century are limitless. Armoires hold clothes, linens, china, bars, stereos, televisions, and more. This particular example (*see photo 99*) from the Whitehall at the Villa, Chapel Hill, was shown in the major exhibition "The American Craftsman and the Eu-

Photo 99. Armoire. (See p. 204)

Photo 100. Dropleaf dining table. (See p. 206)

The CONDITION KEY measures the degree of repair-restoration.

Poor Condition: Missing parts, breaks, and/or very bad restoration (possibly collectible because of some other merit).

Average Condition: Small parts may be missing, and cleaning may be necessary (the condition in which most objects are found).

Good Condition: No parts missing, no major cleaning needed—ready to use or display.

Fine Condition: Near original condition or restored to near original condition.

ropean Tradition, 1620–1820'' and was photographed for the exhibition catalog (p. 177). The piece has a joined carcass and doors (panels "float" in rails that are mortised and tenoned together). Both the doors and the sides have asymmetrical panels (typical Louis XV) that are decorative in their own right and also converge on the doors to create an accented center with fluting and carving. The top and base are generously carved with floral motifs. Short cabriole legs (here original but usually partially or completely replaced) frame off the base, which is scalloped, repeating the curves of the legs. While this example is cherry, armoires frequently are found in walnut, oak, and pine—the wood being helpful in determining area of origin.

Other types of decoration found on period armoires include inlay work, much more flamboyant carving, and various parquet panels. Variations of form include narrow armoires with a central drawer and doors above and below the drawer—called a "standing man" *(homme de bout)* armoire. Bonnetieres are very small, narrow armoires used for hats but also probably used as chimney cupboards and in narrow spots.

TABLES

Country French tables abound—often found in very rough but restorable condition. They come in every size and form imaginable, in various woods, and with varying degrees of decorative elaboration through carving, inlay, and so on. *Photo 100* shows a particularly large, oval cherry drop-leaf dining table sitting in the workshop in Brittany, where I had just acquired it. It needed new casters, and the multiboard top had to be rejoined and smoothed. Oval tables are far less frequently found than simple rectangular forms—all called farmhouse tables but not necessarily found originally in farmhouses. Many of these tables are from workshops, taverns, and inns.

Rectangular dining tables will normally need their aprons reduced in size and their legs tipped up, as they were used with benches—*not* chairs—in the 18th and 19th centuries. Such modification does not decrease the value of these tables, as they are virtually useless without such modification.

Small tables, on the other hand, should not have been altered except for replacement of rotted leg ends by tipping. Tipped feet are almost universal in Country French furniture, as it sat on regularly washed stone floors and then was often relegated to barns with dirt floors. When feet appear to be original, check for rot and other signs of deterioration—if you don't find it, the entire leg is probably replaced.

BUFFETS

The French used buffets such as those in photos 101 and 103 for storage purposes in dining rooms and in various public settings. A buffet with a closed cupboard top is a buffet à deux corps (a buffet in two parts). One with an open rack for dishes is called a vaisselier (a cabinet to show vessels).

In *photo 101* the buffet shows two characteristics highly desired by collectors: iron hinges clad in brass sleeves with turned brass finials, and solid herringbone door panels. Interestingly, little Country French furniture was inlaid or painted; that was the style of the city. Rather, the concept of parquetry (geometric inlay) is expressed as it is in parquet floors: solid pieces of wood set into patterns. (Marquetry, by the way, is floral inlay, as opposed to geometric parquetry.) For those who love fine wood, the French habit of extravagant wood use is very exciting. Not only does Country French furniture often have solid-wood decorative panels, but some pieces were built of solid burl wood, such as the buffet in photo 103, which is made of solid burl elm.

Another interesting aspect of Country French furniture is that one frequently finds construction throwbacks (true of the Country pieces of all nations). *Photo 102* shows the central candle drawer of the rather diminutive buffet in photo 101. Note that this is a "hung" drawer—it runs on boards nailed to the interior sides of the drawer opening; the drawer is literally hung on those boards in the deeply grooved sides of the drawer. This was a construction technique greatly favored in the 17th century and not generally seen again until 20th-century factories re-adopted the technique.

The solid-burl-elm buffet in *photo 103* was photographed before the newly tipped feet were colored and polished to match the rest of the piece. This type of work can be seen on at least 80 percent of the furniture from France found in today's marketplace. Another fun aspect of this piece is the placement of the polished steel or iron escutcheons on the drawers. The left drawer has the escutcheon centered with a ring pull—the drawer has no lock. The right drawer has the escutcheon set at the top edge of the drawer over the keyhole of the lock. To us, it looks slightly silly; to the cabinetmaker, each served a perfectly logical purpose and was thus placed where needed.

The aspects of cabinetmakers' whimsy, extravagant uses of wood, and

Photo 101. Buffet.
(See p. 207)

Photo 102. Central
candle drawer of
buffet. (See p. 207)

Photo 103. Buffet.
(See p. 207)

designs based on the finest city furniture all combine to make Country French furniture one of the most exciting areas of furniture collection. Zippy in design, sturdy in construction, these pieces fit the most modern setting as well as the most traditional.

ASYMMETRY IN FRENCH FURNITURE

© *David P. Lindquist*

Recently, a "dealer" pranced through our shop and loudly declaimed to her friend in tow that a piece was married. Quote: "Any idiot can see the top and bottom are not identical." Well!

Photo 104 shows the piece in question—a Country French Empire buffet à deux corps (a buffet in two parts) with columns, architectural pilasters on the lower case, scalloped skirts, and carved accents. The entire piece is of oak (except the central upper panel carved with cattails, which is cherry). While the novice might see a lack of symmetry and relationship, the experienced dealer or collector will immediately notice the *very* things that say "right," not "wrong"!

DESIGN PERSPECTIVE

Crucial to understanding the design of 18th- and early-19th-century French furniture—showing the influence of the rococo—is the concept of

Photo 104 (left). Buffet à deux corps. Photo 105 (right). Armoire. (See above and p. 210)

asymmetry. In a rococo piece of the ultimate form, curves, carving, medallions, and other design motifs are presented in an asymmetrical form. In fact, 19th-century copies are sometimes unmasked because in the Rococo Revival period (c. 1850–1870) symmetry replaces asymmetry! A Rococo Revival silver piece will usually be perfectly symmetrical—the 18th-century example not symmetrical. Carved aprons on furniture are carefully balanced in the 19th century but unbalanced and asymmetrical in the 18th century. Tops and bottoms of case pieces have different motifs in the 18th century but the same motifs in the 19th century.

A classic example of asymmetry is seen in *photo 105* showing a documented armoire. Inscribed on an inner drawer in French is the statement "Made by Paurais in 1799, the 7th year of the Republic." Note that the general outline is symmetrical, but the upper panels are totally asymmetrical; the relationships of all side and door panels are totally asymmetrical; the relationships of all side and door panels create interesting juxtapositions of varying shapes; the carving is totally different from top to doors to base; and even the escutcheons are asymmetrical cartouche swirls of steel. Steel hardware, by the way, preceded brass hardware on Country French furniture. While more formal pieces and more exuberantly carved pieces may show even greater asymmetry, the point seems well made by an examination of the design of this armoire.

THE BUFFET À DEUX CORPS

Our piece in question shows both expected relationships and design typical of pieces made in the 18th and early 19th centuries. This piece has strong Empire elements, indicating a date of around 1800. Yet it also retains the rococo aspects that hark back to the 18th century. The columns and classical fluted pilasters are stylistically late, the evidence of Louis XVI and Empire styles. The apron, the carved elements, the supports of the upper structure, and the apron of the upper section all reflect rococo-style developments of the mid-18th century.

This amalgam of earlier elements in the early 19th century is typical of Country French furniture. In fact, Country furniture of most nations tends to run later stylistically and retain "out of date" elements longer than do urban pieces, which always reflected the most current fashion.

The relationships that stylistically unite the top and bottom are the apron lines (identical), the moldings on the doors (also identical), and the use of the columns, the top naturally having smaller columns than the base. The finish, cut of wood, and color (original finish, which we had cleaned) all speak in a unified voice. Furthermore, the mass of the piece speaks as a whole, the height and breadth beautifully proportioned.

CONSTRUCTION VERSUS STYLE

While my articles have usually stressed construction, this one has stressed style. I have stressed style because design integrity and design consistency should be the *first* step in analysis of an antique. Before tearing a piece apart from the construction viewpoint, it is imperative to have seen it as a stylistic whole. If it screams that it is ugly, out of character, out of style, out of proportion, or obviously fake, then why bother examining construction? But one must know what to expect stylistically. The dealer who condemned this buffet did so on grounds that should have sent a totally different message to her brain. The visual lessons are clear if one knows what to expect; she didn't and was led to false conclusions.

Having noted, as we now have, that the piece does work stylistically, let's look a little at construction. As noted earlier, much matches. But the proof is often found on the back, especially in multipart pieces. The wood stock (thickness) of the uprights—top and bottom—are identical. The relationship of the back construction—floating panels held by wide-grooved uprights, all framed by heavy timbers—is similar, though the top is more elegantly finished, as it shows from the front. One expects and finds the same construction techniques top and bottom.

Remember—when examining an antique, look for consistency in style and construction. Start with style. And be sure you know what to expect. You can't make a judgment if you do not understand the historical development of trends in style over the past three hundred years.

THE FRENCH COMMODE IN ENGLISH FURNITURE

© *David P. Lindquist*

While we typically study the great styles of France and England, with their translations throughout Europe and America, we seldom study the French-English relationship. Of the many influences of the 18th-century French style on English cabinetmaking, perhaps the most beautiful is the commode.

Louis XV and Louis XVI commodes are some of the most expensive, rarest, and most collected of all furniture forms. *Photo 106* shows a classic Louis XV, c. 1750, bombé commode of two drawers with marble top, ormolu mounts, and fine marquetry (floral inlays). Several features should be noted: the rococo hardware; the serpentine front as well as bombé sides; the use of very simple, straight-grained fruitwood veneered

Photo 106.
Commode.
CREDIT: SOTHEBY'S,
NEW YORK
(See p. 211)

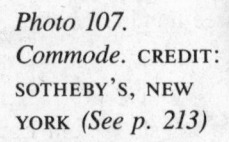

Photo 107.
Commode. CREDIT:
SOTHEBY'S, NEW
YORK *(See p. 213)*

Photo 108. Commode.
CREDIT: SOTHEBY'S,
NEW YORK
(See p. 213)

on a slant to provide background for the flamboyant cartouche panels of the sides and drawers; the contouring of the marble to the base; and the distinctively French use of the lower drawer as part (or sometimes all) of the apron of the piece. In *photo 107* we again find several distinctively French features in an important signed commode by Nicholas Hericourt, who worked during the reign of Louis XV. Note again the use of the lower drawer as the finished apron of the commode and the contrast of the simple, straight-grained wood to highlight the parquetry (geometric inlay). There are, of course, equal numbers of French commodes that have stationary aprons and fully encased drawers, such as those shown in *photo 108.*

Photo 109 shows a very fine English, George III–period mahogany commode in the French taste, c. 1775. Clearly, the pervasive influence of the French pieces we have examined is found in this "Commode Dressing Table" or "French Commode Table," as this piece would have been named by Chippendale or Hepplewhite. The strong—and very un-English—design elements that make this piece quintessentially French in influence are contrasting, simple-grained drawers of light color set off by heavily grained wood inlaid on an angle between and around the drawers; bombé sides with serpentine front (see again photo 106); a base apron created by the bottom of the lower drawer; and a top contoured perfectly as a marble slab might have been. This piece, formerly in the collection of Lady Daphne Straight, has a top drawer fitted for a lady's dressing needs.

Classically English is the fine construction of the piece. The oak drawer liners are finely made. Each drawer has a dust divider. The top is dove-tailed onto the case—it literally slid onto the sides and was then secured by glue and shrinkage. While the rococo brasses show both Louis XV and Chippendale influences, the bails show restraint more typical of 1785, as do the overall smooth lines of the commode.

In the drawing from Chippendale's *Director*, shown as *photos 110 and 111*, we see the 1762 design that presaged this commode. This is Plate 67 of the *Director*, "Two Designs of Commode Tables." While the aprons are stationary in these highly ornamented drawings, it is clear that the choice is open to the cabinetmaker's final option. The body of the left-side commode is bombé with an exaggerated double serpentine front.

In *The Cabinet-Maker and Upholsterer's Guide* by George Hepple-white, published in 1788, 1789, and 1794, we find an even clearer ex-ample. Plate 77 (*photo 112*) shows a design for a painted satinwood "Commode Dressing Table," the top drawer fitted with "partitions or apartments in which are adapted for combs, powders, essences, pin-cushions, and other necessary equipage." The relationship to the com-

Photo 109.
Commode. CREDIT:
WHITEHALL AT THE
VILLA, CHAPEL HILL,
NC, AND SOTHEBY'S,
LONDON *(See p. 213)*

Photo 110.
Design for a
commode. (See
p. 213)

Photo 111 (below, left). Design
for a commode. Photo 112
(below, right). Design for a
commode dressing table. (See
p. 213)

mode in photo 109 is startling, especially the French bombé and serpentine elements. The reason for the dating of the commode before the publication of Hepplewhite's book is the often forgotten fact that Hepplewhite's book—published by his dear wife, Alice, two years *after* he died—was a compendium of styles long current. Hepplewhite compiled ideas from a variety of sources, all predating publication of his work by many years.

Such commodes are rare in Georgian furniture and are avidly sought by collectors; thus, they command prices well above those of their boxier and more typical cousins. This particular commode would bring $25,000–$35,000 depending on the shop offering it; urban shops with higher overhead would obviously be forced to charge at the higher end of the spectrum.

PEMBROKE TABLES

© *David P. Lindquist*

Whether one believes the ninth earl of Pembroke built the first one or the Countess of Pembroke ordered the first one, cute little dropleaf tables with hinged bracket supports have long been known as "Pembroke tables." Such tables must have wooden hinged supports for the leaves and may have one, two, or no drawers. They always have four legs.

Photo 114 shows a typical example. In *photos 113 and 115* we see quite clearly the double bracket supports for the leaves. In 18th-century pieces there will be two brackets (19th-century examples often have only a single centered bracket), and the hinge is five intermeshed wood knuckles (easily seen in photo 115). Pembroke tables are reflective of all periods, from 1750 onward, and the decoration may be enhanced by carving, inlay, or exotic form (serpentine leaves, bow ends, etc.).

QUALITY POINTS

In order of importance, Pembrokes are graded for quality on the basis of size, form, number of drawers, and decorative visual aspects. The smaller the table, the more valuable and desirable. The forms preferred are bow-end or those with shaped leaves. As in photo 114, when the top is oval, the apron should be bowed to be the highest quality level.

Country examples often have no drawers. Simple examples will have a drawer but no opening drawer. More sophisticated examples have a false drawer that exactly mirrors the real one, or they have two drawers.

Of great interest is the overall exterior construction—is it solid wood or veneered? American and English Country examples are made most often of solid mahogany, oak, cherry, maple, or walnut. Citified examples will be veneered. Flame mahogany is highly desired by cabinet-

Photo 113 (left). Bracket supports, Pembroke table. CREDIT:
WHITEHALL AT THE VILLA, CHAPEL HILL, NC. *Photo 114 (right).*
Example of a Pembroke table. CREDIT: WHITEHALL AT THE VILLA,
CHAPEL HILL, NC *(See p. 215)*

Photo 115. Knuckles,
Pembroke table.
CREDIT: WHITEHALL
AT THE VILLA, CHAPEL
HILL, NC *(See p. 215)*

Photo 116. Boxwood edging, Pembroke table. CREDIT: WHITEHALL AT
THE VILLA, CHAPEL HILL, NC *(See p. 217)*

makers, and its use should mark a sophisticated piece. However, it must be used as a veneer to be effective. The large cracks in the surface of this table are carved by the treacherous nature of flame grain—it splits and cracks easily. That's why no sophisticated cabinetmaker would ever use solid flame wood! Veneered pieces of great beauty reflect the highest level of the form.

Design may be additionally enhanced by inlay or carving. *Photo 116* shows a detail of the boxwood edging on each leg and around the real and false drawers. It also shows a line of apron inlay. In American tables one finds bellflower inlays, eagles, lunette borders, and other motifs to enhance the piece. Remember, the more original the inlay, the greater the value; the more *later* inlay, the lower the value!

AGE POINTS

As with all furniture, signs of shrinkage must be found. Also there will be patterns of oxidation of great interest on the underside of the table. Look also for wear, especially where the brackets scrape the underside of the leaves. And perhaps you will even find sewing bird marks such as the ones seen along the edge in *photo 117*. They are small round dents made by the clamp of the screw-on sewing bird favored by ladies of the 18th and 19th centuries. This photo also shows nicely the scoring lines used by the cabinetmaker to plan hinge location. And we see a rather typical variety of early to modern screws as old ones loosened or were lost.

When you look for shrinkage, remember both drawer bottoms and inlay (refer to "Generalities of Furniture Construction" on pp. 197–200). Sometimes the leaves will fly outward or gap outward slightly on a Pembroke. This is because an ignorant cabinetmaker failed to plan his center board wide enough to allow for shrinkage. Such is not good, and there is no truly satisfactory repair: a spline to widen the board is ugly, and replacing the center board destroys its value as an antique.

Photo 117. Sewing bird marks on a Pembroke table.
CREDIT: WHITEHALL AT THE VILLA, CHAPEL HILL, NC *(See above)*

An early table with a bow end will be constructed with blocks or "bricks" of deal or other secondary wood over which veneer is applied. A solid mahogany end of curved form indicates a later piece.

Pieces constructed between 1750 and 1830 will generally have very thin, elegant dovetails and fewer, wider ones at the rear of the drawer. Large handmade dovetails indicate American Centennial furniture. Machine dovetails indicate post-1870 pieces. Tiny dovetails in drawers of solid mahogany with mahogany sides are indicative of English Sheraton Revival and Edwardian furniture (i.e., 1860–1910).

CONDITION POINTS

Examine the legs with care to make sure that they have not been extended (also called "tipped out"). Examine the line of the grain to see that it emerges below inlaid cuffs, overlaid trim, and the like. Check with equal care as to the originality of the top; because of splaying and other damage the top is often replaced or "married" (an old top and base not originally together).

By turning the table upside down as in *photo 118*, you can check for marriage problems. There should be no screw holes to nowhere. Also, look at the oxidation pattern. Where the drawer covers the top, the color should be lighter (less exposure to air). The cross-member below the drawer should leave a light-colored area on the drawer bottom. English Country tables—and even many city pieces—will have very dark oxidation due to the burning of coal for heat. American tables tend to have lighter-colored oxidation as wood was used for heat.

The drawer is another likely replacement. Does the oxidation line up? Is there a matching wear pattern on the drawer edges and table runners?

Add-ins and add-ons, such as inlay, carving, casters, and hardware, should be examined for originality. Do you feel shrinkage in the inlay? Can you see minute gaps between the inlay and the table surface? Are the casters leather (pre-1780) or brass (post-1780) or ceramic (post-1860)?

Photo 118. Pembroke table upside down. CREDIT: WHITEHALL AT THE VILLA, CHAPEL HILL, NC *(See above)*

And, of course, are there holes from other hardware? What about the false drawer hardware? That hardware didn't get much use!

With these tips in mind, examining Pembrokes can be easy and fun. They are so subject to repairs that you will frequently be rewarded by the discovery of repairs or deliberate fakery. Have fun exploring!

ELEGANT INLAY—OR A LITTLE FAKERY?

© *David P. Lindquist*

Over the years I have repeatedly written that easy alterations warm the cockles of a faker's heart. Carving on a plain piece greatly increases the value—*if* the recarving goes undetected or is simply meant to fool the novice. Easier than carving is the addition of inlay (it can be bought from a catalog). However, recent inlay is easily unmasked—just read on!

WHY ADD INLAY?

Many pieces of old or antique furniture have been and are still being enhanced by the addition of inlay to originally simple pieces. Undetected enhanced pieces sell for double or more what simple ones bring.

The great ages of inlay were the late 17th to the early 18th centuries and the late 18th century (the neoclassical styles of Adam, Hepplewhite, Sheraton, etc.). During these periods simple pieces with little or no inlay were also made, in greater quantity than the inlaid examples. Remember—one paid dearly in those days for inlay. Thus, inlaid pieces *of the period* are scarce and valuable.

With the popular revival of the styles of the late 18th century after 1860, vast quantities of "lookalike" furniture were produced for the middle class in England (after 1860) and in the United States after 1885 or so. These new antiques added to the store of genuine simple examples, creating a veritable feast for the 20th-century faker! It was and is a relatively simple matter to enhance these pieces with inlay.

RECOGNIZING ORIGINAL INLAY

Inlays are nothing more than the addition of various elements to the surface of another substance. While one occasionally finds inlay of ivory, bone, pewter, copper, silver, brass, and gold, most inlays we encounter are made of wood. To determine the originality of inlay, one must know something about the properties of the inlay material.

Wood, whether in large or small pieces, is subject to shrinkage with age. As moisture is lost and gained through the interaction of porous wood with its surroundings, wood shrinks and expands. Thus, the key to recognizing old inlay is understanding that it will have shrunk. Examine closely *photo 119*. These are fan inlays of perhaps 1½" on the doors of a sideboard. The fans are set off and structured by line inlays. Both types of inlay are typical of furniture dating as early as 1775 and as late as yesterday (or today!). Just because it looks correct stylistically for the period doesn't mean it is. Most inlay found on antiques at auction and in shops is not original—it just looks stylistically correct. The inlay in this photo is right.

Visual examination will show signs of cracking and shrinking of each small piece creating the fan, as well as contraction (shrinkage) of the narrow line inlays. These fissures have been filled over the years by dirt, wax, and other surface treatments. Not only can you see the signs of shrinkage, you can *feel* it.

Let your fingers do the walking, and you will feel ridges, gaps, and bumps on all areas of antique inlay. It takes a very long time for these flaws to be seen and felt. Their presence is a strong sign of originality.

KNOW WHAT TO EXPECT

Beyond feeling for bumps and gaps in inlay, one should also know what to expect in terms of style and construction. Through examination of proven pieces, through the study of books on antiques, through visits to museums and historic homes (with original furnishings, please!) one learns what to expect.

While knowledge of style is learned variously, knowledge of construction requires careful study *and* physical examination. *Photo 120* shows a number of possible errors regarding inlay in one example: correct style

Photo 119 (left). Fan inlays on the doors of a sideboard. CREDIT: WHITEHALL AT THE VILLA, CHAPEL HILL, NC. *Photo 120 (right). Example of inlay errors.* CREDIT: WHITEHALL AT THE VILLA, CHAPEL HILL, NC *(See above)*

joined with incorrect construction; correct style joined with a lack of proper signs of age; and correct style that *could*, if properly constructed, have marked yet another type of fakery.

The banding—or apparent banding—around the lower leg of this piece is often found on c. 1780 pieces, which, like this piece, have tapered legs and are most often made of mahogany. Thus, we have a logical case that such banding is right. It *is* stylistically correct; however, the banding is not constructed in an 18th-century manner.

Rather than inlaying a wide band with narrow trim horizontally across or around the leg, only narrow line inlays were added on this leg. One sees the mahogany grain pattern preceding directly down the leg right through the supposed banding! Furthermore, there is no shrinkage. This fakery dates from about 1920, and in seventy years no shrinkage has become evident. As I said earlier, it takes a long time for tiny pieces of wood to shrink.

Had the faker done his job in the 18th-century manner and used a wide inlay, we would have one more problem to examine. After checking for shrinkage, we would need to follow the vertical mahogany grain pattern above and below the banding. Broken and repaired or lengthened legs are usually hidden by the addition of banding to cover the joint of new tips to old legs. While we do not want to see the vertical grain where banding should be, we *do* want to see the vertical grain enter at the top of the band and reemerge directly below the band.

OTHER INLAYS

We cannot discuss in detail all other materials used for inlay, but a few important aspects are universal. While other inlays may not shrink, the wood they are set into does have a universal property. All wood shrinks. (And yes, I do know you're tired of reading this line.)

This means that with time the piece of furniture changes its shape slightly as it shrinks across the grain. As it shrinks, it tends to expel a nonshrinking substance, such as metal, and severely cracks a brittle substance, such as ivory. Look for bulges. Look for ends curling up. Look for multiple breaks and black lines in ivory and bone. Look for signs of resetting of inlays. If you don't find such signs—beware.

A FINAL WARNING

Don't just examine the inlays; examine the surface beneath and around the inlays. If you find a crack in the structure of a piece, the inlay over it should *also* be cracked or damaged. When shrinkage tears the body of an antique (as it usually does), it always tears the inlays as well. Inlays over cracks were put there *after* the cracks occurred.

CURRENT TRENDS IN
AMERICAN FURNITURE

The trend in prices in American furniture over the last several years has been that quality continues to command strong prices, although little of great merit has been seen at auction. This trend, which began in 1991, shows no sign of abating.

There has been a softening of prices in the market for the mid-range to near-great American furniture, American decorative arts, and American folk art. This mid-range area has been soft for several years in a manner reflective of the 1970s, which had a sagging of prices in the American market. This is a very startling turnaround from the 1980s and up to 1990, when we saw this range increasing for the first time in quite a number of years. Whether or not the later 1990s will see this mid-range begin to go up again in value or whether it will remain stagnant is very difficult to assess at this point. My personal analysis is that it probably will be 1994 or 1995 before we see the mid-range begin to escalate in value again. The low price ranges of American furniture have been extremely strong. This is not surprising since this is the one market that anyone who wants American things and has a little bit of money can afford to buy in. It is the entry level arena of the American furniture market and, as such, sells quite strongly. With the movement towards a more formal life style in the 1980s and early 1990s, the interest in primitive and painted furniture of an unsophisticated nature has waned. However, High Country furniture—pieces such as tiger maple, curly cherry, and other interesting native woods used in a sophisticated manner, but not an urban manner—have risen in price over the last several years, and in the last year in particular, reflective of both the interest and quality, which remains strong, and the suitability of such High Country pieces for relatively sophisticated homes, which have a fairly high formal decorative motif.

FAKES ALERT

Married highboys and chests-on-chests that were part of something larger, simple pieces made more elegant with inlay, simple pieces given regional inlay designs, and so on, are major problems. Out-and-out fakes are not major contemporary problems because of a lack of craftsmen. The fakes and enhanced pieces made from 1885 to 1940 are now looking very good indeed.

Chests made into desks—especially butlers' chests made into slant-front desks—were a favorite conversion of the early 20th century. Simple rectangular tables were made oval—thus, more valuable then and now if undetected. The old line of American dealers often included rogues. Many were trained cabinetmakers; others had large workshops to restore, create, and transform. Beware.

CONDITION KEY

Fine Condition: glowing finish; all hardware intact; all repairs of high quality.

Good Condition: nice finish; hardware intact but not necessarily correct stylistically; some obvious repairs.

Average Condition: acceptable finish, may need cleaning; hardware intact; some repairs needed and old repairs may be overly obvious.

Poor Condition: poor finish; may be painted over; missing pieces of hardware; needs a number of minor repairs: old repairs of poor quality.

Originality is *not* considered in condition statement but is specified in each individual description.

QUALITY KEY

Good Quality: a nice piece worthy of collecting but having no distinguishing characteristics.

Very Good Quality: a very good example of the type, reflecting several of the most desirable characteristics.

Superior Quality: a superlative example that has nearly all desired characteristics of the type.

This is not a condition statement but strictly a measure of the stylishness of the piece.

Armoire Classical 1845–1865 United States
Mahogany 2-door armoire with 2 columns and paw feet.
Very Good Quality/Good Condition $2420 (A)   **$1500–$3500**

> American armoires or wardrobes are generally well priced compared to other American furniture. A bargain area!—*DL*

Bed 9′9.75″ H Classical 1845–1865 United States
Carved mahogany full tester bed; Southern origin; shortened feet.
Good Quality/Good Condition $7770 (A)   **$5000–$9000**

Bed, 4-poster 75″ H × 62″ W × 64″ D Sheraton 1800–1820 United States
Mahogany turned and reeded 4-poster with canopy (replaced); bottom posts turned and reeded, 2 top posts just turned; unusual size; Massachusetts.
Very Good Quality/Good Condition $4800 (D)   **$4000–$6000**

Candlestand   28″ H × 20.5″ Dia.   Chippendale   1750–1780   United States
Mahogany; molded circular dish top tilting and revolving above birdcage support
with ball; cabriole legs; ball-and-claw feet. *(See photo 121, right)*
Superior Quality/Fine Condition $14,300 (A)   **$10,000–$18,000**

Candlestand   29.5″ H × 22″ W × 17″ D   Hepplewhite   1780–1800   United
States
Mahogany; oval top with urn-shaped pedestal terminating in spider legs with
spade feet; Maryland.
Superior Quality/Fine Condition $1950 (D)   **$1200–$2000**

Chair, arm   45.75″ H   Pilgrim   1700–1750   United States
Bannister back, shaped bannister uprights and shaped arms ending in mushroom
grips; rush seat, turned legs and stretchers, 1″ added to feet.
Superior Quality/Good Condition $3025 (A)   **$2500–$4500**

Chair, arm   36″ H   Windsor   1780–1800   United States
Bowed crest rail connected by 7 spindles with bulb bottom sections; eliptical
seat; knuckles carved of single piece of oak forming bent arm rail; turned legs
and stretchers.
Good Quality/Good Condition $1100 (A)   **$1200–$2500**

Chair, arm   Windsor   1780–1800   United States
Turned and painted; comb back; bowed crest rail supported by 7 spindles, saddle
seat, rakish vine-turned legs conjoined by shaped H-form stretcher. *(See photo
122)*
Very Good Quality/Good Condition $3500 (A)   **$3000–$4500**

Chair, arm   Rococo Revival   1845–1865   United States
Carved and laminated rosewood armchair in the "Henry Ford" pattern; by J. &
J. W. Meeks.
Superior Quality/Good Condition $6050 (A)   **$5000–$7500**

Chair, arm   Renaissance Revival   1885–1900   United States
Walnut and burl walnut; female heads carved on arms; attributed to John Jelliff.
Superior Quality/Fine Condition $605 (A)   **$475–$900**

Chair, easy   45″ H   Federal   1800–1830   United States
Country; birch; beaded front legs, old red linen toile upholstery; retains old red
wash; New England; minor structural repairs to frame.
Very Good Quality/Good Condition $3200 (A)   **$1800–$4500**

Chair, side   38″ H   Chippendale   1750–1780   United States
Mahogany; carved with 4 shells; needlework slip seat (imperfections); old refin-
ish; Philadelphia.
Superior Quality/Fine Condition $13,000 (A)   **$8500–$12,000**

Chair, side   Chippendale   1750–1780   United States
Mahogany; upholstered over the sides with front brackets in the Chinese mode;
backsplat nicely shaped and carved with rosette and well-executed crest rail;
attributed to George Bright, Boston. 1770.
Very Good Quality/Fine Condition $1950 (D)   **$1500–$2500**

Chair, side   40.5″ H   Queen Anne   1750–1780   United States
Mahogany; crest rail with carved shell above shaped splat over balloon slip seat,
cabriole legs with shell-and-tassel carved knees, ball-and-claw feet; Rhode Island. *(See photo 121, left)*
Superior Quality/Fine Condition $12,650 (A)   **$8500–$20,000**

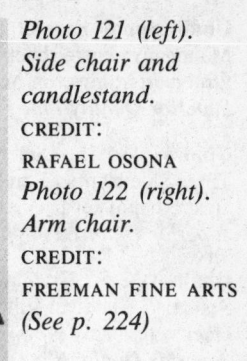

*Photo 121 (left).
Side chair and
candlestand.*
CREDIT:
RAFAEL OSONA
*Photo 122 (right).
Arm chair.*
CREDIT:
FREEMAN FINE ARTS
(See p. 224)

Photo 123. Group of chairs. CREDIT: ELIZABETH R. DANIEL ANTIQUES
(See p. 226)

Photo 124 (left). Dining chair. CREDIT: WHITEHALL AT THE VILLA,
CHAPEL HILL, NC. *Photo 125 (right). Side chairs and dropleaf table.*
CREDIT: ELIZABETH R. DANIEL ANTIQUES *(See p. 226)*

Chair, wing   Federal   1800–1830   United States
Mahogany; barrel back; with flaring wings; horizontal turned arms and nicely
turned front legs; on original casters; Pennsylvania; 1810.
Superior Quality/Fine Condition $4800 (D)   **$3000–$5000**

Chairs   43″ H   Queen Anne   1750–1760   United States
Three side chairs (2 are a pair) and 1 armchair of maple and ash; nicely detailed
crests; bannister backs with bulbous turnings. *(See photo 123)*
Superior Quality/Fine Condition $3000 (D)   **$3500–$4500**

Chairs   32.5″ H   Classical   1800–1830   United States
Set of 12 classical gilt and stencil-decorated side chairs; 2 splats with minor
cracks; probably New York.
Superior Quality/Fine Condition $5000 (A)   **$7500–$15,000**

> An original set of twelve is very rare; these were a bargain—*DL*

Chairs   32″ H   Windsor   1830–1845   United States
Set of 6 painted, decorated, thumb-back side chairs, painted to simulate rosewood; crest rails with stenciled foliage and scrolls; New England; repainted,
paint loss on seats.
Good Quality/Average Condition $700 (A)   **$900–$1500**

Chairs, dining   38″ H × 21″ W × 17″ D   Centennial   1885–1900   United
States
Set of 8 (2 arms); Chippendale style in Philadelphia manner; mahogany; serpen-
tine shell-carved front rail; pierced, carved backs; cabriole legs, with carved
knees and ball-and-claw feet. *(See photo 124)*
Very Good Quality/Fine Condition $9500 (D)   **$9000–$11,000**

> Note the dating here for "Centennial" furniture. It was a backwater exhi-
> bition in 1876—not much was made before 1885. After 1920, we call it
> "Colonial Revival"—a second and important period of reproduction mak-
> ing in the United States.—*DL*

Chairs, side   Queen Anne   1750–1780   United States
Pair; mahogany; stepped vasiform splat, simple curved crest rail; cabriole legs,
pad feet; original undisturbed finish; Queen Anne transitional; Rhode Island.
(See photo 125)
Very Good Quality/Fine Condition $10,000 (D)   **$12,000–$15,000**

Chairs, side   37.5″ H   Chippendale transitional   1780–1800   United States
Pair of carved mahogany side chairs; refinished and restored; transitional, with
tapered, molded legs; Massachusetts.
Good Quality/Good Condition $500 (A)   **$1200–$1800**

Chairs, side   Rococo Revival   1845–1865   United States
Pair of carved and laminated rosewood side chairs in the "Rosalie" pattern by
John Henry Belter.
Superior Quality/Good Condition $2640 (A)   **$2500–$4000**

Chairs, side   Rococo Revival   1845–1865   United States
Pair of carved and laminated rosewood side chairs in the "Henry Ford" pattern;
by J. & J. W. Meeks.
Superior Quality/Fine Condition $4125 (A)   **$5000–$7500**

Chest of drawers 50″ H × 36″ W × 19″ D Queen Anne 1750–1760 United States
Maple; 2 over 4 graduated drawers; molded top, slipper feet; brasses replaced; Rhode Island.
Superior Quality/Fine Condition $8500 (D) **$5000–$10,000**

Chest of drawers 35″ H × 40″ W × 21″ D Chippendale 1750–1780 United States
Cherry; replaced hardware; Philadelphia.
Very Good Quality/Good Condition $11,500 (D) **$10,000–$15,000**

Chest of drawers 32″ H × 36″ × 20″ D Chippendale 1760–1770 United States
Mahogany; block front, molded top above case with rounded, blocked, and graduated long drawers; molded base with central pendant; short cabriole legs ending in ball-and-claw feet; 1 foot restored; minor repairs needed; later brasses.
Superior Quality/Good Condition $42,900 (A) **$50,000–$75,000**

> With minor repairs made, brasses restored to correct form, and a better replacement for the rear foot, this price may easily reach $75,000!—*DL*

Chest of drawers 32.5″ H × 33″ W × 17.5″ D Chippendale 1780–1800 United States
Birch; molded, overhanging top over 4 graduated drawers; ogee feet with slightly shaped apron; left back foot pieced, breaks in front feet. *(See photo 126)*
Good Quality/Good Condition $4500 (D) **$4000–$7500**

Chest of drawers 32.5″ H × 34″ W × 20″ D Chippendale 1770–1810 United States
Mahogany; block front with molded top above 4 graduated drawers with rounded blocking over conforming carved apron; backboard stamped T. H. Balch (working in Massachusetts 1771–1817); brasses original.
Superior Quality/Fine Condition $48,000 (A) **$35,000–$65,000**

Chest of drawers 41″ H × 38″ W × 21.5″ D Hepplewhite 1780–1800 United States
Bowfront; mahogany; small patch in top; Virginia.
Good Quality/Average Condition $6200 (D) **$3500–$5000**

Chest of drawers 36″ H × 40.5″ × 22″ D Hepplewhite 1780–1800 United States
Cherry inlaid bowfront with striped cherry veneer on drawer fronts; brasses replaced; line inlay on drawers and inlaid around base; banded top; Pennsylvania, 1790.
Superior Quality/Fine Condition $7200 (D) **$4000–$7500**

Chest of drawers 37.5″ H × 36″ W × 19″ D Hepplewhite 1780–1800 United States
Inlaid mahogany; straight front; unusual patterned inlay around base and string inlay on drawers; some inlay repair; brasses old but not original; Maryland, 1790.
Very Good Quality/Fine Condition $4800 (D) **$2500–$4500**

Chest of drawers 37″ H × 39″ W × 21.5″ D Hepplewhite 1780–1800 United States
Cherry with tiger maple inlay around top and base; French feet; single-board top and sides; Pennsylvania.
Very Good Quality/Good Condition *$5800 (D)*   **$5200–$6500**

Chest of drawers 38″ H × 42″ W × 18″ D Hepplewhite 1790–1800 United States
Mahogany and cherry; 4 graduated drawers, line inlay around drawer; inlaid medallion in top; original brasses; Connecticut.
Superior Quality/Good Condition *$12,000 (D)*   **$7000–$12,000**

Chest of drawers 40″ H × 41″ W × 21″ D Sheraton 1800–1810 United States
Bowfront; replaced hardware; attributed to the Seymours; virtually identical to chest in the Boston Museum of Fine Art.
Superior Quality/Fine Condition *$15,000 (D)*   **$25,000–$35,000**

Sold by one dealer to another—thus the law price. Originally purchased at an estate sale for $400. It's been owned by four dealers so far—and this one is keeping it!—*DL*

Chest of drawers 44.5″ H × 46.5″ W × 22″ D Federal 1800–1830 United States
Inlaid mahogany; 1 deep drawer over 3 graduated drawers; French feet; northern New Jersey or New York; scalloped apron.
Good Quality/Good Condition *$1540 (A)*   **$1500–$2500**

Chest of drawers 37.5″ H × 41″ W × 21″ D Hepplewhite 1800–1830 United States
Inlaid cherry; string inlay on drawer fronts and band of inlay around base; some repair to 2 front feet; Connecticut, 1800.
Very Good Quality/Good Condition *$3800 (D)*   **$2200–$3600**

Chest of drawers 38″ H × 39.25″ W × 20.5″ Sheraton 1800–1830 United States
Mahogany, bowfront, top with outset corners over reeded columns ending in turned legs, centering 4 drawers over shaped and inlaid shirt. *(See photo 127)*
Good Quality/Good Condition *$1650 (A)*   **$1300–$2500**

Chest of drawers 37.5″ H × 42.25″ W × 21.5″ Sheraton 1800–1830 United States
Mahogany; rectangular top with bow front having parallel string inlay, above 4 conforming, graduated, cockbeaded drawers with string inlay; bracket feet; replaced hardware.
Very Good Quality/Fine Condition *$1980 (A)*   **$2000–$3800**

Cupboard, corner 80″ H × 38.5″ W × 26″ D Federal 1800–1830 United States
Cherry; glazed upper section (old glass) with dentil crown molding (restored); reduced in size, replaced brasses; mid-Atlantic region.
Good Quality/Average Condition *$3600 (D)*   **$3500–$4500**

Cupboard, corner 87.25″ H × 52″ W × 32″ D Federal 1800–1830 United States
Walnut; glazed-door upper section; cabinet below; pine secondary; Southern.
Good Quality/Good Condition *$3800 (D)*   **$3500–$5000**

Cupboard, corner 8′8″ H × 38″ W Federal 1800–1810 United States
One-piece painted corner cupboard in ochre and brown paint with glass door of
9 panes over 1 drawer over 2 flat-paneled doors.
Good Quality/Good Condition $3800 (D) **$3000–$4600**

Cupboard, 2-part 76″ H × 48″ W × 18″ D Country Sheraton 1820–
1830 United States
Cherry stepped-back cupboard in old finish, the top part with glass doors, each
with panes over 2; cutlery drawers and cutout area; bottom section with 2 drawers over 2 doors; round feet; Pennsylvania.
Superior Quality/Fine Condition $12,500 (D) **$8500–$13,500**

Desk 60″ H × 42″ W × 18″ D Hepplewhite 1800–1810 United States
Two-part secretary desk on high, flared French feet; top: 2 doors with
string inlay and book-matched veneer concealing 2 drawers and 6 open sections; bottom: 3 drawers flanked by bottle drawers; Massachusetts; replaced
brasses.
Very Good Quality/Good Condition $6800 (D) **$5000–$7500**

Desk, slant-front 42″ H × 40″ W × 20.5″ D Chippendale 1770–
1780 United States
Mahogany; carved shell in cabinet flanked by flame finials; interior with removable document drawer; original brasses; original finish; Massachusetts.
Superior Quality/Fine Condition $10,000 (D) **$7500–$15,000**

Desk, tambour 43.5″ × 36.75″ × 18″ D Federal 1800–1810 United
States
Mahogany; 2-part; top with line-inlaid prospect door, revealing drawers and
divided compartment, flanked by 2 tambour doors; bottom with flap above 2
line-inlaid drawers; tapering bellflower-inlaid legs; Massachusetts.
Very Good Quality/Good Condition $4600 (A) **$3500–$6500**

Étagère Gothic Revival 1845–1865 United States
Mahogany; 3 arched fret-carved shelves; base with doors enclosing shelves; on
shaped plinth base.
Superior Quality/Fine Condition $4125 (A) **$3500–$6500**

Highboy 72″ H × 37.5″ W × 21″ D Queen Anne 1700–1750 United
States
Curly maple with shell carving on base; 2 over 4 drawers in top section; wood
nicely striped, with old finish; some lip repair to drawers; brasses replaced;
Pennsylvania, 1740.
Very Good Quality/Fine Condition $26,000 (D) **$15,000–$28,000**

Highboy 71.5″ H × 38.5″ W × 19.25″ D Queen Anne 1750–1760 United
States
Maple, flat top with molded cornice, fluted quarter-columns flanking 2 short
over 4 graduated drawers; lower section with 1 long over 3 short drawers; highly
scalloped apron, drop finials, cabriole legs, slipper feet. Probably Newport, RI.
Brasses probably original; minor imperfections.
Very Good Quality/Fine Condition $18,700 (A) **$18,000–$25,000**

Highboy 6′3″ H × 38″ W Queen Anne 1750–1780 United States
Maple, flat top, molded cornice, 5 graduated drawers; lower section with 1
long over 3 short drawers, central one with fan carving; shaped apron, cabriole legs, pad feet. New England. Refinished, but otherwise, no major
restoration.
Very Good Quality/Good Condition $11,000 (A) **$12,000–$18,000**

Highboy 7'9" H × 43" W Chippendale 1750–1780 United States
Cherry; upper part: swan's neck pediment, finial, 2 short drawers flanking fan-carved thumb-molded drawer over 4 graduated drawers flanked by fluted pilasters; lower part: 1 long over 3 short drawers, center drawer fan-carved. Cabriole legs with carved C-scroll knees, ball-and-claw feet. Restorations: drawer in 1 lower part, drawer facings. Good design and proportions. Eastern CT.
Very Good Quality/Good Condition $14,125 (A)   **$12,000–$18,000**

If not so heavily restored, this could be $25,000–$45,000.—*DL*

Highboy 5'7.25" H × 38" W Queen Anne 1780–1800 United States
Maple; upper part: flat top, molded cornice, 4 thumb-molded graduated long drawers; lower section: 1 long over 3 short thumb-molded drawers; shaped apron, cabriole legs, pad feet. New England. Married. Poorly proportioned top to bottom.
Good Quality/Good Condition $2,500 (A)   **$2500–$4000**

Lowboy 28.75" H × 35" W × 20.75" D Chippendale 1750–1780 United States
Walnut; rectangular top (with corner repair) over straight front fitted with 1 wide and 2 small thumb-molded drawers; shaped apron; Pennsylvania; drawer chips, minor loss to talons. *(See photo 128)*
Very Good Quality/Average Condition $22,000 (A)   **$20,000–$40,000**

Secretary-bookcase 87" H × 42" W × 21.5" D Federal 1820 United States
Mahogany and mahogany veneer; in 4 parts; arched glazed doors above 3 short drawers and slide-out writing board; curved lid over writing area; 3 long drawers; Massachusetts; no repairs. *(See photo 129)*
Superior Quality/Fine Condition $12,000 (D)   **$10,000–$15,000**

Settee 35" H × 73" W × 24" D Painted 1830–1845 United States
Three splatbacks with shaped crest rails decorated with birds and fruit above deep plank seat; turned legs with slat stretchers; all with yellow line decoration.
Superior Quality/Fine Condition $1760 (A)   **$1200–$2400**

Settee/bed 36.5" H × 84" W × 26" D Windsor 1800–1830 United States
Painted and stenciled; fold-out hinged sleeping area; allover original yellow paint with gold and black fruit and leaf decoration; seat replaced, minor surface abrasions and enhancements.
Good Quality/Fine Condition $1600 (A)   **$1500–$3000**

Shaving stand 32.5" H × 28.5" W × 8" D Federal 1806 United States
Mahogany; in original condition, including mirror glass and brasses; branded by James G. Blake, Boston.
Superior Quality/Fine Condition $1200 (D)   **$1500–$2400**

Sideboard 41.5" H × 71" W × 26.5" D Hepplewhite 1800–1805 United States
Mahogany; serpentine top with conforming case; central convex frieze drawer over 2 recessed and convex doors flanked by 2 large doors, all with line inlaid panels; inlaid cuffed legs; original brasses; Maryland.
Very Good Quality/Average Condition $17,600 (A)   **$15,000–$25,000**

Photo 126 (left). Chest of drawers. CREDIT: ELIZABETH R. DANIEL
ANTIQUES. *Photo 127 (right). Chest of drawers.* CREDIT: RAFAEL OSONA
(See pp. 227, 228)

Photo 128 (below). Lowboy.
CREDIT: FREEMAN FINE ARTS
(See p. 230)
Photo 129 (right).
Secretary–bookcase.
CREDIT: ELIZABETH R.
DANIEL ANTIQUES *(See
p. 230)*

Sideboard 64″ L × 21.5″ H   Federal   1800–1830   United States
Satinwood and ebony inlaid mahogany; projecting center section with 1 long
drawer over pair of side cupboard doors flanked by cellarette compartments and
all raised on turned and reeded round tapering legs.
Very Good Quality/Good Condition $4,400 (A)   **$3000–$5000**

Sideboard 5′8″ L   Sheraton   1800–1830   United States
Mahogany, with lunette inlays, 6 turned and reeded legs; central section with
middle drawer flanked by 2 bottle drawers, over cabinets; flanked by cellarette
compartments. Outline of top incorporates shape of the turned legs. Completely
untouched, original finish. Provenance: Mary Ropes Trumbull of the Essex Institute, MA.
Superior Quality/Fine Condition $8,800 (A)   **$6000–$9000**

Sideboard 6′8″ L   Hepplewhite   1800–1830   United States
Inlaid mahogany, serpentine front, 6 legs with inlay and banded cuffs, beautifully
figured wood. Central section with 1 drawer flanked by bottle drawers and cutlery drawers, conforming cabinets below (lower central cabinets slightly recessed). New York. Refinished, but otherwise, no major restorations. Good size.
Superior Quality/Good Condition $20,900 (A)   **$20,000–$30,000**

Sideboard 60″ L   Classical   1830–1845   United States
Mahogany; good proportions; middle section of 1 drawer over 2 doors, flanked
by 1 drawer over 1 door on each side; figured veneer; 4 columns fitted with
ormolu capitals on paw feet.
Very Good Quality/Good Condition $1760 (A)   **$1200–$2400**

Sofa 32″ H × 76″ W × 23″ D   Hepplewhite   1800–1830   United States
Mahogany; tapered legs (4 front and 4 rear); nicely shaped back and arms; no
repairs to frame; Boston, 1800.
Superior Quality/Fine Condition $13,500 (D)   **$7500–$14,000**

Stand 28″ H × 18.5″ W × 16.5″ D   Sheraton   1800–1810   United States
One drawer; original pull; Connecticut.
Good Quality/Good Condition $2500 (D)   **$850–$3000**

Stool 18″ H × 22″ W × 14″ D   Federal   1800–1830   United States
Mahogany and mahogany veneer curule-form stool; New England.
Very Good Quality/Fine Condition $950 (D)   **$850–$1200**

Sugar chest 29″ H × 22″ W × 15″ D   Hepplewhite   1810–1815   United
States
Walnut; combination cellarette and desk; some inlay missing; hinge and lick
patches; Southern. *(See photo 130)*
Superior Quality/Good Condition $10,000 (D)   **$8000–$12,000**

Table, banquet 30″ H × 46″ W × 104″ D   Sheraton   1800–1830   United
States
Mahogany; 3 sections (dropleaf center and 2 D-shaped ends) with finely turned
and reeded legs on original casters; Philadelphia, 1800.
Superior Quality/Fine Condition $19,500 (D)   **$17,500–$26,000**

Table, card 29″ H × 36″ W × 18″ D   Hepplewhite   1780–1800   United
States
Inlaid mahogany; D-shaped with ormolu corners; string inlay on skirt and legs;
banded legs; inlay on base of skirt.
Very Good Quality/Fine Condition $6800 (D)   **$6200–$7200**

Photo 130. Sugar chest.
CREDIT: ELIZABETH R. DANIEL
ANTIQUES *(See p. 232)*

Photo 131. Card table.
CREDIT: RAFAEL OSONA *(See p. 234)*

Photo 132.
Pembroke table.
CREDIT:
ELIZABETH R.
DANIEL ANTIQUES
(See p. 235)

Table, card   29.25″ H × 36″ W × 17″ D   Hepplewhite   1790–1795   United States
Mahogany with flaming birch panels; line inlay and checker inlay; Massachusetts.
Superior Quality/Fine Condition $7000 (D)   **$9000–$12,000**

Table, card   28.5″ H × 35.5″ W × 18″ D   Hepplewhite   1800–1805   United States
Mahogany; tapering reeded legs, gouged carving in apron; hinge patches; Massachusetts.
Good Quality/Average Condition $4500 (D)   **$4500–$8000**

Table, card   29.5″ H × 35″ W × 17.5″ D   Hepplewhite   1800–1805   United States
Inlaid mahogany; D-shaped top with inset rounded corners and line-inlaid edges; frieze has oval mahogany panel within a satinwood tablet; legs are line-inlaid and cuffed with conch shell paterae; some inlay losses.
Very Good Quality/Average Condition $2800 (A)   **$2000–$6500**

Table, card   30″ H × 38″ W × 19″ D   Sheraton   1800–1810   United States
Mahogany and satinwood; Salem, Massachusetts.
Superior Quality/Good Condition $16,500 (D)   **$8000–$25,000**

Table, card   29.5″ H × 35.75″ W × 17.5″ D   Federal   1800–1830   United States
Mahogany and mahogany veneer inlaid card table; refinished; minor veneer cracking; New York; slightly warped top.
Good Quality/Good Condition $2600 (A)   **$2500–$3500**

Table, card   29″ H × 36″ W × 17.25″   Federal   1800–1830   United States
Mahogany; bow top with outset corners and hinged leaf; conforming frieze with rectangular inlaid panels of bird's-eye maple, on ring and reeded tapering legs. *(See photo 131)*
Very Good Quality/Fine Condition $3850 (A)   **$3000–$5500**

Table, card   29.75″ H × 38.5″ W × 17″ D   Federal   1800–1830   United States
Mahogany; hinged kidney-form top with double stringing on edge above a frieze skirt with patterned stringing centering inlaid shell medallions on square tapering legs with bellflower inlay; veneer damage.
Very Good Quality/Average Condition $3080 (A)   **$3000–$5500**

Table, card   29.75″ H × 38″ W × 18.6″ D   Federal   1800–1830   United States
Inlaid mahogany; top outlined in double band of stringing with conch inlay outlining skirt; 4 inlaid paterae; refinished; minor repairs; probably Baltimore.
Very Good Quality/Fine Condition $2500 (A)   **$2600–$4200**

Table, center   30″ H × 44″ W × 28″ D   Renaissance Revival   1865–1885   United States
Ebonized and gilt incised; inlaid central panel of winged griffins flanking classical urns; curving X-stretcher with central urn; casters.
Very Good Quality/Good Condition $1100 (A)   **$1000–$1500**

Table, dropleaf   45″ × 47″ open   Queen Anne   c. 1750–1780   United States
Oval; central board 15″ W; cabriole legs, pad feet; scalloped apron; mahogany; Massachusetts. *(See photo 125, p. 225)*
Superior Quality/Fine Condition $10,000 (D)   **$15,000–$18,000**

Table, dropleaf 29″ H × 46″ W × 58″ D Chippendale 1780–1800 United States
Cuban mahogany; swing leg; band along base of skirt; single board top and leaves; transitional Chippendale-Hepplewhite; Maryland, 1785.
Superior Quality/Fine Condition $2200 (D) **$2000–$3500**

Table, dropleaf 29″ H × 48″ W × 18.88″ D Hepplewhite 1780–1800 United States
Mahogany with white pine secondary wood; mahogany and boxwood banding and stringing and cuffing; dramatically tapered legs typical only of Massachusetts; refinished.
Very Good Quality/Fine Condition $2600 (D) **$2000–$3500**

Table, games 29″ H × 33″ W × 16.25″ D Chippendale 1770–1780 United States
Mahogany; top with serpentine front and sides; upper edge carved with flutes; lower edge molded; conforming skirt with beaded edge; bracketed stop-fluted legs; 2 brackets; restored; Goddard-Townsend School, Rhode Island.
Superior Quality/Good Condition $30,000 (A) **$25,000–$40,000**

Table, hall 29″ H × 42″ W × 42″ D Hepplewhite 1780–1800 United States
Inlaid mahogany; single leaf; with swing leg; inlay along base of skirt; tapered legs banded; this form is indigenous to the South—Virginia or Maryland, 1790.
Very Good Quality/Fine Condition $1450 (D) **$1200–$1600**

Table, Pembroke 29″ H × 35.5″ W × 21.5″ D Federal 1810–1815 United States
Mahogany; clover-shaped leaves, long central drawer, reeded legs, original brass terminals; New York.
Superior Quality/Fine Condition $4500 (D) **$2500–$4800**

Table, Pembroke 29″ H × 16″ W × 36″ D Hepplewhite 1800–1815 United States
Mahogany; 2 drop leaves (9″ each); crossed stretchers; drawer; in original condition with original bale handle; Massachusetts. *(See photo 132)*
Superior Quality/Fine Condition $7800 (D) **$5000–$8500**

Table, tea 28.25″ H × 24.75″ W × 18″ D Queen Anne 1700–1750 United States
Cherry and tiger maple, tray top over shaped apron with acorn drops, cabriole legs terminating in paw feet; New England.
Very Good Quality/Good Condition $25,000 (A) **$20,000–$35,000**

Table, work 30.5″ H × 28.5″ W × 17″ D Classical 1800–1830 United States
Mahogany veneered with central fitted drawer above frame drawer for wooden work bag; acanthus-carved base joining 4 splay feet with casters; original turned pulls; replaced top; Boston.
Very Good Quality/Fine Condition $1800 (A) **$1000–$1500**

Replaced top severely reduces value.—*DL*

Table, work 28.5″ H × 20″ W × 18″ D Sheraton 1800–1830 United States
Mahogany and cherry; 2 drawers with book-matched veneer on drawers fronts; brasses replaced; New York, 1820.
Very Good Quality/Fine Condition $1450 (D) **$1100–$1650**

Table, work 29″ H × 17.5″ W × 18″ D Classical 1825–1835 United States
Mahogany; rectangular top with drop leaves above 3 drawers; top drawer with fitted interior, flanked by 2 pairs of columns on plinths joined by columnar stretcher; arched, splayed supports, casters; Massachusetts.
Superior Quality/Good Condition $1650 (A) **$1200–$3500**

AMERICAN FURNITURE—WICKER

Advisors: **BILL and LEE STEWART**

Bill and Lee Stewart have specialized in handwoven wicker for nearly two decades. Their vintage wicker shop, The Collected Works, is located at 1405 Lake Ave., Wilmette, IL. For a tour of their workshop, where their master restorers preserve 19th-century techniques, please call ahead; (708) 251-6897.

In the early 19th century, wicker furniture made in the Orient was first imported to the United States. These pieces inspired some of the first designs used by American manufacturers around mid-century. Wicker became very popular in the 1870s as Americans, desiring the health benefits of fresh air, enjoyed the advantages of furniture that could easily be moved outside. Wicker was cool in the summer, providing ventilation not available in upholstered furniture. In the 1870s, the concern for the benefits of ventilation led to production of great quantities of children's furniture, especially cribs, chairs, and perambulators. Designs for all types of furniture from this period were very ornate, in keeping with Victorian tastes, with an abundance of curlicues. Most of the wicker furniture was stained rather than painted, although this period saw the introduction of reeds painted or dyed and then interwoven. People began using wicker inside on enclosed sun porches and even in living rooms, mixing it with more formal furniture. As wicker came inside, upholstered cushions were added, and wicker pieces were painted to match interiors.

Gustav Stickley began producing Mission-style wicker furniture around 1900, in designs of straight-lined simplicity that contrasted dramatically with Victorian ornamentation. "Cape Cod" wicker, which was closely woven in the Mission style, gave way to the less expensive "Bar Harbor" weave, which used a pattern of open latticework. The "Bar Harbor" style soon overtook Mission-style wicker in popularity. Within the onset of World War I, it became too costly to import rattan from the Orient, and new alternatives had to be found in America. By 1920, half of all American wicker furniture was made from fiber—tightly twisted wood pulp. Pieces made of fiber do not hold up well and are not considered collectible.

When collecting wicker, the best investments are pieces that are in their original condition. Stripping old paint can weaken wicker, so it is important to make sure the piece is structurally sound. Chairs are the easiest to find, but tables, shelves, and plant stands are also widely available, with matching sets having more value than single pieces. Natural, unpainted pieces are at a premium because of rarity. To distinguish between antique and modern wicker, weight is a good guide. Antique American wicker uses hardwoods as a base and is consequently heavier than modern Asian counterparts that use bamboo or rattan for a base. Most modern pieces use staples somewhere in the construction, while antique pieces will have only nails. The 1970s and 1980s established the collectibility of antique American wicker. There now exist specialty shops that deal only in wicker, and these can be good sources of sound antiques and advice to beginning collectors.

CURRENT TRENDS

With museums and major antique shows now including prime examples of wicker furniture in their exhibits, wicker is being properly recognized as an important element of American decorative art. Prices for fine wicker are still higher on the East and West Coasts than in the Midwest, with unique individual pieces bringing the highest dollar. Proliferation of reproductions from cheap (in all aspects) to enormously expensive have only accelerated the appreciation of fine 19th- and early-20th-century hand-woven wicker. Designs may be copied, but the quality cannot be duplicated.

CONDITION KEY

Poor Condition: wobbly, heavily painted or worn finish; missing ornamentation.

Average Condition: finish requires attention; structure needs minor strengthening; some replacement of broken spokes and weavers necessary; ornamentation incomplete.

Good Condition: original finish or professionally restored and painted; structurally sound; minor wrapping and restoration of hand weaving needed; ornamentation near perfect.

Fine Condition: original finish, or if recently painted, professionally sprayed; structurally sound, hand weaving intact; ornamentation (curlicues, "birdcages," medallions, braid, etc.) pristine.

QUALITY KEY

Good: a sturdy, useful piece with some distinguishing features, such as diamond design; aprons and arm supports on most chairs, rockers, and sofas; reed, willow, or fiber.

Very Good: design representative of the period in which item was woven; reed, willow, or fiber.

Superior: representing the finest of the wicker worker's craft, with elaborate ornamentation (Victorian or Art Nouveau), dramatic styling (Arts and Crafts or Art Deco), or classic cottage lines (turn of the century); usually reed.

REFERENCES

Richard Saunders, *Wicker Furniture: A Guide to Restoring and Collecting*, Crown, 1976, rev. 1990; this comprehensive survey of the field of wicker furniture is a delightful "must" for both novice and advanced collector.

Chair   43.5″ H   Heywood Wakefield   1885–1900   United States
Piano chair with serpentine pierced back, circular adjustable seat, cabriole legs joined by stretchers; paper label "Heywood Brothers and Wakefield Company, Wakefield, Mass. USA no. 3901″; rare.
Superior Quality/Fine Condition $750 (A)   **$600–$1200**

Chair, arm   46″ H × 26″ W × 19″ D   Victorian   1885–1900   United States
Fanciful shell back with ornate curlicue back panel, stick-and-ball work, twist trim on rosettes at end of arms; motifs include fish scaling, birdcages, lattice-work; restored arms and seat; natural finish.
Superior Quality/Fine Condition $950 (D)   **$850–$1500**

Chair, arm   36.5″ H × 27″ W × 28″ D   Victorian   1885–1900   United States
Rolled arms; rosettes at end; set-in cane seat, braid trim, full apron, brass caps on feet; reed, painted white.
Very Good Quality/Fine Condition $550 (D)   **$450–$750**

Chair, arm   38″ H × 20″ H × 17.75″ D   Victorian Revival   1885–1900   United States
Elaborate beading, including band around seat frame; hand-caned back panel; originally had hand-caned seat; birdcaging, graduated curlicues, twist-trimmed balls; horizontal figure 8's; natural. *(See photo 133)*
Very Good Quality/Fine Condition $1150 (D)   **$750–$1500**

Chaise longue   37″ H × 32.5″ W × 60″ D   Bar Harbor   1900–1910   United States
Chaise with closely woven seat, high slanted back, magazine pocket and drink holder set in wide arms; heavy braid trim, pineapple feet; natural finish; reed.
Superior Quality/Fine Condition $1750 (D)   **$1250–$2000**

Chaise longue   30″ H × 26″ W × 17″ D   Mission   1900–1910   United States
Square, padded-back armchair with spring construction and original spring cushion; wide, closely woven arms, lattice apron; fiber, painted white.
Superior Quality/Fine Condition $450 (D)   **$350–$595**

Photo 133. Arm chair. CREDIT: STEVE DONISCH. *Photo 134. Loveseat.* CREDIT: STEVE DONISCH *(See pp. 238, 239)*

Desk 42.5″ H × 37″ W × 75″ D Heywood Wakefield 1885–1900 United States
Painted wicker desk with shelved superstructure above a rectangular writing surface above single frieze drawer; splay legs joined by pierced X-stretcher; affixed label.
Very Good Quality/Fine Condition $800 (A) **$600–$1200**

Étagère 62.5″ H × 25″ W × 10.5″ D Heywood Wakefield 1815–1900 United States
Pierced scrolled crest above 4 shelves, on cabriole legs, paper label, "Heywood Bros. and Co., Gardner Mass. no. 3919."
Superior Quality/Fine Condition $1200 (A) **$750–$1500**

Lamp, floor 6′ H, shade 34″ Dia. Mission 1900–1910 United States
Reed-wrapped pole base, mushroom shade; 2 bulbs, 2 pulls; original brass fittings, rewired; some replaced spokes; painted white.
Very Good Quality/Good Condition $950 (D) **$750–$1250**

Loveseat 40″ H × 48″ W × 18″ D Victorian 1865–1885 United States
Five wrapped "pillows" surmount hairpin loops to form crest; more "pillows" punctuate hand-caned back panel; wings at top of arms end in curlicues; cane seat; brass foot caps; natural finish. *(See photo 134)*
Superior Quality/Fine Condition $1750 (D) **$1400–$2200**

Loveseat 34″ H × 49″ W × 24″ D Victorian 1885–1900 United States
Crisp lattice weave with 2-stick vertical panels; rolled arms swoop down to rosette ends; braid trim, wrapped frame; set-in cane seat; painted white; reed.
Very Good Quality/Fine Condition $1350 (D) **$1050–$1750**

Rocker, platform 46″ H × 29″ W × 27.5″ D Victorian 1885–1900
United States
Latice back with solidly woven panel, head rest, chain-of-mail trim on top of
arms, curlicues; set of steel rods activate rocking mechanisms; reed.
Superior Quality/Fine Condition $950 (D)   **$950–$1700**
Sofa 36″ H × 6′ W × 23″ D Art Deco 1910–1930 United States
Double hump back with open diamonds in tightly woven back; wide, sweeping
arms; spring construction, original cushions; reed, with natural finish.
Superior Quality/Fine Condition $1850 (D)   **$950–$2400**
Stand, music 36″ H × 17″ W × 16″ D Victorian 1895–1910 United States
Original honeytone finish with some traces of green on beads; graduated curli-
cues form crest; beads and curlicues surround 3 shelves; turned knobs, brass
feet; some wrapping on legs replaced.
Very Good Quality/Fine Condition $750 (D)   **$400–$1100**
Tea cart 30″ H × 16″ W × 30″ D Arts and Crafts 1900–1910 United
States
Reed; handled cart with lift-out serving tray, full bottom shelf, half middle shelf,
both with woven galleries; large front wheels, small back wheels; original dark
stain.
Superior Quality/Fine Condition $750 (D)   **$350–$950**

CURRENT TRENDS IN
CONTINENTAL FURNITURE

The Continental market has met with some of the vicissitudes of the
English market. Despite the fall of the dollar, Continental furniture has
remained steady in value due to price stagnation and even deflation due
to falling demand. This has allowed the remaining American dealers and
collectors to buy abroad on the Continent at prices that are not much
different in 1992 from what they were in 1989.

The only "unbuyable" area in Country French furniture, for instance,
would be Louis XV period commodes. They have soared to astronomical
levels, levels that most Americans seem unwilling to pay. Most other
types of merchandise are readily available, and at prices that have been
quite stable over the last five years. The one impact over the last five
years was the loss of the dollar against the franc; 1991 and 1992, however, have seen great price stability for the dollar, thus easing this prior
situation.

Over the past year or so, the major area of concern to dealers in the
Continental market has been the decline in market for armoires and other
very large case pieces. This decline in sales (the prices haven't dropped)
has been reported from California to Pennsylvania to the South and to
New England. This decline is, of course, due primarily to the lack of
new housing being developed throughout America over the last couple
of years. It was into new houses with ten-foot ceilings that these large

pieces were being consistently sold in the 1980s. It means that for the foreseeable future, with the American housing market deeply depressed, the sale of armoires and other large pieces will be equally depressed.

Formal French furniture still retains its position as the world's most valuable furniture—particularly labeled pieces of the 18th century. This has been true for 200 years and it probably will be true 200 years from now.

Armoire 7′ H × 53″ W × 20″ D Country 1800–1830 France
Cherrywood; flower-carved, shaped apron; molded cornice with rounded edges; fluting on corners and between doors; doors with boldly curving carved panels; cabriole feet.
Very Good Quality/Fine Condition $6000 (D)   **$5000–$6500**

Armoire 7′ H × 4′9″ W Louis XVI Provincial 1800–1830 France
Walnut; projecting cavetto-molded cornice above pair of paneled doors, flanked by rounded stiles above scalloped apron; cabriole supports; restorations; an ordinary example.
Good Quality/Average Condition $2000 (A)   **$1500–$3000**

Armoire 82″ W × 49″ W × 18.5″ D Louis XV style 1845–1865 France
Oak; double door; flower baskets, leaf and floral carvings on cabriole legs; Provincial. *(See photo 135)*
Very Good Quality/Good Condition $2720 (A)   **$5000–$7500**

> A steal! If 18th century, it would be $12,000. It is 19th century due to hinges, height, lack of originality and depth in carving, and conformity in carving. However, it's a very fine 19th-century example.—*DL*

Bérgère 44″ H Louis XV style 1845–1856 France
Gilt bérgère of the finest carving with contrasting gilding colors.
Superior Quality/Fine Condition $2400 (D)   **$1500–$2500**

Bérgères 36.5″ H × 25″ W × 21″ D Louis XV style c. 1920 France
Pair of Aubusson tapestry bérgères with cream-painted frames; yellow fabric with floral motifs; well and deeply carved.
Very Good Quality/Good Condition $2600 (D)   **$2500–$4500**

Bérgères, pair 36″ H × 22″ W Louis XV 1750–1780 France
Arched padded backs, padded scrolling arms, serpentine loose cushion seat in molded frame; cabriole legs with scroll feet; upholstered; restored. *(See photo 136)*
Very Good Quality/Good Condition $7150 (A)   **$6000–$9000**

Buffet 43.5″ H × 54″ W × 21.5″ D Louis XV 1750–1780 France
Provincial; rectangular molded top over 2 drawers, over a pair of paneled cabinet doors, raised on scroll feet; walnut; feet tipped rather crudely instead of concealed by a diagonal cut.
Very Good Quality/Average Condition $2000 (A)   **$4000–$6500**

Buffet 39″ H × 4′7″ W Louis XV 1750–1780 France
Provincial; walnut; 2 frieze drawers over pair of fluted panel cupboards flanked by fluted angles, scroll feet; foliate carved apron; steel escutcheons and hinges; restorations to top, etc.
Very Good Quality/Average Condition $4950 (A)   **$5000–$9000**

Photo 135 (left). Armoire.
CREDIT: RAFAEL OSONA
(See p. 241)
Photo 136 (below). Bérgères.
CREDIT: CHRISTIE'S EAST
(See p. 241)

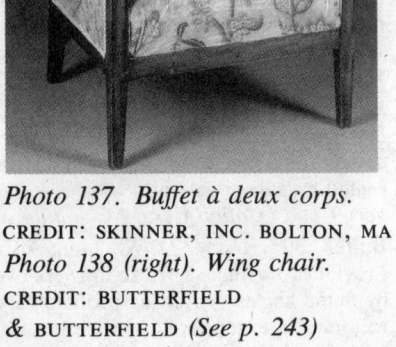

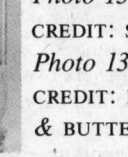

Photo 137. Buffet à deux corps.
CREDIT: SKINNER, INC. BOLTON, MA
Photo 138 (right). Wing chair.
CREDIT: BUTTERFIELD
& BUTTERFIELD *(See p. 243)*

A COLLECTION OF IVORIES

The name "collector" has a whole new meaning when considering the North Carolina lady who owns the fabulous Oriental ivory collection featured in this year's color section. At eighty-five she is as avid in the hunt for fine examples for her myriad collections as she was at sixteen when she bought her first antique.

This particular collection is focused on the ivory carvings of the Orient, especially China and Japan. These pieces were carved primarily between 1850 and 1940—a true golden age in Japan, although a period of rather boring work in China. While the Chinese slavishly copied and still copy the work of master carvers over the centuries, the Japanese went wild with creativity after opening to the West in the 1850s. The pieces shown here feature the great aspects of Japanese carving throughout this period.

In photo 1 the three carvings display a great deal of the breadth of this collection. On the left is a gentle old gardener—with a warm smile revealing some missing teeth. He carries his rake and a basket as he dodders across the yard, a turtle at his feet. He is carved of whale ivory, and his stand is walrus tusk—the dentin adding interesting natural mottling and variety to the "dirt" base.

The central figure is a group piece—a kindly grandfather playing with two children. He is teasingly holding a horse rattle out of reach and has a mask in his other hand. This gentle family scene is touched with whimsey and poignancy, eliciting warm memories in the beholder. Carved of elephant ivory, the piece shows exceptional attention to detail in the beautiful robes, which are elegant and totally realistic, both carved and scrimmed.

The figure on the right is a *fakir*, a begger who performs miracles at fairs and wanders the countryside. He is shown with his child assistant holding a basket of wriggling fish, adding to the atmosphere of anticipation and excitement that always accompanies a *fakir*. With monkeys at his feet and shoulder, he has conjured up a miniature horse and rider, which he holds in his hand.

Through careful examination you can see tiny cracks and fissures in several of these carvings. Ivory is a natural substance that loses moisture with time, cracking and splitting as that process occurs. To retard this process, a bowl or vase of water should be kept in cases where ivory is displayed and proper humidity controls maintained in a house where pieces are displayed out in the open.

The next photo (photo 2) shows a lady riding in a rickshaw. It is a moment of suspended animation; the boy pulling the rickshaw is ready to burst into life. The lady sits regally in the carriage, holding her parasol. If you examine it closely, you can see the striations of the ivory in her parasol. The wheels actually move!

Many ivories celebrate the beauty and grace of women. Such is the ivory pictured in photo 3. This lovely Japanese woman hides rather shyly behind her opened fan. She is caught in the act of turning away from the viewer, her robes twirling out as she turns. Note the design scrimmed into her robes. This kind of extra detail adds to the value of the work.

Another lady is portrayed in photo 4. She is holding a parasol and is depicted with somewhat less skill than the previous figure. Because she is carved with less sense of movement, she does not seem ready to come to life, but she's lovely nonetheless.

The elaborate scene in photo 5 shows a lady swinging, while her lady-in-waiting looks on. This remarkable piece is carved in four pieces: the two side pieces of tracery; the upper section of tracery above the swing; and the ropes holding the swing, and the two women. This is one example of many that demonstrates the intricate art of ivory carving. Imagine being able to carve the ropes, the rings holding the ropes, and the two women—all from one piece of ivory! The movement of the women's robes again gives the piece a sense of immediacy and action.

Sometimes an ivory carver leaves evidence of the original untouched piece of ivory with which he began. One can see quite clearly that the carving in photo 6 was carved from a single piece of walrus tusk, balanced on another piece. The design makes the best use of the shape of the tusk. Note in this wonderful carving how the attention to detail—the man's feet, hands, and the draping of his clothes—all give a sense of naturalism, of real life, to this piece. This is what we look for in a piece of ivory.

We see many scenes from daily life in these carvings and also depictions of animals—often portrayed with whimsey and humor. The two figures in photo 7 show a wonderful slippery mound of frogs on one side, and frogs and turtles on the other. These are playful carvings, which also suggest the productivity of nature. Mama frog and all her babies are carved from one piece of ivory.

The parrot in photo 8 is very carefully carved, with attention given to the detail of every feather. While not as humorous as the frogs (maybe parrots are inherently more boring than frogs!), it certainly captures an aspect of being a parrot. He is somewhat cumbersome and stolid, and doing an awkward bit of preening.

While one usually sees walrus, elephant, or whale ivory, in photo 9 we see a piece carved from a mastodon tooth, thus the darker color. It has not been tea stained; the dark color is a characteristic of mastodon, and the many stained cracks are another sign of mastodon and are due to its great age. Who is this gentleman? One of the immortals—snoozing.

At the same time the Japanese were doing such creative, naturalistic carving in the second half of the 19th century, the Chinese were, in general, turning out pieces of far less quality. The piece in photo 10 is an example of 19th-century Chinese work. It is a procession of horses and warriors all crammed together in a most unlifelike way. It is busy in the extreme, and an uninspired design compared to what we see from Japanese carvers.

Photo 11 shows a whole host of ivories—all the proud possession of our North Carolina collector. One interesting piece is located in the middle of the top shelf. She is a reclining nude woman, rather crudely carved. She is Chinese-carved, and not intended to be viewed as art. She is a "doctor's lady," used by a 19th-century Chinese doctor, who would hand her to an ailing woman patient, modestly hidden from his view. The patient would then mark on the ivory model where she hurt! This workaday object, one of the tools of the trade, is of interest more for social history than artistic merit.

Much more artful are the graceful women featured in photo 12. All are Japanese-carved. The mother and child feeding their rabbits is probably the most winning. It is a winsome, gentle, domestic scene. It is not only lifelike but goes one step further in eliciting an emotional response from the viewer. Japanese ivory carving at its best does not portray or elicit grand emotions, but quieter, more everyday feelings. These carvings are not idealized; instead, they are imbued with feelings of warm humanity.

Photo 13 shows another woman glimpsed in a moment of quiet revery. This carving does not represent the pinnacle of naturalism, since the detail is not as fine as in some of the pieces seen in this collection. However, it is a good example of the Japanese way of conveying a feeling in ivory. In this case we see the restful, dreamy, absent-mindedness of a woman lost in her music.

Finally, photo 14 shows another scene from daily life—basket-makers. These three people are making a basket that will be used to ship goods along the river. If we had no other record of 19th-century Japanese life apart from ivories, we could probably piece together how they lived, what they wore, and what constituted their daily occupations. The beauty of Japanese ivory carving is the charm of everyday life lovingly displayed.

Photo 1.

Photo 2.

Photo 3.

Photo 4.

Photo 5.

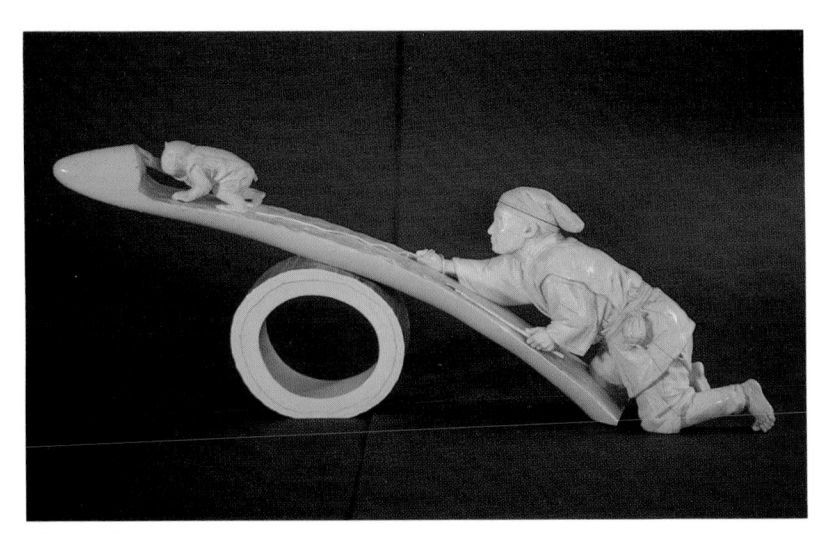

Photo 6.

Photo 7.

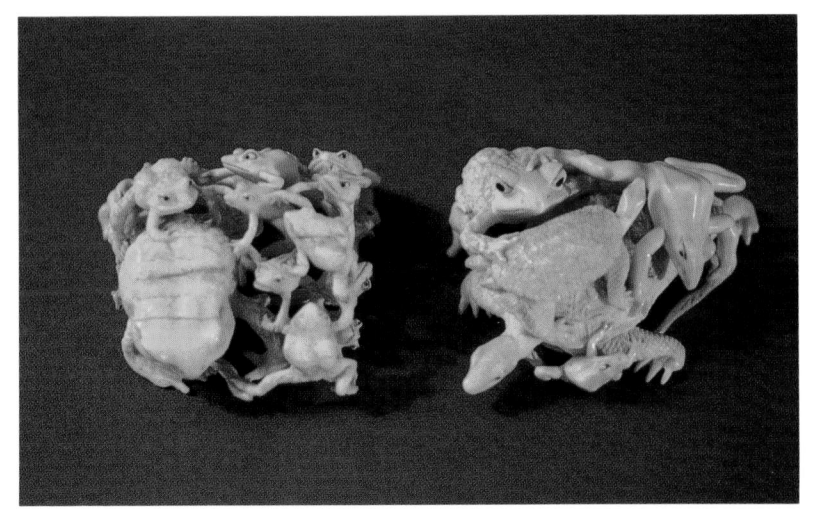

Photo 9.

Photo 8.

Photo 10.

Photo 11.

Photo 12.

Photo 13.

Photo 14.

Buffet 36.5″ H × 54″ W × 23.5″ D Country 1780–1800 France
Walnut; boldly carved with shell-carved apron and cupboard doors; 3 drawers above; steel hardware; swirled feet; reeded corners.
Superior Quality/Fine Condition $7500 (D) **$6000–$9000**

Buffet 40.5″ H × 47″ W × 21″ D Louis XV 1780–1800 France
Small, elegant, carved cherrywood buffet; fully original except tipped feet; shell-carved on base and drawers; deeply molded doors.
Very Good Quality/Good Condition $6800 (D) **$5000–$7500**

Buffet à deux corps 83.5″ H × 56″ W × 25″ D Louis XV/XVI 1780–1800 France
A grand buffet or bahut à deux corps; cherry; original glazed upper section with rare shaped shelves.
Superior Quality/Fine Condition $25,000 (D) **$15,000–$30,000**

Buffet à deux corps 95″ H × 55″ W × 21″ D Louis XV 1780–1800 France
Gray-painted; arched molded cornice above pair of cabinet doors; base with pair of cupboard doors, raised on scroll feet; repainted and restored. *(See photo 137)*
Very Good Quality/Good Condition $4250 (A) **$4500–$6500**

Bureau plat 30.25″ W × 4′6″ L Louis XV style 1900–1910 France
Gilt-bronze mounted tulipwood; top inset with faux leather writing surface and gilt-bronze corner mounts; 3-drawer apron; sides with masks; cabriole legs headed by female busts; chutes and scrolled sabots.
Very Good Quality/Fine Condition $7150 (A) **$5000–$7500**

Cabinet 60″ H × 39″ W × 12″ D Second Empire 1865–1885 France
Dark mahogany, glass sides and doors; brass trim on doors and side lights; brass-trimmed top and base; brass fluting; brass-trimmed turned feet.
Very Good Quality/Good Condition $1850 (D) **$1500–$2500**

Cabinet, display 6′11″ H × 5′8″ L Biedermeier 1800–1830 Germany
Cherry; chamfered frieze projecting over pair of 6-pane glazed doors, shelves in side; set back above base with 7 short drawers; square tapering legs, cuffed feet; vertical crack to right upper section.
Good Quality/Average Condition $3350 (A) **$3000–$5000**

Chair, arm 41″ H Régence style 1885–1900 France
Carved Country French armchair with caned seat, curved X-stretcher; walnut.
Very Good Quality/Fine Condition $1200 (D) **$750–$1250**

Chair, wing 46″ H Biedermeier 1800–1830 Germany
Walnut; high flared back with flaring arms and scrollover padded arms; square tapering legs; upholstery distressed, splits to rear leg, both rear legs with later braces. *(See photo 138)*
Very Good Quality/Average Condition $1430 (A) **$1200–$2500**

Chairs 36″ H × 17″ W × 15″ D Louis XV style 1885–1900 France
Set of 6 Country French rush-seat dining chairs; cabriole legs, shell crest, ladder backs.
Very Good Quality/Fine Condition $3200 (D) **$2500–$3500**

Chairs, dining 33″ H × 19″ W × 18″ D Louis XVI style 1865–1885 France
Set of 6 (2 arm, 4 side) with caned backs and seats; round, fluted legs; such a set may also have been used in a salon; several need recaning.
Very Good Quality/Good Condition $4000 (D) **$3500–$5000**

Chairs, set 35″ H Louis XVI style 1885–1900 France
Set of 12 carved beech chaises en cabriolet, each with ribbon-carved caned oval back and circular seat; tapering turned, stop-fluted supports; old repairs. *(See photo 139)*
Very Good Quality/Good Condition $3300 (A) **$3000–$5500**

> The price of sets of French dining chairs—a late 19th-century concept (benches preceded them)—is low due to their generally poor design, small size (very uncomfortable), and late date.—*DL*

Chairs, side 37.5″ H × 19″ W × 16″ D 1800–1830 France
Pair, fruitwood with fine bellflower and other classical motif carving; carving highlighted with gilding.
Superior Quality/Fine Condition $4100 (D) **$3000–$4800**

Chairs, side Classical 1800–1810 Russia
Pair of Circasian walnut side chairs with parcel gilt decoration, double-serpent-back splats and splayed sabre legs.
Very Good Quality/Fine Condition $3200 (D) **$2600–$3600**

Chaises Louis XVI 1780–1800 France
Pair; rectangular back rests with molded frame above flared seat; drop-fluted tapering legs headed with foliate paterae; losses to gilding; stamped J. Avisse.
Very Good Quality/Good Condition $7700 (A) **$4000–$7000**

Chest 36″ H × 47″ L Biedermeier 1800–1830 Austria
Walnut; rectangular top with bird's-eye maple veneered, beveled edge; projecting frieze drawer upheld by slender ebonized, baluster-turned stiles flanked by 2 long drawers; tapering square feet (repaired).
Very Good Quality/Good Condition $3025 (A) **$2500–$4000**

Chest 34″ H × 42″ W × 22″ D Empire 1820–1840 France
Walnut-veneered 4-drawer chest with flat bracket feet; no hardware (appropriately); veneer well matched up the front; numerous veneer patches.
Good Quality/Good Condition $1980 (D) **$1800–$2600**

Coffer 19.5″ H × 71″ W × 19″ D Louis XV 1780–1800 France
Paneled front; scalloped apron; short cabriole-leg oak coffer with lift-off top; shrinkage and typical worm damage.
Very Good Quality/Good Condition $1400 (D) **$1200–$1800**

Commode 33″ H × 45″ W Louis XV 1725–1750 France
Ormolu-mounted; rosewood crossbanded burl walnut; serpentine-edged marble top over 3 over 2 drawers; outset feet, foliate cast handles and mounts.
Superior Quality/Fine Condition $15,400 (A) **$9000–$18,000**

Commode 33″ H × 37.75″ W × 24.5″ D Louis XV 1750–1780 France
Provincial; liver and gray marble serpentine top over conforming base fitted with writing slide over 2 drawers; floral carved apron; cabriole legs; expected repairs. *(See photo 140)*
Superior Quality/Fine Condition $7150 (A) **$6000–$12,000**

Commode 34″ H × 42″ W × 22″ D Empire 1820–1840 France
Walnut veneered 4-drawer commode with flat bracket feet; no hardware (appropriately); veneer well matched up the front; numerous veneer patches.
Good Quality/Good Condition $1980 (D) **$1800–$2600**

Photo 139 (left). Louis XVI–style chairs. CREDIT: BUTTERFIELD &
BUTTERFIELD. *Photo 140 (right). Commode.* CREDIT: SKINNER, INC.,
BOLTON, MA *(See p. 244)*

Photo 141. Desk. CREDIT:
WHITEHALL AT THE VILLA,
CHAPEL HILL, NC *(See
p. 246)*

Photo 142. Fauteuil.
CREDIT: WOLF'S FINE ARTS
AUCTIONEERS *(See p. 246)*

Commode 38″ H × 4′5″ L Louis XVI style 1865–1885 France
Salmon-veined marble top; long frieze of breakfront outline, over 2 conforming drawers centered with flower-filled basket flanked by diamond parquetry; chipped cabriole legs; ormolu feet.
Good Quality/Fine Condition $2200 (A)   **$2000–$3000**

Commode Beidermeir 1830–1845 Germany
Four-drawer, highly figured walnut; marble top; feet reworked; veneer damage.
Good Quality/Average Condition $1980 (A)   **$2400–$3600**

Console desserte 34.5″ H × 38″ L Louis XVI 1780–1800 France
Brass-mounted mahogany; 3/4 pierced brass gallery enclosing white marble surface, frieze with drawer flanked by concave sides; fluted legs joined by platform stretcher with brass galleries; toupie feet.
Very Good Quality/Fine Condition $9380 (A)   **$6000–$10,000**

Desk Country 1845–1865 Italian
Writing desk on stand; apparently original reading shelf; scalloped apron; delicately curved, tapering legs. *(See photo 141)*
Good Quality/Average Condition $2200 (D)   **$2000–$3000**

Desk, slant-front 42.5″ H × 38″ W × 23.5″ D Marquetry 1865–1885 Holland
Marquetry inlaid fruitwood; ornately inlaid with scrolling flourishes and floral designs; inlaid fitted interior; 1 long over 2 short over 2 long drawers; bracket feet on casters.
Very Good Quality/Fine Condition $6325 (A)   **$4500–$7500**

Dough box 38″ H × 48″ W × 21″ D Louis XVI Provincial 1780–1800 France
Walnut; serpentine molded lifting lid opening to lined interior above 1 drawer, raised on circular turned legs joined by serpentine stretchers; carved throughout in ribbons, vines, flowers; repairs.
Superior Quality/Good Condition $1400 (A)   **$4500–$6500**

Fauteuil 36.5″ H Louis XV 1750–1780 France
Beechwood, serpentine molded crest rail, out-scrolled arms, carved serpentine seat rail, raised on molded cabriole legs ending in scrolled feet; repairs and worm damage.
Very Good Quality/Average Condition $1700 (A)   **$1800–$3500**

Fauteuil 38.5″ H × 26″ W × 23″ D Louis XV style 1865–1885 France
Well-carved, cabriole-leg walnut fauteuil with floral-carved crest rail; all legs well carved; old needlepoint coverings: floral on soft beige background.
Very Good Quality/Fine Condition $2120 (D)   **$1500–$3000**

Fauteuil 38″ H × 22″ W × 22″ D Louis XVI style 1885–1900 France
Dark fruitwood; turned, fluted legs; square back and seat with old silk upholstery; turned, fluted arm supports.
Good Quality/Good Condition $550 (D)   **$400–$640**

Fauteuil 39.5″ H × 24″ W × 23.5″ D Louis XVI style 1885–1900 France
Oval-shaped back rest with leaf border surmounted by carved flowers centered by a ribbon, with inswept arms ending in carved rams' heads; circular seat. *(See photo 142)*
Very Good Quality/Fine Condition $750 (A)   **$600–$1200**

Fauteuils 36″ H Louis Phillipe 1830–1845 France
Pair; rosewood with inlay; molded rectangular upholstered back and bowed seat; raised on sabre legs; repairs.
Very Good Quality/Good Condition $2300 (A)   **$2500–$5500**

Fauteuils 37″ H Louis XV style 1850–1860 France
Pair; carved walnut with caned backs and seats; 1 with hole in cane.
Very Good Quality/Good Condition $3800 (D)   **$3500–$4800**

Fauteuils 37″ H × 23″ W Louis XV style 1845–1865 France
Pair; walnut; caned seats and backs; 1 small damaged area in cane on 1 back; highly carved and robust form.
Very Good Quality/Good Condition $3000 (D)   **$2400–$4800**

Mirror 6′7″ H × 25.5″ W Louis XV 1750–1780 France
Well-carved gilt pine and gesso, rococo, asymmetrical pier mirror with trailing floral vine on the sides and superb cartouches top and bottom; worm damage; some touch-ups and old cracks; minor losses to gilding.
Very Good Quality/Good Condition $4500 (D)   **$3500–$12,000**

Mirror 42″ H × 22″ W 1830–1845 France
Painted white with gilt trim; rectangular.
Good Quality/Average Condition $1000 (D)   **$800–$1500**

Mirror 60″ H × 32″ W Neoclassical style 1845–1865 France
Giltwood wall mirror; flaming urn crest, egg-and-dart and beaded frame; decoration is achieved through extensive gesso over carved pine.
Very Good Quality/Fine Condition $1210 (A)   **$1200–$2500**

Mirrors 35″ H Rococo 1750–1780 Italy
Pair; giltwood girandole mirrors; cartouche shape in deeply molded frame carved and pierced with foliage and wave scrolls; regilt. *(See photo 143)*
Very Good Quality/Good Condition $3300 (A)   **$3000–$4000**

Photo 143 (left). Mirrors. CREDIT: BUTTERFIELD & BUTTERFIELD. *Photo 144 (right). Semainier.* CREDIT: BUTTERFIELD & BUTTERFIELD *(See above and p. 248)*

Salon set   61″ L canapé   Louis XV style   1845–1865   France
Carved and giltwood with original Beauvais tapestry upholstery; 2 fauteuils and a canapé; Louis XV–XVI transitional style; needs tightening.
Superior Quality/Good Condition $8000 (D)   **$6500–$10,000**

Semainier   5′3″ H × 37″ W   Louis XVI   1780–1800   France
Provincial; fruitwood; rectangular top with out-set corners above 7 drawers flanked by fluted engaged columns continuing to form toupie feet. *(See photo 144)*
Very Good Quality/Fine Condition $7150 (A)   **$5000–$7000**

Server   34″ H × 52″ W × 23″ D   Louis XV   1800–1830 France
Country French fruitwood server with cabriole legs, drawers, and paneled sides; reduced depth (as usual).
Very Good Quality/Good Condition $5300 (D)   **$3500–$6000**

Shelf, corner   26″ H   Country   1800–1830   France
Fruitwood with dark inlaid edging; curved front; open shelf above double cabinets.
Very Good Quality/Good Condition $1350 (D)   **$1000–$1500**

Table   30.5″ H × 56″ W × 32.5″ D   Country   1780–1800   France
Rare Country French Alsatian walnut table with shaped apron, cabriole legs, 2 drawers, and tip top.
Superior Quality/Fine Condition $6500 (D)   **$4500–$6500**

Table   28″ H × 27″ W × 65″ L   Provincial   1780–1800   France
Country French applewood and chestnut table with original stretchers; severely warped but untouched except finish.
Superior Quality/Average Condition $2500 (D)   **$2500–$4500**

Table   29″ H × 44.5″ W × 29″ D   Country   1800–1830   France
Country French cherry, rectangular, dropleaf table with tapered legs and rounded leaves; tipped-up legs.
Very Good Quality/Fine Condition $3000 (D)   **$2000–$3500**

Table   30″ H × 36″ W × 80″ D   Louis XV   1800–1830   France
Elegant Country French, cabriole-leg, Louis XV cherrywood dining table.
Very Good Quality/Fine Condition $5500 (D)   **$3500–$5500**

Seldom are cabriole legs original or Country taller, check with great care. Be suspicious and *expect* repairs.—*DL*

Table   31″ H × 49″ Dia.   Country   1820–1830   France
Round cherry table; 7-board top; straight leg; legs tipped; refinished; 1 board replaced.
Good Quality/Good Condition $1800 (D)   **$1500–$2400**

Table   30″ H × 47″ Dia.   Country   1820–1830   France
Round fruitwood table with drawers; repaired cracks in top; chamfered legs.
Very Good Quality/Good Condition $2000 (D)   **$1600–$2500**

Table, bedside   30″ H × 17.25″ W × 12″ D   Country   1800–1830 France
Brass-cuffed feet, heart shape carved in each side, 1 drawer at top with shelf below, tapered legs, mixed woods, Directoire.
Very Good Quality/Good Condition $800 (D)   **$600–$900**

Table, card 29″ H × 29.5″ W Rococo 1780–1800 Holland
Walnut and fruitwood marquetry; serpentine hinged top with flower-filled vase; leather playing surface, candle corners inlaid with cards; 1 long and 2 short drawers; leaf-carved, inlaid cabriole legs.
Superior Quality/Fine Condition $7150 (A) **$4000–$8000**

> While this piece has inlay of the period, later inlay work and c. 1890 copies are also very strong in the market.—*DL*

Table, dropleaf 29.5″ H × 68″ W × 86″ L Country 1800–1820 France
Very large oval cherry dining table with turned legs; brass rollers replaced; dents from meat grinders attached to ends.
Superior Quality/Good Condition $6500 (D) **$5000–$8000**

Table, dropleaf 30″ H × 70″ W × 50″ D Country 1800–1830 France
Oval, cherry, tapered legs, tipped.
Very Good Quality/Good Condition $2200 (D) **$1800–$2800**

> "Tipped" means the feet are repaired (replaced) for several inches from the floor. *Expect* this on *all* forms of Country French furniture and be very suspicious of perfect feet and legs.—*DL*

Table, side 26″ H × 24.5″ W × 18″ D Louis XV 1750–1780 France
Graceful oak cabriole-leg side table with scalloped shaped top and single drawer; drawer has been relined, and there are minor repairs to the top.
Superior Quality/Good Condition $1800 (D) **$1600–$2000**

Table, work 27″ H × 30.5″ W × 26″ D 1800–1830 France
Country French cherrywood work table with a single drawer; remarkably thick wood.
Good Quality/Good Condition $800 (D) **$700–$1200**

Vaisselier 80″ H × 64″ W × 20″ D Provincial 1800–1830 France
Country French oak vaisselier; superb carving; brass hardware; bride's piece.
Very Good Quality/Fine Condition $5200 (D) **$4800–$6500**

Vaisselier 70″ H × 43″ W × 11.6″ D Country 1865–1885 France
Fine, diminutive, painted vaisselier; 3 open shelves above open shelves, 1 drawer and 2 cupboard doors; applied brackets to shelves; paint restored.
Very Good Quality/Good Condition $2800 (D) **$2400–$3500**

CURRENT TRENDS IN ENGLISH FURNITURE

The English furniture market in the United States was wracked by the dual effects of English inflation and a declining dollar in late 1989 and on through 1991. However, 1992 has seen stagnation and deflation in the price of antiques in England, particularly the price of the middle range— that which is most commonly exported to the United States. Combined with that has been a relatively stable dollar value in the 1.70 to 1.80 range. The deflation in England caused by severe recession there, combined with a relatively stable dollar, has put the English market back on the list of choice places where American dealers buy.

Interestingly, English furniture that has been in this country for twenty or thirty years in collections, and that is now coming to market, is often ignored by American dealers. This is, of course, a great mistake, because many of these pieces are selling in the United States for far less than their wholesale value in England. In fact, the retail price of these pieces in America is often less than the wholesale value in England. This has had a dual impact. English dealers have continued to be some of the biggest buyers in America despite the recession in England in the antiques business. What these people are buying, of course, is the very finest English furniture that was imported into this country over the last twenty, thirty, forty, or even fifty years. At the same time, American dealers have, until 1992, been largely ignoring England, and further depressing the prices of English goods in that English market.

There are certain areas that have continued to be strong in the export market to America from England. Those areas are moderately priced furniture—pieces bringing from $3000 to $12,000—pieces that have been extensively reworked so their value is strictly decorative, and shipping goods furniture, which is very inexpensive furniture of the late Victorian to early 20th century.

Bookcase 8′11″ H × 7.5″ W × 24″ D   George III   1780–1800   England
Mahogany; molded cornice with domed central portion, above conforming case of 4 mullioned doors; lower-section central-frieze writing drawer; well fitted.
Very Good Quality/Fine Condition $28,000 (A)   **$25,000–$45,000**

Breakfront 84″ H × 89″ W × 15″ D   George III style   1865–1885   England
Mahogany; stepped, molded cornice above arched-mullioned glazed doors; center section with 2 short and 2 long drawers, flanked by 2 cabinets; reduced in size, glazing added; a classic conversion from a wardrobe! *(See photo 145)*
Good Quality/Good Condition $3850 (A)   **$3500–$7500**

Breakfront bookcase 88.5″ H × 53″ W × 17.5″ D   Regency   1800–1830   England
Mahogany with inlays; fitted writing drawer of satinwood; slide, adjustable shelves; stepped, molded cornice; slightly reduced in size.
Very Good Quality/Good Condition $11,500 (D)   **$9000–$15,000**

Breakfront bookcase 7′6″ H × 8′ L × 24″ D   Georgian style   c. 1990   England
Reproduction (recent!); mahogany; secretaire drawer; 13-pane glazing; remade from an antique wardrobe.
Very Good Quality/Fine Condition $6000 (D)   **$5000–$7500**

Cabinet, display 49″ H × 22.5″ W × 12″ D   1865–1885   England
Small glazed display cabinet on stand; dark oak with fine finish; cross-banded in mahogany; stand of modern date.
Very Good Quality/Fine Condition $2000 (D)   **$1500–$2500**

Cabinet, hanging   35″ H × 15″ D   George III   1780–1800   England
Small mahogany, glazed-door hanging corner cabinet with gothic glazing, rounded doors, repeating gothic arches on molding; minor old repairs to moldings.
Superior Quality/Fine Condition $4800 (D)   **$3500–$5500**

Cellarette   30″ H × 18″ W × 14″ D   Hepplewhite   1780–1800   England
Inlaid mahogany cellarette; fully original; domed top, ebony trim, brass casters.
Very Good Quality/Good Condition $2400 (D)   **$2000–$3500**

Cellarettes   22.5″ H × 26″ Dia.   George IV   1800–1830   England
Pair of mahogany cellarettes or wine coolers; each circular body with egg-and-dart rim and gadrooned lower section, with removable copper liner, on a circular spreading base.
Superior Quality/Fine Condition $19,800 (A)   **$20,000–$40,000**

Bought at Christie's in NY City by a London dealer for sale in England.—*DL*

Chair   31″ H   George II   1740–1750   England
Oak slipper chair of transitional form with flared rear feet and split yoke crest rail.
Good Quality/Good Condition $850 (D)   **$750–$1200**

An unusual but not particularly popular piece—thus the low price for a rarity.—*DL*

Chair   43″ H × 23″ W × 18″ D   Windsor   1800–1830   England
Ash and elm broad-arm Windsor with Christmas tree back; well-figured wood.
Very Good Quality/Good Condition $1400 (D)   **$700–$1500**

In yewwood, the chair sells for $2500–$3500. Sets of elm bring an average for six or more of $1500 each. Sets of six or more in yew bring $3500–$5000 each, depending on the size of the set.—*DL*

Chair, arm   40″ H × 20″ W × 20″ D   Sheraton   1800–1830   England
Mahogany; slip seat; stretcher base.
Good Quality/Good Condition $117 (A)   **$400–$600**

Chair, library   42″ H   George III   1780–1800   England
Mahogany; rectangular upholstered back with downswept arms, raised on square legs, joined by stretchers; repairs.
Good Quality/Average Condition $1100 (A)   **$1800–$4500**

Chair, side   42″ H × 18″ W × 16.5″ D   1780–1800   England
Ladderback side chair of fine mahogany; beautifully carved and well proportioned.
Very Good Quality/Fine Condition $600 (D)   **$500–$750**

Chair, wing   George II   1750–1760   England
Mahogany wing chair with cabriole legs and ball-and-claw feet; wings nicely flared; high curved crest rail.
Very Good Quality/Fine Condition $6800 (D)   **$5000–$7500**

Chair, wing   George II   1750–1760   England
Mahogany wing chair with cabriole legs and ball-and-claw feet; wings nicely flared; high curved crest rail.
Very Good Quality/Fine Condition $6800 (D)   **$5000–$7500**

Chairs   37.25″ H   George III style   1900–1940   Anglo-American
Set of 8 (6 side, 2 arm) dining chairs, with serpentine pierced and carved crest above 3 similarly carved splats, raised on molded square legs joined by stretchers.
Very Good Quality/Fine Condition $1700 (A)   **$3500–$4800**

Photo 145. Breakfront. CREDIT: GROGAN & CO. *(See p. 250)*

Photo 146 (left). Armchairs. CREDIT: SKINNER, INC., BOLTON, MA
Photo 147 (right). Chest of drawers. CREDIT: WHITEHALL AT THE
VILLA, CHAPEL HILL, NC *(See pp. 253, 254)*

Chairs, arm   36″ H   Windsor   1800–1830   England
Pair, fruitwood; small spindle-back, hoop-back Windsors with turned legs; 1 riddled with worm; 1 solid.
Good Quality/Average Condition $950 (D)   (+10% for pair)   **$1000–$1600 pr.**

Chairs, arm   42.75″ H   Provincial   1865–1885   England
Assembled set of 6 elmwood spindle-back armchairs; square backs with turned spindles, out-curved arms over rush seats; turned legs joined by stretchers; pad feet; Lancashire or Cheshire. *(See photo 146)*
Very Good Quality/Fine Condition $2200 (A)   **$4500–$6500**

Chairs, dining   38.5″ H × 20″ W × 16.5″ D   Chippendale style   1865–1885   England
Set of 8, cabriole legs, ball-and-claw feet, well-carved backs; original leather seats; beechwood.
Very Good Quality/Fine Condition $8500 (D)   **$7500–$12,000**

Chairs, side   35″ H × 16.5″ W × 16″ D   Hepplewhite style   1860–1880   England
Pair of inlaid and carved mahogany side chairs.
Very Good Quality/Good Condition $1500 (D)   **$1200–$1800**

Chairs, side   37.5″ H × 20″ W × 16.5″ D   Queen Anne style   1885–1900   England
Pair; mahogany, nicely carved backs, carved back splats.
Good Quality/Average Condition $600 (D)   **$600–$900**

Chest of drawers   37″ H × 36″ W × 20″ D   George I   1700–1750   England
Very rare and desirable size; red walnut 4-drawer chest; restoration to feet; replaced hardware.
Very Good Quality/Good Condition $6000 (D)   **$5500–$8500**

Chest of drawers   39.5″ H × 39.75″ W × 20.5″ D   George II   1700–1750   England
Walnut; crotch veneer; herringbone inlaid banding on drawer fronts; 3 small frieze drawers over 3 graduated drawers; later brasses; bracket feet.
Very Good Quality/Good Condition $2640 (A)   **$2500–$3500**

Chest of drawers   36″ H × 35.5″ W × 20.5″ D   George III   1760–1780   England
Very desirable, small-size caddy-top 4-drawer chest; rich mahogany with oak secondary; form derives from Chippendale tea caddies of the same period; 1 rear foot repaired.
Superior Quality/Fine Condition $6500 (D)   **$5000–$7500**

Chest of drawers   29″ H × 31″ W × 19.5″ D   George III   1780–1800   England
Mahogany, with rectangular cross-banded top above 4 graduated drawers on ogee bracket feet; minor restorations.
Good Quality/Good Condition $2200 (A)   **$800–$2600**

Chest of drawers   35.5″ H × 40″ W × 20″ D   George III   1780–1800   England
Mahogany; serpentine molded top over 4 graduated cockbeaded drawers; reeded quarter columns at corners; molded ogee bracket feet; some restorations.
Superior Quality/Good Condition $8500 (A)   **$7000–$12,000**

Chest of drawers 41.75″ H × 40″ W × 22.5″ D Georgian 1780–1800 England
A stamped "Gillows, Lancaster" mahogany 5-drawer chest with original hardware; minor repairs to feet. *(See photo 147)*
Very Good Quality/Good Condition $3500 (D)   **$3000–$5000**

> The Gillows family have been furniture makers in Lancaster and London since the early 1800s. By the end of the 18th century, they were furnishing some of England's finest houses. From the 1790s on, their furniture was often stamped, as this one is. This practice was not adopted by other furniture makers until Victorian times.—*DL*

Chest of drawers 47″ H × 39″ W × 17.5″ D Late Georgian 1800–1830 England
Well-proportioned mahogany chest with satinwood crossbanding (later) and straight, unmolded top.
Good Quality/Fine Condition $1650 (D)   **$2000–$2800**

Chest of drawers 41.5″ H × 37″ W × 19″ D Late Georgian 1800–1830 England
Bowfront, crossbanded mahogany chest with bracket feet; outstanding matched flame mahogany drawer fronts; feet replaced; crossbanding later.
Good Quality/Fine Condition $1230 (D)   **$2000–$2800**

> Both this chest and the one above have been enhanced by the addition of decorative inlays. Read my article on inlays—real or fake—in the introduction to this furniture section.—*DL*

Chest of drawers 45″ H × 43″ W × 23″ D Late Georgian 1800–1830 England
Bowfront tall chest with 2 over 3 drawers; tall French splay feet; well-matched veneers; deal secondary; replaced brasses and various minor repairs.
Very Good Quality/Good Condition $2600 (D)   **$1800–$2800**

Chest of drawers 43″ H × 21″ W × 21″ D Regency 1830–1845 England
Rare, fitted Wellington-type chest; mahogany; fitted for wine bottles; designed for exceptional security by safe makers Chubb & Son; elaborate lock marked "Chubb & Sons, Makers to Her Majesty."
Superior Quality/Fine Condition $3800 (D)   **$3000–$4500**

Chest-on-chest 77.5″ H × 41.5″ W × 21.5″ D George III 1750–1780 England
Solid mahogany; top section with dentil and blind fret carving, 3 short over 3 long drawers, reeded quarter columns; 3 long drawers below; carved bracket feet; original except for tiny repairs to drawer lips, bracket feet, and side molding. *(See photo 148)*
Very Good Quality/Good Condition $8500 (D)   **$6500–$9500**

Chest-on-chest 75″ H × 44″ W × 22″ D George III 1780–1800 England
Mahogany, well-proportioned, original bracket feet and crown moldings; brasses replaced; simple form with no frills; refinished.
Good Quality/Fine Condition $4050 (D)   **$4500–$6500**

Chest-on-chest 76″ H × 42.5″ W × 22″ D George III 1780–1800 England
Mahogany; in 2 parts; upper section with molded cornice above 3 thumb-molded, aligned drawers and 3 graduated drawers; lower section pull-out writing sleeve above 3 drawers; feet and mid-molding of later period.
Good Quality/Average Condition $1980 (A) **$3500–$6500**

Chest-on-chest 74″ H × 42″ W × 20.5″ D George III 1780–1800 England
Mahogany; rectangular molded cornice with canted corners above 3 short and 3 long graduated drawers; molded waist above secretaire drawer and 2 long drawers raised on later bracket feet; restorations.
Superior Quality/Good Condition $3300 (A) **$6500–$12,000**

Chest, library 42″ H × 65″ W × 12″ D Georgian 1780–1800 England
Mahogany, with central book shelves; originally from an office; bookcase flanked by 8 drawers.
Superior Quality/Fine Condition $6500 (D) **$5000–$8000**

Cupboard, hanging 37″ H × 27″ W × 16″ D George III 1780–1800 England
Oak; flat, molded, dentilated cornice and fluted frieze above panel door inlaid with star; inside shaped shelf flanked by canted, recessed panel sides; stained pine top and stand of a later period.
Good Quality/Average Condition $350 (A) **$1200–$2400**

Cupboard, hanging 48″ H × 35″ W × 17″ D Georgian 1800–1830 England
Mahogany glazed-door hanging corner cupboard; dentil molding at top above band of inlay.
Good Quality/Good Condition $3200 (D) **$3000–$4000**

Cupboard, livery 7′2″ H × 70″ W × 20″ D William and Mary 1680–1720 England
Solid yewwood; crown and waist molding restored; some old patches; brasses replaced.
Superior Quality/Good Condition $18,000 (D) **$12,000–$24,000**

Desk 29″ H × 34″ W × 22″ D Georgian 1780–1800 England
Mahogany kneehole desk; oak secondary wood; original bracket feet of ogee form; shaped kneehole apron is a small drawer; refinished. *(See photo 149)*
Very Good Quality/Good Condition $2000 (D) **$2500–$5500**

Sold wholesale—dealer to dealer—*DL*

Desk 37″ H × 24″ W × 16″ D Queen Anne style 1865–1885 England
A good writing desk on stand; walnut veneer; scalloped apron with shell carving; cabriole legs, pad feet, 1 drawer; minor veneer chips; made of a period top and Victorian base.
Very Good Quality/Good Condition $3000 (D) **$2800–$4500**

Desk 47.5″ H × 60″ L × 32″ D Victorian 1865–1885 England
Mahogany; galleried top over roll top enclosing fitted interior and adjustable writing surfaces above frieze of 3 drawers; pedestals fitted with 3 drawers each.
Very Good Quality/Good Condition $3750 (A) **$3500–$6000**

Desk, partner's 31.5″ H × 66″ W × 47.5″ D Victorian 1845–1865 England

Mahogany; hinged writing slopes revealing drawers and storage; leather writing surfaces. *(See photo 150)*

Superior Quality/Fine Condition $12,500 (D)   **$8000–$14,000**

Desk, partner's 30″ H × 5′ W × 54″ L Georgian style 1845–1865 English

Large mahogany partner's desk with pedestals and drawers on both sides; leather inlaid top; hardware and leather are new; typical alterations.

Very Good Quality/Fine Condition $9000 (D)   **$7500–$12,000**

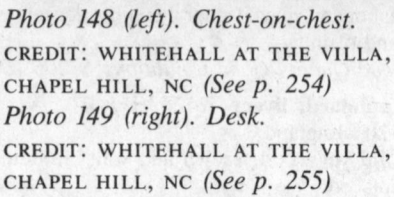

Photo 148 (left). Chest-on-chest.
CREDIT: WHITEHALL AT THE VILLA, CHAPEL HILL, NC *(See p. 254)*
Photo 149 (right). Desk.
CREDIT: WHITEHALL AT THE VILLA, CHAPEL HILL, NC *(See p. 255)*

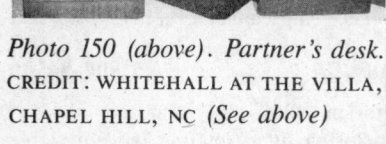

Photo 150 (above). Partner's desk.
CREDIT: WHITEHALL AT THE VILLA, CHAPEL HILL, NC *(See above)*

Photo 151 (right). Slant-front desk.
CREDIT: WESCHLER'S, WASHINGTON, DC *(See p. 257)*

Desk, pedestal 28.5" H × 40.5" W × 22" D Georgian style 1845–1865 England
Mahogany; rectangular top with inset green leather writing surface over central frieze drawer flanked by 4 graduated drawers; new bracket feet; simplified.
Good Quality/Good Condition $700 (A) **$1500–$2800**

Desk, slant-front 40.5" H × 36.25" W × 19.5" D Georgian 1760–1780 England
Red walnut with superb interior: 8 cubbyholes over 8 inlaid drawers, staircase parquet secret drawer; 4 drawers below; ogee bracket feet; rear foot rebraced; brasses replaced.
Superior Quality/Good Condition $7500 (D) **$6000–$10,000**

Desk, slant-front 41" H × 38" W × 19" D 1780–1800 England
Mahogany with flame finial and column-decorated document drawers; replaced back and hardware; numerous veneer patches.
Good Quality/Average Condition $1755 (D) **$1800–$3500**

Desk, slant-front 40" H × 36" W × 40" D Queen Anne 1700–1720 England
Oak; slant front reveals fitted interior; case below with 2 candle drawers flanking 1 long and 2 short drawers below; bracket feet; feet and hardware are old replacements.
Very Good Quality/Good Condition $1320 (A) **$2500–$5500**

Desk, slant-front 42" H × 38" W × 19.5" D George III 1800–1830 England
Mahogany, with molded, cross-banded, and crotch-veneered writing lid; green baize writing surface with pigeonholes and drawers inside; over case having 4 cockbeaded and graduated drawers, on bracket feet. *(See photo 151)*
Good Quality/Fine Condition $1750 (A) **$3500–$4500**

Lap desk Georgian 1845–1865 England
Large and elaborate brass-bound mahogany lap desk on custom-made stand.
Very Good Quality/Fine Condition $1300 (D) **$900–$1500**

Linen press 80" H × 53" W × 24" D 1780–1800 England
Mahogany with dentil molding and bracket feet; line-inlaid doors; original slides; a very fine original piece.
Superior Quality/Good Condition $3700 (D) **$4500–$6500**

Linen press 80" H × 53" W × 24" D Georgian 1780–1800 England
Mahogany with dentil molding and bracket feet; line-inlaid doors; original slides; a very fine original piece.
Superior Quality/Good Condition $3700 (D) **$4500–$6500**

Linen press 72" H 1845–1865 England
Mahogany; figured veneer on raised-panel doors; molded cornice; lower section has 2 short drawers over 1 long drawer; bracket feet. *(See photo 152)*
Good Quality/Good Condition $1375 (A) **$1200–$2400**

> Thoroughly ugly in my opinion; it brought its true value.—*DL*

Linen press Country 1845–1865 England
Upper section with 2 doors under molded cornice; lower section with 2 short over 2 long drawers; knob pulls; pine.
Good Quality/Good Condition $1100 (A) **$1200–$2400**

Lowboy 29.25″ H × 36″ W × 21″ D Queen Anne 1700–1750 England
Red walnut country lowboy with original pulls, cabriole legs, shaped skirt, restorations.
Very Good Quality/Fine Condition $5500 (D)   **$4500–$7500**

Mirrors, pair 41″ H Hepplewhite 1780–1800 England
Each a gilt oval, beaded frame with leaf at bottom, topped by carved flame finial above scrolling acanthus leaf. *(See photo 153)*
Good Quality/Good Condition $4400 (A)   **$4000–$6000**

Secretary-bookcase 92″ H × 59″ W × 21.25″ D George III 1780–1800 England
Satinwood; repeating gothic arch cornice; glazed-mullioned cabinet doors; leather-lined writing drawer flanked by 2 drawers above pair of cabinet doors; rosewood crossbanding throughout; restorations.
Very Good Quality/Good Condition $7500 (A)   **$7500–$12,000**

Secretary-bookcase 8′3″ H × 43″ W × 24″ D Chippendale 1780–1800 England
Mahogany; upper section with swan's-neck bonnet and fretwork; 2 glazed 13-panel doors; slant front opening to pigeonholes and drawers, above 4 graduated drawer bracket feet; recarved and enhanced.
Very Good Quality/Good Condition $4125 (A)   **$7500–$13,000**

Secretary-bookcase 92″ H × 45″ W × 22″ D George III 1780–1800 England
Mahogany; 13-paneled doors; interior with fine inlays; attractively designed; married, both parts period.
Good Quality/Good Condition $8000 (D)   **$7000–$12,000**

Secretary-bookcase 6′10″ H × 39″ W × 23″ D George III 1780–1800 England
Mahogany; slant-front; original bracket feet and bail and rosette brasses (very fine ornate design); intricately glazed doors with chinoiserie overtones; integral crown moldings; minor cornice and foot repairs.
Very Good Quality/Good Condition $16,000 (D)   **$12,000–$18,000**

Secretary-bookcase 94″ H × 62″ W × 22″ D Regency 1800–1830 England
Satinwood-inlaid mahogany; molded cornice over pair of arch-mullioned glazed doors; fitted interior with leather writing surface; over 3 graduated cockbeaded drawers; improved and married; bracket feet. *(See photo 154)*
Very Good Quality/Good Condition $3960 (A)   **$3500–$8500**

Server 38″ H × 44″ W × 20″ D Primitive 1800–1830 England
Ash and oak; heavy, straight legs with stretcher base; single drawer.
Good Quality/Average Condition $450 (D)   **$450–$550**

Settee 37″ H × 48″ L George III 1780–1800 England
Mahogany; arched serpentine upholstered back with out-scrolled arms over a conforming serpentine seat, raised on square molded legs with H-stretcher; silk damask.
Very Good Quality/Fine Condition $2700 (A)   **$3500–$7500**

> This has quite likely been reduced in size. Values listed assume its real. If reduced, value is $2500–$4500.—*DL*

Photo 152 (left). Linen press. CREDIT: NEAL AUCTION CO. *Photo 153 (right). Mirrors.* CREDIT: RAFAEL OSONA *(See pp. 257, 258)*

Photo 154 (left). Secretary–bookcase. CREDIT: GROGAN & CO. *Photo 155 (right, top). Sideboard.* CREDIT: CHRISTIE'S, NEW YORK. *Photo 156 (right, bottom). Card table.* CREDIT: CHRISTIE'S, NEW YORK *(See pp. 258, 260, 261)*

Settle 72″ H × 72″ W × 22.5″ D   Queen Anne   1780–1800   England
Oak; fielded panel back; scalloped seat rail; 3 pad front feet; real—not made from old church paneling!
Very Good Quality/Average Condition $1150 (D)   **$1500–$2400**

Sold in the South, where oak is virtually unsaleable!—DL

Sideboard 37″ H × 6′7″ W × 28.5″ D   George II   1780–1800   England
Mahogany, with massive oblong cross-banded top and serpentine front, above conforming recessed case with central-frieze drawer flanked by a bottle drawer and 2 shallow drawers; tapered legs, spade feet; warping.
Superior Quality/Good Condition $21,000 (A)   **$12,000–$20,000**

Sideboard 37″ H × 66″ W × 28″ D   Georgian   1780–1800   England
Mahogany; decanter drawer on right and pair of drawers on left, curving out to meet central deeper portion; large size.
Superior Quality/Fine Condition $10,500 (D)   **$9500–$12,500**

Sideboard 36.5″ H × 60″ W × 24.25″ D   George III   1800–1830   England
Mahogany; inlaid; bowed rectangular top above conforming case fitted with a drawer flanked by 2 deep drawers; square tapering legs and spade feet; restorations, later inlays.
Very Good Quality/Good Condition $8250 (A)   **$6000–$9000**

Sideboard 36.5″ H × 72″ W × 23.5″ D   George III   1800–1830   England
Mahogany; shaped top over a frieze drawer flanked by a cupboard door and cellarette drawer, on square tapering legs ending in spade feet; split top, chips, and "wrinkled" veneer; probably reduced in depth. *(See photo 155)*
Very Good Quality/Average Condition $7700 (A)   **$6500–$12,000**

Sideboard 36″ H × 54″ W × 22″ D   Hepplewhite style   1900–1910   England
Small mahogany serpentine-shaped sideboard with inlaid crossbanding.
Good Quality/Good Condition $1400 (D)   **$1800–$2800**

Sold wholesale to another dealer. This will retail easily for $2400–$2800.—DL

Sideboard 3.5″ H × 54″ W × 21″ D   Hepplewhite style   1900–1920   England
Small serpentine-front mahogany sideboard with crossbanding and line inlays; spade feet.
Good Quality/Fine Condition $3000 (D)   **$2500–$3800**

Sideboard 40″ H × 36″ W × 19.25″ D   Hepplewhite style   1930–1940   England
Small mahogany serpentine-shaped serving table or sideboard with inlaid crossbanding; lion handles; spade feet.
Very Good Quality/Fine Condition $2400 (D)   **$1800–$3000**

Sideboard 36.5″ H × 58″ W × 22″ D   Hepplewhite   1800–1830   Scotland
D-shaped, with line inlay; use of solid mahogany drawer fronts shows this to be a distinguished yet simple form most likely from Scotland.
Very Good Quality/Good Condition $4700 (D)   **$4500–$7500**

Table, architect's 32.5″ H × 42.5″ L × 26″ D   George III   1780–1800   England
Mahogany; rectangular molded hinged top raised on a ratchet support, above sides fitted with candleholders and various frieze drawers; square, tapering legs with casters.
Superior Quality/Good Condition $7500 (A)   **$5000–$9000**

Table, banquet 11.75″ L × 50″ W × 28″ H William IV 1830–1845 England
Mahogany; double pedestal; strongly turned pedestals with reeded legs and paw feet. Top altered, leaf added.
Very Good Quality/Good Condition $12,500 (D) **$9000–$13,000**

Table, breakfast ·27″ H × 4′2″ L Regency 1800–1830 England
Mahogany; square top with rounded corners, reeded edge, tilting above ring-turned vasiform standard on high, arched quadruple base; foliate gilt-bronze casters; warped top; repairs.
Good Quality/Average Condition $1650 (A) **$1500–$3000**

Table, card 28.5″ H × 31.5″ W × 15″ D George I 1700–1730 England
Walnut; fold-over top with concertina action, oblong top with outset corners above conforming frieze with herringbone cross-banded drawer; tapered legs with lappet collars, pad feet.
Very Good Quality/Fine Condition $4500 (A) **$4000–$6500**

> The drawer is a later alteration, calling the concertina action into question also. If it had no changes or alterations, it would be worth $12,000–$14,000.—*DL*

Table, card 29″ H × 35″ W × 17.25″ D George III 1800–1830 England
Mahogany, with molded, shaped serpentine hinged top enclosing a leather-lined playing surface on later cabriole legs headed by ruffled foliage on hoof feet; restorations. *(See photo 156)*
Very Good Quality/Fine Condition $3300 (A) **$3000–$4500**

> Note the subtle description that casually notes the "later" legs. Range, if real, would be $15,000–$25,000.—*DL*

Table, dining 29.25″ H × 35″ L × 47″ D Regency style 1900–1940 Anglo-American
Double-pedestal mahogany dining table with reeded edge, raised on carved baluster support on tripartite base of carved and reeded splayed legs, brass paw feet; 1 leaf.
Very Good Quality/Fine Condition $1700 (A) **$2500–$4500**

Table, dining 28″ H × 45″ W × 18.75″ D Chippendale 1750–1780 England
Santo Domingo mahogany dropleaf; 6 legs with gold molded design; 1 caster broken.
Very Good Quality/Good Condition $2100 (D) **$1800–$2800**

Table, dressing 29.5″ H × 36″ W × 22″ D George II 1700–1750 England
Pearwood and yewwood table with a cross-banded top and drawers; leaf-carved carbriole legs with pad feet; apparently original hardware; minor inlay and veneer repairs.
Superior Quality/Fine Condition $13,000 (D) **$10,000–$16,000**

Table, dropleaf 27.5″ H × 12.5″ W × 39.25″ D George III 1800–1830 England
Mahogany; the top of oval form, over a scroll-cut frieze; double gateleg design; terminating in pad feet; rough old finish.
Good Quality/Good Condition $1800 (A) **$3000–$5000**

Table, drum   30.5″ H × 38.5″ Dia.   Regency   1830–1845   England
Mahogany; boldly turned shaft with 4 reeded legs terminating in reeded cups
and casters; possibly original green tooled leather; working drawers.
Very Good Quality/Fine Condition $5500 (D)   **$4800–$6500**

Table, games   28″ H × 32.5″ W × 30″ D   George I   1700–1750   England
Concertina action; mahogany; turned legs with carved knees and pad feet; fine
color; minor veneer patches.
Superior Quality/Good Condition $9500 (D)   **$7500–$12,000**

Table, games   29″ H × 35″ W × 16.5″ D   Sheraton   1780–1800   England
Mahogany, with delicately turned legs and perfect proportions; top with line
inlays and crossbanding; slight warp in top.
Very Good Quality/Good Condition $1430 (D)   **$1200–$2000**

Table, miniature   8″ H × 8.5″ Dia.   Regency   1800–1830   England
Carved mahogany miniature tea table with piecrust top; carved, turned shaft.
Superior Quality/Fine Condition $850 (D)   **$750–$1200**

Table, Pembroke   28.5″ H × 32″ W × 19″ D   George III   1780–
1800   England
Mahogany; oak and deal secondary; original hardware; good old finish.
Good Quality/Fine Condition $2000 (D)   **$1800–$2400**

Table, Pembroke   28.25″ H × 39.75″ W × 30″ D   George III   1780–
1800   England
Mahogany, with twin-flap, cross-banded oval top above a frieze drawer fitted
with an adjustable writing surface on square tapering legs with casters.
Very Good Quality/Good Condition $3850 (A)   **$3500–$7500**

Table, Pembroke   28.5″ H × 40.5″ W × 30″ D   George III   1780–
1800   England
Mahogany, with a twin-flap serpentine top above a frieze drawer, on molded
square tapered legs and spade feet. *(See photo 157)*
Good Quality/Good Condition $1760 (A)   **$2500–$4500**

> The leaves are too deep and the feet are too short. The shaped drawer front,
> however, is a real plus.—*DL*

Table, sewing   29″ H × 20.5″ W × 14″ D   Regency   1800–1830   England
Rosewood; lozenge-form top with band of brass bellflowers, above shallow conforming frieze and pleated silk workbag; lyre supports; C-scroll legs, brass toe
caps; minor lifting of brass and veneer splits.
Superior Quality/Good Condition $6500 (A)   **$4500–$7500**

Table, side   27.5″ H × 35″ W × 26.5″ D   Chippendale   1780–
1800   England
Mahogany; rectangular molded top with cut corners above long drawer with
brass post and bail handles; chamfered, square, reeded legs; pierced corner
brackets.
Very Good Quality/Good Condition $1430 (A)   **$1800–$3500**

Table, tea   28.5″ H × 32″ W × 22″ D   George II   1750–1780   Ireland
Mahogany; with rectangular dished top above a serpentine apron raised on cab-
riole legs carved at the knees with foliage and ending in paw feet; restorations.
Superior Quality/Good Condition $6050 (A)   **$6500–$18,000**

Photo 157. Pembroke table.
CREDIT: CHRISTIE'S, NEW YORK
(See p. 262)

Photo 158. Tilt-top table.
CREDIT: WILLIAM DOYLE GALLERIES
(See below)

Remember, the selling price is exactly what the term implies: the object sold for
the stated amount in a shop or show by a dealer (D) or at auction (A).

Table, tilt-top 30″ H × 37″ Dia. Georgian England
Mahogany tea table with birdcage, gun barrel shaft and cage supports; richly
figured single-board top.
Very Good Quality/Good Condition $3500 (D)   **$3000–$5000**
Table, tilt-top 28″ H × 30.5″ Dia. George II 1750–1780 England
Mahogany; circular dished piecrust top tilts and revolves above a baluster-form
standard on tripod base with base carved as cabochons; club feet; several old
breaks to legs at pedestal. *(See photo 158)*
Very Good Quality/Good Condition $4400 (A)   **$2500–$4000**

> Note that the carving all appears to be of later date—it contours perfectly
> to the line of the legs and pedestal instead of leaping out visually and phys-
> ically.—*DL*

Table, tilt-top   29″ H × 13.5″ Dia.   George III   1780–1800   England
Mahogany, with circular galleried top tilting and turning above a baluster-form
standard, raised on tripod base carved with bellflowers and ending in cabochon
and leaf-carved club feet.
Very Good Quality/Fine Condition   *$10,500 (A)*   **$7500–$12,000**

Table, tilt-top   28″ H × 36″ Dia.   George III   1780–1800   England
Tilt-top tea or breakfast table; top is a single board nearly 36″ W; swirled urn
on pedestal; mahogany.
Very Good Quality/Fine Condition   *$5000 (D)*   **$4500–$6000**

Table, tilt-top   27″ H × 31″ Dia.   Georgian   1780–1800   England
Mahogany; piecrust top tilts and revolves above birdcage support; turned tapering standard with leaf carvings; acanthus-carved cabriole legs; carved leaf snake
feet; top and base possibly married.
Very Good Quality/Average Condition   *$1265 (A)*   **$1200–$2500**

If original, *not* married, and in fine condition, $5000!—*DL*

Table, tripod   29″ H × 26.25″ Dia.   George III   1780–1800   England
Mahogany, with scalloped top tilting above a columnar pedestal on cabriole legs
headed by foliage on shell-carved pad feet; some restorations. *(See photo 159)*
Very Good Quality/Good Condition   *$2750 (A)*   **$4500–$7500**

Was this a bargain—or a marriage? The carving *is* original—note how it
leaps off the line of the legs.—*DL*

Table, wake   29″ H × 56″ W × 17″ D   Georgian   1780–1800   Ireland
Small size; faded mahogany; oval with dropleaves, 6 legs (1 repaired); all orig-
inal, original end drawer.
Superior Quality/Average Condition   *$9000 (D)*   **$9000–$12,000**

Table, writing   30.25″ H × 42″ L × 21.5″ D   George III style   1865–
1885   England
Mahogany with inlay; brass gallery above rectangular leather-inset top; frieze
fitted with a long drawer flanked by drawers; circular, fluted legs. *(See photo
160)*
Very Good Quality/Fine Condition   *$2700 (A)*   **$2500–$3500**

Tray-on-stand   21″ H × 36″ W × 23″ D   Regency   1800–1830   England
Cartouche-form papier-mâché tray on custom-made stand of clustered bamboo
form with cross stretchers; black with gilt floral.
Superior Quality/Fine Condition   *$4500 (D)*   **$3500–$6500**

Wardrobe   7′6″ H × 60″ W × 20″ D   George III style   1885–
1900   England
Double-door mahogany 4-drawer wardrobe with fluted crown molding; superior
craftsmanship; solid mahogany secondary with drawer linings of Bermuda cedar;
shrinkage in paneled doors.
Superior Quality/Average Condition   *$3400 (D)*   **$3000–$5000**

Writing cabinet   81″ H × 23″ W × 7′ L   1830–1895   England
Mahogany gentleman's writing cabinet with central butler's desk flanked by large
storage cabinets/wardrobes.
Very Good Quality/Fine Condition   *$5400 (D)*   **$4500–$7500**

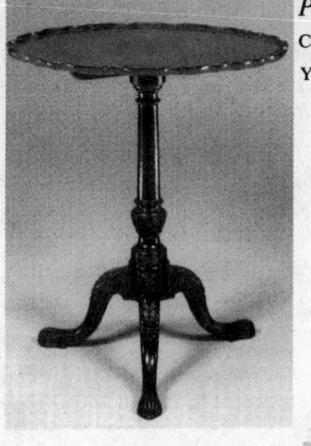

Photo 159. Tripod table.
CREDIT: CHRISTIE'S, NEW
YORK *(See p. 264)*

Photo 160. Writing table.
CREDIT: SKINNER, INC.,
BOLTON, MA *(See p. 264)*

BIBLIOGRAPHY

CARE AND RESTORATION

Kirk, John T. *Early American Furniture: How to Recognize, Evaluate, Buy and Care for the Most Beautiful Pieces*. New York: Alfred A. Knopf, 1974. Delightful, well written, "covers the waterfront."

Marsh, Moreton. *The Easy Expert in Collecting and Restoring American Antiques*. Philadelphia and New York: J. B. Lippincott, 1959. A very useful book.

Williams, Marc A. *Preserving Your Investments: Care and Maintenance of Furniture and Other Wooden Objects*. Haverhill, MA: Furniture Conservation Services.

FURNITURE

Andrews, John. *The Price Guide to English Furniture*. Woodbridge, England: Antique Collector's Club, Baron Publishing. Prices regularly updated. Superb guide to English furniture and to realistic expectations as to dates of construction.

Baillie, Clutton and Ilbert. *Britten's Old Clocks and Watches and Their Marks* (9th ed.). London: Bloomsbury Books, 1986. The single most useful book in the field.

Burton, Eric. *Dictionary of Clocks and Watches*. New York: Bonanza Books, 1963. A valuable reference for tomorrow, great assistance for appraisers.

Edwards, Ralph. *The Dictionary of English Furniture* (rev. ed.); 3 vols. Woodbridge, England: Baron Publishing, 1983. The finest anthology of English furniture.

Fairbanks, Jonathan, and Bates, Elizabeth Birdwell. *American Furniture, 1620 to the Present*. New York: Richard Marek Publishers, 1981. Good photos, good detail, well organized.

Grotz, George. *The New Antiques*. Garden City, NY: Doubleday & Co., 1970. Defines the styles of American Victorian furniture; construction information. Funny, funny, funny!

Gusler, Wallace B. *Furniture of Williamsburg and Eastern Virginia, 1710–1790*. Richmond, VA: Virginia Museum, 1979. Great—blows away many, many misconceptions about American furniture construction.

Huth, Hans. *Lacquer of the West*, Chicago: University of Chicago Press, 1971. Tough to find, absolutely fine scholarship.

Kaye, Myrna. *Fake, Fraud or Genuine*. Boston: Little, Brown, 1987.

Kirk, John T. *American Furniture and the British Tradition to 1830*. New York: Alfred A. Knopf, 1982.

———. *The Impecunious Collector's Guide to American Antiques*. New York: Alfred A. Knopf, 1975. Good, clear, precise, and highly opinionated book on early American furniture.

Loomes, Brian. *The White Dial Clock*. New York: Drake Publishers, 1975. A fine book on the previously neglected area of the white-face, painted-face tall-case clocks.

Miller, Edgar G., Jr. *American Antique Furniture: A Book for Amateurs,* 2 vols. New York: Dover Publishers, 1966. Buy these; you will use them time and again. Thousands of photos, excellent information; splendid for comparing regions, quality, etc.

Montgomery, Charles F. *American Furniture: The Federal Period*. New York: Bonanza Books, 1978. Absolutely essential to understanding this period and to making regional differentiations. The front section on inlay characteristics is worth the price!

Nutting, Wallace. *General Catalogues, Supreme Edition.* Exton, PA: Schiffer Limited, 1977. Reprint. Forget his books on antiques; this catalog's what he made in his factory. You will be surprised at what you thought were antiques but aren't.

Sack, Albert. *Fine Points of Furniture: Early American.* New York: Crown Publishers, 1977. Still essential in every library.

Santore, Charles. *The Windsor Style in America.* Philadelphia: Running Press, 1981. As thorough an analysis as you will find.

———. *The Windsor Style in American Furniture* (Vol. 2). Philadelphia: Running Press, 1987.

Smith, Nancy. *Old Furniture—Understanding the Craftsman's Art.* New York: Little, Brown, 1975. An absolutely perfect book, describes and shows photos of all furniture construction details; essential.

Verlet, Pierre. *French Furniture of the Eighteenth Century* (translated by Penelope Hunter-Stiebel). London and Charlottesville, VA: University Press of Virginia, 1991.

Viaux, Jacqueline. French Furniture (translated by Hazel Paget). New York: G.P. Putnam's Sons, 1964.

Vose, Thomas. M. *Antique American Country Furniture: A Field Guide.* New York: J. B. Lippincott, 1978. A superb paperback guide to every detail of fake versus real.

Hundreds of other valuable reference books are available. You should certainly own one of the many terminology or encyclopedia books readily available at remainder prices. You should also have an English-French dictionary and a good English dictionary. With these tools you should have the essence of a sound library for furniture.

MUSEUMS

Nearly every major and minor museum in the world has furniture in its collections. In the United States several major aggregations exist that are truly exemplary. The five listed below are representatives.

Colonial Williamsburg, Williamsburg, VA. English and American furniture and accessories of all quality levels.

Henry Ford Museum and Greenfield Village, Dearborn, MI. American formal and Country, not to mention everything else under the sun. That man liked to buy!

Museum of Early Southern Decorative Arts (MESDA), Winston-Salem, NC. A superb collection covering all of the South before about 1815.

Sturbridge Village, Sturbridge, MA. A great little collection of New England Americana.

Winterthur, Wilmington, DE. The Rolls Royce of American furniture and decorative arts collections. The "best" of formal and Country is represented.

Garden Accessories

Advisor: MARGARET LINDQUIST

Margaret (Maggie) Lindquist is co-owner and general manager of D-M Enterprises, Ltd., of Chapel Hill, North Carolina, which owns an antiques shop, Whitehall at the Villa Antiques and Fine Art, and participates in numerous antiques shows and sales throughout the country under the name David Lindquist and Associates. She is a co-author of The Official Price Guide to Garden Furniture and Accessories, *currently on the market. Address: 1213 East Franklin Street, Chapel Hill, NC 27514; (919) 942-3179.*

HISTORY AND MARKET TRENDS

Probably as soon as humankind erected shelters and moved "inside"— but certainly as early as the Babylonian, Mesopotamian, and Egyptian cultures—humans have sought to extend their dwellings to incorporate the outside as an integral part of "home." Gardens are the result of attempts to enhance, structure, and showcase nature at her finest. Garden furniture and accessories provide means by which individual tastes can be expressed.

Interest in old, antique, and reproduction garden accessories— including urns, benches, statuary, and fountains—is increasing as our society is becoming more affluent. Consequently, prices are also rising. The current emphasis is on formal homes, large yards, and formal gardens.

Besides the previously mentioned urns, benches, statuary, and fountains, garden accessories also include tables, sundials, gazebos, gates, birdbaths, and an abundance of architectural pieces readily incorporated into distinctive and imaginative gardens. Use of garden pieces is limited only by personal preferences; there are no rules or regulations in designing gardens. However, the rustic, uncultivated, abstract, and primitive looks no longer enjoy the popularity they once had.

Garden furniture and accessories are made of wood (often severely deteriorated), cast iron, wrought iron, lead, bronze, carved and cast stone, carved and cast marble, and terra cotta. What the piece is made of affects its value as much as style does.

Terra cotta, relatively fragile, is enormously popular and somewhat rare, thus commanding a premium price. Lead figures and birdbaths are bringing very high prices; even major new lead pieces sell for thousands of dollars. Cast iron is more popular than wrought iron. Naturalistic Movement styles are very hot right now. Carved marble and stone items sell well to a fairly limited audience because of their rarity (each is one of a kind). Cast marble and stone, affordable and plentiful, include vast quantities of reproductions.

19TH-CENTURY CAST- AND WROUGHT-IRON FURNITURE

The exceedingly long reign of Queen Victoria covered a wide range of furniture styles. We will deal here only with those that relate to the garden: cast- and wrought-iron styles. The basic forms for cast-iron furniture were derived from the furniture styles found indoors in the hall and in the parlor, that is, the best pieces in the house. The Victorian age borrowed heavily from preceding forms and also, as an age of extensive travel, borrowed extensively from different cultures. It was the time of Neoclassical Revival, Gothic Revival, Rococo Revival, and chinoiserie styles.

RUSTIC STYLES

Chinese furniture made from gnarled roots inspired many English adaptations, as was recorded by Matthew Darly and George Edwards in 1754. The last of the 18th-century books to illustrate such rustic furniture depicting more refined designs based on high-style urban chairs was published as *Ideas for Rustic Furniture* about 1790. This was reprinted in the 1830s, probably for manufacturers of cast-iron furniture. Some of the most ambitious designs for wrought-iron furniture are contained in Jean Tijou's 1693 *New Booke of Drawings*. During the 18th century, the number of pattern books published increased as the middle class grew in wealth. The 19th-century craftsmen drew on these designs to create styles for cast-iron furniture.

Unlike indoor furniture, outdoor cast-iron furniture drew stylistic elements from the exotic plants brought from the far ends of the earth. "Passionflower" pattern chairs and settees were characterized by the

Remember, the price range shows what the same item would sell for in average condition (left column) and fine condition (right column). Any item in poor condition has, in general, a value of 50% (or less) of that of the same item in average condition.

passionflower vine woven into a lovely scrolling, symmetrically designed back and apron.

The "Lily of the Valley" pattern seating furniture was distinctive in its broad leaves and large long-petaled flowers. Morning glories, ferns, and grapes were other motifs borrowed from the garden.

In order to disassociate cast iron from its pedestrian, utilitarian image, manufacturers were innovative in their use of decorative shapes and ornamentation. They used both form and surface "bronzing" to make cast iron appear luxurious and ornamental. The mass-produced cast-iron seating furniture evolved over a period of time from the rustic, naturalistic styles found early in the cast-iron era (mid-19th century) to the more conventionalized, artificial, or domestic curtain settees and chairs that were not made until the 1880s.

While there were some twenty-three design patterns found in cast-iron trade catalogs, we will examine only a few of the more prevalent representative styles.

The "Rustic" pattern settee *(photo 161)* first appeared in trade catalogs in the 1840s, and it continued to appear through the 1890s. Its popularity peaked by the third quarter of the 19th century, but by the early 20th century it rarely appeared in trade catalogs.

This style is composed in all parts of naturalistic, realistic elements. Oak branches, twigs, and leaves are tied together by cast-iron rope. The arms are formed by curving forks of a tree, and the legs and feet are in the form of gnarled roots. The seat itself is cast as long, curved, intertwined and knotted branches. It appears to be a wooden creation rather than iron. The best-quality rustic benches, while simplistic in design, are not stark or underembellished.

Grape-pattern settees, chairs, and tables appeared in trade catalogs by 1850 and continued to be produced and sold throughout the rest of the 19th century and into the 20th century. This style was also called "Grape," "Grapevine," "Piazza," or sometimes simply "Iron" because it was the most commonly produced cast-iron garden settee pattern. Different manufacturers produced variations of the basic design, but most examples included three-dimensional bunches of grapes surrounded by connecting leaves, vines, and twisted tendrils. The legs were cast as flowing, raised, veined leaves, bent to form a foot. The "Grape" pattern seat is a plain, flat, architectural grid. This design is more contrived than the Rustic or Naturalistic pattern.

The "Gothic" pattern is even more artificial than the "Grape" pattern. It was first patented in England in 1846 and appeared in American trade catalogs most frequently throughout the 1850s, 1860s, and 1870s. The "Gothic" pattern continued to appear into the early 20th century, gradually appearing less and less often.

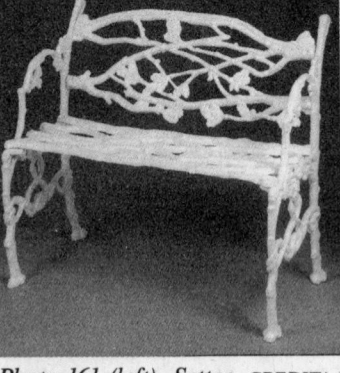 

Photo 161 (left). Settee. CREDIT: LITCHFIELD AUCTION GALLERY. *Photo 162 (right). Settee.* CREDIT: WHITEHALL AT THE VILLA, CHAPEL HILL, NC *(See p. 271 and below)*

It consisted of a curved crest rail decorated with garlands, C- and S-scrolled arms, and cabriole legs ending in volutes and small pads. The back, seat, and arms are fairly flat; the back lancets are encased in a heavy crest rail; and the elaborate pierced-design seat is framed in a rectangular border. It does have foliate motifs and flowing garlands, but they are cast in a subdued and constrained form.

The "Fern" pattern settee *(photo 162)* appeared much later than the preceding styles. It was first found in trade catalogs in the 1870s. Obviously inspired by the fern plant, which was cultivated as decoration in the Victorian home, it consists of a large center frond with other fronds forming the remainder of the back and arms. Fern fronds also decorate the legs. The whole area of vegetation is enclosed by a curving, sometimes vinelike frame that continues into vinelike legs, ending in plain rounded feet. The cast-iron ferns are amazingly realistic, with veining and curving tips. The seat is a geometrically pierced flat grid. While this pattern incorporates a naturalistic motif, it is incorporated in a regulated, controlled, artificial form.

The last and most recent style chronologically is the "Curtain" pattern settee. Also known as a panel settee, an Americus settee, a Columbus settee, or more nebulously, an ornamental lawn settee, it appeared most often in the 1880s, 1890s, and early 1900s. It is rectilinear and geometric in form, with three (or sometimes five) rectangular crested panels. The center panel is often raised, and each panel frames curvilinear foliate designs, scrolls, medallions, and rosettes. The apron consists of several inches of pierced, often Moorish, design work. The legs are fairly plain, and the arms are generally perpendicular to the seat but may curve slightly outward. The Curtain settee style has the most marked variety of style.

The other cast-iron settees varied little in design from one manufacturer to another and generally varied only as to size, finish, and price, with minor design options, but the Curtain settee could vary in the design of the skirt, seat, arms, cresting, back panels, and other elements.

The Curtain settee resembles wooden indoor furniture, particularly Renaissance Revival styles, more closely than any other cast-iron seating furniture. The foliate scrolls and shallow rosettes are extremely stylized, with little depth. The naturalism portrayed in this form is abstracted to a degree of artificiality not seen in earlier cast-iron garden furniture.

TABLES

Tables were not a part of ancient gardens, nor were they used in the garden with any regularity as a permanent fixture until the latter days of the Renaissance. Before that, when tables were needed in the garden, they were simply carried out of the house and then back in when they were no longer needed. Refectory tables from 11th-century abbeys, which were used with their benches in this way, became the prototype for today's picnic tables.

The first tables used permanently in the garden were round and marble-topped, with wrought-iron or cast-bronze pedestal bases. They were not accompanied by chairs but were used for games, with the participants standing. It was not until the late 18th and the 19th centuries that tables were regularly made for the garden for the purpose of having outdoor meals or refreshments. The earliest styles for these tables didn't move far from the Renaissance version. They consisted of a wrought-iron or cast-iron pedestal supporting a separate round marble top. Because the marble top was not attached to the base, the tops tended to get broken or otherwise lost. It is not unusual to find an antique base with no top or with a glass top that is obviously a current addition.

Rectangular marble-topped tables with some version of a four-legged base were developed to provide garden tables large enough for dining. The same style was adapted for a lower coffee table level when that level became fashionable.

During the Victorian era, cast-iron pierced-design tops were made to be attached to cast-iron legs to make single-piece tables with sets of cast-iron chairs to match. These were made in round, square, oval, and rectangular shapes and came in a variety of sizes. They were always complex in design, with a heavy emphasis on the Rococo Revival style as well as the other naturalistic styles associated with the Victorian era.

With the emphasis on simpler design during the Arts and Crafts movement came simpler, almost stark tables with matching chairs. Side tables usually had a lower shelf for storage and in all ways imitated their indoor counterparts. Cast-iron seats, table tops, and shelves were sometimes cast in an open diaper pattern, which at a glance imitates caning. This, combined with the thin legs, gives a lightness and airiness to the pieces that is very different from the heavily decorated Victorian forms.

There are some tables used in today's gardens, porches, patios, and sunrooms that were not made with the intent of gracing gardens. French baker's tables, consisting of cast-iron bases supporting marble slab tops, and baker's racks made of cast and wrought iron were meant for use to make and cool breads in a bakery. They are now commonly pressed into service on patios, decks, and sunrooms.

Architectural building artifacts are also converted to table forms for the garden. Victorian ironwork grills make attractive garden tables once wrought-iron legs are attached. Column capitals are used to provide bases for round, heavy glass tabletops.

FAKES ALERT

The entire field has two problems: constant reuse of old molds for one hundred years and loads of new, fake cast-stone pieces of high quality. In general, be suspicious of any metal item that is not inordinately heavy. Light weight usually means post-1880. Always assume that cast-stone pieces are fake and pay a sensible price. (Figures should be around $200 to $400 each.) Look for aging augmented by yogurt on all stone items (and age your own new pieces by coating them with yogurt—they develop wonderful green curd almost overnight!).

QUALITY KEY

Good Quality: a nice piece worthy of collecting but having no distinguishing characteristics.

Very Good Quality: a very good example of the type, reflecting several of the most desired characteristics.

Superior Quality: a superlative example that has nearly all of the desired characteristics of the type.

CONDITION KEY

Fine Condition: no breaks or cracks in hard metal; only minor bruises on lead items; stone in mint condition; terra cotta with only tiny, old chips. Paint: original and wonderfully peeled, chipped, and rusted (highly desired by many decorators) *or* repainted to a pleasing color without the surface having been sandblasted.

Good Condition: no breaks in hard metal; minor old repairs in hard metal; lead with bruising but not disfigured; stone and terra cotta with discoloration that is not uniform; minor chips. Paint: old or new, as above.

Average Condition: hard metal items well repaired or with very minor loss; lead items with some distortion and normal bruising; stone and terra cotta with losses. Paint: multiple layers in need of cleaning, *not* pleasing in present state or repainted.

Poor Condition: restorable and worth buying at a price *but* hard metal with unrepaired breaks, especially in legs; lead with severe distortion; stone and terra cotta damaged. Paint: do something!

Arbor 80″ H Wrought iron 1800–1830 Anglo-American
Rose arbor with ball finial.
Good Quality/Poor Condition $360 (A)   **$600–$700**

Archway 94″ H × 39.5″ W Cast iron 1845–1865 Italy
Cast and wrought iron; domed top over scroll decoration; sides with flower and leaf decoration.
Good Quality/Average Condition $600 (A)   **$550–$880**

Aviary 70.5″ H × 28.5″ W × 20″ D Wood and wire 1900–1910 France
Rectangular mesh 3-tiered aviary; carrying handles on sides; feeder boxes and perches intact; extra cleaning; slides; painted French blue.
Good Quality/Good Condition $1500 (D)   **$1200–$1800**

Bench 4′6″ L Neoclassical 1865–1885 Anglo-American
Carved stone; lentil and support form with a rectangular top decorated with egg-and-dart border and leaftip-carved apron standing on stylized lion and paw supports on stepped base.
Superior Quality/Good Condition $6655 (A)   **$6000–$7000**

Bench 38″ H × 86″ L × 22″ D Park 1865–1885 England
Twig-form cast-iron wooden park bench with wooden slat seat and back; cast-iron scrolled twig arms and accenting supports.
Good Quality/Fine Condition $1450 (D)   **$1200–$1500**

Bench 30″ H × 36″ L × 13″ D Fern pattern 1885–1900 United States
Cast-iron bench; shaped double back decorated with fern leaves, the conforming fern arms raised on decorated supports; stamped James W. Carr, Richmond, VA. *(See photo 163)*
Superior Quality/Fine Condition $7260 (A)   **$5500–$7500**

Bench 41″ L Rococo Revival 1885–1900 United States
Cast-iron bench with interlacing pierced back and scrolled sides above a pierced scroll-decorated seat, raised on cabriole legs.
Very Good Quality/Good Condition $3630 (A)   **$3000–$4000**

Bench 40″ H × 4′ W × 25″ D Rococo Revival 1900–1910 United States
Park bench with continuous strap iron on back and seat; with arms.
Good Quality/Average Condition $125 (D)   **$100–$350**

Bench 35″ H × 54″ W × 25″ D Wire 1900–1910 United States
Ornate wirework garden bench with scrolled arms and scrolled ornament on back; diapered apron; 6 legs; painted green.
Very Good Quality/Good Condition $600 (D)   **$400–$600**

Bench 45″ W Gothic style 1930–1950 United States
Cast iron; triple lyre patterned back; pierced-lace pattern seat and apron; arms; finial-topped back.
Good Quality/Average Condition $750 (D)   **$750–$950**

Benches Rustic 1885–1900 United States
Pair of cast-iron benches cast with intertwined twig and leaf back, arms, and legs; cast-iron intertwined stick seats.
Very Good Quality/Good Condition $4538 (A)   **$3500–$5500**

Benches, pair 34″ H × 41″ W × 30″ D Victorian 1845–1865 United States
Cast iron; passionflower pattern; parrot-head hand rests; 1 bench signed "The Kramer Bros. Fdy. Co. Dayton, O"; other bench unsigned and without apron.
Superior Quality/Good Condition $4000 (D)   **$3700–$4500**

Birdbath 16″ H Figural 1910–1930 England
Small lead birdbath composed of a cherub and bird seated on an inverted shell, the whole balanced on a rock.
Very Good Quality/Average Condition $1452 (A)   **$1450–$1850**

Birdbath 35″ H × 35″ Dia. Victorian 1865–1885 United States
Cast iron; naturalistic round base decorated with marsh foliage and 3 bowed-necked herons; leaf-decorated bowl with raised rib design; rim alternating with leaves.
Very Good Quality/Average Condition $1800 (D)   **$1800–$2700**

Bough pots 8.5″ L Oriental 1750–1780 China
Rare pair of Chinese export commode-form bough pots modeled in Louis XV style; bombé body molded on front with drawers, turquoise and gold trim; rococo corners; end cartouches of Chinese ladies and flora.
Superior Quality/Fine Condition $12,100 (A)   **$6000–$10,000**

Bulb pots 3.75″ H × 7.75″ L × 5″ W Chippendale style 1900–1910 China
Elegant pair of Grand Peking enamel rectangular bulb planters; original Chinese Chippendale wooden stands; yellow.
Superior Quality/Good Condition $650 (D)   **$600–$750**

Chair, arm Victorian 1885–1900 England
Fern pattern cast-iron armchair.
Good Quality/Fine Condition $500 (A)   **$400–$500**

Chair, arm 48″ H × 30″ W × 30″ D Wrought iron 1830–1845 France
Gracefully carved detail, good proportion; original paint with layers from aqua to salmon to white.
Good Quality/Fine Condition $600 (D)   **$500–$600**

Chair, arm 44.5″ H × 28″ W × 26″ D Naturalistic 1845–1865 Scotland
Tin-glazed, fired earthenware; shaped as a tree stump with branch stumps forming back and arms; foundry mark.
Very Good Quality/Good Condition $2200 (D)   **$1800–$2400**

Chair, arm 40.5″ H × 25″ W Spring steel 1930–1950 United States
Round back and seat, arched steel strips radiating out.
Good Quality/Average Condition $350 (D)   **$300–$400**

Chairs, arm 31.5″ H × 26″ W × 21″ D Naturalistic 1865–1885 United States
Pair; cast iron, Lily of the Valley pattern; old paint.
Very Good Quality/Average Condition $900 (D)   **$700–$1200**

Chairs, arm 3′ H × 26.5″ W × 23″ D Victorian 1865–1885 United States
Pair of wirework armchairs; elaborately scrolled fan back above band inter-
meshed circles; inward-curving legs ending in scrolled feet; St. Louis.
Superior Quality/Good Condition $1500 (D)   **$1250–$1700**

Chairs, arm Fern pattern 1885–1900 United States
Set of 4 cast-iron armchairs with pierced swirl-pattern seats.
Superior Quality/Fine Condition $6655 (A)   **$5500–$6500**

Chairs, set 35.5″ H × 23″ W × 21″ D Wrought iron 1930–1950 Belgium
Four armchairs; intertwined scroll back and arms; X-stretchers.
Good Quality/Average Condition $350 (D)   **$350–$450**

Consoles 28″ H × 10″ D Rococo Revival 1845–1865 France
Pair; cast and wrought iron; interlocking S- and C-scroll bases.
Superior Quality/Good Condition $2400 (D)   **$2000–$3000**

Crane 28″ H × 42″ L × 27″ W Oriental 1750–1780 Japan
Miewa-period granite sculpture; backward-facing crane, perched on a tortoise.
Good Quality/Average Condition $3500 (D)   **$3000–$5000**

Cranes 27″ H Oriental 1865–1885 China
Pair large cloisonné cranes, standing on a root, some enamel damage.
Good Quality/Poor Condition $550 (A)   **$800–$1200**

Finial 45″ H × 16″ sq. 1865–1885 United States
Cast tin cupola finial; crudely hand-crafted; square base; ribbed sphere.
Good Quality/Average Condition $325 (D)   **$275–$425**

Finial Acorn 1885–1900 United States
Pair; cast iron; raised leaf relief molding; round pedestals.
Good Quality/Average Condition $275 (D)   **$275–$350**

Finial 78″ H × 20″ W Dragon 1885–1900 United States
Cast zinc and iron architectural finial or weather vane; possibly J. W. Fiske (see
example in their catalog); dragon above decorated pole with flowers and other
ornamentation.
Very Good Quality/Average Condition $2300 (A)   **$2500–$3500**

Finial 33″ H × 14.5″ sq. 1910–1930 United States
Cast-tin roof finial; square sloped and stepped base topped by squared Hershey
Kiss–shaped body, below sphere and cone.
Good Quality/Good Condition $450 (D)   **$400–$500**

Finials 18″ H 1885–1900 United States
Cast-iron finials; cone shaped above circular baluster ''turning''; scrolled side
ornaments linking top to base.
Good Quality/Average Condition $200 (D)   **$225–$450**

Finials Pineapple 1900–1910 United States
Pair; cast iron; pineapples supported by urn-shaped flower pedal section on round
turned bases.
Good Quality/Good Condition $325 (D)   **$300–$400**

Finials 31.5″ H × 12″ sq. Obelisk 1910–1930 United States
Pair; glazed terra cotta; shaped, stepped square base.
Good Quality/Good Condition $750 (D)   **$675–$825**

Fish bowl 16.25″ H × 18.5″ Dia. Oriental 1865–1885 Japan
Porcelain, decorated on outside with lotus flowers and goldfish on plum ground;
inside with goldfish and green sea grass; carved wooden stand.
Good Quality/Average Condition $495 (A)   **$475–$675**

Fish bowls   18.1″ H × 20.75″ Dia.   Famille rose   1845–1865   China
Pair, Chinese export, painted with 2 pheasants on rock with flowering peonies and prunus with long branches and songbirds; small and large butterflies on reverse; ruyi-scepter border on base.
Superior Quality/Fine Condition $27,800 (A)   **$15,000–$20,000**

Flower basket   73″ H   Neoclassical   1885–1900   Italy
Large sandstone carved basket of flowers; simulated woven body overflowing with flowers and foliage; rising circular foot; square base; flowers broken and missing; basket chipped.
Superior Quality/Poor Condition $4000 (D)   **$7000–$9000**

Fountain   4′7″ H   Spill   1865–1885   Anglo-American
Bronze and marble; leaftip-carved font supporting a cherub whose mouth issues water; raised on a circular, swelled base standard, ending in leaftips and further raised on a plinth.
Very Good Quality/Average Condition $5140 (A)   **$5000–$6500**

Fountain   4′6″ H   Splash   1885–1900   Anglo-American
Cast stone; standing, classically draped, allegorical female supporting an urn on her shoulder that emits spray upward; standing on a round support.
Very Good Quality/Average Condition $2057 (A)   **$2000–$3000**

Fountain   6′ H   Spray   1885–1900   United States
Cast-iron 3-tiered fountain of campagna form, graduated bowls, each gadrooned with egg-and-dart decorated rims on a circular ribbed socle.
Superior Quality/Good Condition $6350 (A)   **$6000–$7000**

Fountain, spill   20″ H   Lead   1845–1865   Anglo-American
Smiling cherub dumping water out of a round jar with a rolled rim, all standing on a rocky base.
Very Good Quality/Good Condition $1155 (A)   **$880–$1320**

Fountain, spill   50″ H   Cast iron   1845–1865   United States
Two tiers; demilune, gadrooned bowls, egg-and-dart rims; winged griffin and dolphin support on round base; probably New Orleans.
Good Quality/Average Condition $1980 (A)   **$2000–$3000**

Fountain, spill   Cast iron   1865–1885   United States
Pedestal and bowl with basin; base cast with 3 bowed-necked herons and grasses; lily pad rimmed bowl.
Very Good Quality/Average Condition $3800 (D)   **$3800–$5200**

Fountain, spill   6′1″ H × 36″ Dia.   Cast iron   1865–1885   United States
Three tiers, gadrooned bowls, each progressively larger. *(See photo 164)*
Very Good Quality/Average Condition $4000 (D)   **$4000–$5000**

Fountain, spill   9′ H × 49″ Dia.   Cast iron   1865–1885   United States
Three tiers with swan fountain head over a petal-form basin over a large embossed basin with lion's-head handles; reeded pedestal; stepped plinth; white paint; by J. L. Mott.
Superior Quality/Poor Condition $8525 (A)   **$12,000–$17,000**

Fountain, spill   87″ H   Cast iron   1885–1900   United States
Three tiers, egg-and-dart rims, semilobed basins; reeded pedestal on plinth; embossed decoration, red paint; possibly by J. W. Fiske & Co. or Adams of Philadelphia.
Very Good Quality/Average Condition $4950 (A)   **$5000–$7000**

Photo 163.
Bench.
CREDIT:
SOTHEBY'S,
NEW YORK
(See p. 275)

Photo 164 (left). Spill fountain. CREDIT: WHITEHALL AT THE VILLA,
CHAPEL HILL, NC. *Photo 165 (right). Statues.* CREDIT: WHITEHALL AT
THE VILLA, CHAPEL HILL, NC *(See pp. 278, 285)*

Fountain, spill   23″ H   Figural   1910–1930   United States
Lead; winged cherub carrying a dolphin over one shoulder, standing on a round, stepped base; water flows from the dolphin's mouth, which is pointed down.
Good Quality/Average Condition $2178 (A)   **$2000–$3000**

Fountain, splash   4′ H × 37″ Dia.   Bronze   1900–1910
Unsigned bronze figure of cloven-hoofed satyr holding a wine jug tipped over arm, sitting atop a short carved pink-marble pedestal rising from shell-carved veined pink-marble basin; dark brown patina.
Very Good Quality/Fine Condition $6350 (A)   **$4500–$6500**

Fountain, splash   24″ H   Stone   1900–1910   France
Carved stone dolphins with their intertwining tails in the air.
Very Good Quality/Fine Condition $4125 (A)   **$3000–$4200**

Fountain, splash   40.5″ H × 35″ Dia.   Cast iron   1865–1885   United States
Fountain manufactured by the Kramer Bros., basin with embossed vine decoration, pedestal with winged griffins and dolphins.
Good Quality/Poor Condition $990 (A)   **$1500–$2500**

Fountain, spray   41″ H   Lead   1885–1900   England
Large classical fountain in the figure of a Grecian maid holding an urn on her shoulder, standing on a low round plinth; water sprays from the top of the urn.
Very Good Quality/Good Condition $1980 (A)   **$1500–$2500**

Fountain, spray   20″ H   Lead   1910–1930   England
Cherub fountain figure holding a jar.
Good Quality/Good Condition $1155 (A)   **$900–$1350**

Fountain, spray   25″ H   Rococo Revival   1845–1865   France
Pair; cast-iron fountains to shoot across a pool; putti amongst cattails, holding jars from which water shoots forth; break on 1 cattail and on 1 base.
Superior Quality/Good Condition $7500 (D)   **$5000–$9000**

Fountain, wall   36″ H   Marble   1650–1700   Italy
Grotesque mask surrounded by a winged ram's mask, on scroll-cast terminal; spill fountain.
Superior Quality/Good Condition $8217 (A)   **$10,000–$18,000**

Fountain, wall   43″ H × 16″ W   Gothic Revival   1900–1910   United States
Long oval shape with wide, pierced, foliate U-shaped border surmounted by a semicircular overhanging rim.
Very Good Quality/Poor Condition $1350 (A)   **$1500–$2500**

Fruit baskets   16″ H × 17″ W   Neoclassical   1900–1910   France
Pair; stone fruit baskets.
Superior Quality/Fine Condition $3000 (A)   **$2200–$3000**

Fruit baskets   24.5″ H × 17.5″ Dia.   Neoclassical   1900–1910   United States
Pair; salt-glazed terra cotta; classical lipped bowl shape filled with various fruits; square base.
Superior Quality/Good Condition $3950 (D)   **$3400–$4000**

Fruit baskets   28″ H   Neoclassical   1885–1900   Anglo-American
Pair, limestone; semilobed, ribbed, and gadrooned bodies, incised circular socle on a square base.
Very Good Quality/Fine Condition $4538 (A)   **$3500–$4500**

Gate   82″ H × 18.5″ W   1885–1900   Anglo-American
Bronze gate (1 of a pair), scroll decoration; ideal for a partition.
Good Quality/Average Condition $220 (A)   **$220–$330**

Gate 39.5″ H × 36.5″ W Cast iron 1845–1865 United States
Four spearpoint-tipped bars alternating with 3 long spearpoint-tipped bars; arched top rail.
Good Quality/Fine Condition $125 (D)   **$125–$300**

Gate 4′ H × 36″ W Victorian 1865–1885 United States
Cast iron; fancy; top pediment; original acorn gate fastener.
Good Quality/Fine Condition $175 (D)   **$150–$175**

Gate 36″ H × 26.5″ W Rococo Revival 1885–1900 United States
Cast iron; floral motif.
Good Quality/Average Condition $375 (D)   **$375–$525**

Gate 40″ H × 35″ W Rococo Revival 1910–1930 United States
Cast iron; 4 foliate symmetrical intertwining scrolled panels, simple rectangular frame, topped by wrought scrolls.
Good Quality/Average Condition $85 (D)   **$85–$125**

Gates 6′2″ H × 49″ W Rococo Revival 1885–1900 England
Pair of cast-iron gates, each rectangular panel cast with scrolling foliate swags, lyre forms, and anthemia; top and bottom quadrants divided by horizontal rectangular panels.
Good Quality/Average Condition $1815 (A)   **$1800–$2500**

Gates 6′6″ H × 5′10″ W Lattice 1910–1930 United States
Pair of wrought-iron gates; spearpointed semicircular top; body in diaper-pattern lattice, florets at each intersection.
Good Quality/Poor Condition $1250 (D)   **$1500–$2500**

Gates, driveway 84″ H × 140″ W Victorian 1865–1885 England
Pair; long spearpoint-tipped shafts above narrow strips of pierced work, above solid rectangular panels embellished with large raised medallions in the centers; painted.
Very Good Quality/Good Condition $2400 (D)   **$1500–$3000**

Gates, driveway 4′ H × 10′ W Wrought iron 1885–1900 United States
Pair; 6 tall posts, 5 with spearpoints; lower portion with short pointed posts.
Good Quality/Average Condition $550 (D)   **$550–$750**

Jardinière 25″ Dia. Ming style 1650–1700 China
Massive blue and white, heavily globular body, incurving mouth, painted vividly with 4 striding 5-clawed dragons above turbulent waves and rocks, cruciform formation clouds and fire scrolls; cracks.
Superior Quality/Good Condition $25,500 (A)   **$25,000–$35,000**

Jardinière 14″ L Famille verte 1800–1830 China
Chinese export, oval, gilded and painted in iron-red, yellow, green, black, and brown; fabulous beasts gamboling in waves; green-edged out-set base on bracket feet; signed.
Very Good Quality/Fine Condition $5140 (A)   **$3500–$5000**

Jardinière 8.5″ W Famille rose 1856–1865 China
Canton famille rose, hexagonal, painted with continuous scene: Mandarin figures at various pursuits in a garden by pavilions; iron-red and gilt-edged rim; green and white flowers and fruit.
Good Quality/Fine Condition $845 (A)   **$650–$850**

Jardinières 14″ Dia. Famille rose 1780–1800 China
Pair, octagonal, each decorated on each facet with seasonal flowers and rockwork
raised on a multicolored pierced foot of conforming section.
Superior Quality/Fine Condition $10,900 (A)   **$5000–$8000**

Jardinières 9.5″, 9.75″ Dia. Famille rose 1885–1900 China
Two similar Canton famille rose, celadon ground jardinières and stands; polychrome on exteriors with overall design of peonies and other flowers, insects
and chilong; stands similarly decorated; wear.
Very Good Quality/Average Condition $5142 (A)   **$4500–$6500**

Jardinières 8.5″, 10.25″ Dia. Oriental 1910–1930 China
Two celadon cylindrical jardinières, both carved with peonies.
Good Quality/Average Condition $1210 (A)   **$800–$1200**

Jardinières 20″ H Louis XVI style 1885–1900 France
Pair; terra cotta; each with continuous panel depicting putti in various pursuits;
rim decorated with urns flanked by putti; fitted on 4 sides with ram's heads;
losses; style copied from Sèvres porcelain.
Superior Quality/Average Condition $9075 (A)   **$9000–$1250**

Lantern 5′9″ H Oriental 1900–1910 China
Cast stone.
Good Quality/Average Condition $2665 (A)   **$2650–$3850**

Lantern 127″ H × 47″ Dia. Oriental 1700–1750 Japan
Hand-carved granite temple lantern with scrolled hexagonal roof; turnip pedi-
ment; pedestal base; Kasugata.
Superior Quality/Good Condition $10,500 (D)   **$7500–$15,000**

Lantern 73″ H × 27″ Dia. Oriental 1865–1885 Japan
Transformation-style Henkei-gata temple lantern ornately carved; hexagonal
scrolled roof, turnip pediment, pedestal base; granite.
Very Good Quality/Average Condition $5000 (D)   **$4500–$7500**

Loveseat 34″ H × 42″ W Wire work 1910–1930 United States
Camelback; scrolling embellishments on back and apron; scroll feet.
Good Quality/Good Condition $450 (D)   **$400–$500**

Plant stand 32″ H × 42″ W × 10″ D Wrought iron 1865–1885 France
Beautifully wrought with quality detail in bent iron; perfect condition.
Very Good Quality/Fine Condition $750 (D)   **$950–$1200**

Plant stand 39.5″ H Rococo Revival 1845–1865 United States
Cast iron; multitiered, composed of conjoined C-scrolls on 3 C-scrolled feet; 6
pierced circular pot trays.
Very Good Quality/Average Condition $1210 (A)   **$1200–$1800**

Plant stand 36″ H × 42″ Dia. Iron, bent 1910–1930 United States
Three tiers; semicircular and made to stand against a wall; each shelf has con-
centric slats with cross pieces.
Good Quality/Good Condition $325 (D)   **$300–$375**

Plant stand 5′2″ H × 32″ W Iron, bent 1930–1950 United States
Diaper pattern; low, ground planter; tall grid pattern; back with round diaper-
pattern planters.
Good Quality/Average Condition $500 (D)   **$500–$700**

Plant stands 7'6" L Wire 1910–1930 United States
Pair; 3 tiers with graduating rounded end tiers, designed to abut a wall; each foot curled into a spiral, each rise of each tier decorated in a different pattern of curved wire.
Superior Quality/Fine Condition $6950 (A) **$6000–$7000**

Planter 18" H × 22" Dia. 1830–1845 England
Large spherical planter; beautifully patinated and decorated pink brass.
Very Good Quality/Average Condition $850 (D) **$850–$1250**

Planter 4.5" H × 4.75" Dia. Wedgwood 1865–1885 England
Small; blue and white.
Good Quality/Average Condition $66 (D) **$65–$125**

Planter 13" H × 28.5" W × 14" D Victorian 1885–1900 England
Cast iron; acanthus leaf legs; unpainted.
Good Quality/Average Condition $325 (D) **$325–$500**

Planter 14" H Oriental 1865–1885 Japan
Naturalistic urn with applied birds and leaves in defined quadrants; incised neck; flared mouth; scrolled feet.
Very Good Quality/Fine Condition $1430 (A) **$1200–$1500**

Planter 16.75" L Oriental 1885–1900 Japan
Rectangular bronze planter, stylized elephant-head handles, bullet-chased sides, short round feet.
Good Quality/Average Condition $188 (A) **$180–$250**

Planters 3" H × 5" W × 3.5" D Oriental 1910–1930 China
Pair; "Made in China" cloisonné; quadruple-lobed bodies, trefoil feet, turquoise, polychrome floral motifs, interior nicks; probably held jade trees.
Good Quality/Good Condition $350 (D) **$250–$450**

Planters 10", 9.12" Dia. Imari style 1950–1970 Japan
Pair; painted in iron red and blue with peonies and birds; gilt highlights; with similar cachepots.
Good Quality/Fine Condition $726 (A) **$500–$750**

Sculptures Oriental 1845–1865 Japan
Pair; standing figures representing thunder and wind; ferocious faces; stylized hair, dressed as barefoot warriors, on rockwork bases; no breaks.
Very Good Quality/Fine Condition $6500 (D) **$4500–$6500**

Seat 13" H Oriental Pre-1700 China
Rare Sancai biscuit garden seat, Kangxi, drum form, applied lion mask handles between rows of bosses; body in openwork formed by conjoined circles; covered overall in green, yellow, aubergine, and white.
Superior Quality/Fine Condition $14,500 (A) **$7000–$10,000**

Seat 11" H Oriental 1750–1780 China
Small blue-and-white porcelain, drum-shaped garden seat, painted with stylized peacocks amid peonies; pierced cash medallions on sides and top surrounded by prunus borders; cracked.
Very Good Quality/Poor Condition $2722 (A) **$3300–$4400**

Seat 19" H Oriental 1885–1900 China
Famille rose single garden seat, barrel form, decorated all over with precious objects; scrolling fretwork bordered top.
Good Quality/Poor Condition $935 (A) **$1500–$2800**

Seat 12.88″ H Oriental 1885–1900 China
Chinese export blue-and-white, drum-shaped seat, painted with stylized peacocks amid peonies; pierced cash medallions on sides and top surrounded by
prunus borders; cracked.
Good Quality/Poor Condition $544 (A)   **$660–$1000**

Seat 19″ H Oriental 1885–1900 China
Chinese export "Green Fitzhugh" decorated with rows of floral clusters and
precious objects; bands of gilt bosses, sides and top pierced with cash medallions; gilt roundels; chipped edge and hairline.
Superior Quality/Average Condition $14,500 (A)   **$7000–$10,000**

Seat 13.5″ H × 11″ Dia. Neoclassical 1845–1865 France
Terra cotta; cylindrical form with classical motifs; ribbons and swags encircling
body; carrying slot chipped.
Good Quality/Average Condition $350 (D)   **$350–$450**

Seat 16″ H × 14″ Dia. Naturalistic 1865–1885 Scotland
Tin-glazed, fired earthenware seat molded in the form of a gnarled tree stump,
cleanly sawn top forms the seat.
Superior Quality/Good Condition $2100 (D)   **$1800–$2300**

Seats 1910–1930 Anglo-American
Pair of brass garden seats.
Good Quality/Average Condition $350 (D)   **$350–$450**

Settee 36″ H × 60.75″ L × 22.5″ D Victorian 1865–1885 England
Fern-pattern cast-iron settee; pierced scrollwork-design seat, fern back and arms;
signed J.PEENE RAYNE FOUNDRY ESSEX.
Very Good Quality/Good Condition $1850 (D)   **$1700–$2000**

Settee 41″ W Spring steel 1930–1950 United States
Double circle back; long oval seat, curved arms, wire legs.
Good Quality/Good Condition $550 (D)   **$500–$600**

Stag and doe 45″ H × 35″ L Oriental 1885–1900 Japan
Pair of large bronze standing deer, 1 male, 1 female, well modeled; male with
full rack of antlers.
Very Good Quality/Average Condition $4200 (D)   **$4500–$6500**

Statue 5′ H Pastoral 1780–1800 England
Carved-stone male hunter carrying game, with feet tied together around his neck;
dog seated between his feet, standing on a square base.
Superior Quality/Average Condition $10,285 (A)   **$10,000–$15,000**

Statue 32″ H Dog 1865–1885 England
Marble figure of a reclining long-haired spaniel lying on a rectangular base.
Very Good Quality/Good Condition $6655 (A)   **$6000–$7500**

Statue 28″ H × 31″ L Dog 1885–1900 United States
Seated terra-cotta retriever on terra-cotta base; crisp detailing of fur; very good
patination; stamped "Hummelstown Terra Cotta Works"; Pennsylvania.
Superior Quality/Fine Condition $9000 (D)   **$5000–$10,000**

Statue 44″ H Pastoral 1950–1970 United States
Cast-stone female figure in 19th-century apparel, leaning on staff, basket of flow-
ers on arm; standing on square base.
Very Good Quality/Good Condition $500 (D)   **$450–$650**

Statue 42″ H Pastoral 1950–1970 United States
Cast-stone male figure in 19th-century apparel posed in front of tree stump, basket of flowers on stump; natural base.
Very Good Quality/Good Condition $500 (D) **$450–$650**

Statues 24″ H Peacocks 1845–1865 Anglo-American
Pair of lead peacocks each standing on a shaped triangular base with outswept tail feathers.
Good Quality/Fine Condition $2540 (A) **$1500–$2500**

Statues 28″ L Lions 1865–1885 Anglo-American
Pair of terra-cotta recumbent male lions with raised heads, tails draped around bodies; on rectangular bases.
Superior Quality/Good Condition $6050 (A) **$4500–$6500**

Statues 22″ H Dwarves 1900–1910 Anglo-American
Group of 3 carved stone dwarves with hump backs.
Good Quality/Average Condition $1089 (A) **$1000–$1200**

Statues 33.5″ H Musicians 1900–1910 Anglo-American
Group of 4 cast-stone figures; curly haired putti playing musical instruments; standing on rocky bases; some repairs.
Very Good Quality/Average Condition $3630 (A) **$3650–$4200**

Statues 5′10″ H Allegorical 1865–1885 England
Pair of carved-limestone female figures, each in classical drapery standing barefoot, holding a flaming urn on cornucopia; on rockform base with tree stump.
Good Quality/Average Condition $4538 (A) **$4500–$6500**

Statues 5′6″ H Classical style 1865–1885 England
Pair of carved-limestone male warriors, each dressed in Roman attire with breastplate and cloak fastened at shoulder with pin, standing on paneled swelled base.
Very Good Quality/Average Condition $6655 (A) **$6000–$8000**

Statues 24″ H × 12.5″ W × 39″ L Lions 1910–1930 England
Pair; carved-limestone reclining lions, chins resting on front paws; curly manes; rectangular base; tails curled around paws.
Very Good Quality/Good Condition $4500 (D) **$3500–$5000**

Statues 29″ H Dogs 1930–1950 England
Pair of seated cast-stone dogs. *(See photo 165)*
Good Quality/Fine Condition $350 (D) **$250–$375**

Statues 24″ H Whippets 1970–1990 England
Pair of well-modeled cast-stone seated whippets.
Very Good Quality/Good Condition $250 (D) **$200–$300**

Sundial 41″ H Victorian 1865–1885 Anglo-American
Cast-iron and cast-stone armillary sphere; iron bands forming hollow sphere; reeded pedestal.
Good Quality/Fine Condition $2725 (A) **$2500–$2800**

Sundial 1910–1930 Anglo-American
Small; lead; horizontal dial plate mounted on carved-stone baluster-shaped pedestal.
Good Quality/Poor Condition $220 (A) **$400–$600**

Sundial 51″ H × 18″ Dia. 1910–1930 England
Bronze sundial with horizontal dial plate on cast-stone pedestal; shaped gnomon on flat dial, attached to baluster-form pedestal on square base.
Good Quality/Average Condition $1450 (D) **$1200–$1600**

Sundial   10″ Dia.   1910–1930   United States
Horizontal cast-iron sundial; round with raised numerals on dial; raised, angled gnomon; on unpriced machine base.
Good Quality/Good Condition $45 (D)   **$40–$65**

Table   29″ H × 36″ sq.   Louis XV style   1845–1865   France
Wrought-iron square table with gracefully curved cabriole legs; original white paint; needs welding.
Good Quality/Poor Condition $460 (D)   **$650–$1000**

Table   27″ H × 28″ Dia.   1885–1900   United States
Cast-iron center table with a circular top and scalloped border, raised on twined standard ending in triform base.
Good Quality/Average Condition $1450 (A)   **$1500–$2000**

Table, baker's   32″ H × 35″ W × 22″ D   Louis XV style   1845–1865   France
Wrought-iron baker's table base; brass ball trim; scrolling iron work; marble probably an old replacement; repainted.
Very Good Quality/Good Condition $1800 (D)   **$1500–$2500**

Table, center   31.5″ H   1885–1900   United States
Cast-iron center table with a lattice top surrounded by foliate border, raised on a rococo triform base.
Good Quality/Good Condition $1450 (A)   **$1200–$1700**

Table, conservatory   30″ H × 27″ sq.   Rococo Revival   1865–1885   United States
Cast iron; square; cabriole legs; elaborate rococo scrolling; curved X-stretcher; glass top missing.
Very Good Quality/Good Condition $1200 (D)   **$1000–$1500**

Table, dining   28″ H × 42″ W × 23″ D   1930–1950   United States
Rectangular; cast iron; scrolled and arched legs connected by a ring.
Good Quality/Fine Condition $350 (D)   **$250–$350**

Table, ice cream   30″ H × 48″ W × 30″ D   Rococo Revival   1910–1930   United States
Granite top; rectangular; cast iron.
Good Quality/Good Condition $155 (D)   **$125–$175**

Table, round   27″ H × 21.5″ Dia.   Rococo Revival   1845–1865 France
Cast iron; triple paw-foot base; heavily embossed with scrollwork; single shaft pedestal splaying out to form triple supports for round top; glass top to replace original.
Good Quality/Average Condition $375 (D)   **$375–$475**

Table, round   29″ H × 20″ Dia.   1865–1885   France
Scrolling steel; layers of old paint; new glass top replaces rusted-out thin metal original top with wrapped-around tubular edges.
Very Good Quality/Good Condition $575 (D)   **$475–$675**

Table, round   27″ H × 34″ Dia.   Gothic   1885–1900   United States
Tripod-based cast-iron table; replaced steel top.
Good Quality/Average Condition $425 (D)   **$400–$500**

Tables, pair   34″ L × 18.5″ W   Rococo Revival   1845–1865   United States
Cast iron; pierced and attenuated posts supporting marble tops; one support had welding repair; New York state.
Superior Quality/Good Condition $2000 (D)   **$1500–$2000**

Trellises 93″ H Cast iron 1900–1910 Anglo-American
Pair; fan shaped with scroll finials; white paint.
Good Quality/Fine Condition $525 (A) **$300–$500**

Urn 19.5″ H × 15.5″ Dia. Neoclassical style 1845–1865 France
Cast iron, semilobed, gadrooned, egg-and-dart rim; cracked.
Good Quality/Poor Condition $275 (D) **$450–$600**

Urn 18″ H × 16″ Dia. Neoclassical style 1845–1865 United States
Cast iron, campagna form, semilobed, gadrooned, ribbed socle, egg-and-dart
decorated rim; signed Buffalo, NY.
Good Quality/Good Condition $425 (D) **$300–$500**

Urn 21″ H × 16.5″ Dia. Neoclassical 1865–1885 United States
Cast iron, semilobed and gadrooned body; decorated rim, handles.
Good Quality/Average Condition $450 (D) **$450–$600**

Urn 25.7″ H × 22″ Dia. Victorian 1865–1885 United States
Cast iron; 3 pieces, ribbon- and swag-decorated body, egg-and-dart rim, em-
bossed bowl, round socle, stepped square base.
Very Good Quality/Average Condition $400 (D) **$400–$750**

Urn 23″ H × 18″ Dia. Neoclassical 1885–1900 United States
Cast iron; ribbed and semilobed body; egg-and-dart rim; square base.
Good Quality/Good Condition $525 (D) **$400–$750**

Urn on plinth 31″ H × 16″ Dia. Neoclassical 1845–1865 England
Cast iron; on low plinth; semilobed and gadrooned; simple socle; square base
and square plinth.
Good Quality/Average Condition $425 (D) **$425–$625**

Urn on plinth 33″ H × 26″ Dia. Neoclassical 1845–1865 France
Cast iron; on iron pedestal; unpainted; grapes and grape leaf vining around
bowl; round, ribbed socle.
Very Good Quality/Fine Condition $3400 (D) **$3000–$3500**

Urn on plinth 40.5″ H Naturalistic 1885–1900 United States
Cast-iron urn on stand; ribbed and foliate cast body flanked by foliate scrolled
handles; on a circular ribbed socle, raised on a tree-trunk-form base.
Very Good Quality/Good Condition $1694 (A) **$1500–$2000**

Urn on plinth 33.75″ H × 21″ Dia. Neoclassical 1885–1900 United States
Cast iron; on low plinth; acanthus leaf handles; ribbed rim, reservoir and socle
embossed "Prize" Pat.; Kramer Bros.
Good Quality/Good Condition $1200 (D) **$1000–$1500**

Urns on plinth 32.5″ H Campagna form 1885–1900 United States
Pair; cast iron; semilobed body decorated with birds and stylized flowers on a
round socle standing on a low plinth base stamped "Washington Iron Works,
Buffalo, NY."
Very Good Quality/Average Condition $2178 (A) **$2250–$2600**

Urns on plinths 42″ H 1845–1865 Anglo-American
Pair; carved marble; gadrooned lip, beaded and paneled frieze; body flanked by
ram heads; foliate swags; paneled and acanthus modeled base with animal heads;
paneled socle; plinth.
Superior Quality/Fine Condition $10,285 (A) **$8000–$10,000**

Urns on plinths 42″ H Neoclassical 1885–1900 Anglo-American
Pair; stone, semilobed campagna form; mask and loop handles; square plinth; 1
foot replaced.
Very Good Quality/Poor Condition $2900 (A) **$4000–$6000**

Urns on plinths Georgian style 1845–1865 England
Pair; cast iron; campagna form; gadrooned, demilune bodies, egg-and-dart rims; on plinths.
Very Good Quality/Average Condition $1000 (D)   **$1050–$1450**

Urns on plinths 4'5" H Victorian 1845–1865 England
Pair of large Codestone urns; double-strap handles; baroque mask of bearded man; raised on square plinth.
Superior Quality/Good Condition $15,400 (A)   **$12,000–$18,000**

Urns on plinths 1865–1885 United States
Pair; cast iron; "Woodbury" vase style; egg-and-dart rims; hexagonal plinths; lion and ring handles; identical to one owned by the Metropolitan Museum of Art, New York, #69.51.1.
Very Good Quality/Average Condition $3000 (D)   **$3500–$4500**

Urns on plinths 44" H × 30" W × 13" sq. Neoclassical 1865–1885 United States
Pair; cast iron; signed "Kramer Bros. Fdy Co Dayton O"; "Prize" style in Kramer catalog; acanthus leaf handles, ribbed rims, leaf-decorated reservoirs, ribbed socles.
Very Good Quality/Fine Condition $2400 (D)   **$2200–$2600**

Urns, covered 54" H × 34" Dia. 1910–1930 Anglo-American
Pair; cast zinc; flame finials; removable tops; deep inverted gadrooning; triple brackets around body.
Very Good Quality/Average Condition $4500 (D)   **$4250–$5000**

Urns, covered 20" H × 12" Dia. Neoclassical 1910–1930 United States
Set of 4; glazed terra cotta; fluted acanthus bases.
Good Quality/Average Condition $450 (D)   **$450–$650**

Urns, pair 16" H Neoclassical 1845–1865 Anglo-American
Fleur-de-pêche marble; campagna shape; molded lips; graduated socles.
Very Good Quality/Good Condition $4840 (A)   **$4000–$6000**

Urns, pair 29" H × 30" W × 18" D Regency 1800–1830 England
Lead; campagna form; leaf-cast double-scroll handles; mythological figures over leaves; circular leaf-decorated foot; minor repairs.
Superior Quality/Average Condition $17,600 (A)   **$16,000–$35,000**

Urns, pair 24" H Rococo Revival 1845–1865 England
Lead; bodies cast with panels of classical figures above acanthus; foliate scrolling handles; circular feet.
Superior Quality/Average Condition $2300 (A)   **$2500–$4500**

Urns, pair 22" H Victorian 1845–1865 England
Semilobed everted form; everted and beaded rim; body molded with fruiting vines masks and ram's head; molded circular base, stamped "Pulham's Terra Cotta, Broxbourne."
Superior Quality/Good Condition $4000 (A)   **$3000–$5000**

Urns, pair 4' H Neoclassical 1830–1845 Italy
Pair; marble, each with outswept trim above body decorated with fruit swags, masks, beading, vining, and acanthus around bowl; on a circular ribbed socle.
Superior Quality/Fine Condition $10,890 (A)   **$6000–$10,000**

Urns, pair 13.5″ H × 19″ Dia. Neoclassical 1845–1865 United States
Cast iron; bodies decorated with acanthus leaves; gadrooned socles, square bases,
leaf decorated rims; low.
Good Quality/Average Condition $250 (D) **$250–$300**

Urns, pair 31″ H × 20″ Dia. Neoclassical 1845–1865 United States
Rare; 2 parts; cast iron; simple lobed form; egg-and-dart rim, laurel leaf han-
dles; original plain square bases; signed ''Mott, NY.''
Very Good Quality/Fine Condition $2400 (D) **$1800–$2400**

Urns, pair 20.75″ H × 15″ Dia. Neoclassical 1865–1885 United States
Cast iron; campagna-form bodies, semilobed and gadrooned; rope and tassle
handles; Kramer Bros.; signed.
Good Quality/Average Condition $775 (D) **$775–$995**

Urns, pair Neoclassical 1865–1885 United States
Two-handled urns, square bases; stylized foliate designs on bodies and rims;
pierced voluté; signed ''J. W. Fiske''; unpainted; no breaks, no plinth.
Very Good Quality/Poor Condition $1750 (D) **$2200–$2800**

Urns, pair 23.5″ H Neoclassical style 1885–1900 United States
Cast iron; gadrooned semilobed body, on round socle, decorated rim, loop han-
dles.
Very Good Quality/Average Condition $2178 (A) **$2250–$2600**

Urns, pair 24″ H × 15″ Dia. Neoclassical 1865–1885 United States
Cast iron; semilobed and gadrooned; ribbed bodies and socles; egg-and-dart
decorated rim and socle top.
Good Quality/Fine Condition $1200 (D) **$950–$1200**

BIBLIOGRAPHY

BOOKS

Barrall, Julia S. *The Garden, An Illustrated History.* New York: Viking
Press, 1966.

Campbell, Marian. *An Introduction to Ironwork.* London: Her Majesty's
Stationery Office, 1985.

Fairbrother, Nan. *Men and Gardens.* New York: Knopf, 1956.

Jekyll, Gertrude. *Garden Ornament.* Woodbridge, Suffolk, England:
Baron Publishing Co., 1918; reprinted, 1982.

PERIODICALS

Journal of Garden History.

MUSEUMS

The Museum of Garden History, Lambeth Palace Road (at St. Mary-at-
Lambeth), London SWI7JU.
Winterthur Museum, DE.

Glass

This chapter is organized by the following categories:
EARLY AMERICAN BLOWN GLASS, BOTTLES AND FLASKS, GEORGIAN AND
REGENCY GLASS, SCENT BOTTLES.

EARLY AMERICAN BLOWN GLASS
Advisor: ALDA LEAKE HORNER

Alda Leake Horner is the author of The Official Price Guide to Linens,
Lace, and Other Fabrics *(New York: House of Collectibles, 1991). She
may be reached at 1213 East Franklin Street, Chapel Hill, NC 27514;
(919) 942–3179*

ORIGIN OF GLASS

We do not know when in prehistory glass was first formed. Perhaps it
was from lightning hitting sandy earth and melting it into a solid mass
of glittering glass. However, we do know from archeological finds that
in 3500 B.C. the Egyptians were glazing their pottery, and from 2000
B.C. have come decorated glass beads as sophisticated as any we can
make today. In 1984 archeologists salvaged a 14th-century B.C. ship-
wreck off the coast of Turkey, the oldest known wreck in the world. The
ship carried mostly raw materials, including glass ingots—the earliest
ever found—of cobalt blue, probably en route to Egypt. These ingots
were to be melted down and shaped into desired forms of the day.

Early finds were in the eastern Mediterranean area, particularly Egypt.
The oldest piece of formed glass extant was found in Damascus. Glass
is another gift in the long list of treasures from that area of the world.

The glass route followed the usual pattern from that area, up to Venice,
one of the first stops in Europe, and then to France, England, Germany,
and the Low Countries, into areas where the proper quality of sand could
be found and where there were workmen who were interested in learning
how to work with this metal. And then eventually glassmaking came to
America.

The first modeled pieces were perhaps made by softened rods of glass
wrapped around a mud or wet sand mold. However, the blow pipe was
used as early as the first century B.C.

WHAT IS GLASS?

Glass is basically sand that has been subjected to extreme heat to produce a liquid molten substance that can, for a brief time, be blown, molded, pressed, or rolled into objects. (Glass gaffers refer to this molten mass as "metal.")

Glass begins as dry, dull-looking sand and chemicals. Sand is refined and purified until it is 100 percent silica; then potash or soda is added to make the melting point lower and the finished glass harder. This is a very lightweight glass, sometimes referred to as window glass. It is the least expensive to make.

Then there is flint, or lead, glass. Lead is pulverized and added to the metal as approximately 24 percent of the batch. This makes the metal heavier and brighter and also softer and easier to cut. Cut glass of the Brilliant Period (1876–1910) was made from flint glass and was indeed brilliant.

Through the years other chemicals have been added to refine the glass, remove the impurities, give it properties that it did not possess earlier, and add color to the metal.

IN AMERICA

The first attempt at glassmaking in this country was at Jamestown, Virginia. Apparently, the works burned and no further attempt was made there. No shards or examples of Jamestown glass have ever been found, only written references in letters sent back to England.

The first successful glassworks in this country was in New Jersey, where Caspar Wistar founded the Caspar Wistar Glass Works at Alloway and was busy making glass as early as 1739. He migrated there from Germany because the sand was found to be the best known for glassmaking at that time. This was the very first successful glassworks in the Western Hemisphere. It was very primitive but turned out free-blown work of great clarity and brilliance because of the quality of the sand. Most of the early pieces were of a pale aquamarine color because of the purity of the sand. Many collectors today refer to all early free-blown aqua glass of great clarity as South Jersey, which in many instances is a misnomer. We really do not know because none was ever signed.

Wistar brought over four German men and their families to help, and he spared no expense to make his primitive glassworks successful. This started the flood of workers from many countries to the United States.

In the meantime, German settlers and their families had moved on to Pennsylvania, where such men as Stiegel (1763–1774) and Amelung (1785–1795) were active, and Pittsburgh glass was becoming as popular as New Jersey glass. The New England Glass Company was founded in 1818 and the Sandwich Glass Company in 1825.

From the mid-1700s to about 1830 all glass was free-blown, including necessary items such as milk bowls, porridge bowls, mugs, salt cellars, bottles, and demijohns for water and liquor.

A great change was made in the glass business when, in 1828, Deming Jarves patented the first successful pressing machine at Boston and Sandwich Glass Co. He has been given credit for inventing the pressing machine; many men worked on developing it, but he was the driving force behind perfecting it. They were working with flint glass, but during the Civil War lead was so expensive that lesser-quality glass was formulated, using soda lime. This allowed for less expensive glassware, and, with the use of the pressing machine, many patterns were developed in every conceivable form. Women could purchase complete services for the table in their favorite pattern. These patterns are still plentiful on the market and are highly collectible.

It is difficult to trace the history of any one company because of the intermarriages of the various families, many switching allegiances as they married into a family and then started new companies. Many carried the patterns they had developed with them, so you will see many patterns that are made by more than one company and at different times. This makes careful study a very important factor to the collector because, as noted, none of the early glass was signed. With the advent of modern-day manufacturing technology many of the old patterns have been reproduced, and that is another headache for the serious collector!

GLASS CARE

Today's inexpensive glass may be washed in the dishwasher—but not crystal or antique glass. Dishwashing detergents will etch and discolor the surface of the glass, and the extreme differences of water temperature will cause it to shatter. *Always hand-wash your fine glassware.* One of the greatest hazards in the sink is the water faucet nozzle. Be sure to turn it away or put on a rubber nozzle guard. *Be sure to place a turkish towel in the sink;* it will protect the glass if it is accidentally dropped. Always use a plastic dishpan. Wash in tepid water with a mild detergent, wash only one item at a time, and rinse well in the same tepid water. Dry only with a soft cloth—never paper—to prevent scratches, and when dusting use only a soft cloth.

To remove stains use an ammonia solution, or if the object is badly stained, swirl a few grains of dry rice and a little water in it. If this doesn't work, fill the stained piece with warm water, break up a denture cleansing tablet in it, and let it soak overnight. If all this fails, take it to a professional!

Be sure to let glassware come to room temperature before using. Never use glassware for extremely cold or hot foods—glass cannot withstand sudden temperature changes.

Never store glass on the top rim as this is the most fragile area of the object. If you must stack plates and other flat objects, be sure to place pads between them. Never let pieces touch each other on the storage shelves; vibrations will cause small chips and, in some instances, cracks.

BIBLIOGRAPHY

Barlow, Raymond E., and Joan E. Kaiser. *A Guide to Sandwich Glass.* (5 vols.). Windham, NH: Barlow-Kaiser, 1985.

Innes, Lowell. *Pittsburgh Glass, 1797–1891: A History and Guide for Collectors.* Boston: Houghton Mifflin, 1976.

McKearin, Helen and George S. *Two Hundred Years of Blown Glass.* New York: Bonanza Books, 1959.

———. *American Glass.* New York: Crown, 1971.

Pepper, Adeline. *The Glass Gaffers of New Jersey and Their Creations from 1739 to the Present.* New York: Charles Scribner's Sons. (Winner of Award of Merit by American Association for State and Local History.)

Wilson, Kenneth M. *New England Glass and Glassmaking.* New York: Thomas Y. Crowell, 1972. (The Corning Museum of Glass.)

Ball   6″ Dia.   1865–1885   United States
Amethyst; blown; hanging chain from open pontil.
Good Quality/Good Condition $60 (A)   **$50–$85**

Bar bottle   12.25″ H   1830–1845   United States
Cobalt blue; applied lip; silverplate cork stopper.
Good Quality/Good Condition $135 (A)   **$110–$150**

Bar bottle   7.5″ H   1830–1845   United States
Violet-cobalt blue; traces of gilt label "Holland"; wear; flared lip is chipped.
Good Quality/Poor Condition $25 (A)   **$35–$50**

Bell jar   12.75″ H   1860–1880   United States
Clear blown; opening in top.
Good Quality/Average Condition $165 (A)   **$150–$200**

Bottle   3.5″ H   1845–1865   United States
Miniature; amber, blown; globular applied lip; Midwestern; minor wear and sickness.
Very Good Quality/Average Condition $555 (A)   **$500–$700**

Bowl   2.2″ H × 14″ Dia.   1830–1845   United States
Shallow; clean blown; applied black glass rim; ground and polished pontil.
Good Quality/Good Condition $25 (A)   **$25–$75**

Bowl   6.5″ H   1830–1845   United States
Clear; applied foot and molded panel bowl with applied rings at lip; top edge recut in a sawtooth design; wear and small flakes on foot.
Good Quality/Poor Condition $25 (A)   **$35–$125**

Bull's-eye   10″ Dia.   1845–1865   United States
Amethyst; folded rim; c. 1850–1860.
Good Quality/Good Condition $100 (D)   **$75–$150**

Candlestick   8.5″ H   1830–1845   United States
Cobalt blue and blown; hollow foot and stem; wide, deep socket.
Very Good Quality/Good Condition $75 (A)   **$75–$150**

Candlesticks   7.5″ H   1830–1845   United States
Pair; clear; with applied foot; hollow stem and bulbous open socket with wide flared rim; similar but not exact match; chip at base of stem; Pittsburgh.
Very Good Quality/Good Condition $600 (A)   **$400–$900**

Chestnut   5.25″ H   1830–1845   United States
Golden amber, blown chestnut; 24 vertical ribs; Zanesville; minor wear and scratches.
Very Good Quality/Average Condition $407 (A)   **$350–$500**

Compote   3.5″ H × 5.25″ Dia.   c. 1815–1850   United States
Amber blown; Zanesville; applied foot; wafer stem and shallow bowl; not very symmetrical; some wear.
Very Good Quality/Good Condition $1540 (A)   **$900–$1800**

Compote   3.5″ H   1840–1850   United States
Amber blown glass; Zanesville; applied foot; wafer stem and shallow bowl; not very symmetrical; some wear.
Very Good Quality/Average Condition $1540 (A)   **$1400–$1800**

Compotes   12.5″ H × 8.75″ Dia.   1830–1845   United States
Pair; blown, amethyst; goblet shape.
Very Good Quality/Average Condition $150 (A)   **$150–$475**

Creamer   5.75″ H   1830–1845   United States
Cobalt blue; applied foot and applied handle that is a bit crooked and misshapen; worn gilded inscription.
Good Quality/Average Condition $95 (A)   **$85–$135**

Creamer   4.5″ H   1830–1845   United States
Clear pillar mold; applied handle; ground pontil; end of handle has small chips and is ground.
Good Quality/Average Condition $110 (A)   **$115–$195**

Creamer   4.25″ H   1830–1845   United States
Violet-cobalt blue; 16 ribs in broken swirl with folded rim; applied handle.
Good Quality/Good Condition $50 (A)   **$45–$80**

Cruet   7.5″ H   1830–1845   United States
Clear, blown; 12 vertical ribs; applied hollow handle; Midwestern; no stopper.
Good Quality/Average Condition $61 (A)   **$50–$150**

Cuspidor   6″ H   United States
Amber, blown, with applied white rim; has surface film; age unknown.
Good Quality/Average Condition $45 (A)   **$35–$95**

Darner   6.5″ H   1860–1880   United States
Dark green blown glass.
Good Quality/Average Condition $37 (A)   **$35–$125**

Decanter   11.25″ H   1830–1845   United States
Canary yellow; blown; pillar mold with ribs swirled in neck; ground pontil; mouth ground for stopper—no stopper; not Pittsburgh but similar.
Very Good Quality/Good Condition $297 (A)   **$250–$500**

Food cover   10.75″ H   1860–1880   United States
Clear, blown Pittsburgh glass; folded and applied knob.
Good Quality/Average Condition $137 (A)   **$125–$150**

Goblets   5.5″ H   1830–1845   United States
Pair; clear flint glass; flute form.
Good Quality/Average Condition $35 (A)   **$35–$75**

Goblets   6″ H   1830–1845   United States
Pair; amethyst; applied foot and stem.
Very Good Quality/Good Condition $90 (A)   **$75–$100**

Goblets   5.5″ H   1830–1845   United States
Five clear rummers; similar shapes with applied foot and stem; flared bowls;
diameter of bowls varies.
Very Good Quality/Good Condition $175 (A)   **$150–$200**

Inkwell   2.5″ Dia.   1845–1865   United States
Clear, blown, 3-mold; probably G-II-18 but not very good impression.
Good Quality/Average Condition $303 (A)   **$250–$500**

Jug   5.25″ H   1845–1865   United States
Amber; blown with applied lip and handle; Midwestern; minor wear and some
interior residue.
Very Good Quality/Good Condition $576 (A)   **$450–$750**

Pipe   15.75″ L   1845–1865   United States
Pale opalescent yellow; applied clear yellow lip on bowl.
Very Good Quality/Good Condition $182 (A)   **$150–$350**

Pipe   19″ L   1845–1865   United States
Medium opaque blue; blown; white lip on bowl; stem is chipped.
Very Good Quality/Average Condition $138 (A)   **$125–$250**

Pitcher   6.5″ H   1830–1845   United States
Clear; Pittsburgh; applied hollow handle with well-detailed attachment;
12 molded panels in base; some wear; lip chips and damage at pontil.
Good Quality/Poor Condition $375 (A)   **$350–$750**

Pitcher   10″ H   1830–1845   United States
Cobalt; blown; applied handle and threading to flared lip; bulbous base has
swirled ribs.
Good Quality/Average Condition $155 (A)   **$150–$395**

Pitcher   5.5″ H   1830–1845   United States
Violet-cobalt blue; applied handle with berry print; threaded lip.
Very Good Quality/Good Condition $100 (A)   **$75–$125**

Pitcher   6″ H   1830–1845   United States
Cobalt blue; applied foot; threaded lip and applied handle with berry print; bowl
has swirled ribs; ground bottom and pontil.
Very Good Quality/Good Condition $125 (A)   **$65–$135**

Pitcher   9″ H   1830–1845   United States
Clear, blown; pillar mold; applied handle; 8 ribs; ground pontil.
Very Good Quality/Good Condition $260 (A)   **$225–$450**

Plant bell   10″ H × 8.5″ Dia.   1845–1865   United States
Free-blown, clear glass; dome shaped; applied knob; folded rim; minor chips
on rim.
Good Quality/Good Condition $150 (D)   **$95–$175**

Powder horn 11.75″ L 1860–1880 United States
Two shades of blue with white looping; chip on applied knob.
Good Quality/Good Condition $182 (A)   **$150–$250**

Rinsing bowls 4.75″ Dia. 1885–1900 United States
Set of 6; amethyst; very heavy.
Good Quality/Average Condition $200 (A)   **$200–$300**

Rolling pin 6″ L 1845–1865 United States
Aqua glass; c. 1860.
Good Quality/Good Condition $115 (D)   **$75–$125**

Rolling pin 13.5″ L 1870–1880 United States
Dark green blown glass.
Good Quality/Average Condition $125 (D)   **$125–$200**

Salt cellar 2.5″ H 1830–1845 United States
Sapphire blue; hexagonal; edge chips.
Good Quality/Average Condition $35 (A)   **$35–$65**

Spill holder 5″ H c. 1850–1860 United States
Clear flint; sandwich star; some edge wear.
Good Quality/Average Condition $20 (A)   **$25–$75**

String holder 4.5″ H × 4.75″ Dia. 1865–1885 United States
Clear; blown; Pittsburgh; with applied cobalt blue vase and finial; area around
hole for string has been ground smooth.
Very Good Quality/Good Condition $267 (A)   **$195–$350**

Sugar and creamer 4.5″ H 1830–1845 United States
Pair; cobalt blue; open sugar; polychrome enamel decoration; creamer has applied handle and foot; sugar has hollow applied feet and applied rim; rim has
chips; missing sugar lid.
Good Quality/Good Condition $250 (A)   **$175–$350**

Sugar and creamer 4″ H × 4″ Dia. 1830–1845 United States
Amethyst; open sugar dish; worn gilded inscription "Be caring with the cream,"
". . . with the sugar"; chip at base of applied handle on creamer; sugar has
applied flared foot with folded rim.
Good Quality/Good Condition $145 (A)   **$125–$175**

Sugar bowl 5.25″ H 1830–1845 United States
Open; violet-cobalt blue; expanded diamond with applied foot; slightly mis-
shapen.
Good Quality/Good Condition $425 (A)   **$300–$475**

Sugar bowl 5.75″ H × 5″ Dia. 1830–1845 United States
Clear; Pittsburgh; applied foot and baluster stem; white loop bowl has folded
lip; no lid.
Superior Quality/Fine Condition $725 (A)   **$550–$900**

Sugar bowl 7″ H 1830–1845 United States
Amethyst; applied foot; galleried rim and domed lid with applied finial.
Very Good Quality/Fine Condition $650 (A)   **$500–$700**

Sugar bowl 3.25″ H × 5″ Dia. 1830–1845 United States
Clear, blown with white looping; open, folded lip, applied foot; ground pontil.
Very Good Quality/Good Condition $83 (A)   **$75–$150**

Sugar bowl 3.75″ H × 4.75″ Dia. 1830–1845 United States
Clear, blown, with white looping; applied blue rim and clear foot.
Very Good Quality/Good Condition $193 (A)   **$125–$295**

Tumbler 5″ H c. 1815–1850 United States
Aqua; blown; applied handle; Zanesville; Ex. Krittle, Ex. Samaha.
Very Good Quality/Fine Condition $1265 (A) **$900–$1500**

Tumbler 4″ H 1830–1845 United States
Cobalt blue; paneled; chips.
Good Quality/Average Condition $30 (A) **$25–$75**

Tumbler 4″ H 1830–1845 United States
Sapphire blue glass; paneled; minor wear.
Very Good Quality/Good Condition $95 (A) **$75–$100**

Vase 11″ H 1830–1845 United States
Clear, blown; pillar mold; applied foot and baluster stem; 8 ribs; scalloped, flared lip; some wear.
Very Good Quality/Average Condition $130 (A) **$125–$475**

Vases 7.25″ H 1830–1845 United States
Pair; clear, blown and cut; applied foot and baluster stem; cut panels, rays and strawberry band.
Very Good Quality/Fine Condition $467 (A) **$350–$475**

Vases 8″ H 1845–1865 United States
Pair; hyacinth; peacock green.
Very Good Quality/Average Condition $135 (A) **$135–$250**

BOTTLES AND FLASKS

Bottles and flasks, primarily of glass, date back hundreds of years. Of primary interest to collectors are 19th-century flasks, 19th- to early-20th-century bottles, and modern "collector" bottles such as Avon or Jim Beam. The last were often made to be collectible from the day of purchase.

Some bottles have remained stable in price (beer bottles, fruit jars, and Avon bottles), and bitters bottles have actually declined since about 1985; but nearly every other area is increasing in value. Furthermore, collectors' clubs keep growing and expanding. Medical bottles, ink bottles, poison bottles, fine antique flasks, spirits bottles, and even soda (pop) bottles are increasing rapidly in value. Jim Beam bottles remain the strongest sellers in the modern area.

QUALITY KEY

Good Quality: ordinary shapes and ordinary colors.
Very Good Quality: unusual sizes, unusual shapes, and interesting colors.
Superior Quality: unusual shapes, interesting colors, rare sizes (not absolutely necessary), artistic merit, and datability.

At all levels, a printed label or intact price enhances value. Contents or partial contents do not enhance value.

CONDITION KEY

Fine Condition: a complete, empty bottle of fine color—bright and clean—showing only slight signs of wear; all spouts, stoppers, and handles complete; labels present.

Good Condition: shows signs of regular wear; gold or silver decoration worn; color may be slightly faded; no damage.

Average Condition: color faded somewhat; labels missing; stoppers, handles, and spouts are complete but worn; a tiny chip is possible.

Poor Condition: severely worn; color faded; sick glass; chips. Don't bother except for rarities.

BIBLIOGRAPHY

Editors of House of Collectibles. *The Official Price Guide to Bottles* (3rd ed.). New York: House of Collectibles, 1987. A pocket guide to old and new bottles—also new miniatures. Good list of bottle dealers.

Editors of House of Collectibles. *The Official Price Guide to Bottles Old and New* (10th ed.). New York: House of Collectibles, 1986. The full-size edition—817 pages of prices, drawings, collector clubs, and so forth.

Kovel, Ralph and Terry. *The Kovels' Bottle Price List* (8th ed.). Excellent, full-scale coverage of the vast panorama of bottle collecting. New York: Crown, 1987.

Munsey, Cecil. *The Illustrated Guide to Collecting Bottles.* New York: Hawthorne Books. An excellent history and includes a bibliography at the end of each category for further research.

Bottle   7.5″ L   Gemel   1845–1865   United States
Double blown gemel bottle; light blue with white looping; South Jersey.
Good Quality/Good Condition $55 (A)   **$50–$100**

Bottle   9.5″ L   Gemel   1845–1865   United States
Blown double gemel bottle; clear with cranberry and white looping.
Good Quality/Good Condition $60 (A)   **$50–$125**

Bottle   8.75″ H   Jenny Lind   1845–1865   United States
Aqua; quart; sheared and fire-polished lip, pontil mark; lip chips; attributed to McCarthy & Torreyson.
Superior Quality/Fine Condition $880 (A)   **$600–$1200**

Bottle   7.25″ H   Scroll   1845–1865   United States
Medium amethyst and streaks of deeper amethyst; pint; sheared and fire-polished lip; pontil mark "J. R. & Son"; hairline to rib of label panel. *(See photo 166)*
Superior Quality/Fine Condition $5225 (A)   **$2000–$6000**

Bottle   4.5″ H   1885–1900   United States
Figural skull poison bottle; deep cobalt; multiple small lip chips.
Very Good Quality/Fine Condition $1045 (A)   **$200–$1200**

Cologne bottle 12″ H Monument 1865–1885 United States
Deep emerald green with turquoise tint; tooled-lip smooth base; small imperfection in neck.
Superior Quality/Fine Condition $1650 (A)   **$1200–$1650**

Demijohn 19.5″ H 1885–1900 United States
Olive green; applied lip.
Good Quality/Good Condition $50 (A)   **$50–$150**

Flask 5″ H × 4.5″ W × 2.5″ D Ribbed 1830–1850 European
Sixteen-ribbed broken swirl; very strong impression; sheared lip, pontil scar; sapphire blue; medial bruise with 2 small cracks; small lower face crack; probably northern European origin.
Good Quality/Average Condition $143 (A)   **$140–$350**

Flask 7″ H Scroll 1845–1865 United States
Deep smoky amber streaked with aqua; pint; sheared and fire-polished lip; pontil mark; the only other example of this extremely rare bottle is in the Corning Museum.
Superior Quality/Fine Condition $6600 (A)   **$2000–$6000**

Flask Portrait 1851–1860 United States
Washington-Taylor; deep blue-green sloping collar with bevel; pontil scar; quart; Philadelphia area glasshouse; high point wear; inner haze.
Good Quality/Average Condition $330 (A)   **$300–$500**

Historical flask 1800–1830 United States
"Success to the Railroad"; bubbly; good color; deep forest green; pint; sheared lip; pontil scar; tiny flake on lip; possibly Mt. Vernon Glassworks.
Very Good Quality/Average Condition $165 (A)   **$175–$250**

Photo 166 (left). Scroll bottle. CREDIT: SKINNER, INC., BOLTON, MA. *Photo 167 (center). Historical flask.* CREDIT: SKINNER, INC., BOLTON, MA. *Photo 168 (right). Pickle bottle.* CREDIT: SKINNER, INC., BOLTON, MA. *(See pp. 298, 300)*

Historical flask 1800–1830 United States
Concentric-ring eagle historical flask; light green; sheared lip; pontil scar; 1 lower rib with tiny flake; light spotty inner haze; approx. 1 pint; New England Glassworks, Cambridge, MA. *(See photo 167)*
Very Good Quality/Fine Condition $4400 (A)   **$4000–$6000**

Historical flask 1800–1830 United States
"Success to the Railroad"; eagle historical flask; deep-green; sheared lip; pontil scar; pint; Coventry Glassworks, CT.
Very Good Quality/Fine Condition $330 (A)   **$150–$350**

Ink bottle 2.5″ H × 2″ W × 1.75″ D 1865–1885 United States
Cabin shape; colorless; squared-off collar; smooth base.
Good Quality/Good Condition $550 (A)   **$500–$750**

Medicine bottle 8″ H 1865–1885 United States
Warners "Log Cabin-Extract-Rochester NY" labeled medicine bottle; with box in mint condition except missing top flap; label 98% intact, booklet and cork-screw; medium blue amber.
Very Good Quality/Fine Condition $143 (A)   **$90–$140**

Pickle bottle 14″ H Cathedral 1865–1880 United States
Three fancy arches, 1 plain; bright bluish finish; rolled mouth; smooth base. *(See photo 168)*
Very Good Quality/Good Condition $330 (A)   **$300–$500**

Pickle jar 11.5″ H 1885–1900 United States
Aqua glass; Gothic mark; lip is rough and irregular; iron pontil.
Good Quality/Average Condition $193 (A)   **$175–$350**

Pictorial flask 1800–1830 United States
Franklin bust; perfect example, almost no wear; aqua; sheared lip; pontil scar; quart; Kensington Glass Works, Philadelphia, PA.
Superior Quality/Fine Condition $110 (A)   **$120–$150**

"Reeds/Bitters" 12.5″ H 1820–1880 United States
Lady's leg; bubbly glass; amber; slipping collar with bevel-smooth base (few burst bubbles, light haze, easily cleanable).
Very Good Quality/Average Condition $193 (A)   **$175–$250**

Whiskey bottle 12.5″ H 1861–1864 United States
"AM Bininger & Co." cannon shape; labeled "Great Gun Gin" with woman holding flag and man with goblet and rifle; label 90% complete; red golden amber; sheared lip; smooth base.
Superior Quality/Fine Condition $1045 (A)   **$750–$1500**

Whiskey bottle 12.5″ H Figural 1870–1880 United States
"Mohawk Whiskey Pure Rye"; Indian figural; original red sealing wax around half lip; medium golden amber; rough sheared lip; pontil scar.
Very Good Quality/Fine Condition $715 (A)   **$700–$1000**

GEORGIAN AND REGENCY GLASS

George Ravenscroft laid the foundation for the cutting and engraving that decorated much Georgian and Regency glass when he developed flint glass—what we now call lead crystal—in the late 17th century. Lead crystal was softer than the earlier Venetian glass, so it was better suited for cutting and engraving. And of course, lead crystal was prized for its ability to refract light beautifully—a property that was not only aesthetically pleasing but also practical in an age before electricity. However, the technical innovations in lead crystal were not fully exploited because of political and economic conditions. In 1745 an excise tax was imposed on glass in England. Glassmakers responded by making thinner walls, and the cutting and engraving was by necessity fairly shallow. The tax also encouraged glassmakers to turn old pieces into "cullet," or broken glass, to be used again. Pieces that do survive from this period were cut with simple geometric designs or with floral engraving. Grapevines with bunches of grapes were often engraved on decanters or wine glasses. Other wine glasses from the mid-18th century were decorated with spiraling air-twists inside the stems. These beautiful glasses are coveted today.

The great period of Irish glass began in earnest during the late Georgian period, when the excise tax on English glass was drastically increased in the 1770s to finance the war against the American colonies. At about the same time the ban on exporting glass from Ireland to England was lifted, in 1780. Irish glass flourished until 1825, when a new excise tax was imposed, and a few years later the American machines for making pressed glass were introduced into England, thus signaling the decline of Irish glass.

No doubt the most famous Irish glasshouse was Waterford, founded by George and William Penrose in 1783. Other important glass factories sprang up in Cork, Dublin, Belfast, and Newry. Unless a piece of Irish glass has the molded factory mark on its base—and that is rare—it is virtually impossible to identify it with certainty. People often assume that any cut crystal with a bluish tint is Waterford and that all Waterford had this bluish tint. Neither of these assumptions is true. The tint is called "Derby Blue" after the region where the lead was mined between 1783 and 1810. After 1810 it disappeared from Anglo-Irish glass.

By the end of the Georgian period deep cutting on thick walls was much in demand. This was even truer during the Regency period in Anglo-Irish glass, which made extensive use of deeply cut designs on heavy classical shapes. Large areas of table glass could be covered in an array of cut diamond patterns. During the first decade of the 19th century a raised, crosshatched diamond, called the strawberry diamond, was a popular motif. Prismatic cutting, or deep parallel steps cut horizontally, was often used to dramatic effect.

The process of cutting involved four steps. First, the design was rough-cut with a soft iron wheel having either a rounded, V-shaped, or flat edge, depending on the kind of cut desired. Then the cut was smoothed by another wheel moistened with water and powdered pumice. At this stage the cut was an opaque white, so a wheel of willow wood was used to make the cut transparent again. Finally, the piece was finished, using a wheel lined with cork or felt.

Cut-glass tableware from this period suited the culinary habits of the time. Decanters were used to serve wine at mealtimes and are now found on the market to suit almost every taste—from the elegantly plain Georgian decanters with three-ringed necks and simple engraving or fluting around the body to the richly cut decanters of the Regency period. Covered sweetmeat urns and open sweetmeat dishes were used for serving a mixture of sweetmeats, fruit, and wine as a "banquet"—an elegant snack between meals or dessert proper. Several types of vessels were developed to keep wine cool at candlelit tables. Monteiths, or large bowls, were filled with iced water to keep wine glasses cool. Their deeply notched rims held the wine glass stems in place while the bowls cooled. Monteiths were later replaced by individual wine glass coolers, or "rinsers," which usually had straight sides with two notches for stems to rest upon. Finger bowls, or "washers," also were used. These were straight-sided, without the notches.

Spectacular cut-glass bowls for fruit or salad graced many dinner tables during this period. Often on pedestal bases, the bowls could be round or boat-shaped, hemispherical on a small foot, or in the shape of a kettle drum. The rims were sometimes rolled over dramatically, rolling back one third of the way down the bowl. When rims were not turned over, they were cut in a variety of different ways, such as a simple scallop or the more elaborate trefoil scallop. After 1800 the fan-cut edge became very popular.

MARKET TRENDS

While glass prices have risen over the past few years in England, in America Anglo-Irish glass continues to be underpriced. In this country interest in Anglo-Irish glass is slowly rising, but prices have remained stable. Compared to other antiques of this period, glass is selling at bargain prices!

Items that are most sought after are wine glasses with air-twist stems, especially if they are colored. Rinsers are beginning to increase in price somewhat and are readily available. Decanters, salad bowls, and sweetmeat dishes are plentiful and reasonably priced, so use discretion in buying them. Decanters should have their original stoppers, and sweetmeat dishes should have their original covers. Look for the best-quality pieces because these will appreciate in value the most over time.

FAKES ALERT

Fakes are not a big problem in this area. The art of cutting and engraving is so difficult to master that it is usually not cost-effective to market fakes. The level of expertise is just too high. The only problem for beginners is to learn to differentiate between antique cut glass and their molded imitations that were first produced in the 1850s. This is easily done. Molded glass does not have the sharp, clean edges of cut glass—use a magnifying glass if it helps. In distinguishing antique cut glass from modern cut glass, one will find signs of wear on the bottoms of old pieces (and the scratches will be totally random); modern pieces will invariably copy late Victorian—not Georgian or Regency—motifs and will be far shallower.

A few chips and flakes are to be expected on Georgian or Regency glass and should affect the price by no more than 10 percent. Naturally, guidelines on condition are stricter on later glass, but when glass has survived for two hundred years, chips and flakes are almost impossible to avoid.

BIBLIOGRAPHY

Crompton, Sydney, Editor. *English Glass*. London: Ward Lock, 1967.

Davis, Derek C. *English Bottles and Decanters 1650–1900*. New York: World, 1972.

Honey, W. B. *English Glass*. London: Victoria and Albert Museum, 1946.

Hughes, G. Bernard. *English, Scottish and Irish Glass from the 16th Century to 1820*. New York: Bramhall House, 1956.

Lloyd, Ward. *Investing in Georgian Glass*. London: Cresset Press, 1969; New York: Clarkson N. Potter, 1969.

Savage, George. *Glass*. London: Octopus Books, 1972.

Thorpe, W. A. *A History of English and Irish Glass*. London: Medici Society, 1929; New York: Saifer, 1970.

MUSEUMS

Baltimore Museum of Art, Baltimore, MD
British Museum, London.
Brooklyn Museum, New York City.
Cleveland Museum of Art, Cleveland, OH.
Colonial Williamsburg, Williamsburg, VA.
Corning Museum of Glass, Corning, NY.
Metropolitan Museum of Art, New York City.
Smithsonian Institute, Washington, DC.
Stourbridge Borough Collection, Stourbridge, England.

Ulster Museum, Belfast, Ireland.
Victoria and Albert Museum, London.

Where the value range clearly exceeds the amount sold for, this reflects price
increases during the last year.

Bowl, covered 8″ H × 8″ Dia. Regency 1800–1830 Anglo-Irish
Diamond pattern and paneled top cut glass; mushroom cut finial on top. *(See
photo 169)*
Good Quality/Fine Condition $475 (D)   **$300–$525**

Compote 8.5″ H × 9″ Dia. Regency 1800–1830 Ireland
Stemmed compote on shaped base with multiple lobed points on flared rim; tiny
chip on 1 point; blown in 3 parts.
Superior Quality/Good Condition $250 (D)   **$200–$450**

Condiment dish 5″ H × 7″ Dia. Late Georgian 1800–1830 England
Cut glass with underplate and cover; mushroom knop; diamond-faceted all over.
Superior Quality/Fine Condition $475 (D)   **$300–$500**

Condiment dish 1.75″ H × 4″ W × 6.5″ D Regency 1800–1830 Ireland
Elegant cut-glass oval dish with shaped and lobed rim.
Superior Quality/Fine Condition $145 (D)   **$125–$175**

Cups, covered 13″ H Late Georgian 1800–1830 England
Pair of faceted crystal covered presentation cups, each in neoclassical taste.
Very Good Quality/Fine Condition $1200 (A)   **$1200–$1800**

Decanter 9″ H Georgian 1800–1830 Anglo-Irish
Two-ringed neck; no cutting; no stopper.
Good Quality/Good Condition $100 (D)   **$75–$150**

Decanters 11.5″ H George III 1780–1800 England
Pair of cut-glass decanters with fluting at base, midbody, and neck; no stoppers.
Very Good Quality/Good Condition $440 (A)   **$400–$600**

Photo 169. Covered bowl.
CREDIT: WHITEHALL AT THE
VILLA, CHAPEL HILL, NC
(See above)

Dishes, covered 6″ H Georgian 1800–1830 Anglo-Irish
Small; pair; amber; covered; faceted sides; button finial on top; rare.
Good Quality/Fine Condition $295 (D) **$250–$325**

Garniture Late Georgian 1800–1830 England
Canoe-form compote (9″ H, 16.5″ L) and pair of smaller compotes en suite (5.5″ H, 10.5″ L); classical form.
Very Good Quality/Fine Condition $1700 (A) **$1500–$2500**

Garniture set 21″ H George III 1780–1800 Anglo-Irish
Cut glass; 3 pieces: pair of covered urns and larger matching covered urn; each with a diamond etched bell-form cover; gadrooned finial above ovoid, fluted and diamond-cut body; on rectangular plinth.
Superior Quality/Fine Condition $26,000 (A) **$18,000–$26,000**

Monteith 9″ Dia. Georgian 1800–1830 England
Cut-glass monteith/fruit bowl; c. 1810.
Superior Quality/Fine Condition $1275 (D) **$800–$1500**

Pitcher 8.5″ H Victorian 1845–1865 Ireland
Blown and cut-glass water pitcher of rather simple form with applied handle.
Good Quality/Fine Condition $115 (D) **$75–$125**

Sweetmeat dishes Regency 1800–1830 Anglo-Irish
Pair; covered; each with silvered handles cast as wreaths; diamond-faceted all over; bases with out-flared trefoil rims; minor chips and flaking.
Superior Quality/Average Condition $1230 (A) **$1200–$2000**

Sweetmeat stands Georgian 1830–1845 England
Pair; cut glass; with liners.
Very Good Quality/Fine Condition $425 (A) **$400–$600**

Tableware 8″ H, 9.5″ L Late Georgian 1800–1830 England
Cut glass; covered cup and stand; pair of oval bowls.
Very Good Quality/Fine Condition $900 (A) **$750–$1200**

Urn, sweetmeat 14.75″ H Georgian 1800–1830 Ireland
Cut-glass sweetmeat urn.
Very Good Quality/Fine Condition $400 (D) **$350–$550**

Urns, condiment 9.5″ H Regency 1800–1830 Anglo-Irish
Pair; cut-crystal covered urns on square bases.
Very Good Quality/Good Condition $875 (D) **$650–$1000**

Urns, sweetmeat 7.5″ H × 6″ Dia. William IV 1830–1845 England
Unusually small pair; covered; with typically faceted sides; covers and bases of hexagonal form.
Superior Quality/Fine Condition $575 (D) **$450–$600**

Urns, sweetmeat 11″ H × 6″ Dia. Regency 1800–1830 Ireland
Pair; swirl-cut; covered; faceted tops and finials.
Very Good Quality/Fine Condition $495 (D) **$450–$750**

Wine rinser 5″ H × 5.5″ Dia. Adam 1750–1780 Ireland
Basket shape; blown and delicately cut (finger bowl with 2 spouts).
Superior Quality/Fine Condition $165 (D) **$125–$165**

Wine rinsers 3″ H × 5″ Dia. Victorian 1830–1845 Anglo-Irish
Rare set of 6; frosted and clear blown glass; c. 1840.
Superior Quality/Fine Condition $900 (D) **$700–$900**

SCENT BOTTLES

Advisor: **JEAN SLOAN**

Jean Sloan is the author of Perfume and Scent Bottle Collecting, *and* Perfume and Scent Bottle Collecting, *2nd edition, published by Wallace Homestead. She has also lectured on the subject and has written numerous articles for various magazines. Jean is an antiques dealer doing business as The Glass House (shows only); (608) 233-9493.*

Perfume has been used since before written history, and its manufacture for personal use and religious reasons has always been costly. Until this century few bottles in which perfume was dispensed by the maker were decorative, and the perfume was decanted into a fantastic variety of wonderful containers. Although glass has been the overwhelming choice of material for the bottles, there have been bottles made of almost every substance that the human mind could conceive. Skilled craftsmen used jewels, precious metals, engraving, and more to enhance the scent within. In this century great glass houses have been employed by the important scent manufacturers to create wonderful bottles, and these too have become very collectible. The interest and demand by the public is growing with each year.

CONDITION KEY

Condition factors in scent bottles can be nebulous in that if a piece is extremely old and you know you will never see another, then the condition can be rather poor and still the price may be high. However, as a general rule of thumb one may consider the following guidelines.

Fine Condition: just about perfect. Perhaps an inner stopper of old scent bottles may be missing (they can generally be replaced), but the outer bottle should be without blemish, and the metal should be in very good shape. The hinge should be unbroken, jewels intact. No chips. One should look for perfection in 20th-century bottles. Atomizers may have the rubber tubing and bulbs replaced. They look better with bulbs than with rotted ends and crumbling rubber. However, if the metal spray head has been replaced with one from another manufacturer or with a new one, this does reduce the value. A dealer should always point out a replacement.

Good Condition: a bottle should be in close to perfect shape. There may be a small chip or bruise or a small dent in the metal mount.

Average Condition: scratched, worn enameling, badly dented metal, etc.

QUALITY KEY

Quality is a very difficult thing to define in scent bottles. Superior quality in this diverse field is in the eye of the collector. One person may be deeply involved with 18th-century scent bottles and feel commercial bottles of the 20th century are extremely uninteresting and of inferior quality, and vice versa. All bottles, whatever their origin, have something that makes them wonderful to someone. A collector, for some reason, becomes enchanted with some aspect, and that makes all the difference. It is the pleasure of the chase, the research, the handling, the beauty, the originality, the history, the design of each piece. This is the joy of collecting.

BIBLIOGRAPHY

Forsythe, Ruth A. *Made in Czechoslovakia*. Galena, OH: Author, 1982.

Launert, Edmund. *Scent and Scent Bottles*. London: Barrie & Jenkins, 1974.

North-Jones, Jacquelyne Y. *Commercial Perfume Bottles*. Chester, PA: Schiffer Publishing, 1987.

Sloan, Jean. *Perfume and Scent Bottle Collecting, with Prices*, 2nd ed. Radnor, PA: Wallace-Homestead Book Company, 1989.

Walker, Alexandra. *Scent Bottles*. Aylesbury, England: Shire Publications, 1987.

Cologne bottle 1900–1910 Bohemia
Clear, blown glass with dark ruby glass overlay; cut to clear in arches, ovals and fans; with facet-cut clear stopper; sold as pair with next entry; see next listing for prices.
Good Quality/Fine Condition
Cologne bottle 1900–1910 Bohemia
Blown, clear glass with dark ruby glass overlay; cut to clear; fine cutting in tiny stars and larger block of deep red alternating; it is topped with deep chased silver cap; sold as pair with above entry.
Good Quality/Fine Condition $240 (A) **$240–$290**
Perfume bottle 8″ L 1885–1900 Austria
Unusually long bottle in cranberry glass; enameled and gilded in intricate floral pattern; screw-on brass top; glass inner stopper; signed in tiny script, "Moser."
Good Quality/Fine Condition $900 (A) **$550–$800**
Perfume bottle 1910–1930 Czechoslovakia
Woman with pompadour hairdo, dressed in hoopskirt of ruffled layers; clear glass; polished areas; often mistaken for R. Lalique; unsigned; came in several sizes.
Good Quality/Fine Condition $75 (D) **$50–$100**
Perfume bottle 4″ L 1885 England
Cameo glass; teardrop shape; sky blue background; white overlay cut in leaves and passionflowers; butterfly; attributed to Webb; mounted with silver; marked 1885 Birmingham; 1 small chip and dent.
Superior Quality/Good Condition $600 (D) **$500–$850**

Perfume bottle 1950–1970 France
Pressed glass; Christian Dior's ''Diorissimo''; never opened; in original oval
pink box with outer box; ½ fluid oz. size; perfect condition.
Good Quality/Fine Condition $165 (D)   **$50–$165**

Perfume bottle 1930–1950 United States
''Dime store'' novelty; golf bag in colorful tartan with 3 scents in glass clubs.
Good Quality/Good Condition $65 (D)   **$50–$75**

Perfume bottle 1930–1950 United States
''Dime store'' novelty; piano-like holder with 2 bottles lying end to end with
simulated piano keys on them.
Good Quality/Good Condition $75 (D)   **$50–$100**

Perfume bottle 5.5″ H 1930–1950 United States
''Dime store'' novelty; floor lamp with plastic shade and base; 3 tiny bottles
suspended under shade.
Good Quality/Good Condition $50 (D)   **$50–$100**

Perfume tester 1″ H × 8.75″ L 1930–1950 France
Perfume tester for 5 scents for D'Orsay by R. Lalique; both D'Orsay & R.
Lalique are incorporated into the decoration; the flower-shaped stoppers are
daubers.
Superior Quality/Fine Condition $2000 (D)   **$1500–$2200**

Scent bottles 3.5″ to 4.5 ″ H 1865–1885 United States
Three; sterling silver with screw-on caps; handles on shoulders to allow chains
to be hung from them; 2 decorated with bright-cut work, another with initials;
1 has hook, others for chatelaine.
Superior Quality/Good Condition $425 (D)   **$350–$500**

Jewelry

Advisor: **ARTHUR GUY KAPLAN**

Arthur Guy Kaplan is a noted dealer of antique jewelry (PO Box 1942, Baltimore, MD 21203) and author of The Official Identification and Price Guide to Antique Jewelry, *6th edition (New York: House of Collectibles, 1990).*

HISTORY

The purpose of this section is to provide an overview of the identifying style and design characteristics of the different periods of antique and collectible jewelry available in today's marketplace.

Georgian jewelry was produced during the reigns of George I through George IV in England, from 1714 to 1830. The French influence was predominant during the Georgian period.

Jewelry produced during the Georgian period consisted of designs of nature—flowers, leaves, insects, birds, feathers, and ribbons—with a fine sense of color, form, and design. Jewelry was delicate and light in appearance. Many articles were *en tremblant*, set on a spring and assembled. Set with precious gemstones, the jewelry was entirely handmade and consequently was individualistic in design; there was no mass production of jewelry during the Georgian period. The small but prosperous middle class that emerged during the mid-Georgian period developed a need for secondary or imitation jewelry. Paste or rhinestones were substituted for diamonds; cut steel or marcasites, for silver; and pinchbeck, for gold. The general characteristics of the Georgian period were an imaginative and delicate use of colored stones and an aesthetically pleasing and lighthearted approach to jewelry.

The Georgian period ended in 1830, and the Victorian period began with the reign of Queen Victoria in 1837. Victoria loved jewelry. If any two words can be characteristic of a period, quantity and variety would stand for the Victorian period. The industrial revolution created a growing middle class, and successful businessmen loaded their wives with jewels to display their newfound wealth. Mechanical processes were developed to mass-produce jewelry, such as the stamping out of gold settings by 1835. France had been the leader of jewelry design, but with the reign of Queen Victoria, Britain became a major jewelry center.

Victoria ruled from 1837 to 1901; she was fond of jewelry and wore it profusely. Her reign is divided into three periods, the first being the early Victorian or Romantic period, 1837 to 1860. During this time jewelry was imaginative and delicate, reflecting a nostalgia for the Middle Ages. Gold was plentiful, especially because of the 1849 California gold rush. The mid-Victorian, or Grand, period ran from 1860 to 1885. Jewelry design became bolder as women became bolder. Women began to work, and in 1870 they gained the right to keep the money they earned. Jewelry continued to be plentiful, though with the growing use of electric light, diamonds began to displace colored gemstones for evening wear.

A greater sense of social responsibility and an even more liberated woman emerged during the late Victorian, or Aesthetic, period, 1885 to 1901. The universities were opened to women, who soon began to question the wearing of jewelry. The lesser gemstones—peridot, alexandrite, tourmaline, garnet, and opal—became fashionable. With the opening of the South African diamond mines and the expanded American tourist trade, large solitaire diamond rings gained popularity. The 1890s brought a revolt against tradition, and a revolutionary style of jewelry was created—Art Nouveau. It is characterized by delicate enamels, sweeping flowers, soft-colored stones, and female heads with long flowing hair. Art Nouveau ended the 19th century in a flourish of originality.

MARKET REVIEW

There has been much publicity over the past few years concerning certain auction sales that have realized record prices, the most notable being the auction of the Duchess of Windsor's jewels. Although the record prices received for her jewels do not accurately establish the value of similar items, this auction did spark a renewed interest in the Art Deco style of jewelry. Art Deco jewelry has been quite popular with collectors for a number of years, but the better signed pieces have greatly increased in value, partly as a result of the Windsor auction.

Other items recently in the news concern the availability for sale of some very special diamonds. An October 1988 sale of diamonds at Christie's, New York, drew outstanding prices for top-quality stones, both traditional and fancy-colored. The largest flawless diamond ever publicly offered for sale, 407.48 carats, received a bid of $13.2 million and was rejected by the seller! A small, .95-carat, rare red diamond set the record price per carat, selling for $800,000. Although these stones are out of the range of most collectors, they do represent a trend toward better stones. Christie's, in a recent market review, stated that the market for diamonds has continued to be strong following the stock market crash of 1987. Also, there has been a continued demand for better-quality colored gemstones. It should be noted, however, that pearls have not been bringing the strong prices that they have brought in the past unless they are of exceptional color and size.

The market for Victorian and Georgian jewelry has gone up steadily as better-quality pieces are becoming more difficult to find. One area of surprise has been the prices old mine cut diamonds have been fetching. A few years ago old mine cut diamonds were only as valuable as their recut weight to the average jeweler or member of the public not interested in antique jewelry. Today there is a demand for these stones, both set and unset, causing the value of antique diamond jewelry to rise significantly. Edwardian jewelry has also increased in value.

Pocket watches, once the darling of the auction sales, declined significantly in value in the early 1980s but now are inching their way up again. The recent 1988 purchase of a Patek Philippe watch (made for James W. Packard in 1922) for $1.3 million by the Patek Philippe company should give specialty pocket watches a boost in the marketplace.

An area of the market that is doing very well currently is the jewelry made in the 1930s and 1940s known as "Retro." Oversize pieces with large stones and items of a whimsical nature are demanding very high prices. Men's wristwatches of this period have gone up in value as they have become very fashionable, although ladies' diamond wristwatches of that period have not fared as well.

A rule of thumb in trying to keep abreast of current market trends without falling short when styles change is to buy better-quality items. Smaller but better stones will hold their value longer than larger, less perfect ones. Pieces that are signed or attributed to a well-known designer will also hold onto their value regardless of fads, as will older, handcrafted pieces of jewelry because of their unique quality, which can never be reproduced.

FAKES ALERT

As with all fields of antiques, there are reproductions and fakes on the antique jewelry market. Art Nouveau– and Art Deco–style jewelry have been mass-produced during the past several years, and the public should be cautious in the purchase of such jewelry. Excellent Edwardian diamond and platinum jewelry is presently being manufactured in Portugal, and fine copies of Victorian Etruscan granulation jewelry are being produced in England. Expose yourself to as many pieces of jewelry as possible in order to educate yourself concerning the reproductions on the market.

CONDITION KEY

Fine Condition: all prongs tight, no chips on facets of stones, no dents in metal, no repairs.

Good Condition: repairs of high quality, no hard solder evident, replaced stones exact match in cut and color.

Average Condition: old repairs with hard solder only evident from reverse, minor dents in metal, loose stones, some replaced stones.

Poor Condition: stones clipped or scratched, stones missing, dents and holes in metal, some prongs missing.

Originality is *not* considered in the condition statement but is specified in each individual description.

QUALITY KEY

Good Quality: a nice piece worthy of collecting but having no distinguishing characteristics; mass-produced, low-end.

Very Good Quality: a very good example of the type, reflecting several of the most desired characteristics; typical of fine merchandise not purchased from a major designer and not caster-made.

Superior Quality: a superlative example that has nearly all desired characteristics of the type; top-quality stones; made by a major maker or designer.

This is not a condition statement but strictly a measure of the stylishness of the piece.

STYLE CHRONOLOGY

Georgian   Edwardian
Victorian   Art Deco
Arts and Crafts   Retro
Art Nouveau

Bracelet   Victorian   1860   England
Seven strands of garnet beads with garnet beads set in clasp.
Very Good Quality/Fine Condition $1000 (D)   **$800–$1200**

Bracelet   Victorian   1865–1885   England
Nuts spaced with 15K gold leaves in fitted box.
Good Quality/Good Condition $600 (D)   **$400–$700**

Bracelet   Art Deco   France
Wide, flexible links with round diamonds set in a geometric pierced motif; diamonds are approximately 12.25 carats; platinum.
Very Good Quality/Good Condition $8800 (A)   **$8000–$12,000**

Bracelet Victorian 1845–1865 Scotland
Rectangular plaques of agate set in engraved mountings; gold.
Good Quality/Good Condition $1100 (A)   **$900–$1400**

Brooch Victorian 1845–1865 England
Bird motif with seed pearls; gold. *(See photo 170)*
Good Quality/Good Condition $900 (D)   **$800–$1200**

Brooch Victorian 1865–1885 England
Peacock on a starburst; set with seed pearls, small round diamonds and 1 large sapphire; 18K gold.
Good Quality/Good Condition $2200 (A)   **$1500–$2400**

Brooch Victorian 1865–1885 England
Star motif set with cabochon-cut moonstones; gold.
Very Good Quality/Good Condition $800 (D)   **$600–$1000**

Brooch Victorian 1885–1900 England
Ivory cameo of an Oriental motif with an engraved gold frame.
Good Quality/Average Condition $400 (D)   **$400–$650**

Brooch Art Nouveau 1890–1900 France
Flower swirl motif with a border of round diamonds; center in *plique-à-jour* enamel; gold.
Superior Quality/Fine Condition $2750 (A)   **$2500–$4500**

Brooch Victorian 1860 Italy
Rectangular *pietra dura* plaque in a flower motif with a bamboo-style frame; silver and gold-filled.
Good Quality/Good Condition $250 (A)   **$200–$400**

Brooch Victorian 1860 Italy
Cameo of a female head carved from black and white onyx; frame with twisted wire and beaded edge; gold.
Good Quality/Good Condition $400 (A)   **$600–$850**

Brooch Victorian 1865–1885 Scotland
Round, faceted citrine in center with fancy carved and engraved frame of Scottish thistles. *(See photo 171)*
Very Good Quality/Fine Condition $650 (D)   **$500–$800**

Brooch Victorian 1865–1885 United States
Oval amethyst surrounded by seed pearls; 14K gold frame.
Good Quality/Good Condition $400 (A)   **$350–$650**

Brooch Art Nouveau 1900 United States
Swirl-motif turquoise set in a carved sterling frame in a swirl and cherub design.
Very Good Quality/Good Condition $300 (A)   **$250–$450**

Brooch Edwardian 1910 United States
Heart-motif pavé set with seed pearls and a sapphire in the center; gold.
Good Quality/Good Condition $550 (A)   **$450–$600**

Brooch Edwardian 1910 United States
Bar pin with a cultured pearl in the center and 1 diamond on either end; diamonds approximately ½ carat each; platinum.
Very Good Quality/Good Condition $710 (A)   **$600–$1000**

Brooch Retro 1940 United States
Large bow set with a spray of 8 round diamonds, approx. .50 carat, and 12 round rubies, approx. 1.0 carat; gold.
Good Quality/Good Condition $1320 (A)   **$1000–$1600**

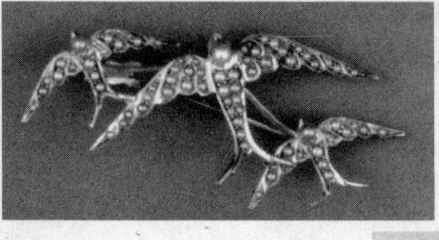

Photo 170. Brooch.
CREDIT: PRIVATE COLLECTION
(See p. 313)

Photo 171. Brooch.
CREDIT: PRIVATE COLLECTION
(See p. 313)

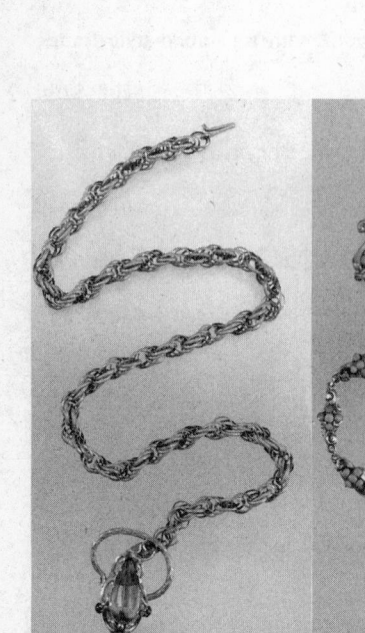

Photo 172 (left). Necklace. CREDIT: PRIVATE COLLECTION. *Photo 173 (right). Suite.* CREDIT: PRIVATE COLLECTION *(See pp. 315, 316)*

Brooch Retro 1940 United States
Motif of car set with an emerald-cut diamond, approx. .17 carat; carved onyx, rubies channel-set, approx. .70 carat, on a row of round diamonds; 18K white gold.
Very Good Quality/Fine Condition $770 (A)   **$900–$1400**

Earrings Victorian 1865–1885
One large sphere with a smaller sphere suspended by chains and with a fishtail tassel at the base of the smaller sphere; Etruscan granulation on the spheres; 14 K gold.
Good Quality/Fine Condition $385 (A)   **$450–$650**

Earrings Georgian 1780–1800 England
Briolette-cut citrine set in a thin gold flower.
Good Quality/Good Condition $360 (A)   **$600–$800**

Earrings Victorian 1830–1845 England
Leaf motif set with rose-cut diamonds; silver-topped gold.
Very Good Quality/Good Condition $550 (A)   **$500–$800**

Earrings Art Nouveau 1885–1900 England
Oval cabochon garnets bezel-set, with snake motif 15K gold frame with 2 small cultured pearls.
Good Quality/Fine Condition $1045 (A)   **$800–$1500**

Earrings Victorian 1865–1885 Italy/France
Center plaque with micromosaic of a bird; mosaic floral designs around border with Etruscan granulation; 18K gold.
Good Quality/Good Condition $800 (D)   **$750–$1250**

Earrings Georgian 1750–1780 Spain/Portugal
Teardrop motif with cutout fancy border set with 12 emerald-cut emeralds.
Good Quality/Fine Condition $660 (A)   **$1000–$1250**

Necklace Georgian 1840 England
Snake motif with citrine set in head and in heart; cabochon garnet eyes; gold.
(See photo 172)
Very Good Quality/Good Condition $1800 (D)   **$1500–$2500**

Necklace Edwardian 1900–1910 England
Cabochon-cut moonstones spaced on 9K gold chain with cabochon and teardrop-cut moonstone drops; 1 oval sapphire.
Good Quality/Good Condition $825 (A)   **$700–$1100**

Necklace Victorian 1860 Italy
Carved coral putti heads, shell, scrolls, and leaves suspended on gold chain.
Very Good Quality/Good Condition $495 (A)   **$400–$800**

Necklace Victorian 1865–1885 United States
Chain with barrel motif slide with black enamel and tassel at end of chain.
Good Quality/Good Condition $1500 (A)   **$1200–$1800**

Pendant Victorian 1845–1865 England
Round with seed pearl border and cluster in center; cobalt blue enamel; locket on reverse.
Good Quality/Good Condition $425 (D)   **$350–$650**

Ring Edwardian 1900–1910 England
Belt motif; 22K gold.
Good Quality/Good Condition $425 (D)   **$350–$550**

Ring Retro 1940 France
Ribbon motif set with round diamonds, approx. 2.40 carats; platinum and 18K gold.
Good Quality/Good Condition $1800 (A)   **$1600–$2400**

Ring Victorian 1880 United States
Navette motif with a row of oval sapphires in the center surrounded by round diamonds; gold.
Good Quality/Good Condition $800 (D)   **$600–$1000**

Ring Victorian 1880 United States
Cluster motif with 1 emerald-cut emerald, approx. .60 carats; surrounded by 12 old mine cut diamonds, approx. .60 carats; platinum and 18K gold.
Good Quality/Good Condition $825 (A)   **$800–$1400**

Ring Victorian 1880 United States
Ruby in center surrounded by 8 pearls in a starburst pattern; 18K gold.
Good Quality/Good Condition $250 (D)   **$200–$400**

Ring Art Nouveau 1890 United States
Freeform flowing motif set with round rubies and sapphires; gold.
Good Quality/Good Condition $425 (D)   **$350–$650**

Ring Victorian 1890 United States
Snake motif set with an oval sapphire in the head; gold.
Good Quality/Good Condition $425 (A)   **$400–$600**

Ring Edwardian 1910 United States
Center round diamond, approx. 1.75 carats, in a cutout and pierced mount pavé with round, rectangular, and baguette-cut diamonds, approx. 1.580 carats; platinum.
Very Good Quality/Good Condition $3500 (A)   **$3000–$4000**

Suite Georgian 1830–1845 England
Necklace, brooch, and earrings in hollow gold settings with turquoise and pearls.
(See photo 173)
Very Good Quality/Good Condition $2500 (D)   **$2500–$3500**

Suite Victorian 1845–1865 England
Brooch and earrings set with sardonyx cameos of a female head; gold frames set with seed pearls in clusters of 3 in 4 places on the frame.
Good Quality/Good Condition $1750 (A)   **$1500–$2250**

Suite Victorian 1845–1865 United States
Brooch and earrings in a geometric motif with a shield design with 3 long drops; black onyx set in gold.
Good Quality/Average Condition $710 (A)   **$800–$1200**

Suite Victorian 1865–1885 United States
Brooch and earrings set with oval plaques of milky quartz with gold matrix; gold frame.
Good Quality/Good Condition $660 (A)   **$500–$800**

Watch key Victorian 1840 England
Watch key in the motif of an eagle's head with a sardonyx intaglio; gold.
Good Quality/Good Condition $800 (D)   **$600–$1000**

BIBLIOGRAPHY

The following books are excellent reference sources for information on antique jewelry.

Armstrong, Nancy. *Jewellery: An Historical Survey of British Styles and Jewels.* London: Luttenworth Press, 1977.

———. *Victorian Jewelry.* London: Cassell & Collier Macmillan Publishers Ltd., 1976.

British Museum. *Jewellery through 700 Years.* London: British Museum Publications, 1976.

Evans, Joan. *A History of Jewellery 1100–1870.* Boston: Boston Book and Art, 1970.

Flower, Margaret. *Victorian Jewellery.* New York: A. S. Barnes & Co., 1967.

Gere, Charlotte. *American and European Jewelry 1830–1914.* New York: Crown Publishers, 1975.

Gere, Charlotte; Rudoe, Judy; Tait, Hugh; and Wilson, Timothy. *The Art of the Jeweller: A Catalogue of the Hull Grundy Gift to the British Museum.* London: British Museum Publications, 1984.

Kaplan, Arthur Guy. *The Official Price Guide to Antique Jewelry* (6th ed.). New York: House of Collectibles, 1990.

MUSEUMS WITH MAJOR COLLECTIONS

British Museum, London.
Metropolitan Museum of Art, New York.
Smithsonian Institute, Washington, DC.
Victoria and Albert Museum, London.
Walters Art Gallery, Baltimore.

KNIVES

Advisor: C. HOUSTON PRICE

C. Houston Price is the author of The Official Price Guide to Collector Knives (10th Ed.), *New York: House of Collectibles, 1991. He is editor and publisher of* Knife World, *a monthly tabloid that features articles of interest to collectors of knives and cutlery-related collectibles. Mr. Price may be contacted at Knife World Publications, PO Box 3395, Knoxville, TN 37927; (615) 523-3339.*

HISTORY

The evolution of knife collecting and trading may have taken centuries or even millennia—perhaps even the caveman swapped their flintstone knives and spears—but the revolution began about two decades ago.

One catalyst was the Gun Control Act of 1968, which made selling and trading guns much more difficult. Since gun shows were already quite popular, the transfer of interest and trading activities from guns to knives was natural. Through the gun show circuits, antique bowie knives and military cutlery items had already found their fanciers; antique pocketknives and modern custom knives would soon follow.

Near this time, one of the nation's major knife manufacturers revamped its marking system, making it easier to understand dates of manufacture of its products and bringing a new charisma to its knives. Before long, growing numbers of bargain hunters and knife traders made their rounds to practically every country store, buying complete dealer displays of Case knives as well as other knives that had been in the dealer's stock for a few years.

Growth of the hobby continued at a rather rapid pace into and through the 1980s as more and more collectors came to recognize the fascination of old knives as pieces of Americana to which most of them could personally relate. And they came to recognize their increasing value. Coincidentally, this period also saw the number of established custom knifemakers increase from a few dozen to hundreds.

Reference books were sorely needed by collectors, and the few published in the early 1970s should be credited not only with providing information but also with increasing public awareness of a new hobby. This same period gave birth to three magazines published especially for the knife collector. Continued growth in numbers of collectors went hand-in-hand during the 1980s, with a substantial increase in published works relating to knives. The cause-and-effect relationship has been good for the hobby.

Collectors are learning that there is something for every budget, and with their investment, regardless of whether it is in knives valued at $5 each or knives that cost several hundred dollars, comes the satisfaction of building a meaningful collection—one that should pay dividends if and when the decision is made to sell.

SPECIALIZATION

Specialization in knife collecting is heartily recommended because it allows for a high level of expertise in the chosen specialty. With the thousands of different knives available to collectors, it is practically impossible to learn much about the majority of them. It is not only possible but entirely feasible for a collector to become an expert in one or a few knife-collecting specialties.

Although true specialization goes far beyond these general categories, areas to consider are older factory-made knives, antique bowie knives, custom-made knives, limited-edition or commemorative knives, and military knives.

THE FUTURE—WHAT'S AHEAD FOR THE 1990S?

One could neither review the progress made during the past few years nor witness the atmosphere of the knife-collecting community without a great deal of optimism. Anticipate prices of desirable antique knives to rise considerably during this decade; finding such knives is becoming increasingly difficult, and whenever they can be found, they are already far from inexpensive. Purchasing knives for investment means that one should acquire the very best examples that the budget will allow. Because the pieces in excellent condition are becoming harder to find, one should expect an increasing demand for and valuation of knives in less than mint or excellent condition. Purchasing a desirable knife rated in good condition is probably the best hedge against future value inflation and for the time when a better piece for the collection may become available.

Custom knives will continue to be an exciting and growing area to watch but one to approach with caution and with the best information available. Selected handmade knives will represent excellent investment opportunities, but as a rule, don't expect the aftermarket for the average custom knife to be especially strong. If your interest in custom knives is primarily for investment, buy the very best knife you can afford—one made by a maker whose work and reputation is already highly regarded. If you simply want to own a custom knife, find one that you like, and if the price is in keeping with its quality and your desire to own it, by all means buy it. But buy it for pride in ownership and not purely for investment.

RECENT MARKET TRENDS

Some exciting and perhaps surprising events during the late 1980s indicate that limited production, and commemorative and reproduction knives may indeed be specialties of opportunity during this decade. In 1988, Randall Knives sold three hundred serial-numbered pieces of their 50th Anniversary knife at $375; the knife is now selling for ten times that amount. With the worldwide reputation and recent death of the pioneering knifemaker founder, W. D. "Bo" Randall, price appreciation was no surprise. Very few collectors, however, would have guessed its magnitude. Factory-authorized Remington Bullet reproductions were introduced and manufactured in quantities of five thousand to ten thousand. Within a year or two, prices had doubled on practically each of the issues and low-serial-numbered pieces were selling for several times the original purchase price. Authorized reproductions of early Winchester knives, made in relatively small quantities, also attracted the interest of collectors, and significant value increases were realized on several of these knives. Cripple Creek was a new brand of limited-production knives entering the collector market in the early 1980s. Several early releases that sold for $35–$50 now demand prices of $300–$500.

To the majority of pocketknife collectors, Case knives have reigned as king of the collectibles for three or more decades. While there are many other brands worthy of collecting—and their values are proof of this fact—Case has been at the forefront of the knife-collecting movement. But due to various factors, the charm began to dwindle during the 1980s. In 1989, W. R. Case & Sons Cutlery Co. was sold by American Brands to well-known importer, distributor, and manufacturer James F. Parker. Within the year, a substantial number of changes were made, including the introduction of new patterns and the revival of popular old ones, new stampings and shields, and combinations of Parker designs and materials with those of Case, among others. Case's introduction of 100th-Year Anniversary knives, produced in limited numbers and available as complete sets or as individual knives, was interpreted by many to be a significant event in the company's long history. These are still definitely knives to watch, especially in view of the Chapter 11 bankruptcy of the parent company that went into effect in mid-1990.

On the whole, the knife-collecting market has been adversely affected by downward turns in our nation's economy. The net effect has been fewer collectors entering the hobby, and those who are already involved have become more selective in their purchases, but this period can offer opportunities for "distress sale" bargains.

FAKES

Fakes are an unfortunate fact of life, and perhaps it is a backhanded compliment about the value of knives as collectibles that we must be concerned with counterfeits. While no single specialty of knife collecting is immune, primary targets for the counterfeiters' forgeries are antique bowies and medium- to high-priced factory pocketknives.

As a rule, pocketknives selling in the $100–$200 range are most subject to deceptive practices. Knives selling for less would hardly be worth the counterfeiter's time and effort; knives selling for higher amounts would normally be subject to greater scrutiny by the prospective buyer.

Guarding against buying counterfeit knives is not unlike caution used with other collectibles. The best rule is to first know your knives and, whenever possible, know the seller. The collector who has done his homework well should be able to spot inconsistencies either in the piece or in the story behind it, perhaps in both. If the knife and/or its bargain price are too good to be true, that's probably the case.

One should learn as much as possible about the tricks of the counterfeiter as well as the craft of knife restoration. There is a difference between a knife that has been restored and is represented as such and one that has been altered with an intent to deceive. Properly restored knives or knives that have been taken apart for cleaning, although valued at less than a true mint piece, are certainly acceptable in the marketplace; counterfeits are not. Fortunately, there are very few counterfeiters who possess sufficient skill and the necessary equipment to make a foolproof counterfeit knife. But there are those who are able to deceive the inexperienced or naive collector, and even the "expert" can be fooled on occasion.

Determine if the knife has been taken apart. If it has, ask what was done with it to determine if its parts are original. Obviously, regardless of how it looks, it is not a mint knife. Use intelligence and common sense to evaluate what your eyes, ears, and intuition are trying to tell you. Don't be shy about asking for second opinions from reputable and knowledgeable collectors. Finally, don't be afraid to ask the dealer for a receipt and for an agreement of return privileges for a reasonable length of time.

CONDITION KEY

Grading the condition of a knife varies with the individual and is almost always interpreted differently by the prospective buyer and the seller. The most widely accepted guidelines, however, are those established by the National Knife Collectors Association and described below.

Mint: a knife that is absolutely original as it came from the manufacturer; never used, carried, sharpened, nor heavily cleaned; an unblemished knife.

Near Mint: a new-condition knife that may show very slight signs of carry or shop wear; blades not worn and snap perfectly; handles show no cracks; most of original finish is obvious.

Excellent: a knife that shows no more than 10 percent blade wear; handles are sound with no cracks; blades snap well; some discoloration of blades or handles acceptable; may have been heavily cleaned.

Very Good: a knife with up to 25 percent blade wear, slight cracks in handles; no blades nor other parts replaced or repaired; stamping clearly visible to the naked eye.

Fair: a knife with up to 50 percent blade wear, cracks or chips in handles; blades "lazy" (lacking snap) and may have been repaired; stamping faint but readable with magnifying glass.

Poor: blades very worn or may have been replaced with ones of same type; handles bad or missing; reading of stamping nearly impossible; a knife valued only for its parts.

Although these grading guidelines directly apply to mass-produced or factory-made knives, they may also be used (with perhaps more generalized interpretations) for antique bowies or custom knives. Grading of recently made custom knives more directly relates to levels of workmanship, fit, finish, and types of materials used in making the knife.

QUALITY KEY

In keeping with the harmony of this book, quality keys of good, very good, and superior are used. These quality keys essentially reflect upon the knife's rarity as well as its desirability or demand among collectors. There are many knives that, although rare because of age or numbers produced, rank low in desirability or collector demand. Just because a knife is old and perhaps of excellent quality (material and workmanship), there is no reason to assume that it has high value. With factory-made pocketknives especially, brand and pattern are of greater importance than age or numbers produced.

Because most knife collectors tend to specialize, one man's junk may truly be another man's treasure. Collectors of antique factory-made knives may have no interest in, and therefore fail to recognize the potential value of, an antique custom knife. A collector of current handmade art knives may be astonished to learn that an old pocketknife, perhaps made in a quantity ranging in the tens of thousands, will sell for several hundred dollars.

An excellent example of this junk/treasure precept at work came to light during a recent visit to a Midwest knife show. A collector, naturally very proud of his good fortune, showed me an old ivory-handled pocketknife in somewhat worn but complete condition. He had found the rare piece while rummaging through a dealer's "junk knife" box and knew that the ivory handles made it worth the $5 price tag. After some cleaning and further examination of the knife, he recognized it as having been made by William Scagel during the first third of this century. With a slight twinge of envy, I shared his exhilaration in the find. At least I was afforded the opportunity, perhaps the only one of my lifetime, to examine and admire the very rare knife. With pride, he showed the old knife to dozens of other dealers and collectors, and I suspect that the majority of them regarded it as a crude "junker," not worthy of their time. But one, a collector of Scagel knives, was willing to part with $1,400 to call it his own.

Recognizing that this scenario is not so unusual, I have tried to approach the Quality Key definitions from the viewpoint of a collector who has a reasonable amount of knowledge about the several specialized areas of collectible knives. The perception of rarity and desirability are, in fact, subjective. One extremely enlightened in any one special area may not necessarily agree with a specific example, but, after all, that's what makes one man's $5 junk another man's $1,400 treasure. And with a reasonable amount of knowledge and a great deal of luck, it's what makes some lives richer.

Good Quality: a knife that may be commonly found through the usual knife-trading channels; recognized as desirable and in reasonable demand by collectors.

Very Good Quality: a knife that is not commonly found for sale; one that is in high demand by collectors familiar with the specialty area of the subject knife.

Superior Quality: a knife that is very rarely found for sale; one that is generally recognized by collectors as rare and desirable; demand far exceeds availability in the marketplace.

Bowie knife Presentation 1861 United States
Classic Civil War bowie by Hassam/Boston; crown stag handle with nickel-silver butt cap; 8″ clip-point blade; original black leather sheath with silver throat engraved "C.C. Hills/from his friend/S.S.M. 1861." *(See photo 174)*
Superior Quality/Very Good Condition $4500 (A) **$2500-$6000**

Bowie knife E. Carver Co. 1850-1860 United States
16.6″ stag-handled bowie with 10.88″ clip blade; steel ferrule and pommel cap; brown leather with nickel silver throat and tip; blade stamped "E. Carver Co.," who also made cotton gins for Eli Whitney.
Superior Quality/Near Mint Condition $2100 (A) **$1200-$2500**

Commemorative pocket Boker Collector 1974-1978 Germany
Set of 12 different knives mounted on Plexiglas-covered wood frame; handles are delrin in various colors, and each knife has different shield.
Good Quality/Mint Condition $134 (D) **$95-$160**

Commemorative pocket Jim Bowie c. 1970 United States
Three-blade stockman pattern with black delrin handles; shield is miniature representation of large bowie knife; made by Schrade Cutlery Co., includes original papers.
Good Quality/Mint Condition $22 (D) **$15-$25**

Custom knife Warther folder 1922 United States
Ivory-handled with numerous decorative pins; bolsters made from U.S. dimes; stamped "E. Warther" and "1922"; made in Dover, OH.
Superior Quality/Excellent Condition $275 (D) **$250-$500**

Custom knife Moran Cinqueadea c. 1960 United States
Stamped "W. F. Moran, Lime Kiln"; very complex dagger, handle has 26 parts; hand-forged; fewer than 7 made; sheath of leather and brass. *(See photo 175)*
Superior Quality/Near Mint Condition $4200 (D) **$3000-$5000**

Custom knife Barlow, handmade c. 1978 United States
Stamped "Cargill"; 1-blade Barlow pattern with genuine stag handles; blade etched "Buckeye Knife Club"; made by custom maker, Bob Cargill; never sharpened, slight tarnish.
Very Good Quality/Near Mint Condition $100 (D) **$85-$130**

Hunting dagger Hunting 1885-1900 Germany
8.88″ spear-point blade with decorative scroll engraving, 13.6″ overall; marked "T.J.I.K.R."; horn handle; black leather sheath with nickel throat and tip.
Good Quality/Very Good Condition $50 (A) **$50-$225**

Hunting knife Remington RH-4 1930-1940 United States
Bone-handled hunting knife with original leather sheath; sharpened but very slight blade wear and tarnish.
Very Good Quality/Near Mint Condition $45 (A) **$25-$75**

Military knife Hunting 1880 United States
Military utility or hunting knife marked "US/Springfield" and serial number "342"; blade shows no use, turned-wood handle excellent; with original leather scabbard. *(See photo 176)*
Superior Quality/Near Mint Condition $700 (A) **$400-$800**

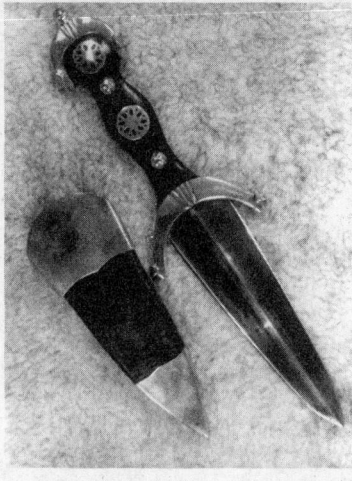

Photo 174 (left). Bowie knife. CREDIT: J. C. DEVINE, INC., AUCTIONEERS. *Photo 175 (center). Custom knife.* CREDIT: C. HOUSTON PRICE. *Photo 176 (right). Military knife.* CREDIT: J. C. DEVINE, INC., AUCTIONEERS *(See p. 324)*

Photo 177 (left). Folding hunter pocketknife. CREDIT: C. HOUSTON PRICE *(See p. 326)*

Photo 178. Case utility pocketknife. CREDIT: C. HOUSTON PRICE *(See p. 327)*

Military knife V-42 Stilletto 1943 United States
Made by W.R. Case & Sons Cutlery; only about 2000 were made on contract to the government and the majority of these were lost; with original sheath.
Superior Quality/Good Condition $1850 (D)   **$1000–$2000**

Pocketknife Fruit knife 1900–1910 England
Hallmarked sterling-silver-blade fruit knife with carved mother-of-pearl handles and chased backspring; English made, probably Sheffield.
Very Good Quality/Near Mint Condition $105 (A)   **$70–$150**

Pocketknife E.C. Simmons 1870–1940 United States
Three-backspring whittler with celluloid handles in candy-stripe design; blades marked with both "E.C. Simmons" and "Keen Kutter"; polished.
Good Quality/Excellent Condition $95 (D)   **$60–$95**

Pocketknife Picture handle 1880–1900 United States
Three-blade whittler with fraternal order emblems beneath celluloid handles; stamped "Vignos, Canton, O."; made by Novelty Cutlery; slight tarnish, no blade wear.
Very Good Quality/Near Mint Condition $100 (A)   **$75–$150**

Pocketknife Advertising c. 1910 United States
Aluminum-handled 2-blade penknife; handle engraved and blade etched "E.H. Best Co. Boston, Mass."; blade tangs stamped "New York Knife Co., Walden, N.Y."
Very Good Quality/Very Good Condition $40 (A)   **$40–$125**

Pocketknife New York Knife Co. c. 1900 United States
Equal-end jackknife with wood handles; made by New York Knife Co., Walden, NY; has bow-tie shield.
Very Good Quality/Excellent Condition $60 (D)   **$45–$65**

Pocketknife Marbles 1902–1931 United States
Stag-handled, single-blade folding hunter with folding guard; "Safety Hunting Knife" made by Marbles Safety Axe Co., Gladstone, MI; blade not sharpened, slight tarnish.
Superior Quality/Near Mint Condition $650 (A)   **$400–$900**

Pocketknife Cattaraugus 1920–1930 United States
Bone stag handle, 2-blade regular jackknife pattern; stamped with "Cattaraugus, Little Valley, N.Y"; slight tarnish on blades, no wear on master blade, pen blade has moderate wear.
Very Good Quality/Excellent Condition $60 (A)   **$55–$145**

Pocketknife Cattaraugus 1920–1930 United States
Cattaraugus Cutlery Co. wrench knife with jigged bone handles; also master spear blade and secondary blade that includes a cap-lifter and screwdriver; minor pitting on wrench; no blade wear.
Very Good Quality/Near Mint Condition $350 (D)   **$250–$375**

Pocketknife Folding hunter 1920–1930 United States
"King of the Woods" model, 5.5″ folding hunter made by Cattaraugus; bone handles, lanyard hole in 1 bolster; slight wear and tarnish on blade. *(See photo 177)*
Superior Quality/Very Good Condition $425 (A)   **$450–$750**

Pocketknife Case penknife 1920–1940 United States
Celluloid-handled 2-blade pen or "office" knife; blades stamped with Case "Circle C" marking; rare with this handle engraving.
Superior Quality/Mint Condition $250 (D)   **$150–$325**

Pocketknife Case utility 1920–1940 United States
Case scout or utility knife handled in jigged bone; master blade stamped with
Case's "Circle C" trademark. *(See photo 178)*
Good Quality/Very Good Condition $45 (A) **$60–$125**

Pocketknife Remington 1925–1935 United States
Five-blade "sowbelly" stockman pattern with bone handles; blades stamped "Remington UMC Made in USA" in circle; very slight blade and handle wear; rare.
Superior Quality/Excellent Condition $750 (D) **$700–$1700**

Pocketknife Cattaraugus 1925–1940 United States
Rare take-apart folding knife and fork, generally known as a "Hobo" knife;
cap-lifter on fork; unique shield inset into brown bone handles; no measurable
blade or handle wear. *(See photo 179)*
Superior Quality/Near Mint Condition $375 (D) **$200–$375**

Pocketknife Jackknife 1925–1940 United States
Stag-handled teardrop jackknife with circle Remington UMC stamping.
Very Good Quality/Fine Condition $45 (A) **$60–$140**

Pocketknife Utility knife 1925–1940 United States
R4243-pattern Remington "Bullet" knife; bullet shield on brown bone handles;
blades worn and slightly lazy.
Superior Quality/Average Condition $225 (D) **$400–$1000**

Pocketknife Case knife-ax 1927–1948 United States
Combination knife/ax (blades interchange into handle) marked "Jean Case Cutlery Co., Little Valley, New York"; wood handle.
Superior Quality/Very Good Condition $185 (D) **$150–$225**

Pocketknife Walkill River 1928–1931 United States
Three-blade penknife with celluloid handles; made by New York Knife Co. in
Walden, NY; striped celluloid handles.
Good Quality/Fair Condition $18 (A) **$40–$90**

Pocketknife Remington 1930–1940 United States
Two-blade penknife with mastodon ivory handles, 1 side carved with totem pole;
blades stamped with Remington's circle trademark.
Superior Quality/Excellent Condition $900 (D) **$450–$1500**

Pocketknife Barlow knife c. 1950 United States
Two-blade Barlow pattern with "RCC" on bolsters; bone handles; made by
Robeson Cutlery Co.
Good Quality/Very Good Condition $25 (A) **$30–$65**

Pocketknife Jim Bowie c. 1970 United States
Commemorative; 3-blade stockman pattern with black delrin handles; shield is
miniature representation of larger knife made by Schrade Cutlery Co.; includes
original papers.
Good Quality/Fine Condition $22 (D) **$15–$25**

Pocketknife NKCA Club knife 1979 United States
Made by W.R. Case & Sons Cutlery in 1979 for National Knife Collectors
Association, membership knife; stag handles; single blade is etched with year
and club name; serial-numbered.
Good Quality/Mint Condition $75 (D) **$65–$85**

Pocketknives Collector set 1947–1978 Germany
Boker collector set of 12 different knives mounted on Plexiglass wood frame;
handles are delrin in various colors and each knife has different shield.
Good Quality/Fine Condition $135 (D) **$95–$160**

Photo 179.
Cattaraugus pocketknife.
CREDIT: SMOKY MOUNTAIN
KNIFEWORKS *(See p. 327)*

Sheath knife Military 1940–1950 United States
KA-BAR military issue utility knife with original sheath; slight wear to blade, handle, and sheath.
Good Quality/Very Good Condition $45 (A) **$40–$85**

BIBLIOGRAPHY

Cole, M. H. *U. S. Military Knives, Bayonets and Machetes*, Book 4. Birmingham, AL: Author, 1990. Considered the standard reference for collectors of these types of knives. Well respected for detailed sketches of desirable knives.

Giles, James S. *Case, the First 100 Years.* Sevierville, TN: Smoky Mountain Knifeworks, 1989. A pictorial and historical review of W. R. Case & Sons Cutlery and the people who were a part of its history.

Goins, John E. *Goins' Encyclopedia of Cutlery Markings.* Knoxville, TN: Knife World Publications, 1986. Most complete listing known of trademarks used in cutlery manufacture. Includes illustrations, dates of use, etc. The standard reference for cutlery historians and hobbyists.

Karsten, Bill. *Silver Folding Fruit Knives.* Knoxville, TN: Knife World Publications, 1986. An in-depth review, including hallmarks, of English-, French- and American-made silver fruit knives. Many excellent-quality photos. Brief price range guides.

Levine, Bernard. *Levine's Guide to Knives and Their Values* (2nd ed.). Northbrook, IL: DBI Books, Inc., 1989. Features a unique system for estimating prices of most types of knives. Excellent editorial content on knife history.

Levine, Bernard R. *Knifemakers of Old San Francisco*. San Francisco: Badger Books, 1978. Extremely well-researched and -written reference on 19th-century knifemakers in the San Francisco area, especially Michael Price and Will & Finck.

McEvoy, Harry. *Scagel, the Man and His Knives*. Knoxville, TN: Knife World Publications, 1985. Booklet with an interesting story about William Scagel, credited by most collectors as being "the father of modern-day custom knives."

Pankiewicz, Philip R. *New England Cutlery*. Gilman, CT: Hollytree Publications, Inc., 1986. Historical sketches of the scores of knife manufacturers and makers located in the New England area. Very informative on older companies.

Platts, Harvey. *The Knifemakers Who Went West*. Longmont, CO: Longs Peak Press, 1978. Traces family histories and the companies they founded. Features the pioneers and prime movers of the U.S. cutlery industry.

Price, C. Houston. *The Official Price Guide to Collector Knives* (10th ed.). New York: House of Collectibles, 1991. Historical information plus pricing guide. A handy reference to thousands of knives of interest to collectors.

Swayne, Allen P. *The Case Knife Story*. Knoxville, TN: Knife World Publications, 1987. Very informative small booklet that traces the history of Case and related knife companies through the many trademarks used, giving illustrations and dates of use.

COLLECTORS' CLUBS

National Knife Collectors
Association
PO Box 21070
Chattanooga, TN 37421

The NKCA is a nonprofit club with approximately 17,000 members throughout the United States and several other countries. In addition to this membership organization, there are scores of regional or local knife clubs. Most are nonprofit clubs, relatively small in membership, that are organized for the purpose of collectors' interaction. Those that meet on a regular basis allow opportunities for buying, selling, and trading knives as well as learning about them. Since club meeting dates, times, and places vary and are subject to change, it is not practical to list them here. Updated information regarding local clubs may be obtained from *Knife*

World (PO Box 3395, Knoxville, TN 37927; (615) 523-3339), a publication with monthly issues that provide a listing of these clubs, their meeting dates, and contact addresses.

MUSEUMS

The National Knife Museum, 7201 Shallowford Road, Chattanooga, TN 37421, is open to the public at a $2 admission charge for adults and no charge for those under sixteen and for senior citizens. Special rates are available for groups. This museum displays a seemingly endless variety of knives and knife-related items, with the total valuation of its contents ranking into several millions of dollars. Although there are no formal tours, individuals as well as groups are welcome Monday through Saturday during the hours of 10 A.M. to 4 P.M.

Lighting Devices

(See also Metalware)

In collecting, it is very important to be able to cite the introduction or change of a style, design element, construction, or function of the subject item. The recognition of these starting points will help the collector date the item. One has the option of starting from the beginning or traveling backward into history to note these developments.

The first revolutionary change in lighting is credited to the ancient Greeks. From the universal saucer lamp they developed a closed-reservoir lamp, which slowly emerged with a spout or two (and more). The budding handle emerged as a ring, about 700 B.C. Although scarce, some of these lamps can be found today.

From the Bronze Age and Iron Age through the great Renaissance, changes were made only in the lighting device, not its function. Lamplight continued to be derived from a flame, wick, and fuel (grease and oils). Torches, torchères, candlebeams, candleholders, fire baskets, float lamps, spout lamps, and grease lamps were carryovers from the earliest times. Metals (iron, silver, and alloys), wood, earthenware, and glass were used, from simple to bejeweled forms. The 17th-century European iron crusie is a surviving form. Our Pilgrim Betty and Phoebe lamps are derivatives of the crusie grease lamp and have continued to be used. The advancement displayed in the oblong, pear-shaped Betty lamp is that the reservoir has a hinged lid for safety against spillage and that the basin is deeper, with upright walls. The attached curved handle with spiked hook allows the user to place the lamp on the table or to hang it from the wall or a chimney crevice. The Pennsylvania German crusie stand is a carryover from early times. America has made iron implements, rush holders, grease lamps, and stands since the 1630s.

Very few iron examples prior to the 17th century have survived. Authentic and reproduced later metal fixtures are at hand. Bettys, hogscrapers, standing lamps, and rushlights are found.

The 18th century was the first "well lighted" century, with candlepower reigning supreme. Wax, tallow, bayberry, and spermaceti candles were dipped or molded. The candleholder became the focal point of design, artistry, and manufacturing. Brass, silver, and faceted glass were produced in abundance. European porcelain makers, followed by the English potters, produced rococo and figural candleholders to please their wealthy clientele. Candlesticks and candelabra of all periods are plentiful although often costly. Fakes are equally prevalent.

The plebeian grease and spout lamps continued to be used but were kept out of the sight of the affluent. These dim and bad-smelling lamps were of importance in the houses of poorer people and in the servants' quarters of the wealthy.

From the 17th to the 19th century spout lamps were made in many shapes and a variety of metals. They could be bucket-shaped, cylindrical, globular, conical, or rounded. One or several wick spouts sprang from the lamps. There were now drip catchers under the closed spouts. Some were made as peg lamps for candleholders, as candlelight was being displaced by whale oil lighting. It is important to note that these lamps still have their spouts mounted to the sides of the reservoir. Spout lamps "of the period" are fairly rare.

The most important development in lighting history was in getting the wick spout to the top of the oil reservoir. This was achieved around the third quarter of the 18th century. One wick was sufficient until Benjamin Franklin discovered the increased yield from two spouts. These burners were used until after the Civil War. Lamps were of metal, including pewter. Their shapes varied, depending on the job at hand: hand lamps, tavern lights, reading lamps with the newly invented bull's-eye lens, gimbals, sconces, peg lamps, and some hanging lamps and lanterns. Whale oil was favored, and later lard oil was used. A typical lamp form would be a cast-pewter or brass candlestick form with a bulged oil reservoir and a screwed-on burner with one or two wick tubes.

Lighting had become of great importance to the now successful glass industry of the early 19th century. From 1820 to 1840 more than one hundred glassworks were in business. The most celebrated 19th-century glasswork in America, the Boston and Sandwich Glass Company of Cape Cod (1825–1888), produced blown glass, mold-blown flint glass, and pressed glass. They and others produced early glass oil lamps that were similar to the metal prototypes. These beautiful lamps were important household items, kept and adapted to the changing fuels and burners. Throughout the century an infinite variety of glass lamps were made, including art glass and stained glass. China lamps did not become popular until the end of the 19th century. Comparatively speaking, very few earthenware and art pottery lamps were made.

This is a period from which examples abound, and fakes are again quite common. With lighting devices, as with all antiques, look for signs of long, regular use!

Innovations to improve illumination, to develop shading and adjustable direction, were made throughout the Victorian era. The Student Lamp encompassed all of these features.

Improved fuel and a more efficient burner were of pressing importance from about 1775 to about 1875. Over this broad but relatively short span much happened to artificial lighting. In 1783 a Swiss chemist, Ami Argand, developed a hollow cylindrical draft burner with glass shade, providing a brighter flame. The Solar and Astral lamps were Argand adaptations.

A disastrous development in fuel was the combination of turpentine and alcohol, patented in 1830 and named Camphene. It was volatile and dangerous. After many explosions and accidents it was removed from the market in 1850.

Natural gas came into general use after the mid-19th century. Fixtures were stationary. They were produced in all of the revival styles of the period. Glass shades, including those from famous Art Nouveau manufacturers, are highly collectible examples from this period.

By 1866 coal oil (kerosene) was plentiful and inexpensive enough to become the most popular of all liquid fuels. A burner had been developed with a flattened wick and with the lamp fonts made larger to accommodate more of the cheap oil. A chimney and shade completed the lamp. Kerosene-fueled lamps and lanterns are still used today. The lamps can easily be converted to electricity without damage. Lamps of this period—kerosene or converted—are available and affordable. Watch for reproductions and fakes, as they are prevalent.

With the advent of the incandescent light bulb (patented by Thomas Edison in 1879) the entire concept of lighting changed. Even so, our primitive form of lighting, fuel-fed flame, has not been abandoned. Also, many, many lighting devices from the Argand period forward have been electrified and are still being electrified today—not, by the way, a good idea, as it cuts the value by at least 25 percent!

Lamp forms, like all of the decorative arts, have followed the styles of historical periods and design movements. Burners can be interchangeable and offer no guarantee of being issued with the lamp. Glass shades for Fairy Lamps are often interchangeable. The collector should keep in mind that overlaps in form occur and that revivals are created. Reproductions and fakes are to be watched for, especially in Early American lighting devices such as tin lanterns. Ships' lights and lanterns of brass are reproduced and imported from Japan. Brass candleholders and lamps are reproduced; many are imports from India. The 1960s and 1970s suffered a flood of reproduction Victorian glass lamps (table size and miniatures) that are often mistaken for antiques.

CONDITION KEY

Fine Condition: glass and china: with clarity, without damage or discoloration.

Iron: negligible corrosion, all parts original.

Alloys: mellow patina, all parts original.

Good Condition: glass and china: with clarity, minor damage or discoloration.

Iron: minor corrosion; tolerate minor restoration.

Alloys: mellow patina; tolerate minor restoration.

Average Condition: glass and china: mellow with use; tolerate some damage.

Iron: mellow with use; tolerate some damage or restoration.

Alloys: mellow patina; tolerate some damage or restoration.

Poor Condition: glass and china: discolored; badly scratched, chipped, or cracked, reflecting a degree of abuse.

Iron: pitted or rusted; broken, missing parts; in need of restoration.

Alloys: patina or surface removed; damaged or broken; missing parts; in need of restoration.

Originality is not considered in the above condition statement.

QUALITY KEY

An overlapping scale of *Superior Quality*, *Very Good Quality*, to *Good Quality* runs from an excellent example of the best style and scale of proportion to a mediocre but collectible example. This is not a condition statement but a measure of the stylishness of the item's form.

Argand lamp   Double arm   1830–1845   United States
With 2 period shades, lacking fitters; labeled "Louis Vernon, Philadelphia."
Very Good Quality/Fine Condition $1300 (A)   **$900–$1500**

Argand lamps   17″ H   Regency   1800–1830   England
Pair of single-arm argand lamps, with later shades.
Good Quality/Good Condition $1210 (A)   **$900–$1500**

Argand lamps   15″ H   Sheffield plated   1800–1830   England
Pair; each having lobed spherical body, removable obelisk finial, lower section with bright-cut floral festooning and 2 gas jets, raised on columnar supports and square plinth base. *(See photo 180)*
Superior Quality/Fine Condition $1550 (A)   **$1500–$3500**

Argand lamps   11.25″ H   1830–1845   England
Pair cast bronze wild boar's-head lamps with original and frosted shades; never altered, totally original.
Superior Quality/Fine Condition $3200 (A)   **$4000–$6000**

Photo 180 (left). Argand lamps. CREDIT: WESCHLER'S, WASHINGTON, DC. *Photo 181 (right). Candlestick lamp.* CREDIT: BUTTERFIELD & BUTTERFIELD *(See pp. 334, 336)*

Photo 182 (left). Grueby lamp. CREDIT: BUTTERFIELD & BUTTERFIELD
Photo 183 (right). Piano lamp. CREDIT: BUTTERFIELD & BUTTERFIELD
(See pp. 337, 338)

Argand lamps   13″ H   1830–1845   England
Pair; gilt and patinated bronze stands; original burner apparatus; no shades.
Very Good Quality/Good Condition $990 (A)   **$900–$1500**

Argand lamps   13″ H   Cornelius   1845–1865   United States
Pair of stand Argand lamps, possibly by Cornelius & Co., Philadelphia; retaining original gilt finish and burner apparatus; no shades.
Superior Quality/Good Condition $1870 (A)   **$1500–$2500**

Astral lamp   15″ H   Cornelius   1845–1865   United States
Brass; marked "Cornelius & Co., April 1, 1845"; on stepped marble base; no shade.
Good Quality/Good Condition $175 (A)   **$150–$250**

Astral lamp   17″ H   Victorian   1845–1865   United States
Reeded brass shaft and white marble base, period foliate cut and etched shade; electrified.
Good Quality/Good Condition $660 (A)   **$450–$750**

Bouillotte   Regency style   1910–1930   France
Brass; painted tole shade; 2-light.
Good Quality/Good Condition $450 (A)   **$450–$850**

Bouillotte   Neoclassical style   1910–1930   France
Classical form; brass; green painted tole shade; 3-light.
Good Quality/Good Condition $375 (A)   **$450–$850**

Candelabra   38″ H   Religious   1900–1910   Italy
Pair; gilded brass with embossed foliage; vines, grains, etc.; enameled porcelain medallions in base with portraits of Jesus with crown of thorns; flowers have colored "jewel" centers; repairs.
Good Quality/Average Condition $110 (A)   **$100–$350**

Candle chandelier   28″ H   1910–1930   United States
Reproduction made from old turning; 18 wire arms with tin sockets and drip pans; includes a chain.
Good Quality/Average Condition $303 (A)   **$300–$500**

Candlestick lamp   12.25″ H   Tiffany   1899–1928   United States
Favrile glass swirl-molded, spreading, cylindrical base; white opaque shaft with green leaves; small amber shade with iridescence and flaring ruffle; base and shade signed "L.C.T." *(See photo 181)*
Very Good Quality/Fine Condition $1760 (A)   **$1500–$2500**

Candlesticks   30″ H   1885–1900   England
Pair of tall, brass candlesticks with open spiral stems.
Very Good Quality/Good Condition $325 (A)   **$275–$500**

Candlesticks   8″ H   1885–1900   United States
Pair; mercury glass; some wear and worn decoration.
Good Quality/Average Condition $145 (A)   **$125–$300**

Fixture   Late Victorian   1885–1900   Anglo-American
Pierced brass and bejeweled gas lighting fixture with beveled glass panels.
Very Good Quality/Fine Condition $660 (A)   **$600–$1200**

Grease lamp   19″ H   1800–1830   United States
Primitive wrought-iron grease lamp on stand; crown base; old dark patina including layers of old wax.
Good Quality/Average Condition $72 (A)   **$70–$195**

Grueby lamp 19″ H × 16″ Dia. Arts and Crafts 1900–1910 United States
White and mustard earthenware lamp base of cylindrical form, spreading to
bulbous base; with relief-molded flowers; domed, leaded, stained glass shade
with floral border base impressed "Grueby Pottery-Boston USA." *(See photo
182)*
Superior Quality/Fine Condition $5500 (A) **$3500–$6500**

Hanging lamp 23.5″ H Empire 1800–1830 United States
Wall lamp; clear blown globe with cut panels and floral design with cranberry
flashing; brass fittings; black patina with traces of original gilt; unmatched smoke
bell with Greek key design.
Very Good Quality/Fine Condition $1870 (A) **$1500–$3000**

Kerosene lamp 26″ H Arts and Crafts 1900–1910 United States
Rookwood incised and floral-painted matte-glazed lamp with Chandler molded
art glass shade; lamp with impressed factory and date marks and no. 429z; shade
has 1 crack.
Very Good Quality/Average Condition $1870 (A) **$1500–$2500**

Lamp 16.5″ H Art Nouveau 1900–1910 France
Brass and bronze; domed, hemispherical shade with repoussé pendant pine cones,
branches; 4 amber glass cabochons; attached to twin arms tapering to raised
circular base; signed G. Leleu.
Good Quality/Fine Condition $1000 (A) **$750–$1250**

Lantern 10″ H 1885–1900 United States
Tin candle lantern with clear globe; impressed label "J. Fleming."
Good Quality/Average Condition $88 (A) **$85–$200**

Lantern, hall 13.5″ H Gothic Revival 1840–1850 England
Tin and pewter; octagonal form; glazed panels set within reticulated borders
displaying gothic tracery.
Very Good Quality/Good Condition $330 (A) **$300–$500**

Lava lamp 23.5″ H Tiffany United States
"Lava" glass and gilt-bronze lamp base of baluster form with gold iridescence
and "bubbled lava" surface, inscribed "L.C. Tiffany-Favrile"; mounted on gilt
base; stamped "Tiffany Studios NY."
Good Quality/Fine Condition $1875 (A) **$1500–$3000**

Lighting stands 55.5″ H Rush light 1800–1830 United States
Pair; wrought-iron finials; 1 with spring clamp, the other with counterbalances;
nonperiod wooden adjustable bases, 1 with worm holes; broken leather thong on
1, wire ratcher on other.
Good Quality/Average Condition $275 (A) **$250–$500**

Marriage lamp 12.5″ H 1885–1900 United States
Ripley marriage lamp; blue and clam broth on mismatched opaque white base;
marked "D.C. Ripley & Co., Pat. Pending"; strawmarks, minor chips and crazing in base.
Very Good Quality/Average Condition $880 (A) **$500–$1500**

Nautilus lamp 13″ H Tiffany 1918–1928 United States
Patinated bronze domed, circular base with bifurcated stem; natural iridescent
shell shade; base impressed "TIFFANY STUDIOS/ NEW YORK/25893" and
monogram.
Very Good Quality/Fine Condition $1650 (A) **$1500–$2500**

The QUALITY KEY measures the stylishness and collectibility of an antique.

Good Quality: Exhibits standard characteristics of the object.

Very Good Quality: A more desirable example because of above-average workmanship and design.

Superior Quality: Exhibits nearly every known feature found on such items, with workmanship and design of the highest quality.

Oil lamp 5.5″ H Wedgwood 1800–1830 England
Black basalt with *rosso antico* applied leaves, handle, and sunburst molded, beaded trim, impressed marks; some nicks.
Very Good Quality/Average Condition $475 (A)   **$400–$750**

Piano lamp 12.5″ H Handel 1910–1930 United States
Cylindrical shade in "chipped" glass, painted with "Tel El Amarna" border in avocado green, brown, and white; pivoting on adjustable bronzed metal branching support on base; shade and based marked "HANDEL." *(See photo 183)*
Good Quality/Fine Condition $770 (A)   **$450–$750**

Sconces 14.5″ H Floral 1910–1930 Italy
Pair; gilded iron candle sconces with floral detail; 3 nozzles each.
Good Quality/Average Condition $190 (A)   **$150–$350**

Sinumbra lamp 31.5″ H 1830–1845 United States
Brass; hexagonal stepped base; cylindrical shaft; fine frosted cut-glass shade with long cut prisms; excellent acanthus cast decoration; electrified.
Superior Quality/Good Condition $1700 (A)   **$1500–$2400**

Sinumbra lamp 28.5″ H Victorian 1830–1845 United States
Brass; square base with molded leaves, vase shaft; fine frosted cut-glass shade with long cut prisms; electrified.
Good Quality/Fine Condition $1300 (A)   **$1200–$1800**

Sinumbra lamp 28.5″ H Victorian 1830–1845 United States
Brass; square base with molded leaves, vase shaft; fine frosted cut-glass shade with cut prisms; electrified. *(See photo 184)*
Very Good Quality/Good Condition $1100 (A)   **$900–$1500**

Sinumbra lamps 24″ H Victorian 1830–1845 United States
Pair; bronze with gilt and gunmetal finish; frosted shades; electrified.
Good Quality/Good Condition $770 (A)   **$700–$1200**

Solar lamp 34″ H Empire 1845–1865 United States
Tall solar lamp labeled Cornelius & Co., supporting a cut and etched globe hung with star-cut crystals; electrified.
Very Good Quality/Good Condition $1430 (A)   **$1200–$1800**

Solar lamp 27″ H Gothic 1845–1865 United States
Gothic design with later cut and etched shade; gilt, polished, and patinated bronze; hung with crystals; electrified; gothic arches heavily entwined with ivy.
Superior Quality/Average Condition $660 (A)   **$600–$1200**

Solar lamp 24″ H Victorian 1845–1865 United States
Fluted columns with Ionic capital supporting a ring of double-jeweled long, faceted crystals and well-cut geometric ball shade; converted to kerosene.
Good Quality/Good Condition $1045 (A)   **$900–$1250**

Solar lamp   24.5″ H   Victorian   1845–1865   United States
Fluted column on marble base; the font, now converted to kerosene, hung with crystals and supporting a cut and etched shade.
Good Quality/Good Condition $410 (A)   **$350–$600**

Solar lamp   22″ H   Victorian   1845–1865   United States
Fluted-column standard plinth base in 2-tone gilt; cut and etched ball globe of gothic design; some crystals missing; now electrified. *(See photo 185)*
Very Good Quality/Good Condition $1210 (A)   **$900–$1800**

Solar lamp   19″ H   Victorian   1845–1865   United States
Gilt bronze, on stepped white marble base, with period foliate cut and etched shade, hung with cut, pointed prisms.
Very Good Quality/Good Condition $880 (A)   **$600–$950**

Solar lamp   28″ H   Victorian   1845–1865   United States
Gilt bronze; converted to kerosene; exceptional pear-shaped, cut and etched gothic shade; hung with prisms; Boston.
Superior Quality/Good Condition $1875 (A)   **$1500–$2500**

Solar lamps   Neoclassical   1825–1830   England
Pair; patinated and gilt-bronze solar lamps, now electrified; no shades.
Superior Quality/Good Condition $2200 (A)   **$2200–$4500**

> Fine would include original shades and no wiring.—*DL*

Student lamp   11.5″ H   Tiffany   United States
Favrille glass and gilt bronze; hemispherical shade decorated with iridescent yellow horizontal banding; inscribed "Tiffany-Favrile"; gilt-bronze harp; stamped "Tiffany Studios, New York 418."
Good Quality/Fine Condition $2850 (A)   **$1500–$3000**

Wax jack   6.5″ H   Neoclassical   1865–1885   England
Brass and pink brass, with snuffer on chain, ring handle.
Very Good Quality/Fine Condition $225 (D)   **$150–$250**

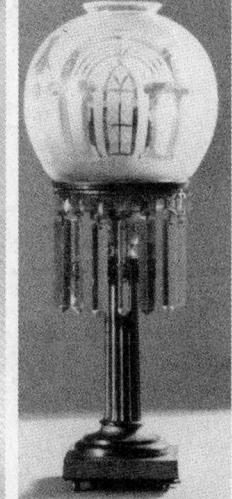

Photo 184 (left).
Sinumbra lamp.
CREDIT: SKINNER, INC.,
BOLTON, MA *(See p. 338)*
Photo 185 (right).
Solar lamp.
CREDIT: ALFORD
AUCTION CO. *(See above)*

BIBLIOGRAPHY

Hayward, Arthur H. *Colonial and Early American Lighting* (3rd. ed.). New York: Dover Publications, 1962. A first-person discussion (with pictures of collections) about lighting devices belonging to noted collectors, including himself.

Hornung, Clarence P. *Treasury of American Design*, vol. 1. New York: Harry N. Abrams, 1950. One of two volumes; illustrations with restrained text.

Lee, Ruth Webb. *Antique Fakes and Reproductions*. Wellesley Hills, MA: Lee Publications, 1966. Discussions, with photographs, regarding glass.

Mitchell, James, R. *Antique Metalware*. New York: Main Street Press, Universe Books. A collection of articles gathered from the magazine *Antiques*; with pictures.

Thuro, Catherine M. V. *Oil Lamps: The Kerosene Era in North America*. Lombard, IL: Wallace Homestead Book Co. Good history and illustrations; also a second volume, *Oil Lamps II*.

MUSEUMS

Henry Ford Museum, Dearborn, MI.
Sandwich Glass Museum, Cape Cod, MA.
Smithsonian Institution, Washington, DC.
Winchester Center Kerosene Lamp Museum, Winchester Center, CT.

Metalware

***Advisor:* GARLAND PASS**

The listings in this chapter are arranged as follows:
PEWTER, BRASS, COPPER, IRON, TIN.

Garland Pass is an antiques dealer specializing in fine antique metal-ware. He has lectured and written articles and book reviews on the subject for national publications. He is a past president of the Pewter Collectors Club of America and corresponding member of the Pewter Society of Great Britain. He and his wife exhibit in a few major antique shows in New England but primarily conduct their antique business via mail order. They can be reached at Garland and Frances Pass, Fine Antique Metalware, 87 Paper Chase Trail, Avon, CT; (203) 673-0787.

In this edition, the section on base metals will feature utilitarian objects made of pewter, brass, copper, iron, and tin, dating mostly from the late 17th century through 1860 and of American, English, or Western European origin. Utilitarian objects are those items made for everyday use. They were used to some extent in almost every public building and home, except for those of the very poor.

Items made during the Art Nouveau, Art Deco, and the Arts and Crafts movements will not be covered here, not only because of their later dates but because they are more closely related to the fine arts, where the emphasis is not on utility. Also excluded here are metalware collectibles, arms and armaments, and scientific instruments.

MARKET TRENDS

Metalware values move with the broad field of antique decorative arts. Record prices have been achieved at auctions within the past few years, and demand for the best pieces remains high. For the broad range of metalware pieces, however, prices continue to move steadily higher but at a slightly slower rate.

There are several reasons for this. One is the peaking of the Country craze—the interest in Country antiques and decorator trends that were enhanced by pieces of utilitarian metalware. Another is the peaking of interest in folk art, which has some effect on wrought iron and decorated tinware. Trends in Country and folk art rise and fall from time to time and have some effect on metalware values.

Another reason for the steady but unspectacular increase in metalware values is that antique metalware is a mature field; that is, most of the major discoveries have already been made and written about. In fact, the best metalware books have not only been written but are now out of print. It is perhaps significant that in three of the five categories of metalware (pewter, brass, and iron), the most recent books have been pictorial surveys with little text.

New information does continue to come to light in articles in the major antiques publications. Also the Americana concept (an appreciation of items used but not made here during and after our colonial period) is now being applied to metalware in the same manner that it has been applied to ceramics for years. This has been especially important in pewter, where a distinction is being made between English export pewter made specifically for this country and English pewter made for the home market. Export items are included in the lists of metalware items that follow.

FAKES

Fakes exist in metalware, although collectors are more likely to encounter reproductions (not originally meant to deceive) and heavily restored items. More metalware is misrepresented by ignorance than by intent. Until one's eye and hand have been trained by experience, it is best to rely on an experienced dealer.

QUALITY KEY

Good Quality: exhibits standard characteristics of the object.

Very Good Quality: above average design and workmanship.

Superior Quality: exhibits the highest level of design and unsurpassed workmanship.

CONDITION KEY

Poor Condition: holes, cracks, or other damage; repairs; heavy oxidation and/or pitting; such pieces would not interest a serious collector.

Average Condition: some dents, light surface oxidation, or roughness; some light pitting and many signs of use and wear.

Good Condition: better than average condition; shows use and wear, but dents and surface roughness are minor.

Fine Condition: all signs of use and wear are minor.

MARKS

Maker's marks are more important on American metalware than on English or Continental metalware. However, a maker's mark (especially if identifiable) will always add a premium to the value of an item. Sometimes only a set of initials will be found. More often than not they will be the owner's initials rather than the maker's. For American extant pewter, somewhat more than half of the pieces are marked; for English pewter, about 90 percent are marked; for Continental pewter, the percentage marked falls somewhere between, depending on the country. For the other base metals, most pieces are unmarked regardless of country. In fact, for some forms in some metals, a marked piece is a true rarity. Dated pieces will also sell at a premium. For this reason, always look very carefully at maker's marks and dates: they may have been put there yesterday.

PEWTER

Pewter is to silver as pottery is to porcelain: an everyday ware of the 18th and 19th centuries found in the home, tavern, and church. Until about 1840, pewter, which is mostly tin with a few alloying agents, was cast in brass on bronze molds. After spinning and stamping techniques were developed in the middle of the 19th century, antimony was added to pewter to strengthen the metal and allow it to be formed into sheets. The resulting ware was named "Britannia" in England, where it was first developed. The important difference between the metals is not in how they were formulated but in how the wares from the two metals were made: pewter items were cast; Britannia items were fabricated from sheet.

Because Britannia was a late development, items fabricated in this manner show an increasing Victorian influence in their design. It is this deterioration of form, rather than the method of fabrication, that causes the serious collector to favor the earlier pieces.

At the time of the American Revolution, it has been estimated that for every piece of American-made pewter in this country there were one hundred pieces of British pewter. That ratio still holds today. It has been compounded by the large quantities of post-Imperial (i.e., post-1826, when England adopted the Imperial capacity standard) measures and tavern mugs brought here by dealers and collectors following World War II.

In recent years, collectors have begun to appreciate the difference between English pewter that is rightfully a part of our colonial heritage and the post-1826 English pewter that is not. Many of the export forms were made specifically for this country and are not found in England. Several of the English pewterers used a different mark on exported pewter. This important subset of English pewter is now generally referred to as English export pewter.

Most American pewter made during this period copied the English export pieces. Their forms are practically identical. For those who collect pewter for its form, the English export pieces offer a decided advantage: they sell for one-third to one-tenth of what their American counterparts bring, depending upon the rarity of the form.

Although the quantity of Continental, or European, pewter in this country is less than that of English or American pewter, its popularity is growing among American collectors. Ironically, there are more Continental reproductions on the American market than authentic period pieces. Most were sold to unsuspecting American tourists. When genuine pieces of Continental pewter can be found, they can usually be purchased for bargain prices.

Basin 8″ Dia. 1817–1856 United States
Signed by William Calder, Providence, RI; normal wear and some dents.
Good Quality/Average Condition $330 (A)   **$350–$500**

Basin 8″ Dia. 1844–1845 United States
Signed by Boardman & Hall; Philadelphia, PA; one of several partnerships of the Boardman family of Hartford, CT, where most of the pewter was believed made but marked for point of sale.
Good Quality/Good Condition $413 (A)   **$350–$500**

Beaker 3″ H 1808–1835 United States
Signed by Ashbil Griswold; Meriden, CT; short 3″ beakers are the typical 19th-century American beaker form.
Good Quality/Average Condition $154 (A)   **$150–$300**

Burning fluid lamp 6″ H Beehive form 1830–1860 United States
Unsigned; a late form; the burner is a possible replacement, although this was commonly done when manufactured burning fluids replaced the more expensive whale oil.
Good Quality/Average Condition $132 (A)   **$100–$150**

Coffeepot 11.5″ H Pear-shaped 1808–1835 United States
One of the most common of the tall coffeepot designs; made by several pewterers in this period; Meriden, CT.
Good Quality/Fine Condition $465 (A)   **$350–$525**

Photo 186.
Coffeepots.
CREDIT:
GARLAND PASS
(See below)

Coffeepot 12″ H Lighthouse 1813–1856 United States
Signed by Isreal Trask; Beverly, MA; his typical bright-cut engraving can be found on most of his hollowware; his are the most sought after lighthouse coffeepots. *(See photo 186, right)*
Very Good Quality/Fine Condition $950 (D) **$650–$950**

Coffeepot 11″ H Lighthouse 1817–1856 United States
The "lighthouse" type is the most popular with coffeepot lovers; signed by William Calder; a dull surface due to the removal of oxidation; Providence, RI. *(See photo 186, left)*
Good Quality/Average Condition $475 (D) **$450–$650**

Creamer, 3-footed 4″ H 1740–1785 English Export
Signed by Henry Joseph of London, a major exporter to this country; the "Best" of the creamer forms, although some can have better, fancier legs and feet.
Superior Quality/Fine Condition $2450 (D) **$1800–$2500**

Dish 12.25″ Dia. 1755–1782 United States
Signed by Thomas Danforth II of Middletown, CT; considerable wear and some repairs.
Good Quality/Poor Condition $303 (A) **$600–$1000**

Dish 13.25″ Dia. 1761–1793 United States
A very rare dish designed by Henry Will, brother of the more famous William Will; New York City and Albany, NY; all pewter made by any of the Wills is sought after.
Good Quality/Good Condition $1320 (A) **$1000–$1750**

Dish 13″ Dia. 1790–1816 United States
Deep dish; signed by Samuel Danforth; Hartford, CT: shows considerable wear and overall light denting.
Good Quality/Poor Condition $495 (A) **$600–$1000**

Flagon 12″ H 1825–1830 United States
The most common and one of the best-designed American flagons; signed by Boardman & Co.; Hartford, CT; bold "SJ" or "broken" handle and a triple-disk or tiered lid finial. Flagons are the largest hollowware form found in American, English, and English Export pewter. They were used as serving vessels in the home and tavern and in communion services in churches. The earlier forms do not have pouring spouts. *(See photo 187)*
Very Good Quality/Fine Condition $2450 (D) **$2000–$2500**

Measure 8.25″ H Tappit Hen 1730–1826 Scotland
The most popular pewter form in Scotland; this one the "Chopin" size; owner's
initials on lid; found in many sizes and capacities, usually unmarked by maker.
Good Quality/Fine Condition $1200 (D)   **$900–$1200**

Measures 1840–1860 France
Cylindrical form with rectangular handles; 7 sizes, from centiliter to liter; many
very late and reproduction sets around—be careful of these; authentic ones have
government capacity verification marks; assembled set.
Good Quality/Fine Condition $450 (D)   **$300–$450**

Open salt, footed 3″ H 1795–1819 United States
Positive attribution to Parks Boyd of Philadelphia, PA, based on use of form as
a portion of another signed piece; beaded rim and base; never found signed.
Unsigned American pewter usually sells for ⅓ to ½ the price of signed pieces
depending on rarity and demand for the form; exceptions are items such as the
Parks Boyd salt and sugar bowl, never found signed, but with positive attribu-
tions.
Superior Quality/Fine Condition $950 (D)   **$600–$950**

Pitcher 1837–1861 United States
Signed by Rufus Dunham; Westbrook, ME; open-top water pitcher; good pitch-
ers are always in demand because they can still be used on a daily basis; 2-quart.
Good Quality/Fine Condition $525 (A)   **$350–$500**

Plate 9″ Dia. 1751 England
Made to commemorate a marriage between "H" and "L"; wriggle-work is a
type of folk art decoration that gives these plates appeal; signed by A. Carter,
c. 1730–1770.
Very Good Quality/Good Condition $1500 (D)   **$1000–$2000**

Plate 7.75″ Dia. 1740–1780 United States
Signed "Semper Eadem" and "Boston," marks used by John Skinner and others; Ex Kerfoot collection (an early collector/dealer/author); a scarce item from
a desirable collection.
Good Quality/Good Condition $770 (A)   **$500–$800**

Plate 8.25″ Dia. 1755–1793 United States
A pre-Revolutionary plate from Newport, RI; with single-reed rim design that
must have been more popular than the plain rim, as many more exist.
Good Quality/Good Condition $413 (A)   **$350–$450**

Plate 9.25″ Dia. Smooth rim 1760–1790 United States
Signed by John Skinner; Boston, MA; smooth rim, pre-Revolutionary plates are
rare; when made by a desirable pewterer from Boston—what more could you
want!
Very Good Quality/Good Condition $853 (A)   **$600–$1200**

Porringer 5.5″ H Flowered handle 1815–1825 United States
Signed by Thomas Danforth and Sherman Boardman; Hartford, CT; one of the
most attractive and popular handle designs found on American porringers.
Very Good Quality/Fine Condition $1000 (D)   **$650–$1000**

Salt and pepper c.1800 England
Two-piece lot: pepper pot and open salt; unsigned; small items display well when
intermixed with larger items, so there is always a demand, regardless of origin;
usually inexpensive.
Good Quality/Average Condition $99 (A)   **$50–$100**

Set of measures 1826–1875 England
Assorted set; bulbous shape; quart, pint, half-pint, gill, half-gill, quarter-gill; in
post-Imperial capacities; most with government verification marks; most common form of English hollowware. Many English, Scottish, and Irish post-Imperial
capacity (i.e. after 1826) measures and tavern mugs are found on the American
market. These were never exported to this country. All have been brought over
by dealers and collectors after World War II. They are not part of the subset of
English pewter known as "English export" pewter.
Good Quality/Average Condition *$660 (A)*　　　　　　**$650–$800**

Sugar bowl, covered 5.5″ H 1795–1819 United States
Positive attribution to Parks Boyd of Philadelphia, PA, based on use of same lid
on a signed piece; decorative beading on lid, rim, and foot; never found signed.
Superior Quality/Fine Condition *$6500 (D)*　　　　　**$5000–$7000**

Tall beaker 5.25″ H 1795–1816 United States
Signed by Samuel Danforth, Hartford, CT; most tall beakers were made
in the 18th century. The Boardmans made them in the first quarter of the
19th.
Very Good Quality/Fine Condition *$550 (A)*　　　　　**$400–$550**

Teapot 5.5″ H Queen Anne 1748–1801 English Export
Made without feet; signed by John Townsend, a major exporter to America; the
wooden handle and lid finial are replacements but do not affect value more than
10%; some pitting inside, as usual. *(See photo 188, left)*
Superior Quality/Fine Condition *$2500 (D)*　　　　　**$2000–$2500**

Teapot 6″ H Queen Anne 1748–1801 English Export
Footed; signed by John Townsend; same replacements and condition as above;
Queen Anne teapots with feet will sell for ⅓ more than those without feet. *(See
photo 188, right)*
Superior Quality/Fine Condition *$3250 (A)*　　　　　**$2600–$3250**

Teapot 7″ H Queen Anne Revival 1804–1810 United States
Signed by Thomas Boardman of Hartford, CT; beaded lid; beehive lid finial
with ivory button; cast metal handle originally painted black to simulate ebony;
faceted spout; extended dome lid.
Very Good Quality/Fine Condition *$2750 (D)*　　　　　**$1750–$2750**

Photo 187. Flagon. CREDIT: GARLAND PASS. *Photo 188. Teapots.*
CREDIT: GARLAND PASS *(See p. 345 and above)*

Teapot 8″ H 1817–1856 United States
Signed by William Calder, Providence, RI; 19th-century teapots with a "Federal" style and simpler handle are more desirable than later models.
Good Quality/Good Condition $303 (A)   **$250–$495**

Whale oil lamp 7″ H 1830–1835 United States
Original burner; made in Malden, MA; a lamp with its original burner is best; a good-fitting, not original, burner is acceptable; a missing burner: deduct $50 from the value.
Good Quality/Good Condition $303 (A)   **$250–$400**

Whale oil lamp 7″ H Chamber type 1830–1860 United States
Unsigned; gadrooned rim on saucer base; original burner replaced with burning fluid burner; acceptable.
Good Quality/Average Condition $165 (A)   **$165–$185**

BRASS

Brass is the most sophisticated of the base metals. When highly polished, its goldlike color gave a touch of elegance to any colonial interior no matter how drab the surroundings. The same is true today, and both collectors and dealers are aware of just how much a good pair of candlesticks can enhance a piece of furniture. Because of their decorative appeal and continued use in today's home, candlesticks are the most popular item of antique brassware. More candlesticks have been made of brass and bronze than any of other material. Their durability has made it possible to find, without too much difficulty, candlesticks from the 16th, 17th, and 18th centuries on today's market. Last year a rare 15th-century bronze English candlestick brought a record $12,950 at auction. At major antique shows it is not unusual to find two to three dozen pairs of 18th-century brass candlesticks for sale. All are of English or European origin.

To date, no authenticated 18th-century American brass candlestick has been discovered. If one is found, chances are that it will have been made by one of the American brass founders who made brass andirons, the second most popular brass antique in this country. Over thirty founders signed their andirons, and probably several times that number made them. Period andirons have cast halves, seamed construction similar to 18th-century English brass candlesticks.

Another bass item of American origin, probably made by the andiron founders, is the brass whale oil lamp, c. 1800–1835. It also has cast-in-halves and seamed construction. To date, only one maker, William H. Webb of Warren, Maine, is known to have signed his lamps. American brass whale oil lamps are much scarcer than 18th-century English petal-base candlesticks or American andirons. However, they sell for less, not only because of a lack of knowledge on the part of the average collector but because they lack the utilitarian ease of use that the other two items possess. Collectors don't like to be bothered with messy fuel oils and wicks.

Most brass items found on the American market are of English or European origin. Popular items include bed warmers (only a half dozen or so have been authenticated as American), snuff and tobacco boxes, ink stands, cookware and hearth items, and lanterns. A rare and much sought-after category of brass antiques is referred to as "silver-form" brass: brass items identical in form to silver items of the 18th and early 19th centuries. Many will have traces of silver, indicating that they were once silver-coated. This should not be confused with a coating of silver or tin on the inside surface of brass and copper items used to hold food or consumable liquids. That type of coating was used to prevent the contamination of food by contact with toxic copper oxide.

Andirons 24″ H Revere type 1775–1800 United States
Once believed made by Paul Revere but now known not to be; one of the most sought-after types; if swirl design of finial continued to column below, the quality would rise to superior; New York. *(See photo 189)*
Very Good Quality/Fine Condition $17,600 (A) **$15,000–$25,000**

Andirons 14″ H Ball top 1800–1820 United States
Signed: John Molineux; the ball top is the least popular and never reach the height, in size of price, of the other forms, yet these were a bargain; Boston. Assuming good-to-fine condition the 3 most important factors affecting value in andirons, in descending order: form, height, and maker's mark (signed).
Good Quality/Fine Condition $770 (A) **$500–$1500**

Andirons 23″ H Urn top 1800–1820 United States
A wonderful pair of andirons with pierced gallery and matching log stops; attributed to Richard Wittingham; New York.
Superior Quality/Fine Condition $4950 (A) **$2500–$5000**

Andirons 21″ H Steeple top 1800–1825 United States
Pair; with matching tools and jab hooks; signed "J. Davis"; extremely rare to find a complete set with signed andirons; one of the tools doesn't match; repair to 1; Boston.
Very Good Quality/Poor Condition $2200 (A) **$3500–$10,000**

Candlestick 6.5″ H Trumpet base 1660–1680 England
Single candlestick; restoration period with multiring stem and mid-drip pan; very much in demand; height is everything, with price increasing at more than $1000 per half-inch!
Very Good Quality/Fine Condition $3500 (D) **$2500–$3500**

Candlestick 8.25″ H Georgian 1745 England
Single candlestick; undoubtedly the most popular stick on the market today; not at all rare but much in demand; look for cast-in-half, seamed construction, although some later models are unseamed. Several years ago, single sticks of this type sold for ⅓ the price of a pair, but recently demand has increased the price of pairs to about 8 times the price of a single.
Very Good Quality/Good Condition $385 (A) **$350–$450**

Photo 189 (above, left).
Andirons. CREDIT: SKINNER,
INC., BOLTON, MA *(See p. 349)*
Photo 190 (above, right).
Candlesticks. CREDIT: SKINNER,
INC., BOLTON, MA *(See below)*
Photo 191 (left).
Whale oil lamps.
CREDIT: GARLAND PASS *(See p. 351)*

Candlesticks 7″ H Georgian 1740 England
A transitional form between Queen Anne and the fully developed Georgian petal-base design; pair.
Good Quality/Fine Condition $1100 (A) **$900–$1200**

Candlesticks 8.5″ H Georgian 1740–1755 England
One of the pair marked "Geo Grove," a Birmingham founder; swirl-base sticks are in big demand and signed are very rare; perhaps 1 in 1000 are signed. *(See photo 190)*
Very Good Quality/Good Condition $3025 (A) **$2500–$4500**

Candlesticks 11″ H Beehive type 1840–1850 England
Pair; typical multiknop design with the prominent beehive knop at mid-height; original push-up ejectors; reproductions abound; be very careful with these.
Good Quality/Good Condition $185 (D) **$150–$200**

Candlesticks 8″ H Heemskerk 1700–1725 Holland
Named for a Dutch sea captain who lost a cargo of these sticks (also often called "mid-drips"); made for over 100 years; earlier forms have cylindrical sockets, larger ejection holes; pair.
Good Quality/Fine Condition $1750 (D) **$1350–$1750**

Muffineer   3.5″ H   1725–1750   England
Muffineer or dredger: kitchen shaker for flour, spices, etc.; found in a half-dozen or more sizes; seamed construction in heavy sheet brass; strap brass handle.
Good Quality/Fine Condition $325 (D)   **$250–$325**

Pitcher   7″ H   1725–1750   England
Beautiful form in heavy sheet brass; seamed construction; strap brass handle; found in several sizes; may be Scandinavian.
Very Good Quality/Fine Condition $750 (D)   **$500–$750**

Pocket tobacco box   5.5″ H × 2″ W   1750–1775   Holland
Typical folk art–style engraving with agricultural scene; engraving still sharp, not worn away from polishing; avoid boxes with worn engraving.
Very Good Quality/Good Condition $475 (D)   **$300–$600**

Posnet   6″ H × 21″ L × 10″ Dia.   1800   United States
Signed by J. Davis; Boston; posnets from England are common, but signed American ones are extremely rare; probably less than a dozen are known; watch out for English reproductions.
Good Quality/Fine Condition $1500 (D)   **$1000–$1500**

Rush light   8.5″ H   1750–1800   England
Rare in brass (most are wrought iron); counterweight is a candle socket; twisted stem; tripod base.
Good Quality/Good Condition $750 (D)   **$500–$1000**

Tea caddy   4″ H   1780   England
Beautiful form; nicely decorated with geometric and punched engraving; sheet brass body with cast brass feet.
Superior Quality/Fine Condition $450 (D)   **$500–$750**

Whale oil lamps   8.5″ H   1810–1835   United States
Pair; signed by William H. Webb, only known American brass founder who signed his lamps; cast-in-halves, seamed construction; original copper burner tubes; rare; singles sell for ⅓; Warren, ME. *(See photo 191)*
Very Good Quality/Fine Condition $2400 (D)   **$1800–$2400**

COPPER

It is more difficult to find early American copper items than items in any other base metal. Other than the superbly designed American copper teakettle, the open cooking pots with long wrought-copper handles, and a few rare measures, it is impossible to determine the origin of many copper items found on the American market. Some items of English or European origin can be identified by their distinctive forms. These include English and Scandinavian teakettles, English coffeepots, Dutch chocolate pots, and most English copper cookware. Continental copperware tends to be less well made and often will be decorated with repoussé and punched designs. English and French food molds are popular.

Eighteenth- and early-19th-century copperware has seams joined by a process called dovetailing. See the reference book, *American Copper and*

Brass, by Kauffman for a good explanation of how this was done. Also look at the bottom of any period teakettle—American, English, or European—to learn what dovetailing looks like. Similar in appearance to dovetailed joints found on furniture, period dovetailing exhibits the less uniform characteristics of hand-fabricated workmanship.

In recent years a large quantity of new-but-made-to-look-old copperware has been imported from the Middle East. Pieces that have dovetailed seams will have dovetails about the size of human teeth. They will be uniform in size and spacing, having been cut mechanically. Overall workmanship runs from good to poor. At one time, large quantities were being sold by the pound in department store decorating departments.

Some American cookware will be found signed, but most of this dates from the last half of the 19th century into the 20th century. About one out of seven American copper teakettles was signed; it sells for twice the price of an unsigned one.

Brandy warmer 4″ H × 3″ Dia. 1800–1825 England
Small, open, tapered drum shape with original wood; side-mounted handle; dovetailed construction.
Good Quality/Good Condition $195 (D)   **$175–$225**

Candy kettle 13.5″ Dia. 1845–1865 United States
Hemispherical dovetailed bowl with wrought-iron handles; signed A. Elsingham & Buffalo, NY; dovetailed construction.
Good Quality/Good Condition $225 (D)   **$200–$250**

Coffeepot 10″ H 1800–1830 England
hanTapered drum-shaped body with lid; straight, side-mounted original wood handle; graceful, goose-neck pouring spout; dovetailed construction.
Very Good Quality/Fine Condition $650 (D)   **$500–$750**

Cooking pot 8″ Dia. 1800–1830 United States
Typical copper cooking pot with copper strap handle joined to body with wrought-iron copper rivets; dovetailed construction.
Good Quality/Good Condition $125 (D)   **$100–$150**

Dredger 3.5″ H 1800–1830 England
Similar to the brass dredgers but later and more scarce; strap copper handle; dovetailed construction.
Good Quality/Good Condition $125 (D)   **$100–$150**

Mug 7″ H × 4″ Dia. 1780–1820 United States
Large capacity, 57 oz.; with a great copper strap handle; dovetailed construction with a dovetailed patch in the body, probably original to the copper sheet.
Very Good Quality/Good Condition $250 (D)   **$225–$275**

Mug 5″ H 1850–1875 United States
Ceremonial mug; with outward-flaring sides and 2 handles, 90 degrees apart; also found with 3 handles; probably made by East European immigrants; dovetailed construction.
Good Quality/Good Condition $175 (D)   **$150–$200**

Pocket tobacco box 5.5″ L × 2″ W   1775–1800   Holland
Copper with rare brass inlays on cover; lid and bottom engraved with agricultural scenes and Dutch writing; typical folk art–quality engraving in good-to-fine condition, with little wear.
Very Good Quality/Good Condition $550 (D)   **$400–$600**

Saucepan 5″ H × 7″ Dia.   1850–1875   United States
Covered, 2-quart size; copper lid; both lid and pan have long iron handles; marked "V. Olac & Sons, Phila."; dovetailed construction.
Good Quality/Fine Condition $250 (D)   **$200–$250**

Teakettle 5″ Dia.   1825–1850   Scandinavia
Scarce, small size (1 liter); typical short pouring spout with hinged lid at end of spout; round, bulbous body.
Good Quality/Good Condition $150 (D)   **$125–$175**

Teakettle 7″ H   c. 1852   United States
Two-quart size; marked "W. Heiss No. 213 North St. Phila."; copper rivets at swivel handle replaced with crude bolts; otherwise condition is good; smaller and larger sizes will sell for twice the price.
Very Good Quality/Good Condition $413 (A)   **$400–$600**

IRON

Blacksmiths outnumbered other metal craftsmen twenty to one in early colonial communities. Yet considering their numbers, a surprisingly small quantity of their wares survive. The explanation lies in the types of items produced. Most were made for horses, farm implements, and tools—all having a high attrition rate. Also, because scrap iron is used in the production of steel, large quantities were melted down, especially during periods of war. Also, when unprotected, iron will corrode at a fast rate and be lost forever to the rust pile.

Collector interest today is primarily centered on cooking utensils and other items for the open hearth and early lighting devices. Many of the cooking pots and kettles were made of cast iron. The majority of these are American, some signed and identifiable as such. A large number were exported from England. This is especially true of forms such as cast-iron porringers, many signed "Kenrick and Sons," "Clark," "Baldwin,"—all from the mid-19th century and almost all from England. Very few have been authenticated as American.

Most cooking utensils and lighting devices were made of wrought iron. Unlike cast iron, which is the product of the mold maker, each piece of wrought iron is fashioned by the blacksmith and reveals his skill or lack of it. It is the most expressive of the base metals, and, in the best pieces, rises to the level of folk art sculpture. Decorative details were often added by twisting the shafts of utensils, notching and filing the edges of handles, and shaping the terminals of handles into bold geometric shapes or hearts and ram's-horn designs. So-called white work—punched designs, incised lines, and inlaid designs of copper or brass—is found on some pieces and adds substantially to their interest and value.

Signed and/or dated pieces are rare. Very few of the makers of signed pieces have been identified, and probably because of that, dated pieces tend to bring higher prices. It is often difficult to determine if initials are those of the maker or the owner.

Open-hearth cookware utensils that are in much demand include top examples of revolving toasters and griddles, long-handled "flesh forks" (this term was not invented by an enterprising dealer but is actually found in early inventories and invoices), and skewer holders. Watch out for fake skewer holders. They have increased in number as the value of authentic ones has risen.

Wrought-iron lighting devices in demand include Betty lamps and a variety of grease lamp forms, together with the adjustable lighting trammels used to suspend them from the ceiling. Rush lights, the clamplike devices used to hold burning grease-soaked rushes, are popular. Some may have been made in this country, but most are from England. Few, if any, have been authenticated as American, although it is common to find them labeled as such at antiques shows and in auction catalogs. The highest-priced lighting device is the American double-arm, floor-mounted candle stand. Single-arm models or those with rush holders are believed to be English. The best American ones sell for $2500 and higher.

Andirons 18″ H 1750–1800 United States
Pair; wrought iron; tall shaft topped by ball finial; simply elegant and elegantly simple; some wear on feet, otherwise fine condition; some bargains do slip through at auctions.
Very Good Quality/Fine Condition *$165 (A)*   **$150–$750**

Betty lamp 4″ H 1800–1850 United States
Wrought-iron closed-font grease lamp with hinged font cover, wick support, hanging rod and wick pick.
Good Quality/Good Condition *$250 (D)*   **$225–$275**

Candlesticks 7″ H × 8″ H 1800–1830 England
Five single "Hogscraper" candlesticks with brass "wedding band" decorative ring; some signed; although American ones may exist, none known to have been positively identified; fakes abound.
Very Good Quality/Average Condition *$2090 (A)*   **$1500–$2000**

Chandelier 1750–1800 United States
Country; double arm with single socket at each end; twisted arms; hanging bar is an adjustable trammel; closed height 26″
Good Quality/Good Condition *$695 (D)*   **$500–$750**

Flesh fork 18″ L 1780–1800 United States
Good flesh forks are becoming scarcer; there are better ones than this around, but a prominent heart in the design always adds a premium to the price.
Very Good Quality/Fine Condition *$2000 (D)*   **$1000–$2000**

Frying pan 54 " L × 14 " Dia. 1780–1820 United States
Long handle; wrought-iron construction; marked; possibly English.
Good Quality/Fine Condition $275 (D)   **$225–$275**

Porringer 4 " Dia. 1845–1865 England
Cast iron with integral cast handle with splayed rib designs; marked "pint," "Kenrick & Son"; exported to the United States in large numbers; found in several sizes by several makers.
Good Quality/Fine Condition $150 (D)   **$100–$150**

Saucepan 6 " Dia. 1845–1865 English Export
Cast iron with lid; tapered, tubular-iron straight handle set at an angle to the bulbous body; quart size; marked "A. Kenrick & Son": for exportation.
Good Quality/Fine Condition $150 (D)   **$100–$150**

Toaster 5 " H × 13 " L 1780–1800 United States
Wrought-iron swivel toaster; each piece of wrought iron is unique, and value is determined by the folk art quality of this most expressive of the utilitarian base metals.
Good Quality/Good Condition $440 (A)   **$350–$1200**

Toaster 7 " H × 18 " L 1780–1800 United States
Wrought-iron swivel toaster; another unique piece of folk artwork.
Good Quality/Good Condition $605 (A)   **$350–$1200**

Toddy stick 18 " L 1780–1820 United States
After heating in fire, used to impart carmelized flavor to beverage; wrought iron with heart terminal; incised line and notched-edge decorations; a rare form.
Very Good Quality/Fine Condition $250 (D)   **$250–$350**

TIN

Tinware is actually sheet steel coated on both sides with a thin layer of tin. It has been produced in Europe and England since the 15th century. However, due to the oxidation of the tin and steel, plus the easily damaged sheet metal construction of every item, few pieces on the market today date prior to 1800.

Kitchen tinware (shakers, plates, baking pans, cups, etc.) are the most common forms found and usually are of undetermined origin. Some writers have estimated the majority may be from England. Serious collector interest lies with three categories that can be more easily identified as American. They are (1) lighting devices, (2) Pennsylvania punch-decorated forms, and (3) paint-decorated tinware.

In lighting devices, all of the grease lamps and whale oil lamps are American. Most (probably 98 percent) of the sconces and candlesticks also were made here. It is more likely that reproductions and late-made items will be encountered than those of foreign origin. Some reproductions have an artificially produced patina that is very convincing. Items made in the first quarter of this century have acquired more than sixty-five years of oxidation. If they have been stored in a barn or attic, it is almost impossible to determine their true age. If in doubt, it is best to walk away or limit your purchases to a dealer or auction gallery that will guarantee their items.

A similar caveat applies to Pennsylvania punch-decorated tinware. The forms and decorations are easily learned and recognized. Reproductions and outright fakes are much more prevalent than non-American forms. Look very carefully at the punched decoration to make sure it has not been added to a genuinely early, but plain, piece.

As for paint-decorated tinware, large quantities from England and France were imported into this country in the 19th century. Strictly speaking, only the French pieces should be called "tole." Pieces from both countries are easily distinguished from American pieces. Both countries produced a more formal decoration, consisting of realistically painted floral arrangements, still lifes, and scenic views, all done with a well-trained, very professional hand. In contrast, the American paint-decorated pieces are done in bright colors with bold, rythmic brush strokes that give them an appealing folk art quality.

Since the appeal is in the painted decoration, value is determined not only by the quality of the decoration but by the condition of the paint (sometimes referred to as paint loss). Serious collectors will not consider items that have more than 5 percent paint loss. Restoration can be detected with ultraviolet light and can greatly reduce and often kill the value of an otherwise good piece. The question of whether or not to restore is best left to the buyer.

Coffeepot   11″ H   1800–1830   United States
Punch decorated; from Pennsylvania; worn old black paint and light rust; value is determined by the quality of the folk art punch decoration and condition.
Very Good Quality/Good Condition   *$2600 (A)*   **$1500–$3000**

Document box   6.25″ H × 9.5″ W   1825–1850   United States
Brightly colored, hand-painted decoration; the colors and quality of the folk art decoration plus condition of the paint determine value; very little loss on this example. It is not difficult to distinguish American painted tinware from English or French versions. American decoration has a vigorous folk art quality, while the English and French decoration is more formal and academic. See illustrations of both in the listed reference.
Very Good Quality/Fine Condition   *$550 (A)*   **$250–$1200**

Document box   4.75″ H × 8″ W   1825–1850   United States
Brightly colored, hand-painted decoration; very little paint loss.
Very Good Quality/Fine Condition   *$330 (A)*   **$250–$1200**

Dredger   4.5″ H   1850–1900   United States
Typical kitchen castor or dredger used for flour, corn meal, sugar, etc.
Good Quality/Good Condition   *$25 (D)*   **$15–$35**

Photo 192. Chamber-type lamp and sconces. CREDIT: SKINNER, INC., BOLTON, MA *(See below)*

Lamps 11″ H   Chamber type   1830–1860   United States
Pair of whale oil lamps; although they were made in greater numbers, exact pairs of tin lamps are rarer than pairs in pewter, but the demand for them is far less. *(See photo 192, center)*
Very Good Quality/Good Condition $413 (A)   **$400–$600**

Sconce 15″ H × 9″ W   1800–1850   United States
Single sconce; oval back with crimped edge; the large sconces tend to be earlier than the smaller ones. *(See photo 192, left)*
Very Good Quality/Good Condition $220 (A)   **$200–$350**

Sconces 14″ H   1830–1850   United States
Pair; rare form with coffin-shaped backplates; small crimped-edge candle socket support plate.
Very Good Quality/Fine Condition $1195 (D)   **$900–$1200**

Sconces 11.75″ H   1840–1860   United States
The spiderweb design of the backplates and the smoke bells are sophisticated developments not found on the earlier sconces; pair *(See photo 192, right)*
Very Good Quality/Good Condition $330 (A)   **$300–$600**

Teakettle 1800–1830   United States
Two-quart size; dovetailed construction; similar in form and construction to American copper teakettles; cast-iron swivel handle; rare in tin.
Very Good Quality/Fine Condition $175 (D)   **$125–$175**

Tray 10″ W × 8″ D   1830–1850   United States
Paint-decorated; rectangular with outward curving sides; stylized fruit forms, predominately red and yellow; 95% intact.
Good Quality/Good Condition $300 (D)   **$200–$400**

BIBLIOGRAPHY

An asterisk before the title indicates the book is out of print but can usually be obtained from antique book dealers on search liens.

PEWTER

Montgomery, Charles F. *A History of American Pewter*. New York: Praeger, 1973 (hardcover); New York: E. P. Dutton, 1978 (paperback). The best introduction to the subject.

Peal, Christopher. *Pewter of Great Britain*. London: John Gifford Ltd., 1983. The best introduction to the subject and the only book that contains a chapter on English export pewter made for the American market.

BRASS AND COPPER

Kauffman, Henry J. *American Copper and Brass*. Camden, NJ: Thomas Nelson and Sons, 1968. Contains a good discussion of American copper teakettles and American brass andirons, with lists of craftsmen in each metal.

Schiffer, Herbert, et al. *The Brass Book: American, English, and Europeans, 15th Century Through 1850*. Exton, PA: Schiffer Publishing, Ltd., 1978. Invaluable for the 2,000+ items pictured. The section on andirons is especially good.

IRON

Kauffman, Henry J. *Early American Ironware, Cast and Wrought*. Rutland, VT: Charles E. Tuttle, 1966. Provides a good understanding of the difference between cast iron, wrought iron, and steel, as well as the various craftsmen who worked them.

Schiffer, Herbert, et al. *Antique Iron: Survey of American and English Forms*. Does for iron what *The Brass Book* did for brass.

TIN

DeVoe, Shirley Spaulding. *The Art of the Tinsmith*, Exton, PA: Schiffer Publishing, Ltd., 1981. The most recent book on tin and the only one that gives equal space to English and American items.

Coffin, Margaret. *American Country Tinware, 1700–1900*. New York: Galahad Books, 1968. The first and still the best book on Country painted tinware.

MIXED METALS

Michaelis, Ronald F. *Old Domestic Base-Metal Candlesticks*. Woodbridge, Suffolk, UK: Antique Collectors Club, 1978. The best book ever written on the subject. For serious collectors.

MUSEUMS

Winterthur, Winterthur, DE
Brooklyn Museum, New York, NY

Museum of Fine Arts, Boston, MA
Yale University Art Gallery, New Haven, CT
Smithsonian Institution, Washington, DC
Williamsburg, Williamsburg, VA

Also be sure to visit historic homes found in almost every state east of
the Mississippi; most will have several examples of each of the base
metals.

COLLECTORS' CLUBS

For those who would like to keep abreast of the latest discoveries and
research in pewter, membership in the Pewter Collectors Club of America is highly recommended. Benefits include twice yearly issues of the
Bulletin, which reports on the latest research, and twice yearly issues of
the *Newsletter*, which reports on club activities. There are both national
and regional meetings with hands-on inspections of public and private
collections. For membership information write William G. Paddock, 29
Chesterfield Road, Scarsdale, NY 10583. There are no collectors' clubs
for any of the other base metals.

Movie Posters and Lobby Cards

Advisor: **RICHARD DE THUIN**

Richard De Thuin's work has appeared in American Film, Ford Times, Soho News, *and the* Village Voice. *He is the author of* The Official Identification and Price Guide to Movie Memorabilia *(House of Collectibles, 1990). His collecting interests include inserts and lobby cards, magazines with star covers, movie tearsheet ads, sheet music, and other movie memorabilia. Mr. De Thuin may be reached at Crouch International, Ltd., 1156 6th Avenue, Suite 710, New York, NY 10036.*

INTRODUCTION

The most actively collected movie memorabilia is movie paper; this includes posters, banners, lobby cards, and window cards.

Poster sizes include the one-sheet ($27'' \times 41''$), half-sheet ($22'' \times 28''$), two-sheet ($45'' \times 59''$), three-sheet ($41'' \times 81''$), six-sheet ($81'' \times 81''$), and twenty-four-sheet ($109'' \times 236''$). There is also a mini one-sheet that bears identical art to the one-sheet and is $17'' \times 24''$.

Some collectors prefer to classify all movie paper as posters; other collectors differentiate posters from the following movie paper: banners ($24'' \times 82\frac{1}{2}''$), inserts ($14'' \times 36''$), lobby cards ($11'' \times 14''$), and window cards ($14'' \times 22''$). Window cards were printed in three different sizes: mini, regular, and oversize. The mini window card carried the same art as the one-sheet poster but in a reduced size of $8'' \times 14''$. The regular window card measured $14'' \times 22''$, and the oversize window card was $14'' \times 28''$, about the same size as a half-sheet.

Lobby cards were produced in sets of eight (a title card and seven scene cards). Lobby cards are either color photos that measure the full $11'' \times 14''$ size of the card or $8'' \times 10''$ color stills bordered by a film's logo and credits; films released by United Artists, Universal, and Warner Brothers prior to 1981 were bordered $11'' \times 14''$ sets.

One-sheet and half-sheet posters, inserts, and lobby cards are the most popular types of movie paper. They are easiest to display or store (a collector would need a palace the size of Versailles to hang a collection of six-sheet or twenty-four-sheet posters) and tend to be exceptionally beautiful in design, particularly movie paper produced during the 1930s and 1940s.

Title cards are more desirable and usually more expensive than scene cards. Scene cards that picture a major star in a close-up bring the highest prices, while scene cards with the major star(s) pictured in the background, with supporting players and a major star, or just supporting players alone are less expensive and less popular with collectors. At the bottom of the price scale are scene cards that picture objects such as an airplane, a farmhouse alongside a hill, or a group of extras. Such scene cards are the least desirable to collectors unless they are needed to complete a set. However, scene cards of monsters, spaceships, or robots are an exception. For example, a scene card picturing the giant ants from the 1954 Warner Brothers film *Them* or of Robby the Robot from the 1956 Metro-Goldwyn-Mayer film *Forbidden Planet*, would bring a high price and strong collector interest.

Poster and lobby cards that are free of any noticeable flaws (and there are few in mint condition) usually realize the highest prices. But even pinholed, soiled, taped, folded, or creased movie paper and, to some extent, water-damaged paper can also be expensive. Posters that are faded or trimmed or are missing large chunks of paper are almost always off-limits to the more serious collector.

Linen-backed posters, along with cotton and other materials, are collectible, as they were used to preserve the paper. Original movie paper is preferred to reissues (printed when the movie was released), but reissues of movies like *Gone With the Wind, Casablanca*, and several of the Disney animation films would entice many a collector. If given the choice, however, between an original poster and a reissue, choose wisely. Make sure that the reissue has the letter ''R'' somewhere in the border of the poster or lobby card. Otherwise, it is questionable what a collector will be acquiring for his or her money.

In the listings below, you will often notice that the value ranges are higher than the actual price realized. Most of these items sold at auction. It just goes to show that items will often sell for below their true value at auction.

Abbott and Costello Meet the Killers 18″ × 14″ 1955 Belgium
Boris Karloff; Universal; title card, linen-backed.
Good Quality/Good Condition $50 (A) **$100–$150**
Adventures of Sherlock Holmes, The 27″ × 41″ 1939 United States
Basil Rathbone, Ida Lupino; one-sheet; 20th Century Fox; linen-backed; rare.
Superior Quality/Fine Condition $4000 (A) **$4000–$4500**

Alice in Wonderland 22″ × 28″ 1933 United States
Gary Cooper, W. C. Fields, Charlotte Henry; Paramount; half-sheet.
Superior Quality/Good Condition $700 (A) **$1000–$1200**

All of Me 22″ × 28″ 1933 United States
Miriam Hopkins, Fredric March, George Raft; Paramount; half-sheet.
Very Good Quality/Fine Condition $300 (A) **$400–$500**

Andy Hardy's Double Life 11″ × 14″ 1942 United States
Mickey Rooney, Esther Williams; MGM; scene card; a fairly high price paid for
this particular scene card from the Andy Hardy series.
Good Quality/Fine Condition $165 (D) **$15–$40**

Andy Hardy's Private Secretary 11″ × 14″ 1941 United States
Mickey Rooney, Lewis Stone, Kathryn Grayson; MGM; scene card.
Good Quality/Good Condition $10 (D) **$10–$25**

Anna Karenina 14″ × 22″ 1935 United States
Greta Garbo, Fredric March; MGM; window card.
Superior Quality/Good Condition $500 (A) **$1200–$1400**

Auntie Mame 27″ × 41″ 1958 United States
Rosalind Russell, Peggy Cass; Warner Bros.; one-sheet.
Very Good Quality/Fine Condition $100 (A) **$150–$200**

Babes in Toyland 14″ × 22″ 1934 United States
Stan Laurel, Oliver Hardy; MGM; window card. Auction fever in this case.
Superior Quality/Fine Condition $5000 (A) **$1500–$2000**

Baby Takes a Bow 11″ × 14″ 1934 United States
Shirley Temple, James Dunn; Fox (later 20th); scene card.
Very Good Quality/Fine Condition $250 (A) **$250–$350**

Bambi 11″ × 14″ 1942 United States
Title card and 7 scene cards (complete set); RKO (Walt Disney).
Very Good Quality/Fine Condition $1100 (A) **$1000–$1500**

Bar 20 41″ × 81″ 1943 United States
William Boyd (Hopalong Cassidy); three-sheet; United Artists; framed.
Good Quality/Average Condition $175 (A) **$50–$100**

Bengal Brigade 11″ × 14″ 1954 United States
Rock Hudson, Arlene Dahl; Universal; scene card.
Good Quality/Good Condition $6 (A) **$5–$10**

Birds, The 11″ × 14″ 1963 United States
Rod Taylor, Tippi Hedren; Universal; scene card.
Good Quality/Good Condition $63 (A) **$40–$50**

Blue Skies 27″ × 41″ 1946 United States
Bing Crosby, Fred Astaire, Joan Caulfield; Paramount; one-sheet.
Good Quality/Good Condition $275 (A) **$200–$300**

Boogie Man Will Get You, The 11″ × 14″ 1942 United States
Boris Karloff, Peter Lorre; Columbia; title card.
Good Quality/Good Condition $122 (A) **$75–$100**

Bride of Frankenstein, The 27″ × 41″ 1935 United States
Boris Karloff, Elsa Lancaster; Universal; one-sheet.
Superior Quality/Good Condition $3250 (A) **$3500–$4500**

Broadway Limited 11″ × 14″ 1941 United States
Victor McLaglen, Patsy Kelly; United Artists; title card.
Good Quality/Good Condition $10 (D) **$10–$20**

Bus Stop 27″ × 41″ 1956 United States
Marilyn Monroe, Don Murray; 20th Century Fox; one-sheet.
Very Good Quality/Good Condition $192 (A) **$150–$200**

Canary Murder Case, The 11″ × 14″ 1929 United States
William Powell, Louise Brooks; Paramount; scene card.
Very Good Quality/Good Condition $127 (A) **$75–$100**

Casablanca 27″ × 41″ 1942 United States
Humphrey Bogart, Ingrid Bergman, Claude Rains; Warner Bros.; linen-backed;
one-sheet.
Superior Quality/Fine Condition $6600 (A) **$6000–$7500**

Casablanca 22″ × 28″ 1956 United States
Reissue (pictures famous scene at airport); half-sheet; Warner Bros.
Superior Quality/Good Condition $400 (A) **$250–$500**

Cinderella 14″ × 36″ 1950 United States
Animated film; RKO (Walt Disney); insert.
Very Good Quality/Fine Condition $94 (A) **$50–$75**

City That Never Sleeps, The 27″ × 41″ 1953 United States
Gig Young, Mala Powers (Republic), and *The Frightened City* (also called *The
Killer That Stalked New York*)', Evelyn Keyes, Charles Korvin (1950, Columbia);
one-sheet.
Very Good Quality/Good Condition $150 (A) **$250–$350**

Creature Walks Among Us, The 14″ × 36″ 1956 United States
Jeff Morrow, Rex Reason; Universal; insert.
Good Quality/Average Condition $101 (A) **$75–$100**

Dancers in the Dark 22″ × 28″ 1932 United States
Miriam Hopkins, Jack Oakie; Paramount; half-sheet.
Very Good Quality/Good Condition $175 (A) **$250–$350**

Dancing Lady 22″ × 28″ 1933 United States
Joan Crawford, Clark Gable; MGM; half-sheet.
Superior Quality/Fine Condition $2250 (A) **$2000–$2500**

Day the Earth Stood Still, The 27″ × 41″ 1951 United States
Michael Rennie, Patricia Neal; 20th Century Fox; one-sheet.
Superior Quality/Fine Condition $850 (A) **$600–$750**

Day the Earth Stood Still, The 41″ × 81″ 1951 United States
In 2 sections; three-sheet.
Superior Quality/Fine Condition $2086 (A) **$1500–$2500**

Deadline, USA 11″ × 14″ 1952 United States
Humphrey Bogart; 20th Century Fox; title card and 7 scene cards (complete set).
Very Good Quality/Good Condition $165 (A) **$100–$125**

Dracula 14″ × 36″ 1931 United States
Bela Lugosi, Helen Chandler; insert; framed; very rare poster; the artist's (Karoly Grosz) design of Count Dracula emerging from a spiderweb places this
insert among the crème de la crème of movie paper.
Superior Quality/Fine Condition $11,000 (A) **$15,000–$18,000**

Duel in the Sun 22″ × 28″ 1946 United States
Jennifer Jones, Gregory Peck, Lillian Gish; Selznick; half-sheet.
Superior Quality/Fine Condition $200 (A)   **$200–$300**

Dumbo 22″ × 28″ 1941 United States
Animated film; RKO (Walt Disney); half-sheet; poster had extensive damage,
but apparently that didn't deter the collector from placing an exaggerated bid.
Good Quality/Poor Condition $363 (A)   **$95–$125**

Empire Strikes Back, The 27″ × 41″ 1980 United States
Mark Hamill, Harrison Ford; 20th Century Fox; one-sheet.
Very Good Quality/Good Condition $82 (A)   **$75–$95**

Female Jungle 11″ × 14″ 1956 United States
Jayne Mansfield, John Carradine; American Releasing; scene card.
Good Quality/Good Condition $10 (D)   **$10–$20**

Flying Down to Rio 22″ × 28″ 1933 United States
Dolores Del Rio, Fred Astaire, Ginger Rogers; RKO; rare poster; half-sheet.
Superior Quality/Fine Condition $4000 (A)   **$4000–$6000**

Follow the Fleet 27″ × 41″ 1936 United States
Fred Astaire, Ginger Rogers; Morgan lithographed, linen-backed; RKO; one-
sheet. *(See photo 193)*
Superior Quality/Fine Condition $2950 (A)   **$2500–$3000**

Forbidden Planet 27″ × 41″ 1956 United States
Walter Pidgeon, Anne Francis, Robby the Robot; MGM; one-sheet, one of the
best posters from the 1950s, the movie has attained a cult following.
Superior Quality/Fine Condition $850 (A)   **$500–$600**

Frankenstein 11″ × 14″ 1951 United States
Boris Karloff, Mae Clarke, Colin Clive; reissue; Universal; linen-backed; scene
card.
Superior Quality/Fine Condition $356 (A)   **$100–$200**

Gasoline Gus 41″ × 81″ 1921 France
Fatty Arbuckle, Lila Lee; Paramount; three-sheet; linen-backed.
Superior Quality/Good Condition $950 (A)   **$1500–$2000**

Giant 22″ × 28″ 1956 United States
Elizabeth Taylor, Rock Hudson, James Dean; Warner Bros.; half-sheet.
Very Good Quality/Good Condition $302 (A)   **$150–$200**

Great Lie, The 11″ × 14″ 1941 United States
Bette Davis, Mary Astor; Warner Bros.; scene card.
Very Good Quality/Fine Condition $150 (A)   **$150–$200**

Hellcats of the Navy 11″ × 14″ 1957 United States
Ronald Reagan, Nancy Davis (only card in the set picturing both stars); Colum-
bia; scene card.
Very Good Quality/Fine Condition $80 (A)   **$100–$150**

Invasion of the Body Snatchers, The 11″ × 14″ 1956 United States
Kevin McCarthy, Dana Wynter; Allied Artists; scene card.
Very Good Quality/Fine Condition $66 (A)   **$40–$50**

Invisible Man, The 22″ × 28″ 1933 United States
Claude Rains, Gloria Stuart; Universal; half-sheet; one of the most sought-after
posters.
Superior Quality/Fine Condition $11,000 (A)   **$10,000–$15,000**

King for a Night 27″ × 41″ 1933 United States
Helen Twelvetrees, Chester Morris; Universal; one-sheet.
Very Good Quality/Good Condition $245 (A) **$250–$350**

King's Row 27″ × 41″ 1942 United States
Ann Sheridan, Ronald Reagan, Robert Cummings; Warner Bros.; one-sheet.
Very Good Quality/Good Condition $300 (A) **$500–$700**

Love Me Tender 27″ × 41″ 1956 United States
Elvis Presley, Debra Paget, Richard Egan; 20th Century Fox; one-sheet.
Very Good Quality/Good Condition $225 (A) **$150–$200**

Lucky Devils 11″ × 14″ 1940 United States
Richard Arlen, Andy Devine; Universal; title card.
Good Quality/Good Condition $10 (D) **$10–$25**

Madame Mystery 11″ × 14″ 1926 United States
Theda Bara, Tyler Brooke; complete set of black and white lobby cards; Pathe.
Superior Quality/Fine Condition $300 (A) **$300–$500**

Maltese Falcon, The 63″ × 47″ 1941 France
Humphrey Bogart, Mary Astor, Peter Lorre; linen-backed poster; Warner Bros.
(See photo 194)
Superior Quality/Fine Condition $1400 (A) **$300–$400**

Menace of the Mystery Metal 11″ × 14″ 1951 United States
Chapter 10: ''Master of the Stratosphere'' (Captain Video); Columbia; scene
card.
Good Quality/Average Condition $25 (A) **$25–$35**

Photo 193 (left). Movie poster. CREDIT: RICHARD DE THUIN. *Photo 194 (right). Movie poster.* CREDIT: RICHARD DE THUIN *(See p. 364 and above)*

Misleading Lady, The 22″ × 28″ 1932 United States
Claudette Colbert, Edmund Lowe; Paramount; half-sheet.
Superior Quality/Fine Condition $2500 (A)   **$700–$900**

Mummy, The 11″ × 14″ 1932 United States
Boris Karloff, Zita Johann; Universal; title card; pinhole in mummy's forehead; some reports have it that this is the finest title card in existence. Buyer got this at a bargain price.
Superior Quality/Fine Condition $8784 (A)   **$10,000–$15,000**

Nob Hill 11″ × 14″ 1945 United States
George Raft, Joan Bennett; 20th Century Fox; title card and 7 scene cards (complete set).
Good Quality/Average Condition $25 (A)   **$150–$200**

North by Northwest 11″ × 14″ 1959 United States
Cary Grant, Eva Marie Saint, James Mason; MGM; scene card.
Very Good Quality/Fine Condition $72 (A)   **$45–$60**

On the Waterfront 22″ × 28″ 1954 United States
Marlon Brando, Eva Marie Saint, Rod Steiger; Columbia; half-sheet, framed.
Very Good Quality/Good Condition $300 (A)   **$300–$500**

Palm Beach Story, The 41″ × 81″ 1942 United States
Claudette Colbert, Joel McCrea, Mary Astor; linen-backed three-sheet; signed by McCrea; Paramount.
Superior Quality/Fine Condition $1000 (A)   **$1000–$2000**

Pals of the Saddle 41″ × 81″ 1938 United States
John Wayne, Ray "Crash" Corrigan; linen-backed three-sheet; Republic.
Superior Quality/Fine Condition $1250 (A)   **$1200–$1400**

Picnic 27″ × 41″ 1955 United States
William Holden, Kim Novak, Rosalind Russell; Columbia; framed one-sheet.
Very Good Quality/Good Condition $200 (A)   **$200–$250**

Possessed 11″ × 14″ 1947 United States
Joan Crawford, Van Heflin, Raymond Massey; Warner Bros.; scene card.
Good Quality/Average Condition $10 (A)   **$10–$20**

Princess and the Pirate, The 27″ × 41″ 1944 United States
Bob Hope, Virginia Mayo; RKO; one-sheet.
Good Quality/Good Condition $80 (A)   **$75–$95**

Revenge of Frankenstein 11″ × 14″ 1958 United States
Peter Cushing, Eunice Grayson; Columbia; title card and 7 scene cards (complete set).
Good Quality/Average Condition $125 (D)   **$90–$150**

Road to Bali 22″ × 28″ 1952 United States
Bing Crosby, Bob Hope, Dorothy Lamour; Paramount; half-sheet.
Good Quality/Good Condition $93 (A)   **$50–$70**

Road to Utopia 11″ × 14″ 1945 United States
Bing Crosby, Bob Hope, Dorothy Lamour; Paramount; scene card.
Good Quality/Good Condition $25 (A)   **$40–$50**

Romeo and Juliet 8″ × 12″ 1936 United States
Norma Shearer, Leslie Howard; MGM; mini window card; rare card.
Superior Quality/Fine Condition $155 (A)   **$80–$100**

Saigon 27″ × 41″ 1948 United States
Alan Ladd, Veronica Lake; Paramount; one-sheet.
Good Quality/Good Condition $125 (A)   **$150–$200**

Second Chance 14″ × 36″ 1953 United States
Robert Mitchum, Linda Darnell, Jack Palance; RKO; insert.
Good Quality/Good Condition $250 (A)   **$25–$75**

Shall We Dance 27″ × 41″ 1937 United States
Fred Astaire, Ginger Rogers; RKO; one-sheet; linen-backed; rare.
Superior Quality/Fine Condition $3250 (A)   **$3500–$4000**

Snow White and the Seven Dwarfs 11″ × 14″ 1937 United States
Walt Disney animated feature; RKO; scene card.
Superior Quality/Fine Condition $275 (A)   **$250–$350**

Suddenly It's Spring 27″ × 41″ 1946 United States
Paulette Goddard, Fred MacMurray; Varga art; Paramount; one-sheet.
Very Good Quality/Good Condition $61 (A)   **$95–$125**

Suzy 11″ × 14″ 1936 United States
Jean Harlow, Cary Grant, Franchot Tone; MGM; scene card.
Superior Quality/Fine Condition $275 (A)   **$250–$350**

Ten North Frederick 11″ × 14″ 1958 United States
Gary Cooper, Diane Varsi, Suzy Parker; 20th Century Fox; title card.
Good Quality/Good Condition $10 (D)   **$8–$20**

To Have and Have Not 41″ × 81″ 1944 United States
Humphrey Bogart, Lauren Bacall; Warner Bros.; three-sheet; linen-backed.
Very Good Quality/Fine Condition $1500 (A)   **$700–$900**

Two-Faced Woman 22″ × 28″ 1941 United States
Greta Garbo, Melvyn Douglas, Constance Bennett; MGM; half-sheet.
Very Good Quality/Good Condition $250 (A)   **$200–$300**

Vertigo 27″ × 41″ 1958 United States
James Stewart, Kim Novak, Barbara Bel Geddes; Paramount; one-sheet.
Superior Quality/Fine Condition $325 (A)   **$200–$250**

When Worlds Collide 41″ × 81″ 1951 United States
Richard Derr, Barbara Rush; Paramount; three-sheet; linen-backed; rare.
Superior Quality/Fine Condition $600 (A)   **$1000–$1500**

Wizard of Oz, The 11″ × 14″ 1939 United States
Judy Garland, Jack Haley, Bert Lahr; MGM; scene card.
Superior Quality/Fine Condition $2700 (A)   **$2000–$3000**

Woman in the Window, The 27″ × 41″ 1944 United States
Edward G. Robinson, Joan Bennett; Universal; one-sheet.
Very Good Quality/Good Condition $150 (A)   **$200–$300**

Women, The 11″ × 14″ 1939 United States
Norma Shearer, Joan Crawford, Joan Fontaine; MGM; scene card.
Superior Quality/Fine Condition $450 (A)   **$300–$400**

BIBLIOGRAPHY

JOURNALS

Paper Collector's Marketplace, PO Box 127, Scandinavia, WI 54977.

P.A.C. (The Paper and Advertising Collector), PO Box 500, Mount Joy, PA 17552.

Paper Pile Quarterly, Box 337, San Anselmo, CA 94960.

MUSEUMS

American Museum of the Moving Image, 35th Avenue and 36th Street, Astoria, NY.

COLLECTORS' CLUBS

Gone With the Wind Collector's Club, PO Box 503, Walkersville, MD 21793; (301) 254-2461.

The Shirley Temple Club, c/o Rita Dubas, 8811 Colonial Road, Brooklyn, NY 11209; (718) 745-7532.

Universal Autograph Collector's Club, PO Box 6181, Washington, DC 20044-6181.

Studio Collectors Club, PO Box 1566, Apple Valley, CA 92307.

Wallace Nutting
Photographs

Advisor: **MICHAEL IVANKOVICH**

Michael Ivankovich has been collecting Wallace Nutting pictures for fifteen years. Today he is this country's largest collector/dealer of Wallace Nutting—including pictures, books, and furniture—and a frequent lecturer on Wallace Nutting. Mr. Ivankovich has written articles for most major trade papers, has appeared on various radio and television programs, and is frequently consulted by antiques columnists throughout the country. As part of his antiques business, he provides Wallace Nutting appraisal services, exhibits at various antiques shows, and conducts regular Wallace Nutting auctions throughout the Northeast. Mr. Ivankovich has numerous publications, including The Price Guide to Wallace Nutting Pictures *(3rd ed., 1989),* The Wallace Nutting Expansible Catalog *(1987; a reprint of Wallace Nutting's 1915* Salesman's Catalogue*),* The Alphabetical and Numerical Index to Wallace Nutting Pictures *(1989), and* The Guide to Wallace Nutting Furniture *(1990). Mr. Ivankovich can be reached at PO Box 2458, Doylestown, PA 18901; (215) 345-6094.*

BACKGROUND

Wallace Nutting was probably the most famous photographer of the early 20th century. Between 1900 and his death in 1941, his hand-colored photographs of pastoral America achieved such enormous popularity that hardly an American middle-class household was without one.

Beginning in 1897, Wallace Nutting went on to take nearly fifty thousand pictures. Most failed to meet his high standards and were destroyed. Of the ten thousand that he did keep, most were sold in limited numbers, while others were not sold at all. Wallace Nutting would simply take photos for use in his lectures, for research, or for his friends, and those particular pictures would never be hand-colored or sold to the general public.

By most estimates, only 2500 different titles were sold commercially. Some of these titles were extremely successful and sold in very large numbers. Titles like *The Swimming Pool, Larkspur, A Barre Brook, An*

Afternoon Tea, and *Honeymoon Drive* were so popular that tens of thousands of each picture were sold.

Other titles were introduced commercially, failed to generate any significant sales, and were withdrawn. For example, titles like *The Belles of San Gabriel, Southbury Water*, and *Mohonk House from Spring Path* appear in the 1912 *Picture Catalog*, but do not appear in the 1915 *Expansible Catalog*, indicating low sales in the 1912–15 period.

Wallace Nutting would always take his own photographs. His keen sense for composition and taste and his ability to locate and construct beautiful settings enabled him to shoot pictures that he knew Americans would enjoy.

Once back in the studio, Nutting would develop his pictures through a glass negative onto a special platinum paper (hence the name Wallace Nutting Platinotype Pictures). This platinum paper would be sized with a special coating of banana oil and then colored entirely by hand. The first picture would be colored by one of Nutting's head colorists, following his strict instructions. Once this first model picture was approved by Nutting, it became the standard that all the other colorists strived to duplicate.

Pictures that met Nutting's high standards were then mounted upon a tan or beige mat, and signed with the title and the Wallace Nutting name by the head colorist. Wallace Nutting signed very few pictures himself.

Literally millions of these hand-colored pictures were sold. They were beautiful, inexpensive, and provided many people with the opportunity to decorate the walls of their homes at a very affordable price.

The peak of Wallace Nutting picture popularity was 1915–1925. As with other things, however, people eventually began to tire of them after twenty to thirty years. Because of their initial low price, many were simply thrown away; others were stored in attics and basements. Only within the past twenty to twenty-five years, as they have been recycled through auctions and estate sales, have they regained much of their previous popularity.

The CONDITION KEY measures the degree of repair-restoration.

Poor Condition: Missing parts, breaks, and/or very bad restoration (possibly collectible because of some other merit).

Average Condition: Small parts may be missing, and cleaning may be necessary (the condition in which most objects are found).

Good Condition: No parts missing, no major cleaning needed—ready to use or display.

Fine Condition: Near original condition or restored to near original condition.

In the 1960s they could sometimes be purchased for as little $.50 and $1 each or, for all practical purposes, for the price of the frame. By the early 1970s, prices had increased to the $10–$50 level. Some people assembled fabulous collections during this period of low prices. Collections of several hundred were not uncommon. One individual assembled a collection of nearly one thousand pictures, all framed and hanging in one house.

By the 1980s, Wallace Nutting pictures had caught on and prices began to escalate. In fact, prices more than doubled in some categories between 1986 and 1988 alone. Today, the Wallace Nutting auction record picture is *The Guardian Mother*, selling at Michael Ivankovich's September 1989 auction for $4950.

DETERMINING VALUE

The value of a Wallace Nutting picture depends upon several factors.

Subject Matter: What is the topic or theme of the picture? Is it common or rare? How many people are interested in owning the same picture?

Condition: What is the quality of the picture itself? Does the matting have any water stains, foxing, or other damage? What is the condition of the frame? How difficult will it be to find the same picture in the same condition?

Size: How big is the picture itself? The matting? The frame?

Each of these items must be considered in arriving at the final estimated value.

SUBJECT MATTER

There are three main categories of Wallace Nutting pictures.

Exterior scenes are what most people associate with Wallace Nutting, and they comprise the largest segment of his pictures. These include pictures of apple blossoms, birches, country lanes, streams, rivers, ponds, lakes, and fall scenes.

Wallace Nutting worked out of Framingham, Massachusetts, and sold a large percentage of his pictures in New England. Winters were very long and cold, and people generally desired pleasant, optimistic signs of the warmer weather ahead. As a result, these nice warm-weather pictures were the most popular, sold the best, and account for the largest percentage (85 percent) of exterior pictures that may be found.

Since they were so popular then and since so many were produced, they are fairly common today. The fact that they are more common and readily available is the reason for their relatively low price when compared to other types of Wallace Nutting pictures.

Interior scenes were pictures taken inside old houses and usually had women dressed in long dresses and bonnets. Some were done in primitive settings, others in more formal surroundings. They included period furniture and were quite charming.

Although these were popular, they were not nearly as popular as the exterior scenes, accounting for only approximately 10 percent of all Wallace Nutting pictures. Thus, the law of supply and demand holds true here. Since fewer were originally done, fewer are available today. With so few available, demand has pushed the prices of some up to two or three times higher than comparable exterior scenes.

All things being equal (i.e., size and condition), a basic rule of thumb is that interior scenes are worth approximately two to three times as much as exterior scenes.

Miscellaneous unusual pictures, a third category, somewhat overlaps the exterior and interior categories but is the most desirable subject for the serious or advanced collector. It is also the category least understood by beginning collectors and dealers.

Collectors usually begin buying exterior scenes because of their lower price and then progress to buying interior scenes. But once the collector is hooked on Wallace Nutting, the real search begins for rare and unusual pictures.

Wallace Nutting collectors are like any other collectors; they are always looking for rare and unusual items to add to their collection. They travel long distances, scour flea markets and antique shows, and pay whatever it takes to acquire a special picture.

Few collectors will go too far out of their way to purchase an exterior scene. They are too common and easy to obtain.

Even interior scenes must be something very unusual before the serious collector becomes motivated to buy. But once you have a rare and unusual picture in your hands, you have something very desirable to all levels of Wallace Nutting collectors.

Some of the unusual topics would include seascapes, pictures with animals, foreign scenes, exteriors with people, floral arrangements, and snow scenes.

All unusual topics combined account for only about 5 percent of all Wallace Nutting pictures.

EVALUATING CONDITION

Once you have determined the type of picture you have, the next step in determining the value is to assess its condition because condition is the most important determinant of value. The rarest picture in poor condition has very little value; a common exterior in excellent condition is

still a very desirable piece. There are several important characteristics
to look for when evaluating condition.

The Picture Itself

Many pictures are nearly one hundred years old, and, as time has
passed, their condition has deteriorated. Some hung on walls that received years of direct sunlight, causing the colors to fade. Others were
stored in damp basements where condensation formed and caused spots
and blemishes to occur.

Second, each picture was individually hand-colored, not colored by
machine. Whenever something is manually produced in large numbers,
some items are inevitably going to look better than others.

Finally, although quality standards were set, some hand-colored pictures were almost masterpieces, while others barely met the minumum
standards. Wallace Nutting also sold the business at one time, so different minimum quality standards were in place at various times between
1900 and 1941.

It should therefore be understood that the quality of pictures can vary
widely. Experience is your best guide. The more pictures you see, the
better you will be able to differentiate between a good and excellent
piece.

Matting

The matting is the beige or tan backing that the picture is mounted on
and that contains the title and signature. This is really the most susceptible to damage. All too often, as pictures were stored in basements or
attics, water would get on the matting because of basement floods or
attic leaks. Once a matting becomes water-stained, it is almost impossible to remove.

Severe water stains are very unsightly and definitely detract from the
beauty and value of a picture. Although some collectors will still buy a
picture with a water-stained mat, other collectors will shy away unless
the picture itself is very rare and of high quality. Therefore, a water-
stained mat decreases the value of a picture, sometimes by as much as
25 percent to 50 percent.

Another problem that can occur with the matting is yellowing from
the sun. It was not uncommon for a picture to hang in direct sunlight
for many years. A yellowed mat is usually accompanied by a faded picture, thus significantly reducing the value.

Spotting, or foxing, on the mat is another problem but not as severe
as water stains. Spots form because of age, dampness, fungus growth,
the type of backing used, or for any of several other reasons. Spots can

sometimes be removed, but this should be attempted only by a qualified, experienced individual.

It goes without saying that a torn mat will significantly reduce the value of a picture. Sometimes mat damage may be camouflaged by an overmat. There is nothing wrong with this because the picture itself is the most important part, and if overmatting will enhance the beauty of a picture, fine. But just be aware that an overmat is probably a sign of a damaged mat and is no substitute for a mat in excellent condition. It will also reduce the value of the picture. As a general rule, overmatted pictures may be worth as much as 50 percent less than pictures with clean, original mats.

Sometimes you will see a picture with a black border instead of an indented mat. Stories that the black border represents pictures done after Wallace Nutting's death are not true. These are also not reproductions. Rather, this was just another style that Wallace Nutting tried to market in the late 1920s. Most black-bordered pictures are 100 percent hand-colored (vs. only partial coloring on most earlier pictures). Frequently, original labels can be found on the backs of these pictures. Some people love these black-bordered pictures; others do not. As a general rule, pictures with black borders are somewhat less desirable to some collectors than those without it.

Frame

The frame is very important to the overall beauty of a picture. The solid brown wooden frame is the most common and desirable type. Wallace Nutting framed many of the pictures he sold, but some of his large customers (e.g., some department stores) preferred to buy their pictures unframed. They would then frame them according to their customer's taste (and presumably save shipping charges as well). This accounts for the wide variety of frames you may see.

Only when you have seen a Wallace Nutting picture in a perfect original frame do you realize the importance of the frame to the overall picture. Chipped, pitted, painted, or unsightly frames can spoil an otherwise perfect picture. Although frames are replaceable (whereas the picture and original mat are not), the cost of replacing a frame can turn a good buy into a bad buy.

Other Miscellaneous Considerations

Other things to look for in determining value are original wavy glass, original paper backing, and original copyright labels. These things are not absolutely necessary for an excellent picture, but they may represent the difference between an excellent picture and a mint condition piece.

SIZE

After analyzing the subject matter and condition of the picture, the third key to determining value is size. With only a few exceptions, the larger the picture, the greater the value. A large exterior is usually more valuable than a smaller exterior; a large interior is usually more valuable than a smaller interior.

There are two sizes to consider: the picture size and the mat size. Some people lend particular importance to the size of the picture itself; others do not. I personally feel that the mat size is the primary determinant of value. However, a disproportion between picture and mat could indicate that a mat has been cut down to eliminate water stains or other damage.

There are two exceptions to this general rule regarding size. Miniatures (4″ × 5″ pictures) seem to command a higher price because of their relative rarity than comparable pictures of a somewhat larger size. Second, unusually large pictures (more than 20″ × 28″) seem generally to sell for less than some of the smaller sizes. This is most likely because such large pictures are usually of the more common exterior scenes, they take up a prohibitive amount of wall space, and they are quite difficult to transport.

PROCESS PRINTS

During the 1930s, Wallace Nutting began producing what he called "process prints." These were reprints of some of Nutting's most popular hand-colored pictures, except they were machine-produced rather than hand-colored. This cost-cutting measure occurred during the Depression years in an attempt to bolster declining picture sales.

Process prints are not considered reproductions because they were produced by Wallace Nutting and sold as such. They were all 12″ × 15″ and included only twelve scenes. Some were framed as is; others were matted on 16″ × 20″ mats before framing. Some have a Wallace Nutting copyright on the picture or a "process print" label on the back.

These are not highly prized by most collectors. I have seen them priced from $5 to $75 each. In reality most collectors who are willing to spend a fair amount of money on a picture would prefer a hand-colored picture to a process print. Thus, their value is well below comparable hand-colored pictures.

FAKES ALERT

It happens in every field. As soon as something is successful and widely collectible, someone else tries to reproduce it. Wallace Nutting pictures are no exception. One company reproduced some Wallace Nutting pictures during the 1920s but excluded the Wallace Nutting signature and copyright. He fought them in court and won but not until many had been reproduced. The quality was not good, and they are easy to detect. Look closely with a magnifying glass. An original Wallace Nutting picture will not have a series of little dots visible. Also, the "Wallace Nutting" name was excluded, and the title was moved to the lower right corner below the picture. These have no real value as Wallace Nutting pictures except as a piece of reference.

Another series of Wallace Nutting reproductions appeared about ten years ago and are still in circulation. These were relatively good reproductions. They are usually interior scenes and contain the title and signature in its normal position. An experienced collector can detect a reproduction relatively easily, but a new collector might be fooled.

Most reproductions I have seen possess several obvious characteristics:

- A glossy picture with a dark tint
- A title and signature with a purple tint
- An almost paper-thin mat
- A new frame

You should be aware that these reproductions were photographs of a photograph, *not* a machine-printed picture as in the 1920s reproductions. As a result they will fail the magnifying glass test. After you have seen a few of these reproductions, you will know what to look for. Fortunately, I have seen relatively few of these over the past three years.

A more recent series of reproductions has appeared within the past year. Actually, these might more correctly be described as fakes. Some unscrupulous individual has selected approximately ten actual, but unusual, Wallace Nutting titles from *The Alphabetical and Numerical Index to Wallace Nutting Pictures* (see Bibliography), found non–Wallace Nutting pictures that seem pertinent to the title (i.e., an Italian picture for the title *Tivloi*; a picture of the Washington Monument and cherry blossoms for *Washington Cherry Blossoms*, etc.), mounted them on a mat board, and signed the title and the Wallace Nutting name. These fakes even include a stamp on the back of the picture that says: THIS PICTURE IS ___ BY WALLACE NUTTING IN PROCESS COLOR, with the studio hand-stamped into the blank area. These pictures have been framed in old frames, which adds to the deception. And because these are photographs of photographs, they also fail the magnifying glass test. These pictures seem to be priced at less than $50, which makes them even more tempting to the unsuspecting buyer.

You should also be aware that dozens of other photographers were selling hand-colored pictures during the early 20th century. The work of some of these photographers was nearly as good as Nutting's, while others were simply awful. Occasionally you will see a picture done by one of these other photographers, with the original name replaced by the name "Wallace Nutting." Usually this is done by erasing the original signature and simply writing in the Wallace Nutting name.

Although Wallace Nutting reproductions and fakes are very limited in scope, collectors should be aware that they are out there.

A Sip of Tea 13″ × 16″ 1915–1925 United States
Girl reaches for teapot over fire.
Superior Quality/Fine Condition $150 (D) **$150–$200**

A Warm Spring Day 14″ × 17″ 1910–1920 United States
Several dozen sheep graze beside a blue lake; note: although animal pictures are generally considered rare, sheep are more common than cats, dogs, birds, cows. *(See photo 195)*
Superior Quality/Fine Condition $231 (A) **$175–$350**

An Afternoon Tea 13″ × 16″ 1910–1925 United States
Two girls have tea near fireplace; note: a very common interior.
Very Good Quality/Average Condition $150 (D) **$125–$250**

Decked as a Bride 14″ × 17″ 1915–1925 United States
Country lane winds through orchard.
Very Good Quality/Good Condition $135 (D) **$100–$150**

Dog-on-it 7″ × 11″ 1910–1925 United States
Eight little puppies sit on garden bench; signed lower right, title on picture; mat stains, lower right.
Good Quality/Average Condition $1292 (A) **$600–$1500**

Photo 195. Wallace Nutting photograph. CREDIT: MICHAEL IVANKOVICH *(See above)*

Dutch Sails 16″ × 10″ 1930–1935 Holland
Two sailboats sail along canal past windmill: note: black border around picture dates picture around 1930.
Superior Quality/Good Condition $220 (A) **$175–$325**

Four O'Clock 17″ × 14″ 1910–1925 United States
Fifteen cows graze by stream at foot of hill; held Wallace Nutting record price for a brief period.
Superior Quality/Fine Condition $1430 (A) **$750–$1500**

Larkspur 17″ × 14″ 1915–1925 England
Girl stands in flower garden near thatch-roofed cottage; note: a very common picture.
Very Good Quality/Good Condition $125 (D) **$85–$175**

Pasture Dell 13″ × 16″ 1910–1925 United States
Close-up view of 7 cows grazing in a field; early pencil signature; note: this was the first Wallace Nutting picture to sell for more than $1000 at auction.
Superior Quality/Fine Condition $1182 (A) **$600–$1200**

Returning from a Walk 17″ × 14″ 1915–1925 United States
Girl in purple dress climbs stairs in early hallway.
Superior Quality/Fine Condition $242 (A) **$175–$350**

Sea Ledges 11″ × 17″ 1915–1925 United States
White waves crash upon large shoreline rocks.
Superior Quality/Fine Condition $450 (A) **$275–$475**

Silhouette 4″ × 4″ 1927–1935 United States
Girl stands near garden urn; Nutting produced around 30 different silhouettes after 1927; all are marked "WN" or "EJD" for Ernest John Donnelly, his employee who actually drew the original silhouette.
Superior Quality/Good Condition $45 (A) **$40–$60**

The Dahlia Jar 20″ × 16″ 1930–1935 United States
Large, close-framed picture of stoneware pitcher filled with colorful flowers; unusually large size; signed on picture; original copyright label on back.
Superior Quality/Fine Condition $374 (A) **$250–$450**

The Guardian Mother 16″ × 12″ 1910–1920 United States
Little girl in white dress stands beside mother who also wears flowing white dress; mint condition; even has "Guardian Mother" label on back; note: this picture currently holds WN auction record.
Superior Quality/Fine Condition $4950 (A) **$1500–$4950**

The Maple Sugar 14″ × 17″ Cupboard 1915–1925 United States
Girl reaches into cupboard above fireplace.
Very Good Quality/Good Condition $175 (D) **$150–$200**

The Meeting Place 15″ × 19″ 1910–1925 United States
Four cows and 1 horse drink from opposite sides of stream; note: on 2 occasions this picture sold for a Wallace Nutting record price.
Superior Quality/Fine Condition $2750 (A) **$1000–$2750**

The Swimming Pool 14″ × 17″ 1910–1920 United States
Blue stream flows between rocky banks; mat stain lower right; note: this is one of the most common WN titles.
Good Quality/Average Condition $85 (D) **$75–$150**

The Way It Begins 13″ × 16″ 1905–1910 United States
Man in red jacket stands beside woman playing piano; early pencil signature.
(See photo 196)
Superior Quality/Fine Condition $715 (A) **$500–$800**

The Whirling Candles 14″ × 11″ Candlestand 1915–1920 United States
Little girl stands near mother by whirling candlestand in early setting; children
pictures, except for *The Coming Out of Rosa*, are very rare.
Very Good Quality/Fine Condition $302 (A) **$250–$375**

Three Chums 13″ × 16″ 1915–1925 United States
Two girls near fireplace with sitting cat.
Superior Quality/Fine Condition $462 (A) **$275–$475**

Untitled Cottage 7″ × 9″ 1915–1925 England
Thatch-roofed cottage stands beside green garden.
Very Good Quality/Good Condition $75 (D) **$50–$125**

Untitled Exterior 12″ × 8″ Scene 1915–1925 United States
Tall birch trees stand beside blue lake.
Very Good Quality/Good Condition $60 (D) **$35–$65**

Untitled Exterior 7″ × 9″ Scene 1921 United States
Blossoming apple trees stand beside country lane.
Very Good Quality/Average Condition $45 (D) **$35–$50**

Photo 196. Wallace Nutting photograph. CREDIT: MICHAEL
IVANKOVICH *(See above)*

Untitled Interior   7″ × 9″   Scene   1910   United States
Girl reaches for teapot over fire.
Superior Quality/Good Condition $110 (D)   **$75–$125**
Untitled Interior   12″ × 8″   Scene   1915   United States
Girl stands near tall grandfather's clock; major water stain on mat.
Good Quality/Poor Condition $45 (D)   **$75–$135**

BIBLIOGRAPHY

The following books, all written by Michael Ivankovich, are available
from Diamond Press, Box 2458, Doylestown, PA 18901, or by calling
(215) 345–6094.

The Alphabetical and Numerical Index to Wallace Nutting Pictures, 1988.
The Guide to Wallace Nutting Furniture, 1990.
The Price Guide to Wallace Nutting Pictures (3rd Ed.), 1989.
Wallace Nutting, 1984.
Wallace Nutting General Furniture Catalog, Supreme Edition, 1984 (re-
   print).

COLLECTORS' CLUBS

The Wallace Nutting Collectors' Club, c/o George and Justine Monro,
186 Mountain Avenue, North Caldwell, NJ 07006.

AUCTIONS

Michael Ivankovich conducts periodic Wallace Nutting specialty auctions
featuring Wallace Nutting pictures, books, and furniture. If you would
like to contact him regarding upcoming Wallace Nutting auctions, about
buying or selling any Wallace Nutting material, or simply to be put on
his mailing list for any future Wallace Nutting updates, you can write to
him at Diamond Press, Box 2458, Doylestown, PA 18901, or call (215)
345–6094.

Oriental Fine and Decorative Arts

This chapter is arranged by the following subcategories: BRONZES, CLOISONNÉ, FURNITURE, IVORY, JAPANESE PRINTS, PORCELAIN.

The finest pieces of Oriental fine art—especially Chinese and Japanese—have continued to increase astronomically this year. Although great values were to be found (with 20-20 hindsight) at shows and in fine shops, auction prices again shot to new highs. Fine porcelains, great bronzes, Tang horses—all have again increased dramatically.

Additionally, prices for the lower levels of fine art, the fine Japanese prints, and many areas of the decorative arts have increased significantly. A new appreciation of Japanese ivories—and to a lesser extent Chinese ivories—as well as the recent trade laws regarding ivory, has led to a price surge for small ivory sculptures. Netsukes have always been in high demand; now Okimono have joined the category of highly collectible items.

Of course, good values and very affordable areas remain, but the bargain category is shrinking. Blue and white porcelains are suffering a price decrease at the moment, while the once stagnant Famille Rose group is appreciating in value. Long dormant interest in Ming and later bronzes has been aroused. All of these areas will be well worth watching this year.

CONDITION KEY

Fine Condition: glowing finish; all original hardware intact; no repairs.

Good Condition: nice finish; hardware intact but not necessarily original; some high-quality repairs.

Average Condition: acceptable finish; may need cleaning; hardware intact; some repairs may be obvious.

Poor Condition: finish poor or painted over; missing pieces of hardware; needs a number of minor repairs; old repairs of poor quality.

QUALITY KEY

Good Quality: a nice piece having only ordinary characteristics.

Very Good Quality: a very good example of the type, reflecting several of the most desired characteristics.

Superior Quality: a superlative example that has all of the characteristics of the type; few examples remaining.

BRONZES

Ku vase   9.5″ H   1850–1860   China
Flaring cylindrical form with raised geometric design; after the archaic.
Good Quality/Good Condition $175 (A)   **$175–$275**

> All but the earliest Oriental bronzes remain a depressed market. Their last "hot" period was the late 1970s.—*DL*

Ku vase   7.5″ H   1850–1860   China
Circular, turned, flared form with geometric decorations; after the archaic.
Good Quality/Fine Condition $50 (A)   **$125–$225**

Teapot   8.5″ H × 8.5″ L   Edo period   Japan
Rare iron teapot with steel bead and tracery decoration; artist signed; bronze lid and knob.
Superior Quality/Fine Condition $2400 (D)   **$1500–$2500**

Vase   12″ H   1885–1900   Japan
Ovoid with figure of a child riding an ox in relief beneath an inlaid gold crescent moon; impressed inscription.
Very Good Quality/Fine Condition $650 (A)   **$500–$900**

CLOISONNÉ

Carp   6.5″ L   1890–1900   Japan
Gilt silver and enamel carp with articulated scales; swirling tail; orange and yellow eyes.
Very Good Quality/Fine Condition $1200 (D)   **$900–$1500**

Cup   4″ H   1900–1910   Japan
Cylindrical; enameled with various insects on a light blue ground with gold flecks, domed base with bracket feet; by Takeuchi Chubei, signed and inscribed with studio name.
Superior Quality/Fine Condition $225 (A)   **$225–$275**

Vases   7″ H   1910–1920   Japan
Pair; each ovoid with a rose on a yellow ground; silver rims.
Good Quality/Fine Condition $225 (A)   **$150–$250**

> Cloisonné, like bronzes, remains depressed, but with some surges in signed Japanese pieces of the 1900 to 1930 period.—*DL*

CHINESE FURNITURE CONSTRUCTION

© *David P. Lindquist*

While we in the West constantly examine our antique furniture for construction techniques and tirelessly admire the advances in technique made between the crude pre-1700 work and later work that grew ever finer, the Chinese were simply continuing sophisticated work already extant for hundreds of years. It was not only in porcelain production that China led the world. By 1600, China was producing furniture of superlative craftsmanship.

The pieces photographed for this article have their roots in period Chinese furniture of the Ming and early Qing (Ch'ing) Dynasties, and the construction techniques used are identical to the early techniques.

Photo 197 is of a child's chair—it is pure mid-19th century and relates closely to adult chairs that we often see in so-called ancestral portraits of that period. The arms and apron are carved with prunus blossoms; the feet are fiery dragons. In this piece the entire construction is mortise and tenon. The feet are triangular with concealed tenons (see photos of this technique below). The clever use of the carved head totally conceals this joint where the hair streaks away from the head.

In *photo 198* we find a superb example of a *yuanyi* chair—literally, "round chair" and known in the West as a horseshoe-armchair for obvious reasons. The chair is sublimely comfortable and made of tight, beautifully grained Ju wood (a very dense, heavy Chinese elm). Note the triangular joints on the back splat *(photo 199)* and the lapped joints on the top rail *(photo 200)*. The seat frame is mortise and tenon with an exposed joint with a side pin or peg that is large and rectangular *(photo 201)*.

A very clever design element in this chair is the use of decorative aprons as spandrels around the openings created by the legs, seat rails, and stretchers. These aprons are purely decorative, giving a sense of weight and proportion to a chair that would otherwise appear spindly.

Age is a very difficult judgment in superb-quality Chinese furniture such as this chair. Such chairs were made identically for several hundred years. This chair has great shrinkage; splines and other tightening devices have been inserted in the floating seat panel and in many joints. The dense Ju wood shrinks very slowly, so considerable age is evidenced.

The bottoms of the legs of this chair show a very open grain and deterioration due to cleaning of floors and other natural wear. Again, this is judged as it is on *all* chairs from all countries. One finds open grain and real wear, and one judges accordingly. The rules of age that I

Photo 197 (left). Child's chair. CREDIT: WHITEHALL AT THE VILLA, CHAPEL HILL, NC. *Photo 198 (right). Yuanyi chair.* CREDIT: WHITEHALL AT THE VILLA, CHAPEL HILL, NC. *(See p. 383)*

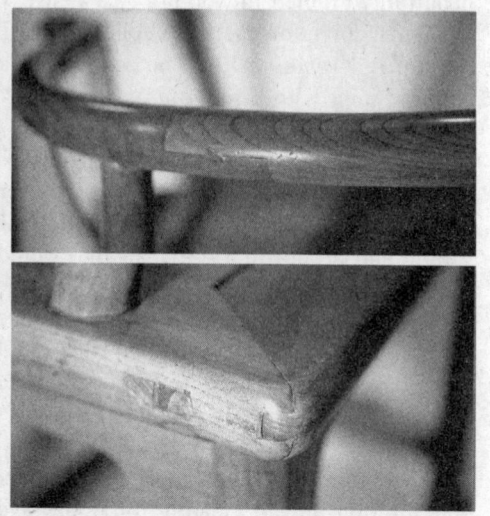

Photo 199 (left) and photo 200 (top right). Details of yuanyi chair. CREDIT: WHITEHALL AT THE VILLA, CHAPEL HILL, NC. *Photo 201 (bottom right). Detail of seat frame.* CREDIT: WHITEHALL AT THE VILLA, CHAPEL HILL, NC *(See p. 383)*

have incorporated in so many articles on Western furniture are equally operable on Oriental furniture.

To further explore furniture joinery or construction, I include a photo of a miniature Chinese armchair in red lacquer, *photo 202*, which I have totally dismantled to show how the joints are made. This chair is in the "lamp hanger's," or *dengguayi*, form. In the late-19th-century manner, it is heavily embellished with dragon carving.

The remarkable thing is that all of those fancy triangular joints are an optical illusion—they conceal straight mortise-and-tenon joints. *Photo 203* shows a close-up of the joint between the arm and the rear back upright and the lower stretcher—both triangular. *Photo 204* shows the arm joint pulled apart, and we see that it is in fact an illusion to make it appear more elegant and less obvious. *Photo 205* shows the "triangular" joint of leg and stretcher.

At each opportunity you find, study the superb and rather exotic construction found in Chinese furniture. For those of us who love furniture, it's a joy. For those who thought the West made great furniture, think about who may have taught them. The English learned fine furniture construction techniques from the Dutch with the accession of William and Mary to the throne. Guess whom the Dutch learned from? China.

Photo 202 (left). Miniature Chinese armchair. Photo 203 (center). Side view of armchair shown in Photo 202. Photo 204 (top right). Detail of arm joint. Photo 205 (bottom right). Detail of triangular joint. CREDIT: WHITEHALL AT THE VILLA, CHAPEL HILL, NC *(See above)*

FURNITURE

Altar table   38″ H × 55″ W × 16″ D   1885–1900   China
Hardwood, with molded top and scrolled ends above a pierced and grapevine-carved frieze, raised on pierced and carved legs.
Good Quality/Fine Condition $1400 (A)   **$1200–$1800**

Bonheur du jour   56.5″ H × 28.5″ W   Lacquer   1830–1845   China
Chinese export; recessed cabinet top with 2 doors opening to drawers and cubbyholes; resting on rectangular case with fold-out writing surface; shaped skirt, cabriole legs, paw feet; usual lacquer cracking. *(See photo 206)*
Superior Quality/Good Condition $5750 (A)   **$4500–$7500**

Chair   1910–1930   China
Carved rosewood armchair with cloisonné plaque in a vaguely Ming style; for the Western market.
Very Good Quality/Fine Condition $240 (A)   **$450–$750**

Picnic box/table   24″ H × 24.5″ W × 17″ D   Black lacquer   c. 1860   China
Gilt-decorated fitted picnic box; on later stand. *(See photo 207)*
Superior Quality/Fine Condition $3025 (A)   **$2400–$3500**

Screen   84″ H × 108″ L   1885–1900   China
Six-panel paper screen with village scene on the water and various figures engaged in activities, set on a silver ground.
Good Quality/Fine Condition $1200 (A)   **$750–$1500**

Screen   40.5″ H × 130″ L   1780–1800   Japan
Six-panel paper screen with open fans depicting various landscape, figural, and animal scenes.
Good Quality/Fine Condition $4250 (A)   **$3000–$4500**

Screen, table   12″ H × 34.5″ W   1780–1800   Japan
Six-panel paper table screen; noble women in a palace garden viewing cherry blossoms, on goldleaf ground; slight wear; framed.
Good Quality/Good Condition $1000 (A)   **$800–$1200**

Table, center   34.5″ H × 23″ W × 20″ D   Lacquer   1780–1800   China
Oblong top with incurvate sides; recessed pierced frieze and draped apron; scrolling legs and whorled feet on molded dais; black ground with gilt and bronze landscape and foliage; for export; cracked base panel.
Very Good Quality/Average Condition $3000 (A)   **$2500–$3500**

IVORY

Ivory is most commonly associated with elephant tusks, but historically, marine ivory has also been used extensively both for carving and for scrimming (scratching and then coloring the lines with India ink). The Japanese, in particular, were (and unfortunately still are) great whalers, and they brought back vast quantities of whale teeth and walrus tusks. While the Oriental carver preferred elephant ivory for its evenness of color, grain pattern, and size range, he would also use marine pieces.

Photo 206 (left). Bonheur du jour. CREDIT: WILLIAM DOYLE GALLERIES
Photo 207 (right). Picnic box/table. CREDIT: GROGAN & CO. *(See p. 386)*

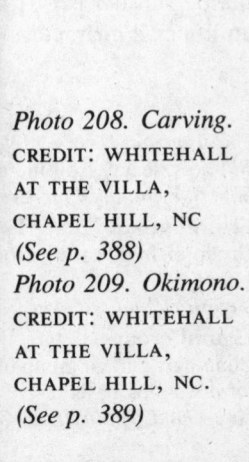

Photo 208. Carving.
CREDIT: WHITEHALL
AT THE VILLA,
CHAPEL HILL, NC
(See p. 388)
Photo 209. Okimono.
CREDIT: WHITEHALL
AT THE VILLA,
CHAPEL HILL, NC.
(See p. 389)

Today value can be enhanced by discussing with collectors the interesting contrasts among the types of ivory and how the artist used the advantage of each and often disguised any problems.

DIFFERENTIATING TYPES

Ivory is found in a huge size range. Truly monumental pieces will, of course, be elephant; small pieces, however, require discernment.

Elephant ivory has a crosshatch pattern in the growth of the tusk that *invariably* appears on each carved piece. This crosshatching creates small diamond patterns that even the most casual observer can spot.

Walrus and whale ivory do *not* have a crosshatched grain pattern. However, walrus has an iridescent dentin that is very distinctive: a range of brown tones that, to the Oriental mind, mars the quality of the ivory. However, we find artful disguising of the dentin through carving and scrimming—efforts that ironically can *increase* the value of a piece carved from "inferior" ivory!

Whale ivory shows no dentin and has a soft, almost invisible growth pattern that is rather like concentric tree rings. The pattern is basically indiscernible.

Thus, crosshatching equals elephant ivory; dentin equals walrus ivory; neither indicates whale ivory.

FAKES ALERT

There are many resin-based ivory substitutes found in the market—modern faux ivory. This is plastic! Check each piece with great care. If in doubt, test the bottom with a heated needle (it slips right into *most* plastic substances). If still in doubt, consult an expert or buy only with an ironclad guarantee.

Carving 8.5″ H   1900–1910   China
Bijin, or beauty, spilling a basket of flowers; on stand. *(See photo 208)*
Superior Quality/Fine Condition $875 (D)   **$600–$900**
Figural group 2.5″ H × 5″ W   Naturalistic   c. 1880   Japan
Group of frogs carved from a single block of ivory; Meiji period; small nick on 1 foot.
Superior Quality/Good Condition $1800 (D)   **$1500–$2800**
Figural group 12″ H   Naturalistic   c. 1920   Japan
Cunningly carved group of 3 monkeys that hang from a natural tree on a natural-form wooden base.
Very Good Quality/Fine Condition $1000 (D)   **$800–$1500**

Figure 2.5″ H × 3.5″ W c.1890 China
Ivory horse on naturalistic wood stand; prancing animal; well carved but not fully developed.
Good Quality/Fine Condition $215 (D) **$150–$250**

Okimono 3.75″ H c.1920 Japan
Family group of a rope maker, wife, and baby; child is going for his thongs; arranged on a stand that is not original.
Good Quality/Fine Condition $2800 (D) **$2000–$3500**

Okimono 5″ H c.1920 Japan
Man with pipe and hat; fine, mellow color; signed; good, but not fine carving.
Very Good Quality/Fine Condition $1850 (D) **$1500–$2000**

Okimono 2.75″ H c. 1890 Japan
Meiji period; man with a child in lap playing with a puppy.
Very Good Quality/Fine Condition $1650 (D) **$1200–$1650**

Okimono 5.25″ H c. 1930 Japan
Barefoot fisherman with net; good and interesting carving, but lacking great detail.
Very Good Quality/Fine Condition $1850 (D) **$1200–$2000**

Okimono 4.5″ H Realistic 1830–1845 Japan
Early-19th-century okimono; god of wealth with traditional symbols; minutely carved details with fine engraving; signed.
Superior Quality/Fine Condition $3000 (D) **$2500–$3500**

Okimono 9″ H Naturalistic c.1880 Japan
Extraordinary, finely sculptured man with frogs, walking through the waters; artist and owner marks on base.
Superior Quality/Fine Condition $6000 (D) **$4500–$7500**

Okimono 8″ H Realistic c.1880 Japan
Carved, early Meiji period; man with a walking stick and a bird on his shoulder; Tokugawa crest on his robe; signed. *(See photo 209)*
Superior Quality/Fine Condition $3000 (D) **$2500–$4000**

Okimono 7.5″ H 1870–1890 Japan
Wise man in flowing robes; exceptional detail on face, hands, and feet.
Superior Quality/Fine Condition $4500 (D) **$3500–$5000**

Okimono c.1880 Japan
Two boys reading scrolls; lovely color and excellent carving; signed; Meiji period.
Very Good Quality/Fine Condition $1700 (D) **$1200–$2200**

Okimono 8.5″ H 1885–1900 Japan
Superb carving of a warrior on his camel; very detailed; signed.
Superior Quality/Fine Condition $12,500 (D) **$8000–$12,500**

Okimono 11.5″ H 1885–1900 Japan
Man carrying boy and basket on his head.
Superior Quality/Fine Condition $6000 (D) **$4500–$7000**

Okimono 5.5″ H c.1890 Japan
Meiji period; group at the water wheel to irrigate the rice paddles.
Superior Quality/Fine Condition $2000 (D) **$1200–$2500**

Okimono 5″ H 1900–1910 Japan
Little boy with movable flag; signed.
Superior Quality/Fine Condition $1800 (D) **$1500–$2400**

JAPANESE PRINTS

Advisors: **MITZIE and MICHAEL VERNE**

Mitzie and Michael Verne are a mother-and-son team who have had a gallery of Japanese art for thirty-seven years. They have lectured and participated in major art shows throughout the country. Mitzie is the author, in collaboration with Betsy Franco, of The Emperor Was My Neighbor in Japan: The Mitzie Verne Collection. *The Vernes are members of International Fine Print Dealers Association. The Mitzie Verne Collection of Japanese Art is located in the Grasselli Library Gallery of John Carroll University, 20700 North Park Blvd., University Heights, OH 44118; (216) 397-4551.*

SURVEY OF THE FIELD

Ukiyo-e

Ukiyo-e, or antique Japanese woodblock prints, reflected the history of Japan from 1660 to the end of the 19th century. The term *ukiyo-e* literally translates to "pictures of the floating world," the world that passes before your eyes.

Japan was a feudal country up to 1860, closed to the Western world from 1620 to 1853. The woodblock prints mirrored the rise to power of the merchant class, which was low on the social totem pole; they reflected the taste of the common man.

Ukiyo-e were the posters, the picture postcards, the prints of the favorite courtesans of the common merchants, the handbills for the Kabuki theater. The woodblock prints of sumo wrestlers might be compared to baseball cards.

These prints sold for a few sen (a few cents) on the streets of Edo (Tokyo). As a result, they were held in very low esteem. People threw them out as we throw out the Sunday supplement to the newspaper. Thus, there are very few *ukiyo-e* extant in good condition even though they were never limited in edition.

The full-color woodblock print came into being in 1730. There were four people involved in the creation of *ukiyo-e*. First was the artist, whose name comes down to us. The master artist made the original sketch on a tissue-thin sheet of paper, which he then gave to the woodcarver. The woodcarver placed the artist's sketch on a kiln-dried piece of cherrywood and carved up every detail of the artist's sketch to create the key block. Thus, if someone wishes to sell you an original sketch of an antique woodblock print, be wary! The original drawing was carved up to create the key block. The third person involved was the printer, who printed the key block twenty to thirty times. The artist then indicated where he wanted each of the colors. A separate woodblock was carved for each color in the print so that as many as twenty to thirty separate blocks could have been carved for one print. The publisher also played an important role. The best publishers could afford the best stable of artists, the finest woodcarvers and printers, the finest pigments, sun-dried cherry blocks, and handmade mulberry paper. Even though *ukiyo-e* sold for very little, a great deal of work went into their creation.

TRENDS IN COLLECTING *UKIYO-E*

Until the value of the *ukiyo-e* was recognized by the Western world, the Japanese did not realize what they had in their own backyard. Today it is the Japanese collector who is buying *ukiyo-e* by such artists as Sharaku (fl. 1794–1795), Utamaro (1754–1856), Hiroshige (1797–1858), and Hokusai (1760–1849), just to name a few. They want the *ukiyo-e* returned to their country of origin. It is the Japanese collector who is responsible for the escalation of prices at auction today. One Sharaku went for almost half a million dollars at Christie's!

Until recently, *ukiyo-e* scholars were not interested in any artists after Hiroshige and Hokusai, who worked in the mid-19th century. They considered most of the prints after Perry's arrival in Japan in 1853 to be decadent. After Perry opened Japan to the Western world, German analine dyes came into Japan. Instead of the pleasing muted tones of natural vegetable and mineral pigments, harsh purples and reds were used in creating woodblock prints. Attitudes about these Meiji Period prints changed after Julia Meech-Pekarik wrote *The World of the Meiji Print* in 1986. They are now looked upon as an important record of the history of the late 19th century.

Another artist who has achieved great esteem in the past few years is Yoshitoshi (1839–1892). He is considered the last great artist of the 19th century. His *One Hundred Aspects of the Moon* series, done between 1886 and 1892, is eagerly sought by knowledgeable collectors.

Shin Hanga

The *shin hanga*, or New Print movement, began in the early part of the 20th century. The publisher Watanabe wanted to revive an interest in the traditional Japanese print, and he chose artists such as Hasui (1883–1957) and Hiroshi Yoshida (1876–1950) to start this movement. The subject matter was the same as 19th-century "famous places," but Western perspective came into play. Goyo (1880–1921) and Shinsui (1898–1972) were noted for their *bijin*, or beautiful women, prints in this *shin hanga* period. Ohara Koson (1877–1945), later known as Shoson, did handsome bird and flower subjects.

TRENDS IN COLLECTING *SHIN HANGA*

There is a tremendous interest in collecting prints from this early-20th-century movement. Especially sought after are prints by Hasui that were issued before the earthquake in Japan in 1923. Most of Hasui's woodblocks and prints were destroyed in the ensuing fire that burned his studio to the ground. Thus, his pre-earthquake prints are extremely rare. *The Complete Woodblock Prints of Hiroshi Yoshida*, a retrospective volume of his *shin hanga*, was published in 1987. His watercolor-like woodblock prints have set new highs at Christie's and Sotheby's. Goyo's and Shinsui's beauties have also escalated in value.

Sosaku Hanga

Sosaku hanga, the Creative Print movement, was born in 1904. In these contemporary prints the artist is involved from start to finish. Because the prints do not have mass appeal but sell only to the discerning, most are done in extremely limited editions. In the *sosaku hanga* movement the artists work in every medium, not just the woodblock print. They create silkscreen prints, etchings, lithographs, mixed media, wood engravings, monoprints, and woodblock prints. *Sosaku hanga* is international in scope. Art always reflects what is going on in a country at any given time, and today the Japanese are influenced by their own traditions and those of the West. It is in their tradition to be great printmakers. Thus, the most important printmaking in the world is going on in Japan today.

Among the important contemporary printmakers are: Umetaro Azechi (b. 1902), famous for his woodblock prints of mountain men; Yoshitoshi Mori (b. 1898), hand-stencil-dyed prints of traditional subjects; Reika Iwami (b. 1927), abstract woodblock prints of water themes; Mayumi Oda (b.1941), Matisse-like "goddesses" done in the silkscreen medium; Shigeki Kuroda (b. 1953), etchings of "bicycles and umbrellas"; Tetsuro Sawada (b. 1935), silkscreen prints of "skyscapes"; Kiyoshi Saito (b. 1907), wood-grain effects in prints of traditional subject matter; Ryohei Tanaka (b. 1933), mind-boggling detailed etchings of thatched-roof farmhouses; Toko Shinoda (b. 1913), the grande dame of Japanese women artists, calligraphic lithographs; and Jun'ichiro Sekino (1914–1988), appealing portraits of his fellow *sosaku hanga* artists.

TRENDS IN COLLECTING *SOSAKU HANGA*

Contemporary Japanese prints are still very much within reach. Especially collectible are the early works of the pioneers in the *sosaku hanga* movement. When James Michener wrote *Japanese Prints* in 1959, which concentrated on antique Japanese woodblock prints, he devoted one chapter to contemporary Japanese graphics. Michener suggested that there were three up-and-coming young artists: Kiyoshi Saito, Jun'ichiro Sekino, and Shiko Munakata. Kiyoshi Saito is the only one still living. Munakata's prints have greatly increased in value since his demise. Sekino passed away in 1988, and prices for his prints have more than doubled since that time.

New stars such as Mayumi Oda, Reika Iwami, Ryohei Tanaka, Daniel Kelly (an American living in Japan), Shigeki Kuroda—only thirty-six years old and chosen the number-one printmaker by the Japanese government four years ago—are well worth collecting. Japanese collectors once again are ignoring their own great modern printmakers. Usually, the Japanese will collect only the prints of artists who have achieved success as painters. The Western world is the audience for the *sosaku hanga*. Even though the exchange rate for the American dollar is poor at present, contemporary Japanese printmakers have adjusted their prices to their Western market. Thus, their very limited edition prints are a bargain.

The first important auction of *sosaku hanga* was held at Sotheby's in June 1990. It was the Roy G. Cole Collection of Fine Sosaku Hanga. Record prices were recorded for such artists as Koshiro Onchi (1891–1955), who was one of the leaders of the Creative Print movement; for Kiyoshi Saito (b. 1907); and Jun'ichiro Sekino (1914–1988). This auction established the importance of *sosaku hanga* throughout the world.

Japanese Folk Art—Mingei

Japanese folk art, or *mingei*, is the "sleeper" for the collector who wishes to find important prints that are still very much within reach. The Japanese government was concerned that with the industrialization of Japan in the 1950s all of the traditional folk arts and crafts would disappear. In 1956 they designated their top thirty-three craftsmen "Living National Art Treasures." They were given a small stipend to train two or three apprentices each year, so that after the master was gone, the art form would continue.

Keisuke Serizawa (1895–1984) was designated a Living National Art Treasure, Master of Stencil Dyeing (*kataezome*), a process that was originally used for dying kimono fabric and thus considered a folk art. Serizawa and his apprentices used a paste-resist stencil method to create hand-stencil-dyed prints on handmade *kozo* (mulberry) paper. The artists whom Serizawa trained—Tokujiro Kojima (b. 1912), Choko Tachibana (b. 1913), Samiro Yunoki (b. 1922), and Kichiemon Okamura (b. 1916)— have carried on the *kataezome* craft. All of Serizawa's former apprentices are in their late sixties and seventies, so their hand-stencil-dyed work will soon be out of print.

Just think of collecting the works of a man designated as a Living National Art Treasure, Master of Stencil Dyeing, for as little as $25 for a 6″ × 4″ print, or $225 for a 13″ × 17.5″ print. The works of Serizawa's apprentices range from $45 to $125 for Okamura's whimsical "Japanese Alphabet."

COLLECTING INFORMATION

Since really good examples of *ukiyo-e*, the antique Japanese woodblock prints, by such artists as Sharaku, Utamaro, Kiyonaga, Hiroshige, and Hokusai are now priced from tens of thousands and even hundreds of thousands of dollars, we recommend that the collector concentrate on *shin hanga* (the early-20th-century traditional prints) and, especially, *sosaku hanga* (contemporary Japanese graphics) and Japanese folk art. They are all excellent "finds" in today's high-priced art market.

FAKES ALERT

When antique Japanese woodblock prints look too pristine, be wary, for many of the original prints date from the 18th and 19th centuries. Reproductions of classic *ukiyo-e* have been on the market for well over one hundred years. The works of artists such as Harunobu, Kiyonaga, Utamaro, Hiroshige, and Hokusai, to name just a few, have been reprinted from recut woodblocks or rolled off a press. Even today the Adachi Print Institute is producing excellent copies, which it sells as reproductions. The paper is just not right in the copies. It is usually much thicker than the paper used for the original woodblock prints, and the texture is not the same. If there is a thin tissue over the print, printed in English and Japanese, it is sure to be a reproduction. If the color does not come through to the back of the print, this is often an indication that it has been rolled off a press. However, sometimes the print has been backed to preserve it.

Shin hanga, the early-20th-century traditional woodblock prints, are very much in demand these days. One word of caution about prints by Hasui and Hiroshi Yoshida; the collector must be on the lookout for posthumous prints by these artists. The posthumous prints are aesthetically pleasing but are worth less than one-third of the original prints. Twenty years ago we visited the studio of Toshi Yoshida, the son of Hiroshi Yoshida, who still had his father's woodblocks. When we were in the studio, they were printing the father's woodblock prints—he had been dead for more than twenty years—and were selling them as posthumous prints. However, there are many dealers who are either not knowledgeable or are unscrupulous and are passing them off as originals.

Insofar as contemporary prints are concerned, most of the artists are still living, so it is not yet necessary to produce fakes. After Munakata died in 1975, his prints escalated in value tremendously, and there are copies of his prints in existence. The prints of Kochiro Onchi (1891– 1955), another pioneer of the contemporary print movement, have been produced posthumously.

CONDITION KEY

Condition is most important in collecting Japanese prints. Because the Japanese considered *ukiyo-e* as little more than posters or picture post-cards when they were originally issued in the 18th and 19th centuries, they did not take good care of them. Even though these prints were never limited in edition, there are very few extant in good condition.

The Japanese thought so little of these antique woodblock prints that when Perry opened Japan to the Western world in 1853, they used the prints to wrap their porcelains in when they were shipped to France. The French Impressionist artists found this unusual wrapping paper to their liking, and "Japonisme" (the influence of the Japanese woodblock prints on the French Impressionists) was born.

Fine Condition

1. Of the period.
2. By the specified artist.
3. Original fine condition.
4. Not faded from exposure to light.
5. Untrimmed (many borders were cut on the *ukiyo-e*).
6. No worm holes in the paper (unfortunately, insects had very good taste and tended to eat the best prints).
7. An early impression from the blocks in *ukiyo-e* (there usually were 250 prints in an edition of *ukiyo-e*; the nose lines and hair lines show wear first).
8. Provenance—most important.
9. Register (sometimes the prints were so popular that care was not taken to print them well).
10. Not mounted down (some collectors did not like wrinkles in the paper, so framers dry-mounted them).
11. No mat burn (only recently have collectors recognized the impor-tance of the use of 100 percent acid-free mat board and hinges).
12. Clean.
13. No masking tape marks causing thinness in the paper.
14. No foxing (caused by excessive moisture).

Good Condition

1. Of the period.
2. By the specified artist.

3. Print cleaned and restored by a good paper conservator.
4. Laid-down print lifted by paper conservator.
5. Slight fading.

Average Condition

1. Of the period.
2. By the specified artist.
3. Some amount of normal wear due to age.
4. Not restored.
5. Faded.
6. Borders trimmed.
7. Print dry-mounted.

Poor Condition

1. Of the period.
2. By the specified artist.
3. Badly faded.
4. Mat burn.
5. Mounted down.
6. Poor restoration.
7. Many worm holes.
8. Corners missing.
9. Trimmed borders.
10. Badly soiled.
11. Foxing.
12. Poor register.

QUALITY KEY

Quality is difficult to define in the field of Japanese prints. Prints of a certain period or by a certain artist do not go in and out of fashion, but prints that were not considered important thirty years ago are now seen as good reflections of the history of that period in spite of their somewhat garish colors. Even Utamaro's prints, which are now being auctioned at very high prices, were criticized as decadent not so many years ago.

When a Japanese art scholar writes a book on an artist or period that has previously been neglected, a new awareness of the printmaker or the period is evoked. For example, Osaka actor prints were not regarded very highly by collectors in Japan or the Western world until *The Theatrical World of Osaka Prints* by Roger Keyes and Keiko Mizushima was published by the Philadelphia Museum of Art in 1973. When we were visiting Japan in 1973, the prices on Osaka prints had more than doubled as the result of this book.

Superior Quality: the most famous prints and series by the prominent artists of their own period. For example, Japanese collectors value snow and rain scenes by such artists as Hiroshige more than any other subject done by him. Hiroshige's *Fifty-Three Stations of the Tokaido Road* is an extremely important series. The theme was so popular that sixteen different series were published. The most valuable series is the first published by Hoiedo. In *ukiyo-e*, if a print was very popular when the original blocks wore out, a second edition would be published. Of course, the first edition is the most important one. Superior-quality prints are included in major museum collections throughout the world.

Very Good Quality: The lesser works of the number-one printmakers and the best works of those considered medium-caliber artists.

Good Quality: Average works by artists who have achieved little renown at this time; in contemporary prints, the works of young artists who are just gaining worldwide recognition from art scholars and knowledgeable collectors.

This key is not a condition statement but strictly a measure of the stylishness of the piece.

BIBLIOGRAPHY

Binyon, Laurence, and Sexton, J. J. O'Brien. *The Japanese Colour Prints*. London: Faber & Faber, 1960 (first published in 1923). One of the early introductions to the subject of Japanese prints; great reference material for studying seals on *ukiyo-e*.

Blakemore, Francis. *Who's Who in Modern Japanese Prints*. New York, Tokyo: Weatherhill, 1975. Covers many younger contemporary artists who are not written about in earlier books on the subject.

Franco, Betsy, with Verne, Mitzie. *The Emperor Was My Neighbor in Japan: The Mitzie Verne Collection*. Ann Arbor, MI: Edwards Brothers, 1986.

Kawakita, Michiaki. *Contemporary Japanese Prints*. Tokyo, Palo Alto, CA: Kodansha International, 1967. An excellent early volume on contemporary prints.

Keyes, Roger, and Mizushira, Keiko. *The Theatrical World of Osaka Prints*. Philadelphia: Philadelphia Museum of Art, 1973. This catalog put the Osaka actor prints on the map.

Lane, Richard. *Images from the Floating World*. New York: G. P. Putnam's Sons, 1978. Contains many photographs of important *ukiyo-e*.

Meech-Pekarik, Julia. *The World of the Meiji Print*. New York, Tokyo: Weatherhill, 1986. This former Metropolitan Museum of Art curator has set up the Meiji print as an important reflection of the history of that time.

Michener, James. *The Floating World*. New York: Random House, 1954. A very readable book and a wonderful introduction to the world of *ukiyo-e*.

———. *Japanese Prints*. Tokyo, Rutland, VT: Charles E. Tuttle, 1959. Beautiful reproductions of classic *ukiyo-e* plus an important chapter on the contemporary graphics we've referred to.

———. *The Modern Japanese Print: An Appreciation*. Tokyo, Rutland, VT: Charles E. Tuttle, 1968. The winners of an unusual competition Michener organized among the most important contemporary Japanese printmakers to gain worldwide recognition for them.

Petit, Gaston. *44 Modern Japanese Print Artists*. Tokyo, New York, San Francisco: Kodansha International, 1973. Two volumes, well documented with color and black-and-white reproductions of the artists who Petit feels are the best contemporary printmakers.

Roberts, Laurance P. *A Dictionary of Japanese Artists*. Tokyo, New York: Weatherhill, 1976. An indispensable reference volume.

Smith, Lawrence. *The Japanese Print since 1900*. New York: Harper and Row, 1984. A catalog of the British Museum collection of Japanese prints. Lawrence Smith is the Keeper of Oriental Antiquities at the British Museum, but his main focus of interest is contemporary Japanese graphics.

———. *Contemporary Japanese Prints: A Symbol of a Society in Transition*. New York: Harper and Row, 1985. The British Museum neglected to collect any Japanese prints from 1920 to 1980, a hiatus of sixty years. Thanks to the author, they are filling up the gap with a vengeance. This too is a catalog of the contemporary Japanese print collection in the British Museum.

Statler, Oliver. *Modern Japanese Prints: An Art Reborn*. Tokyo, Rutland, VT: Charles E. Tuttle, 1956. This was the first book written in English about Japanese contemporary prints after World War II. Oliver Statler introduced these important printmakers to the Western world.

Stern, Harold P. *Master Prints of Japan*. New York: Abrams, 1969. Harold Stern was Director of the Freer Gallery of the Smithsonian Museum in Washington, DC, and a brilliant scholar.

Stevenson, John. *Yoshitoshi's 36 Ghosts*. New York, Tokyo: John Weatherhill, 1983. We have referred to this series by Yoshitoshi.

Stewart, Basil. *Japanese Colour Prints*. New York: Dodd, Mead, 1920. An early view of *ukiyo-e*.

Strange, Edward F. *The Colour Prints of Hiroshige*. New York: Frederick A. Stokes Co., 1919. Best early reference listing all of Hiroshige's prints.

Wright, Frank Lloyd. *The Japanese Print: An Interpretation*. New York: Horizon Press, 1967. Frank Lloyd Wright had an extremely important collection of *ukiyo-e*.

MUSEUMS WITH MAJOR COLLECTIONS

Albertina, Vienna.
Art Institute of Chicago, IL.
Boston Museum of Fine Arts, MA.
Bridgestone Art Museum, Tokyo.
British Museum, London.
Brooklyn Museum, NY.
Cincinnati Museum of Art, OH.
Cleveland Museum of Art, OH.
Fogg Art Museum, Harvard University, MA.
Freer Gallery of Art, Washington, DC.
Kyoto National Museum.
Los Angeles County Museum of Art, CA.
Metropolitan Museum of Art, NY.
Mingei International Museum of World Folk Art, San Diego, CA.
Musée Guimet, Paris.
Musée National d'Art Moderne, Paris.
Museum of Modern Art, NY.
National Museum of Modern Art, Tokyo.
Nelson Gallery, Atkins Museum, Kansas City, MO.
New York Public Library, NY.
Ohara New Art Museum, Kurashiki, Japan.
Philadelphia Museum of Art, PA.
Riccar Art Museum, Tokyo.
Rijksmuseum, Amsterdam.
Royal Ontario Museum, Toronto.
Springfield Museum, Springfield, MA.
Staatliche Museum, Berlin.
Tokyo National Museum.
University of Michigan Museum of Art, MI.
Victoria and Albert Museum, London.
Yale University Art Gallery, New Haven, CT.

In the listings that follow, prints are arranged by period: *ukiyo-e, shin hanga, sosaku hanga*, and folk art. Within each period, items are arranged by date. Also, note on artists' names: The artist's first name is given first. The surname follows. The name the artist is known by is printed in capital letters. —*DL*

Woodblock print   9″ H × 13.75″ W   Ukiyo-e   1843   Japan
"Station Kuwana" #43 from *53 Stations of Tokaido Road* by Ando HIROSHIGE (1797–1858); first series, publisher Hoiedo; corners and print trimmed; center fold; 2 sailing boats in foreground against Kuwama castle wall; 3 sailboats in background on choppy green-blue sea. *(See photo 210)*
Superior Quality/Average Condition $1000 (D)   **$1000–$10,000**

Woodblock print   14.5″ H × 9.5″ W   Ukiyo-e   1888   Japan
"The Fireman's Wife" by Taiso YOSHITOSHI (1839–1892) from series *32 Aspects of Women*; portrait of woman dressed in brown checkered kimono clutching a pipe; her husband's fireman's coat hangs in upper left corner; slight soiling and wrinkles.
Superior Quality/Good Condition   *$1250 (D)*   **$800–$1500**

Woodblock print   13″ H × 8.5″ D   Ukiyo-e   1898   Japan
"One Hundred Roles As Played by Kabuki Actor Ichikawa Danjuro IX Kezori Kyuenom" by KUNICHIKA (1835–1900); bust portrait of bearded, curly-haired figure dressed in a plum robe decorated with orange, yellow, and red dragons on a greenish blue ground.
Very Good Quality/Fine Condition   *$300 (D)*   **$150–$300**

Woodblock print   11.5″ H × 8″ W   Ukiyo-e   1900   Japan
"Kimono Design—Autumn" from series *Layers of Kimonos*, artist unknown; autumn flowers in rust and green along flowing blue river on pink-violet ground. *(See photo 211)*
Very Good Quality/Fine Condition   *$150 (D)*   **$100–$150**

Woodblock print   20″ H × 14.5″ W   Shin Hanga   1926   Japan
"Sailing Boats, Morning" by Hiroshi YOSHIDA (1876–1950) from his classic series *A Study of How Light Hits the Sails at Different Times of Day and Night*; orange hue on 3-masted sailboat with small boat in tow; reflection of sails in gray-blue water; shadow of boats in distance.
Superior Quality/Fine Condition   *$10,000 (D)*   **$5000–$10,000**

Woodblock print   9.5″ H × 14.5″ W   Shin Hanga   1927   Japan
"Snow at Kansa Shrine at Lake Tazawa" by HASUI Kawase (1883–1957) from series *Souvenirs of Travel—3rd Series*; snow falling on wooden shrine located on greenish blue lakeside; snow-covered branches; paper slightly toned.
Superior Quality/Good Condition   *$1000 (D)*   **$750–$1500**

Woodblock print   14.25″ H × 9.5″ W   Shin Hanga   1928   Japan
"Twilight" by Yamakawa SHUHO (1898–1944); bust portrait of a *bijin* (beauty) dressed in a blue kimono holding a fan, plum-colored obi, jet black hair, on mica ground.
Superior Quality/Fine Condition   *$1400 (D)*   **$750–$1500**

Woodblock print   15″ H × 9.75″ W   Shin Hanga   1937   Japan
"Yomei Gate—Nikko" by Hiroshi YOSHIDA (1876–1950); single figure in foreground on steps against elaborate background of intricately carved Yomei Gate in gold and grays, green-blue cryptomeria trees behind the gate. *(See photo 212)*
Superior Quality/Fine Condition   *$1500 (D)*   **$750–$1500**

Woodblock print   9.75″ H × 14.75″ W   Shin Hanga   1940   Japan
"Omuro Ninnaji Temple, Kyoto" by Hiroshi YOSHIDA (1876–1950); 2 kimono-clad women in left foreground; Omuro Temple, in pinkish hues with deep pink pillars, looms very large in background; soft pastel colors give a painterly effect; this print in British Museum collection.
Superior Quality/Fine Condition   *$1250 (D)*   **$500–$1250**

Etching   9″ H × 8.5″ W   Sosaku Hanga   1988   Japan
"Summer Day #4" by Ryohei TANAKA (b. 1933); farmhouse with thatched roof in background with grasses and flowers and 1 tree in foreground; black and white; limited edition.
Very Good Quality/Fine Condition   *$175 (D)*   **$150–$175**

Photo 210 (left). Woodblock print.
CREDIT: THE MITZIE VERNE COLLECTION
(See p. 399)
Photo 211 (right). Woodblock print.
CREDIT: THE MITZIE VERNE COLLECTION
(See p. 400)

Photo 212 (left). Woodblock print. CREDIT: THE MITZIE VERNE
COLLECTION. Photo 213 (right). Hand-stencil-dyed print. CREDIT: THE
MITZIE VERNE COLLECTION (See p. 400, 402)

Remember, the selling price is exactly what the term implies: the object sold for the stated amount in a shop or show by a dealer (D) or at auction (A).

Etching 22.75″ H × 14″ W Sosaku Hanga 1989 Japan
"Blow" by Shigeki KURODA (b. 1953); bicycles and umbrellas converging from left foreground, 3 umbrellas right foreground, photo engraving of "Mission" building in Seattle, WA, in background; drypoint; limited edition of 50.
Superior Quality/Fine Condition $350 (D)   **$250–$350**

Hand-stencil-dyed print 17.25″ H × 13″ W Sosaku Hanga 1960 Japan
"Comic Shinto Dancers" by Yoshitoshi MORI (b. 1898); 2 comic figures in black *sumi* ink and brown; limited edition; illustrated in Michener's *The Modern Japanese Print—An Appreciation*, 1 of 10 Michener competition winners. *(See photo 213)*.
Superior Quality/Fine Condition $1000 (D)   **$750–$1000**

Hand-stencil-dyed print 19.25″ H × 12.5″ W Sosaku Hanga 1960 Japan
"Listening" by Sadao WATANABE (b. 1913); "voice of heaven"; his face is white; on deep red ground, some black and ochre in the print done on handmade, hand-wrinkled *kozo* paper; natural mineral and vegetable dyes.
Superior Quality/Fine Condition $1000 (D)   **$750–$1000**

Silkscreen print 31″ H × 22.75″ W Sosaku Hanga 1975 Japan
"Storyville VII" by Mayumi ODA (b. 1941); Matisse-like figure clothed in white, orange hair, looking in a mirror, seated on brown velvet couch, light teal patterned wallpaper background.
Superior Quality/Fine Condition $700 (D)   **$500–$700**

Silkscreen print 27.75″ H × 20″ W Sosaku Hanga 1990 Japan
"Tropical Kimono" by Karyn YOUNG (b. 1955); shading of kimono from top to bottom goes from deep red to pink, green sleeves, vermilion birds with green wings; border pattern green and orange, feather with gold veins; limited edition; Young is a Canadian living in Kyoto. *(See photo 214)*.
Very Good Quality/Fine Condition $425 (D)   **$425**

Woodblock print 14.12″ H × 10.88″ W Sosaku Hanga 1934 Japan
"After a Bath" by Koshiro ONCHI (1891–1955), from series *8 Figures of Modern Women*; profile of black-haired woman drying her back with a white towel patterned with violet-colored leaves.
Superior Quality/Fine Condition $18,700 (A)   **$10,000–$15,000**

Woodblock print 37.25″ H × 15″ W Sosaku Hanga 1955–1961 Japan
"Twelve Great Disciples of Sakyamuni (Buddha)" by Shiko MUNAKATA (1903–1975); "Mokkenren" and "Ragora" shown; stark black on white ground; series won Grand Prize at São Paulo Biennale in 1955, alerting the Western world to the importance of contemporary Japanese printmakers.
Superior Quality/Fine Condition $990,000 (A) (series of 12)
                                          $30,000–$50,000 *(single prints)*

Woodblock print 24″ H × 17″ W Sosaku Hanga 1957 Japan
"Rejoicing at Reaching the Summit" by Umetaro AZECHI (b. 1902); mountain man in black and gray against a deep turquoise ground; rapelling hooks; white arms; limited edition.
Superior Quality/Fine Condition $2000 (D)   **$1000–$2000**

Photo 214 (left). Silkscreen print. CREDIT: THE MITZIE VERNE COLLECTION. *Photo 215 (right). Woodblock print.* CREDIT: THE MITZIE VERNE COLLECTION *(See pp. 402, 404)*

Photo 216 (left). Woodblock print. CREDIT: THE MITZIE VERNE COLLECTION. *Photo 217 (right). Woodblock print.* CREDIT: THE MITZIE VERNE COLLECTION *(See pp. 404, 405)*

Woodblock print 17.25″ H × 11.25″ W Sosaku Hanga 1959 Japan
"Lakeside at Byodo-in" by Un'ichi HIRATSUKA (b. 1895); black peace lantern in middle ground in raked sand in front of steps of Byodo-in, lakeside in black in foreground; limited edition; 1 of 10 prize winners of 1959 Michener competition.
Superior Quality/Fine Condition $1500 (D)   **$1000–$1500**

Woodblock print 15.25″ H × 10.75″ D Sosaku Hanga 1959 Japan
"The Lamp" by Maekawa SEMPAN (1888–1960), 1 of 10 prize winners in Michener competition in 1959; young woman with jet-black hair dressed in brown vest, touch of deep pink, holding lantern with green cicada on rim; striped brown on black sleeve; beige ground. *(See photo 215)*
Superior Quality/Fine Condition $1500 (D)   **$1000–$1500**

Woodblock print 15″ H × 10.5″ W Sosaku Hanga 1959 Japan
"Tori B (Birds B)" by Tamami SHIMA (b. 1937); 1 of 10 prize winners in 1959 Michener competition; black and grays, 3 stylized birds on beige and brown ground, strong grain of wood; limited edition.
Superior Quality/Fine Condition $1000 (D)   **$600–$1000**

Woodblock print 15.75″ H × 10.75″ W Sosaku Hanga 1959 Japan
"Winter Composition" by Reika IWAMI (b. 1927), 1 of 10 winners of 1959 Michener competition; abstract composition—white circle surrounded by vertical black and rust lines, mica mixed into black and red; gray background.
Superior Quality/Fine Condition $750 (D)   **$450–$750**

Woodblock print 16″ H × 7.75″ W Sosaku Hanga 1959 Japan
"Earth" by Masaji YOSHIDA (b. 1917), 1 of 10 winners of 1959 Michener competition; brick red triangular shape at base of print with parallel pinkish-brown vertical lines; gives a sense of the boundless expanse of earth.
Superior Quality/Fine Condition $600 (D)   **$350–$600**

Woodblock print 17″ H × 10.75″ W Sosaku Hanga 1959 Japan
"Ox" by Haku MAKI (b. 1924), 1 of 10 winners in Michener competition; calligraphy character in black *sumi* ink symbolizes "ox" on beige natural ground; small red seals provide color; limited edition.
Superior Quality/Fine Condition $600 (D)   **$350–$600**

Woodblock print 14.5″ H × 9.5″ W Sosaku Hanga 1960 Japan
"Mountaineer in the Snow" by Umetaro AZECHI (b. 1902), 1 of 10 winners in Michener competition; single abstract figure, black mountain in background, head of "Snowman" set off by white ground, dressed in black and grayish teal. *(See photo 216)*
Superior Quality/Fine Condition $1000 (D)   **$600–$1000**

Woodblock print 15″ H × 20.5″ W Sosaku Hanga 1961 Japan
"Gion in Kyoto" by Kiyoshi SAITO (b. 1907); entrance to tea house with large red lantern in right foreground; much wood grain, which he is noted for; limited edition.
Superior Quality/Fine Condition $1250 (D)   **$750–$1250**

Woodblock print 27.5″ H × 18.5″ W Sosaku Hanga 1973 Japan
"Waiting to Go on Stage" by Jun'ichiro SEKINO (1914–1988); portrait of Sato Takako, Okinawan dancer, red sleeve lining and inner kimono, darkened red background, outer kimono of brightly colored floral design.
Superior Quality/Fine Condition $4500 (D)   **$3000–$4500**

Woodblock print   10.5″ H × 7.5″ W   Sosaku Hanga   1990   Japan
"The Old North Church" by Sachiko FURUI (b. 1950) and Keiji SHINOHARA (b. 1955) from series *8 Views of New England Old North Church;* light green, white steeple, gold windows, flanked by olive-green buildings, red lamppost in foreground. *(See photo 217)*
Superior Quality/Fine Condition $175 (D)   **$175–$200**

Hand-stencil-dyed print   13″ H × 17.5″ W   Folk art   1960   Japan
"Fish Symbolize Everything You Might Wish For" by Keisuke SERIZAWA (1895–1984); 9 fish, 3 in each row; fish are white, rust, and black on gray ground; all natural mineral and vegetable dyes.
Superior Quality/Fine Condition $225 (D)   **$200–$225**

> The folk art prints are so recent that they are all in the same fine condition.—*DL*

Hand-stencil-dyed print   6″ H × 4″ W   Folk art   1980–1984 Japan
"Drying of the Silks" by Keisuke SERIZAWA (1895–1984); 3 bolts of hand-stencil-dyed fabrics in mustard, vermilion, blue, and green drying in the wind; top portion with man dyeing fabric; brown.
Superior Quality/Fine Condition $25 (D)   **$25**

Hand-stencil-dyed print   13″ H × 17.5″ W   Folk art   1989   Japan
"Cranes Symbolize Longevity" by Samiro YUNOKI (b. 1922); 3 light brown cranes against dark chocolate brown background.
Superior Quality/Fine Condition $45 (D)   **$40–$45**

Hand-stencil-dyed print   13″ H × 17.5″ W   Folk art   1989   Japan
"Fish for Boy's Day" by Tokujiro KOJIMA (b. 1912); a carp, symbolizing strength, in blue and rust, swims against a white ground; blue borders, stream, and flowers.
Superior Quality/Fine Condition $45 (D)   **$40–$45**

Hand-stencil-dyed print   17.5″ H × 13″ W   Folk art   1989 Japan
"Kotobuki" by Kichiemon OKUMURA (b. 1916); crane with blue wings, black tail, pink body, gold neck; head and tortoise in mustard, pink, and blue are incorporated into brush strokes of the character.
Superior Quality/Fine Condition $125 (D)   **$120–$125**

PORCELAIN

Bowl   4″ H × 8″ Dia.   Kutani   1880–1900   Japan
Octagonal, with overall rust and gilt decoration; wild boar in center.
Very Good Quality/Fine Condition $700 (D)   **$500–$750**

Bowl, punch   5″ H × 10.5″ Dia.   1845–1865   China
Chinese export; rust decoration on outside; rust and aquamarine fishes inside.
Very Good Quality/Fine Condition $600 (D)   **$500–$750**

Bowl, punch   5.5″ H × 13″ Dia.   Rose medallion   1845–1865   China
Small bowl with panels of figures and birds.
Very Good Quality/Fine Condition $750 (A)   **$600–$1200**

> A 15″ diameter would be $1800–$2400; an 18″ diameter would be $2400–$3500.—*DL*

Bowls   10″ Dia.   1780–1800   China
Pair of Chinese export bowls in Mandarin palette, with figural reserves on an orange diaper ground; restored.
Superior Quality/Average Condition $1300 (A)   **$1200–$4500**

Bowls   2.5″ H   Guangxu   1875–1908   China
Pair; with dragon and phoenix chasing a flaming pearl in multicolor enamels; Guangxu mark.
Superior Quality/Fine Condition $900 (A)   **$500–$1000**

Brushwasher   4.6″ Dia.   Kangxi   1662–1722   China
Peachbloom; compressed circular form, supported on a shallow tapering foot; side with mottled mushroom-pink glaze; interior and base glazed white; firing crack, pinhole glaze gaps; this auction was the "crash" in NYC auction prices.
Superior Quality/Good Condition $2570 (A)   **$4000–$6000**

Cachepots   8″ H × 8.5″ Dia.   Rose mandarin   1845–1865   China
Pair; original underplates; hexagonal. *(See photo 218)*
Superior Quality/Fine Condition $10,000 (D)   **$8000–$12,000**

> Rose mandarin is the finest quality famille rose porcelain of the period.
> —*DL*

Canisters   5.75″ H to 3″ H   Rose medallion   1885–1900   China
Rare graduated set of 5 canisters; square with slightly domed covers, alternating floral and figural panels; rim chips.
Superior Quality/Good Condition $2100 (A)   **$2000–$4000**

Censer   9″ H   Late Edo   1846–1865   Japan
Kakiemon cylindrical censer with reserves of dragon and phoenix, on bracket feet; domed silver cover with cloud relief; signed Sekichuan.
Very Good Quality/Fine Condition $325 (A)   **$250–$450**

Photo 218 (left). Cachepots. CREDIT: WHITEHALL AT THE VILLA, CHAPEL HILL, NC. *Photo 219 (right). Covered jar.* CREDIT: SKINNER, INC., BOLTON, MA. *(See above and p. 407)*

Charger 19.25″ Dia. Imari 1885–1900 Japan
Central landscape scene with a floral and swag border, traditional colors with gold accents; old restoration, yellowed finish.
Very Good Quality/Poor Condition $400 (A)   **$750–$1200**

Charger 18.5″ Dia. Imari 1900–1910 Japan
Figural landscape in underglaze blue and polychrome enamel flowers, gilt accents.
Good Quality/Good Condition $250 (A)   -   **$400–$750**

Cranes 16″ H Ming style 1885–1900 China
Pair of nicely modeled cranes, each with 1 foot resting on a stump.
Very Good Quality/Fine Condition $1200 (D)   **$800–$1200**

Cups 3″ H × 4.5″ L Ceremonial 1800–1830 China
Pair of libation cups with the important symbols of bats and peaches; on wooden stands of a later date.
Superior Quality/Fine Condition $4000 (D)   **$3500–$4500**

Equestrian figure 15.5″ H Tang dynasty 618–907 China
Rider with unglazed head, dressed in green, cream, and ochre glazed robes astride a dappled saddle blanket; chestnut horse standing foursquare.
Good Quality/Good Condition $15,000 (A)   **$12,000–$18,000**

Equestrian figure 15.5″ H Tang dynasty 618–907 China
Foreign rider with unglazed head, dressed in green and ochre coat and pants, seated on a dappled saddle blanket, his well-modeled horse cream-glazed with splashes of green and ochre.
Very Good Quality/Good Condition $21,000 (A)   **$15,000–$25,000**

Jar, covered 18″ H Famille rose 1800–1830 China
Baluster form enameled in polychrome with floral sprays, blue double-circle mark. *(See photo 219)*
Very Good Quality/Fine Condition $750 (A)   **$600–$1000**

Platter 17.5″ L 1800–1830 China
Chinese export; rectangular; decorated in the Mandarin palette with figures beside a lake; some rubbing, especially on border vignettes.
Very Good Quality/Average Condition $1000 (A)   **$900–$1600**

Platters 15.75″ L × 13″ W Rose mandarin 1800–1830 China
Pair; magnificent enameled decoration of individual figures. *(See photo 220)*
Superior Quality/Fine Condition $7500 (D)   **$6000–$9000**

Soup plates 9.75″ Dia. Rose medallion 1800–1830 China
Set of 6, bearing arms of Grant, with ribbed mottos "Craigelachie" and "Steadfast"; varying central figural courtyard scenes; wide floral and butterfly borders; wear.
Very Good Quality/Good Condition $2800 (A)   **$2400–$3600**

Teapot Japan
Pottery monkey teapot with raffia handle.
Very Good Quality/Fine Condition $235 (D)   **$200–$300**

Urn and cover 15″ H Rose medallion 1885–1900 China
Low, domed cover with onion finial, alternating floral and figural panels; interior rim chip.
Very Good Quality/Good Condition $650 (A)   **$800–$1200**

Photo 220. Platter. CREDIT: WHITEHALL
AT THE VILLA, CHAPEL HILL, NC
(See p. 407)

Photo 221. Vase. CREDIT: SKINNER,
INC., BOLTON, MA *(See below)*

Vase 22 " H Archaic Hu-form 1736–1795 China
Large blue-and-white vase of archaic Hu-form with overall scene of dragons
among clouds; Qianlong period; rim fritting, base hairline.
Superior Quality/Good Condition $5000 (A) **$3500–$6000**

Vase 13 " H Meiping 1736–1795 China
Blue-and-white vase decorated in early Ming style with pomegranate peach and
finger citrus; Quianlong period.
Very Good Quality/Fine Condition $3750 (A) **$3000–$4500**

Vase 22 " H Blue and white 1750–1780 China
Baluster vase with tapering body and flowering and scrolling vines; pierced wood
cover.
Good Quality/Fine Condition $1300 (A) **$1200–$1800**

Vase 12 " H Rose mandarin 1845–1865 China
Bottle vase of squat, globular form with long neck. *(See photo 221)*
Superior Quality/Fine Condition $950 (A) **$750–$1200**

Vases 25 " H Famille verte 1846–1865 China
Pair; hexagonal; with figural reserves and flowers in green, red, blue, and other
enamels; repaired.
Very Good Quality/Average Condition $2000 (A) **$2000–$4500**

BIBLIOGRAPHY

The reference works that follow are readily available at most bookstores
and museum gift shops.

Brown, Claudia, and Rabiner, Donald. *Chinese Glossary of the Qing
  Dynasty 1644–1911.* Phoenix, AZ: Phoenix Art Museum, 1987.
Ecke, Gustav. *Chinese Domestic Furniture.* Tokyo: Charles E. Tuttle
  Company, 1985.

Hobson, R. L. *Chinese Pottery and Porcelain*. New York: Dover Publications, 1976.

Koizumi, Kazuko. *Traditional Japanese Furniture*. Japan: Kodansha International, 1986.

Man Sill Pai, and Wright, Edward Reynolds. *Korean Furniture: Elegance and Tradition*. Japan: Kodansha International, 1984.

Minnich, Helen Benton. *Japanese Costume and the Makers of Its Elegant Tradition*. Tokyo: Charles E. Tuttle, 1986.

Page, Amy. "Chinese Art," *Art and Auction*, September 1988, pp. 134–135.

Schiffer, Herbert, Peter, and Nancy. *Chinese Export Porcelain Standard Patterns and Forms, 1780 to 1880*. Exton, PA: Schiffer Publishing, 1975.

Shixiang, Wang. *Classic Chinese Furniture: Ming and Early Qing Dynasties*. San Francisco, CA: China Books and Periodicals, 1986.

MUSEUMS

Asia Society of New York, NY.

Los Angeles County Art Museum, Japanese Pavilion, Los Angeles, CA.

Metropolitan Museum of Art, The Weber Wing and the Astor Court, New York, NY.

National Gallery of Art, Sackler Wing, Washington, DC.

Royal Ontario Museum, Toronto, Ontario, Canada.

Oriental Rugs

Advisors: ROBERT FRITZ and DOUGLAS LAY

Dr. Robert Fritz is a dealer in and lecturer on Oriental rugs. He has traveled extensively in the United States and to many countries abroad and spent several years studying in Afghanistan. Dr. Douglas Lay is a professor at the University of North Carolina at Chapel Hill, a nationally respected lecturer, and an owner with his wife, Nelda, of The Persian Carpet, 5634 Chapel Hill Blvd., Durham, NC 27707; (919) 489-8362.

SURVEY OF THE FIELD

The Pazyryk carpet, excavated from a Scythian burial mound in the Altai mountains of Soviet Central Asia, dates to c. 500 B.C. Many fragments of similar age have been recovered from these sites. Numerous carpet fragments, at least one intact carpet, and many kelim weavings dating to c. 200 B.C. have been recovered from Scythian sites in Sinkiang Province, China. These specimens were constructed by using the same weaving techniques that are employed in weaving handknotted carpets today—symmetrical or asymmetrical knots, flat warp, warp depression, or warp doubled under.

Essentially, no examples of carpetry are known to have survived from the period of 200 B.C. to the 15th century. Examples from the 15th, 16th, 17th, and 18th centuries and the first half of the 19th century are relatively rare. More examples are known to have survived from the latter portions of this period than from the earlier portions.

It is impossible to categorize today's collector of Oriental carpets. Collector interests span the entire gamut of age and carpet types. Most private collections cover the range of types of 19th- and 20th-century carpets.

Trends and information on collecting may be gleaned from the appropriate sections of the journal *Hali* and the *Oriental Rug Review*. Data on national and international market values may be obtained by study of the numerous auction catalogs (Sotheby's, Christie's, Skinner's, Butterworth's, etc.) and if possible by studying the pieces to be auctioned at the previews. Local prices may be determined by attending estate auctions and visiting local Oriental rug shops that deal in antique and semi-antique carpets.

More designs and color combinations in new handmade rugs from China, Egypt, India, Pakistan, Rumania, and Turkey are available now than ever before. Some of these examples may become collectible in time, although they are certainly not and never will be comparable to antique and semiantique carpets of the 19th and 20th centuries.

FAKES ALERT

Recently there were reports of excellent fake examples of late 19th-century Shahsevan bag faces, constructed with old yarns, being sold at auction in Europe.

CONDITION KEY

Fine Condition: essentially as new; full pile, selvedges and end finishes intact, no blemishes; small but excellent repairs acceptable.

Good Condition: essentially full pile but slight even wear over entire surface is acceptable; selvedges may need repair or have been restored; end finishes (fringe, web, or kelim) may have been lost or reduced in length but restored to stable condition; modest areas of good restoration to pile (virtually unnoticeable) are acceptable.

Average Condition: pile worn considerably below perfect condition, with noticeable areas where pile is worn unevenly; selvedge in need of repair; reduction or loss of end borders of piled surface; small areas of moth damage front or back; small areas of painting (retinting—always check painted areas with a wet rag; if dye is water-soluble, reconsider carefully for downgrading); considerable restoration of pile of good or average quality.

Poor Condition: pile showing extensive wear; foundation (warp and weft) visible in areas as large as 36 square inches or more; large unrepaired holes or tears, extensive moth damage, dry rot (brittle foundation); major losses to ends or sides; large painted areas; restoration of pile unfeasible.

QUALITY KEY

Beauty and uniqueness of design represent the most significant criteria of quality and must be judged by comparing any specimen to the best-known contemporaneous examples of the specific type of carpet (e.g., Kazak Caucasians of the 1880–1900 period, Farahan Sarouks of the 1880–1900 period, Sarouks of the 1920–1935 period, etc.). Some consider quality in Oriental carpets to be directly proportional to increasing knot density per square centimeter or inch. This is an invalid generalization and cannot be usefully applied in any general way for making comparisons among all carpet types. However, this concept may be useful for making without-group comparisons among finely woven city carpets (i.e., Isfahan, Na'in, Tabriz, silk Hereke, etc.). If two carpets are identical in color, design, and age but one exhibits a higher knot density, then it would probably be regarded as the better quality. Vegetable dyes were employed almost exclusively until around 1910, though there was limited and unsatisfactory use of the synthetic fuchsin from about 1880 to 1900. Synthetic chrome dyes replaced most natural dyes after 1910. Type of dyestuff does not connote quality. Comparisons should be made within contemporaneous groups, as there are poor and excellent examples made with all dyestuffs.

Good Quality: good colors and design, technicalities of weave above average for its group.

Very Good Quality: good colors, design more unusual or better executed than in "good" category, technicalities of weave above average for its group.

Superior Quality: exceptional colors, design outstanding and rare for type. In some groups white field color may help place a piece in this category, whereas navy blue may be the criterion in others.

> KPSI = knots per square inch. It is valuable only when comparing the same type of rug. One might compare KPSI on two Bachtiari rugs; one would not compare KPSI between a Bachtiari and a Kashan.—*DL*

Bachtiari 4′8″ W × 6′9″ L Floral After 1930 Iran
Cream field; rose red border and center medallion; lapis corners; green, rose, blue, gold, maroon, and ivory accents; no wear; minor restorations to selvedge and pile on one end; approx. 125 KSPI.
Very Good Quality/Good Condition $2875 (D)   **$2000–$4500**

> Spellings vary on many Oriental rugs—all are phonetic variations of Farsi or other Mideastern languages.—*DL*

Bachtiari 4′8″ W × 6′6″ D Floral 1920–1930 Iran
Large ivory medallion on brick red field; indigo blue corners; narrow ivory major borders; rose red minor borders; gold and medium green accents; minor areas of pile restoration; approx. 80 KPSI.
Very Good Quality/Good Condition $2250 (D)   **$1800–$3500**

Baluch 2′10″ W × 5′2″ D Geometric 1890–1900 Iran
Camelhair ground covered by diagonal rows of leaves; surrounded by a rust major border; 3 minor borders; both ends intact; approx. 90 KPSI.
Good Quality/Average Condition $770 (A)   **$600–$2000**

> These rugs are often referred to as Baluchi, Baluchis, or Baluchistan rugs.—*DL*

Bergama 3′2″ W × 3′9″ D Geometric 1910–1930 Turkey
Large deep red medallion on navy blue field fitted with small red and navy octagonal shields; striped major border; 6″ end skirts; 2 areas of fold wear; minor loss to selvedge; approx. 80 KPSI.
Good Quality/Fine Condition $1200 (D)   **$600–$1500**

Bidjar 3′8″ W × 5′3″ L Floral 1900 Iran
Cherry red cartouche; covered by a medium blue medallion; rose red border; medium blue minor borders; navy blue corners in field; major restorations not evident; approx. 120 KSPI. *(See photo 222)*
Very Good Quality/Good Condition $2750 (A)   **$1500–$4000**

Photo 222. Bidjar rug. CREDIT: CHRISTIE'S, NEW YORK *(See above)*

Hamadan 2'8″ W × 4'1″ D Geometric 1910–1920 Iran
Lapis blue geometric medallion on rust red field; navy blue corners; navy blue and coral major border with ivory minor borders; slight loss to both ends; approx. 120 KPSI.
Good Quality/Average Condition *$450 (D)*   **$450–$1200**

Heriz 9'8″ W × 12' L Geometric 1910–1930 Iran
Navy blue field, rust border, large medallions of navy and rust; coral corners; accent colors: green, blue, and gold; all natural dyes; full pile; minor restorations to selvedge; 75 KPSI.
Very Good Quality/Fine Condition *$12,250 (D)*   **$8500–$20,000**

An antique Heriz (made before 1910) is called a Serapi.—*DL*

Isfahan 4'11″ W × 7' D Floral 1920–1930 Iran
Rust red, lozenge-shaped medallion on cream field of Arabesque floral vines; floral sprays of medium blue in corners; rust red major border of multicolor floral motifs; approx. 450 KPSI.
Good Quality/Good Condition *$6500 (D)*   **$3000–$10,000**

Jason Sarouk 4'6″ W × 6'10″ D Floral 1910–1920 Iran
Navy blue field with modified zuli-sultan latticework design; centered medallion of rose red and medium blue; rose red major border; minor loss to end border guards; approx. 160 KPSI.
Superior Quality/Average Condition *$3600 (D)*   **$3000–$7500**

Kashan 4'3″ W × 6'7″ D Floral 1930–1940 Iran
Diamond-shaped navy medallion with ivory center on rust red field of multicolored arabesque floral vines; navy blue major border with ivory minor borders; excellent accents; approx. 260 KPSI.
Very Good Quality/Fine Condition *$5000 (D)*   **$2500–$6000**

Kazak 3'8″ W × 6'7″ D Geometric 1908 Russia
Prayer rug with double panels showing a date of 1324 (approx. 1908); rust red field, ivory medallion; multicolored major border of gold, teal, medium blue, red, and ivory; minor restorations; 45 KPSI.
Very Good Quality/Fine Condition *$3650 (D)*   **$2000–$4500**

Kerman 8'6″ W × 12'11″ D Floral 1940–1950 Iran
Green and medium blue elongated center medallion on semiopen red field with multicolored detached floral sprays; navy blue major border with rose and blue minor border; approx. 200 KPSI.
Good Quality/Good Condition *$4500 (A)*   **$3000–$6000**

Khamseh 4'10″ W × 6'9″ D Geometric 1890–1900 Iran
Navy blue field with an allover pattern of horizontal rows of multicolored abstract floral bouquets with assorted geometric symbols; brick red primary border of vines and roses; approx. 90 KPSI.
Very Good Quality/Good Condition *$3850 (A)*   **$2500–$7000**

Mahal 9'1″ W × 12' D Geometric 1910–1920 Iran
Dark navy blue field with allover multicolored Herati design; unusual coral corners; deep red major border with stylized floral motifs; minor uneven surface wear; approx. 50 KPSI.
Very Good Quality/Average Condition *$6650 (D)*   **$5000–$12,000**

Peking Chinese 7′8″ W × 9′6″ D Floral 1900–1910 China
Indigo blue field with a medallion of a coral central flowering vase; scattered floral sprays; medium blue primary border with urns and birds; indigo blue outer border guard.
Very Good Quality/Good Condition $7150 (A)   **$3000–$10,000**
Saumak 4′10″ W × 5′8″ D Geometric 1860–1880 Russia
Brick red ground with 3 intersecting diamond-shaped medallions; brown major border with multicolored stepped octagons; multiple minor borders; some wear; small repairs and slightly ragged end borders.
Very Good Quality/Average Condition $7700 (A)   **$7000–$20,000**
Yomud Turkanan 5′9″ W × 9′5″ D Geometric 1860–1880 Russia
Lattice motif; ivory major border, multicolor narrow minor borders; full end skirts of stylized flowers; some small stains and moth damage.
Superior Quality/Fine Condition $18,700 (A)   **$4000–$20,000**

BIBLIOGRAPHY

Hundreds of books have been published on the subject of Oriental rugs. The great majority of these titles offer illustrations of carpets with little substantive discussion of the technicalities of identification.

BOOKS

Bennett, I. *Oriental Rugs: Vol. 1. Caucasian.* Austria: Oriental Textile Press Ltd., 1981. (376 pp.). Well-illustrated volume that covers all types of Caucasian carpets. More illustrations of Caucasian carpets than any other single source.

Eiland, M. I. *Oriental Rugs: A Comprehensive Guide.* Boston: Little Brown, 1981. (294 pp.). Probably the best book available for the beginner. Systematic discussion of most types of Oriental rugs with careful structural descriptions. Good presentation of the basic techniques used in rug identification.

Iten-Maritz, J. *Turkish Carpets.* New York: Kodansha International, 1977. (353 pp.). Well-illustrated book on Turkish carpets. Place nomenclature varies from that used by most other references.

Loges, W. *Turkoman Tribal Rugs.* Atlantic Highlands, NJ: Humanities Press, 1980. (239 pp.). Good illustrations of the various types of Turkoman carpets.

Mackie, L., and Thompson, J. (eds.). *Turkmen.* Washington, DC: The Textile Museum, 1980. (239 pp.). Essays on various topics of Turkoman rugs with many good illustrations.

Opie, J. *Tribal Rugs of Southern Persia.* Portland, OR: James Opie Oriental Rugs, Inc., 1981. (223 pp.). Valuable for illustrations of the various types of tribal rugs of southern Iran; does not teach you how to distinguish the various types.

Schurmann, U. *Caucasian Rugs*. Accokeek, MD: Washington International Association, 1964; reprinted 1974. Illustrations of the "classic" types of Caucasian carpets.

Ware, Joyce C. *The Official Price Guide to Oriental Rugs*. New York: House of Collectibles, 1992.

CATALOGS

Sotheby's Auction Catalogs, Sotheby's, 1334 York Avenue, New York. Catalogs for all auctions of Oriental rugs. These present descriptions and/or illustrations of the sale items with sales estimates. After a sale each subscriber receives a list of prices for which each item sold. An excellent means for keeping current with international auction prices, but examination of the carpets at the preview exhibition greatly increases the usefulness of these publications.

JOURNALS

Hali: The International Journal of Fine Carpets and Textiles. Hali Publications Ltd., Kingsgate House, Kingsgate Place, London NW6 4TA, UK. A bimonthly publication with feature articles on a wide range of carpet and textile subjects, reports on carpet exhibitions, reviews of and titles of new books on carpets, market news, gallery reviews of dealer shows, reports on auction prices with descriptions and illustrations of selected goods, beautiful color illustrations primarily by advertisers.

Oriental Rug Review. Oriental Rug Auction Review, Inc., PO Box 709, Meredith, NH 03253. A bimonthly publication with feature articles on Oriental rug topics, notes on carpet exhibitions and rug societies, auctions previews and reviews, market reports.

Rug News. Museum Books, Inc., 6 West 37th Street, New York, NY 10018. A monthly trade publication by the Oriental Rug Importers Association. Emphasis on new rugs, some articles of general interest, market reports.

The Textile Museum Journal. The Textile Museum, Washington, DC. An annual publication that features excellent academic studies of textiles.

Paintings—Miniature

Advisor: **LESTER E. SENDER**

Lester E. Sender is owner of Sender's Gallerie Nouvelle, 3482 Lee Road, Shaker Heights, OH 44120, (216) 752-2935, and president of the National Association of Dealers in Antiques, a member of the International Society of Appraisers, and a member of the American Institute of Conservation.

WHAT IS A MINIATURE PAINTING?

A miniature painting is a scene or portrait painted on a surface of paper, vellum, metal, canvas, wood, bone, ivory, or cellulose, small in scale and perspective appropriate to the subject, using techniques adapted and handed down through the years. The terms *limnings*, or "paintings in little," which derives from the illuminations in manuscripts of the 15th and 16th centuries, was initially used to describe the product of the artist/illuminator/limner. The term limnings prevailed into the 17th century, when the word *miniature*, derived from the Latin word *minimum* (the red lead or vermilion pigment used by illuminators on manuscripts) came into popular use. These little portraits and/or scenes were executed in any medium, and sizes varied from 1 inch to 8 inches in height, the largest acceptable size being one that could be held comfortably in one hand.

There are two main categories of miniatures. *Portrait miniatures* are portraits and/or scenes small enough to be carried by an individual as a memento of a beloved person or place. *Cabinet miniatures* are larger and usually encased in heavier frames. They were wall-hung or placed on a table or in a cabinet.

HISTORY

Historians generally agree that the earliest recorded miniatures were painted in England during the 16th century. The first known miniaturist was Lucas Horenbout, who died in 1544. His student, Hans Holbein, became painter to the court of Henry VIII and was sent to Cleves to paint the Lady Anne's portrait. The Holbein miniature of Anne of Cleves is now in the collection of the Victoria and Albert Museum in London.

As the British Empire expanded and other European nations rushed to compete for territory and markets, the popularity of miniature painting spread throughout the world. Sailors, merchants, soldiers, and missionaries went out from their homelands carrying portraits of their loved ones, images of their homes or the countryside, and reminders of their faith. The miniature served all mankind in its day as the wallet or table photo serves us today.

DATING MINIATURES

From the 16th century to the beginning of the 18th century the most commonly used material for miniatures was vellum (sheep or calf skin), followed by paper (playing card or having playing card backing), metal, porcelain, wood, and pottery. Pigments used on these surfaces included gouache (opaque tempera), watercolor, oil paint, plumbago, and enamel. At the beginning of the 18th century ivory and bone became the base material of choice. Ivory in particular gave a certain quality of luminosity and dimension to the small miniatures that had never been achieved with the previous surfaces. Also, watercolors and transparencies replaced opaque pigments and oils to give more palpable realism to skin tones and some clothing in portraits.

During the Colonial period, technique, materials, and style in American portrait miniatures closely paralleled those used in Great Britain, as most prominent American painters-in-little were either English transplants or had gone to England for training. After the Revolution, however, itinerant painters with little formal training roamed the countryside creating charming miniatures for whoever would pay by giving lodging and a small wage. Indigenous techniques and schools of art grew from the sharing of applications and methods in wayside inns where these naive painters or traveling artists lodged and collaborated.

Rule of Thumb: Prior to 1700 no ivory or bone was used in miniature painting. After 1700 watercolor and some gouache pigments on ivory or bone became the mainstay of miniature painting. Porcelain, metal, canvas, and eglomise (painting behind glass) were also in use for the larger cabinet miniatures but seldom for portrait miniatures. In American miniatures there is an abrupt change in hair and clothing styles after 1812, which can help in dating portraits painted here.

MARKET TRENDS

English and Continental miniatures have always held a certain stature among museums and investors. Recently, American miniatures have started to gain status as investment art. Some judicious study prior to starting a collection is advised. Trial-and-error buying can be costly for the novice collector.

1. Become familiar with the basic history of miniatures.

2. Learn which pigments, supports, mediums, and techniques were used by the various artists and schools of art in Great Britain, America, and Europe.

3. Become familiar with price structures in different marketplaces.

4. Learn about fakes and forgeries.

5. Learn what differentiates a good-quality miniature from a best-quality miniature.

NEW DEVELOPMENTS

During 1990 a number of lengthy and detailed articles on the subject of portrait miniatures have appeared in prominent periodicals. In addition, a number of eastern museums have had special shows both from their own collections and borrowed from private and other museum collections. The Metropolitan Museum of Art in New York has initiated a major show and tour complete with a special catalog in which the entire collection being shown is reproduced in photographs. This exhibit of portrait miniatures will travel to other sections of the country. It is an extraordinarily comprehensive presentation both educationally and visually for collectors and art lovers alike. The national galleries and other major institutions are picking up the tempo of interest as well. Major movement is occurring in the portrait miniature field with asking prices increasing by up to 300 percent during the past year.

OPINION

Although there is much movement in the market and the prices of portrait miniatures have risen up to three times what they were several years ago, my research indicates that the buyers of these art pieces are in many cases speculating dealers. I have also found that these speculating dealers rarely have the knowledge of history, quality, and distinguishing characteristics that should be conveyed to the potential buyer. I caution potential buyers to tread lightly and cautiously when purchasing portrait miniatures for investment. I believe that, as has so often happened in the past when an art form is heavily promoted and prices surge, values will settle at lower levels after the initial rush to "get in."

I caution buyers not to "read in" or attribute finished works to artists too hastily. More often than not, the investor will be disappointed. During revival periods many original works by prominent artists of the past were duplicated and signed with the original artist's name or last name in order to take advantage of the market. In the late 19th century an English pharmacist, for example, had a thriving business selling "hot" antique miniatures that were actually copies produced in his back room.

FAKES ALERT

Beware! Beware! We have recently become aware of significant numbers of fake antique miniatures in the marketplace. If a piece seems too good to be true, it very well may be. These pieces are signed with last names only of well-known, highly collectible artists and are on ivory or an ivorene material. They come in rectangular and oval shapes, with the rectangular predominating. Frames are usually oxidized brass or black, and the glass is fine domed crystal.

Art that approaches worldwide investment quality will have forgers blatantly copying masterworks. Throughout history all important original art, whether large paintings or small miniatures, has been copied by forgers seeking to defraud the unsuspecting buyer. In the mid-19th century a London dealer did a thriving business employing a miniaturist to make three or four copies of originals in his possession, which he then sold in addition to the originals. Those copies are so notorious that reference books present as much information on the copies as they do on the original miniatures. Signature, technique, style, and materials must all be checked before investing. Provenance often plays an important role in the authentication and valuation of a miniature and should accompany it throughout its lifetime.

CONDITION KEY

Examination can be accomplished with a magnifying glass, black light, infrared light, and/or phosphorus light to determine if the item has been altered, restored, cracked, or damaged. A determination of condition can then be made as follows:

Fine Condition: of the period, by the specific artist, without restoration or in "as is" original fine condition; provenance papers of documentation add to the value.

Good Condition: of the period, by the specified artist, with some amount of properly completed restoration and a letter describing work done by a recognized conservator; provenance or papers of documentation add to the value.

Average Condition: of the period, by the specified artist or school of art, with some amount of normal wear due to age and conditions; not restored yet not really damaged; provenance or papers of documentation add to the value.

Poor Condition: of the period, by the specified artist or school of art, with damages such as cracked ivory or base material, peeling pigment, poorly restored areas, miniature loose in the framework, with seepage of air and dirt; without provenance.

Originality is not normally a condition statement but must be considered when an attribution or designation of artist or school of art is made and the conditions do not fit the norm of that artist or school.

QUALITY KEY

This key is a scale for placing the work of an artist in its proper position within the entire lifetime output of the artist. All works completed by a given artist are not equal to each other. Neither are they of the same quality. The reason for this could be as simple as having had a "bad day." Still, differences do exist. This key is not a condition statement but strictly a measure of the stylishness of the piece.

Good Quality: (1) in a good hand of the artist of record, (2) of a personage of the period, (3) in the style and technique of the period, (4) proper costuming appropriate to sitter's station, (5) in a proper period frame and in good condition, (6) in a good coloration and perspective with dimensional stability.

Very Good Quality: (1) in the fine hand of the artist of record, (2) of an important or recognized person of the period, (3) costuming depicting the office/station of the sitter, (4) in the proper technical and innovative style of the period, (5) showing some degree of individuality in pose or position, (6) properly framed and in excellent condition.

Superior Quality: (1) in the high period of the artist's recognized work, (2) of a personage of great importance in the period, (3) in fashionable Continental-style costume befitting the station of the sitter, (4) important framing in the best original condition, (5) the artist's highest concept in posing, sculptural dimension, and luminescent portraiture, (6) exceeds the artist's personal norm in style and technique (establishes new definition of excellence for the artist and furthers growth in the category).

PRESENTATION OF RECORDS OF MINIATURE PAINTINGS

For the most part, early miniature paintings are already in museums, institutions, and collections and are not likely to be available to the modern collector unless they are offered privately or in an important auction offering as part of an estate. Some of the artists are listed for those who are interested in the early, important limners:

Nicholas Hillard	Jean Fouquet
Hans Holbein	Henri Toutin
Isaac Oliver	Henry Bone
John Smart	John Hoskins
William Wood	Bernard Lens
Charles Hayter	Rosalba Carriera
Charles Boit	Richard Cross
Sr. T. Lawrence	C. F. Zincke
Lucas Horendout	Jean Petitot
Sidney Cooper	Jacques Bordier
Richard Cosway	John Simpson
George Engleheart	Rowland Lockey

The following section lists artists and schools of art that one may expect to find, if diligent and observant, when prowling the galleries, shops, and marketplaces of the world.

Boy 2.36″ × 1.7″ Naive 1800–1810 United States
"Garrick Darby, Aged 6″; boy in blue shirt with gathered balloon sleeves, lace collar, unkempt blond hair; watercolor on ivory; in detailed, carved wood frame; by Isabella Waters; rectangular.
Superior Quality/Good Condition $2100 (D)   **$1200–$2500**

Bride 3.12″ × 2.5″ Realistic 1885–1900 United States
Watercolor on ivory of a bride in white dress, wearing dress veil on hair; turquoise background, natural coloration; no restoration; signed by Caprioli; oval.
Superior Quality/Fine Condition $425 (D)   **$250–$500**

Double portraits 2.6″ × 2.12″ Naive 1780–1815 United States
One side: itinerant portrait of teenage girl with hair braided as laurel wreath, in blue gown; other side: woman in blue cape, white dress, with hair woven as laurel wreath; watercolor on ivory; 14K frame.
Superior Quality/Fine Condition $3400 (D)   **$1600–$5000**

Duchess of Devonshire 3.36″ × 2.5″ Realistic 1780–1790 England
Grayed values of full coloration in this magnificent portrait—very fine details, enameled highlights; watercolor on ivory; gilded metal frame; signed by Samuel Shelley; oval.
Superior Quality/Fine Condition $10,000 (D)   **$6000–$15,000**

Gentleman 3″ × 2.5″ Realistic 1844 United States
Seated gentleman, American actor W. M. Sedley Smith (sat for a series by the artist); oil on vellum; in black wood frame with brass liner; by Thomas Ball; oval.
Superior Quality/Fine Condition $1800 (D)   **$1000–$2200**

Girl 3.25″ × 2.5″ Realistic 1900–1905 Germany
Oil on porcelain of girl with very curly hair, white blouse, very detailed; in ornate frame with brass finish; signed by Fr. Till, Dresden; oval.
Superior Quality/Fine Condition $625 (D) **$350–$1000**

Group portrait 3.25″ Dia. Naive 1740–1760 United States
Family at tea, with dogs and toys; furniture and technique seem to be American; bronze frame; perfect condition; watercolor on ivory; not signed or dated. *(See photo 223)*
Superior Quality/Fine Condition $5600 (D) **$3500–$8500**

Interior scene 3″ Dia. Realistic 1820–1840 England
Watercolor on ivory drawing room scene with furniture, a woman, and 2 men (1 seated); crack across upper central area; frame with gold wash; muted colors with blue dominating; signed "Agar (John Samuel) R.A."
Very Good Quality/Average Condition $385 (D) **$300–$1500**

Lady 2.12″ × 1.6″ Realistic 1810–1820 France
Lady in ornate costuming and dress hat; soft colors, lace work as trim all over; watercolor on ivory, in ornate brass frame; velvet around oval reserve; signed "Drea"; Spanish school technique; oval.
Superior Quality/Good Condition $950 (D) **$500–$1200**

Lady 2.75″ Dia. Realistic 1810–1815 Germany
Lady with low bodice, lace jewelry, tight hairdo; red detailed jewelry at bodice perimeter; lace sleeves; watercolor on ivory; no restoration; unsigned; European school.
Very Good Quality/Fine Condition $325 (D) **$200–$450**

Lady 2.5″ × 2″ Naive 1800–1810 United States
Watercolor on ivory of a lady in red vest with gold color details, white costuming with blue shading; black wood frame with brass liner; fine condition—no restoration; attributed to J. Brown.
Very Good Quality/Fine Condition $725 (D) **$600–$1200**

Lady 2.25″ × 1.6″ Naive 1830–1845 United States
Watercolor on ivory of a lady with fine lace work and jewelry, fine detail; in wood frame inlaid with mother-of-pearl and brass; perfect condition; attributed to Joseph Whiting Stock.
Superior Quality/Fine Condition $3100 (D) **$2000–$5000**

Lady in hat 3.25″ × 2.25″ Realistic 1770–1780 England
Lady with large hat seated at window, hands folded on table, cape over chair back; watercolor on ivory, in gilded bronze frame; perfect condition; signed by George Moreland; oval.
Superior Quality/Fine Condition $1425 (D) **$900–$1500**

Lady of royalty 3.12″ × 2.36″ Realistic 1735–1740 France
Gouache on ivory; lady in white wig, lace-trimmed hat, red velvet gown with roping details; landscape background, in bronze frame with coiled details; oval; signed "Pesne" (Antoine, 1683–1757).
Superior Quality/Fine Condition $8200 (D) **$3000–$10,000**

Lady, side view 2″ × 1.5″ Very realistic 1850–1860 England
Lady with off-the-shoulder blouse, large pearl necklace, hair pulled tight with braided tresses; ornate brass frame; watercolor on ivory; oval; signed "H.K."; English school.
Superior Quality/Good Condition $440 (D) **$250–$600**

Photo 223.
Group
portrait.
CREDIT:
LESTER
SENDER
(See p. 423)

Photo 224.
Portrait.
CREDIT:
LESTER
SENDER
(See p. 425)

Lady wearing a hat 2.75″ × 2.12″ Realistic 1800–1810 England
"Mrs. Montgomery"; lady in wig and hat, open-neck blouse; sitter in casual position; watercolor on ivory; black frame with brass liner; slight provincial feel, not signed or dated; oval.
Very Good Quality/Good Condition $450 (D)   **$250–$600**

Man 2.75″ × 2.25″ Realistic 1780–1790 England
Middle-aged man in wig, navy jacket with gold buttons, white collar, gathered shirting; watercolor on ivory; 14K gold frame; seems to be a professional man; unsigned; oval.
Superior Quality/Fine Condition $1700 (D)   **$625–$2000**

Portraits 4.5″ Dia. Realistic 1770–1780 England
Pair of fine portraits of ladies wearing hats; each with full, subtle coloration; watercolor on ivory; black frames with brass liners; no restoration; both signed "Russell" (John, 1744–1806). *(See photo 224)*
Superior Quality/Fine Condition $10,000 (D)   **$6000–$15,000**

Woman of royalty 2.75″ × 2.12″ Realistic 1795–1810 France
Watercolor on ivory of woman with green brocade hairpiece and matching blouse, ruby jewelry, pink damask wrap, pearls at neck; no restoration; signed by Jean Baptiste Jacques Augustin; oval.
Superior Quality/Fine Condition $4300 (D)   **$3000–$7500**

Young woman 2.6″ Dia. Realistic/formal 1720–1730 France
Young woman in 17th-century costume and ornate paneled hat, necklace with cross; watercolor on ivory with enameled highlights; in liner frame; signed "B. Laveau."
Superior Quality/Fine Condition $2600 (D)   **$950–$3000**

BIBLIOGRAPHY

In-depth research in the field of miniature painting is best done in an art museum library, as the best references are limited editions published before World War II. The following books are suggested for a general overview.

Foskett, Daphne. *Miniatures: Dictionary and Guide*. London, Faber and Faber, 1972.

Murdoch, Murrell, Noon, Strong. *The English Miniature*. New Haven, CT: Yale University Press, 1981.

Noon, Patrick J. *English Portrait Drawings and Miniatures*. New Haven, CT: Yale Center for British Art, 1979.

Wehle, Harry. *American Miniatures: 1730–1850*. Garden City, NY: Garden City Publishing Co., 1927.

MAJOR COLLECTIONS

Great Britain: The national galleries of Scotland and Ireland contain examples of miniature art. In England the finest and most complete collection is in the Victoria and Albert Museum in London. Most English miniatures remain in private collections.

The Continent: The Louvre, the Rijks Museum, National Museum of Denmark, National Museum of Sweden, National Museum of Poland in Cracow, the Uffizi and Pitti Palace museums in Florence, the Prado, and the Hermitage Museum contain interesting collections.

The United States: There are many examples of miniature art in museums in the United States but few complete representational collections. Some of the best are in the Metropolitan Museum of Art, New York; the Smithsonian National Collection, Washington, DC; the Cleveland Museum of Art, Cleveland, OH; the Walters Gallery, Baltimore, MD; the Huntington Gallery, San Marino, CA; the William Rockhill Nelson Gallery of Art, Kansas City, MO; Museum of Art, New Orleans, LA.

Peanuts Collectibles

Advisors: ANDREA PODLEY and FREDDI MARGOLIN

Freddi Margolin and Andrea Podley have authored The Official Price Guide to Peanuts Collectibles *(New York: House of Collectibles, 1990). Mrs. Podley is the owner of one of the world's largest Peanuts collections, which has been featured in a number of publications in the United States, Europe, and Japan. In 1983 she formed the Peanuts Collectors' Club, and she continues to edit its newsletter. Ms. Margolin owned and operated one of the country's only boutiques devoted exclusively to Peanuts from 1979 to 1985. Her extensive personal collection is housed in a private museum in her home. The following introduction is based on the* Official Price Guide to Peanuts Collectibles *by Freddi Margolin and Andrea Podley.*

The *Peanuts* comic strip first came out in 1950, and it has grown in popularity ever since. *Peanuts* products can be found in the form of dolls, clothes, home furnishings, music boxes, toys, games—even TV specials (63 in 12 languages). Most of us either grew up with *Peanuts* or our children did. Collecting *Peanuts* can be a wonderful way to relive childhood memories.

If you are a beginning *Peanuts* collector, the following tips will be helpful. It's a good idea to do some initial reading on *Peanuts*. You will find a selected bibliography following the listings. You may want to start collecting in a particular area. If so, there are many ways to shape a *Peanuts* collection: by the character, by the material used (ceramics, glass, metal), by pose, by category (music boxes, plates, mugs, etc.), to name a few possibilities. Even though you may be looking for older *Peanuts* items, don't overlook current products, as they will be the collectibles of tomorrow. Remember, *Peanuts* items are not antiques, and age is not the major determinant of value.

Peanuts collectibles can be found in thrift shops, gift and toy shops, and at toy shows and flea markets. If you go to shows, it's always a good idea to arrive well before the show opens because the best items tend to sell quickly. To be really prepared, take along batteries for testing toys. Finally, when you make a purchase, keep a record of when you bought the item, how much you paid for it, and what the condition was. These records will be invaluable to you as your *Peanuts* collection expands.

AUTHENTICITY

Every authentic *Peanuts* item has Charles Schulz's personal imprimatur. On every licensed item you will find a copyright date and the words "United Feature Syndicate, Inc." They own the copyright. You may also find the name of the manufacturer or distributor who has been granted the license. Some of the major licensees include Determined (the largest), Hallmark, Avon, Aviva, Hungerford (rubber dolls), Ideal, Arni, and Schmid (plates, bells, and music boxes). Finally, if the product features a drawing, it will usually be signed "Schulz."

Once you have determined the authenticity of an item, discovering when the item was produced is another matter. The copyright date on the item should not be confused with the year the item was produced; the copyright date refers to the year the *character*, in its own distinct pose, first appeared in the cartoon strip. For example, a two-dimensional Charlie Brown item always bears a 1950 copyright date, no matter when the item itself was manufactured, because Charlie Brown made his first appearance in the comic strip in 1950. Three-dimensional *Peanuts* items have different copyright dates, but again, the copyright date does not refer to the year of manufacture. One further thing to know is that if a character—Snoopy, for instance—changes radically over the years, each time that character appears in a very different pose he is considered a "new work," and he gets a new copyright date. Of all of the *Peanuts* characters, Snoopy is the one with the most incarnations—the Flying Ace, Joe Cool, Snoopy with his nose in the air doing his exuberant dance, to name a few. See Freddi Margolin and Andrea Podley's book for more details on the intricacies of copyright.

Since copyright doesn't tell when an item was made, it is best to be familiar with how the look of the cartoon characters evolved over the years and to know when a character first appeared in the strip. The kind of material used is another helpful clue. For example, plastic was not used much until the 1970s, when wood was being phased out. Age is not of primary importance when determining value. Condition and rarity are more important.

CONDITION

Ideally an item should be as unspoiled as possible. If it came in a box, it should still have the box. It is most valuable if the box has never been opened and the item is in perfect condition. This condition is known as "mint in the box." If an item in mint condition is missing its box, it is called "mint" rather than "mint in box." In the listings below, an asterisk (*) indicates that the item came with a box or package, and it should be "mint in the box" (or package) to get top dollar. "Good" condition means that the item has a few minor blemishes, only limited signs of wear and tear. The box, if there is one, should also show only minor signs of wear. All parts should be there. "Poor" indicates major wear and tear. Parts may be missing. From a monetary standpoint, items in poor condition are not worth collecting. For this reason, the price ranges in the following listings refer to items in good to mint condition.

Availability is another factor that affects price. Items that are plentiful do not command high prices. Some of the *Peanuts* banks, for example, were made in large numbers, and their prices have not increased. In general, the same is true of dolls, except for Schroeder and Pigpen dolls by Hungerford, which are difficult to find. Categories that are in demand include metal toys (especially those made by Chein), wooden toys, mirror pictures, music boxes, ceramic items, and Christmas ornaments.

Please remember that these prices are meant to serve as a guide, not a bible. If an item seems somewhat overpriced according to this guide, but you really feel it would improve your collection and give you pleasure (and you can afford it), then go for it. Money isn't everything!

Album, photograph Hallmark 1972
Charlie Brown sits at a school desk with raised hand. Caption: "Don't You Just Love School?" #250PHA 106-1. **$15–$20**

Bank, doghouse 3.25″ × 6″ Determined Early 1970s
Snoopy lying on roof of house. This is a Bank of America premium. It is the box only that indicates "Bank of America" on 2 of its 4 sides. There is no special marking on the bank itself. Determined for Bank of America.
$25–$35*

Bank, egg-shaped 2″ × 3″ 1976
Snoopy is lying on top of his doghouse. Woodstock is sleeping in his nest, which is on Snoopy's tummy. Caption: "This Has Been a Good Day." **$12–$17**

Banner Determined 1970
"Happiness Is Loving Your Enemies." Snoopy and the bunnies. **$20–$25**

Banner Determined Early 1970s
"Merry Christmas From All of Us." Sally, Charlie Brown, Violet, Schroeder, Lucy, Linus, Snoopy. **$20–$30**

Book 1964
The Gospel According to Peanuts, by Robert Short. The author lends a theological interpretation to the *Peanuts* cartoons. John Knox Press.
Soft cover **$3–$4**
Hard cover **$10–$12**

Book 1952
Peanuts, by Charles M. Schulz. Cover: Patty taking picture of Schroeder and Snoopy on piano; a frowning Charlie Brown stands behind. Rinehart & Co., soft cover. **$4–$8**

Photo 225.
Canister set.
CREDIT: PETER
TORRES *(See below)*

Book 1966
Snoopy and the Red Baron, by Charles M. Schulz. Cover: Snoopy as the Flying Ace on roof of his doghouse. Holt, Rinehart & Winston, Canada, 1966, 1st ed.   **$4–$6**

Book 1962
Happiness Is a Warm Puppy, by Charles M. Schulz. Cover: Lucy hugging Snoopy. Determined; hard cover.   **$3–$5**

Canister set Determined 1979
Triple-nested; wraparound cartoon art; metal. Large canister: Snoopy is sitting at a table in a café, 6.25" × 7.75" dia. Medium canister: Snoopy as a chef holds a frying pan and Woodstock is sitting in it, 5" × 6.75" dia. Small canister: Snoopy looks out from underneath a tablecloth, 4.36" × 5.75" dia. #0367. *(See photo 225)* Set   **$30–$45**

Clock, alarm (tabletop) 3.5" × 5.5" 1972
A dancing Snoopy decorates the face of the clock. His hands are used to tell the time. This style came in a variety of color combinations. Made in West Germany; metal. Blessing/Determined, #353.   **$20–$30**

Clock, wall 7" Equity Early 1980s
In the center of the clock Snoopy as a chef carries food, with Woodstock flying behind him. Caption on face: "Bon Appetit." The case is white metal with an orange face and white letters; battery operated. #402 250.   **$40–$50***

Coloring book 14" × 19.5" Determined Early 1960s
The Colorful World of Snoopy, Linus, Schroeder, Lucy, and Charlie Brown. Cover: in addition to the wording, orange and green cover includes pictures of Linus with his blanket, Charlie Brown in baseball gear, Snoopy in his dancing pose, Schroeder at his piano, and Lucy skipping rope.   **$30–$45**

Coloring book Saalfield 1965
Peanuts: A Book to Color. Cover: Snoopy and Charlie Brown on a skateboard. #4629.   **$20–$30**

Doll 15" Determined 1971
Snoopy, sitting. Felt eyes, eyebrows, and nose, black spot on back. Red plastic tag around his neck has a picture of Snoopy. Captioned: "A Peanuts Character Plush Dog From the Peanuts Comic Strip." #883.   **$15–$30***

Doll, Hungerford 8.5" 1958
Charlie Brown in a red shirt with zigzag black design and black pants. Clothes are painted on. Hard rubber. Hungerford Plastics Corp.   **$20–$75***

Doll, Hungerford 7″ 1958
Schroeder and his white piano (which is not attached to Schroeder). He is wearing red pajamas; clothes are painted on. Hard rubber. Hungerford Plastics Corp. **$150–$200***

Game Selchow & Righter Late 1960s
Peanuts, The Game of Charlie Brown and His Pals. The first player to form a complete sequence of cards numbered 1, 2, 3, 4, and 5 or any 4 of these numbers, plus the Peanuts card, is the winner. Cover of the box: Charlie Brown, Violet, Patty, Schroeder, Lucky, Pigpen, Shermy, and Linus chasing Snoopy, who is running with a ball in his mouth. #86. **$20–$30***

Game Milton Bradley 1977
Snoopy's Doghouse Game. A plastic doghouse is completely built in the course of playing the game. Box cover shows all the pieces of the house apart and together; Snoopy is walking toward the house with a hammer. #4704.
$20–$30*

Lunch box King Seeley Thermos 1976
Metal, red. Charlie Brown is leaning back to pitch. Reverse: Snoopy and Woodstock as scouts are off on a fast hike. Plastic thermos with Charlie Brown swinging his bat. #1448. **$10–$20**

Lunch box King Seeley Thermos 1968
Metal, house shape in yellow; Snoopy is lying on his back eating a sandwich. Reverse: Snoopy is on his tummy reading a book. The metal thermos pictures Snoopy, Charlie Brown, Schroeder, Linus, and Lucy, each with their names printed beneath them. Caption on front: "Have Lunch With Snoopy." #658. **$20–$30**

Megaphone J. Chein & Co. 1970
Caption: "Head Beagle." Pictured: Snoopy as a director, Lucy, and Charlie Brown. Written beneath their pictures: "Stars of the Movie *A Boy Named Charlie Brown*." This came in a variety of colors; metal with plastic mouthpiece.
$10–$20

Mirror picture 10.5″ × 8″ Determined Mid-1970s
Peppermint Patty holds hands with Charlie Brown; Snoopy is hugging Woodstock; large hearts in background. Caption: "Love." **$25–$30**

Mug, ceramic 3.5″ Determined Mid-1970s
Snoopy wears a red football helmet; he's standing in front of Woodstock. Snoopy's thought balloon: "There's Always That Chance We Might Not Even Get Invited to the Rose Bowl." **$8–$12**

Music box, wooden 5″ ANRI 1971
Schroeder at his piano, bust of Beethoven on top. There is a little bird near the piano, but it is not Woodstock. "Beethoven's Emperor's Waltz." #819 030. *(See photo 226)* **$125–$130**

Patch 3″ Dia. Determined 1970
Snoopy with skis and ski cap. Caption: "To the Bunny Slope." #730
$3–$4*

Remember, the price range shows what the same item would sell for in average condition (left column) and fine condition (right column). Any item in poor condition has, in general, a value of 50% (or less) of that of the same item in average condition.

Patch 3″ Dia. Determined 1970
Lucy. Caption: "World's Crabbiest Female." #727. **$5–$6***

Pencil sharpener, Snoopy's Kenner 1974
Snoopy is at the typewriter on the roof of his house; directly behind him is the pencil sharpener. The entire item stands on a green base that holds pencils. Box cover: Lucy is using the sharpener, and Charlie Brown is waiting his turn. Plastic; battery operated. #3550. **$35–$45***

Piano Ely Late 1960s
Pictured on top is Schroeder at the piano, Lucy leaning on it, Snoopy standing on it playing a fiddle, and Linus with his blanket. Wood. **$90–$150***

Pin, Bicentennial Aviva 1976
Snoopy as an Indian holding a package of tea. Caption: "1776–1976."
$15–$20

Pin, cloisonné Aviva
Snoopy as the Flying Ace. **$8–$10**

Pinback 2.25″ Dia. Butterfly Originals Early 1980s
Snoopy is lying on top of a pumpkin. Cloth front, metal back. **$5–$9**

Pinback 6″ Dia. Simon Simple Early 1972
"All Secretaries Need a Little Compliment Now and Then." Woodstock is on Snoopy's house typing a letter; Snoopy pats him on the head. Thought balloon: "That's Very Nice." Metal. **$20–$30**

Puzzle 24″ × 24″ Determined 1971
Love Is. Four scenes, each with a different "Love Is" theme and each occupying one quarter of the puzzle. Features Charlie Brown and Snoopy ("Love Is Having Someone to Lean On"), Linus and Sally ("Love Is Tickling"), Shermy and Patty ("Love Is Walking Hand-in-Hand"), and Schroeder and Lucy ("Love Is Mussing Up Someone's Hair"). 1000 pieces; #711-4. **$25–$35***

Scrapbook 10.75″ × 9″ Early 1970s
Cover design: Snoopy with a book shares the roof of his house with Woodstock. Cover is green, white, and blue. Caption: "Scraps." Hallmark, #450 PA 60 5-5. **$15–$25**

Photo 226 (left). Wooden music box. CREDIT: PETER TORRES. *Photo 227 (right). Train set.* CREDIT: TABARANZA *(See pp. 431, 433)*

Thermometer 11″ × 12″ 1979

For indoor and outdoor use. Snoopy and Woodstock in their dancing poses are in the center of the face. Sybron/Taylor, #5374. **$35–$50***

Train set Aviva 1977

Schroeder is driving the locomotive captioned "Snoopy Express." Behind the blue locomotive is Charlie Brown in a coal tender (which is meant to look like a baseball mound). Caption: "Charlie Brown." Snoopy's doghouse car follows with Snoopy lying on top; caption: "Snoopy." Woodstock is in his tree car; caption: "Woodstock." To complete the set, railroad signs, doghouse ticket booth, blue tracks, and a green tunnel are included. #3000. Battery operated. *(See photo 227)* **$75–$95***

Watch 1.75″ Dia. Determined 1969

Snoopy Time. Snoopy in his dancing pose. Silver or gold case; second hand. Available in various color faces and bands. **$45–$80***

Watch .88″ Dia. Determined Early 1970s

Charlie Brown All Star Watch. Charlie is dressed in baseball gear. The watch comes with a green patch of Charlie captioned "I Need All the Friends I Can Get." Watch face is yellow; band is black. **$75–$140***

BIBLIOGRAPHY

Margolin, Freddi, and Andrea Podley. *The Official Price Guide to Peanuts Collectibles*. New York: House of Collectibles, 1990.

Johnson, Rheta Grinsley. *Good Grief: The Story of Charles M. Schulz*. New York: Pharos Books, 1989.

Schulz, Charles M. *Peanuts Jubilee*. New York: Holt, Rinehart & Winston, 1975.

———. *You Don't Look 35, Charlie Brown*. New York: Holt, Rinehart & Winston, 1985.

Schulz, Charles M., and Lee Mendelson. *Charlie Brown and Charlie Schulz*. New York: World Publishing Co., 1969.

Schulz, Charles M., and R. Smith Killiper. *Charlie Brown, Snoopy & Me*. New York: Doubleday, 1980.

COLLECTORS' CLUB

Peanuts Collector Club, PO Box 94, North Hollywood, CA 91603; publishes a bimonthly newsletter. Send a self-addressed stamped envelope for information on how to join.

Political Memorabilia

Advisor: **RICHARD FRIZ**

Richard Friz is a nationally recognized author of many books and articles, including The Official Price Guide to Political Memorabilia, The Official Price Guide to World's Fair Memorabilia, The Official Price Guide to Toys, *and* The Official Identification and Price Guide to Toy Trains *(New York: House of Collectibles). For information on all phases of collecting political memorabilia, see Mr. Friz's book, listed in the bibliography at the end of this chapter. Mr. Friz is a member of the New Hampshire Appraisers Association. He can be reached at RFD 2, Box 155, Peterborough, NH 03458; (603) 563–8155.*

HISTORY

The purposeful collection of political artifacts had its origins in the late 1860s following the assassination of Abraham Lincoln. Single-sheet prints of party favorites lined the walls of Victorian homes; Currier & Ives made a fortune selling their Grand National Banner prints, which quickly became "collectible."

The Centennial Exposition in 1876 and the Columbian Exposition in 1893 played a major role in rekindling our patriotic spirit; posters, ceramics, glassware, and textiles honoring presidents, statesmen, and military heroes were popularized in those two international fairs, instilling a collecting mania that is with us to this day.

Perhaps the biggest stimulus to political memorabilia collecting came in the form of coins, medals, and medalettes struck in the likenesses of politicos. In the 1920s, Robert T. King's *Lincoln in Numismatics* appeared, listing over a thousand medalia issues. Bessie M. Lindsey's *American Historical Glass* appeared in 1948, and J. Doyle DeWitt's *A Century of Campaign Buttons* was published in 1959; both focused attention on many of the fascinating artifacts from campaigns past.

The American Political Items Collectors, now numbering over 2000 members, was founded in 1945. The nonprofit organization today includes more than 30 local chapters and clubs across the United States.

RECENT TRENDS

A few years ago it could be said of campaign pinbacks and political memorabilia in general that the hobby was dominated by four or five very affluent collectors. Times have changed; as opposed to a few free spenders, the market now has a broad, solid base, attesting to the ever-increasing growth and vigor of the hobby. We have been able to chart fierce competition at all levels for political memorabilia, even in the $50 to $100 range.

Subcategories of campaign memorabilia where intensified activity has been noted include items relating to holding various public offices prior to springboarding a specific candidate to the national scene—for example, a "Harry Truman For Judge" cello, which now lists in the $300-plus range, and "FDR for Senator" (New York) from his 1910 race, which sold recently for $1200 at auction. Campaign posters and prints, particularly those from the first half of the 19th century, are beginning to bring the prices they so justly deserve. Another trendsetter seems to be *anything* that relates to the century-long woman's suffrage movement.

FAKES AND FANTASIES ALERT

The majority of spurious pieces discovered in this hobby fall into the "fantasy" category. A fantasy is classified as not campaign-related nor of the period but usually commemorative in nature—for example, a John Frémont celluloid ribbon badge, issued by the Republican League in 1906 to celebrate the 50th anniversary of the GOP, or a ceramic "Keep Cool With Coolidge Near Beer" bottle issued in the 1950s.

The biggest culprits to confuse entry-level collectors were the various promotional sets issued (rather innocently, we can assume) by such advertisers as Kleenex, Proctor & Gamble, Liberty Mint, and Pepsin Gum through the years. Some are fakes, and others are pure fantasy; but most examples differ in size and differ considerably in color from the originals. Repros featuring candidates from 1896 to 1916 are invariably in lithographed tin, whereas the originals were celluloid on tin. The most important aid in recognizing fakes is education. By familiarizing yourself with as many original artifacts as possible, your visual and tactile skills will be sharpened—your sense of what is "right" or "bogus" becomes almost intuitive. Visit the collections listed at the end of this chapter, and study their contents.

CONDITION GRADING OF POLITICAL CAMPAIGN PINBACKS

Condition, as it relates to value as well as aesthetic appeal, includes mention of deep scratches, celluloid cracking, surface bumps, structural damage and staining, flaking of celluloid, and oxidation of metal parts.

As with stamps, fine prints, textiles, and even baseball cards, proper centering, with uniform borders on all sides, is a critical factor.

Fine Condition: the visual impact of the pinback and its physical condition are of such high quality that there are no visible flaws detracting from collector's overall appreciation of the piece.

Good Condition: defects are immediately apparent on the face of the pinback.

Average Condition: pieces have apparent flaws of a more serious nature.

Poor Condition: items have critical defects (bear in mind that there is no real way to bring back a celluloid pinback with severe foxing to "as new" condition).

Ceramics   Benjamin Butler   1870s   United States
Porcelain toothpick holder with lid; 4-sided with bas-relief heads of Butler on each side; Civil War military kepi on lid serves as handle; white.
Good Quality/Good Condition $325 (D)   **$275–$325**

Ceramics   12″ oval   Henry Clay   1851   United States
Bas-relief bust by Jones & Drennon Studio; nicks on edge; ivory color.
Good Quality/Good Condition $225 (A)   **$250–$275**

Ceramics   James Garfield   1880   United States
Milkglass shaving mug with caricature of Garfield in bas-relief.
Fine Quality/Fine Condition $1200 (D)   **$1000–$1200**

Ceramics   12″ L   William McKinley   1900s   United States
Ceramic tile cribbage board; double portrait; multicolor.
Good Quality/Good Condition $350 (D)   **$250–$350**

Ceramics   Alfred Smith   1932   United States
Stangl pottery mug; bas-relief caricature on barrel-shaped mug; mustard color.
Good Quality/Good Condition $50 (D)   **$35–$45**

Ceramics   Zachary Taylor   c. 1850   United States
Bennington pottery figural bust pitcher; "Rough & Ready" embossed on opposite sides; glazed dark brown.
Superior Quality/Fine Condition $4400 (A)   **$3500–$4000**

Ceramics   6″ H   Woodrow Wilson   1916   United States
"Strange Bedfellows" glazed earthenware pocket flask; caricatures of Woodrow Wilson and his newly appointed secretary of state, William Jennings Bryan, snuggled under bedcovers; pale blue.
Superior Quality/Fine Condition $500 (A)   **$500–$600**

Lapel device   2″ Dia.   William Jennings Bryan   United States
"My Hobby—A Winner" 1896 campaign; Bryan riding an ostrich with broom attached at lower end; waves a palm branch; multicolor.
Superior Quality/Fine Condition $4200 (A)   **$1500–$2000**

Lapel device   .8″ Dia.   Calvin Coolidge   United States
"Home Town Coolidge Club" pinback portrait; red, white, blue, and black.
Good Quality/Fine Condition $161 (A)   **$100–$200**

Lapel device .8″ Dia. Calvin Coolidge United States
"Firm as the Rock of Ages" pinback portrait; red, white, black.
Very Good Quality/Fine Condition $196 (A) **$100–$200**

Lapel device 2″ Dia. Herbert Hoover United States
"For President/Herbert Hoover" centerpiece portrait item; black and white.
Good Quality/Fine Condition $573 (A) **$450–$550**

Lapel device 2″ Dia. William McKinley United States
"My Hobby—A Winner" 1896 campaign; McKinley riding hobby horse with
broom at one end; multicolor.
Superior Quality/Good Condition $4100 (A) **$1500–$2000**

Lapel device 1.5″ H William Howard Taft United States
"The Gunnison Tunnel Opening"; illustration of eagle, with small inset of Taft
above tunnel view; black and white oval.
Very Good Quality/Fine Condition $660 (D) **$500–$600**

Lapel device 1.25″ Dia. Woodrow Wilson United States
"Man of the Hour" pinback portrait; black, purple, orange.
Good Quality/Fine Condition $506 (A) **$450–$500**

Lapel device 1.5″ Dia. Woodrow Wilson United States
"Man of the Hour" pinback portrait; black, purple, orange.
Good Quality/Fine Condition $524 (A) **$450–$500**

Snuff box 5″ L Henry Clay 1844 United States
Papier-mâché handcolored with black rim; Clay is seated at desk with document
in hand; multicolor.
Good Quality/Good Condition $750 (D) **$650–$750**

Snuff box 3.25″ W × 2″ H William Harrison 1840 United States
Log cabin, trees, cider barrel; pewter; metal finish.
Good Quality/Good Condition $450 (D) **$350–$400**

Snuff box William Harrison 1840 United States
"W.H. Harrison/Ninth President of the U.S."; papier-mâché; three-quarter por-
trait; black transfer against pale orange background.
Good Quality/Good Condition $1000 (A) **$850–$950**

Snuff box Andrew Jackson 1829 United States
"Jackson & No Corruption"; pasteboard box with glass-enclosed portrait inside
lid; outer lid has velvet pin cushion; rainbow colors.
Fine Quality/Good Condition $1100 (A) **$1000–$1500**

Snuff box 2.25″ Dia. Andrew Jackson 1844 United States
Portraits of Jackson, Martin Van Buren, Henry Clay, and Daniel Webster; papier-
mâché; multicolor.
Good Quality/Good Condition $800 (D) **$700–$900**

Textile James Garfield 1880 United States
"Hurrah For Garfield & Arthur" cotton banner; illustration of large rooster
crowing; blue, white.
Good Quality/Good Condition $1000 (D) **$800–$1000**

Textile Benjamin Harrison 1888 United States
Benjamin Harrison–Levi Morton Republican cotton bandanna; cameo portraits
from H. B. Hall engraving; red, blue, white.
Good Quality/Good Condition $325 (A) **$300–$350**

Textile   William Harrison   1840   United States
William Henry Harrison on horseback (center) bandanna with 6 vignettes highlighting career; reddish brown on buff.
Good Quality/Good Condition $225 (D)   **$200–$250**

Textile   21.5″ L   Andrew Jackson   1832   United States
Andrew Jackson "Glorious Victory of New Orleans/Jackson Leading Troops to Victory" bandanna; small oval of Washington at top; historical vignettes and battle scenes; brown, white.
Fine Quality/Good Condition $1500 (D)   **$1200–$1500**

Textile   24″ Sq.   Theodore Roosevelt   1904   United States
Theodore Roosevelt "First in War, First in Peace" canvas banner, honoring Theodore Roosevelt as recipient of Nobel Peace Prize; multicolor.
Good Quality/Good Condition $500 (A)   **$450–$550**

Thread box   5″ W × 3″ W   John Adams   1824   France
John Quincy Adams "Adams & Liberty" pasteboard box with flag design in rope border; hinged lid with ribbon supports; paper engraving of Adams mounted under glass; rainbow colors.
Good Quality/Good Condition $1100 (D)   **$1000–$1200**

Thread box   5″ W   Andrew Jackson   1828   France
Bust portrait in ruffled shirt; black coat; eagle on reverse with banner inscribed "Gen'l Andrew Jackson Jan 8" (inaugural item); white enameled papier-mâché.
Good Quality/Good Condition $1800 (D)   **$1500–$1800**

BIBLIOGRAPHY

Fischer, Roger A. *Tippecanoe and Trinkets Too*. Urbana and Chicago: University of Illinois Press, 1988.

Friz, Richard G. *Political Memorabilia*. New York: House of Collectibles, 1988.

Hake, Theodore. *The Encyclopedia of Political Buttons: 1896–1972*. New York: Dafran House Publishers, 1974.

———.*Political Buttons, Book II: 1920–1976*. York, PA: Hake's Americana Press, 1977.

———.*Political Buttons, Book III: 1789–1916*. York, PA: Hake's Americana Press, 1978.

The three books above by Theodore Hake have been updated, including a revised price guide, and are available from Hake's Americana Press, PO Box 1444, York, PA 17405.

Sullivan, Edmund B. *Collecting Political Americana*. New York: Crown, 1980.

COLLECTORS' ORGANIZATIONS

American Political Items Collectors (APIC)
PO Box 340339
San Antonio, TX 78234

In addition, over thirty local clubs and chapters are sponsored by APIC. There are special chapters for Hopefuls and Third Parties as well as for the following past candidates for president:

Carter Political Items Collectors
Gerald R. Ford Chapter
Warren G. Harding Chapter
John F. Kennedy Chapter
Franklin D. Roosevelt Chapter
Theodore Roosevelt Chapter
Harry S. Truman Chapter
Nixon Political Items Collectors
George C. Wallace Chapter
Wendell L. Willkie Chapter

PUBLIC COLLECTIONS

The following museums and institutions offer permanent collections of presidential memorabilia:

Clark Historical Library at Central Michigan University, Mt. Pleasant, MI.
Museum of American Political Life at University of Hartford, West Hartford, CT (collection of the late J. Doyle DeWitt).
National Museum of History and Technology, Smithsonian Institution, Washington, DC.
Paul Perlin Collection of Political Americana at University of Louisville, Louisville, KY.
(The) Presidential Museum, Odessa, TX.
Western Reserve Historical Society, Cleveland, OH.
Wisconsin State Historical Society, Madison, WI.

Postcards

This chapter is arranged by the following subcategories:
VIEW CARDS, GREETINGS, ARTIST-SIGNED POSTCARDS, AND TOPICALS.

Advisor: **DIANE ALLMEN**

Diane Allmen is partner with David Long in Modern Postcard Sales, a business specializing in selling current-issue postcards to collectors. She is the former publisher and founding editor of Postcard Collector *magazine. She has published a number of National Postcard Week postcards. She keeps abreast of current trends while attending postcard club meetings and selling at postcard shows across the United States. Her collecting specialties are pioneer views of Chicago, woman suffrage, vinegar valentines, Century of Progress, and contemporary events. Diane Allmen can be reached at Modern Postcard Sales, PO Box 644, Elkhart, IN 46515; UPS address: 513 Baldwin, Elkhart, IN 46514; (219) 264-0013.*

HISTORY

In 1869, based on a proposal by Dr. Emanuel Herrmann, Austria introduced the first government-issue postal card. This postal stationery for brief open communications offered a more economical means of sending a message than a letter. Postal cards were an instant hit, and many other European countries (in 1870, 1871, and 1872) rapidly adopted them, as did the United States in 1873.

The first widely distributed pictorial postal cards in the United States were the official Goldsmith issues—souvenir items for the Columbian Exposition of 1893. The colored artwork was printed on the "backs" of U.S. postal cards. Pictorial series were also issued by other firms, some on plain nongovernment, privately printed cards that required the higher postage of letter mail.

In the United States, this disparity in postage between government postal cards and privately printed cards was eliminated in 1898 by the Private Mailing Card Act (this occurred earlier in Europe). Freed from unfair competition, private publishers offered view cards, holiday greetings, topicals, and artist-signed picture postcards in ever-increasing numbers.

The craze for picture postcards, which began in Europe, caught on rapidly in the United States. Additional reduction of postal restrictions in 1902 and 1907 helped more. One statistic from this "golden age" of postcards offers a glimpse of postcard popularity: the official figures from the U.S. Post Office for the fiscal year ending June 30, 1908, cite 677,777,798 postcards mailed in this country. That was at a time when the total population of the United States was 88,700,000!

The majority of "old" picture postcards found in collections today date from the period 1902 to World War I. Post–World War I postcards are now surfacing in ever-increasing numbers as collectors look at more recent issues and as a new generation of "saved" items is recycled in the collectibles market.

WHAT MAKES A POSTCARD VALUABLE?

Postcards from the earliest pioneers to the current-issue designs can have value as collectibles. But not all postcards are "collectible" and fewer still are valuable! Collectibility depends largely on subject matter. Besides subject, factors affecting value include condition, age, scarcity, design, printing, originality, authenticity, and usage.

CONDITION IS IMPORTANT!

Postcards are made of fragile paper. After 50–100 years of handling and storage, it's no wonder that not all postcards have survived or are in "collectible" condition! The following are widely used definitions for grades of postcard condition.

Mint: a perfect card just as it comes from the printing press.

Near Mint: very, very light aging or discoloration from being in an album for many years; not quite fresh looking.

Excellent: no bends, creases, or rounded or blunt corners; may be postally used or unused with writing or postmark only on the address side; a clean fresh card on picture side.

Very Good: corners a bit blunt or rounded; barely detectable crease or bend that does not detract from overall appearance of picture side; writing or postal usage only in appropriate place; still very collectible.

Good: noticeable wear.

Fair: excess soil and wear; postal markings or writings may affect picture; collectible only if very scarce in any condition.

HOW RARE IS RARE?

The field of postcards is so large that it is very difficult to define relative rarity. The following terms offer only a framework for comparison:

Unique: only known surviving copy.
Very Rare: countable in the single digits.
Rare: seldom seen, even by expert dealers.
Scarce: desirable card; low frequency of its appearance may be partly a factor of high collector appeal.
Not Common: available, possible to acquire with some effort.
Common: easy to acquire.
Very Common: very easy to acquire.

COMMON TERMS IN DELTIOLOGY

This brief listing highlights some frequently used terminology.

Artist-signed: The artist's signature is reproduced with the artwork on the postcard. (Do not confuse with an original *autograph*, which is written on the postcard itself.)

Back: The address side of the postcard. Unfortunately, students of postal history and collectors of postal stationery use the term ''back'' for the picture side, as they assign more importance to the side with evidence of postal usage.

Chrome, chrome era: The first color postcards produced from color film and printed with the photomechanical halftone process. The beginning of the ''chrome era'' dates from the publication of the first series of Union Oil advertising postcards in 1939.

Continental size: Postcards measuring 4" × 6". Most of the postcards published today are continental size.

Deltiology: The collecting and study of postcards. The word *deltiology* comes from *delti* (little picture) and *logy* (the theory, science, or study of).

Divided back: Beginning in 1907 in the United States (earlier in Europe), the address side of the postcard (the back) was divided so that a message could be written on half of the space.

DRGM: Deutsches Reichsgebrauchsmuster—Design registered in Germany. (These initials appear on the backs of many early quality greetings and are often mistakenly assumed to be the name of a publisher.)

Fantasy: Postcard image created from the imagination.

Front: Picture side of a postcard.

Greeting: Postcard mailed as a greeting, in celebration of a holiday or special day.

Gruss aus: Literally, "Greetings from." The picture side of many pioneer views contained the words "Gruss Aus" with a location's name and one to three vignetted images of the location joined by loose scrollwork illustrations. A large area was left blank for a message.

Hold-to-light (HTL): A postcard that glows in certain areas or where a hidden image appears when held to the light. In die cut hold-to-lights, the surface layer has been cut away to reveal a thin colored layer of paper through which light can shine. In transparency hold-to-lights, an intermediate paper layer carries the hidden image.

Leather: Postcard made of leather; the design was burned in and sometimes coloring was added.

Linen, Linen era: Linens are typically printed in vivid colors on paper with a linen-textured surface, and they tend to have a shadowless airbrushed appearance. Linen-style cards were printed from the 1920s through the 1950s.

Novelty: Postcard made of unusual materials or with attachments, moving parts or cutouts. Hold-to-lights and leather postcards are two types of novelty postcards. Other examples are metal attachments or silk attachments.

Pioneer: A postcard mailed or produced prior to the effective date (July 1, 1898) of the Private Mailing Card Act of May 19, 1898. The early pictorial images had to be printed on government postal cards to benefit from the one-cent postcard rate. Before 1898, images privately printed on plain card stock required two-cents postage.

Postal card: A card supplied by the U.S. Postal Service, with postage imprinted on it.

Postcard: Privately printed mailing card for transmission of an open message at the first-class postcard rate.

Private mailing card (PMC): A card produced for mailing between 1898 and 1902. The Private Mailing Card Act of 1898 required the following wording to appear on the cards: "Private Mailing Card—Authorized by Act of Congress, May 19, 1898." Private mailing cards could be sent through the mail for one-cent postage.

Real photo: A picture postcard made directly on photographic paper with a "postcard" back. (See Section on "fakes"!)

S.A.S.E.: Self-addressed stamped envelope. Any query that does not include remittance but to which a reply is expected should be accompanied by an S.A.S.E.

Silk: Novelty postcard. These are applied silks—a layer of silk covers part of the picture, e.g., Santa's suit. The image may be printed on silk cloth, or the image may be embroidered silk or woven silk.

Standard size: Postcard measuring 3.5″ × 5.5″; most postcards published in the United States between 1902 and the 1960s were standard size.

Topical: Subject matter of postcard such as person, place, or object; may be real or imaginary.

Undivided back: Postcard published before 1907 (in the United States), when only the address could be written on the back of a picture postcard. The message had to be written on the picture side, and often a space was left blank for that purpose.

View: Postcard based on realistic images showing people, places, events, and things identified with a specific geographic location.

PHOTOGRAPHIC POSTCARDS:
BE ALERT FOR FAKES!

Postcards created directly from photographic negatives and printed onto photographic paper are termed "real photo" postcards. They are difficult to date when they have not been postally used. Fake backs as well as reproduced images may exist.

For some guidelines on production and usage periods for various postcard photographic papers, see *Prairie Fires and Paper Moons*, by Hal Morgan and Andreas Brown (Boston: David R. Godine, 1981), and "Dating Post-1920 Real Photo Postcards," by Ernest G. Covington (*Postcard Collector*, July 1986, pp. 26–28).

Demand for real-photo postcards is high. It is particularly important to study unused real-photo postcards carefully to be assured that the age of the card corresponds to the picture on the card! Some postcards have been reproduced by private photographers and are not marked appropriately. They should be added to a collection only if they are inexpensive and the image is needed.

POSTCARD VALUATIONS AND LISTINGS

In the following listings, all valuations offered are for postcards in excellent+ condition. For postcards in near mint to mint condition, add 20 percent–50 percent. For very good condition, deduct 20 percent. For good and fair condition, deduct 50 percent–90 percent.

All listings and illustrations are American subjects and publishers unless stated otherwise.

VIEW CARDS

View cards show realistic images of people, places, events, and things identified with specific geographic locations. View cards, as a group, are the most widely collected type of postcard in the United States today. However, as most collectors concentrate on postcards of their hometown and places they have lived or visited, any specific view is in demand by a limited number of people.

Views of major U.S. cities are the most common and the least valuable. Views of foreign tourist attractions have no collector value. Foreign view cards of topical interest are valued much like U.S. topics.

Pioneer view cards are scarce. Even the most frequently seen series of pioneer views—those published by the American Souvenir Card Co.—are valued at $15-$35 each.

Most common views, regardless of their age, are very moderately priced—at $3 or less. There can be great competition for less common views.

Pre-World War I small-town real photos are the most avidly sought after of view cards. It is not unusual for real-photo depot postcards to change hands at $35-$75. Values for some of the more bizarre subjects on real-photo postcards can exceed $100.

Here are some general guidelines for view cards:

State views (pioneer, common)	$15-$35
State views (pioneer, uncommon)	$20-$50
State views (1898-1920, common)	50¢-$3
State views (1898-1920, uncommon)	$2-$10
State views (real photo, 1898-1920)	$5-$20
State views (1920s-1960s, common)	25¢-$3
State views (1920s-1960s, uncommon)	$2-$8
State views (1970s-present, common)	25¢-$1
State views (1970s-present, uncommon)	$1-$2

Many views are collected more avidly for their subject matter than for their location. The listings that follow represent some of the more popular topical aspects of view cards.

Albertype: U.S. publisher of handtinted views. Undivided back   **$2-$15**
Divided back   **$1-$8**
Alligator border: c. 1909, published by S. Langsdorf, a series of 165 postcards numbered S500 to S664.   **$25-$35**
Breweries: 1898-1920   **$8-$25**
real photo   **$10-$80**
1920s-1960s   **$3-$20**
1970s-present   **$1-$5**

Carousels: 1898–1920   **$5–$10**
real photo   **$10–$50**
1920s–present   **$1–$20**
Court houses: 1898–1960s   **50¢–$5**
1970s–present   **25¢–$1**
Covered bridges: 1898–1960s   **$1–$5**
1970s–present   **25¢–$1**
Detroit: Publisher using the patented Phostint process. Views: PMCs–
1920s. (See also "Artist-signed, Schmucker.")   **$2–$20**
Horse-drawn commercial: 1898–1920   **$2–$20**
real photo   **$10–$100**
Horse-drawn commercial vehicle, real photo advertising: The sign on the
vehicle reads, "Dr. Ward's Remedies, Stock, Food." Postally used in 1907; the
printed message on the back reads: "I will call on you soon with a full line of
Dr. Ward's remedies. Yours truly, Olaf Gullikson, Waupaca, Wis." A superb
example. *(See photo 228)*   **$100**
Hotels: Pioneer   **$10–$30**
1898–1920   **$3–$10**
1920s–1960s   **$1–$5**
1970s–present   **25¢–$1**
Jos. Koehler: Publisher of a series of 113 die cut hold-to-light views of 11 American cities and locales, c. 1909   **$35–$60**
Large letter: 1898–1920   **$1–$5**
1920s–1960s   **$1–$5**
Lighthouses: 1898–1960s   **$1–$3**
1970s–present   **25¢–$2**
Main streets: 1898–1920   **$3–$10**
real photo   **$5–$25**
1920s–1960s   **$1–$3**
1970s–present   **2 5¢–$3**
Maps: **$1–$5**
Military bases: Buildings   **$1–$3**
Men   **$2–$5**
Women   **$2–$10**
1970s–present   **25¢–$2**
Mitchell: California publisher of views. PMCs   **$2–$10**
1902–1920   **$1–$5**
Fruit exaggeration   **$1–$3**
Motorcycles: 1898–1920   **$5–$20**
real photo   **$15–$50**
1920s–1960s   **$3–$35**
1970s–present   **$1–$5**
Railroad depot, in Pulaski, WI: Excellent real photo. Postally used
1909. *(See photo 229)*   **$35**
Railroad depots: 1898–1920   **$3–$20**
real photo   **$15–$75**
Restaurant interior. Corey's cafe, Las Vegas, NV. A fine example of linen
advertising. Note slot machines. Collectors also look for postcard racks as subject matter in interior views. Probably early 1950s.   **$8**

Photo 228. Postcard.
CREDIT: DIANE
ALLMEN
(See p. 446)

Photo 229. Postcard.
CREDIT: DIANE
ALLMEN
(See p. 446)

Restaurants: 1898–1960s	$1–$5
Interior	$2–$10
Diner	$20–$30
1960s–present	50¢–$2
Stadiums/arenas: 1898–1920 professional baseball	$15–$40
1920s–1960s	$3–$20
1970s–present	$1–$5
State capitols: 1898–1920	$3–$6
1920s–present	50¢–$3
Teich: Most prolific U.S. publisher, especially of views and advertising. 1898–1960s	$1–$20
Theaters: 1898–1920	$3–$10
real photo	$5–$35
1920s–1960s	$1–$5
1970s–present	50¢–$2
Tuck: Raphael Tuck & Sons, most prolific British publisher of postcard views, artist-signed, greetings and topicals. PMC views	$5–$15
Undivided-back views	$2–$10
Divided-back views	$2–$5

GREETINGS

Most of the vast quantities of postcard greetings mailed before 1920 have quite unremarkable designs. Often called "junk cards," they have little value for collectors. Some exceptions are described and illustrated here, and the listings represent desirable greetings produced in Europe for the American market, 1902–1920.

Ground-Hog Day and Labor Day postcards are rare and eagerly sought after. Halloween postcards and Santas are the most widely collected. Jewish New Year greetings also have a strong following.

April Fools' Day:	**$10–$20**
Christmas: No Santa	**$2–$20**
Hold-to-light	**$15–$35**
Easter: Sentimental	**$1–$5.**
Published by Paul Finkenrath, Berlin	**$3–$20**
Swedish witches	**$10–$25**
Ground-hog Day: c. 1909	**$150**
Halloween:	**$8–$20**
Signed Clapsaddle	**$8–$15**
Clapsaddle black background	**$30–$40**
Clapsaddle mechanical	**$150–$200**
Signed Freixas	**$35–$50**
Attributed to Schmucker	**$50–$150**

Halloween novelty greeting: Artist-signed Ellen H. Clapsaddle, published by International Art. The arm/hand holding the jack-o'-lantern is riveted to the card and rotates to cover the child's face. A scarce and desirable novelty mechanical, this is one in a series of 4 designs. The rarest is a black child **$200** White child. *(See photo 230)* **$150**

Photo 230 (left). Postcard.
CREDIT: DIANE ALLMEN *(See above)*

Photo 231 (right). Postcard.
CREDIT: DIANE ALLMEN *(See p. 449)*

Halloween, Winsch: Unsigned, attributed to Samuel L. Schmucker. The combination of glamour and Halloween on a Winsch greeting makes this a highly desirable postcard greeting. A scarce postcard. **$75**

Hanukkah:	**$5–$20**
Independence Day:	**$5–$15**
Signed Bunnell	**$25–$50**
Jewish New Year:	**$5–$50**
Labor Day: Published by Lounsbury	**$250**
Published by Nash	**$100**
Leap Year:	**$2–$10**
Lincoln's Birthday:	**$3–$20**
Memorial Day:	**$3–$20**
New Year's Day:	**$3–$20**
Santas:	**$5–$50**
Krampus	**$25–$50**
Die cut hold-to-light	**$100–$200**
Transparency hold-to-light	**$50–$100**
Mechanical	**$50–$250**
Uncle Sam	**$200–$250**
Uncle Sam hold-to-light (estimate)	**$1000–$1500**

Silk Santa. Delightful design of silk appliqué over Santa's robe and the reindeers' cinch. Not common. *(See photo 231)* **$50**

St. Patrick's Day: Sentimental	**$2–$10**
Comic ethnic	**$2–$5**
Winsch silk	**$20–$40**
Thanksgiving:	**$1–$10**
Valentine's Day: Sentimental	**$1–$5**
Comic insult	**$2–$8**
Signed Clapsaddle	**$5–$15**
Attributed to Schmucker	**$15–$50**
Washington's Birthday:	**$3–$20**
Year dates: pre-1901	**$30–$50**
1901–1903	**$18–$20**
1904–1906	**$12–$15**
1907–1908	**$8–$10**
1909–1913	**$5–$8**
After 1913	**$8–$10**

ARTIST-SIGNED POSTCARDS

Thousands of illustrators created work that was reproduced on postcards. Much of the work cannot be attributed to a specific artist. Only a fraction of identifiable work actually bears the artist's signature itself. Of this group, a relatively small number of artists are avidly collected for the artwork rather than for the subject. The following is a selective list of postcard artists popular with today's collectors.

Atwell, Mabel Lucie (English, 1879–1964): Children	**$5–$30**
Bishop, C. (American): Humor	**$3–$15**
Boileau, Philip (Canadian-American, 1864–1917): Glamour	**$15–$45**
Breger, David (American, 1908–1970): Military humor	**$5–$15**
Brown, Ken (American): 1980s humor	**$1–$5**
Browne, Tom (English, 1872–1910): Humor	**$5–$20**
Brundage, Frances (1854–1937): Halloween greetings published by Gabriel	**$10–$15**
Undivided back published by Tuck	**$30–$40**
Divided back	**$5–$20**
Bunnell, C.B. (American):	**$5–$40**
Burd, Clara M. (American): Children	**$5–$10**
Nursery rhymes published by Fralingers Taffy	**$25–$30**
Carr, Gene (American, b. 1881): Humor/greetings	**$5–$12**
Christy, F. Earl (American):	**$10–$15**
College Girl Series	**$70–$75**
Christy, Howard Chandler (American):	**$5–$15**
Jamestown Expo Navy and Army girl	**$70–$75**
Clapsaddle, Ellen H. (American, 1865–1934): Greetings	**$3–$20**
Suffrage-related	**$50–$100**
Halloween mechanicals	**$150–$200**
Clay, John Cecil (American):	**$10–$30**
Corbett, Bertha (American): Children	**$5–$20**
Davis, Jim (American): Garfield	**50¢–$2**
Dixon, Dorothy. Children	**$5–$20**
Drayton (See Wiederseim.)	
Dwiggins, Clare Victor (American, 1874–1959): Humor	**$5–$35**
Halloween series 981	**$25–$35**
Ebner, Pauli: Children/greetings	**$10–$30**
Fisher, Harrison (American, 1875–1934): Glamour	**$10–$30**
Advertising postcards	**$75**
900 series	**$75–$100**
Flagg, James Montgomery (American):	**$5–$15**
Gassaway, Katharine (American):	**$8–$20**
Gear, Mabel: Animals	**$5–$15**
Geary, Rick (American, b. 1946): Humor, National Postcard Week	**$1–$10**
Gibson, Charles Dana (American, 1867–1944): Glamour	**$8–$35**
Greenaway, Katherine A. (English, 1846–1902):	**$60–$100**
Greiner, Magnus:	**$8–$25**
Griggs, H. B.: Greetings	**$5–$20**
H.B.G. (See Griggs.)	
Hesse, Hermann: Humor	**$5–$10**
Humphrey, Maude (American):	**$8–$25**
Hutaf, August (American, b. 1879):	**$5–$15**
Josza, Carl (Art Nouveau):	**$300–$800**

Kaber, G. F.: "Lovely Lilly" $45–$50

King, Hamilton (American): Bathing beauties $8–$20
Coke advertising $300–$500

Kirchner, Raphael (Austrian, 1876–1917): Early glamour $80–$250
Later glamour $40–$100
Hold-to-lights $250
Invitation to join Paris postcard club $2000

Klein, Catharine. Advertising $10–$30
Alphabet $8–$15
Flowers $4–$15

Koehler, Mela (Austrian, 1885–1960): Glamour $30–$300
Art Deco $30–$100
Wiener Werkstätte $100–$300

Kokoschka, Oskar (Austrian, 1886–1980): $500–$3000

Larsen, Gary (American): Humor $1–$2

Larsen, L. H. "Dude" (American): Western humor $1–$5

Leyendecker, Joseph Christina (German-American, 1874–1951): Advertising
$15–$50

McCay, Winsor Zenie (American, 1869–1934): Little Nemo $25–$30

McGill, Donald (English, 1875–1962): Humor $5–$15

McMannus, George (American, 1884–1954): $20–$40

Moser, Koloman (Austrian, 1868–1918): $200–$500

Mucha, Alphonse (Czechoslovakian, 1860–1939): Glamour, advertising
$50–$500
Waverly Cycles advertising $12,500

Nystrom, Jennie (Swedish, 1854–1946): Greetings $5–$50

O'Neill, Rose (American, 1874–1944): Kewpies published by Gibson
$40–$60
"Klever Kards" published by Campbell Art $35–$75
Rock Island RR advertising $50–$75
Suffrage published by Campbell Art $150

O'Neill, Rose: "Votes For Our Mothers," artist-signed O'Neill. Copyright 1915
and published by National Woman Suffrage Pub. Co. A rare and exceptional
woman suffrage postcard. *(See photo 232)* $300

Opper, Frederick Burr (American, 1857–1937): Humor $5–$15

Outcault, Richard Felton (American, 1863–1961): Humor/advertising.
Buster Brown $10–$30
Rockford Watch calendars $15–$30
Yellow Kid $50–$75

Parrish, Maxfield (American, 1870–1966): $40–$100

Payne, Harry (English, 1858–1927): $10–$50
Military $10–$20

Penfield, Edward (American): $15–$20

Phillips, Coles (American, 1880–1927): $20–$40

Remington, Frederic S. (American, 1861–1909): Western art, early cards
$40–$80
Contemporary reproductions 50¢–$2

Robinson, Florence: $15–$20

Rockwell, Norman (American, 1894–1978): $20–$80

Russell, Charles Marion (American, 1865–1926): Western art $10–$25

Sager, Xavier (French): Early glamour $20–$50
Later glamour $20–$30

Schmucker, Samuel L. (American, 1879–1921): Glamour published by Detroit $150–$250
Halloween greetings published by Winsch $40–$150

Shinn, Cobb (American, 1887–1951): Humor/greetings $5–15

S.L.S. (See Schmucker.)

Smith, Jessie Willcox (American, 1863–1935): $15–$20

Twelvetrees, Charles H. (d. 1948): Humor $2–$12

Vargas (Peruvian, b. 1896 Joaquin A. Vargas Y Chavez): Glamour
$30–$50

Wain, Louis (English, 1860–1939): Cats and animals $30–$100
Paper doll cats $300–$400
Santa Claus cats $200–$250

Wall, Bernard E. (American, 1872–1956): Children/humor $3–$10
Suffrage $15–$25
Sunbonnets $12–$15

Wellman, Walter (American, 1879–1949): Humor $5–$40
Suffragette series $30–$40
"The Suffragette," artist-signed Walter Wellman. Card #4000 of the rare 16-card suffrage humor series. $40

Wiederseim-Drayton, Grace Gebbie. Cute kids $10–$40
Campbell Kids (unsigned) $60–$100

Photo 232 (left). Postcard. CREDIT: DIANE ALLMEN (See p. 451) Photo 233 (right). Postcard. CREDIT: DIANE ALLMEN (See p. 453)

TOPICALS

Advertising postcards of all ages are avidly sought and carry premium values. Entertainment, sports, world's fairs, and transportation all have large numbers of followers. There is great competition for political postcards and woman suffrage; carousels and amusement parks; Coca-Cola and McDonald's; and diners, Americana, and roadside attractions on postcards.

Actors/actresses: Pre-1920	$8-$20
1920s-present	$1-$10
Aircraft: Air meets pre-1920	$5-$35
Commercial 1920s-1960s	$1-$5
1970s-present	50¢-$2
Advertising 1920s-1960s	$2-$25
1970s-present	$1-$5
Amusement parks/carousels: Real photo	$10-$75
Pre-1920	$3-$25
1920s-present	$1-$10
Animals:	25¢-$5
Anti-Semitism:	$5-$75
Automobiles: 1900-1920	$1-$10
Advertising 1900-1920	$10-$50
1920s-1960s	$4-$30
1970s-present	$1-$6
Ballparks/stadiums: Pre-1920	$15-$40
1920s-1960s	$3-$20
1970s-present	$1-$5
Blacks: Pre-1920	$2-$20
Racist comics	$1-$5
Bull Durham tobacco advertising:	$30-$50
Cabbage Patch Babies: Pre-1920	$6-$12
Campell's Soup advertising: Vertical designs	$90-$100
Horizontal designs	$40-$50
Campell's Soup advertising: Rare vertical design. Unsigned Grace Wiederseim Drayton. *(See photo 233)*	$100
Century of Progress: Elusive series of real photos combining exposition buildings, pinups, and Art Deco graphics. Published by Arena. Scarce.	$8
Century of Progress Exposition: 1933-1934	$1-$10
Chautauqua: Pre-1920	$5-$25
Cherry Smash advertising:	$200-$300
Circus: Pre-1920	$5-$30
1920s-present	$1-$10
Coca-Cola advertising: Pre-1920	$300-$500
1920s-1960s	$10-$80
1970s-present	$1-$15

Coins: $2–$20

College Girls: Pre-1920 $5–$20

Columbian Exposition: 1893. Official issue from Goldsmith. Common. Printed on the back of a postal card, these designs are often found trimmed to conform to European mailing requirements. $15

Columbian Exposition, Chicago: Goldsmith pre-official $100–$150

Goldsmith official series $12–$18

Published by Koehler $40–$50

Cracker Jack bears: $25–$35

Dean, James: $1–$25

Dickens: $8–$15

Dionne quintuplets: 1930s–1940s $4–$20

1950s–present 50¢–$5

Disney: 1930s–1960s $2–$20

1970s–present $1–$3

Dressed bears: $8–$30

Roosevelt bears $15–$75

Dressed cats: Mainzer $1–$5

Wain $30–$250

Du Pont Powders advertising: Birds $50–$60

Dogs $60–$75

Elvis: 1950s–1960s $5–$15

1970s–present $1–$5

Embroidered silk: $8–$50

Ships $40–$100

Erotic: Pre-1920 $15–$30

1920s–1960s $10–$20

1970s–present $1–$10

Exaggeration: Pre-1920 $5–$75

Frogs $100

1920s–1960s $1–$15

1970s–present 50¢–$2

Fairy tales: Pre-1920 $5–$35

1920s–present $1–$8

Farm equipment: Pre-1920 $1–$25

1920s–present $1–$8

Garbo: Pre-1970 $10–$25

1970s–present $1–$10

Garfield: 1970s–present issued in U.S. 50¢–$2

Issued elsewhere $2–$5

Glamour: Pre-1920 $10–$400

1920s–1960s $3–$20

Gold Dust Twins soap advertising: $40–$60

Hershey chocolates: Pre-1920 $4–$8

1920s–present $1–$5

Hitler: $5–$20

Hold-to-lights:	$15–$200
Koehler views	$35–$60
Die cut Santas	$100–$200
Uncle Sam Santas (estimate)	$1000–$1500
Indians: Pre-1920	$2–$20
1920s–present	50¢–$5
Jamestown Exposition: 1907	$5–$25
Warships	$15–$30
Christy army/navy girls	$75
Illustrated postcard, embossed	$40–$50
Job cigarettes advertising:	$300–$500
Kellogg's: Pre-1920	$15–$20
1920s–present	$1–$8
Kewpies: Signed O'Neill	$35–$60
Kornelia Kinks:	$10–$12
Rare (kite in air, no 5¢)	$30
Lincoln:	$2–$25
Little Nemo:	$25–$30
Lord's Prayer:	$2–$15
Lovely Lilly:	$45–$50
Lovers/romance: Pre-1920	$3–$15
1920s–present	$1–$4
McDonald's: Early bulk-mail advertising for this fast-food pioneer. 1960s. An excellent advertising postcard. Scarce. *(See photo 234)*	$25
McDonald's advertising: 1950s–1960s	$10–$30
1970s–present	$1–$15
Men's fashion:	$1–$20
Metamorphic: Pre-1920	$30–$60

Photo 234 (left). Postcard.
CREDIT: DIANE ALLMEN *(See above)*
Photo 235 (right). Postcard.
CREDIT: DIANE ALLMEN *(See p. 457)*

Mickey Mouse: 1930s–1960s $3–$30
1970s–present $1–$5

Monroe, Marilyn: Pre-1970 $5–$20
1970s–present $1–$5

Motels: 1920s–1960s $2–$20
1970s–present   50¢–$5

Motorcycles: Pre-1920 $5–$50
1920s–present $1–$20

Nesbit, Evelyn: Pre-1920 $5–$15

Novelty attachments: $2–$30

Nudes: Pre-1920 $15–$30
1920s–present $1–$20

Ocean liners: Pre-1920 $3–$10
Advertising $10–$30

Passion play: 1890–1900 $10–$20
1910–present   50¢–$5

Paul Bunyan: 50¢–$8

Presidential campaigns: Pre-1920 $10–$250
1920s–1960s $5–$125
1970s–present $1–$5

Queen's doll house: $8–$10

Quiz Kids: $8–$10

Rail transport: Real photo $5–$35
Real photo depots $25–$75
Trains 1900–1960s $1–$10
1970s–present   25¢–$2

Roadside attractions: 50¢–$20
real photo $5–$40

Rock 'n' roll performers: 1960s–1970s $4–$10
Concert advertising $10–$20

Roosevelt, Theodore: $8–$50

Roosevelt bears: $15–$75

Route 66: $1–$5

Royalty: Pre-1920 $5–$30
1920s–present $1–$10

Sambo's restaurants advertising: $2–$4

Scouting: $1–$15

Space: 50¢–$5

St. Louis World's Fair: 1904 $5–$15
Cupples hold-to-light $30–$40
Inside Inn $100
Illustrated postal card, woven silk $100–$200

Stamps: Pre-1920 $10–$40
1920s–present $1–$10

State girls: Pre-1920 $8–$12
Silk $30–$40

Statue of Liberty: Pre-1920 $3–$20
1920s–1960s $1–$5
1970s– present $1–$2
Sunbonnet Babies: Pre-1920 $12–$20
Sunbonnet Baby: "Thursday," from the Days of the Week series. Published by Ullman, design by Bernhard Wall, copyright 1905. All of the Sunbonnet series are seductive examples of sexual-steering or gender-based activities. Common. $15
Swift's Pride soap advertising: Shadows $15–$20
Children, signed Wiederseim $30–$40
Titanic: $20–$200
Uncle Sam: Pre-1920 $5–$25
real photo $15–$100
1920s–1960s $3–$15
1970s–present $1–$5
Vin Fiz grape drink: Roger's Flight $75
Water craft: Pre-1920 $3–$10
1920s–present   50¢–$5
Waverly Cycles advertising: Signed Mucha $12,500
Woman suffrage: $10–$15
Cargill #111 $200
Signed Clapsaddle $35–$100
Signed O'Neill $150–$300
Women's fashion: $1–$20
World's fairs: Pre-1898 $15–$200
1898–1920 $5–$100
1920s– 1960s $1–$10
1970s–present   50¢–$2
World War I: $5–$20
World War II: $1–$20
World War II propaganda: Linen comic shows Uncle Sam spanking the naughty Japanese. Published by E.C. Kropp. Not common. *(See photo 235)* $8
Yellow Kid: Signed R. F. Outcault $50–$75
Zoos: 25¢–$5

INFORMATION SOURCES

Two specialty periodicals contain articles and advertising as well as up-to-date listing of U.S. postcard clubs and postcard shows. They are *Barr's News* (a weekly auction newspaper), 70 South Sixth Street, Lansing, IA 52151, and *Postcard Collector* (a monthly magazine), PO Box 37, Iola, WI 54945.

A bookstore that carries books about postcards and sells by mail is the Gotham Book Mart, 41 West 47th Street, New York, NY 10036.

The Curt Teich Postcard Collection at the Lake County Museum,

Lakewood Forest Preserve, Wauconda, IL, is administered by a department dedicated solely to postcards, their study and preservation.

WHERE TO BUY POSTCARDS

Two specialty postcard periodicals, *Barr's News* and *Postcard Collector*, offer a national market for buying and selling new and previously owned postcards by mail. Almost every town in the country offers brand-new postcards at its variety stores, gift shop, drugstore, newsstand, or souvenir shop. At least one shoebox-full of previously owned postcards is available at almost any antique store in the country! Flea markets are another good source. Nearly one hundred active U.S. postcard clubs offer a casual environment for buying, selling, and trading postcards of all ages. The briskest buying-selling activity is found at annual (or more frequent) postcard shows held in many major cities. Dealers and collectors may travel considerable distances to participate in this competitive environment.

WHERE TO SELL POSTCARDS

Previously owned postcards can be sold to antiques dealers, to dealers at postcard shows, or directly to other collectors if the person decides to become a dealer. *Barr's News* and *Postcard Collector* are two primary sources for selling directly or for finding information on dealers, clubs, and shows. A national postcard dealer association with an annual directory is the International Federation of Postcard Dealers, John McClintock, Executive Secretary, PO Box 1765, Manassas, VA 22110. Send a self-addressed business-size envelope for a free list of dealers, and contact the ones in your area.

Silhouettes

Advisor: **ALDA LEAKE HORNER**

Alda Leake Horner is an author, consultant, and dealer. She is the author of The Official Price Guide to Linens, Lace, and Other Fabrics *(New York: House of Collectibles, 1991). She may be contacted at Whitehall at the Villa Antiques and Fine Art, 1213 East Franklin Street, Chapel Hill, NC 27514; (919) 942-3179.*

Silhouettes were very popular in America from the late 18th century until about 1850, when the daguerreotype was developed. It was a very inexpensive method for the average person to have a profile likeness made of himself or herself or family members.

A silhouette is a profile paper cutting, usually a negative in black laid down on a white background. Some referred to them as "shades," as Benjamin Franklin did when he wrote home from London in 1767, sending his family a small copy of one, presumably reduced from a life-size cutting. The earliest shade cutting was made by placing the subject between a wall and a candle and using the outline of the shadow to reproduce a likeness. This eventually gave way to greater artistic skill by a silhouettist who clipped the likeness without means of a shadow outline or the use of a pantograph.

The term *silhouette* was derived from Etienne de Silhouette, a minister of France, who was reputed to be rather frugal with his money and that of his country as well; he cut shades as an inexpensive pastime. The popularity spread quickly throughout France, England, and the United States. Many notables in this country became subjects, including George Washington and his family, who were cut many times.

Those who took up this pastime eventually used several methods: hollow cutting, mechanical tracing, and painting, as well as cutting by sight (this method was referred to as "scissorgraphics"). In the hollow-cutting method the likeness was cut from white paper and then laid down on a black background of paper or occasionally fabric. Mechanical tracing used a pantagraph, an instrument to copy, enlarge, or reduce the likeness. Some silhouettes were fully painted and embellished with additions of ink. Frequently, the silhouette was cut from black paper and laid down on white. Often the black paper remaining, which ordinarily was discarded, was put on white paper or silk, with the features added in ink or color.

459

Silhouettes took many forms: single profile busts, family groups, and full-length figures. Some show various backgrounds and landscapes done in ink or engraving, often showing a design of the person's interest or profession.

Among the many artists who became popular in this country were Augustin Edouart, of France, the Peale family, and William Bache, all highly sought after today. Look for the stamp of "Peale Museum" or "Peale." Also look for signatures that include "cut by mouth" or "cut by foot." Some artists in the United States were physically handicapped and learned to use scissors by various means, giving them an outlet for their talents as well as a new means for financial support. A recent ad in a trade paper pictured a rare silhouette of a man signed "Cut by M. Honeywell with the mouth"—it was only 2 inches by 4 inches.

Many collectors are interested in one category, such as famous people cut during their lifetime, signed examples, children (very collectible because fewer were made), or full-length figures or groups. The most important consideration when beginning a collection is to select the subject that appeals most to you. Go to museums and legitimate antiques shops and study the various techniques, quality, and sharpness of cutting; ask about age and whether the item is original or a later copy made years after the subject had passed away. It is difficult to know if a frame is original because many silhouettes were not framed in the beginning but tucked away in the family Bible until a later date. If an example is a later rendering but appealing to you, then it is collectible, but the value may not be that of an original.

A silhouette should always be examined out of the frame if it represents a major investment. The edges of the paper covered by the frame should be lighter because they have not been exposed to various lighting conditions. All of the exposed paper should show signs of age and be proper for the period of supposed execution. Study the outline of the subject to determine if it was executed by mechanical means—often a drawn line or indentation will show close to the cut area. Silhouettes made by mechanical means frequently do not have the sharpness and artistic freshness of those done freehand.

Silhouettes enjoyed a renewed popularity for a brief time during the late 1930s and 1940s in this country and in France. Most silhouettists were itinerant and appeared at resorts and in department stores. Many of their works are now coming on the market through estate sales and auctions, and this makes putting together a collection less prohibitive than older examples.

TRENDS

With the tremendous interest in American folk art, this form of expression is enjoying a renewed life of its own. There are still a large number of the older shades available, many undervalued, but most of the signed examples by known artists can be expensive, and they will most likely continue to appreciate in the future.

Some current artists are now advertising their services. One recent ad stated: "Hollow cut silhouettes are rendered by hand using small scissors. No copying devices used." Now is the time to add your family shades to those of your ancestors or to start a new family tradition. In time these family treasures will be just as collectible.

QUALITY KEY

Good Quality: cut crisply with clean outlines from good quality stock, showing recognizable likeness of subject.

Very Good Quality: showing all of the above and extra attention to details such as hair style, eyelashes, and clothing.

Superior Quality: exhibits finest scissoring, shows personality of subject, charm and visual impact. Uses finest materials, and signed either by artist or studio stamp or both. Appropriately framed.

CONDITION KEY

Average Condition: shows fading and foxing. Fabrics, if used, have begun to fray. Paper shows splits, tears, and soil. Damaged or missing frame.

Good Condition: shows age on edges when removed from frame. Clean, near-mint condition, little damage, which may be restored.

Fine Condition: mint or near mint, all elements bright and clean, shows proper age to back and to obverse edges when removed from frame. Original frame or appropriate to period, in excellent condition.

Children 7″ × 15.6″ Cut and mounted c. 1842 United States
Silhouette of 3 children with toys, cat, and dog; inscribed "Elizabeth 7 years/ Fay/ Henry, 9 years/ Blaze/ Alice, aged 6″; signed "Aug. Edouart pint. 1842"; cut and applied to watercolor and ink background.
Superior Quality/Fine Condition $2310 (A)   **$2000–$2500**

Couple 1838 United States
Portrait of Mr. and Mrs. Thomas Cottrell Scholefield; he is standing and has a cane, she is seated; framed.
Very Good Quality/Good Condition $495 (A)   **$400–$700**

Family Cut 1942 United States
"The Cary Family" portrait; Col. Thomas Cary, Mary, Richard and Emma Cary; framed; Boston. *(See photo 236)*
Very Good Quality/Good Condition $615 (A) **$500–$800**

Family 12″ H × 19″ W Hollow-cut 1840–1850 United States
Mother and father facing each other, with 3 children in between; in gilt wood frame; some discoloration.
Very Good Quality/Average Condition $825 (A) **$700–$1000**

Family 4.5″ H × 4″ W Hollow-cut 1845–1865 United States
Six members of the Swain family, Concord, MA; 3 have pencil detail (not all by the same artist); similar frames have some veneer damage; backs of frames have been marked with family names.
Good Quality/Average Condition $495 (A) set **$400–$600**

Gentleman 1840–1850 United States
Gentleman in top hat, cane, and umbrella; in antique gold frame; by Samuel Metford, an Englishman working in Charleston and New York. *(See photo 237)*
Very Good Quality/Good Condition $440 (A) **$350–$600**

Gentleman 9.75″ × 7.5″ Cut and mount 1840–1860 United States
Silhouette of a gentleman in a library, American school; cut and mounted to watercolor and ink background; unsigned; restored.
Good Quality/Average Condition $220 (A) **$200–$350**

Gentleman and lady 7.25″ × 6.25″ Hollow-cut 1850–1860 United States
Pair; with ink detail; lady also has bits of green and pink watercolor in dress; black paper backing; minor stains; framed.
Good Quality/Average Condition $330 (A) pair **$300–$500**

Group 2.75″ × 3.88″ Cutout 1840–1850 United States
Group of 4: 3 children and 1 lady; unsigned; each cut out, backed with fabric and enhanced with watercolor; framed.
Very Good Quality/Good Condition $2200 (A) set **$1800–$2500**

Groups, duplicate 11.75″ H × 9.25″ W 1830–1845 United States
Two pages from August Edouart's collection of duplicates (he always made 2 copies); each has 9 silhouettes of men and women with good detail; in narrow black frames.
Superior Quality/Good Condition $934 (A) **$800–$1500**

Man 5.36″ H × 3.88″ W Hollow-cut 1840–1850 United States
Young man, in ebonized frame.
Good Quality/Average Condition $154 (A) **$125–$225**

Photo 236 (left). Silhouette. CREDIT: NEAL AUCTION CO. *(See above)*
Photo 237 (right). Silhouette. CREDIT: NEAL AUCTION CO. *(See above)*

Man 3.75″ × 2.5″ Hollow-cut 1840–1850 United States
Silhouette of John Blake, Jr.; hollow-cut head and upper shoulder, painted jacket lapel and waistcoat collar, printed label identifying sitter below; backed with black silk; watercolor and ink on paper; framed.
Good Quality/Average Condition $660 (A) **$600–$800**

Man in top hat 5″ H × 3.5″ W 1865–1885 United States
Hollow-cut; minor tear; old gilt frame.
Good Quality/Average Condition $83 (A) **$75–$250**

Memorial 6.25″ × 6.88″ c. 1850 United States
Paper cutout memorial with tombs, trees, and serpent on green coated paper; tree trunk also has 2 reverse silhouettes of faces; stains; gilt frame.
Good Quality/Average Condition $357 (A) **$350–$500**

Officer 4.5″ Dia. 1885–1900 United States
Eglomise; portly officer; reverse painted on convex glass; round alabaster frame; paint is flaked.
Good Quality/Average Condition $75 (A) **$50–$150**

Old woman 6.25″ × 4.88″ Cut and paste 1840–1850 United States
Cut silhouette of an old woman; black cut-out is frayed, and pigment is worn and crazed; black lacquered frame is crazed to match.
Good Quality/Average Condition $49 (A) **$45–$150**

Old woman 8″ H × 6.75″ W 1865–1885 United States
Cut and paste; old woman with elaborate coiffure; white paper ground is replaced; oval pine frame is refinished and has a chip.
Good Quality/Poor Condition $55 (A) **$150–$300**

Woman 5″ H × 4.5″ W Hollow-cut 1840–1850 United States
Young woman; minor stains and faint embossed stamp (probably Peale Museum); molded pine frame.
Good Quality/Average Condition $165 (A) **$125–$225**

Woman 5.75″ × 4.75″ Hollow-cut c. 1850 United States
Silhouette of young woman; embossed seal "Peale's Museum"; stained; in frame.
Good Quality/Average Condition $137 (A) **$125–$300**

Woman 6.6″ × 5.75″ Cut and mount 1850–1860 United States
Cut silhouette of a young woman with gold highlights; old black lacquered frame with gilded trim; frame has some damage.
Good Quality/Good Condition $93 (A) **$90–$200**

BIBLIOGRAPHY

Carrick, Alice Van Leer. *Shades of Our Ancestors*. Boston: Little, Brown.

Comstock, Helen (ed.). *The Concise Encyclopedia of American Antiques* (pp. 545–565). New York: Hawthorne Books.

Jackson, Mrs. E. Nevill. *Silhouettes, A History and Dictionary of Artists*. New York: Dover Publications. Unabridged re-publication, 1981.

Rifkin, Blume, J. *Silhouettes in America, 1790–1840: A Collectors' Guide*. Burlington, VT: Paradigm Press, 1987.

Silver

The listings in this chapter are arranged by the following subcategories: COIN SILVER, CONTINENTAL SILVER, ELECTROPLATE, SHEFFIELD PLATE, STERLING FLATWARE, STERLING HOLLOWWARE.

Advisors: **WILLIAM PILLSBURY and ROBIN MICHEL**

William Pillsbury and Robin Michel (Pillsbury-Michel, Inc.) are nationally recognized museum curators and shop dealers. They can be reached at 2620 S. Shepherd #174, Houston, TX 77098; (713) 522-4790.

IDENTIFYING ANTIQUE SILVER
© *David P. Lindquist*

Of all antiques, silver is perhaps the easiest to understand, date, and evaluate, and yet many aspects are utterly misunderstood by customers and dealers. Terminology is grossly misused by the trade—not by silver specialists but by dealers and auctioneers who also sell silver in addition to other objects. When you finish reading this article, you will be able to avoid those terminology pitfalls.

ALLOY OR PLATE

There are only two basic types of silver—alloy and plate. An alloy is a mixture of silver with a base metal of *copper* (and traces of other metals). Plated pieces are items made of a base metal and then disguised by a layer of silver.

Silver in its pure form lacks tensile strength; it will not hold its shape. To strengthen it, people learned thousands of years ago that they needed to melt it together with copper, the result having considerable tensile strength. The most common alloy found in this country is sterling silver, followed closely by coin silver. It is the alloy content that creates some of the greatest confusion and deepest prejudice in the field of silver collecting. The alloy called sterling is simply a combination of 925 parts of silver and 75 parts of copper out of every 1000 parts of metal. It is the standard of English alloy most common since the late 1300s. Sterling has been the common standard in the United States since the 1860s.

There is nothing sacred about the sterling standard! Other standards have been used constantly throughout the world. In our own country the common name for our standard until the 1860s was coin silver. Coin silver is approximately 900 parts of silver, a fraction less pure than sterling. This was very, very approximate. Tests of coin silver in this country show that even the same silversmith might make one batch of silver at 900 standard and another at 875 or 915. The levels were very inconsistent. Pieces of important American silver have been tested and found to be as low as 700 level of purity. It is *not* purity that affects value in coin silver, as we shall see.

On the Continent the standards vary considerably. French silver is either second standard (.800) or first standard (.950). German silver is most often .800, but other standards are found. Other countries use standards ranging from .700 to .835 to .9479. The range in Europe is enormous.

EXTRINSIC VERSUS INTRINSIC VALUE

One of the deepest prejudices that permeates the dealer and retail population is the idea that "only sterling is real silver" and everything else is suspect—except for coin silver. This is hogwash. Silver should be valued on the basis of workmanship, age, rarity, and appropriateness of weight when compared to similar pieces. These are all *extrinsic* values, values *added* to the metal by outside sources and processes.

The alloy content—the *intrinsic* value—should have no bearing on collectibility and value unless you plan to melt the piece. All pieces of silver alloy have a verifiable intrinsic value—a quantity of pure silver can be melted out of a piece and exchanged for the currency of the realm. This intrinsic value fluctuates due to international trade pressures. It has little to do with true value except for silver that has no extrinsic value.

A heavy teaspoon of sterling silver has only 5 cents more intrinsic value than an equally heavy .800 silver teaspoon. It seems pretty strange to me to pay a huge premium for a sterling piece, as Americans usually do. Silver pieces should be judged on the basis of extrinsic qualities, not scrap value.

THREE TYPES OF PLATED SILVER

Silverplate is the second type of silver. There are only three types of silverplate: French, or close, plate; Sheffield plate; and electroplate. The terminology of plating is grossly misused by dealers and terribly misunderstood by the public.

The earliest form of plating is termed French, or close, plate. This is a process identical to gold leaf in which pure silver is burnished onto a cold base metal object already totally formed. It is a laborious and expensive proposition. Because it is pure silver, not an alloy, it wears away very quickly. It was, however, a method used extensively during the period of Sheffield plating (1750–1850) for touching up areas of plated pieces, as it was an ideal method of hiding small cracks, seams, pits, and the like.

Another common use for this method was to cover steel items with silver, especially knife blades, skewers, scissors, and so forth. These pieces had to be forged of steel to create a tempered blade of useful strength. Silver leaf applied to the steel hid the steel, creating a more beautiful item. Unfortunately, you cannot heat such objects greatly because the silver will run off, and you cannot let them become damp because the steel will rust and bubble the silver.

The most common type of antique silverplate is called Old Sheffield plate, Sheffield plate, rolled plate, or fused plate. All are terms for the same process, which was discovered about 1740 and was in common use within ten years. The accidental discovery that sterling silver and copper are identically malleable led to this process.

In Sheffield plate a sheet of silver *alloy* is fused on one or two sides of an ingot of copper. It is then rolled until sheets of thin copper with very thin silver alloy are ready for working into useful and decorative objects. The important point here is that this is a hand and machine process requiring considerable time and skill. The pieces created were identical to their solid alloy cousins but far cheaper, as only a tiny amount of the valuable silver alloy was needed for each piece.

IDENTIFYING SILVER ALLOYS: ENGLAND, SCOTLAND, AND IRELAND

One of the reasons British silver—the product of England, Scotland, or Ireland—has been forever collectible is the ease of identification. All British silver is *hallmarked*, and every detachable section of a piece is partially hallmarked. A teapot will carry a full set of hallmarks on the body, and the hinged lid will carry a full or partial set as well. A muffineer will have a full set on the body and a full or partial set on the detachable top. Every piece of a chatelaine may be marked, or only the hook may be marked.

What are these hallmarks? They are symbols, originally of guild or town marks, to indicate the origin of a gold or silver piece. First required in France in 1275, a system was adopted in England about 1300. It was at the Hall of the Goldsmiths' Company in the City of London that the first English assaying and marking was done—thus, "hallmark."

Hallmarks on British silver will always have a purity mark, a city (assayer's) mark, a date mark, and usually a maker's mark. In addition, certain other symbols are found during various periods and special celebration years.

CITY MARKS

(1)   (2)   (3)   (4)

Shown above are *examples* of city marks: (1), the crowned animal, is called "leopard's head crowned" and was used from 1497 to March 27, 1697, and again from 1719 through 1820; (2), London mark, was used after 1820; (3), "lion's head erased," was used between March 27, 1697, and 1719 as the symbol of London; (4), the present mark, is the "leopard's head" or "leopard's head uncrowned." Each city where an assay office is located has its own separate mark. Learn to recognize them: there are only half a dozen common ones.

DATE MARK

Of equal importance to identification is the date mark, allowing precise dating of a piece of British silver. Every twenty years a new series of date marks is begun at each assay office, always in a different script and background block than the series before and alternating upper/lowercase every twenty years. Again, with a book showing all hallmarks (always organized by city) you can quickly date any piece. The hallmark books are available in small handbook size—great for dating and worthless for makers—and in complete guides with all known makers. Go and buy Seymour B. Wyler's *The Book of Old Silver*, Crown Publishers, New York, which is reissued regularly. It's all you really need for British silver.

PURITY MARK

Yet another essential mark for identification is the purity mark. British silver is made in two standards—sterling and Britannia. Sterling is .925 quality, and Britannia is .958.

Shown is the lion mark associated with the sterling standard and the symbol of Britannia associated with the Britannia standard. The lion is found standing, reclining, and facing various ways at various times with various assay offices. Whether the lion is rampant, passant (shown and most common), or guardant, it always indicates the sterling standard. Furthermore, this mark is essential and will always be found on even the smallest piece (assuming a tax cheater didn't make the piece).

The purity mark in Edinburgh was the assay master's initials until 1759 and a thistle after that time. The major Irish center was Dublin, where Hibernia symbolized the city and a crowned harp indicated sterling purity.

MAKER'S MARK AND SOVEREIGN'S HEAD

Yet two more marks may be found: a maker's symbol (his, her, or their initials in some format) and the head of the reigning monarch. The maker's marks are listed year by year in the major guides such as Wyler's. The sovereign's head was used from 1784 to 1890 in England, from 1784 to 1890 in Edinburgh, from 1819 to 1890 in Glasgow, and from 1807 to 1890 in Dublin. It is also found in Jubilee and Coronation years, making those years particularly collectible.

While there are many problems involving fakery to be aware of in the collecting of English silver, the majority of those will concern only the advanced collector buying major pieces by rare makers. Collectibility and value are greatly influenced by the maker, whether English, Scottish, or Irish (the first being generally less expensive), and by condition, provenance, and rarity.

SILVER IN THE UNITED STATES

Coin silver was the standard until about 1860–1870 in the United States. It is a varying level of purity approximating .900. In addition, in the 1850s several fine firms led by Tiffany and Company began an early adoption of the sterling standard, Tiffany often using a .950 standard.

Coin silver is readily recognized by one of two marking characteristics. Most frequently, only a maker's name or initials will be on the piece.

MOOD, JOSEPH
Charleston, S. C. .... 1806 { I MOOD I MOOD J MOOD J.*P.MOOD }

Occasionally the name is accompanied by a city name. Also, one may find pseudo-hallmarks or fake hallmarks, alone or with a name. These hallmarks were designed to make purchasers in the 18th and 19th centuries believe they were getting something of equal quality to imported English sterling silver, and they will make no sense if you try to research them in an English hallmark book!

To research American coin silver you can start with one book, then add two others later as you budget them into your library. The essential is *Kovel's American Silver Marks* by Ralph and Terry Kovel (Crown Publishers, New York, 1989). This includes line drawings, as above, and an extensive list of names and cities. Two other invaluable resources are *Marks of American Silversmiths in the Ineson-Bisell Collection* by Louise Conway Belden (University of Virginia Press, 1980) and *Marks of American Silversmiths, 1650–1900* by Robert Alan Green (revised; Robert Alan Green Publishers, 214 Key Haven Road, Key West, FL 33040). The Belden book has a photograph of every mark in the Winterthur collection and lists variations as well. Green's book does a great job with pseudo-hallmarks. It also has a good introduction to all details of coin silver.

American coin silver prices are greatly influenced by maker, rarity, and regionalism. The rarest pieces are 18th-century hollowware, and 18th-century flatware is far from common. Nineteenth-century hollowware has a vast price range; most often prices are little more than for comparable sterling pieces of the late 19th and 20th centuries. Nineteenth-century spoons are very, very common and worth about what modern sterling pieces are worth. Forks and knives are rare, especially sets.

Regionalism can have a great influence on price. Southern silver brings an enormous premium because of its original rarity combined with the loss of vast quantities during the Civil War and Reconstruction. As a rule of thumb, pieces sell best the closer they are to the city in which they were made.

AMERICAN STERLING SILVER

After 1870 all American silver alloy was sterling standard. The purity was and is the same as in England—.925. The major mark always found is the word *sterling*. In addition, a maker's mark, a patent date, the weight, and a year mark will sometimes be found. The vast majority of pieces have the maker's mark.

Research on American sterling silver makers is easily pursued in *Encyclopedia of American Silver Manufacturers* (3rd ed.) by Dorothy T. Rainwater (Schiffer Publishing, West Chester, Pennsylvania, 1986). This superb book covers the post-1865 period and includes manufacturers *and* the small shops still producing hand-wrought silver.

CONTINENTAL SILVER

On the Continent silver and gold have been equally important socially and decoratively. From early times, crowns, scepters, hollowware, and jewelry were wrought from gold and silver. The French invented the hallmark concept. Because of the profusion of nations and cities of importance—unlike backwater England and America—the amount of silver produced is enormous, and the alloy varied greatly from nation to nation, city to city, maker to maker.

The range of Continental silver purity is generally .800 (the most plentiful) to .950. The four nations producing the most silver, and whose products are most commonly found, are Austria, France, Germany, and Russia.

The Austro-Hungarian Empire used the rank of the commoners, which had four weights and corresponding marks, shown below.

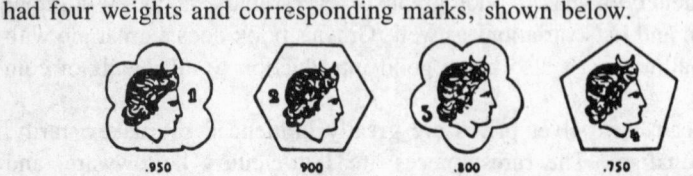

.950   900   .800   .750

French silver is of two standards: First Standard of .950 and Second Standard of .800. The purity mark for second standard is shown on the left, for first standard on the right.

.950

In addition, city marks and maker marks are also found on almost all French pieces.

German alloy silver is almost always .800 and carries a purity mark of "800" or a standard mark such as
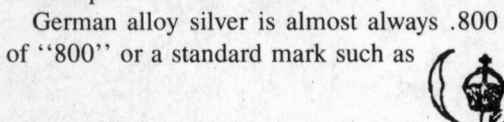
.

In addition, city or state marks and makers' marks are generally present.

Russian silver is most often marked with an "84" (zolotniks), which translates to a standard of .875. Additional standards are "88" for .9166 purity and "91" for .9479 purity. City marks are usually found, Moscow and St. Petersburg being the most common. A maker's mark is almost always included.

The most useful book—in addition to some help in Wyler's book, cited earlier—is *International Hallmarks on Silver*, collected by Tardy (English translation; Paris, 1981). This book will identify nearly every Continental city, country, and purity mark, as well as full dating information. For identification of makers you must buy books for each country, written in the language of that country and sold only in that country. Good luck!

It is, of course, the difficult identification process for European silver that has suppressed the market value *except* in the countries of origin. It also means that if you want to own beautiful silver to use and enjoy, you can buy Continental pieces for a fraction of the cost of American or English goods. A good pair of early-19th-century French candelabra can be purchased for $1800 to $2500. The same thing from England is $12,000 or more (possibly much more—in the $100,000 range for rare makers). American examples are not available at any price. So if you want to live in champagne style on a beer budget, buy Continental silver!

IDENTIFYING ANTIQUE SILVERPLATE
© *David P. Lindquist*

OLD SHEFFIELD PLATE

The social background for the discovery of the methods of plating on copper used in the Sheffield process is interesting. It was a time of rising expectations for an emerging merchant class distinct from the upper class in England. These newly wealthy families wished to live with silver luxuries befitting their new status. Unfortunately for them, solid silver hollowware objects were totally beyond their means. Only the aristocracy could afford sterling silver tureens, vegetable dishes, salvers, and the like. But that didn't keep the merchants from wanting those objects. In 1742 a discovery credited to Thomas Boulsover of Sheffield led to the Sheffield plating business.

Boulsover discovered that when sterling silver is fused to copper the two metals are identically malleable. You could pound out a piece and have the silver and copper retain the same geometric ratio to one another as the metal was worked. This led rather quickly to the development of a very large industry based on the fusing of ingots of sterling silver to one or both sides of ingots of copper—small ingots of the costly sterling and large ingots of cheap copper. The new merchant class—and down-on-their-luck members of the aristocracy—could now have terrific pieces of hollowware that appeared to be made of sterling silver but were in fact made of thinly veiled copper!

The keys to identifying Sheffield silver are strictly related to the methods of manufacturing it and to the need to disguise the underlying copper. Because the silver, not the labor, was the expensive part of the process, large pieces of Sheffield silver were tinned rather than silvered on unseen surfaces. Areas such as the inside of a meat cover, the bottom of a large tray, even the bottom of a large tureen, will often be tinned, not plated. When you find such a tinned area on a piece, you know for a fact that it is old Sheffield plate, unless it's a tinned bottom added to electroplate with rolled edges. Then you have fake Sheffield!

Another major characteristic of Sheffield plate is that all exposed edges must be covered with a rim of silver; otherwise the copper middle layer would show through, giving away the fact that the piece is not solid sterling silver. This is referred to as a wrapped edge. One of two processes was used: either the applied silver decorative motif was bent over the edge, or a thin band of silver was wrapped and fused around the edge. In both cases you can get a fingernail virtually under this edge. You will also find a seam where the ends of the strip of silver or applied moldings meet.

In the 18th and 19th centuries most families purchasing large pieces of hollowware had their family crest engraved on the item. If you were to engrave a piece of Sheffield plate, the copper would show because of the thinness of the silver layer. Engraving shields or plaques were therefore inlaid into the side of a piece in the appropriate spot for engraving. If you blow either at the engraved area or at the appropriate areas on an unengraved piece, the engraving shield will "jump out" at you. This is caused by the differing rates of condensation on the solid silver plaque versus the plated areas. Any piece with an engraving plaque will invariably turn out to be Sheffield plate.

On any item formed out of a cylinder of plated metal, such as candlesticks, pots, vases, and so on, the metal was joined together by crimping or dovetailing. This left an obvious seam, often with a little copper showing. Originally, this was carefully burnished, but with wear and aging you can often spot such seams. The presence of these seams is a guarantee that the items are old Sheffield.

There were many fascinating processes involved in the making of fused plate, well beyond those discussed here. They do not, however, leave any telltale marks that specifically identify a piece of Sheffield plate as opposed to solid silver or electroplate. You can learn most readily about those processes by reading the major books that detail all of the processes involved in the creation of fused plate.

The value determinants of Sheffield silver are similar to those for all antiques, but with some unique exceptions. Aesthetic factors are identical to those for similar pieces of sterling silver. Provenance and rarity also have an impact on value. The originality of the pieces making up a multipart piece, such as a covered vegetable or entrée dish with separate water reservoir, is as crucial to value on Sheffield pieces as it is to all other sterling or electroplated items. Anything made in multiples and of more than one part had each separate piece numbered in series. Thus, you would have cover, dish, and undertray number 1, number 2, and so on. Because the pieces were not always perfectly compatible, the numbering system allowed servants to get the correct cover on the correct base. If the pieces no longer are 3 to 3 or 1 to 1 but are cover 3 with base 4, then an incestuous relationship has developed, and the value is no more than 75 percent of a completely original piece. Marriages of work by two makers would have even less value, perhaps only 25 percent of the value of a perfect piece.

Approximately 90 percent of old Sheffield silver pieces are completely unmarked. In fact, the lack of marks can often make one first think an item might be a piece of Sheffield plate! In the very early days a few makers put on pseudo-hallmarks to suggest the high quality of their goods. The guilds of silversmiths sent up an immediate howl, and Parliament quickly established severe penalties for the hallmarking of plated wares. As the companies making Sheffield plate grew stronger, they began to lobby for some allowable marking system, and the end result was that either a name or a small symbol could be used as an identification device. Because marked pieces are rare, a premium of 24 percent or more adheres to a marked piece over an identical unmarked piece.

Finally, of utmost importance to value is the level of originality of the actual plating. Old Sheffield silver is often in remarkably good condition, with little or no bleeding (copper showing through). This is because it is the unique property of Sheffield plate that it is sterling silver over copper, not pure silver, as is the case with both close plate and electroplate. Remember—sterling is an alloy, and the point of making an alloy is that it is hundreds of times more durable than pure silver. Whereas pure silver wears away quickly with regular polishing, sterling wears away very, very slowly.

Related to this condition problem is the question of electroplating old Sheffield plate. Never do it unless the condition is so bad that it has no value as an antique. Electroplating adds a process totally foreign to the early piece, and it covers the mellow sterling with the more harshly colored pure silver. Values of overplated pieces are about half that of an original piece in good to fine condition.

ELECTROPLATED SILVER

In approximately 1840 the Elkington Company of Birmingham, England, began production of electroplated silver. They had cleverly bought up all patent rights related to the experimentation then taking place throughout England in addition to their own work. This far simpler method—by which a completed base metal object is suspended in a vat, a charge introduced, and pure silver fused onto all surfaces—quickly put the old method out of business.

Electroplated wares are coated with a thin layer of pure silver, which, as noted earlier, wears away far more quickly than an alloy would. The base metal also impacts on adherence, the preferable base metals being copper, brass, or nickel-brass alloy (commonly called nickel silver). Britannia and other similar white metals are inferior because they lose their shape more readily and because they provide a poor base for the silver to adhere to.

Electroplated items lack all of the distinctive aspects discussed in the Sheffield section. They are commonly marked by their markers and usually have marks indicating the quality of plating and the type of base metal. Marks commonly seen include EP (electroplate), EPNS (electroplated nickel silver), EPBM (electroplated Britannia metal), A-1, quadruple plate, triple plate, and so on. As with all silver, value is influenced by age, rarity, desirability of style and type, provenance, condition, and additionally by base metal used.

Because they were competing with the old Sheffield platers who had earned wonderful reputations for fine quality, electroplating companies have often used the word "Sheffield" in their company names or as a descriptive adjective for their plating. Thus, one sees on objects such words and phrases as "Sheffield, England," "Sheffield Silver on Copper," "Sheffield Plate," "Sheffield Silver," and so on. In each and every instance the presence of the word "Sheffield" on a piece of silver is your absolute, iron-clad guarantee that the piece is electroplate, having nothing in common with the magnificent pieces of genuine old Sheffield plate!

RECENT TRENDS

Once again the adage remains true—blue chip areas of collecting remain strong through thick and thin. In a generally skittish market deeply affected by a weak dollar, silver has been remarkably strong. Oriental, English, Continental, and American silver—all areas have been very solid. And it has nothing to do with raw silver value, which has reached new lows in the past twenty-five years.

FAKES ALERT

The detection of fraudulent or fake silver is not easy to describe. As with any object of value, whether furniture, paintings, or silver, the greater the value, the higher the chance of deception. Very early silver, items made by important names such as Paul deLamerie, Hester Bateman, Paul Storr, Paul Revere, and Joseph Richardson, Jr., can be suspect until examined by an experienced dealer, appraiser, or collector. Desirable makers' marks may be lifted from insignificant pieces and inlaid on important unmarked or newly fabricated forms. Fake punches exist for important American and English smiths' marks. Early seal-top and apostle spoons have been cast from originals, as have important serving pieces from such desirable patterns as Whiting's "Lily." The greater the experience and access to experience the collector may have, the less chance exists that he or she will be deceived.

CONDITION KEY

Condition is a very important aspect of collecting silver and determining the value of a given piece. Condition is strictly the physical well-being of a piece and should not be confused with its originality of design. The following four condition standards for silver should clarify these designations in the price guide:

Fine Condition: retains original surface appearance, not buffed to mirror finish; outstanding patina with fine color and appearance; little, if any, wear; no visible repairs; engraved or applied decoration, if any, in crisp state; no surface disturbance such as dents, deep scratches, obvious removal of initials; clear makers' marks, if any.

Good Condition: relatively unblemished surface appearance; any wear visible should be normal to the piece depending on function and age; no obvious repairs such as blobs of solder, poorly reattached finials or handles; no thin metal areas from overbuffing or initial removal; no disturbing dings, dents, or gouges; markings, if any, should be clear or legible.

Average Condition: acceptable surface appearance but may require removal of minor dings, dents, or blemishes; minor repairs visible on close examination but do not mar the overall appearance of the object; easily repairable problems of minor nature; markings, if any legible enough for identification.

Poor Condition: unacceptable surface appearance marred by abuse, obvious and ineptly done repair work, serious dents, deep scratches, tears or breaks in the metal; markings, if any, may or may not be legible.

QUALITY KEY

Quality, too, is another important aspect in the collecting and appraisal of a piece of silver. This standard may sometimes be subjective depending on individual taste, but at no time does it infringe on condition. Quality is strictly related to the design and stylishness of the piece and is basic to value—bad form cannot be overcome! The following three levels of quality are fairly standard within the antiques market:

Good Quality: a piece with average or below average design, weak proportions, passable workmanship but no better; obviously ordinary in concept and boring in appearance; any combination of the above.

Very Good Quality: a piece by a good or fine craftsman but lacking in real excitement or "pizzazz"; competent design and manufacture but not imaginative.

Superior Quality: a piece of good-quality craftsmanship or manufacture with perfect proportions, good weight and balance; one that could pass as a standard for similar items; a piece that "speaks" or "sings" because of its successful overall appearance and quality. Excellent provenance, such as royal, presidential, or fine period coat of arms, if traced, improves the value.

The majority of pieces the collector may see are not of superior quality. When applied to a piece of pattern flatware, the use of that designation means imaginative design, heavy weight, good balance, and finish. In other words, the above three designations are used to grade items only within their own form.

COIN SILVER

Butter knives 6.5″ L Rococo Revival 1845–1865 United States
Pair, master butter knives; pointed oval thread style with foliate sprigging around edges; by T. Steel, Hartford, CT.
Very Good Quality/Fine Condition $225 (D)   **$100–$250**

Dessert spoons 1800–1830 China
Four; fiddle, thread, and shell; Canton, China, by Wang Shing; engraved initials "CCT" script; heavy, fine quality.
Superior Quality/Fine Condition $400 (D)   **$300–$500**

Gravy ladle 6.25″ L 1845–1865 United States
Plain fiddle; by William H. Ewan, Charleston; heavy.
Superior Quality/Fine Condition $250 (D)   **$200–$400**

> It's Southern—in Charleston it would have sold for $400.—*DL*

Ladle, sauce 9.25″ L Renaissance Revival 1845–1865 United States
Wood & Hughes, NY; high-relief medallion female bust on oval, foliate-trimmed plaque; 3.5 oz. troy.
Superior Quality/Fine Condition $575 (D)   **$350–$650**

> Medallion pieces have become increasingly popular as pristine style pieces representing the Renaissance Revival period.—*DL*

Mustard ladle   4.75″ L   1830–1845   United States
Plain fiddle; by Nathaniel Olstead (1785–1860), Farmington and E. Hartford, CT.
Very Good Quality/Fine Condition $58 (D)   **$35–$70**

Punch ladle   13.25″ L   Plain fiddle   1830–1845   United States
Script engraved initials on handle, by Robert and William Wilson, Philadelphia.
Superior Quality/Fine Condition $350 (D)   **$250–$400**

Sugar tongs   4.75″ L   Plain fiddle   1830–1845   United States
Plain fiddle with round tip ends; by Smith & Sill, New York City.
Very Good Quality/Fine Condition $79 (D)   **$50–$90**

CONTINENTAL SILVER

Box, sugar or tea   5.5″ H × 7″ W   1845–1865   Continental
"800" silver; rounded oval; rope-motif feet with rope-motif handle; small geometric decoration in bands around base and lid; gilt interior.
Very Good Quality/Fine Condition $600 (D)   **$450–$750**

Cigarette case   4.36″ × 3.12″   Deco   1925   Germany
Relief Pegasus on lid; gilded interior; by K. Huebler.
Superior Quality/Fine Condition $275 (D)   **$200–$350**

Claret jugs   9.25″ H   1890   Germany
Globular threaded-glass bases with silver tops and handles; hinged lids with ball thumbpieces; glass and silver perfect; .800 standard; pair.
Very Good Quality/Fine Condition $1250 (D)   **$800–$1600**

Jewel box   4.88″ H × 5.75″ W × 4.25″ D   Rococo Revival   1850–1880   European
Marks undecipherable; silver near coin standard (88–90%); repoussé decoration, flattened ring handle (hollow).
Very Good Quality/Fine Condition $475 (D)   **$225–$500**

Ladle, punch   1851   Russia
Moscow; with Imperial double mark for items made for the Kremlin.
Very Good Quality/Fine Condition $650 (D)   **$600–$900**

Pot, chocolate   6.75″ H   c. 1870   Continental
Small; "800" silver; with widely spaced ribbed lines on bulbous body; ivory insulators on hinged lid and handle.
Very Good Quality/Fine Condition $500 (D)   **$450–$650**

Poultry skewer   7.75″ L   1780   France
Plain, tapered small skewer with loose rings on ends; by G. M., city unknown; French, 1st standard.
Very Good Quality/Fine Condition $235 (D)   **$150–$275**

Sauceboat   Repoussé   1885–1900   Germany
"800" silver; repoussé floral and swag designs.
Very Good Quality/Fine Condition $285 (D)   **$275–$375**

Wine tasting cup   3.5″ Dia.   1838   France
1st standard mark; double snake handle.
Very Good Quality/Fine Condition $280 (D)   **$250–$375**

Wine tasting cup   3.5″ Dia.   1838   France
Snake handle and grapevine motif; 1st standard. *(See photo 238)*
Superior Quality/Fine Condition $360 (D)   **$300–$450**

Wine tasting cup   3.75″ Dia.   1920   France
1st standard mark; E. Puiforcat, Paris.
Superior Quality/Fine Condition $156 (D)   **$125–$195**

ELECTROPLATE

> Condition note: One should demand the highest quality finish condition in
> electroplate. Replating—if the design is not muddied in the process—should
> have no negative impact on value. Replating is simply reapplication of the
> original process and does not thereafter alter the originality of the piece.
> —DL

Bride's basket   4″ H × 8.5″ W   Neoclassical style   1865–1885 England
Fluted form, beaded handle, oval.
Very Good Quality/Fine Condition $165 (D)   **$125–$185**

Butter spreaders   4.75″ L   1890–1910   United States
Set of 6, with mother-of-pearl handles, floral ferrules, plated steel paddle blades.
Very Good Quality/Fine Condition $135 (D)   **$90–$150**

Candelabra   18″ H × 13.5″ W   Adam style   1850–1860   England
Pair; 3-light candle arms (removable) on Corinthian columns, with removable
central finial; fine-quality electroplate in late-18th-century style.
Very Good Quality/Fine Condition $2600 (D)   **$1400–$3200**

Candlesticks   10.75″ H   Rococo Revival   1850–1860   England
Pair; cast decoration, with scrolled and foliate bases, stems, and nozzles; bo-
beches follow lines of base. *(See photo 239)*
Very Good Quality/Fine Condition $700 (D)   **$500–$800**

Chafing dish   10.75″ H   1920–1940   United States
International; heavy plate on heavy copper base; unusually good quality; with
alcohol burner.
Superior Quality/Fine Condition $300 (D)   **$125–$350**

Coffeepot   11.25″ H   1845–1865   England
Heavily constructed with engraved banding, cast quatrefoil finial, faceted spout;
plated handle with insulators; by W. G. & Co.
Very Good Quality/Fine Condition $295 (D)   **$200–$300**

Dessert stand   17″ H   Rococo Revival   1845–1865   England
Unmarked but superb quality; 2 glass circular shelves with plated metal frames,
on central stem connected to circular base; grape-motif cast decoration.
Superior Quality/Fine Condition $1200 (D)   **$700–$1400**

Egg set   7.5″ H   Rococo Revival   1860–1880   England
4 cups, 4 spoons; sides of egg cups with chased and crimped floral decoration;
4 Scottish sterling egg spoons with engraved crests (Edinburgh, 1836); by Walker
& Hall, Sheffield.
Superior Quality/Fine Condition $450 (D)   **$325–$600**

Fruit bowl   13″ L   1870–1890   England
Silverplated frame with engraved decoration on platform; ball feet; holding finely
cut and scalloped-edge glass oval bowl.
Superior Quality/Fine Condition $375 (D)   **$200–$400**

Muffineer   7.25″ H   Queen Anne style   1940–1960   England
Sheffield-made, octagonal. *(See photo 240)*
Very Good Quality/Fine Condition $85 (D)   **$35–$90**

Photo 238 (left). Wine tasting cup. CREDIT: WHITEHALL AT THE VILLA, CHAPEL HILL, NC. *Photo 239 (right). Candlesticks.* CREDIT: ROBIN MICHEL *(See pp. 477, 478)*

Photo 240 (left). Muffineer. CREDIT: ROBIN MICHEL. *Photo 241 (right). Quaich.* CREDIT: ROBIN MICHEL *(See pp. 478, 480)*

Photo 242. Candlesticks.
CREDIT: ROBIN MICHEL *(See p. 481)*

Mug   5.25″ H   Rococo style   1845–1865   England
Electroplated, gilded interior in c. 1750–1760 style, with fruit and foliage "berry spoon" repoussé work on sides.
Very Good Quality/Fine Condition $195 (D)   **$100–$225**

Pitcher   7.75″ H   Rococo Revival   1845–1865   England
Marked "Tavern Plate"; heavy white metal, silverplated, with engraved floral, foliate, and scroll designs; interior gilded; heavy, solid cast handle.
Very Good Quality/Fine Condition $125 (D)   **$75–$150**

Quaich   3″ H × 7.25″ Dia.   1890–1900   Scotland
Heavy quality bowl marked by Scottish retailer Cameron of Kilmarnock; finely pierced handles in early-18th-century style. *(See photo 241)*
Very Good Quality/Fine Condition $175 (D)   **$75–$175**

Relish dish   6.5″ H × 6.5″ Dia. × 8.75″ L   1900–1910   England
Two-part; plated frame with loop handle holding 2 half-oval molded glass dishes.
Very Good Quality/Fine Condition $110 (D)   **$75–$130**

Salver   18″ Dia.   Renaissance Revival   1865–1885   England
Round, footed salver with openwork border of masks of gods and goddesses and other Roman mythological scenes.
Superior Quality/Fine Condition $2400 (D)   **$1500–$2500**

Tray   16″ W × 21″ D   1885–1900   England
Oval, footed, and silverplated tray.
Very Good Quality/Fine Condition $400 (D)   **$300–$550**

Vase   8″ H   1930–1940   United States
Finely cast circular foot in Danish style; flared lip with cast dot-dash decoration; heavily made; by Wallace.
Superior Quality/Fine Condition $55 (D)   **$25–$65**

SHEFFIELD PLATE

CONDITION KEY

Fine Condition: little or no bleeding plus the other characteristics for all silver.

Good Condition: bleeding is evident but not obtrusive—it simply shows the antiquity of the piece; other characteristics the same as above.

Average Condition: very noticeable bleeding, which begins to detract aesthetically.

Poor Condition: little silver repairs; suitable only for electroplating or sale as a decorative "copper" piece (electroplating will restore decorative value but *not* antique value).

Candle snuffer   10.25″ L   Neoclassical   1780–1800   England
With stand; original silverplate; tray with piercing and bright-cut engraving at ends; tinned-over copper bottom; snuffer scissors with reeded decoration; unusual to find in excellent condition.
Superior Quality/Fine Condition $450 (D)   **$200–$600**

Candlesticks 10.5″ H Adam 1780–1800 England
Pair; weighted bases and stems, pierced work in capitals, removable bobeches, original wood bases; replated over copper. *(See photo 242)*
Superior Quality/Fine Condition $1200 (D) **$800–$1200**

> In original state with applied sterling silver, these sticks would have brought $2200. Electroplating of Old Sheffield is always damaging to value—see my article at the beginning of this section.—*DL*

Candlesticks 12″ H Adam 1790 England
Set of 4; weighted, with felt covering on square bases; plating in perfect condition (protected by years of lacquer); rare set of 4.
Very Good Quality/Fine Condition $2300 (D) **$1600–$4000**

Entrée dishes 7″ H × 12″ W × 9″ D 1800–1830 England
Pair of good old Sheffield plate covered entrée dishes, in 4 parts, by Blagden, Hodgson & Co. Each rectangular; edges with foliate scrollwork; flat dome lid. Bottoms with separate warming compartment; raised on ornate scrolled feet; replated.
Very Good Quality/Average Condition $715 (A) **$1200–$2500**

Tea urn 16.25″ H × 14.5″ W Regency 1820–1830 England
Old Sheffield plate; lion's-paw feet on square base; lobed body; egg-and-dart and gadrooned borders; acanthus-leaf decoration on handles and finial; 1 finial on pouring handle is replaced.
Very Good Quality/Good Condition $1350 (D) **$900–$1500**

Wine cooler 9.50″ H 1800–1830 England
By Matthew Boulton Manufactory; campagna form with a rim of gadrooning and shells; with foliate loop handles; on pedestal base. Engraved with noble crest.
Very Good Quality/Good Condition $825 (D) **$800–$1200**

Wine coolers 11″ H × 5.25″ Dia. Regency 1800–1830 England
Pair of highly ornate coolers by J. Watson and Son; marked by maker; original coats of arms; pristine, unretouched condition.
Superior Quality/Fine Condition $11,000 (D) **$8000–$12,000**

Wine trolley 13.75 L Neoclassical 1790–1800 England
"Jolly Boat" wine trolley; rare 3-bottle boat form with original wood and baize cloth bottom, working wheels; engraved at stern "Jolly Boat," where plating is slightly worn.
Superior Quality/Good Condition $3000 (D) **$1600–$3500**

STERLING FLATWARE

Berry spoon 8.25″ L Rococo Revival 1823 England
Handle with chased floral and foliate decoration (applied on old English spoon), bowl chased with repoussé in fruits and foliage; bowl gilded; London, Robert Rutland.
Very Good Quality/Fine Condition $145 (D) **$125–$200**

Child's set "King's" pattern 1845–1865 England
Three-piece (knife, fork, and spoon) set; in fitted box.
Very Good Quality/Fine Condition $225 (D) **$125–$225**

Fish set 1885–1900 England
Walker & Hall ivory-handled fish service for 12 with sterling ferrules and plated blades; original mahogany case (cracked); service condition is perfect.
Very Good Quality/Fine Condition $850 (D) **$600–$850**

Fork, pickle 3.75″ L 1939 United States
Relish or pickle fork; "Prelude" pattern by International.
Very Good Quality/Fine Condition $22 (D) **$14–$26**

Fork, sardine 4.25″ L Arts and Crafts 1900–1910 United States
By Shiebler, New York; hammered surface with stylized short tines and gold appliqué, Greek-style male medallion head at handle end; "mixed metals."
Superior Quality/Fine Condition $240 (D) **$200–$300**

Forks, dinner 7.5″ L 1874 United States
Set of 12 Gorham "Raphael"-pattern dinner forks.
Very Good Quality/Fine Condition $395 (D) **$250–$425**

Forks, fish 1900–1910 United States
Four individual forks in "Chantilly" pattern by Gorham.
Very Good Quality/Fine Condition $260 (D) **$200–$300**

Forks, ice cream 4.75″ L 1910–1930 United States
Set of 6; half-spoon and fork combination; Whiting, now part of Gorham; "Louis XV" pattern.
Very Good Quality/Fine Condition $295 (D) **$225–$300**

Knives, dinner 9.88″ L Reed & Barton 1901 United States
Original silverplated steel blunt-end blades in perfect condition; "Six Fleurs" pattern; 6 knives.
Superior Quality/Fine Condition $475 (D) **$300–$500**

Ladle 14.25″ L 1800–1830 United States
Handle terminus with monogram; by Allen Armstrong, Philadelphia; 8 troy oz.; simple.
Very Good Quality/Good Condition $357 (A) **$300–$375**

Ladle, gravy 1930–1950 United States
"Strasbourg" pattern; monogrammed; vermeil bowl.
Good Quality/Fine Condition $70 (D) **$60–$90**

Ladle, punch 1885–1900 United States
Engraved; vermeil bowl.
Good Quality/Good Condition $160 (D) **$125–$175**

Service for 12 Modern 1955 Denmark
"Sparta" pattern, by Cohr, Copenhagen; 60 pieces.
Very Good Quality/Fine Condition $2100 (D) **$1200–$2500**

Spoon 1873 England
Presentation spoon, London.
Good Quality/Good Condition $85 (D) **$60–$95**

Spoon, mote 6.88″ L 1760 England
Unusually large and fine, with elaborately pierced bowl and barbed end; London, by William Turner.
Superior Quality/Fine Condition $325 (D) **$275–$350**

Spoon, serving 1930–1950 England
Ornate, large lobed bowl.
Good Quality/Good Condition $55 (D) **$45–$75**

Spoon, serving 8.75″ L 1893 United States
Heavy Art Nouveau "Chrysanthemum" pattern by Gurgin, now Gorham.
Superior Quality/Fine Condition $225 (D)   **$175–$275**

Spoon, serving 9.5″ L Art Nouveau 1903 United States
Large-bowl serving spoon; heavy, high style; "Frontenac" by International.
Superior Quality/Fine Condition $200 (D)   **$150–$250**

Spoon, serving 9.25″ L c. 1935 United States
Stieff "Rose" large-bowl serving spoon; Baltimore, MD.
Superior Quality/Fine Condition $110 (D)   **$85–$150**

Spoons, dessert 7.25″ L 1896 Denmark
Set of 6; threaded upturned Old English style; Copenhagen, by Michelson.
Superior Quality/Good Condition $275 (D)   **$200–$325**

Spoons, dessert 7.25″ L 1871 United States
Set of 12; rare Gorham pattern, "Corinthian."
Very Good Quality/Good Condition $350 (D)   **$200–$400**

Spoons, salt 3″ L George III 1750–1780 England
Pair, master salt spoons; upturned end, late-Hanoverian style by Hester Bateman;
maker's mark with lion passant (usual).
Superior Quality/Fine Condition $325 (D)   **$175–$375**

Sugar shell 7″ 1930–1950 United States
Rose motif; shaped bowl; by Wallace.
Good Quality/Fine Condition $55 (D)   **$40–$60**

Sugar tongs 5.5″ L Adam 1785 England
Bright-cut engraved decoration; slender oval grips; London, by Hester Bateman.
Superior Quality/Fine Condition $375 (D)   **$200–$400**

STERLING HOLLOWWARE

Bottle tag 2.25″ H × 1.5″ D George II 1700–1750 England
Butterfly-like escutcheon backplate form with engraved grape and vine decoration and "white wine" in Roman engraving; with chain; by John Hugh LeSage.
Superior Quality/Fine Condition $350 (D)   **$250–$400**

> A very early example—most are late George III to Victorian—thus a very high price for a very small item.—*DL*

Candlesticks 12.5″ H George III 1772 England
Set of 4, each of Corinthian column form with a stop-fluted shaft and cavetto-form base ornamented with raised husk, ribbon, and paterae devices; weighted, minor dents; John Carter, London. *(See photo 243)*
Very Good Quality/Good Condition $6000 (A)   **$5000–$7500**

Candlesticks 11.5″ H George III 1775 England
Set of 4, each of Ionic column form with a stop-fluted shaft and resting on a cavetto-ornamented base, with sash drawn through bow-knotted corner loops; John Carter, London.
Very Good Quality/Fine Condition $8000 (A)   **$5000–$8000**

Candlesticks   10.5″ H   Rococo Revival   1905   United States
Set of 4; hand-chased and repousséd with roses, each pair by different craftsmen
with slight variations but made at same time; weighted, silver bottoms, heavy-
gauge silver; S. Kirk., Baltimore; rare in set.
Superior Quality/Fine Condition $7400 (D)   **$5000–$8500**

Card case   3.75″ W × 4.73″ H   Rococo Revival   1889   England
Fine engraved foliate and floral decoration, in original silk-lined leather case;
Birmingham, 1889, maker C.C.
Superior Quality/Fine Condition $250 (D)   **$150–$300**

Chamber taperstick   Neoclassical style   1904   England
Made in Chester by GN & RH; with original extinguisher; gadrooned border
and removable bobeche; all pieces marked.
Very Good Quality/Fine Condition $395 (D)   **$300–$550**

Coffeepot   7.25″ H   1900   United States
Made by Shiebler; slightly concave faceted sides, wood handle.
Very Good Quality/Fine Condition $200 (D)   **$125–$300**

Coffeepot   10″ H   Tiffany   1900–1920   United States
Tapering quatrefoil form with alternating panels of basketweave and cartouche
motifs; 36 troy oz. *(See photo 244)*
Superior Quality/Fine Condition $2750 (A)   **$1800–$3000**

Compotes   7.5″ H   Jensen   1925–1932   Denmark
Pair; flared bowls with grape bunches hanging down; spiral stem, vintage detail,
model #263B; rim imperfection; not monogrammed; George Jensen; 37 troy
oz.
Superior Quality/Average Condition $6500 (A)   **$4500–$7500**

Cup   12.5″ H   George III   1765   England
Two-handled cup and cover; baluster body with gadrooned foot and domed cover
with bud finial, leafy double-scroll handles; engraved coat-of-arms in rocaille
and motto; maker "IS" London; body dents; 48 troy oz.
Very Good Quality/Average Condition $2750 (A)   **$3000–$5000**

Cup, covered   16″ H   Georgian style   1899   United States
Two scrolled handles, baluster body, and domed cover, repoussé with spiral
flutes and scrolling acanthus; inscription; Howard and Co., New York; 70 troy
oz. *(See photo 245)*
Superior Quality/Fine Condition $1800 (A)   **$1500–$3000**

Egg set   8″ H   Oriental   1845–1865   China
Chinese export; egg set and stand with 6 cups and spoons on wirework stand,
spoons and cups marked "KHC"; Khecheong, Canton; 28 troy oz.
Very Good Quality/Fine Condition $2600 (A)   **$2000–$3500**

Epergne   16.5″ H × 16.5″ W   Rococo Revival   1910   England
Central vase retains bracket supports for 3 removable baskets and vases; totally
disassembles for cleaning and storage; fine pierced decoration; Sheffield, 1910,
by Harris Atleins; 72 troy oz.
Superior Quality/Fine Condition $4400 (D)   **$3600–$5000**

Letter holder   5″ H × 6.25″ W   Rococo Revival   1890   European
Cast decoration, hand-chased work, no legible marks.
Very Good Quality/Fine Condition $125 (D)   **$85–$150**

Lorgnette   Victorian   1900–1910   United States
Prince-nez style; folding into overlapping lenses; short handle, long chain.
Superior Quality/Fine Condition $75 (D)   **$40–$80**

Photo 243. Candlesticks. CREDIT: WILLIAM DOYLE GALLERIES *(See p. 483)*

Photo 244 (left). Coffeepot. CREDIT: SKINNER, INC., BOLTON, MA.
Photo 245 (right). Covered cup. CREDIT: SKINNER, INC., BOLTON, MA *(See p. 484)*

Photo 246. Dressing mirror. CREDIT: GROGAN & CO. *(See p. 486)*

Loving cup 7.25″ H × 5″ Dia. 1884 England
Three hollow "C" handles, 3 ball feet, molded banding at edge; London, by
J.A. and T.S.; 21 troy oz.
Superior Quality/Fine Condition $650 (D)   **$400–$725**

Mirror, dressing 17.5″ H Victorian 1895 England
Cartouche form; border pierced and chased with putti and satyrs amid rocaille
and floral scrolls, surmounted by putti bearing cartouche; purple velvet easel
back; William Comyns, London. *(See photo 246)*
Superior Quality/Fine Condition $1210 (A)   **$1200–$2400**

Mustard pot 2.6″ H Regency 1818 England
Boat shape with ball feet, pierced thumbpiece; blue glass liner (original); Lon-
don, William Bateman.
Very Good Quality/Good Condition $375 (D)   **$300–$500**

Mustard pot 2.75″ H Rococo Revival 1885 England
Circular with double-scroll handle, domed lid, carved thumbpiece, engraved dec-
oration, gilded interior; London, 1885, by J.A. and T.S.
Very Good Quality/Fine Condition $275 (D)   **$200–$400**

Mustard pot 3.12″ H Rococo Revival 1890 France
Finely chased floral and foliate decoration, cast handle and scroll feet; gilded
interior; Paris.
Superior Quality/Fine Condition $325 (D)   **$225–$400**

Pitcher, water 10″ H Repoussé 1905 United States
"Rose Repoussé" pattern, by Schofield, Baltimore; hand-chased, fine quality.
Superior Quality/Fine Condition $2200 (D)   **$1400–$2500**

Ringholder 3.36″ H × 4.12″ Dia. Repoussé 1890 United States
Unmarked, evidently a custom order; hand-chased and repoussé work in tradi-
tional Baltimore style; rare form.
Superior Quality/Fine Condition $275 (D)   **$225–$400**

Salt and pepper 4.25″ L 1935 Japan
Pair; in the shape of perfectly crafted mandolins with strings; .950 standard.
Superior Quality/Fine Condition $125 (D)   **$85–$140**

Salt and pepper 3″ H 1935 Japan
In form of Japanese water buckets; salt cellar with clear glass liner and sterling
salt spoon (American); pepper with bottom filling slide; highly detailed; .950.
Superior Quality/Fine Condition $175 (D)   **$100–$200**

Salt and peppers 3.25″ H 1935 Japan
Set of 4 finely detailed pagodas with slide for filling on bottom; .950 standard.
Superior Quality/Fine Condition $275 (D)   **$160–$300**

Salt and peppers 4.75″ H Baltimore Rose 1910 United States
Set of 4; deep repoussé rose decoration, finely chased and finished, cast feet;
Baltimore, by Heer-Schofield.
Superior Quality/Fine Condition $650 (D)   **$350–$700**

Salver 12.6″ Dia. George II 1752 England
Scroll and scalloped rim, scrolled feet, contemporary engraved heraldic crest
(worn down by polishing), inscription on reverse; surface scratches, illegible
maker's mark; 35 troy oz. *(See photo 247)*
Very Good Quality/Average Condition $1700 (A)   **$1500–$3500**

Photo 247 (left). Salver. CREDIT: SKINNER, INC., BOLTON, MA. *Photo 248 (right). Tankard.* CREDIT: SKINNER, INC., BOLTON, MA *(See pp. 486, 488)*

Photo 249.
Tea service.
CREDIT:
GROGAN & CO.
(See p. 489)

Photo 250. Wine jug.
CREDIT: SKINNER, INC., BOLTON, MA *(See p. 489)*

Salver 16.5″ Dia. George II style 1932 England
Heavy cast and chased edge with shells, gadrooning in style of Paul de Lamerie (c. 1735); London, by Atkin Bros; 1932; 84 troy oz.
Superior Quality/Fine Condition $2300 (D)   **$2000–$2300**

Shaving mug 3.6″ H × 3″ Dia. Whiting 1880 United States
"Heraldic" pattern; gilded interior, strainer compartment opposite handle; hollow cast handle in double "S" curve.
Very Good Quality/Fine Condition $250 (D)   **$100–$275**

Shell dish 9.25″ W × 8.5″ D 1957 United States
Scallop-shell form; dated; Gorham; weight: 14 oz. troy.
Very Good Quality/Fine Condition $300 (D)   **$125–$300**

Snuff box 3.25″ W × 2.25″ D George II 1750–1780 England
Silver-mounted cowrie shell; unmarked, with finely engraved (wear) English armorial with unicorn on silver lid; inside with original gilding.
Superior Quality/Fine Condition $500 (D)   **$300–$750**

Soup cups 1900–1930 United States
Set of 12 Lenox white porcelain and gold banded; sterling frames by Watson; pierced, with handles.
Superior Quality/Fine Condition $575 (D)   **$400–$650**

Sugar and creamer 4.25″ H creamer Stieff 1942 United States
Heavy, hand-chased "Rose" pattern by Stieff Co., Baltimore.
Superior Quality/Fine Condition $550 (D)   **$400–$650**

Tankard 8″ H George III 1788 England
Domed molded cover with pierced thumb rest (repaired); baluster body and molded foot with scrolled handle; maker "BM" (not traced), London; 26 troy oz. *(See photo 248)*
Very Good Quality/Average Condition $3250 (A)   **$3000–$5000**

Tea caddy 5.25″ H × 4.5″ W × 2.75″ D Adam 1794 England
Bright-cut engraved decoration on flat lid; glass with typical shallow-cut fluting and banding; good documentation for Newcastle glass; by John Langland, Newcastle.
Superior Quality/Fine Condition $2100 (D)   **$1400–$2500**

Tea service Kettle 13.5″ H Oriental 1900–1910 Japan
Kettle on stand, teapot, tea caddy, creamer, and sugar; each globular form with repoussé design of dragon, signed by maker; marks "SM" and impressed characters and seal; dents; 93 troy oz.
Very Good Quality/Good Condition $3250 (A)   **$3000–$4800**

The QUALITY KEY measures the stylishness and collectibility of an antique.

Good Quality: Exhibits standard characteristics of the object.

Very Good Quality: A more desirable example because of above-average workmanship and design.

Superior Quality: Exhibits nearly every known feature found on such items, with workmanship and design of the highest quality.

Tea service   Teapot 9.25″ H   Federal   1800–1830   United States
Teapot, covered sugar, creamer, waste bowl; each of lobed oval form on pedestal
foot with die-rolled borders and pineapple finials; unmarked; some shapes out
of true. *(See photo 249)*
Good Quality/Average Condition $1265 (A)   **$1200–$2500**

Tea set   Teapot 5.5″ H   George IV   1822   England
Hot water kettle and stand, teapot, sugar, and creamer; each heavily repousséd
with scrolling flowers and foliage; scrolling legs with espagnolette capitals; William Reid, London.
Very Good Quality/Good Condition $4100 (A)   **$3500–$5000**

Teapot   12″ H   Neoclassical   1794   England
Baluster form with bands and medallions of bright-cut ornaments, resting on
similarly ornamented foot and delicately molded spout; treen arched, looped
handle; Samuel Howland, London.
Superior Quality/Fine Condition $2500 (A)   **$2000–$3500**

Toast rack   6″ H   Rococo Revival   1844   England
Unusual arrangement of toast slots, limiting height of bread; London, by Charles
T. Fox.
Superior Quality/Fine Condition $500 (D)   **$350–$600**

Tray   26.5″ W   Chippendale style   c. 1930   Mexico
Large oval sterling silver tray with handles and monogram in center; hand raised;
Taxco marks.
Good Quality/Fine Condition $1500 (D)   **$1000–$1800**

Tray, card   8.5″ Dia.   Chippendale style   1910   England
Goldsmiths & Silversmiths Ltd., London; sterling silver card tray; shell and
scrolled border; scrolled feet.
Superior Quality/Fine condition $375 (D)   **$250–$450**

Wine cups, footed   3.75″ H × 2.5″ Dia.   Regency   1800–1830 England
Pair; London, by Samuel Hennell; slight downward slant on circular foot; original interior gilding; engraved Greek key banding at lip; marked on edge of foot;
contemporary crests; weight of pair is 6 oz.
Superior Quality/Fine Condition $875 (D)   **$600–$950**

Contemporary crests mean crests engraved when the piece was made, not
something engraved recently. Contemporary refers to the item, not the present time. It is very detrimental to value to have engraving of crests, mon-
ograms, etc., that were made after the piece was made. It is also damaging
to remove a monogram—leaving a blank area.—*DL*

Wine jug   George III   1795   England
Covered wine jug by Peter and Ann Bateman, London; paneled baluster form,
bright-cut decoration, wooden handle, monogrammed; minor dents; 31 troy oz.
(See photo 250)
Very Good Quality/Good Condition $2000 (A)   **$1800–$3500**

Wine taster   2.88″ Dia.   Rococo   1890   France
Paris, first standard silver (95%) with cast leaf at top of ring handle; fine chasing
and repoussé decoration.
Superior Quality/Fine Condition $475 (D)   **$300–$525**

BIBLIOGRAPHY

Banister, Judith, ed. *English Silver Hall-marks*. Des Moines, IA: Wallace-Homestead Book Co., 1970. Handy pocket-size reference for marks of British Isles silver with concise explanation of their use and list of important makers' marks.

Belden, Louise Conway. *Marks of American Silversmiths in the Ineson-Bissell Collection*. Charlottesville, VA: University Press of Virginia for The Henry Francis du Pont Winterthur Museum, 1980. Good reference for collectors of American silver although it contains some misattributed marks.

Bennett, Douglas. *Irish Georgian Silver*. London: Cassell, 1972. A necessity for the collector of Irish silver because Jackson and Wyler are incomplete and sometimes inaccurate on this subject.

Carpenter, Charles H., Jr. *Gorham Silver: 1831–1981*. New York: Dodd, Mead, 1982. Useful and informative study, well illustrated, of the largest silver manufacturer and its products.

———. *Tiffany Silver*. New York; Dodd, Mead. 1978. Well illustrated and researched insight into this famous company and its silver.

Delieb, Eric. *Silver Boxes*. New York: Exeter Books, 1979. Informative study of the highly collectible and numerous special-purpose boxes, with descriptions of decorating and manufacturing techniques together with backgrounds of the principal Birmingham makers.

Forbes, H. A. Crosby. *Chinese Export Silver 1785 to 1885*. Milton, MA; Museum of the American China Trade, 1975. The standard reference on this subject although far from complete.

Grimwade, Arthur G. *London Goldsmiths 1697–1837*. London: Faber & Faber, 1976. For the collector of London silver, indispensable for identification of makers' marks.

Holland, Margaret. *Silver: An Illustrated Guide to American and British Silver*. Secaucus, NJ: Derby Books, 1973. Extensively illustrated, with sound advice and information regarding the entire realm of collecting British and American silver (more pertinent to former, however).

Hood, Graham. *American Silver: A History of Style, 1650–1900*. New York: Praeger, 1971. Good overview of evolving American silver forms and their history.

Jackson, Sir Charles James. *English Goldsmiths and Their Marks*. New York: Dover, 1964. The standard work on British silver marks and history of subject; every collector should have either this volume or Wyler, which is basically a reprint of Jackson. New edition available as of 1991.

Jeweler's Circular Keystone. Sterling Flatware Pattern Index. Radnor, PA: Chilton, 1970. Available in periodically updated printings, the best quick visual reference to American pattern flatware.

Jones, Kennedy Crisp, ed. *The Silversmiths of Birmingham and Their Marks 1750–1980*. London: N.A.G. Press, 1981. A necessity for the advanced collector of Birmingham silver.

Kovel, Ralph M., and Terry H. *Kovel's American Silver Marks*. New York: Crown, 1989. Although this contains listings for many retailers, undifferentiated from makers, it is still useful for American makers' identification; collectors of American silver should have a copy.

Pickford, Ian. *Silver Flatware: English, Irish and Scottish 1660–1980*. Woodbridge, England: The Antique Collectors' Club, 1983. The best guide to British flatware, with sound collecting advice and well illustrated.

Rainwater, Dorothy T. *Encyclopedia of American Silver Manufacturers*. West Chester, PA: Schiffer, 1986. Best reference for American silver manufacturers' marks from mid-19th century to present.

Silver Magazine. Published by Silver Magazine, Inc., PO Box 1243, Whittier, CA 90609. Informative and useful to collectors for researched articles and specialized information; advertising of silver dealers.

Turner, Noel D. *American Silver Flatware 1837–1910*. South Brunswick, NJ, and NY: A.S. Barnes, 1979. Comprehensive work on American sterling and plated flatware, with numerous illustrations, explanations of forms, directory of makers, and patterns; well indexed.

Wilkinson, Wynyard R. T. *Indian Colonial Silver: European Silversmiths in India (1790–1860) and Their Marks*. London: Argent Press, 1973. Standard reference work on this specialized aspect, useful to the general collector of silver.

Wyler, Seymour B. *The Book of Old Silver*. New York: Crown, 1937. The best single volume for British, American, and European silver, although confusing for European marks and outdated for the others; still, a very handy single reference.

COLLECTIONS

Albany Institute of History and Art, Albany, NY.
Art Institute of Chicago, Chicago, IL.
Baltimore Museum of Fine Art, Baltimore, MD.
The Brooklyn Museum, Brooklyn, NY.
The Cleveland Museum of Art, Cleveland, OH.
Colonial Williamsburg, Williamsburg, VA.
Currier Gallery of Art, Manchester, NH.
The Detroit Institute of Arts, Detroit, MI.

The Fogg Art Museum, Harvard University, Cambridge, MA.

Henry Ford Museum, Dearborn, MI.

The Henry Francis du Pont Winterthur Museum, Winterthur, DE.

Henry Huntington Library, San Marino, CA.

The Heritage Foundation, Old Deerfield, MA.

Maryland Historical Society, Baltimore, MD.

The Metropolitan Museum of Art, NY.

The Minneapolis Institute of Arts, Minneapolis, MN.

Museum of the City of New York, NY.

Museum of Fine Arts, Bayou Bend Collection, Houston, TX.

Museum of Fine Arts, Boston, MA.

New-York Historical Society, NY.

Philadelphia Museum of Art, Philadelphia, PA.

Rhode Island School of Design Museum of Art, Providence, RI.

Smithsonian Institution, Washington, DC.

The Sterling and Francine Clark Art Institute, Williamstown, MA.

Virginia Museum of Fine Arts, Richmond, VA.

Wadsworth Atheneum, Hartford, CT.

Worcester Art Museum, Worcester, MA.

Yale University Art Gallery, New Haven, CT.

Stoneware— American

(see also Folk Art—American)

***Advisor:* GEORGE SULLIVAN**

George Sullivan is a full-time freelance writer and author of more than 100 books. His work on antiques and collectibles includes books on collecting autographs and sports memorabilia. He is also the author of the forthcoming House of Collectibles Official Price Guide to American Stoneware. *In addition to his many articles on collecting, his column "Collecting" appears regularly in* Memories *magazine.*

Year in, year out, American salt-glazed decorated stoneware continues to grow in popularity as a fascinating collectible. From New York to California, stoneware fanciers descend on roadside antique shops, besiege dealers, and crowd auction galleries in search of attractive and unusual crocks, jugs, jars, and other treasures.

Stoneware is a type of pottery produced from a special clay that is fired only once, but at such intense heat that it becomes vitrified, that is, very hard and nonporous. It does not require glaze to be usable but, almost without exception, salt is thrown into the kiln to give the ware a glossy finish, an impervious coating, and thereby increase its utility. Most pieces are decorated with a pigment containing an oxide of cobalt, deep blue in color.

Much of the pleasure to be derived from collecting stoneware comes from its social history. Before home canning or ice refrigerators—"ice boxes"—stoneware vessels were desperately needed by the pioneer homemaker for food storage. In the kitchen were stoneware butter churns and batter jugs, bottles and jars, pitchers, bowls, and beanpots. The bedroom had stoneware foot warmers and chamber pots. In the barnyard were waterers and poultry fountains.

Many stoneware pieces have aesthetic appeal as folk art. Decorating was often done by itinerant artists who used cobalt, a dark blue metallic oxide that fired to a glasslike finish. Applied with a slip cup or stiff brush, it made possible a wide range of unusual or elaborate designs.

Collectors pay high prices for stoneware featuring rare and handsome decoration. The number of people who will pay more than $10,000 for a piece has "increased dramatically" in the past few years, according to Betty and Joel Schatzberg, well-known Connecticut dealers in folk art. The current stoneware auction record is $31,900, the amount paid for a large butter churn at the Robert F. Skinner auction house in Bolton, Massachusetts, on November 1, 1986. Manufactured by John Burger of Rochester, New York, around 1860, the piece is decorated with a masterfully drawn rooster.

Most collectors, of course, content themselves with the lower end of the market, paying $300 to $500 for pieces featuring stylized birds, simple floral designs, or geometric patterns. There are thousands of such pieces available.

DECORATING

From the very first, American stoneware was incised, stamped, brushed with slip, and, later, stenciled to give the ware color and dramatic appeal. Decorative techniques and styles were almost as varied as the pots themselves.

Incising was a decorating technique that involved cutting the outline of a design into soft clay with a thin metal rod or wooden-handled instrument that had a sharp blade or tip. In its simplest form, the incised decoration took the form of a band at or near the top of the pot. Such bands were not only decorative; they aided the potter in positioning the vessel's handles.

For incised designs, leaves, flowers, and birds were popular subjects. Large designs, sometimes depicting sailing ships or the American flag, are also seen, but these are rare. Incised designs, large as well as small, were frequently highlighted with cobalt blue.

Impressing, another method of decorating, was faster and more mechanical than incising. Impressing involved the use of either a coggle wheel or a hand stamp.

The simplest coggle was a coin that had been notched around the edge with a knife or sawblade. The coin was pierced in the center, and a nail was then inserted in the hole and used as an axis in rolling the coin and forming a decorative band. More sophisticated coggles took the form of a small wheel with a sunken or incised design. A handle was attached to the center of the wheel with a cotter pin.

The most popular decorating technique was the application of surface glazed color. An oxide of cobalt, which produces blue, was the most commonly used. It blended well with stoneware grays and, unlike other oxides, proved remarkably stable in high firing temperatures. And a little bit went a long way, meaning it was economical. Manganese oxide, producing brown, also found use, but only on rare occasions. The same can be said of copper oxide, which produces green.

TYPES

Jugs, jars, crocks, and churns were the standard pieces offered by every 19th-century stoneware potter. Manufactured in huge quantities, they sold at prices that seem unreal in today's marketplace. While each of the standard vessels had a basic form, countless variations of each type were produced.

JUGS

Of all the many types of stoneware, the jug is the most common. A tall, rounded vessel with a narrow neck meant to be stopped with a cork or wooden plug, the jug ranged in size from one-half gallon to six gallons, although jugs with eight and ten-gallon capacities are seen occasionally. All true jugs have handles. Most have merely a single handle, but those that are four gallons or larger are double-handled.

CROCKS

Another extremely popular stoneware form, the crock is a tall, rounded, and wide-mouthed vessel, which was used for storing butter, lard, salted meat, and many other foods. Crocks were also used in processing and storing pickled foods, such as cucumbers.

As in the case of jugs, early crocks were ovoid, with greater girth in the middle than at the base or top. By the 1850s, crocks had become straight-sided.

JARS

Like crocks, jars are wide-mouthed containers, but they're slimmer. They, too, were used for preserving and storing foods. Some had lug handles; others did not.

Some early jars are slightly ovoid in shape, but jars are usually straight-sided, with the neck slightly smaller in diameter than the body and base. Jars were made in sizes from one gallon to five gallons. They were almost always fitted with lug handles.

CHURNS

Usually tall, cylinder-shaped, and topped with a simple neck or collar, stoneware churns were not produced until the 19th century. Before that time, milk or cream was churned into earthenware vessels or ones made of staved wood.

Churns were made in two-gallon, three-gallon, four-gallon, five-gallon, six-gallon, eight-gallon, ten-gallon, and twelve-gallon sizes. They were fitted with wood or ceramic lids. The lid had a central hole to accommodate the handle of the dasher. Lug handles were typical.

BATTER JUGS

Rather like a pitcher in use and a pail in form, the batter jug was a slightly ovoid, wide-mouthed vessel with a tubular pouring spout. It was used to mix and pour pancake batter.

PITCHERS

Pitchers are most common in one-quart, half-gallon, one-and-a-half-gallon, and two-gallon sizes. Three-gallon pitchers, used in farm homes for storing milk, are seen occasionally.

Most pitchers have a bulbous body that tapers into a cylindrical neck and collar. The collar usually represents about one-third of the vessel's height. There are also straight-sided pitchers, but they are rare. Pitcher handles are always strap handles.

BOTTLES AND FLASKS

Produced in great quantity and variety during the 19th century, bottles and flasks were widely used because they kept liquids cool before refrigeration was common.

Bottles were turned out in a variety of cylindrical shapes until the 1850s. From that time on, they were made with straight sides and a cone-shaped neck that tapered to a heavy lip. This allowed wire to be tightly tied beneath to hold the cork in place.

Only a relatively few bottles and flasks are decorated. What they do have, however, are imprints bearing the name of the brewer, bottler, tavern, or storekeeper who purchased the piece.

Bottles were usually made in one-quart size, although one-pint bottles are common, too.

BOWLS

Deep, round dishes used for holding liquids or foods were very popular in the middle Atlantic states but scarcely manufactured at all in some other areas. Before 1860 or so, bowls were made with sloping sides. Some were deep; others shallow. They were often called pans, not bowls. Such vessels were one, one-and-one-half, and two gallons in size.

MUGS

Manufactured in one-half pint and one-pint sizes, mugs were usually cylinder shaped and, aside from banding or combing, were not elaborately decorated.

CHAMBER POTS

Chamber pots were short, wide, and slightly globular in form, with broad flattened rims. Each was fitted with a stout strap handle. Two sizes, adult and child, were manufactured.

COLANDERS

Used for draining or straining a variety of foods, colanders usually took the form of perforated bowls, although there were some that resembled wide-mouthed jars. They were made as ordinary jars or bowls, then pierced by the potter before the clay dried.

WATER COOLERS

These large, cylinder-shaped jugs usually date to late in the 19th century. They were fitted with a small neck that could easily be corked, a pair of strap handles, and an opening for a spigot near the base.

FLOWERPOTS

Flat-bottomed with slightly flared sidewalls, and with a central drainage hole in the bottom, flowerpots were produced by most of the larger potteries. Since they were rarely decorated, they are seldom sought by the serious collector.

Because of the enormous quantity of stoneware pieces produced during the 19th century, examples of every type are still available to the collector. They can be purchased in a great range of shapes and sizes, with all manner of decoration, and at prices to suit every budget.

FAKE ALERT

During the 1980s, when stoneware prices began to take off, the field attracted counterfeiters. They produced high-priced fakes by taking an inexpensive, undecorated crock or jug, adding some blue to it, and then refiring it. They then sought to sell what might have been a $30 or $40 piece for many hundreds, or even many thousands, of dollars.

One way dealers have learned to spot such fakes is by examining the inside walls of a piece. In the refiring, the brown-slip coating on the interior blistered and was no longer smooth.

When buying an expensive piece, it's a good idea to close your eyes and feel it. "Your eyes can lie to you," says Joel Schatzberg. "But with your fingers, you can sometimes feel variations in the surface materials that can tip off a piece has been tampered with."

"If you have any doubt of the authenticity of a piece," says Schatzberg, "take a key or a coin out of your pocket and ask the seller whether you can scratch the surface. If he says no, don't buy the piece. It it's an authentic salt-glazed piece, you can't scratch it, not even with the point of a knife. Practically nothing can penetrate the surface. But if the item has been tampered with, you can probably carve your initials in it.''

In an effort to spot fakes, some collectors use black light, that is, ultraviolet or infrared radiation. Black light shows tampered-with areas in bright purple. ''Unless you really trust the person you're buying from,'' says one dealer, ''you should black-light anything over $3000 or $4000.''

One way to avoid getting burned is to buy from a reputable dealer. You're almost certain to have the option of being able to return any piece you find unsatisfactory. Another advantage in buying from a dealer is that you'll be offered only those pieces in which you specialize and in the price range you've designated.

For any item you purchase, ask for a bill of sale. Be sure it includes the date, a description of the piece (including any defects), the amount paid, and any other conditions of sale. You'll want the bill of sale for your own records as well as for insurance and resale purpose.

CONDITION

As in any field of collecting, the matter of condition is all-important. What about cracks, a somewhat common flaw? A piece may have a hairline crack—called a ''line''—or a deeper, wider, more serious crack, one that can catch a fingernail when you draw it over the surface. Naturally, the bigger the crack, the more the piece is devalued. But the location of the crack is just as critical as the size. If the crack cuts through the decoration, ruining the appearance of the piece, it can diminish the value by as much as 40 or 50 percent, even more. But a line on the back or at the base of a crock or jug, where its scarcely noticed, may reduce the value by only 10 percent or so.

Blistering or flaking that occurred during firing, or base chips or rim chips that resulted from careless use, can also lessen the value of a piece. Again, what's important is whether these imperfections mar the decoration.

GLOSSARY

Albany Slip. A brownish clay used by potters to seal the interior walls of stoneware vessels.

Blistering. A swelling or bubbling that formed in the clay during firing, usually caused by overheating of the kiln.

Capacity Mark. The number either stamped or painted on a crock, jug, or other vessel to indicate its capacity in gallons.

Cobalt. A metallic element that occurs in compounds that provide blue coloring substances.

Cobalt Blue. Any of a number of pigments containing an oxide of cobalt.

Coggle, Coggle Wheel. A small wheel bearing a sunken or incised design that was rolled over the surface of the clay before firing to form a decoration.

Earthenware. Pottery made of baked or hardened clay, usually fired at below 1100 C.

Greenware. Vessels that have been formed by the potter, dried, but not fired.

Impressing. A method of decoration in which a design was pressed into the damp clay with a hand stamp or coggle.

Incising. A decorating technique in which a design was outlined in the damp clay with a thin metal rod or other sharp-pointed instrument. Incised decoration often took the form of a band or bands near the top of the vessel.

Line. A very thin crack in a stoneware vessel (short for hairline).

Lug Handle. Common to stoneware crocks, handles mounted in pairs on opposite sides of the vessel, and attached to the crock side along their entire length.

Ocher. An earthy mineral oxide of iron that, when combined with clay and sand, produces a reddish or brownish mixture.

Ovoid. Egg-shaped.

Pinholes. Tiny holes that appear in the glaze, caused by escaping gases during firing.

Popout. A defect in a stoneware vessel that results when particles of lime in the clay burst open during firing.

Porringer. A small-handled bowl or cup.

Salt Glaze. The smooth, glossy surface on stoneware pieces that resulted from vaporization of salt during the firing process.

Slip. A creamy mixture of clay and water used in pottery decoration.

Stoneware. Pottery produced from a special clay that was fired only once, but at such high temperature (above 1200 C) that it became vitrified.

Strap Handle. A free-standing handle formed of a looped band of clay.

Swag. A decoration that gives the appearance of a suspended wreath, drapery, or the like.

Batter jug c. 1880
These jugs were used to mix and pour pancake batter. Marked ''WHITE'S BINGHAMTON'' with only a few strokes of blue around the handles. Wire bale handle missing. Minor hairline cracks at base and top.
Good Quality/Average Condition $225 (A)

Bottles

Two bottles, one quart and one pint size, typical of the type produced in great quantities in the 1800s. Wholesaler's mark stamped into the clay. *(See photo 251)*
Good Quality/Average Condition $15 each (D)

Butter churn

A finely proportioned five-gallon butter churn by Thompson Harrington. Decorated with a realistic partridge on a delicate branch. The thick dark blue enhances the value of this piece.
Very Good Quality/Good Condition $4500 (D)

Churn

A five-gallon churn from the pottery of J. and F. Norton in Bennington, Vermont. Exceptional peacock design, noted for its size and deep blue color.
Superior Quality/Fine Condition $25,800 (A)

Cookie jar

Six-quart cookie jar with modernistic design of a large bird sitting in a tilted tree. Cookie jars were seldom decorated with such elaborate design. Dark cobalt blue.
Superior Quality/Fine Condition $2800 (D)

Cream pot   c. 1881

A one-gallon cream pot by Daniel Goodale, Hartford, Connecticut. Usual flock decoration, an incised drawing of a large house. Minor lines and small chips at base.
Very Good Quality/Good Condition $3500 (D)

Crock   c. 1870

A five-gallon cylindrical crock by Thompson Harrington, with elaborate floral design.
Good Quality/Good Condition $275 (A)

Crock   c. 1861

A four-gallon crock with folksy decoration depicting two men—barely more than stick figures—in conversation. New York Stoneware Company, Ft. Edward, New York. Some rim chips.
Very Good Quality/Good Condition $6500 (D)

Crock

Three-gallon, straight-sided crock with delicate pastoral scene. By Seymour and Bosworth, Hartford, Connecticut.
Good Quality/Good Condition $4000 (D)

Crock   Late 1800s

Three-gallon crock with undistinguished floral design. Marked with an "X," trademark of Madison Woodruff of Cortland, New York.
Good Quality/Average Condition $275 (D)

Cuspidor   c. 1880

Also called a spitoon, the cuspidor has a circular opening in the side to facilitate cleaning. Nicely decorated with Albany slip at the top and within. No potter's mark, but attributed to White's pottery of Utica, New York. Some minor chipping at top and inside.
Good Quality/Average Condition $200 (D)

Jar   c. 1855

A three-gallon, wide-mouthed jar by J. & E. Norton of Bennington, Vermont. Peacock design done in thick glaze. Slight kiln burn near bird's head.
Good Quality/Good Condition $1900 (D)

Photo 251 (left). Stoneware bottles. CREDIT: GEORGE SULLIVAN. *Photo 252 (right). Stoneware jar.* CREDIT: GEORGE SULLIVAN *(See p. 500 and below)*

Jar

A three-gallon, wide-mouthed jar by J. F. Brayton of Utica, New York. Decorated with a floral motif that incorporated the jar's capacity into the design. Minor chips at top. Purchased at a Connecticut flea market.
Good Quality/Good Condition $150 (D)

Jar c. 1800
Double-handled, two-gallon jar with incised swag design coated in blue. David Morgan, potter. *(See photo 252)*
Good Quality/Good Condition $4500–$5000 (D)

Jar c. 1840
Wide-mouthed jar with folk bird decoration. Excellent condition, but potter unknown, which reduces its value.
Good Quality/Fine Condition $500–$600 (D)

Jar
A one-gallon jug, exceptional for its unique beehive shape and unusual design of a bird in its nest with a tree in the background. Potter and date unknown. *(See photo 253)*
Very Good Quality/Good Condition $4000 (D)

Jug c. 1804
A rare marked jug bearing a bird design from the pottery of Jonathan Fenton. Also decorated with a neck band. *(See photo 254)*
Very Good Quality/Good Condition $5000 (D)

Jug c. 1902–1905
A four-gallon jug with simple floral design by the Lyons Cooperative of Lyons, New York, from the waning days of American stoneware.
Very Good Quality/Good Condition $400 (D)

Jug
A one-gallon jug by Jonathan Fenton of Boston. Condition is only fair, but unusual, because Fenton's name is impressed upside down. *(See photo 255)*
Very Good Quality/Average Condition $1050 (A)

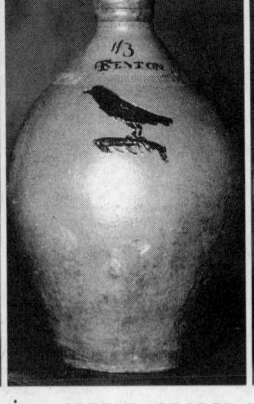
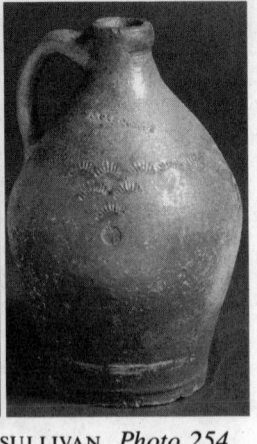

Photo 253 (left). Stoneware jug. CREDIT: GEORGE SULLIVAN. *Photo 254 (center). Stoneware jug.* CREDIT: GEORGE SULLIVAN. *Photo 255 (right). Stoneware jug.* CREDIT: GEORGE SULLIVAN *(See p. 501)*

Jug c. 1838
One-gallon jug, marked "CLARK," probably for Lyman Clark of Lyons, New York, and "38" presumably for the year of manufacture, 1838 (the Clark pottery operated between 1822 and 1852). Minor cracks and kiln damage.
Good Quality/Average Condition $800 (D)

Jug c. 1860
Three-gallon jug with a tornado-like design by Frank Norton, Worcester, Massachusetts.
Good Quality/Fine Condition $750–$1000 (D)

Jug c. 1880
Very rare straight-sided four-gallon jug by the Fulper Brothers' pottery of Flemington, New Jersey. Decorated with performing acrobats. Probably worth more than its auction price.
Very Good Quality/Fine Condition $28,600 (A)

Milk pan
A two-gallon milk pan, or milk bowl, 12½ inches in diameter at the top, used for separating cream from milk. By Nathan Porter of West Troy, New York. Some chips at the rim.
Very Good Quality/Good Condition $250 (D)

Mug c. 1830
A one-pint mug, standard design but attractive decoration. Potter unknown.
Good Quality/Good Condition $1800 (D)

Pitcher c. 1850
Bulbous pitcher, Germanic in style and form. Floral decoration. Believed to be the work of Jakob Wingender of New Jersey.
Good Quality/Good Condition $375 (A)

Water cooler c. 1825
Rare two-handled water cooler of classic ovoid design by Israel Seymour, Troy, New York.
Very Good Quality/Good Condition $6000 (A)

BIBLIOGRAPHY

Barret, Richard Carter. *Bennington Pottery and Porcelain.* New York: Bonanza Books, 1958.

Branin, M. Lelyn. *The Early Potters and Potteries of Maine.* Middletown, CT: Wesleyan University Press, 1978.

Greer, Georgeanna H. *American Stonewares.* Exton, PA: Schiffer Publishing Ltd., 1981.

Guilland, Harold F. *Early American Folk Pottery.* Philadelphia: Chilton Book Co., 1971.

Ketchum, William C., Jr. *Early Potters and Potteries of New York State.* New York: Funk and Wagnall, 1970.

Osgood, Cornelias. *The Jug and Related Stoneware of Bennington.* Rutland, VT: Charles E. Tuttle Co., 1971.

Ramsey, John. *American Potters and Pottery.* Clinton, MA: Hale, Cushman and Flint, 1939.

Spargo, John. *Early American Pottery and China.* Rutland, VT: Charles E. Tuttle Co., 1974.

Watkins, Laura Woodside. *Early New England Pottery.* Sturbridge, MA: Old Sturbridge Village, 1966.

Webster, Donald Blake. *Decorated Stoneware and Pottery of North America.* Rutland, VT: Charles E. Tuttle Co., 1980.

Teddy Bears—Antique and Modern

Advisors: **KIMBERLY BREWER (Antique) and
CAROL-LYNN RÖSSEL WAUGH (Modern)**

ANTIQUE TEDDY BEARS

Kimberly Billings Brewer is a woodcarver and artist specializing in oil painting. In addition, she is a restorer of fine art. As a noted carousel horse restorer, she often works with The New England Carousel Museum of Bristol, CT. Her fascination with antique teddy bears has turned her into one of the most highly respected appraisers in the field, and she is frequently consulted by major auction houses. When not at home in Simsbury, CT, she is lecturing and exhibiting her collection throughout the United States. She is also the co-author of The Official Price Guide to Antique and Modern Teddy Bears *(New York: House of Collectibles, 1990).*

HOW THE TEDDY BEAR GOT HIS NAME

Who made the first bear actually called a "teddy bear"? And what is the story behind it?

In November 1902, President Roosevelt was invited by Southern friends to go bear hunting in Mississippi. The president was in trouble with some Southern Republicans and national Republicans for his sponsorship of progressive social programs. He had further antagonized them by inviting Booker T. Washington to dine at the White House with his family and to advise him on the appointment of blacks to federal posts in the South. There was a move among Republicans to dump Roosevelt as their candidate in 1904 in favor of Senator Mark Hanna. Ever the politician, Roosevelt decided that he could consolidate his supporters in the South by appearing among them in the relaxed atmosphere of a hunting party, knowing well that the press would be following every aspect of the trip.

On the second day of the hunt the pack of hounds struck the trail of a bear, and the hunting party gave chase. After several hours of pursuit and waiting for the quarry to emerge from the dense brush, the president returned to camp. When the bear was finally cornered by the hounds, it was captured and tied to a tree and the president was summoned. When Roosevelt saw the animal, he refused to shoot it in such an unsportsmanlike way and ordered the bear put out of its misery. The bear weighed 235 pounds.

News of the day's events quickly reached the papers. Two days later, on November 16, 1902, a cartoon montage was published on the front page of *The Washington Star*. It was drawn by the *Post*'s political cartoonist, Clifford K. Berryman, and comprised five separate cartoons, one of which showed the president refusing to shoot an unhappy bear cub tied by a rope around its neck. The caption read: "Drawing the line in Mississippi."

The public was enchanted by the little bear and wanted more of it. Berryman obliged and soon was drawing a bear in every cartoon in which the president appeared. Often the bear carried a motto or spoke. "Teddy's Bear" became Berryman's trademark.

It was not long before stuffed toy bears called "Teddy Bear" began to appear, in response to an obvious market opportunity. One of the first was made by Morris Michtom, a Brooklyn candy store owner, and his wife. It was displayed in the window of their shop with a price tag of $1.50. Michtom's grandchildren tell the story of how Michtom wrote to the president, asking for permission to use the name "Teddy's Bear" for his toy and of Roosevelt's reply that it was all right with him but that he didn't see how it would help the bear business! Little did Roosevelt—or Michtom—guess that the teddy bear would propel Michtom and his family into big business in the form of the Ideal Toy Co., which used as its motto "Excellence in Toy Making Since the Teddy Bear."

At the same time, the Steiff jointed bear was transformed through the mysteries of marketing into "Teddy's Bear," and by the end of 1904 Steiff had sold 12,000 of them. This number increased to nearly a million by 1907, when it was finally known as the "teddy bear."

In 1905 the first of the "literary" teddy bears made its debut. English writer Paul Piper (writing as Seymour Eaton) wrote a series of books about "The Roosevelt Bears" that stimulated a flow of commercial products, including stuffed bears called "Teddy G" (for gray) and "Teddy B" (for brown). These were the first in a continuing tradition of literary-cum-toy bears that includes Pooh, Paddington, Little Bear, Yogi, and Smokey.

THE ANTIQUE BEAR MARKET: ONWARD AND UPWARD

Eighty years have passed since an alarmed customs inspector in Kansas City reported that he had cleared the import papers of 609 bears, 5 goats, 6 cats, and other animals and that he feared "this place won't be fit to live in!" Worse was yet to come—he was informed that 15,000 other bears had already been inspected. "It will be positively dangerous to spend the winter in Kansas City!" was his chilling conclusion.

The interesting phenomenon that this reveals, however, is one we tend to forget today. And that is that the teddy bear was big business in the first decade of the 20th century, in spite of annual predictions that the bottom would drop out "next year."

The chances of finding a mint-condition antique bear for a bargain price at a flea market or auction, either here or in Europe, has become more and more remote; but the possibility of finding an exact replica of an antique bear is becoming more promising. This is because there are modern bear artists and bearmakers whose extraordinary artistry creates handcrafted bears of great beauty and distinctiveness. Some are replicas of antique bruins; others are entirely original. Many are signed and numbered, assuring their value as collectors' delights.

The antique bear market and the modern artist bear market are reflections of each other. One inspires the vision of the other; both fulfill the needs of collectors—and the longings of children. Together they form an expanding market with a wonderful history and a bright future.

Christie's London started selling teddy bears "seriously" in 1983, according to Olivia Bristol. "I noticed that as people really got interested, prices took off. When offered a large teddy bear collection, we decided to hold our first ever teddy bear and soft toy sale. That was in December 1984. The media response was incredible. We had nine television stations represented in the room, with barely two yards of space for each. They were queued up outside on the pavement at half past eight in the morning, fighting for a place. It was very exciting. Nothing like that had happened before, and we were really amazed at the interest. At first we thought it a sort of phenomenon, that it wouldn't last; but people are still buying. There are very serious collectors. A good bear (an early Steiff bear in good condition and rare color) will bring £10,000 or £15,000.

"Although the future of the bear market is difficult to predict, we suspect the top-quality bears will hold their value. Even the cheaper end of the market—Chad Valley, Merrythought, and 1950s' bears—are now bringing £100 or £150. And those can still be picked up at jumble sales for 10p. So it's quite an interesting market."

In 1989 a major American newspaper reported that top-of-the-line antique teddy bears had been performing at an investment rate equal to or above that of the top collectible European sports cars. The prediction was made by a noted critic and market analyst that over the next half decade prices for fine-quality antique bears would more than double.

WHAT DETERMINES PRICE?

There are several criteria that knowledgeable collectors and dealers can apply when deciding how much to pay for a teddy bear. Among these are *condition, rarity, color, provenance*, and *price per inch*. Let's look at each in turn:

Condition

It is obvious that a bear in excellent condition—all original parts, little wear, etc.—will be priced at the top end of each category, whereas the bear with a "sorrow"—in a much-loved and worn condition—will be at the lower end.

Of critical concern to the serious teddy collector today is the condition, type, and length of the mohair "fur." A bear with a luxurious pelt will nearly always command a higher price than his balding brother. Even with two fully furred and otherwise equal bears, the one with the longer mohair will rise to the top of the price range.

Rarity

Although mint condition is usually a prediction of premium price, an important corollary is rarity, or the frequency with which a certain bear appears on the market. If 20,000 bears of a certain type were manufactured but only a handful ever appear for sale, they are considered rare, and their price will rise accordingly. The bottom can drop out quickly, though, when a pack of identical bruins comes to market. This happened in 1983 when a huge Steiff display bear brought $9000. Suddenly, four more surfaced and were sold. When a sixth—in mint condition—was put up for sale at a prestigious auction house, it went for only a fraction of the price of the first one. Why? It was no longer a "rarity."

Color

A horse of a different color is a rarity, and bears of a different color—lavender, black or red, for example—are among the most sought-after toys in the world, leaving their cinnamon, beige, and golden brother bears in the dust.

When a lavender Chad Valley bear went up for auction at Marvin Cohen's in 1986, tremendous excitement built as the bidding rose to $600. A little earlier in the same auction, a bear that was identical, except that it was golden in color, had brought only $100!

Schuco miniature bears are great ambassadors of color, traveling from collector to collector in their elegant deep cinnamon and bright orange furs, rarely pausing to be admired on a dealer's shelf. Mechanical Schuco bears, especially in turquoise and kelly green, are a toy dealer's dream.

Recently a lavender "Tumbler" sold for $2000, despite its diminutive size, and a lavender "Perfume" in its original shade and condition was plucked by a British fancier for $2200. Color, in these cases, was obviously the reason for the high prices because at the same time a Midwestern dealer tried unsuccessfully to sell a "Compact" Schuco mechanical bear at the Atlantic City Show for $500 and finally sold it for a slightly lower price a year later. The bear was a common color.

Since 1985, prices in Europe have skyrocketed: a Schuco "Perfume" priced in the United States at $500 would bring $1000 in England. Dealers and collectors are learning, with difficulty, to live with this international disparity. And they must also adjust to the fact that the Northeast corridor of the United States is a true "bear market," where the game seems to call for records to be topped at each sale.

Provenance

Because teddy bears are usually family pets before they become collectors' items, most would have long and interesting stories to tell if they could just talk! It is natural, therefore, to put a higher value on a bear whose owner was a famous person or who participated in some historical event. Imagine owning Christopher Milne's Pooh! (The original Pooh Bear, by the way, is greeting friends at his new home in the children's room of the Donnell branch of the New York Public Library.) In May 1989 a much-worn little bear that a cousin of Czar Nicholas II once played with brought the highest price then paid for a bear: nearly $20,000. As with all antiques, a provenance that documents where it has been and who has owned it is a valuable asset for a teddy.

Price Per Inch

For years I supplied bear dealers and pickers with a sliding scale showing how various factors affected what I would pay for antique teddies. The graphs had columns for percentage of mohair, color of mohair, and height of bear. Later I incorporated columns for length of arm and size of foot. It was an interesting concept but doomed to failure because of wide variations in human perceptions.

In one instance I bought a white bear for top dollar sight unseen because the auctioneer who described it to me as of pristine quality could not see the slight patches of mohair missing all over the toy and the stained shade of "white."

Once you have your hands on the bear, the primary concerns for price differentials are general condition, amount of mohair present, length of mohair, regional preferences, color, and size.

Bears are measured from the top of the head to the heel. Do not measure from the ears because ears can stand several inches above the skull peak.

A toy is considered "mint-in-box" when it retains all of its original tags, pamphlets, and so on, and is virtually unplayed with.

CONDITION KEY

Poor Condition: under 65% fur still evident; more than two pads replaced; excessive minor repairs, such as ankle seams redone; enough of original bear has been altered so that original integrity of the piece is no longer represented, or else so many additions made to item that basic character is irreversibly compromised.

Average Condition: 80–90% mohair present; pads often replaced but acceptable.

Good Condition: 85–90% mohair with some small repairs allowable; some fading to fabric present.

Fine Condition: overall 95% hair present with minimal fading of original color.

QUALITY KEY

Good Quality: a toy with more than average appeal, healthy overall mohair condition, and retaining much of its original color, expression, and parts.

Very Good Quality: hair or mechanism in toy is exceptionally nice; fur density high; symmetry of features and balance of item quite noticeable.

Superior Quality: item has provenance, color, condition, and some extraordinary charm to offer; it may therefore be scarce and highly desirable and hard to find.

FAKES

The current popularity of teddy bears has made the reproduction—and faking—of antique bears into a lucrative business. Along with the public's willingness to pay high prices for good reproductions came an awareness of the tremendous potential for forgeries passed off as original. As is the case with other collectibles, such as Tiffany lamps and folk art, forgeries have become so prevalent in the last few years that there is a need for some basic guidelines to help the purchaser separate the real from the fake antique.

When purchasing an old bear, in particular one that has no noticeable restoration, look at the pads for telltale hints of fraud. Most fakes lack overall wear on the pads but instead exhibit dark-stained central sections only. Many fakers use leather to eliminate this problem, but you should know that leather was rarely used on old bears. One fraudulent Ideal bear purchased in 1985 for $750 had been "christened" in herb and clove scents that gave it a suspiciously unauthentic aroma. Old bears have a unique odor that comes from the combination of old straw, wood shavings, and the canvas and mohair fabric.

Lately, I have seen several examples of "wear" made by crude horizontal scissor cuts on some carefully formed bears. Uneven wear and thick-ended mohair tufts revealed the fact of mechanical distress rather than of natural wear.

Noses in the fake teddies are often too thick in thread, and the thread is sometimes dark in color instead of worn to a grayish color. Eyes are often tiny old shoe buttons because authentic glass eyes and large old shoe buttons are difficult to obtain. One giveaway is the turn of the seam on the newly produced critter. In many cases fur on old bears, Steiff in particular, is carefully plucked out of the seams, and a fluffy, even appearance is evident on the seam line. Repros' seams are usually clumped with mohair, the result of hasty handiwork.

Stuffing is not often a good indicator of falsified goods. Some fine old bears are restuffed with nylon stockings, cotton, and acrylic. Over the years some collectors have indicated to me that a certain percentage of restuffing is acceptable; the advanced collector may prefer to buy bears without any stuffing if the disks, seams, and other elements are original.

AMERICAN BEARS—IDEAL TOY CO.

Until quite recently it has been virtually impossible to identify antique bears of American origin. One of the reasons is that American bears in the early years of the century were almost never marked by their manufacturers. Sometimes it is this absence of any tags that most clearly points to an American bear. But to determine the company that made it is an additional problem.

In some cases definite attributions have been made through the fortunate combination of historic documentation and company records, as in the identification of the Teddy Roosevelt campaign teddies as Ideal Toy Co. bears.

The Ideal Toy Co. makes claim, along with others, to having been the first company to make the teddy bear. However, the phenomenal success of the company has been due more to its original ideas and creative marketing than to any one product. It has acquired the licenses for innumerable toys from the movie and entertainment industry and has become a giant manufacturer with a modern plant in Newark, NJ, and subsidiary operations worldwide. The company went public in 1968 and was purchased by CBS, Inc., in 1982.

American, Ideal, 12″, golden mohair. Firsthand accounts of two girls, now in their 80s, place this bear with the ambitious Roosevelt campaign around 1904. This is the model and painted "Googley eyed" Ideal that was thrown from trains into the waiting arms of elated children. Note the spear-shaped tops of the toes, a certain mark of the Ideal Co. It is likely that the few surviving examples of this bear lost the white and black top paint laid over the shoe button eyes. As yet, we have no absolute indication of the reason for the comical gesture. (A premium investment example in folk art, political, historical, and Americana.) *(See photo 256)*
Value (with original painted eyes): $1500 (D)

ENGLISH BEARS

Chad Valley

Chad Valley bears are classic examples of English toymaking. Created from fine-quality mohair in beautiful natural and rainbow colors, these bears have been popularly priced for decades. Examples of this "bear from Birmingham" regularly turn up at sales because of their great numbers and wide distribution pattern.

To date, few Chad Valleys have reached the striking prices of the most desirable German bears; but these bright English bruins, with their unique kaleidoscope of mohair hues, are an absolute necessity for a well-balanced collection.

1823—founded as a family printing and bookbinding company in Birmingham, England, by Anthony Bunn-Johnson.

Photo 256. American Ideal teddy bear. CREDIT: DOTTIE AYERS *(See above)*

Photo 257. *Chad Valley teddy bears.* CREDIT: DOTTIE AYERS *(See p. 513)*

Photo 258. Merrythought specialty bears. CREDIT: DOTTIE AYERS *(See p. 514)*

Photo 259 (left). Hermann and Steiff bears. CREDIT: DOTTIE AYERS.
Photo 260 (right). Steiff display bear. CREDIT: DOTTIE AYERS *(See pp. 515, 517)*

1919—product line expanded to include soft toys, dolls, and games; name was changed to Chad Valley.

1920s—Chad Valley expanded by purchasing other toy companies; began labeling all bears—to the delight of today's collectors!

1938—Chad Valley appointed "toymakers of the queen."

1950—Chad Valley became a public company.

1978—Chad Valley purchased by Palitoy, subsidiary of General Mills.

Chad Valley Clan, 28″, 10″, and 20″. These display the most recognizable of English features. *(See photo 257)*
Value: Left, $800 (D); Right, $600 (D); Small, $75 (D).

Chiltern

The Chiltern teddy bear is quite different from any other English bear. Although it exhibits the same velveteen or canvas paw pads found in his Anglo brothers, there is an exceptionally soft touch to the mohair. An almost silky sensation is derived from the sweet-faced Chiltern.

The short feet and wide head proclaim his British bloodlines, but the overall design of this pretty bruin makes it easy to identify and separate from the average English bear. Some Chilterns were made in extremely large sizes, such as 38″–40″. In 1986 a 40″ bear was offered at an antique show in New Haven, CT, for $1500, but it remained unsold.

Dean's

Dean's Rag Book Co., Ltd. was founded in London in 1903 by Samuel Dean. Its 1910 trademark shows two dogs tugging for possession of one of its cloth books. These washable, durable books ("for children who wear their food and eat their clothes") were part of a line of soft toys that included printed cloth dolls sold as kits for home assembly. Teddy bears were an early favorite in the Dean's line, and they patented a unique joint called "Evripose" that allowed the bears unlimited positioning.

In the 1920s, Dean's began making bears and other animals on wheels and in the 1930s a series of named animals based on cartoon or storybook characters (Peter Rabbit, Mickey and Minnie Mouse, Dismal Desmond, etc.). By the end of World War II soft toys that included teddy bears, golliwogs, and other animals became Dean's main products. In 1972, Dean's Rag Book Co. merged with Dean's Childsplay Toys and purchased Gwent Toys of South Wales.

J. K. Farnell

The pioneering English company of J. K. Farnell (c. 1840–1968) claimed, along with others, to have made the first teddy bear. It was developed as part of a series of rabbit-skin animals that were marketed in various countries, including Germany, where—according to one story—they inspired Margarete Steiff.

One of the founders of the company was Agnes Farnell, sister of J. K. Farnell, and it was her creative genius, along with that of animal designer Sybil Kemp, that was responsible for such Farnell favorites as "The Alpha Bears." When A. A. Milne went to Harrod's department store in London to buy a toy bear for his little boy Christopher, it is thought that he purchased a Farnell bear, which Christopher named "Pooh." The rest is history!

Merrythought

Merrythought of England has produced some of the most entertaining and whimsical teddies in the world since its founding in 1930 by former employees of Chad Valley and J. K. Farnell in partnership with Holmes, Laxton & Co. spinning mills. The smiling expression and childlike eyes of the Merrythought bears make them very popular in the collectibles market, even though the earliest ones are scarcely in the semiantique category yet.

The first Merrythought line in 1931 was designed by Florence Atwood, who learned the craft while attending the Deaf and Dumb School in Manchester. A classmate of hers was the daughter of a Merrythought founder. Florence Atwood served as chief designer for the company until her death in 1949. Customer and employee satisfaction are high on Merrythought's priority list; a number of their employees have worked their entire careers with the company. A high quality of English knitted plush, an imported woven plush, and felt and fur are the materials from which Merrythought animals are constructed—still almost entirely by hand. Most of its production is sold within the United Kingdom.

Two Merrythought specialty bears, 1928 and 1930. *(See photo 258)* *Value: Left, $850 (D); Right, $400 (D).*

GERMAN BEARS

Gebrüder Hermann

Johann Hermann and his children began to manufacture teddy bears in 1907 near Sonneberg, Germany. Sonneberg became a world center of toy manufacturing, where important American purchasers (such as Woolworth, Kresge, Borgfeldt, Louis Wolf, etc.) maintained offices.

Gebrüder Hermann relied somewhat on the handwork of the cottage industry and was one of the first toy manufacturers to encourage this kind of independent labor. In the early years a cottage worker would fill a basket with his finished toys, and the baskets would be picked up by the company on a regular schedule; the worker did not have to leave his home.

In 1948, Gebrüder Hermann moved its headquarters to Hirschaid near Bamberg. Teddy bears continue to be their top-selling product. Early Hermann bears are true collectors' items. Unfortunately, they did not have permanent markers and can be somewhat difficult to identify.

Left. Hermann, 22″, 1940. **Right. Steiff**, 1984. Beautiful brown Hermann sits beside his German rival, Anniversary Papa Bear, by Steiff. *(See photo 259) Value: Left, $450-$600; Right, $600-$1000*

Steiff

The Steiff toy company (officially Margarete Steiff, GmbH) of Giengen-on-the-Brenz, Germany, played a unique role in the development of the teddy bear and other stuffed toys. The story begins with its founder—yes, there really was a Margarete Steiff—who overcame daunting physical handicaps to initiate and lead her company for more than 30 years.

She made her first stuffed toy in 1879 from a pattern she found in the German fashion magazine *Modenwelt*. She gave the little felt elephants stuffed with lambswool as gifts, but they were so popular that she made more to sell. By 1883, her price list showed several sizes of felt elephants for sale as children's toys.

Steiff's first stuffed toy—the elephant—was the work of Margarete, but its first jointed bear (the prototype for teddy bears) was the inspiration of Richard Steiff. According to Steiff archives, the company was making stuffed, nonjointed bears as early as 1892. By 1899 its catalog offered polar bears, dancing bears with handlers, and "Roly Poly" bears on rocking platforms. In 1902 a series of animals, including bears, was made with movable joints. The limbs were simply attached to the body by string. The animal shapes seem to have come from Richard Steiff's sketch pad, but it is not known who first thought of the jointed limbs. It was certainly Richard who devised the method used, however. When Richard's brother Paul carried the new toys to the United States early in 1903, he met with disappointment. The bear was obviously too hard, heavy, and large (21½″) for the American toy buyers. Margarete herself had feared the bear was too high priced to sell well.

It was in November of 1904 that the Steiff button-in-ear trademark was devised by Franz Steiff. Until that time, Steiff products had carried a cardboard label marked with the company's logo of an elephant with an upraised, S-shaped trunk. It is interesting to note that it is the motto "button in ear" that was given the German patent on May 13, 1905, not the button itself.

It was apparently a coincidence that Steiff began to produce the popular jointed bear at precisely the same moment in history when the teddy bear craze was sweeping America (following the November 1902 cartoon of President Theodore Roosevelt and the bear cub). Steiff built on the demand for their toy by aggressively advertising "the original teddy bear series." Their application for copyright of the name "teddy" and "teddy-bear" was denied, however (as was an application for a growler voice box); and many other companies in Germany and elsewhere competed with them for the bear market. The competition was exacerbated in 1907 by large orders being suddenly canceled during a deep but short recession in the United States.

Margarete Steiff died in 1909 at the age of 62, leaving her nephews and nieces as owners/managers of the prospering company that bears her name.

During the next 20 years Steiff continued to develop new lines of toys and dolls, including some truly original items: the "Roloplan," an air and wind toy that was part kite and part glider; a plush chimpanzee radiator cap and a felt "Michelin Man" and animals with snap-off limbs. The Steiff factory was allowed to produce only war supplies during World War I, but by the mid-1920s was expanding again with the installation of conveyer belts and modern machinery.

Richard Steiff, whose genius had created the teddy bear, died in 1939 in the United States, where he had lived since 1923 as representative of the firm and developer of its outstanding production and advertising methods.

Miraculously, Steiff's archival material, which included crates of prototype toys, production documents, and other treasures, escaped the ruptures of the war and postwar periods and today provide both a museum display and a historic record of the firm.

Not until 1947 was Steiff allowed to make a public offering of toys again. But since then, Steiff has regularly introduced new toys to a worldwide market and today also does a thriving business in reproducing, from its original patterns, teddy bears and other toys for the collector.

Its motto continues to be the words of Margarete Steiff, the remarkable founder, who wrote in her 1902–03 catalog: "For children only the best is good enough."

Steiff, display bear, 5′5″, c. 1948 (U.S. war zone Germany).   All original tags and labels present. Excellent mohair throughout. All jointed with original threads on mouth and nose. Pictured beside a young girl measuring 5′ 4″. Investment potential: Six of these bears have been sold in the United States and in Europe in the last five years. The range of value has been quite extensive, and the last one to sell went for $2400 at Sotheby's, London, 1986, from the author's collection. This bear failed to sell at auction, and negotiations after the sale

resulted in Steiff of Germany purchasing the bear for a special room and exhibit in their museum. Two similar bears were sold in the $1200–$1500 price range, and prior to the Sotheby's auction one identical bear, missing both his button and chest tag, sold for $8500 in 1985. It is clear that the potential for investment is great for large display items and that hidden values such as the fact that this bear is actually considered a logo bear for the Steiff Co. can create tremendous opportunities to bank on. In some cases such toys may appear on the market after the first one sells for a large sum. Only then will similar models surface, and the price usually drops accordingly. This bear represents a wonderful potential investment even for the beginning collector. *(See photo 260)*
Value: $8500 (D).

MODERN TEDDY BEARS

Advisor: CAROL-LYNN RÖSSEL WAUGH

Carol-Lynn Rössel Waugh was trained as an art historian and was one of the first American teddy bear artists. Today she is considered the foremost authority on contemporary American teddy bears. Carol-Lynn is the author of several books and countless magazine articles about dolls and teddy bears, and she co-edits a series of mystery anthologies and writes children's books. She is also the co-author of The Official Price Guide to Antique and Modern Teddy Bears *(New York: House of Collectibles, 1990). In addition to creating handmade teddy bears for collectors, she designs bears commercially for manufacturers, including the House of Nisbet in England (now part of Dakin) and Effanbee Dolls. Carol-Lynn lives with her husband and son in Winthrop, ME.*

CONTEMPORARY HANDMADE BEARS

Are you prowling antiques shops and boutiques, flea markets and sales, searching to replace the teddy bear you foolishly abandoned in adolescence? Do the paucity and prices of antiques make you growl? Take heart; the bear of your dreams may become reality.

The teddy bear market's character is rapidly changing. As old bears grow scarce and pricey, "designer teddies" are taking their place as today's hottest ursine collectible.

Except for age, these charming bruins sport the same desirable attributes as antiques: rarity, originality, and "name value," offering buyers the added bonus of "art patron" status.

Although artists have been quietly designing and making original bears since the early 1970s, awareness of their work has only recently reached the general public. Today's bear buyer has the luxury of a wide variety in style, size, materials, and price.

Since we are dealing here with a product that is currently being produced under widely diverse circumstances, for different subaudiences under one collector canopy, it is unwise to predict whose work will be a good investment, if that is your goal.

Collectors of contemporary handmade bears have, I believe, an advantage over antique-bear collectors. They can keep up to date on the latest trends and artisans through shows and trade magazines. They can compare and contrast work either by mail or in person, and they can specially commission work to meet their needs.

On the other hand, they are at a disadvantage if they want a time-proven "sure bet." There aren't many. However, as in any field of collecting, there are basic guidelines to follow and things to look out for. The following suggestions should make bear hunting less risky.

TEDDY BEAR ARTISTS

The reputation of the bearmaker is a good starting point for making purchasing decisions. Many people seek out "name" bearmakers. However, newer, less established people also produce superb work, and these may just be the ones to watch. As in any field, a bearmaker's longevity often equates with quality, but only if his or her work is constantly evolving. One basic design in 17 different colors, fabrics, and sizes, with new clothes and story lines every six months, does not qualify.

The contributions an artist has made to the field outside bearmaking add to his or her résumé, giving credibility and value to the work, as does professional recognition in terms of awards and commercial contracts.

The fewer bears an artist makes, the more valuable each one is. Thus, a bear made by a prolific artist (one who makes lots of bears) may not, down the road, have as much investment value as one by an artist with limited production. Of course, much depends on the bears in question. Outstanding design can override these parameters.

Is the bearmaker an innovator or a follower? Do his or her designs stand out because of appealing facial expression perhaps, or daring or innovative use of materials, techniques, or colors?

Upper-echelon teddy bear-makers have recognizable, personal style. Like Seurat's pointillist dots or Van Gogh's brush strokes, a bearmaker's "signature" shows in the way a nose is stitched, the way the eyes are set, in the bear's persona.

The best designers are daring, whimsical, and outrageous, playing with new concepts and new fabrics; yet their personal style, their way of expressing the "teddy bear essence," shines through all of these experiments. The past may inspire them, but they use it in unexpected, offbeat ways, not reproducing or copying bears designed by others. (Why waste time with retreads when there are wonderful new things to make?) Usually, they do limited editions or one-of-a-kind designs.

In time (and today the time lag can be the few weeks between teddy bear shows), innovators are copied. Their ideas filter down as diluted rip-offs selling to the less discriminating. The most desirable handmade bears are "all original," made entirely by the designer. Their freshness of concept, their flair, their fine workmanship set them apart. Reputable bearmakers mark work "designed by" if they did not actually handmake every part of it. If this is important to you, if you're paying for the bear to be "artist-made," ask.

Some "name" artists have begun designing for well-known toy companies in the United States and abroad. Their involvement varies, and hang tags should be checked to see to what extent the artist actually was involved in the development of the toy bearing his or her name. The involvement of some "celebrities" consists of lending a name to a product designed by in-house designers. Some provide sketches from which the product is made. This is *not* designing; it is merely offering inspiration.

PURCHASING GUIDELINES

Now that you have a whetted appetite and an idea of your prey, how can you track down these rare bears? Start looking at gift, speciality, and toy shops. Many now have a "stable" of bearmakers and are proud of the people whose work they have elected to represent. A knowledgeable owner can introduce bears by a favorite artist, recommend books and magazines, and even take special orders.

Look at "bear events": conventions, rallies, or sales. Here collectors can often meet bearmakers and compare work on the spot. The interaction with other arctophiles you'll experience at even one "bear rally" is invaluable, resulting in leads, solace, and inspiration. Word of new designers rockets through the bear world's extensive underground network. Become a part of it. Sharing the hunt is fun; it could be profitable.

Look in collector magazines such as *Teddy Bear Review* or *Teddy Bear and Friends* for up-to-date information on bearmakers, shows, supplies, and sales. Shops offering exclusive and limited-edition bears often advertise in such magazines, and they welcome phone calls and special orders.

But don't look for bargains. Although some cost under $100, teddies by "name artists," when available, can fetch well over $2000.

Before making such an investment, ask yourself why you are buying this bear. For interior decoration? Status? Resale? Love? I hope your motive is the last. If you fall in love with a bear, buy it. There will never be another exactly like it. Don't worry about resale; you're adopting a friend, not a portfolio.

Keep in mind that Teddy will likely remain with you for years. Look

The CONDITION KEY measures the degree of repair-restoration.

Poor Condition: Missing parts, breaks, and/or very bad restoration (possibly collectible because of some other merit).

Average Condition: Small parts may be missing, and cleaning may be necessary (the condition in which most objects are found).

Good Condition: No parts missing, no major cleaning needed—ready to use or display.

Fine Condition: Near original condition or restored to near original condition.

for a personality in tune with yours. Wait till he speaks to you, looks at you in a special way, before picking him up. Whatever your aesthetic standards, sometimes the most technically imperfect bear, the silliest one on the shelf, will say "take me home." If this happens, follow your heart.

Otherwise, look for workmanship. Are the ears sewn on well? They should appear to grow out of the head. Are the seams finished, with no thread showing? Has the fur been brushed from seam lines? Is the design excellent, original? Is it signed? Is its face wonderful? Of what is it made? Today mohair is "status," promising durability, huggability, and a large price tag. Real fur is a poor choice, as it can disintegrate.

Once you've found a bearmaker whose work you admire, who captures the teddy bear essence exactly for you, ask if he or she does commissions or special orders and how long one might take. Share your dreams, your hopes, your memories. Just maybe, working together, you'll be able to approximate (but never replace) that love-worn teddy you stashed, and lost, so many years ago.

A Buyer's Checklist

Questions to consider before buying a handmade bear:

1. What is the reputation of the bearmaker, including contributions to the field? How long has he or she been making bears?

2. Is the design original?

3. How rare is the bear? The work of a prolific artist (one who makes many bears) will, in general, be less valuable than one with very limited production.

4. Is it well made?

5. Exactly who made the bear? Was it completely made and dressed by its designer?

6. Is it signed?

7. Is its face wonderful?

8. Am I in love?

THE REV. CHESTER D. FREEMAN, JR.—"BASKETS AND BEARS"

"**The Freeman Backpacker Bear**" (logo and trademark of the classic Freeman Bears, copyright © 1983 by Chester Freeman) is 13″ tall. He is made of pure silver gray German mohair and has antique black shoe-button eyes, embroidered nose and mouth, and pure wool felt pads. He wears a handmade black ash splint Adirondack basket with red and green straps. *(See photo 261)*

Chester Freeman began making bears in 1982 during his chaplaincy at the University of Massachusetts in Amherst in response to a challenge from a friend. He found such acceptance for his work, both as a solacing object in hospital ministry and as a commercial product, that he went into the bear business full-time in 1985.

Chester's bears are classic in style, using a pattern he designed and refined until he felt it matched his idea of the "perfect teddy bear." Perhaps his best-known teddy wears a handmade basket backpack made by his partner, John Maguire, the other half of "Baskets and Bears."

They come in three sizes—10″, 13″, and 16″—are fully jointed, and are made from specially dyed imported mohair. Half are dressed, a new development for the upstate New Yorker. He handproduces from 250 to 300 a year. Special editions, when done, are limited to 100 or 150. He also produces charming teddy bear muffs.

Chester, whose work in two sizes has been produced commercially by Merrythought Ltd. in England, sees making bears as a logical outgrowth of his ministry: "I design and make bears as a symbol of love," he says, "a love that is patient and kind, always ready to excuse, to trust, to hope, and to endure."

Freeman bears are available at selected shops or by mail order.

Value: They range in price, *$98–$145.*

DOLORES GROSSECK—"BEARS OF SOUTHAMPTON"

Dolores Grosseck's 24″-tall mohair bear with felt paw pads is fully jointed and wears a fur-trimmed winter coat, a feather-trimmed picture bonnet, and lots of jewelry (copyright © 1989 by Dolores Grosseck). *(See photo 262)*

Whenever one of Dolores Grosseck's bears says what she wants it to say artistically, she credits the design education she received at Drexel University in Philadelphia. "The department stressed stretching ideas and integrating heretofore unrelated objects into a project and making them relate," she says. "As a result, I try to mix media, such as putting clay noses on bears."

She began making her large (20″ to 24″ tall) bears in 1986, using them as a vehicle for design concepts. "I've kept the body somewhat traditional," she says, "and choose to rely on the basic form relating to other media. There are many ways to reinterpret an art form, to reillustrate it. I use environmental props and relate them to my bear. A hat, bird, button, etc., will provide the springboard."

Often Dolores's bears wear clothing reminiscent of gentler times. Their props seem to come from already-established personalities. "I feel I do bears that come with a script," she says. "They're playing a role already, almost as if they had a life before the customers buy them. It is up to the customer to continue the play."

The Pennsylvania designer completes fewer than 100 bears a year and offers them for sale at shows or selected shops. Most are one-of-a-kind or in "editions" of two or three.

Value: "Bears of Southampton" range in price, *$250–$300.*

DEBBIE KESLING—"GRANNY'S LOCKET BEARS"

"Bellhop" by Debbie Kesling is 2″ tall, fully jointed, and made of upholstery fabric. He has enameled eyes, 14K-gold buttons, and Ultrasuede pads. He is stuffed with cotton batting. The costume is a permanent part of the bear. *(See photo 263)*

Since making her first bear in 1982, Debbie Kesling's teddies have undergone many evolutionary changes. Ranging upward in size from ³/₄″, they are fully jointed. Her "standard-size" bears are made from mohair or alpaca and have antique shoe-button eyes; tiny teddies are fashioned from special low-nap upholstery fabric and have special eyes Debbie developed.

Debbie loves making her bears, and it shows. She spends hours developing new patterns and personalities, searching for accessories and matching them with fabrics to enhance each bear's character. She stitches into each bear's face a sweet imploring innocence. But she rarely dresses them, except when the "fur" costume is part of the body. "I'm not a dressmaker," she said when asked about costuming. "I'm involved in birthing bears, not making their wardrobes."

In 1988 Debbie left her job as a corporate personnel manager to devote all of her time to bearmaking. She sells her bears directly—by mail or at shows—and rarely accepts wholesale accounts.

Value: "Granny's Locket" bears range in price, *$120–$220.*

MARGORY HOYA NOVAK

A trio composed of 16″ "Toby," 14″ "Delia, the Wood Nymph," and 12″ "Toby" is by Margory Hoya Novak. They are fully jointed and made of mohair, with glass eyes. *(See photo 264)*

Margory Hoya Novak came to bearmaking in 1980 from the world of

Photo 261 (left). Freeman Backpacker bear. CREDIT: DALE DUCHESNE.
Photo 262 (center). Dolores Grosseck mohair bear. CREDIT: RICHARD
HEGGS. *Photo 263 (right). Debbie Kesling "Bellhop" bear.* CREDIT:
CAROL-LYNN RÖSSEL WAUGH *(See pp. 521, 522)*

Photo 264 (left). Trio of bears by Margory Hoya Novak. CREDIT:
MARGORY HOYA NOVAK. *Photo 265 (right). Beverly Matteson Port bear.*
CREDIT: CAROL-LYNN RÖSSEL WAUGH *(See p. 522, 524)*

*Photo 266 (left).
Kimberlee Port
bear.* CREDIT:
CAROL-LYNN
RÖSSEL WAUGH

*Photo 267 (right).
Carol-Lynn Rössel
Waugh bear.*
CREDIT: CAROL-LYNN
RÖSSEL WAUGH
(See pp. 525, 526)

dolls. She still teaches porcelain dollmaking and gives workshops in bearmaking techniques when time permits. Beginning in 1973, she designed original award-winning dolls in porcelain and occasionally created plush animals to accompany them.

Her fully jointed mohair or synthetic plush teddies range in size from 7″ to 24″ and are easily identifiable by the signed self-fabric name tag that doubles as the bear's tail. Most are undressed. "I think it's harder to cuddle and take a dressed bear to bed with you for fear of messing it up," she says. "I like to give my bears the illusion of being dressed by using head coverings and collars, leaving their cute bare bodies soft and huggable."

Two of Marge's bears, "Toby" and "Delia," were inspired by a *National Geographic* special on Alaska's grizzlies. "All my sketches for them were done that day on my morning paper," she says. "The body has a rounded belly and hump on its back, while its arms are bent with paws intricately inserted, and the legs are curved in front with fetlocks in back like real bears have."

In 1988 she was selected to present two of her bears as a goodwill gesture to a delegation from the Russian "sister city" to Santa Rosa, CA.

Marge has won many awards for dollmaking, and her bears have been accepted as an art form by the exclusive Sausalito, CA, arts festival. But she doesn't make many of them—perhaps 30–40 a year, with a little help in stuffing from a young friend. "An edition of three bears is big for me," she says. "Then I'm ready to move on to something else."

"Marganova" bears are available from their designer at shows or by direct mail.

Value: They range in price, *$20–$175.*

BEVERLY MATTESON PORT

"**Raggedy Muffin Cubcake,**" a Forgotten FabriBear (copyright © 1987 by Beverly Matteson Port), is made of vintage and recycled fabrics. Her body, upper legs, and arms are vintage flour and cake sacks. Her hands have leather palms and wired separate fingers. Her head, hands, and feet are made of curly pink wool. She holds her "security bear" by the paw. She won the Golden Teddy award in 1988 and was shown at the Incorporated Gallery, New York, in 1987. *(See photo 265)*

Beverly Port has been an innovator in the doll and teddy bear field since she made her first teddy bears in the 1950s. Skilled in many art forms, she has combined media since the early 1970s to produce porcelain-faced soft-bodied dolls and teddies and is the first professional teddy bear artist of record.

In the late 1960s she introduced teddy bears as an art form in the doll world. Gradually breaking through "old guard" resistance, Bev paved the way for acceptance for subsequent waves of bearmakers, many of whom she taught and inspired. Her articles about teddy bears and their history were published years before collecting bears became fashionable, and she is well known for her lectures on the subject.

Beverly's work, which bridges the gap between plaything and sculpture, has won many awards, including Golden Teddy awards, for both handmade and commercial versions, and has been featured in art galleries. She designed successful teddy bear and gift lines for Gorham-Textron from 1985 to 1988. In 1989 the House of Nisbet, Ltd. produced a yes/no version of her "co-author," "Theodore B. Bear."

Ranging in size from 1″ to life-size, Beverly's repertoire ranges from fantasy bears to high-fashion teddies with swivel waists and armatured arms, to mechanical bears and nostalgic "Time Machine Teddies," who wear her well-known medallion with the logo: "Won't you be my teddy bear?" Others are trademarked with a "Bee" for "Bearverly."

Many Port designs are musical; some contain secret compartments or feature unexpected juxtapositions of fibers and ideas, such as patchwork leather paws or underbodies made of cake sacks, sweaters, or recycled memorabilia.

Because Bev works slowly, does all of her work alone, and is always experimenting, her production is very limited and her waiting list is lengthy. Her teddies are occasionally available by direct mail or through Emily's Cottage in Bremerton, WA, and other select stores.

Value: "Beverly Port Originals" range in price, *$295–$5000.*

KIMBERLEE PORT—"KIMBEARLEE KREATIONS"

"**Little Gold**" (copyright © 1984–89 by Kimberlee Port) is 2″ tall, fully jointed, and made of mohair with felt paw pads. She is dressed in vintage ribbon. *(See photo 266)*

When Kimberlee Port began making bears in 1974, she was an anomaly. Few people made art bears then, and fewer still made miniatures. But bears were a family concern, and Kim came up with her first original that year as a Christmas present for her mom. She was 14. By the time she was 16, her family of Christmas teddies had graced the cover of *Doll News*, receiving national acclaim.

Her work, which has won many awards, including the Golden Teddy award, has been displayed in several art galleries, including the Incorporated Gallery in New York City, and was on permanent display at the London Doll and Toy Museum. She is widely known for the entertaining cooking column she writes for *Teddy Bear Review* magazine and for the seminars she gives at bear conventions.

Always an innovator, Kim consistently produces designs stretching the definition of "teddy bearness," introducing such subsequently imitated concepts as "bearterflies," "Fleur" (a flower bear), and "Teddy, Teddy Tree," a green, mohair Christmas-tree bear with working miniature ornaments and "teddy star" on top. The latter has no precedent, antique or modern.

The first artist of record to create tiny, full-jointed teddies as an art form, her work ranges in size between ½" and 21" tall.

Kim is renowned for using the seamline joining body pieces in her smallest teddies as a design element. These entail 19–34 individual minute fabric pieces and hundreds of tiny handstitches. Larger teddies have turned pieces.

Because of the slow, painstaking way in which she creates her work, Kim's editions never exceed ten bears. She produces fewer than 50 annually. They are easily recognizable by their appealing faces ("I often spend four to five hours just on the face, to get the expression right," she says) and by their outstanding workmanship and attention to details. All of Kim's bears sport a signed clear-plastic heart; she was the first bear artist to use a heart as her signature. Some of her tiny teddies come in custom-made boxes designed to complement their contents.

"Kimbearlee Kreations" are available directly from the artist and occasionally from shops or at shows.

Value: They range in price, *$150–$950.*

CAROL-LYNN RÖSSEL WAUGH

"Noelle," a 22" mohair original by Carol-Lynn Rössel Waugh, limited edition, *$695. (See photo 267)*

Carol-Lynn Rössel Waugh (author of this section) grew up in New York City loving dolls, art, and books and has made them her life's work. She taught herself to sew doll and teddy bear clothes at six, designing originals at an early age, and went on to earn two degrees in the history of art.

A prolific writer, mystery anthologist, and award-winning photographer, the Winthrop, ME, resident is adept in many media, from watercolors to sculpture. She is best known in the doll and teddy bear worlds for her many photo-illustrated books and articles chronicling the work of contemporary artists. She is also an internationally respected teddy bear designer, producing work for three commercial firms as well as handmade originals for collectors.

A self-taught award-winning doll artist, she made her first jointed "teddy bear dolls" of porcelain in the mid-1970s, graduating to latex composition in the 1980s.

Her first mohair design, "Yetta Nother Bear," made in September 1985, was produced commercially by the House of Nisbet Ltd. in 1987 and was a best-seller, leading to other designs, including a yes/no bear named "Maybe." Her successful work for Effanbee Dolls ("Gilda and Gordon") has further proved her versatility in the commercial marketplace.

Carol-Lynn's originals range in size from 2″ to 22″, are fully jointed, and are distinguished by their sensitive, intelligent expressions, derived through a combination of needle sculpture and embroidery. Most have contented smiles and prominent noses. All sport distinctive embroidered eyebrows and wear a heart-shaped pendant around the neck. Most of her collector bears, as opposed to her commercial work, are undressed.

Because she is primarily a writer/photographer and because she works very slowly, believing an artist's bear should be completely handmade by its designer, Carol-Lynn's annual production is usually less than 50 teddies. That is why she has designed for home crafters an ongoing line of patterns for making bears and clothing centering on "Yetta Nother Bear" and her extensive family. Bears and patterns are available directly; selected shops infrequently carry Waugh teddies. Carol-Lynn also sells at two or three shows a year.

Value: Carol-Lynn Rössel Waugh's originals range in price, *$100–$1000.*

BIBLIOGRAPHY

ANTIQUE BEARS

Bialosky, Peggy and Alan. *The Teddy Bear Catalog*. New York: Workman, 1985.

Brooks, Jacki. *Teddy Bears on Parade Down Under*. Australian Doll Digest, 1986.

Bull, Peter. *The Teddy Bear Book*. Cumberland, MD: Hobby House, 1986.

Cieslik, Jurgen and Marianne. *Button in Ear: The History of the Teddy Bear and His Friends*. Jürlich/West Germany: Marianne Cieslik Verlag, 1989.

Gottschalke, Elke. *Geliebte Steiffe-Tiere*. Laterna Magica, 1984.

Hebbs, Pam. *Collecting Teddy Bears*. William Collins and Sons, 1988.

Hutchins, Margaret. *Teddy Bears and How to Make Them*. New York: Dover Books, 1977.

Mandel, Margaret Fox. *Teddy Bears and Steiff Animals*, 2nd series. Collector Books, 1987.

Mullins, Linda. *The Teddy Bear Men, Theodore Roosevelt and Clifford Berryman*. New York: Hobby House, 1987.

Schoonmaker, Patricia N. *A Collector's History of the Teddy Bear*. New York: Hobby House, 1981.

MODERN TEDDY BEARS

Green (Venturino), Joan, and Ted Menten. *Complete Book of Teddy Bears.* Publications International, 1989.

Maddigan, Judi. *Learn Bearmaking.* Open Chain Publishing, 1989.

Menten, Ted. *The Teddy Bear Lovers Companion.* Running Press, 1989.

Mullins, Linda. *Teddy Bears Past and Present.* New York: Hobby House, 1986.

Volpp, Rosemary; Paul, Donna Harrison; and Dottie Ayres. *Teddy Bear Artist Annual.* New York: Hobby House, 1989.

Waugh, Carol-Lynn Rössel. *Teddy Bear Artists: Romance of Making and Collecting Teddy Bears.* New York: Hobby House, 1984.

MAGAZINES

Bear Tracks: The Magazine of the Good Bears of the World, PO Box 8236, Honolulu, HI 96815.

Collector's Showcase, 1018 Rosecrans Street, San Diego, CA 92106.

Teddy Bear and Friends, 900 Frederick Street, Cumberland, MD 21502.

Teddy Bear Review, Collector Communications Corp., 170 Fifth Avenue, New York, NY 10010.

The Teddy Tribune, 254 West Sidney, St. Paul, MN 55107.

TEDDY BEAR ORGANIZATIONS

The Iowa Teddy Bear Makers Guild
4817 Dakota Drive
West Des Moines, IA 50265
Contact: Charlotte Joynt, Secretary

Westchester Teddy Bear Club
PO Box 329
Lake Peekskill, NY 10537
Contact: Vincent A. Tannone, President

TEDDY BEAR SHOWS

There are many teddy bear shows throughout the year. For current listings, see *Teddy Bear Review* and *Teddy Bear and Friends*. Also see the listing in Kim Brewer and Carol-Lynn Rössel Waugh's *The Official Price Guide to Antique and Modern Teddy Bears* (New York: House of Collectibles, 1990).

MUSEUMS

Museum of Childhood, Edinburgh, Scotland.

Textiles

(See also Arts and Crafts Movement, Vintage Clothing)

This chapter is arranged by the following subcategories:
COVERLETS, LACE, LINENS, QUILTS.

Advisor: ALDA LEAKE HORNER

Alda Leake Horner is an author, consultant, appraiser, and dealer. She is the author of The Official Price Guide to Linens, Lace, and Other Fabrics *(New York: House of Collectibles, 1991). She can be reached at Whitehall at the Villa Antiques and Fine Art, 1213 E. Franklin St., Chapel Hill, NC 27514; (919) 942-3179.*

When we think of handmade textiles in America, we must reflect on centuries of many cultures. Every country that sent settlers to our shores sent with them their special gifts and talents, which continue to influence our culture today. We have many objects remaining to enrich our lives and our knowledge of the lives they lived and the difficulties they surmounted. Their progeny have continued the arts and crafts to this day.

Textiles are essentially those things made from cloth or fabric, things that are woven, knitted, crocheted, or embroidered. We have coverlets; quilts; hand-woven blankets; samplers showing the exquisite, almost painful, expertise of young girls only nine or ten years old; bed rugs; floor rugs; tapestries; household linens; and clothing for the family, which was also handmade in the 18th and 19th centuries.

When shopping for such objects today, look for the brightest colors and best fabric condition, because the finest items were kept in trunks and closets and used only for "best company," which means that many were probably never out in daylight. That is why they are with us today!

Many of these items are collected today because there is a nostalgic feeling in this country for their decorative uses. There is also a professional interest in the study of textiles and related items of all kinds as part of our historic record.

MARKET TRENDS

This market is now in an upswing because of the interest shown in various professional home and decorator publications and because of the very high sales results in auction houses. Nostalgia for the lovely and the handmade, and the *honest*, is at an all-time high. Our feeling is that this trend will be with us for the coming decade and beyond because collectors are interested in this form of history for the pure honesty and integrity woven into the very fabric of the objects, and now the popular market wants them for their decorative value.

In this chapter ''ES'' means the item was purchased at an estate sale. The value level is similar to that found at flea markets.—*DL*

COVERLETS

Woven coverlets were made in England before the first settlers came to this country. It is thought that coverlets came over with them as part of their household necessities; and when those coverlets began to wear out, the housewife was forced to weave replacements.

The first looms in this country were very basic, and no fancy patterns could be woven on them. They could produce fine linen cloth, thin material for baby clothes and underwear, wool for clothing, wool and cotton coverlets for the beds and heavy tow for bed and feed sacks and other farm use. Most produced narrow strips of fabrics no more than 40 to 45 inches wide maximum, so it was necessary to seam strips together for beddings and tablecloths.

Coverlets were not made to be used as counterpanes but as a utilitarian necessity—a warm bed cover, or cover-lid (from the French *covrir lit*). The earliest made in this country were of a homespun linen warp with homespun and dyed wool weft. A few were made with wool in both the warp and weft, but unfortunately, very few of these have survived. Not many coverlets from the 17th and early 18th centuries have survived that may be definitely documented. The majority of what we see in the market today are made with cotton weft and wool warp from the late 18th century and the 19th century.

Machine-made coverlets date from the mid-19th century. The mills were fully mechanized by that time, using water power. During the Civil War, factories were busy weaving blankets for the war effort, and few had time to weave coverlets. When the war ended, handwoven coverlets had lost favor to the manufactured blanket; however, hand weaving continued in some rural areas for some time.

To avoid any misconceptions in terminology, quilts and coverlets are not the same, and the terms are not interchangeable. A quilt is made by sewing fabrics together in three layers: A top, a middle batting for warmth, and a backing. These three layers are held together by stitching through all layers in a decorative or simple manner. Some of the more decorative quilts that are used especially for show have little or no middle batting and are in only two layers. A coverlet is made by weaving yarns together on a loom. Both are intended for use as warm bed coverings.

There are four types of coverlets: overshot, double weave, summer and winter, and jacquard. Listings are arranged by these categories.

OVERSHOT

This is considered the first type of coverlet made in America. It was made on the simple, small hand loom in strips of no more than 40- to 45-inch widths. Early coverlets had homespun linen as the warp thread and homespun and home-dyed wool as the weft. The most popular colors for the wool were various shades of indigo blue. The availability of cotton yarn caused it to replace linen, and very few coverlets with linen warp are found today.

The overshot pattern was achieved by having the wool weft skip over several of the warp threads at given spaces to create a pattern. The skip thread would lie on top of the warp and could be lifted up with a small implement or a fingernail, very much like a long stitch in bargello needlework. It was possible to weave many different designs and color combinations; however, all were geometric or plaids. None were signed in the loom; sometimes there were cross-stitched initials or numbers worked on a corner.

DOUBLE WEAVE

These coverlets were also made on a small, narrow hand loom and had to be seamed up the center. The weaving incorporated two warp yarns and two weft yarns, back to back. Where there was a color change, the weft yarn would go through to the other layer of fabric, thus joining the two layers together at that color change. This produced a coverlet with a dark background and a light pattern on one side and a light background on the other with the dark pattern showing. The two layers may be separated with the fingers. These two layers made a very warm bedcover. All patterns were geometric and in colors available at the time. A few were initialed.

SUMMER AND WINTER

This is a single-weave, double-face coverlet. This type of weave has the design in reverse from front to back. One side is light and presumably used in summer; the other side is dark and used in winter. Since this is lighter in weight than the double weave, it would be suitable for summer use. The designs were more elaborate than those of the overshot but still geometric. They were more closely woven, having the overshot pass over no more than three warp threads at a time.

JACQUARD

This type of coverlet was made possible when a Frenchman, Joseph Jacquard, invented an attachment for the loom that would make possible patterns of curvilinear designs on large *unseamed* coverlets.

Jacquard coverlets could be woven in a variety of patterns and with fanciful borders. These borders were often specialized designs of one particular weaver and usually contained his name, date, town, and customer's name in a corner block. This has greatly aided research into the history, area of manufacture, and provenance of this type of coverlet. There have been hundreds of Jacquard weavers documented, many being Germans who emigrated to this country.

MARKET TRENDS

Coverlets are a very popular item in the antiques and collectibles fields at present. The renewed interest in all textiles recently has caused the market to appreciate considerably. This trend has been helped along tremendously by various decorator and home magazines, as well as by interior decorators. Many coverlets are more modestly priced than quilts of the same age and condition. It is still possible to collect some very attractive coverlets for under $500. Prices are stable at this time and probably will remain so for a while. But, just remember, as with all antique textiles, they are becoming more scarce, and with time, they will appreciate in value along with market demands. Always buy the very best for the amount you have to invest.

CONDITION KEY

This listing measures only the physical condition of the article, not the quality of design, materials used, or workmanship.

Fine Condition: as close to mint as possible; no stains or visible repairs; bright colors; no thin areas; no losses.

Good Condition: few repairs, using period threads and not obvious if repaired; all seams and hems are strong; original fringe or of the period if replaced; colors good, with slight fading of dyes; some overall wear.

Average Condition: some repairs, fading, and thinning; minor breaks and losses; may need cleaning; this is the condition in which most coverlets are found.

Poor Condition: thinning and breaks in wool; some losses, especially at top; fading; needs cleaning; not collectible for investment; if not valuable due to provenance, will be suitable for pillows, stuffed toys, and framed sections.

QUALITY KEY

This listing measures the stylishness and collectibility of the piece within its category.

Good Quality: nice piece worthy of collecting but not for investing.

Very Good Quality: appealing design; good color selection; workmanship is excellent; all elements stylistically correct for period.

Superior Quality: high visual impact; expert workmanship of highest quality; all elements are superb and of the period.

Overshot   72″ × 76″   c. 1820   United States
Natural homespun linen warp, homespun indigo wool weft; 2-part, center seam restitched; top and bottom rehemmed; wear to wool, linen breaking; clean. *(See photo 268)*
Good Quality/Poor Condition $100 (ES)   **$50–$250**

Overshot   72″ × 84″   c. 1830   United States
Two-piece; blue, red, and natural white cotton; end fringe original, side fringe has been added and could be easily removed; optical type pattern.
Good Quality/Average Condition $198 (A)   **$150–$350**

Overshot   64″ × 86″   c. 1830–1835   United States
Two-piece; red and natural white with sewn-on fringe.
Good Quality/Average Condition $165 (A)   **$150–$350**

Overshot   66″ × 82″   c. 1830   United States
Two-piece; two shades of blue and natural white cotton; self fringe on sides; top and bottom hemmed; some losses to top edge.
Good Quality/Good Condition $325 (D)   **$250–$500**

Double weave   68″ × 84″   c. 1835   United States
Two-piece; cross motif pattern; deep blue and natural white cotton; self fringe on sides, sewn-on bottom fringe; center seam restitched; heavy.
Very Good Quality/Good Condition $525 (D)   **$350–$750**

Double weave   72″ × 76″   c. 1835–1840   United States
Two-piece; blue, rust, and natural white; geometric design; side weft fringe; top and bottom hand-hemmed; some losses at top edge; overall wear.
Good Quality/Average Condition $275 (D)   **$150–$350**

Summer-winter   70″ × 90″   c. 1840   United States
Two-piece; rust, black, gold, and natural white; weft fringe on two sides; sewn-on fringe on bottom; good colors; center seem needs restitching. *(See photo 269)*
Very Good Quality/Good Condition $350 (D)   **$250–$500**

Jacquard   85″ × 91″   Patriotic   c. 1850   United States
One piece; single weave in two shades of green, two shades of brown, red, and natural white; star and floral medallion center with eagles and banners: ''Virtue, Liberty & Independence''; borders have compotes and flowers, trees, stags, etc.; very minor stains.
Very Good Quality/Average Condition $440 (A)   **$250–$600**

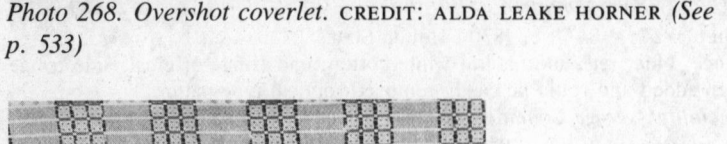

Photo 268. Overshot coverlet. CREDIT: ALDA LEAKE HORNER *(See p. 533)*

Photo 269.
Summer-winter coverlet.
CREDIT: ALDA LEAKE
HORNER *(See p. 533)*

Jacquard 76″ × 82″ Patriotic c. 1876 United States
One piece; single weave; "Centennial, Memorial Hall, 1776–1876"; good bright colors of red, green, blue, grayish brown, and white; minor wear, some very minor stains, a few small faded spots.
Good Quality/Average Condition $250 (A)   **$150–$400**

Jacquard 78″ × 96″ 1852 Trexlertown, PA
One piece; double weave; green, red, navy blue, and natural white; star and floral medallion with floral border and corners marked "Made by E. Hausman, Trexlertown, 1852"; stains; Ephriam Hausman (1813–1901, son of Jacob, also a weaver).
Very Good Quality/Good Condition $660 (A)   **$500–$750**

Jacquard 82″ × 84″ c. 1850 United States
Two piece; double weave; blue and white; birds feeding young; Christian and heathen borders showing Boston houses and Oriental houses with palm trees; some wear.
Superior Quality/Good Condition $935 (A)   **$750–$1200**

Jacquard 78″ × 88″ c. 1850 United States
Two piece; double weave; deep blue and natural white floral and fruit pattern; edge wear and stains with minor overall wear; unsigned.
Good Quality/Good Condition $500 (A)   **$300–$700**

LACE

The four main types or "families" of lace can be more or less broken down into the centuries in which they were developed: 16th century— embroidered laces; 17th century—needlepoint laces; 18th century— bobbin laces; 19th century—machine-made laces, "imitation" laces, chemical laces, mixed laces, and in the 20th century—the now very popular "crazy quilt" mix of laces in household linens and fashion items.

Embroidered laces were mostly openwork or drawnwork in handmade linen using handspun linen thread and an ordinary sewing needle. Some of the threads were drawn and/or removed from the fabric's counted spaces, and the remaining threads were then bundled together and held in place by sewing together to create a simple design. Since this was worked into fabric, it was used mainly as an edging such as a ruff for collars and cuffs, also for altar cloths and vestments. Modern-day equivalents are Ayrshire, broderie anglaise, and Madeira.

Needlepoint laces are recognized by the buttonhole stitch and are made with a single thread and an ordinary sewing needle. The basis of all needlepoint lace is the buttonhole stitch, which makes it immediately recognizable. It is considered by many to be the earliest form of lace. The two earliest needlepoint laces were *reticella* and *punto in aria*.

Bobbin laces are produced by a process of weaving with bobbins— from which its name is derived. It is also known as "bone" lace and "pillow" lace. A design is pricked into parchment or cardboard and attached to a pillow; pins are placed in the pricked design to hold the threads as they are woven, plaited, twisted, and formed into a patterned motif that closely resembles woven fabric. The thread is first wound around bobbins, and the lacemaker manipulates these around the pins, sometimes using two hundred or more bobbins, depending on the design and width of the lace being made. The width was limited by the width of the pillow before the advent of machine-made lace. "Bone" lace refers to the fact that many of the early bobbins were made of bones from chickens, birds, or small animals.

The fourth type includes *machine laces*, *chemical laces*, and *"imitation" laces*. These date from the 19th century with the development of many new technologies.

The era of glorious handmade laces ended with the French Revolution in 1789. Clothing was suddenly very plain. Most people became puritanical, considering lace frivolous and unpatriotic.

Machine-made lace was a product of the Industrial Revolution. By 1840 machine technology had progressed to producing very good imitations almost undetectable from most handmade laces. This was greatly helped by the French invention of the Jacquard "card" system. The Great Exhibition of 1851 and the International Exhibition of 1867 had a great influence on the use of machine-made lace, designs, and manufacture.

With the introduction of machine-made products, the use of lace was no longer the status symbol of the wealthy, as it was soon available to all classes.

Chemical lace was an invention of both the Swiss and Germans in 1883, at about the same time. It was derived from machine-made cotton embroidery on silk; the silk was then dissolved by chlorine or caustic soda wash. This technique was used to imitate almost all forms of lace, obviously making it much less expensive than the original handmade or machine lace.

Now less drastic processes are used, such as blasting with hot air, making it possible to produce more delicate embroidery and therefore a more delicate lace. It is easy to detect chemical lace by the fuzzy appearance of the edges and brides, the lack of definite lace stitches, and a matted look on the reverse.

Imitation laces were popular during the late Victorian era and the early 20th century. There was a fascination with amateur crafts, and this led to the home production of what is termed "imitation laces." Many of these were not new methods but were based on old processes:

"Battenberg" was made from machined braid or tape basted down on a paper or fabric-printed pattern, then turned and twisted into curves or angles to follow the outlines. Tapes are then joined by brides and fillings to hold the tapes together. The earlier work had a fineness to the brides and fillings that is not evident in recently made battenberg.

Some form of "crochet" has been mentioned since the 14th century, though not becoming popular as an art form until the early 19th century; the Irish first produced it in the mid-1840s. It was an important cottage industry during the potato famine (1846), when even men and boys joined the women and girls in this endeavor. It is worked with a crochet hook using cotton thread and is identified by the tiered rose petals in the design and the frequent use of the shamrock. The first lace to be copied by the chemical lace method was Irish crochet, in the 1880s.

"Filet crochet" was extremely popular in the late 1880s and 1890s, up through the early 20th century to about 1940. It was worked to resemble needle-run net. The basic pattern was net form with stitches crocheted in to fill the square holes, creating a pattern. Crochet has been designed to imitate many other forms of lace as well.

"Knitting" dates from the early 1800s. It is worked with one to four needles, making horizontal rows of loops from a continuous thread. Knitted lace came into popularity during the Victorian era.

"Macramé" differs from knotted lace in that it is not made with a needle but by hand, usually using very heavy or coarse threads.

"Tambour," as a lace, is made with a hook and a basic chain stitch on net to create a design. This method is also used on fabric and is considered an embroidery stitch. It is now machine-made.

"Tatting" dates from the 18th century. It is made with a shuttle and a continuous thread. It uses one basic knot to secure the loops and picots.

"Mixed laces" are pieces containing different styles of laces in one object, such as a combination of needle and bobbin laces or different laces stitched onto net. Frequently, this will include embroidery as well.

A new use for lace in the past few years is referred to as "crazy quilt." This is not a process or method of construction but a clever way to use all of those beautiful snippets of lace that we collect and can't possibly discard.

As you delve into the mysteries of lace history, you will find it to be fascinating. Its development has spanned one of the most interesting, intriguing, and explosive periods of our documented history. It is at once a social, political, and industrial history of its time.

COLLECTING TIPS

Examine the article and try to place it in the proper family. Is it a bobbin lace that has *woven*-appearing *toiles*? Does it appear to be needlepoint with toiles and brides of buttonhole stitch? Check through the other various categories until you have a feel for its identity. A magnifying glass will be of enormous help. Machine-made lace is almost impossible to distinguish from handmade lace—with the exception that the designs will all be exactly alike and even; handmade lace will show stitches and designs that are less uniform, and some will be tighter or looser in execution and perhaps more random. Until you have learned to spot chemical lace by sight, examine the reverse with the glass. It will seem matted, and you will not be able to follow a thread through the design. The edges will appear less smooth and more fuzzy than other lace. Using the glass, check for minor breaks and losses and also the type of thread used. Early lace was made from linen or silk. After the advent of the machine, cotton was used almost exclusively until the 20th century and the development of manmade fibers. That should help you put it in the proper *time* frame. Compare it with the condition and quality keys to assist with a decision of putting it in the proper *value* scale.

You will not see very much handmade lace on the market today. Machine-made lace dates from 1830, and since that date until today it has been, and still is, made in great quantities. The finer and older machine-made lace is highly collectible; it is lovely and is just as desirable as—and certainly more affordable than—early handmade lace, if and when you find it.

MARKET TRENDS

For many years lace was out of fashion, but now, considered an art form, it is making a dramatic comeback. Since the late 1970s and through the 1980s there has been a considerable upsurge in the market. Interest among collectors has been higher than at any time since the early days, when royalty and the gentry vied with each other for the most lavish use of lace. Many workshops have been formed around this country and in Europe to research and teach the early techniques of handmade lace.

We are using lace for clothing fashions as never before in this century and also for home decoration. Every fashion magazine or advertisement shows clothing with some touch of lace—collars or cuffs—not only in adult fashions but for children and babies. We still feel a great love for the christening gowns made with yards and yards of lace trim, and we still hold onto these family traditions. Many young women today want handmade Victorian wedding gowns with all of the white work and lace frothings.

Home decorators use lace in household fashions because it is compatible with quilts, coverlets, antique linens, and the wonderful reproduction fabrics on the market now. Is there any wonder that lace is a big market today?

CONDITION KEY

This listing measures only the physical condition of the article, not the quality of design, material, or workmanship.

Fine Condition: complete and original or restored to original condition; retains its original ground; without stains, fading, or losses; most desired condition for collecting.

Good Condition: restored or replaced ground, as near to original as possible; no breaks, fading, or stains; may need cleaning.

Average Condition: needs minor mending; may have weak spots; some losses; minor stains and fading; needs cleaning; this is most often the condition in which lace is found.

Poor Condition: most often found in fragments or pieces removed from an article; frequently will show weak spots, stains and fading; needs cleaning; collectible for doll clothes, "crazy quilt," and other small articles where the good sections can be utilized with other fabrics. Usually found in "box lots" at flea markets and estate sales; often a bargain—but not for investment!

QUALITY KEY

This listing measures the stylishness and collectibility of the piece within its category.

Good Quality: exhibits standard characteristics of the piece, whether handmade or machine-made.

Very Good Quality: more desirable example because of above-average design, materials, and workmanship.

Superior Quality: exhibits every known feature found for such items, handmade or machine-made, with design, material, and workmanship of highest quality; most desirable for collecting.

EMBROIDERED LACE

Banquet cloth 72″ × 144″ Drawn and cut c. 1935 Italy
Ivory linen; border of cut and drawn floral designs attached by brides; deep pointed edges; the entire center is of drawn work in ¼″ square filets; all needlework done in brown thread; with 12 matching napkins, 24″ × 24″. *(See photo 270)*
Superior Quality/Fine Condition $1800 set (D)   **$900–$1800**
Bridge cloth 52″ × 52″ Drawn work c. 1920 China
Silk pongee; natural color; wide hem is hemstitched; design has been worked from threads after planned warp and weft threads have been removed; all handmade.
Very Good Quality/Fine Condition $85 (D)   **$45–$85**

Doily 18″ × 24″ Cut work c. 1930–1940 Madeira
Oval white linen with pale blue embroidery edges; needlepoint brides and toiles in cut spaces; filet lace edging.
Good Quality/Average Condition $15 (D)   **$12–$35**

Tablecloth 68″ × 102″ Cut work 1920–1930 Italy
Natural-colored linen; needlepoint lace toile inserts and machine embroidery; machine-hemstitched border.
Good Quality/Fine Condition $125 (D)   **$75–$150**

Tablecloth 68″ × 84″ Cut work c. 1935 Madeira
White linen; insets of floral design; border of white filet lace 2″ wide; with 8 napkins with corner motif and filet lace edging, 20″ × 20″.
Good Quality/Average Condition $195 set (D)   **$165–$225**

Table runner 18″ × 54″ Drawn work c. 1920 China
White linen; all handwork.
Good Quality/Average Condition $18 (D)   **$15–$45**

Table runner 18″ × 60″ Drawn work c. 1930 Italy
White linen; classical design of peacocks and flower vases; filet background, all hand-drawn and hand-stitched; designs on both ends.
Very Good Quality/Good Condition $95 (D)   **$45–$125**

Tea cloth 56″ × 56″ Drawn work c. 1900 Italy
White linen; all designs are drawn and whipped by hand; a fine example. *(See photo 271)*
Superior Quality/Fine Condition $175 (D)   **$125–$225**

Tea cloth 56″ × 56″ Cut and drawn work c. 1935 Philippines
White linen; "Army-Navy" type, having alternating squares of cut and drawn work with floral filet insertions on linen and squares of floral-design filet lace; 2″ filet lace border; no losses.
Very Good Quality/Average Condition $95 (D)   **$65–$125**

NEEDLEPOINT LACE

Border 54″ × 64″ × 4″ Gros Point c. 1900 Italy
Ecru; border removed from worn linen tablecloth; outer border with a center strip; special attention to corners; machine-made toiles, hand-assembled; no losses; a bargain from an estate sale. *(See photo 272)*
Very Good Quality/Average Condition $25 (ES)   **$15–$50**

Doilies 18″ Dia., 24″ Dia. Rose Point c. 1900 Italy
Ivory color; allover rose design; scalloped edges; machine-made; no losses; 2 minor breaks that may be tacked.
Very Good Quality/Average Condition $95 pair (D)   **$50–$125**

Napkins, dinner 26″ × 26″ Point de Venise trim c. 1900 Italy
Set of 12; ecru linen; large motif with putti and flower in 1 corner; 1.5″ matching lace border; machine-made lace, hand-assembled and hand-applied to linen; very elegant.
Superior Quality/Fine Condition $550 (ES)   **$450–$600**

Place mats 11″ × 15.5″ Alençon c. 1935 France
Set of 8, luncheon size; ivory; machine-made; allover floral pattern; scalloped edges; with 8 napkins, 14.5″ × 14.5″; edged in narrow matching lace.
Good Quality/Average Condition $75 (D)   **$50–$95**

Where the value range clearly exceeds the amount sold for, this reflects price increases during the last year.

Photo 270 (left). Banquet cloth lace. CREDIT: ALDA LEAKE HORNER.
Photo 271 (right). Tea cloth lace. CREDIT: ALDA LEAKE HORNER *(See pp. 539, 540)*

Photo 272 (left). Border needlepoint lace. CREDIT: ALDA LEAKE HORNER. *Photo 273 (right). Lace cap.* CREDIT: ALDA LEAKE HORNER *(See pp. 540, 542)*

Photo 274. Lappet.
CREDIT: ALDA LEAKE HORNER
(See p. 542)

Scarf 17″ × 45″ Alençon c. 1930–1935 France
Ecru; allover floral design; machine-made.
Good Quality/Fine Condition $23 (D)   **$18–$25**
Tablecloth, banquet 84″ × 144″ Point de Venise c. 1940 China
Ecru cotton thread; allover design of leaves and medallions surrounded by bor-
ders of flowers; hand-assembled; few stains, no losses; with set of 12 napkins of
ecru linen with a corner motif and 1″ matching lace on edges; quality of lace
superior to workmanship of napkin construction; lace machine-applied to raw
edge of fabric; 24″ × 24″; napkins unused, paper labels still attached.
Good Quality/Average Condition $750 set (ES)   **$500–$2500**

BOBBIN LACE

Bridal veil 48″ × 80″ Brussels c. 1940 Belgium
White, scrolling border (8″ deep) on net field; some breaks in net field; machine-
made.
Very Good Quality/Average Condition $235 (D)   **$150–$250**
Cap, adult size Valencienne c. 1850 France
Ivory color; very fine threads; hand-sewn. *(See photo 273)*
Good Quality/Good Condition $25 (ES)   **$15–$50**
Cape 45″ Dia. Chantilly c. 1890–1920 France
Black, complete circle; showing typical floral, ribbon, and swag pattern; no
losses or breaks.
Very Good Quality/Good Condition $225 (D)   **$150–$250**
Collar, Bertha 6″ × 24″ Brussels probably c. 1900 United States
Ivory color; machine-made; fine; lightweight.
Very Good Quality/Fine Condition $175 (D)   **$125–$225**
Cloth 32″ Dia. Cluny c. 1900–1920 United States
Ivory color; machine-made lace, hand-applied to linen center; slight fold-line
stain, will launder; probaby made from a kit.
Good Quality/Good Condition $50 (D)   **$25–$75**
Doilies 12″ × 16″ Bobbin c. 1920 France
Pair; ivory color; oval; center motif in form of lady with a basket of fruit;
machine-made toiles attached to edging by handmade plaited brides.
Very Good Quality/Good Condition $95 pair (D)   **$75–$125**
Dress trim 14″ × 12″ Buckinghamshire c. 1900 England
Ivory cotton thread; neck trim and frontal combined; machine-made; typical
Bucks design.
Good Quality/Average Condition $18 (ES)   **$12–$45**
Flounce 5″ × 72″ Lille c. 1900 France
Ivory color; machine-made; Lille is often very similar to Bucks; few minor breaks
in net.
Good Quality/Average Condition $15 (ES)   **$10–$35**
Handkerchief 14″ × 14″ Honiton c. 1920 England
Ivory color; very fine linen with 1.5″ machine-made lace; hand-applied.
Good Quality/Average Condition $18 (D)   **$10–$25**
Lappet 6″ × 45″ Brussels c. 1850–1870 Belgium
Cream color, extremely fragile, fine, and lightweight; appears to be handmade,
although pieces of this quality were machine-made at this time; shows flowers,
leaves, and scrolls. *(See photo 274)*
Superior Quality/Fine Condition $195 (D)   **$95–$225**

Pillow cover 18″ × 34″ Chantilly c. 1910–1920 France
Cream-color lace with inserts of embroidered batiste, all machine-made and hand-assembled; lined and backed with peach-colored iridescent taffeta; label reads: "Made in France."
Superior Quality/Fine Condition $225 (D) **$150–$275**

CHEMICAL AND IMITATION LACES (MACHINE-MADE)

CHEMICAL LACES

Bodice Medium size Chemical c. 1920–1930 United States
White; lace front and collar on a net bodice to be worn under a dress or blouse; collar is fully ruffled; side ties at waist.
Good Quality/Average Condition $25 (D) **$15–$50**

Doily 24″ Dia. Chemical c. 1940 United States
White cotton; allover pattern of flowers, leaves, and swirls.
Good Quality/Good Condition $4 (ES) **$2–$15**

Handkerchief 10″ × 10″ Chemical c. 1950 United States
White cotton lace on batiste center; machine-attached.
Good Quality/Average Condition $3 (D) **$1–$10**

Lappet 6″ × 48″ Chemical c. 1880 England
White cotton net with 2″ ruffled lace edging.
Good Quality/Good Condition $15 (ES) **$10–$35**

IMITATION LACES

Doily 27″ Dia. Battenberg c. 1880–1890 United States
All white; fine linen center; very well-defined bunches of grapes with well-padded rings; leaves are of very narrow tapes and fine threads; spaces filled with spiderweb-like brides; hand-sewn to center; very fine example. *(See photo 275)*
Superior Quality/Fine Condition $135 (D) **$50–$150**

Photo 275 (left). Doily. CREDIT: ALDA LEAKE HORNER. *Photo 276 (right). Tea tray cover.* CREDIT: ALDA LEAKE HORNER *(See above and p. 544)*

Luncheon cloth   54″ × 60″   Battenberg   c. 1880–1890   United States
All white; linen center; leaf and swirl design; well-defined rings; hand-constructed and hand-applied to linen.
Very Good Quality/Good Condition $95 (D)   **$50–$125**

Scarf   18″ × 44″   Battenberg   c. 1920   United States
All white; designs of daisy-like flowers and leaves with circular corner motifs; needs minor tacking; no losses.
Good Quality/Average Condition $35 (D)   **$25–$50**

Tablecloth   68″ × 84″   Battenberg   c. 1930   United States
All white linen; rectangular center motif and outer edges of floral, leaf, and vine pattern; needs minor tacking; no losses.
Good Quality/Average Condition $75 (ES)   **$50–$150**

CROCHET

Antimacassar   12″ × 15″   Filet crochet   c. 1910   United States
Cream color; design has cat encircled in scrolls; 3 pieces, including back and 2 arm covers.
Very Good Quality/Good Condition $45 set (D)   **$25–$65**

Bedspread   88″ × 104″   Crochet   c. 1930   United States
Cream-color cotton thread; hexagonal shape; 6-point star shapes and shield motifs; 6″ hand-tied fringe on 3 sides.
Good Quality/Average Condition $285 (D)   **$195–$375**

Bodice insert   6″ × 12″   Irish crochet   c. 1910–1920   Ireland
White mercerized cotton, fine thread; handmade with picots on brides; heavy toiles with double raised leaves.
Good Quality/Average Condition $12 (ES)   **$10–$25**

Edgings, assorted   Filet crochet   c. 1890–1930   United States
White cotton thread; assorted patterns of handmade filet crochet; each removed from worn pillow cases; these are examples of lot bargains available at various sales, found along with items that may be a total loss; use for pillow cases, towel edgings, little girl's skirt trim, collar and cuff sets, etc.
Good Quality/Good Condition $3 lot (ES)   **$1–$15**

Napkin envelope   12″ × 24″   Filet crochet   c. 1890–1910   United States
White; rose motif and monogram.
Very Good Quality/Good Condition $18 (D)   **$10–$35**

Tea tray cover   18″ × 24″   Filet crochet   c. 1935   United States
White; showing tea accessories and "Take a Cup For Auld Lang Syne"; 4 linen napkins with teapot motif in 1 corner. *(See photo 276)*
Good Quality/Good Condition $35 set (D)   **$25–$50**

KNITTED LACES

Bedspread   85″ × 106″   Knitted   c. 1920–1930   United States
Ivory mercerized cotton thread; 6″ geometric squares in assorted pattern samples; crocheted edging 4 sides plus 6″ hand-tied fringe on 3 sides.
Very Good Quality/Fine Condition $375 (D)   **$250–$425**

Doily   12″ Dia.   Knitted   c. 1910–1920   United States
White, fine mercerized cotton thread; floral-and-spoke pattern; scalloped edging; would be lovely backed with fabric and framed.
Good Quality/Average Condition $15 (ES)   **$5–$25**

Pillow cover 14ʺ Dia. Knitted c. 1950 United States
Natural-color cotton thread; knitted in a pinwheel pattern with scalloped edging; underlined and backed with fabric to match; button back.
Very Good Quality/Average Condition $18 (ES) $10–$45

TAMBOUR LACES

Curtain panels 36ʺ × 90ʺ Tambour c. 1935 United States
Ivory; machine-made; allover floral, leaf, and spray design on net; scalloped edges on 3 sides; pocket top; some losses of design.
Good Quality/Average Condition $65 pair (ES) $50–$250

Tablecloth 64ʺ × 86ʺ Tambour c. 1920 France
White; machine-made; floral-and-spray design on net with elegant cartouche in center; losses to design and minor tears in net. *(See photo 277)*
Good Quality/Poor Condition $25 (ES) $25–$250

TATTED LACES

Handkerchief 12ʺ × 12ʺ Tatted c. 1950 United States
White linen center with hemstitched edge with 1ʺ tatted lace attached, ruffled; somber shades of lavender.
Very Good Quality/Fine Condition $10 (D) $5–$35

Lace edging 1ʺ × 72ʺ Tatted c. 1940 United States
White; lovely lace pattern suitable for baby clothes or lingerie; another bargain find!
Very Good Quality/Fine Condition $5 (ES) $2–$15

Photo 277 (left). Tablecloth. CREDIT: ALDA LEAKE HORNER. *Photo 278 (right). Lace blouse.* CREDIT: ALDA LEAKE HORNER *(See above and p. 546)*

MIXED LACES

Collar 3″-W lace   Mixed lace   c. 1930   Ireland
Ivory; main portion of collar is Carrickmacross lace (appliqué) mixed with Chantilly at front tabs and edging; cutwork is filled with a variety of brides; machine-made.
Good Quality/Good Condition $18 (ES)   **$12–$35**

Tea cloth 42″ Dia.   Mixed lace   c. 1900–1910   Italy
All white; center is fine-quality linen; inner insert is needlepoint; outer border is exquisitely worked in bobbin-lace figures in reliefs, attached by brides to needlepoint floral-and-leaf toiles with a scalloped edge of bobbin lace; a truly fine example of very high quality.
Superior Quality/Fine Condition $325 (D)   **$250–$350**

CRAZY QUILT LACE

Blouse Size 8/10   Mixed laces   United States
Ivory; a collection of at least 7 kinds of laces stitched together into a very attractive lady's blouse in a Victorian style; this blouse was put together on a net base to help support and stabilize the fragile lace; cuffs have ribbons run through and tied in a bow at the wrist. *(See photo 278)*
Superior Quality/Fine Condition $285 (D)   **$150–$450**

Tablecloth, banquet 84″ × 144″   Crazy quilt   c. 1940   United States
Off-white; a variety of laces and strips of 2″-wide net trim assembled into a very exciting banquet cloth; no under-lining; all laces are hand-assembled onto each other; center medallion and swag trim; other laces filling in spaces and a medallion of Brussels lace in each of the corners.
Very Good Quality/Fine Condition $1200 (D)   **$500–$1500**

LINENS

Due to the fragile nature of linens and because so many were stored improperly through the years, fewer and fewer of the lovely old pieces are appearing for sale on the market. The finest and earliest will be found in museums and in private collections and not available to the average collector. However, there is a great interest in linens today, thanks to the many home and decorator magazines and other publications that are showing them being used lavishly in home settings and because of the feeling of nostalgia that seems to pervade our culture at this time. There is a tremendous upswing in the manufacture of new linens at present, coming from Europe and China and also being made here in the United States. Although some are very well made by hand, most are machine-made but can easily be used with the older pieces. Most will not show the intricate handwork and the fresh and naive designs that our great-grandmothers and great-aunts lovingly worked into each precious object. It is those linens that have, fortunately, survived and have been passed down through the years to us that we will be discussing.

We owe much to the banks of the Nile. Not only did they give us the world's finest long-staple cotton but also linen from the flax plant. The word *linen* has been borrowed from the Latin *linum*, flax. Linen has been known to exist for many centuries, dating back to wrappings for Egyptian mummies. Linen as a table cover has been mentioned in the Bible and other writings of an early age. We have seen "borde" cloths in early drawings and paintings showing sharply pressed creases in the fold lines. History tells us that tablecloths were in common use among the wealthy in England before the Norman Conquest in 1066.

Today the word *linen* has become a generic designation for our household dressings for the table, bed, kitchen, and bathroom, whether made of linen, cotton, lace, silk, or manmade fibers. So when we refer to "household linens," it can be any of those fibers, and their use will be in the home's adornment and dressing.

COLLECTING TIPS

If we are interested in collecting linens, it is important to place these various lovely things in their proper time frame. In that way we can determine, within a period of a few years, if a piece really is as presented; and considering the three important criteria of *quality*, *condition*, and *provenance*, plus the current market, we will be able to make an educated decision as to adding it to our collection. What we have to remember is that when given a time period for introduction of anything— textiles, furniture, glass, or porcelain—the introduction never started on one given date and became obsolete on another certain date. That is why we should have some idea of differing time frames for consideration. We do have documented dates as to when various machines were invented and registered. However, whatever started in England, France, or other European countries usually had a time lag of a few years before reaching our shores. And even in this country the processes found their way into the hinterlands many years after the introduction into the major cities. It is reasonable to assume that a stylish fad in England certainly did not reach the backwoods of Kentucky or Tennessee until quite a few years later.

When shopping for linens, visit yard sales, flea markets, tag sales, estate sales, and the usual auctions, antiques shops, and shows. There are so many avenues open to collectors that the hunt can be very exciting. Be sure to do your homework first; be prepared by having some knowledge of what you are most interested in. Museums are a great source of information, and most libraries are stocked with all of the necessary references.

Always look in the box lots. Almost always there will be one or two items that will more than pay for the lot. Last year a major auction house had two box lots of linens with an estimate of $150 each. Apparently there was something very special in each of those boxes that had escaped the scrutiny of the firm's appraiser, and several bidders were aware of it. The final bid on each was $1200! If these had been at an estate sale or where each had a set price, someone would have had a banner day. It pays to know what you are shopping for.

If you are collecting for investment, always buy the very finest you can afford and take into consideration quality, condition, and provenance. Be sure to get a written receipt with all of the pertinent information included, and keep accurate and complete files.

The average collector should also consider quality, condition and provenance but can have more latitude in selecting things he or she likes but that may need laundering, a simple repair, or replacement of some of the lace or trim. These are the things you can use and enjoy and not be totally desolate if the puppy chews the lace edge off the pillow cover.

MARKET TRENDS

The trend toward collecting these treasures from the past has escalated in the past several years and seems to be firmly entrenched. There appears to be a plentiful supply of late-19th- and early-20th-century pieces to keep the market viable for some time to come and to make the search easy as well as fun. Of course, there will always be a market for museum- and top-quality linens. This is a good time to shop for the top-quality pieces because the exquisite trousseaus put together in the early 20th century, when it was popular for the wealthy to shop in Europe or to commission handmade objects in this country, are now coming into the marketplace through estate sales and from grandmothers' trunks. There have been a number of publications recently that specialize in all kinds of textiles. Keep a check on the advertisements of firms in major cities. And of course, watch for estate sales, tag sales, small antiques shops, and the large antiques shows in your area—there are always bargains to be found if you have done your homework!

CONDITION KEY

This listing measures only the physical condition of the article, not the quality of design, material, or workmanship.

Fine Condition: mint, no stains or visible repairs; colors are bright; no thin areas; all lace and trim are intact.

Good Condition: few repairs and not obvious; no stains; all seams are strong; colors good.

Average Condition: some repairs; minor fading; slight thinning; minor spots in fabric; may need new ribbons if applicable; may need laundering.

Poor Condition: fading; spotting; rips; tears; incomplete; not collectible, but sections may be used for making doll clothes or other small objects.

QUALITY KEY

This listing measures the stylishness and collectibility of the piece within its category.

Good Quality: nice piece worthy of collecting, but not for investment.

Very Good Quality: fine fabric and trims, workmanship is excellent; all elements stylistically correct for period.

Superior Quality: exquisite fabric and some handwork; expert workmanship of highest quality; all elements are superb and of the period.

> ''ES'' means the item was bought at an estate sale. The value is on the same level as if bought at a flea market.—*DL*

Bedspread 46″ × 62″ Appliqué c. 1935 United States
Baby bed size; white muslin appliquéd with animals and flowers, touched with embroidery, edged with a band of pale blue fabric.
Good Quality/Good Condition $65 (D)   **$50–$75**

Blanket 60″ × 69″ Jacobs c. 1930 United States
All-wool blanket or robe; geometric pattern in green, red, white, black, and gold; ''Jacob,'' Oregon City label.
Very Good Quality/Good Condition $192 (A)   **$100–$300**

Blanket cover 74″ × 90″ c. 1930 United States
Pale yellow rayon crepe with 2 rows of 4″-wide ecru lace inserted in side seam lines.
Good Quality/Good Condition $45 (D)   **$18–$50**

Bolster case 16″ × 58″ White work c. 1890–1900 United States
Linen, Victorian white work; open both ends, each end scalloped and with heavily padded, embroidered floral design; minor thin areas.
Very Good Quality/Average Condition $45 (D)   **$15–$50**

Bridge set 32″ × 32″ c. 1920–1930 United States
Ivory linen; hand-embroidered with purple grapes and green leaves in shaped corners, matching center design; set with 4 napkins (12″ × 12″).
Superior Quality/Fine Condition $45 set (D)   **$25–$50**

Fragment 14″ × 88″ c. 1860 Russia
Unfinished fragment of a bedcover, unhemmed edges; Russian Suzini, Usbeck tribe; handwoven fabric, natural-color background; design is all of needlework in shades of mauve and turquoise.
Good Quality/Average Condition $325 (D)   **$200–$400**

Remember, the selling price is exactly what the term implies: the object sold for the stated amount in a shop or show by a dealer (D) or at auction (A).

Fragment 36″ × 42″ Homespun 1836 United States
Piece of homespun linen; 2 sides hemmed by hand; 1 corner embroidered in red "RCB, 1836"; Easton, PA.
Good Quality/Good Condition $45 (ES)   **$25–$75**

Handkerchief 11″ × 11″ Appenzill c. 1910–1920 Switzerland
Sheer white linen; hemstitched edges; floral design and drawn work in 1 corner; all done in pale blue thread.
Very Good Quality/Average Condition $15 (D)   **$7–$25**

Handkerchief 10.75″ × 18″ c. 1920 United States
Printed children's handkerchief; red on white cotton, "Old Mother Hubbard . . ." etc.; minor stains, wear, and small holes; framed.
Good Quality/Poor Condition $50 (A)   **$10–$65**

Handkerchiefs 14.75″ × 13.75″ c. 1920 United States
Two printed handkerchiefs; red on white cotton; "birds" and "wild beasts"; stained; "birds" has slight bleeding of color; "beasts" has repair; in matching frames.
Good Quality/Poor Condition $145 both (A)   **$60–$130**

Napkins, cocktail 5″ × 7″ c. 1940 Madeira
Six with lavender linen bunch of grapes, green linen leaves, cut work, no backing; handmade; very unusual.
Superior Quality/Fine Condition $45 set (D)   **$25–$50**

Napkins, cocktail 9″ × 9″ c. 1930 Madeira
Six of white linen; flower basket embroidered in 1 corner; scalloped edges.
Very Good Quality/Good Condition $30 set (D)   **$25–$45**

Napkins, luncheon 14″ × 14″ c. 1940 United States
Four of cream-colored linen, pink cross-stitched rose in 1 corner, pink embroidered edges; handmade.
Good Quality/Average Condition $20 set (D)   **$15–$35**

Pillow case 15″ × 17.5″ c. 1900 United States
Amish, pieces in simple squares and 1 square on pinwheel pattern in center; machine-sewn with button back.
Good Quality/Average Condition $27 (ES)   **$20–$45**

Pillow cases 22″ × 30″ c. 1880–1900 United States
Pair, white linen with heavy, padded satin-stitch chrysanthemums and swirls embroidered on each end; ends are scalloped; minor thinning. *(See photo 279)*
Very Good Quality/Average Condition $35 pair (ES)   **$25–$45**

Pillow cases 20.5″ × 27″ c. 1860–1880 United States
Pair, homespun cotton, with pieced and appliquéd quilt square designs in pink and green calico; designs on both sides; each has a star flower on 1 side, Carolina lily on other; minor stains.
Very Good Quality/Average Condition $330 pair (A)   **$200–$400**

Pillow sham 28″ × 28″ c. 1910–1920 United States
Single; white muslin; embroidered in tan design of leaf and spray; hemstitched border 4 sides; throw type.
Good Quality/Good Condition $18 (ES)   **$15–$35**

Place mats 12″ × 18″ c. 1935–1940 United States
Four; linen; woven checks of red and tan with self fringe on 4 sides; napkins to match, also fringed.
Good Quality/Average Condition $25 set (D)   **$15–$35**

*Photo 279.
Linen pillow
cases.*
CREDIT: ALDA
LEAKE HORNER
(See p. 550)

Sheet 72″ × 76″ Homespun c. 1850–1860 United States
White; hand-sewn hems and center seam; red embroidered initials "M.K."
Good Quality/Average Condition $44 (A) **$15–$65**

Sheet 84″ × 104″ Bride's c. 1920 Madeira
White, fine linen; top end has 18″-deep embroidery in all-white designs of flowers, doves, ribbon bows, and vining; hand-sewn sides and bottom hem; beautifully done.
Superior Quality/Fine Condition $195 (D) **$125–$225**

Tablecloth 72″ × 102″ c. 1935–1940 Italy
Ecru linen; machine embroidery in brown and small amount of cutwork; machine-hemstitch edges; with 8 matching napkins (18″ × 18″).
Good Quality/Average Condition $95 set (D) **$65–$150**

Tablecloth 70″ × 76″ Homespun c. 1850 United States
White; hand-sewn center seam and hand-hemmed edges; gold and white plaid.
Superior Quality/Fine Condition $225 (A) **$125–$300**

Tablecloth 72″ × 74″ Homespun c. 1880 United States
White homespun cotton with blue and tan plaid borders; hand-sewn edges.
Good Quality/Average Condition $50 (D) **$25–$65**

Tablecloth, luncheon 52″ × 54″ c. 1935–1940 United States
White cotton with boldly printed flowers with printed blue border; machine-hemmed.
Good Quality/Average Condition $45 (D) **$15–65**

Tea cozy Small c. 1900–1910 England
Insulated flannel-covered liner with 2 separate white linen covers; each cover embroidered with white flowers and having scalloped bottom edge; for 2-cup pot; liner has minor interior stains; covers with label: "Made in England."
Very Good Quality/Average Condition $35 (ES) **$25–$75**

Towel, commemorative 19″ × 34″ plus fringe c. 1920–1930 United States
Linen; white-on-white woven scene of Washington on horseback; red border with "Washington"; mint.
Very Good Quality/Fine Condition $60 (A) **$25–$75**

Towel, guest 14″ × 24″ c. 1935–1949 United States
White linen; 1 end with band woven in royal blue showing "Our Guest" in white and a daisy on each side; other end machine-hemmed.
Good Quality/Average Condition $15 (D) **$2–$20**

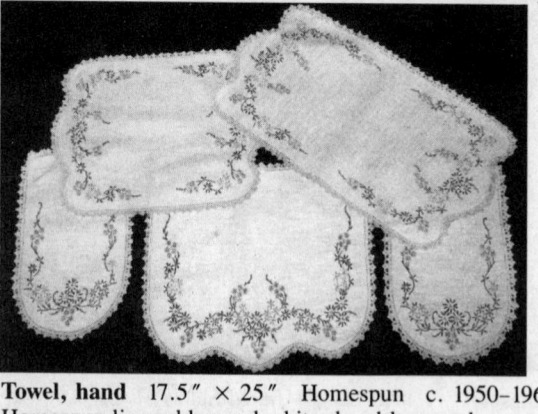

Photo 280.
Vanity set.
CREDIT: ALDA
LEAKE HORNER
(See below)

Towel, hand 17.5″ × 25″ Homespun c. 1950–1960 United States
Homespun linen; blue and white; hand-hemmed; wear and small holes.
Good Quality/Poor Condition $60 (A)   **$25–$75**

Towel, show 18″ × 60″ Homespun 1838 United States
White homespun linen; drawn work and embroidery in red: "KLD," "1838,"
and "ALD"; self fringe both ends.
Superior Quality/Fine Condition $195 (D)   **$125–$225**

Vanity set center piece 15″ × 16″ c. 1920–1930 United States
White heavy linen; bright embroidery; edged with narrow crochet; 5 pieces;
from a kit. *(See photo 280)*
Good Quality/Average Condition $50 (D)   **$35–$65**

QUILTS

Interest in American quilts is now at an all-time high. The proliferation
of quilt societies and clubs is staggering; museums are having special
quilt exhibitions; and antiques shows are awash with quilts of every hue
imaginable, of all styles and periods. Newsstands are flooded with quilt
magazines of all types, and every decorator magazine has space devoted
to the display and use of quilts, not only in the home but in business
establishments and institutions as well. This new appreciation of the quilt
and the time-consuming efforts of the early homemaker has raised the
quilt from a household necessity and craft to that of an art form.

By the early 18th century in this country, quilting had become a social
event, even in Boston among the wealthier classes. It was one of the few
social events of the less wealthy folk; quilting bees were one of their
special times for getting together. Women would gather at a home where
there was room enough to put up a quilting frame and would work on
quilting by day and then be joined by the men, from the fields, to have
a hearty supper spread followed by dancing.

On the long trek westward the quilt was an important part of the cargo.

After the trials of moving westward, quilt patterns achieved new names as women were influenced by their new surroundings, but many of the traditional patterns were cherished and passed on to their daughters and friends.

Patchwork. It is difficult to research which came first in America, the appliquéd or the pieced quilt, because no 17th-century examples have survived.

The most basic patterns for pieced quilts are the "four-patch" and the "nine patch." The four-patch is a square made from four pieces of equal size; when stitched together, they make a perfect square. The nine-patch square is composed of nine blocks of equal size making the square. By differing the arrangement, color, and fabric within the square, many different patterns are achieved. Some of the blocks may be made with triangles forming the block, but the square will always contain the basic four or nine blocks.

White Work. White work is another whole-cloth quilt. Originating in Europe in the 16th century, it was popular in this country from about 1790 to 1820. The fine white fabric was woven in two or three strips on narrow looms and had a backing of coarser linen. These rarely had a center stuffing and were used as spreads. Being of a solid color, this gave the quilter leeway to be artistic and creative with the design for an allover stitched pattern.

Album Quilts. These quilts were usually created by a number of women, who would each make a square; each square had an *appliquéd* design of their choice. These would often be made as a friendship effort, and each square would be signed by one woman who "had a fine hand," some in ink and some embroidered.

It is said that the most beautiful quilts made in America are the "Baltimore" album quilts, made by a group of women in that area who were expert in needlework. They have several characteristic designs, including baskets of flowers, fruits, animals, and Baltimore monuments.

Sampler Album. These quilts are very much like the above, except the squares are *pieced* instead of being appliquéd. They were made by groups of women or by one woman, not necessarily in the Baltimore area; some signed, some not.

Amish–Mennonite. The Amish settled in Lancaster County, Pennsylvania, and some eventually moved into Indiana, Ohio, Illinois, Missouri, and Iowa. Because of their plain ways, their quilts have a simplicity of pattern that is relieved by the striking colors and the exquisitely designed and stitched quilting. The Amish religion forbade certain bright colors for clothing, such as pink, orange, and bright red, so the women expressed themselves in the colors used in their quilts. And because of that strict life-style, very few quilts were made before 1860. Before this time, it is believed that the women wove stout wool blankets, or they stitched several layers of fabric together for extra warmth.

Friendship. Friendship quilts are in the same category as the earlier Album quilts, *pieced*, instead of being appliquéd, signed, and dated. Most were made for friends or the rector of a church. Many were raffled to raise money. Whatever small amount was realized from the sale was always used for a charitable cause. These quilts were also referred to as Autograph, Signature, Tithing, and Charity.

Commemorative–Patriotic. From the late 18th century to the late 19th century there were quilts made to honor famous people or some special event in our country's history. Many were pieced-work quilts; and in the late nineteenth century some were crazy quilt designs with the person's image in the center or in some other way worked into the design. At the time of this country's Centennial, Patriotic quilts were popular; all of these quilts had flags and/or eagles as the major design element.

Hawaiian. Until the early 19th century sewing was unknown to these island people. In 1820, women of rank were given sewing lessons by Mrs. Lucy Thurston, an American missionary. Sewing was allowed only to the most important women, according to rigid social standards. The majority of Hawaiian quilts will be made in two colors; they may be patriotic, showing their flag, or represent some special event. The work is always appliquéd, frequently using reverse appliqué. Many of the stylized floral quilts are evenly balanced by folding the fabric four ways and cutting the design, similar to paper cutting, producing an original motif to appliqué onto the ground cloth.

Crazy Quilts. When or why women in the United States started making crazy quilts seems to be debatable. Some may have been influenced by the Japanese displays at the Centennial Exhibition in Philadelphia, where many beautiful silks were shown for bed dressings, as well as elegant silk screens. And many were influenced by the Aethestic movement. Whatever the reason, by the middle of the 1880s, there was tremendous interest in making these quilts, using silks, satin, velvets, painted fabrics, ribbons, and clothing. Freeform pieces of silk were basted down with edges turned under and whipped into place. When the square was covered, the seams were then worked over with a variety of embroidery stitches, using silk floss. Frequently, the pieces in the square had a design embroidered with the floss or chenille.

Kits and Patterns. After the craze of the crazy quilt had died down in the early part of the 20th century, interest in quilt making waned. Women had lost their desire for making the traditional patterns after the excitement of the crazy quilt, and at this time machine-made blankets and bedcoverings were available. By 1920 kits and printed patterns for both pieced and appliquéd quilts were made popular by many of the magazines published for the homemaker. Many quilts show great originality in the manner in which the quilter used these patterns and fabrics. With the war effort at that time, quilt making again lost favor, only to reemerge in popularity during the 1960s and 1970s. Now it has developed into an exciting and thriving business.

CONDITION KEY

This listing measures only the physical condition of the article, not the quality of design, material, or workmanship.

Fine Condition: near original condition or expertly restored to near original condition.

Good Condition: no losses; no obvious major restorations; no cleaning needed; ready to use or display.

Average Condition: small areas may need restitching; minor losses to fabric or binding; cleaning may be necessary; this is the condition in which most quilts are found.

Poor Condition: missing binding; losses to squares; fading, thinning, poor restorations, if any; not collectible, but small areas may be used to make pillows, stuffed animals, pincushions, etc.

QUALITY KEY

This listing measures the stylishness and collectibility of the piece within its category.

Good Quality: attractive, but fabrics and workmanship may not be of acceptable quality; worthy of collecting for use but not for investment.

Very Good Quality: fine fabrics, excellent stitchery in piecing and quilting; colors and fabrics arranged in an artistically pleasing manner.

Superior Quality: workmanship of highest quality; all elements are superb and of the period; has stunning visual impact.

PATCHWORK

Apple trees 79″ × 92″ 20th century United States
Appliquéd apple trees, birds, and meandering border in brown, red, green, and yellow; embroidered stems; somewhat faded.
Good Quality/Average Condition $440 (A)   **$300–$600**

Blocks 76″ × 86″ c. 1920 North Carolina
Quilt top; hand- and machine-pieced; 3″ blocks on diagonal, assorted jewel tones of rich blues, reds, and gold cotton fabrics; unlined and unquilted.
Very Good Quality/Fine Condition $125 (ES)   **$50–$200**

Bow tie 80″ × 88″ c. 1910 United States
Pieced; red, teal green, and white; scalloped border is teal green with red binding; some faded areas in border.
Good Quality/Average Condition $247 (A) **$200–$400**

Carolina lily 92″ × 101″ c. 1890–1910 United States
Appliquéd and pieced; the lily in red calico, solid green with green and blue sawtooth borders, and red calico binding; beautifully quilted with vintage border; signed in ink: "Sarah Elizabeth Beams"; very minor wear.
Very Good Quality/Fine Condition $1237 (A) **$1000–$2000**

Diamond in square 79″ × 79″ c. 1860 United States
Pieced; all calico and other prints in reds and other colors on a blue and white ground; sawtooth border; blue and white homespun backing.
Very Good Quality/Good Condition $880 (A) **$500–$1200**

Dresden plate 14″ × 14″ c. 1920–1930 United States
Twenty-five quilt squares, unassembled; hand-pieced of 1920s' calicos in assorted colors of yellows, reds, and greens.
Very Good Quality/Fine Condition $5 each (ES) **$3–25 each**

Eight-point star 80″ × 80″ c. 1900 Northampton County, PA
Variation of 9-patch square; pieced and quilted by hand; polka dots and prints in pinks, reds, and greens; sashed in pink polka dots and green; triple border of pink, polka dots, and green; backed with pink striped cotton. *(See photo 281)*
Superior Quality/Fine Condition $1250 (A) **$750–$1500**

Floral 92″ × 90″ c. 1860 United States
Stylized floral medallions, appliquéd and pieced, in reds and greens; some wear and fading; reds are more worn and have holes.
Good Quality/Poor Condition $160 (A) **$150–$500**

Photo 281.
Eight-point
star quilt.
CREDIT: ALDA
LEAKE HORNER
(See above)

Floral 82″ × 82″ c. 1830–1850 United States
Appliquéd stylized flowerpots of vining flowers in pink and green calico, with
solid red and yellow.
Good Quality/Average Condition $715 (A) **$500–$1000**

Floral 82″ × 96″ c. 1870–1880 United States
Appliquéd; 26 green flowerpots, each with a different-colored flower and 2 blue
calico birds; green Greek key border; minor stains.
Good Quality/Average Condition $770 (A) **$500–$1000**

Geese in flight 84″ × 84″ c. 1890 United States
Pieced; 4 barred, blue and white; very good quilting; overall wear.
Good Quality/Average Condition $550 (D) **$350–$750**

Lone Star 78″ × 78″ c. 1875 United States
Pieced in red, goldenrod, and khaki on white ground; red backing and binding;
well quilted; overall wear, minor staining.
Good Quality/Average Condition $450 (D) **$300–$600**

Poinsettia 72″ × 90″ c. 1900–1910 United States
Appliquéd and pieced; red, green, and gold on white ground; 12 blocks of stylized poinsettias interspersed with white blocks similarly quilted; floral swag border quilted on diaper stitch.
Very Good Quality/Average Condition $1331 (A) **$1200–$2200**

Sawtooth 68″ × 75″ c. 1860–1870 United States
This pattern also known as Kansas Troubles; pieced in alternating triangles with
sawtooth edges on 2 sides; blue calico and white homespun.
Good Quality/Average Condition $715 (A) **$500–$800**

Schoolhouse 69″ × 85″ 1900–1910 United States
Pieced; each house has 2 shades of brown, blue sky, red chimney, and windows
are in calico and ecru; brown print background with ruffled edge; summer weight,
quilted without batting; ¼″ burn hole.
Good Quality/Average Condition $440 (A) **$350–$750**

Sixteen patch 68″ × 80″ c. 1890 North Carolina
"Hired hand" quilt; all-wool squares from clothing; dark colors, hand-pieced,
crudely quilted; backed wtih Alamance County cotton plaid in navy and brown;
all corners have been rounded off when repaired.
Poor Quality/Average Condition $150 (D) **$50–$150**

Star 88″ × 88″ 1900–1910 United States
Pieced, all in calico; yellow and pink on green ground; reversible with yellow
and pink bars on back.
Very Good Quality/Average Condition $935 (A) **$500–$1500**

Sunshine and shadow 76″ × 76″ 1885–1900 Berks County, PA
Machine-pieced, hand-quilted; all solid colors of cotton in a variety of shades;
backed with 7″ strips of blue and brown calico prints; seeds in thin cotton
batting.
Good Quality/Fine Condition $900 (D) **$750–$1200**

Triangles 84″ × 84″ 1885–1900 Pennsylvania
Also known as Thousand Pyramids; all blocks are triangles of assorted calico
and solid fabrics in light and dark shades; browns predominate; hand-pieced and
hand-quilted.
Very Good Quality/Fine Condition $2000 (D) **$1500–$2500**

Tumbling blocks 48″ × 60″ 1885–1900 New Jersey
Hand-pieced; all velvet and silk in tones of burgundy, mauve, and rose; the
backing is of burgundy cotton, exquisitely quilted in allover floral design with
princess feather border; not quilted to front; sleeved for hanging; several of the
silk pieces are beginning to split.
Very Good Quality/Good Condition *$450 (D)*   **$350–$750**

WHITE WORK—WHOLE CLOTH

Bride's quilt 86″ × 86″ 1885–1900 United States
White work, whole cloth; all white muslin, finely quilted all over with highly
designed center of floral and vining motif; border with princess feather quilting;
thin batting.
Superior Quality/Fine Condition *$2500 (D)*   **$1000–$5000**

Whole cloth 72″ × 90″ c. 1940 United States
Mauve rayon; hand-quilted overall in geometric design; scalloped edges; thin
cotton batting.
Good Quality/Average Condition *$50 (ES)*   **$25–$150**

ALBUM QUILT

Album 85″ × 95″ c. 1850 Maryland
Appliquéd and pieced; centering a square reserve with a lemon tree, the inner
border with 38 pictorial squares including tulips, roses, oak leaves, flower baskets, wreaths, birds, and flags; surrounded by a floral swag border; slight staining; 1-dimensional tree.
Superior Quality/Fine Condition *$6050 (A)*   **$5000–$10,000**

AMISH—MENNONITE

Barred 80″ × 94″ c. 1880 Berks County, PA
Amish; cotton in shades of dark green, light orange, and mahogany brown,
bordered in dark green; backed with red calico print; allover diamond quilting
in 18 stitches per inch; thin cotton batting.
Very Good Quality/Average Condition *$1200 (D)*   **$750–$1500**

Checkerboard 85″ × 87″ c. 1900 United States
Amish; pieced quilt; black and maroon; some wear, maroon is frayed in places
and black wool has some moth holes; black squares are of a variety of fabrics
including sateen, wool, and crepe.
Good Quality/Poor Condition *$165 (A)*   **$100–$500**

Joseph's-coat-of-many-colors c. 1880 Lancaster County, PA
Mennonite; pieced quilt; bars in a spectrum of bright fabrics with rope-twist
stitching, the border similarly stitched, with purple binding.
Superior Quality/Fine Condition *$6050 (A)*   **$2500–$7500**

Old Maid's puzzle 80″ × 94″ c. 1900 United States
Amish; pieced quilt; 2 shades of blue and light green; hand-sewn with machine-
sewn binding; some loose seams; small holes, minor stains.
Good Quality/Poor Condition *$75 (A)*   **$50–$250**

Photo 282. Friendship quilt.
CREDIT: ALDA LEAKE HORNER
(See below)

FRIENDSHIP

Friendship 77″ × 78″ 1904 Lehigh County, PA
Hand-pieced; light blue and white blocks, 5½″ blue calico border, backed in rich red and orange calico in 8″ strips; almost all of the blocks are signed and dated in ink; corner block shows "Presented to Charles G. Beck, Pastor, St. Peter's Lutheran Church, North Wales, Pa., 1904." Later inscription to grandson (of same name) "Presented to Charles G. Beck, 1914, by Great-Great Grandmother Herman"; finely hand-quilted; thin cotton batting. *(See photo 282)*
Very Good Quality/Good Condition $900 (D) **$750–$1200**

Friendship 65″ × 78″ 1890–1900 Kentucky
Pieced; multicolored prints and white with penciled names; good overall condition except for olive brown fabrics, which are faded and frayed.
Good Quality/Average Condition $650 (A) **$750–$1200**

COMMEMORATIVE

Trip around the world 77″ × 80″ 1876 Philadelphia
Pieced quilt; with several patches having busts of Washington, "Union" 1776–1876, etc.; back has colorful red paisley print; made at the Centennial.
Good Quality/Average Condition $440 (A) **$300–$750**

HAWAIIAN

Floral 78″ × 80″ c. 1850 Hawaii
Appliquéd and pieced; worked with 4 enlarged floral and vine urns in blue fabric with white dots on a white ground with echo stitching and slate blue binding.
Very Good Quality/Fine Condition $5500 (A) **$3000–$7500**

Patriotic 74″ × 74″ 1860–1880 Hawaii
Appliquéd and pieced; centering a square reserve depicting the crest of the Hawaiian monarchy and inscribed "KUU HAE" (My beloved flag) above and "ALOHA" below; surrounded by 4 stylized Hawaiian flags completed with 4 blue triangles and a white binding (worn).
Very Good Quality/Good Condition *$8800 (A)* **$5000–$10,000**

CRAZY QUILTS

Crazy quilt 84″ × 86″ c. 1900 United States
Charming primitive; pieced of old dark wool fabrics, probably from men's suits; wool embroidery between each square; family members' hands embroidered on pieces; signed "Willia Mae"; slight wear.
Good Quality/Average Condition *$150 (ES)* **$100–$350**

Crazy quilt 76″ × 80″ 1900–1910 North Carolina
Pieced; all wool, dark colors, probably from clothing; each piece with wool embroidery of flowers; much damage to wool; Orange County.
Good Quality/Poor Condition *$25 (ES)* **$25–$150**

Crazy quilt 84″ × 92″ c. 1890 United States
Pieced; combination of silks, wools, and velvets in various rich colors; silk floss embroidery of birds, butterflies, animals, fans, etc.; bound in dark red silk; some wear to silk pieces.
Very Good Quality/Average Condition *$750 (D)* **$500–$1200**

KITS/PATTERNS

Checkerboard 78″ × 92″ c. 1930–1935 United States
Pieced; from a pattern; blue and white squares alternating; the white squares are embroidered with bright flowers and butterflies; blue binding; hand-quilted; cotton batting.
Good Quality/Average Condition *$375 (D)* **$250–$500**

Sunflowers 78″ × 94″ c. 1945–1950 United States
Appliquéd; sunflowers and border stripe in green, yellow, and brown on a white ground; unused condition with pencil quilting pattern intact; small tear near one corner.
Good Quality/Average Condition *$385 (A)* **$250–$500**

CRIB QUILTS

Amish 30″ × 45″ Contemporary Ohio
Pieced; blue, black, and gray; machine-pieced and hand-quilted.
Good Quality/Average Condition *$247 (A)* **$150–$350**

Amish 43″ × 43″ 1965 Ohio
Lone Star in bright colors on a black ground; made by Sarah Miller, Holmes County, Ohio.
Good Quality/Average Condition *$165 (A)* **$150–$350**

Blocks 35″ × 41″ 1930–1940 United States
Pieced; printed chintz, floral pattern with patchwork design, in shades of brown and green on white, alternating dark and light; 1 end faded.
Good Quality/Average Condition *$82 (A)* **$50–$125**

Monkey wrench 31″ × 42.5″ 1900–1910 Indiana
Pieces; reversible; monkey wrench in blue, red, and white on one side, 9 patch on the other in various-color prints on the same blue ground; made by Edythe Cole.
Very Good Quality/Average Condition *$495 (A)* **$350–$600**

DOLL QUILTS

Flying geese 21.5″ × 26″ 1930–1940 United States
Pieced; flying geese pattern in orange and white; machine-sewn; overall wear, fading and tear to one "goose."
Good Quality/Poor Condition *$66 (A)* **$50–$100**

Four patch 17″ × 25″ 1920–1930 United States
Pieced and knotted; 4 patch in blue and other prints.
Good Quality/Poor Condition *$22 (A)* **$20–$50**

Tumbling blocks 16.75″ × 19.5″ c. 1920 United States
Hand-pieced; colorful satins; wear and stains with some damage; red has bled in places.
Good Quality/Poor Condition *$50 (A)* **$25–$75**

BIBLIOGRAPHY

Bacon, Lenice Ingram. *American Patchwork Quilts.* New York: Bonanza Books, 1980.

Bath, Virginia Churchill. *Lace.* Chicago: Henry Regnery Co., 1974.

———. *Needlework in America: History, Designs and Techniques.* New York: Viking Press, 1974.

Belden, Louise Conway. *The Festive Tradition: Table Decoration and Desserts in America, 1950–1900.* New York: W. W. Norton, A Winterthur Book, 1983.

Bishop, Robert. *New Discoveries in American Quilts.* New York: E. P. Dutton, 1975.

Bishop, Robert, and Elizabeth Safanda. *A Gallery of Amish Quilts: Design Diversity from a Plain People.* New York: E. P. Dutton, 1976.

Bishop, Robert, William Secord, and Judith Reiter Weisman. *The Knopf Collector's Guides to American Antiques, Quilts, Coverlets, Rugs and Samplers.* New York: Alfred A. Knopf, 1982.

Brackman, Barbara. *Clues in the Calico.* McLean, VA: EPM Publications, 1990.

Buchanan, Rita. *A Weaver's Garden.* Loveland, Colorado: Interweave Press, 1987.

Burnham, Harold B., and Dorothy K. *"Keep Me Warm One Night": Early Handweaving in Eastern Canada.* Toronto and Buffalo, NY: Toronto Press with the Royal Museum, 1972.

Caulfield, S. F. A., and Blanche C. Saward. *Encyclopedia of Victorian Needlework.* New York: Dover Publications, 1972.

Dolan, Maryanne. *Old Lace and Linens Including Crochet, An Identification Guide.* Florence, AL: Books Americana, 1989.

Duke, Dennis, and Deborah Harding, eds. *America's Glorious Quilts.* New York: Park Lane, distributed by Crown Publishers, 1989.

Eanes, Ellen Fickling, et al. *North Carolina Quilts,* edited by Ruth Haislip. Chapel Hill: University of North Carolina Press, 1988.

Earnshaw, Pat. *A Dictionary of Lace.* Aylesbury, Bucks, UK: Shire Publications, 1984.

———. *The Identification of Lace.* Aylesbury, Bucks, UK: Shire Publications, 1989.

Finch, Karen, O. B. E. and Greta Putnam. *The Care and Preservation of Textiles.* London: B. T. Batsford, 1985.

Hall, Dorothea, ed. *The Gentle Arts.* New York: The Lace Guild, Exeter Books, 1986.

Hall, Eliza Calvert. *A Book of Handwoven Coverlets.* New York: Little, Brown, 1912, 1925.

Harbeson, Georgiana Brown. *American Needlework: The History of Decorative Stitchery and Embroidery from the Late 16th to the 20th Century.* New York: Bonanza Books, 1938.

Heisey, John W. *Checklist of American Coverlet Weavers.* Williamsburg, VA: Colonial Williamsburg Foundation, 1978.

Henneberg, Alfred F. A. von. *The Art and Craft of Old Lace.* Berlin: Ernest Wasmuth, 1931.

Hinson, Delores A. *A Quilter's Companion.* New York: Arco, 1973.

Horner, Alda Leake. *The Official Price Guide to Linens, Laces, and Other Fabrics.* New York: House of Collectibles, 1991.

Kraatz, Anne. *Lace: History and Fashion.* London: Constable and Low, 1875; New York: Dover, 1984.

Marich, Lilo, and Heinz Edgar Kiewe. *Victorian Fancywork.* Chicago: Henry Regnery Co., 1974.

Montgomery, Florence H. *Textiles in America, 1650–1870.* New York: W. W. Norton, A Winterthur Book, 1984.

Palliser, Bury. *History of Lace.* New York: Dover, 1984.

Safford, Carleton, and Robert Bishop. *America's Quilts and Coverlets.* New York: E. P. Dutton, 1972.

Swan, Susan Burrows. *Plain and Fancy, American Women and Their Needlework, 1700–1850.* New York: Holt, Rinehart & Winston, 1977.

Warnick, Kathleen, and Nilsson, Shirley. *Legacy of Lace: Identifying, Collecting and Preserving American Lace.* New York: Crown, 1988.

Woodward, Thomas K., and Blanche Greenstein. *Classic American Quilts.* New York: E. P. Dutton, 1984.

———. *Crib Quilts and Other Small Wonders.* New York: E. P. Dutton, 1981.

MUSEUMS

Cleveland Museum of Art
11150 East Boulevard
Cleveland, OH 44106

Cooper-Hewitt Museum of Design
Smithsonian Institution
Fifth Avenue at 91st Street
New York, NY 10018

Daughters of the American
Revolution (DAR) Museum
1146 D Street, NW
Washington, DC 20006

Metropolitan Museum of Art
Fifth Avenue at 82nd Street
New York, NY 10028

Museum of Early Southern
Decorative Arts (MESDA)
Winston-Salem, NC 27108

National Museum of History and
Technology
Smithsonian Institution
Washington, DC 20560

Rockwood Museum
610 Shipley Road
Wilmington, DE 19809

Valentine Museum
1015 East Clay Street
Richmond, VA 23219

Toys and Toy Trains

(See also Character Collectibles, Ephemera, Peanuts Collectibles, Teddy Bears)

Advisor: **RICHARD FRIZ**

Richard Friz is a nationally recognized author of many books and articles, including The Official Price Guide to Toys, The Official Price Guide to Political Memorabilia, The Official Price Guide to World's Fair Memorabilia, *and* The Official Identification and Price Guide to Toy Trains. *(New York: House of Collectibles). Mr. Friz is a member of the New Hampshire Appraisers Association. He can be reached at RFD 2, Box 155, Peterborough, NH 03458; (603) 563–8155.*

HISTORY

Although single-movement, string-worked toys date from as early as 5000 years ago in the Indus Valley in southern Asia, it was not until the 16th century that the toy centers of Nuremburg and Sonnenburg, Germany, developed wooden and tin toys as we know them today.

Metal toys were produced in quantity after 1840, following the decline of the forests and the shortage of wood in Germany. By the 1870s, Germany was exporting toys to France, Great Britain, and the United States.

The first clockwork toys were train sets, produced in Germany from 1865 to 1867. In France quality tin toy production reached its zenith in La Belle Epoque, from 1903 to 1914.

The first manufacturer of wooden toys in the United States was William Tower, who organized The Tower Guild, a tradesman co-op in the early 1850s. A. Schoenhut & Co., eminent producer of circus and comic jointed wooden toys, opened its doors in 1872. Lithographed paper-on-wood toys were first popularized by Charles Crandall and Sons in 1867, followed by R. Bliss, W. S. Reed, and Morton Converse.

The earliest clockwork toys produced in the United States were the "Walking Zouave" by Stevens & Brown and "Autoperipatetikos" by Martin & Runyan, patented in 1862. By midcentury stencil-decorated tin menageries on wheels were produced by Philadelphia Toy Co. and George W. Brown. Other premier makers or jobbers of tin toys were Althof Bergmann, Ives & Blakeslee, James Fallows, Hull & Stafford, American Toy Co., and Merriam Manufacturing.

Dominant manufacturers of cast-iron toys and banks in the "Golden Era" of the late 19th century included F. W. Carpenter, John Hubley, E. R. Ives, James Wilkins, Pratt & Letchworth, Harris Toy Co., Kaiser & Rex, Gong Bell, and A. C. Williams.

Considered the earliest producer of cast-iron toys (truly an American innovation) was J. & E. Stevens, with their firecracker and cap pistols in 1859. Stevens, along with James Fallows, J. Hall, and J. Serrell, initiated tin and cast-iron still and mechanical banks in the late 1860s. Cast-iron toy enthusiasts will be inclined to extend their collecting parameters to include Dent, Hubley, Kenton Hardware, and a handful of others who produced superb replicas up to World War II.

Many tin toy "purists" focus their attention exclusively on the 19th century, but delightful tin windups, particularly of the comic and character variety, abound from the modern era as well. Leading manufacturers include Louis Marx, J. Chein, and Ferdinand Strauss. The German firms of Ernest Lehmann, Gebruder Bing and Maerklin, Georges Carette, S. G. Gunthermann, Carl Bubb, and Tipp & Co. excelled in enameled tinplate transportation toys. From France, JEP (Jouets en Paris), Charles Rosignol, Fernand Martin, and Andre Citroën produced nicely detailed toys in the first quarter of this century.

Lack of accessibility to uncommon vintage toys has helped trigger a whole new subgroup of collectors in pursuit of contemporary space and robot toys, many of them battery operated; also exact renderings of real automobiles and trucks, c. 1950s and 1960s, by Japanese, English, and German makers, are sought.

RECENT TRENDS

In the final year of the decade, a number of auction and sale records were set in the toy world: $125,000 for a "Charles" hose reeler by George Brown at Alex Acevedo's Tag Sale of the Bernard Berenholtz Collection in New York City. At the same sale, a "Pull for Shore" litho-paper-on-wood toy by W. S. Reed brought $10,000; a "Tally-Ho" cast-iron rig by Carpenter sold for $25,000. At Sotheby's in London, a teddy bear sold at $77,000; at Sandwich Auctions in Massachusetts, a 1929 fire truck pedal riding toy by National set a new high in that category at $77,000. Mechanical banks, however, continue to top the toy world aristocracy, with several of the ultrascarce versions, such as the "Freedman's" and the "Darky with Watermelon," ascending to the $250,000 plateau.

It can truly be said that the more uncommon, exceptional toys, in top condition, will continue to escalate in value as we enter the 1990s—perhaps well up into seven figures.

FAKES ALERT

The only major toy and bank category in which to be constantly on the alert is the cast-iron version. Even then, there are certain dead giveaways that can help you to avoid getting stung.

1. Reproduced cast-iron toys and banks tend to be heavier, thicker, and slightly smaller than originals.

2. The finish on a bogus toy has a rough, grainy feel; most modern usurpers have yet to master the smooth, almost soapstone-like feel of the old-timers.

3. Other telltale repro signs include bright, shiny paint; dead black or shiny gold finish; and no signs of wear, except in suspicious places where a repro identification may once have appeared but is now obliterated. Watch also for mismating, where parts do not fit together snugly; new screws are also a clue to authenticity or lack of same.

4. Watch the price. If it is uncommonly low, this is often your first indication that it has no real pedigree.

5. Don't be shy about seeking advice from knowledgeable dealers and collectors. Above all, deal only with reputable individuals who, without hesitation, back up anything they sell.

QUALITY KEY

Good Quality: a desirable toy, bank, or game that manages to appear with some frequency on the market; for example, the tin Toonerville Trolley by Nifty.

Very Good Quality: a classic and more elusive piece, combining superior graphics, cleverness, and a touch of whimsy; for example, Punch and Judy Bell Ringer.

Superior Quality: an extremely uncommon or possibly unique example that seldom, if ever, surfaces in the hobby; for example, the Freedman's Bank by Jerome Secor.

This is not a condition statement but strictly a measure of the stylishness and desirability of the piece.

CONDITION KEY

Toys, banks, games, puzzles, and other collectible playthings are under intense scrutiny as prices have escalated within recent years. Condition of the item dramatically affects value. Whether made of wood, lithographed paper-on-wood, tin, composition, or cast iron, the following grading code would apply:

Gradations of Fine:

Mint (unused or unplayed with): no chips, flaking, tears, or wear; if mechanical, the item is completely operable; very few specimens are ever found in this condition.

Near Mint (pristine): chips, flaking, tears are *minimal* and do not affect the most visible (faces, torsos) parts of the item.

Fine: still in superb condition, with at least 90% of the original finish; nothing to detract appreciably from overall aesthetics.

Good: in nice condition, still appealing to the eye, with at least 70% of the finish intact.

Average: only 50% of the finish remains; overall aesthetic appeal is diminished; most discerning collectors would probably pass on specimens in this state; if the item is extremely uncommon, restoration is a consideration.

Poor: possesses too many flaws for possible resale unless the item is particularly scarce; generally with less than 30% paint; usually sold only at rock-bottom prices and then only as a filler until the specimen can be up-scaled by a better example.

Originality is not considered in the condition statement but is implicit with each individual description.

TOYS

Aircraft 1920s Germany
Rocking steering airplane by Gunthermann; painted tinplate windup; open cockpit with pilot figure; tan and red.
Good Quality/Fine Condition $675 (D)   **$600–$700**

Aircraft 1920s German
Guntherman, lithographed, windup, tin roll plane; red and blue.
Good Quality/Fair Condition $220 (A)   **$200–$250**

Aircraft 22″ H 1920s German
Spiraling bi-wing gravity toy; painted tin; maker unknown; red and yellow.
Fine Quality/Fine Condition $1540 (A)   **$1200–$1600**

Aircraft 1930 Italy
Cardini *Nord Sud* bi-wing plane; red and blue.
Good Quality/Good Condition $275 (D)   **$250–$300**

Aircraft 13″ L 1930s United States
Girard *Air Mail* twin-engine bi-wing; tin windup; blue and yellow; mechanism frozen; a few dents.
Good Quality/Fair Condition $132 (A)   **$150–$175**

Clockwork tin 9″ L 1890s United States
Steeplechase racers, maker unknown; 2 horsemen, each on a single wheel that
revolves around base; red, blue, yellow, and black.
Fine Quality/Good Condition $3300 (A)   **$2500–$3500**

Clockwork tin 9″ L 1890s United States
Camel with rider on wheeled platform; maker unknown; offset wheels produce
realistic motion; brass bell; yellow, red, and brown.
Good Quality/Fine Condition $4070 (A)   **$3500–$4000**

Clockwork tin 14″ H 1890s German
Carousel with equestriennes and passengers in swings; painted tin; musical; mul-
ticolored.
Good Quality/Good Condition $2640   **$1000–$2000**

Clockwork tin 7″ L 1890s United States
Jockey on horse rocker; maker unknown; painted tin; multicolored.
Good Quality/Good Condition $990 (A)   **$700–$1000**

Clockwork tin 6″ L 1890s United States
Circus dog (poodle) pushing ball, maker unknown; painted tin; brown, blue;
some flaking.
Good Quality/Fair Condition $467 (A)   **$500–$700**

Disneyana 1930s Japan
Borgfeldt Mickey, Minnie Mouse motoring 3-wheel cart; celluloid windup with
original box, Minnie missing 1 ear, red, black, and yellow.
Good Quality/Fair Condition $7700 (A)   **$8000–$10,000**

Disneyana 1930s German
KW Mickey Mouse tap dancer, lithographed-tin mechanical; red, black, and
yellow. The selling price was an auction record for a Disney toy, set at Christie's,
New York, on Oct. 30, 1990.
Fine Quality/Good Condition $17,600 (A)   **$12,000–$15,000**

Penny toy 2.5″ Dia. 1890s German
Four-place mini carousel; painted tin; gravity powered; multicolored.
Good Quality/Fine Condition $935 (A)   **$600–$700**

Penny toy 4.5″ L 1890s German
Gunboat on wheels manned by Captain; maker unknown; painted tin push toy;
blue, metallic.
Good Quality/Good Condition $550 (A)   **$400–$500**

TOY TRAINS

HISTORY

Toy trains are one of the oldest and most widely collected subcategories of the toy hobby, arriving almost simultaneously with the first real-
life railroads in the 1830s and 1840s. Early wood, tin, and pewter toy
trains were highly stylized, more surreal than authentically detailed.
George Brown & Co. of Forestville, Connecticut, is believed to be the
first major U.S. maker, concentrating on clockwork tinplate models.
Cast-iron trains and brass model steam trains originated in the United
States in the 1880s; litho paper-on-wood versions, c. 1850.

The main focus in the hobby, however, is the electric train, which was introduced in the form of a rather crude Elevated Railway in 1884 by Novelty Electric Co. of Philadelphia. Major U.S. train makers are most popular on these shores and include the big four: American Flyer, Ives, Lionel, and Marx, with some attention devoted to Boucher and Dorfan.

Toy railroaders frequently collect by manufacturer, by type of gauge (i.e., large standard or wide guage vs. miniaturized O-gauge), or by prewar (early 1900s–1940) or postwar (1945–to present) periods. A recent survey by *Classic Toy Trains* magazine revealed that over three-quarters of those polled considered themselves toy train operators as well as collectors; a surprising 84 percent concentrate on trains manufactured after 1945.

Locomotive 2.88″ 1901 United States
Lionel No. 100 locomotive; clockwork; black.
Fine Quality/Good Condition $2500 (D)   **$3000–$4000**

Locomotive 1901 United States
Ives No. 0 engine with No. 1 tender; clockwork tin; black.
Good Quality/Good Condition $135 (A)   **$125–$150**

Locomotive Early 1900s United States
Ives cast-metal clockwork engine with Limited Vestibule Express tender; black, gilt lettering and trim; F.A.O.S. (designating F.A.O. Schwarz, NYC toy emporium). *(See photo 283)*
Good Quality/Good Condition $200 (D)   **$200–$250**

Locomotive 1925 United States
Dorfan No. 51 New York Central locomotive, 0-4-0; green.
Good Quality/Fine Condition $135 (D)   **$125–$150**

Locomotive 7.5″ L 1920s United States
Dorfan Loco-Builder engine No. 52; electric headlight and hand rails: red; also in green (No. 51).
Good Quality/Good Condition $125 (D)   **$125–$150**

Locomotive 1927 United States
Ives President Washington with No. 40 tender, 4-4-0; black and olive.
Fine Quality/Fine Condition $900 (D)   **$750–$800**

Photo 283. Locomotive. CREDIT: MADALINE FRIZ *(See above)*

Locomotive 1927–1930 United States
Marx No. 350 mechanical; black, yellow, red, and blue.
Good Quality/Good Condition $400 (D)   **$300–$350**

Locomotive 1930–1931 United States
Marx No. 101 Joy Line; cast iron, electric, 0-4-0 configuration; black.
Good Quality/Good Condition $125   **$125–$150**

Locomotive 1930s United States
Ives No. 3238 New York City locomotive; with Santa Fe and Swift refrigerator cars; New York, New Haven, and Hartford box car; No. 1025 tanker and gondola.
Good Quality/Good Condition $600 (D)   **$650–$750**

Locomotive 1931–1932 United States
Ives No. 10E engine, electric outline; tin; standard gauge (Lionel's designation after acquiring Ives), peacock blue.
Good Quality/Fine Condition $350 (D)   **$300–$350**

Locomotive 21.5″ c. 1930 United States
Boucher Blue Comet No. 2500; standard-gauge electric; 4-6-2 wheel configuration; with tender (black, 2 have been repainted).
Good Quality/Fair Condition $1980 (A)   **$2000–$2500**

Locomotive 1939 United States
Marx No. 897; 0-4-0 configuration; black, gray, and white lithography.
Good Quality/Good Condition $50 (D) **$35–$50**
(Color variation of above—olive, black, and white.)   **$110–$125**

Locomotive 1934–1937 United States
Marx 100000 No. 732 Union Pacific diesel streamliner; 4 wheels; brown top; yellow sides.
Good Quality/Good Condition $35 (D)   **$35–$50**

Locomotive/Tender 1954 United States
Marx No. 1895E with No. 4551 Santa Fe tender.
Good Quality/Good Condition $50 (D)   **$50–$75**

Train set 1916–1918 United States
American Flyer Type 1 Hummer set.
Good Quality/Good Condition $150 (D)   **$100–$125**

Train set 1917–1921 United States
Lionel armored set, with ammunition cars; one of Lionel's scarcest sets. *(See photo 284)*
Very Good Quality/Good Condition $4000 (A)   **$2500–$3500**

Train set c. 1925 United States
American Flyer Presidential set; locomotive No. 4689.
Superior Quality/Good Condition $8500 (D)   **$7000–$9000**

Train set 1925 United States
American Flyer Empire Express 0-gauge locomotive and No. 328 tender; Chicago Hummer-type passenger car; yellow and red. *(See photo 285)*.
Good Quality/Good Condition $150 (D)   **$125–$175**

Train set 1926 United States
American Flyer wide-gauge, The President's Special; Nos. 4039, 4080, 4081, and 4081 passenger cars; locomotive No. 4089; dark blue; gold trim.
Very Good Quality/Fine Condition $7500 (A)   **$6000–$8000**

Photo 284 (top). Train set. CREDIT: MADALINE FRIZ. *Photo 285 (bottom). Train set.* CREDIT: MADALINE FRIZ *(See p. 570)*

(See p. 570)

Train set 1927 United States
Ives Green Mountain Express; No. 3258 with Nos. 551 and 552 chair and parlor cars.
Good Quality/Good Condition $220 (A) **$175–$225**

Train set 1928 United States
Dorfan No. 890 Champion Limited locomotive, orange; with 2 Pleasant View pullmans; 0-4-0 wheel arrangement; orange with green roofs.
Good Quality/Fine Condition $800 (A) **$700–$800**

Train set 1929 United States
Ives Prosperity Special No. 1134; No. 40 tender; Nos. 241, 242, and 243 club, parlor, and observation cars; standard gauge; copper-plated. (Ives's last and greatest train set.)
Superb Quality/Fine Condition $9500 (A) **$8000–$10,000**

Train set 1930s United States
Ives Seneca No. 00; with No. 11 tender; Nos. 50, 51, 51, 1 baggage and 2 chair cars.
Good Quality/Good Condition $400 (D) **$450–$500**

Train set 1931–1940 United States
Lionel Twentieth Century Limited 400E, No. 400 tender, Nos. 412, 414, 416 State green cars with dark green ventilators; black locomotive.
Fine Quality/Fine Condition $6000 (A) **$5000–$6000**

Train set 1932 United States
American Flyer clockwork Dictator locomotive; No. 940T Chief tender; black.
Fair Quality/Good Condition $600 (D) **$500–$550**

Train set 1935 United States
Lionel No. 250E Hiawatha with No. 250WX tender, No. 782 coach, No. 783 coach, No. 784 observation car.
Fine Quality/Fine Condition $700 (D) **$650–$750**

Train set 1936–1937 United States
American Flyer No. 1741W Hiawatha locomotive, No. 1683; gray and orange tender and coaches; type-8 trucks; matching colors and gray roof; yellow on maroon decals; beveled end observation car; with 1741-RW passenger set, 1936.
Good Quality/Fine Condition $2200 (D) **$2000–$3000**

Train set 1936 United States
American Flyer Union Pacific streamliner, power car, 2 coaches, and observation car, with whistle.
Good Quality/Fine Condition $100 (D) **$50–$75**

Train set 1938 United States
American Flyer No. 15 Blue Car Train Set; 4 streamliner cars with 4-wheel trucks, No. 4622-6 locomotive; 2-toned blue.
Good Quality/Fine Condition $175 (D) **$150–$200**

Train set 1948 United States
Lionel Santa Fe No. 671; 0-gauge diesel scale model of General Motors prototype with Nos. 4452, 4454, 5459, and 4357 cars.
Good Quality/Good Condition $400 (D) **$400–$450**

Train set 1950 United States
Lionel (2) Union Pacific Alco Diesel No. 027 series, Anniversary Set; orange and black locomotives: one pulls 3 passenger coaches, the other pulls freight car, tanker, coal car, and caboose.
Good Quality/Good Condition $400 (D) **$450–$500**

Train set 1955 United States
Lionel Pennsylvania R.R. Congressional with No. 2340 Tucson red GG1; Molly Pitcher, William Penn, Betsy Ross, and Alexander Hamilton passenger cars.
Good Quality/Good Condition $1100 (D) **$1300–$1500**

Train set 1956 United States
Lionel No. 2341 Jersey Central Train Master with Nos. 2533, 2532, and 2531 wide-channel passenger cars.
Good Quality/Good Condition $900 (A) **$800–$900**

Train set 1964 United States
Lionel No. 9820 Military Train Set, made for Sears; includes No. 240 engine, flat car with tank, No. 3666 cannon box car, and No. 347 cannon firing range set with toy soldiers.
Good Quality/Good Condition $550 (D) **$500–$600**

Train set 1957 United States
Lionel No. 2037-500SLT-engine Lady Lionel set; Nos. 6462, 6464, 6436, 6464, and 6427 cars; engine in pink; rainbow-colored cars.
Fine Quality/Fine Condition $1100 (A) **$1100–$1200**

Train set 1959–1962 United States
Lionel No. 1862 General; Civil War classic prototype; steam outline, 4-4-0; No. 1862 tender; black.
Fine Quality/Good Condition $200 (D) **$175–$225**

Train set 1955–1966 United States
Lionel Virginian Trainmaster; double engine; yellow with blue roof.
Good Quality/Good Condition $425 (A) **$350–$500**

Train set 7.5″ L Locomotive 1902 Germany
Marklin MK gauge-1 clockwork locomotive; 0-4-0 locomotive and tender, dark green with orange trim; blue passenger car, orange freight car.
Good Quality/Fine Condition $935 (A) **$900–$1000**

Train set 1938 Germany
Marklin gauge P.L.M. locomotive; 4-8-2 wheel arrangement; original box, transformer, controls; 3 Mitropa gauge-0 passenger cars, c. 1926.
Very Good Quality/Fine Condition $3080 (A) **$2500–$3000**

Train set 1981 Germany
Lehmann Gross Bahn 100th Anniversary Set, G scale.
Good Quality/Fine Condition $500 (D) **$400–$500**

BIBLIOGRAPHY

Barenholtz, Bernard, and McClintock, Inez. *American Antique Toys*. New York: Harry N. Abrams, 1980.

Friz, Richard. *The Official Price Guide to Toys* (5th ed.). New York: House of Collectibles, 1990.

——. *The Official Price Guide to Toy Trains* (1st ed.). New York: House of Collectibles, 1990.

Gottschalk, Lillian. *American Toy Cars and Trucks*. New York: New Cavendish Books, Abbeville Press, 1985.

Moore, Andy and Susan. *The Penny Bank Book: Collecting Still Banks*. Exton, PA: Schiffer Publishing, 1984.

Norman, Bill. *The Bank Book: The Encyclopedia of Mechanical Bank Collecting* (standard ed.). San Diego, CA: Accent Studios Collector's Showcase Library Publication, 1984.

Whitten, Blair. *Toys*. New York: Alfred A. Knopf, 1984.

COLLECTORS' ORGANIZATIONS

Antique Toy Collectors of America*
Route 2, Box 5A
Baltimore, MD 21120

Mechanical Bank Collectors of America
PO Box 128
Allegan, MI 49010

National Association of Miniature Enthusiasts
PO Box 2621, Brookhurst Center
Anaheim, CA 92804

*Membership in this and certain other groups may be contingent on recommendation by at least two members in good standing at that club or society.

MUSEUMS

Children's Museum, Indianapolis, IN.

Children's Museum, Salem, MA.

Essex Institute, Sandwich, MA.

Forbes Museum, New York, NY.

Henry Francis Du Pont Winterthur Museum, Wilmington, DE.

Margaret Woodbury Strong Museum, Rochester, NY.

Mary Merritt Doll and Toy Museum, Douglasville, PA.

Museum of the City of New York, NY.

National Museum of American History, Smithsonian Institution, Washington, DC.

Shelburne Museum, Shelburne, VT.

Washington Doll's House and Toy Museum, Washington, DC.

Vintage Clothing

Advisor: **CYNTHIA GILES**

Cynthia Giles—author, editor, and teacher—has been collecting vintage clothing for a number of years. She is the author of The Official Identification and Price Guide to Vintage Clothing *(New York: House of Collectibles, 1989). Address: 1106 Cain Court, Cedarhill, TX 75104; (214) 291-8628.*

OVERVIEW OF THE FIELD

These days, when new clothes are designed by the cookie-cutter method (and are often cheaply made even if the price tag is staggering), it's not surprising that so many people miss the delicate detail and generous line of Victorian and Edwardian clothes; the outrageous wit and the flattering fit of clothes in the thirties; the ultrasophistication of high fashion in the fifties; and the experimental passion that hit the streets in the sixties. But the romance of the past is just one reason for collecting vintage clothing. Another is aesthetic interest. Some vintage garments were true works of art, made in a time when creative imagination could be expressed almost without limit in fashion because labor was incredibly cheap and fabulous materials were plentiful.

It's not only the Chanel suits and the *broderie anglaise* petticoats and the silk-velvet evening capes that have become collectibles, though. Even everyday clothes—work clothes, play clothes, children's clothes—all can have great interest for the collector because they reveal, in their lines and colors and textures, a great deal about how people saw themselves at a particular time in history. Clothing expresses the values and customs of a society and therefore is collectible from a historical as well as an aesthetic point of view.

There is also an economic aspect to collecting clothes. Vintage clothing is in limited supply, and without careful preservation what remains will deteriorate. Therefore, well-chosen items that are also well preserved will generally appreciate in value—which makes vintage clothing potentially a good investment and an attractive collecting field.

It's still a relatively open field as well. Until fairly recently, vintage clothing was looked upon by almost everyone as merely old and out of fashion, rather than "collectible," so the countryside hasn't yet been thoroughly scoured for every last remnant. There are plenty of treasures—from both an aesthetic and financial standpoint—left to be found at affordable (even bargain) prices.

The types of treasure that remain available, however, are progressively changing. Items from before 1880 are now so scarce and expensive that the average collector will not be able to acquire them; pre-1880 garments may be considered "antique" rather than "vintage." The late Victorian (1880–1900) and Edwardian (1900–1914) periods can still be collected today, but a substantial outlay of time, money, and/or luck will be required to assemble more than a few items.

The time span between the two world wars (1919–1939) has up to now been the most "collectible" period for vintage clothing. However, really interesting items from this period are becoming more and more difficult to acquire. The much sought-after beaded dresses of the 1920s and the bias-cut evening gowns of the 1930s, for example, are almost all in the hands of dealers, where they fetch a very good price. The collector interested in this period will have to be diligent to find the remaining good examples of between-wars design.

Not everyone agrees that clothes from the post–World War II period should be considered collectible, but by and large, the trend seems to be toward increasing interest in fashion collectibles from the late 1940s, the 1950s, and the 1960s. Excellent items from this period are still readily available, which means that a new collector can still build a very good collection with a reasonable investment in this area.

It's important to keep in mind, however, that although there are many 1950s and 1960s items available, few of them are truly collectible. Here's a general principle: nearly 100 percent of the clothing that remains from the 1880s is collectible, simply because of its age, but the proportion of collectible items to existing items declines steadily as age diminishes. At the near end of the scale, probably only between 5 percent and 10 percent of the clothing that remains from the 1960s is really collectible.

To put it another way, age alone can make a garment collectible but only if it is *both* at least 50 years old *and* in good condition; garments less than 50 years old should have significant design values and/or obvious historical interest in order to be considered seriously collectible. Successful collections from the post–World War II period will be those that are very selective, focusing on strong design, high quality, and uniqueness.

Among the especially collectible post–World War II items are

• Authentic imported, ethnic, and regional clothes (dramatic Hawaiian shirts, richly embroidered rodeo outfits, and handpainted Mexican skirts, for example).

• Heavily beaded cashmere sweaters.

• Garments made from unusual fabrics, such as Abstract Expressionist prints.

• "Hippie" clothes (such as painted denims, real tie-dyed T-shirts, neo-Edwardian dresses homemade from scraps of silk and velvet and lace).

• Designer clothing (including not only the European designers, such as Givenchy and Balenciaga but also the prestigious American sportswear designers like Vera Maxwell and Pauline Trigère).

MARKET TRENDS

The popular interest in vintage clothing began in the 1960s, when eccentricity became an important fashion statement. Flea markets and thrift shops were rummaged for artful wearables, and old fabrics were pieced together into new boutique items; vintage accessories—from hats to handkerchiefs—were also sought.

Since then, the vintage clothing market has become much more sophisticated. In the 1970s and early 1980s, there were a number of elegant shops devoted entirely to expensive vintage clothing, as well as many stores featuring less expensive items that appealed to young people in search of the "retro" look.

In the mid-1980s, the number of vintage clothing stores decreased, but more recently, there has seemed to be a resurgence of interest. Surviving dealers are doing better than ever, and new stores are opening across the country. Many vintage clothing customers are still looking for wearable items, but a growing number are buying for collecting purposes.

During the past several years, prices for designer items have risen substantially. The greatest price appreciation has been in the creations of fashion pioneers like Poiret and Vionnet, in the unique designs of artists such as Fortuny and Gallenga, and in the garments of designers—like Charles James or Boué Soeurs—whose output was relatively small. Clothes from high-production houses such as Chanel and Balenciaga hold their value but don't show dramatic increases.

The vintage market, therefore, continues strong in almost all areas, but hats—particularly early ones—seem to be especially in demand. Twenties' dresses are also much sought after, along with anything for men. Sixties' clothing, however, is not yet attracting a lot of interest.

Among vintage items that have either leveled off or decreased in value are Victorian whites, 1920s/1930s silk lingerie, and 1950s "poodle" skirts. Men's and children's clothing, on the other hand, are showing steady gains, as are ethnic costumes.

FAKES ALERT

There are two principal categories of clothing that can be mistaken as to period or value, even though they were never intended to be "fakes." The first category is clothing from the 1960s that was made to resemble Edwardian or 1930s styles. These "revival" pieces are usually easily detected because they have one or more of the following characteristics: modern paper or printed-fabric labels or care tags, synthetic fabric (other than rayon, which actually was used as early as the teens), nylon lace or other synthetic trimmings, zippers (which were not in general use until after 1935).

The second category is clothing that has a designer label but does not have designer value from a collecting standpoint. Only one-offs (garments made to order for a particular patron by the design house) and limited-production designs have true designer value. However, most of the major houses also sold partially or completely ready-made clothing in their own boutiques, and these items—though they may be wonderful pieces and quite collectible in their own right—have only the minimal value added by the designer name.

Further, from the 1950s on, many houses licensed the designer name for use on mass-produced clothing; this type of label adds no collecting value to the garment. In general, the only way to tell couturier-quality garments from ready-made and mass-produced garments is by the quality of fabric and workmanship, which are far superior in the former. Couture garments also may have design numbers on the label or sewn into the garment.

CONDITION KEY

Here are the conditions in which vintage garments may be found: *poor* (in very deteriorated condition overall and/or having irreparable damage), *average* (visibly worn, with some noticeable repairs), *good* (some wear, no visible repairs), and *fine* (very little wear, no repairs).

"New-old" merchandise was never worn because it was never sold; it sat in a warehouse somewhere, perhaps for decades. New-old stock is not necessarily in "mint" condition, however; there may be fading, weakening of the fabric, set-in creases, and the like. As a rule, new-old merchandise is valued much like "good" merchandise.

QUALITY KEY

Both workmanship and design are determining aspects of value in vintage clothing. The following characteristics indicate high quality in a garment; and the more of these characteristics that are present, the higher the quality that may be assigned.

Techniques used to make the garment hang or fit properly; these might involve extra sewing by using several separate pieces instead of one, or they might utilize large, shaped pieces that are more difficult and expensive to cut.

Seams that are finished on the inside by frenching or some other method.

Labor-intensive detailing (such as pin tucks, covered buttons, faggoting, insets, beaded seams, etc.).

Print or plaid fabrics carefully matched at seams and closures.

Print design that is distinctive, with a pleasing or arresting composition.

Strong dyes with little fading and no bleeding of one color into another.

Good colors (i.e., pale colors that are subtle and delicate, as opposed to weak, muddy, and/or nondescript, and bright colors that are vivid and rich rather than harsh and flat).

Good textures (soft fabrics should not be limp, and crisp ones should not be stiff; heavy fabrics should drape well and should not seem bulky; wool should not be scratchy).

Well-made trimmings that are carefully attached to the garment; high-quality trimmings include handmade lace, beading, unusual buttons, silk or velvet ribbons, and fine embroidery.

Blouse   1900–1910
Beaded all over; pigeon-breast front; ¾ sleeves with beaded fringe.
Superior Quality/Good Condition $185 (D)   **$150–$300**

Chemise   1910–1930
Black silk georgette; straps and sash of 2-sided ribbon; lace borders; trimmed in pastel silk rosettes.
Very Good Quality/Fine Condition $20 (D)   **$20–$45**

Coat   c. 1940
Gabardine topper with large Bakelite buttons.
Good Quality/Good Condition $50 (D)   **$35–$75**

Dress   1874
Print; 2-piece with bustle; apron front; velvet trim; steel-cut buttons.
Good Quality/Good Condition $195 (D)   **$150–$600**

Dress   c. 1900
Wedding dress of dotted swiss with lace inserts; 2 heavily trimmed petticoats; much detail. *(See photo 286)*
Superior Quality/Fine Condition $2400 (D)   **$1000–$2500**

Dress   1910–1918
White satin and lace court dress with ostrich-feather fan.
Very Good Quality/Good Condition $165 (D)   **$150–$500**

Dress   c. 1920
Pleated silk trimmed with Venetian glass beads; floor length; Fortuny label.
Superior Quality/Good Condition $715 (A)   **$700–$1200**

Photo 286 (left). Dress.
CREDIT: CYNTHIA GILES
Photo 287 (right). Dress.
CREDIT: CYNTHIA GILES
(See p. 579 and below)

Dress c. 1920
Black and pink chiffon and silk; silver beaded trim. *(See photo 287)*
Very Good Quality/Fine Condition $828 (A)   **$300–$1000**

Dress c. 1930
Crepe; floor-length bias-cut skirt; dropped waist; sleeveless blouson bodice with attached scarf; Molyneaux label.
Superior Quality/Good Condition $504 (A)   **$350–$600**

Dress c. 1930
Rayon; mid-calf bias-cut skirt; puffed sleeves; celluloid buttons.
Very Good Quality/Good Condition $48 (D)   **$30–$80**

Dress c. 1930
Floor length; peach crepe; tiny straps; maroon velvet leaves; maroon beading.
Very Good Quality/Good Condition $65 (D)   **$40–$250**

Hat c. 1890
Red velvet; with large brim; many red flowers.
Very Good Quality/Fine Condition $250 (D)   **$100–$300**

Hat c. 1930
"Toy" hat; crown about 3" across; small brim; many curly feathers; long velvet ties; all aqua.
Superior Quality/Fine Condition $20 (D)   **$20–$40**

Nightgown c. 1890
Handmade; cotton with fine white work; long sleeves; button yoke.
Very Good Quality/Good Condition $75 (D)   **$50–$150**

Remember, the price range shows what the same item would sell for in average condition (left column) and fine condition (right column). Any item in poor condition has, in general, a value of 50% (or less) of that of the same item in average condition.

Photo 288. Sweater.
CREDIT: CYNTHIA GILES
(See below)

Pantaloons c. 1910
White cotton; with cotton lace.
Very Good Quality/Fine Condition $25 (D)   **$20–$35**

Petticoat c. 1950
Pastel crinoline; 3 tiers.
Very Good Quality/Good Condition $20 (D)   **$15–$35**

Shirt c. 1940
Western style; peach gaberdine with brown yoke, cuffs, and piping; colorful
embroidery on yoke.
Good Quality/Fine Condition $80 (D)   **$40–$80**

Shirt c. 1950
Men's; Hawaiian; rayon, burgundy background with gray and white pineapple
print; Kamehameka label.
Superior Quality/Fine Condition $75 (D)   **$55–$100**

Shoes c. 1890
Burgundy; leather; high-laced.
Good Quality/Good Condition $100 (D)   **$75–$200**

Shoes 1950–1960
Clear Lucite platforms with ankle strap.
Good Quality/Average Condition $7 (D)   **$7–$35**

Suit, lady's c. 1910
Black wool; ankle-length skirt; fur-trimmed jacket; frog closures.
Good Quality/Good Condition $155 (D)   **$100–$200**

Sweater c. 1950
Cashmere cardigan; navy with all-over pattern of intricate white beading. *(See
photo 288)*
Superior Quality/Fine Condition $210 (D)   **$100–$225**

BIBLIOGRAPHY

BOOKS

Batterberry, Michael and Ariane. *Fashion, the Mirror of History.* New
    York: Greenwich House, 1977. An absolutely fascinating and first-rate

overview of the development of fashion; wonderful illustrations. (This book is also found under the title *Mirror, Mirror.*)

Bond, David. *The Guinness Guide to 20th-Century Fashion.* Middlesex, UK: Guinness Superlatives Limited, 1981. Terrific pictures; covers the 1960s much better than most books do, and even skims the 1970s.

Giles, Cynthia. *The Official Identification and Price Guide to Vintage Clothing.* New York: House of Collectibles, 1989.

Kemper, Rachel H. *A History of Costume.* New York: Newsweek Books, 1977. This beautiful book relates fashion to the political and cultural factors that have shaped history. An unusually thoughtful and wide-ranging book, yet very concise, it covers the entire history of costume in 150 pages! (The chapter on the 20th century, however, is very unsatisfactory.)

Milbank, Caroline Rennolds. *Couture: The Great Designers.* New York: Stewart, Tabori & Chang, 1985. A beautiful and informative book with an excellent bibliography.

Nunn, Joan. *Fashion in Costume 1200–1980.* New York: Schocken Books, 1984. Pleasant sketches provide a well-organized visual catalog of styles for each period. Most useful is the fact that men's and children's clothing are treated, along with accessories.

Robinson, Katherine. *The Clothing Care Handbook.* New York: Fawcett Columbine, 1985. Excellent all-around guide to techniques of clothing care.

PERIODICAL

Vintage Clothing Newsletter. This newsletter arrives six times a year, full of interesting notes about vintage clothing and the people who buy, sell, collect, and wear it. There are useful advertisements, too, along with news of books and shows. Well worth $15 a year. Write: Terry McCormick, PO Box 1422, Corvallis, OR 97339

COLLECTIONS

The major costume collections in this country are wonderful repositories of antique and vintage clothing, but for the most part, the many thousands of garments held in these collections are available for viewing to "serious" students and design professionals only. Most collections do, however, mount public exhibitions periodically.

Local, state, and regional historical societies frequently have costume collections (some quite large), as do many art museums.

The Costume Institute
The Metropolitan Museum of Art
Fifth Avenue at 82nd Street
New York, NY 10028

The Goldey Paley Design Center
at the Philadelphia College of
Textiles and Science
4200 Henry Avenue
Philadelphia, PA 19144

Indiana Fashion Design
Collection
Indianapolis Museum of Art
1200 West 38th Street
Indianapolis, IN 46208

The Arizona Costume Institute
The Phoenix Art Museum
1625 North Central Avenue
Phoenix, AZ 85004

The Doris Stein Research and
Design Center for Costumes and
Textiles at the Los Angeles
County Museum of Art
5905 Wilshire Boulevard
Los Angeles, CA 90036

Historic Costume and Textile
Collection
University of Washington
Seattle, WA 98195

The Texas Fashion Collection
University of North Texas
Denton, TX 76203-3677

Walking Sticks and Canes

A field of minor interest for many years, the intensity of collecting fervor has increased enormously in the past several years. "Sticks" have been a very good investment in that prices have climbed steadily for five years, increases for very good to superior examples averaging 20 percent or more each year. This year has been equally hot.

Examples range from the practical to the sublime, from the ridiculous to the exquisite. Both ladies' and gentlemen's sticks are desired by collectors. People who need a stick are also tending to buy attractive, sturdy examples, not just the hospital specials.

Sticks often contain secrets! An ordinary stick may contain a fine-quality corkscrew, a whiskey flask, a pen, or a pencil. An elegant stick may contain an inelegant sword or gun. A delicate lady's stick may conceal a gold vinaigrette. It is the additional intrigue of hidden goodies that greatly increases value.

And of course, obvious beauty is highly desired. Fine carved ivory, elegantly hand-chased gold or silver, carved animal heads of exotic wood, tortoiseshell with inlays—all are desired. The shaft of the stick is very important—it should enhance the handle.

FAKES ALERT

The greatest areas of fakery involve the addition of flasks to originally solid sticks and the conversion of umbrellas to walking sticks (by removing fine handles and placing them on new shafts). The very exotic pieces are seldom faked. Ivory heads must be examined with great care, as many are brand-new, made of plastic! Horn and brass handles are also highly suspect.

CONDITION KEY

Fine Condition: glowing finish, totally intact; any repairs are of high quality; original.

Good Condition: nice finish on shaft; intact with no missing parts; repairs are not obvious; original.

Average Condition: acceptable finish; ivory greatly lined; needs additional cleaning and polishing; repairs easily noted; if married, a successful marriage of all old parts.

Poor Condition: broken; badly scarred; missing parts; obvious marriage.

QUALITY KEY

Good Quality: a nice piece worthy of collecting but having no distinguishing characteristics.

Very Good Quality: a very good example of the type, reflecting several of the most desired characteristics.

Superior Quality: a superlative example that has nearly all desired characteristics of the type.

Cane 36″ L 1880–1890 United States
Rosewood cane with engraved silver head and horn tip; silver content not marked.
Good Quality/Average Condition $330 (A)   **$300–$500**

Ivory cane Art Nouveau 1910–1930 United States
Graceful, ivory, long-haired female nude reclining and shackled to a bed of rocks, on wood shaft. *(See photo 289, A)*
Superior Quality/Fine Condition $2200 (A)   **$1500–$2200**

Shooting stick Bamboo c. 1920 England
Simple shooting stick with metal seat; worn disk won't release.
Good Quality/Average Condition $125 (D)   **$125–$185**

Shooting stick Bamboo c. 1920 England
Leather grip handle folds out to make a seat; bamboo shaft, small dish flips out at top and is installed on point as a stop.
Very Good Quality/Fine Condition $165 (D)   **$125–$185**

Walking stick 33.75″ L 1880–1890 United States
Lignum vitae, with tooled silver head engraved "Sallie Burton"; brass top.
Good Quality/Average Condition $85 (A)   **$80–$200**

Walking stick 34.25″ L 1880–1890 United States
Figured walnut or mahogany with carved ivory head of a bearded man with indistinct inscription and gold-colored band; minor age cracks in ivory.
Good Quality/Average Condition $110 (A)   **$100–$300**

Walking stick 43.5″ L Blown glass 1880–1890 United States
Blue and brown swirl, "End of Day Cane."
Very Good Quality/Good Condition $33 (A)   **$30–$150**

Walking stick 36.5″ L 1890–1900 United States
Curly maple with good old brown patina; tip has chip.
Good Quality/Average Condition $60 (A)   **$50–$150**

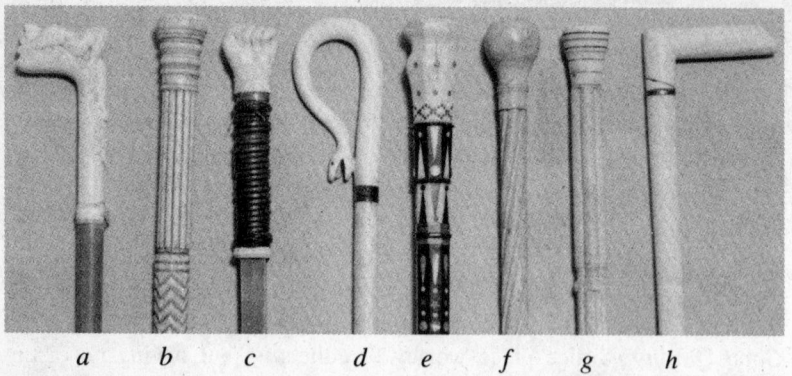

a   b   c   d   e   f   g   h

Photo 289. Group of canes. CREDIT: RAFAEL OSONA *(See pp. 585, 586, and below)*

Whale ivory 1865–1885 United States
Solid whale ivory octagonal knob inlaid at top with 1781 coin; connected to octagonal hardwood shaft with inlaid abalone teardrops, silver stars, and diamonds, ivory and tortoiseshell triangles. *(See photo 289, E)*
Superior Quality/Fine Condition $3300 (A)   **$2500–$3500**

Whale ivory 1865–1885 United States
Ivory handle shaped in the form of a serpent with metal tongue and baleen eyes and collar; shaft of tapering whalebone. *(See photo 289, D)*
Superior Quality/Fine Condition $2850 (A)   **$2000–$3000**

Whale ivory 1865–1885 United States
Whale ivory turned knob with round tortoiseshell inlay, joined to a carved whalebone shaft of reeded carving to a parallel zigzag carving to a deep swirl carving. *(See photo 289, B)*
Very Good Quality/Fine Condition $1650 (A)   **$1200–$2000**

Whale ivory 1865–1885 United States
Whale ivory and bone, with ivory knob top with mother-of-pearl inlay, joined to carved, twisted whalebone shaft, merging to a grid pattern carving; tapering end. *(See photo 289, F)*
Very Good Quality/Fine Condition $1225 (A)   **$800–$1500**

Whale ivory 1865–1885 United States
Carved solid whale ivory clenched fist and cuff joined in a 4″ baleen-wrapped section with chamfered square ivory spacer; shaft is 2 riveted baleen pieces. *(See photo 289, C)*
Very Good Quality/Good Condition $1650 (A)   **$1200–$2000**

Whale ivory 1865–1885 United States
Whale ivory and bone cane with solid whale ivory L-shaped handle with carved star end, joined by a narrow collar to a round tapering whalebone shaft; crack near collar joint. *(See photo 289, H)*
Good Quality/Poor Condition $775 (A)   **$600–$1200**

Whalebone 1865–1885 United States
Whalebone and ivory with whale ivory knob with red and black scribe lines and mother-of-pearl star inlay; whalebone shaft designed in 4 columns. *(See photo 289, G)*
Very Good Quality/Fine Condition $1650 (A)   **$1000–$1800**

BIBLIOGRAPHY

Dike, Catherine. *Cane Curiosa from Gun to Gadget*. Geneva: Catherine
  Dike Publishers, 1983.
Stein, Kurt. *Canes and Walking Sticks*. York, PA: 1974.

MUSEUMS

No major collections are known, but nearly every historic home and museum has one or more examples.

Watches

(See also Clocks)

Advisors: **COOKSEY SHUGART and RICHARD E. GILBERT**

Mr. Shugart and Mr. Gilbert are co-authors of The Complete Price Guide to Watches. *Both authors have been active watch buyers since the early 1960s. The authors have been horologists and members of the National Association of Watch and Clock Collectors since the early 1970s. Both have searched for fine timepieces all over the world and are the foremost experts in the field of antique pocket and wristwatches. Mr. Shugart resides in Cleveland, TN, and Mr. Gilbert lives in Sarasota, FL. They can be reached at Cooksey Shugart Publications, PO Box 3147, Cleveland, TN 37320-3147; (615) 479-4813.*

MARKET REPORT

Pocket watches are on an upward trend today, with European and Japanese buyers still being the strong buyers and keeping demand high. The wristwatch fever, however, has stabilized, with some high-grade, very expensive wristwatches falling in price. Repeaters or pocket watches with complications are still underpriced compared to time-only-style watches. Most buyers for these high-grade and complicated watches are looking for top-grade condition in dial, case, and movement, with the dial and case all original. Most dealers have faith in the market with no panic selling.

EXAMINATION AND INSPECTION OF A WATCH BEFORE PURCHASING

The examination and inspection of a watch before purchasing is of paramount importance. This is by no means a simple task, for there are many steps involved in a complete inspection.

The first thing you should do is to listen to a watch and see how it sounds. Many times the trained ear can pick up problems in the escapement and balance. The discriminating buyer will know that sounds cannot be relied on entirely because each watch sounds different, but the sound test is worthwhile and is comparable to the doctor putting the stethoscope to a patient's heart as the first source of data.

Check the bow to see if it is securely fastened to the case and look at the case to see if correction is necessary at the joints. The case should close firmly at both the back and front. (Should the case close too firmly, rub the rim with beeswax, which will ease the condition and prolong the life of the rim.)

Take note of the dents, scratches, wear, and other evidences of misuse. Does the watch have a generally good appearance? Check the bezel for proper fit and the crystal to see if it is free of chips.

Remove the bezel and check the dial for chips and hairline cracks. Look for stains and discoloration, and check to see if the dial is loose. It is important to note that a simple dial with only a single-sunk dial is a stronger unit than a double-sunk dial, which is constructed of three separate pieces.

If the watch is a stem-winder, try winding and setting. Problems in this area can be hard to correct. Parts are hard to locate and may possibly have to be handmade. If it is lever-set, pull the lever out to see if it sets properly into gear. Also check to see that the hands have proper clearance.

Now that the external parts have been inspected, open the case to view the movement. Check to see that the screws hold the movement in place securely. Note any repair marks and any missing screws. Make a visual check for rust, discoloration, dust, dirt, and general appearance. If the movement needs cleaning and oiling, this should be deducted from the price of the watch, as well as any repair that will have to be made.

Note the quality of the movement. Does it have raised gold jewel settings or a gold train (center wheel or all gears)? Are the jewels set in or pressed in? Does it have gold screws in the balance wheel? Sapphire pallets? Diamond end stones? Jeweled motor barrel? How many adjustments does it have? Does it have overall beauty and eye appeal?

Examine the balance for truth. First look directly down upon the balance to detect error in the roundness. Then look at it from the side to detect error in the flat swing or rotation. It should be smooth in appearance.

Examine the hairspring in the same manner to detect errors in truth. When a spring is true in the round, there will be no appearance of jumping when it is viewed from the upper side. The coils will appear to dilate and contract uniformly, in perfect rhythm, when the balance is in motion. Check the exposed portion of the train wheels for burred, bent, or broken teeth. Inspect pinions and pivots for wear. If a watch has complicated features, such as a repeater, push the slides, plungers, and buttons to see that they are in good working order.

After the movement and case have been examined to your satisfaction and all errors and faults have been found, talk to the owner about the history of the watch and elicit his or her personal thoughts about it. Is the movement in the original case? Is the dial the original one? Just what has been replaced? Has the watch been cleaned? Does it need any repairs? If so, can the seller recommend anyone to repair the watch?

Finally, see if the seller makes any type of guarantee, and get an address and phone number. It may be valuable if problems arise or if you want to buy another watch in the future.

APPRAISING WATCHES

Watch collecting is still young when compared to fields of the standard collectibles: coins and stamps. The watch-collecting field is growing, but information is still scarce, fragmented, and sometimes unreliable. To be knowledgeable in any field, one must spend the time required to study it.

The value of any collectible is determined first by demand. Without demand there is no market. In the watch trade, the law of supply and demand also holds. The supply of the American watches has stopped, and the demand among collectors continues to rise. There are many factors that make a watch desired or in demand. Only time and study will tell a collector just which watches are most collectible. After the collector or investor finds out what is desirable, then a value must be placed on it before it is sold. If it is priced too high, the watch will not sell; but on the other hand, if it is priced too low, it will be hard to replace at the selling price. The dealer must arrive at a fair market price that will move the watch.

No two watches are alike. This makes the appraising more difficult and often arbitrary. But there are certain guidelines one can follow to arrive at a fair market price. When watches were manufactured, most companies sold the movements to a jeweler, and the buyer had a choice of dials and cases. Some high-grade movements were placed in a low-grade case, and vice versa. Some had handpainted multicolored dials; some were plain. The list of contrasts goes on. Conditions of watches will vary greatly, and this is a big factor in the value. The best movement in the best original case will bring the top price for any type of pocket watch.

Prices are constantly changing in the watch field. Gold and silver markets affect the price of the cases. Scarcity and age also affect the value. These prices will fluctuate regularly.

APPRAISING GUIDELINES

Demand, supply, condition, and *value* must be the prime factors in appraising an old watch.

Demand, which is the most important element, can be determined by the number of buyers for that particular item. And a simple but true axiom is that value is determined by the price someone is willing to pay.

To obtain a better knowledge in appraising and judging watches, the following guidelines are most useful. Consider all of these factors before placing a value on the watch. (There is no rank or priority to the considerations listed.)

1. Demand: Is it high or low?
2. Availability: How rare or scarce is the watch?
3. What is the condition of both the case and movement? Very important.
4. Low serial numbers: The first one made would be more valuable than later models.
5. Historical value.
6. Age.
7. Is it an early handmade watch?
8. Type of case: beauty and eye appeal, value of metal content.
9. Is it in its original case? Very important.
10. Complications: Repeaters, for example.
11. Type of escapement.
12. Size, number of jewels, type of plates (¾, full, and bridge), type of balance, type of winding (keywind, lever-set, etc.), number of adjustments, gold jeweled settings, damaskeening, gold train.
13. What grade of condition is it? Pristine, Mint, Extra-Fine, Average, Fair, or Scrap?
14. Identification ability.
15. Future potential as an investment.
16. Quality (high or low grade) or low-cost production watches (dollar watch).
17. How much will this watch scrap out for?

GUIDE TO ABBREVIATIONS

★ ★ ★ ★ —Extremely rare; fewer than 20 known to exist

★ ★ ★ —Rare; fewer than 100 known to exist

★ ★ —Scarce; fewer than 500 known to exist

★ —Uncommon; fewer than 2500 known to exist

ADJ—Adjusted (to temperature, heat and cold, also isochronism)

BASE—Base metal used in cases; e.g., silveroid
BC—Box case
BRG—Bridge plate design movement
COIN—Coin silver
DB—Double back
DES—Diamond end stones
DMK—Damaskeened
DS—Double-sunk dial
DR—Double roller
DWT—Penny weight: $^{1}/_{20}$ troy ounce
ETP—Estimated total production
EX—Extra nice; far above average
FULL—Full plate design movement
   $^{3}/_{4}$—$^{3}/_{4}$ plate design movement
   1F brg—One-finger bridge design and a $^{3}/_{4}$ plate
   2F brg—Two-finger bridge design
   3F brg—Three-finger bridge design
GF—Gold-filled
GJS—Gold jewel settings
G#—Grade number
GT—Grade train (gold gears)
GCW—Gold center wheel
GRO—Good running order
HC—Hunter case
HCI-P—Adjusted to heat, cold, isochronism, and positions; e.g., HCI5P
HL—Hairline crack
J—Jewel (as 21J)
K—Karat (as 14K solid gold—not gold filled)
KS—Keyset
KW—Keywind
KW/SW—(Keywind/stemwind) transition
LS—Lever-set
MCBC—Multicolor box case
MCC—Multicolor case
MCD—Multicolor dial
MD—Montgomery-type dial
M#—Model number
Mvt. Only—Dial and movement only; no case
NI—Nickel plates or frames
OF—Open face
P—Position (5 positions adj)
PS—Pendant-set
PW—Pocket watch

Q—Quartz
RGP—Rolled gold plate
RR—Railroad
RRA—Railroad approved
RRG—Railroad grade
S—Size
SBB—Screw back and bezel
SRC—Swing ring case
SS—Stainless steel
SW—Stemwind
S#—Serial number
TEMP—Temperature
TP—Total production
2T—Two-tone
WGF—White-gold-filled
WI—Wind indicator (also as up and down indicator)
WW—Wristwatch
YGF—Yellow-gold-filled

Watches listed in this book are priced at the retail level and as complete watches, having an original 14K gold-filled case with an original white enamel single-sunk dial. The entire original movement is in good working order with no repairs needed, unless otherwise noted. Watches listed as 14K and 18K have solid-gold cases. Coin or silveroid-type and stainless steel cases will be listed as such. Keywind and keyset watches are listed as having original coin silver cases. Dollar-type watches or low-cost production watches are listed as having a base-metal-type case and a composition dial. Wristwatches are priced as having original gold-filled case with all-original movement in good working order, the wristwatch band made of leather except where bracelet is described.

Many of the watch manufacturers were commissioned to put jewelers' or jobbers' names on their movements in place of their own. Because of this practice, the true manufacturers of these movements are difficult to identify. These watch models are listed under the original manufacturer and can be identified by comparison with the model sections under each manufacturer.

The prices shown were averaged from dealers' lists just prior to publication and are an indication of the retail level or what collectors will pay. Prices are provided in three categories—average condition, extra-fine condition, and mint condition—and are shown in whole dollar amounts only. The values listed are a guide for the retail level and are provided for your information only. Dealers will not necessarily pay full retail price. Prices listed are for watches with *original* cases and dials.

POCKET WATCHES

AMERICAN WALTHAM WATCH CO.

18 Size

GRADE OR NAME, DESCRIPTION	AVERAGE	EXTRA-FINE	MINT
American Watch Co., 17J, ¾, KW, M#18KW ★ ★ ★	$1400	$1700	$2200
American Watch Co., 19J, M#1883, HC, silver ★ ★	$800	$1000	$1400
American Watch Co., 17J, M#1883	$75	$100	$150
American Watch Co., 21J, M#1883, ADJ, GJS	$400	$500	$700
American Watch Co., 15J, M#1870, KW	$200	$250	$350
American Watch Co., 17J, M#1857, KW, KS ★	$200	$250	$350
American Watch Co., 14K, HC, heavy box hinged, multicolor (4 colors)	$2200	$2400	$3200
American Watch Co., 15 & 17J, M#1870, KW, ADJ	$150	$200	$300
American Watch Co., 11J, M#1883, SW or KW	$55	$75	$125
American Watch Co., 17J, M#1892, LS	$75	$100	$150
American Watch Co., 21J, M#1892, PS	$150	$175	$225
American Watch Co., 7J, M#1877	$50	$70	$100
American Watch Co., 7J, M#1883, KW	$75	$100	$150
American Watch Co., 11J, M#1883, KW	$50	$85	$150
American Watch Co., 15J, M#1857, SW ★	$200	$300	$450
Crescent Street, 21J, M#1892, SW, Adj.5P, GJS	$100	$125	$170
Warren, 15J, M#1857, KW, KS, S#18–29, original 17S silver case ★ ★ ★	$18,000	$23,000	$28,000
Warren, 15J, M#1857, KW, KS, S#30–60, original 17S silver case	$12,000	$16,000	$20,000
Warren, 15J, M#1857, KW, KS, S#61–90, original 17S silver case ★ ★ ★	$10,000	$14,000	$18,000
Warren, 15J, M#1857, KW, KS, S#91–110, original 17S silver case ★ ★ ★	$9000	$12,000	$15,000

(Warren not in original silver case: deduct $1000 to $2500)

16 Size

GRADE OR NAME, DESCRIPTION	AVERAGE	EXTRA-FINE	MINT
Crescent Street, 19J, M#1908, Adj. 5P, LS, OF	$100	$125	$150
Crescent Street, 21J, M#1908, Adj.5P, PS, OF	$100	$125	$150
Crescent Street, 21J, M#1908, Adj.5P, PS, HC	$125	$150	$200
Crescent Street, 21J, M#1908, Adj.5P, LS, wind indicator	$350	$400	$450
Park Road, 11–15J, M#1872, PS	$90	$110	$135
Premier, 9J, M#1908, PS, OF	$50	$55	$70
Premier 11J, M#1908	$50	$60	$75
Premier, 15J, M#1908, LS, OF	$70	$85	$100
Premier, 17J, M#1908, PS, OF, silver-oid	$75	$90	$100
Premier, 21J, M#1908, silveroid	$55	$60	$70
Premier Maximus, 23J, M#1908, GT, gold case, LS, GJS, Adj.6P, WI, DR, 18K Maximus case, box and papers ★ ★	$8000	$9000	$10,000
Premier Maximus, 23J, M#1908, GT, gold case, LS, GJS, Adj.6P, WI, DR, 18K Maximus case, no box ★ ★	$6000	$7000	$8000
Premier Maximus, 23J, M#1908, GT, gold case, LS, GJS, Adj.6P, WI, DR, 18K Maximus case, sterling box and papers, extra crystal and main-spring ★ ★	$9000	$9500	$11,000
Premier Maximus, 23J, M#1908, GT, YGF recased ★ ★	$2000	$2500	$3000
Railroader, 17J, M#1888, LS, NI ★ ★	$300	$350	$535
Railroad King, 17J, 2-T ★	$195	$240	$375
Railroad Watches with RR names on dial and movement, such as Canadian Pacific RR, Santa Fe Route, etc., M#s 1888, 1899, 1908 ★	$255	$450	$750
Repeater, 16J, M#1872, original coin case, 5 min ★ ★ *(See photo 290)*	$2000	$2500	$3000
Repeater, 1 min. moon phase, M#1872, Perpetual Cal., 18K case, all orig. ★ ★ ★ ★	$30,000	$35,000	$45,000

14 Size

GRADE OR NAME, DESCRIPTION	AVERAGE	EXTRA-FINE	MINT
Chronograph, 13J, M#1884, 14K HC with register, Am. W. Co. case	$850	$950	$1350

GRADE OR NAME, DESCRIPTION	AVERAGE	EXTRA-FINE	MINT
Chronograph, 13J, M#1884, 18K HC with register, Am. W. Co. case	$1200	$1400	$1600
Chronograph, 13J, M#1884	$175	$225	$300
Chronograph, 17J, M#1884	$195	$270	$385
Chronograph, 15J, M#1874, split second, 14K, HC ★ ★	$1200	$1350	$1600

DUDLEY WATCH CO.

12 Size—"Masons" Model

GRADE OR NAME, DESCRIPTION	AVERAGE	EXTRA-FINE	MINT
12S, Dudley, 19J, 14K, flip-open back, Serial #1 (made 5 experimental models with Serial #1) ★ ★ ★	$5000	$7000	$10,000
12S, M#1, 19J, OF, 14K, flip-open back ★	$3000	$3200	$3500
12S, M#1, 19J, OF, 14K, flip-open back, with box and papers ★	$3000	$3500	$4000
12S, M#2, 19J, OF, flip-open back, GF ★	$1600	$1800	$2200
12S, M#2, 19J, OF, 14K, flip-open back case ★	$2000	$2200	$2600
12S, M#3, 19J, OF, 14K flip-open case ★	$2000	$2200	$2500

ELGIN WATCH CO.

18 Size

GRADE OR NAME, DESCRIPTION	AVERAGE	EXTRA-FINE	MINT
Elgin W. Co., 7J, OF, SW	$50	$75	$100
Elgin W. Co., 7J, KW, gilded, HC	$75	$100	$150
Elgin W. Co., 11J, LS, SW, HC, 9K–10K	$325	$375	$475
Elgin W. Co., 11J, LS, SW, HC, silveroid	$40	$50	$65
Elgin W. Co., 13J, SW, PS/LS, silveroid	$40	$50	$65
Elgin W. Co., 15J, SW, LS, OF	$50	$75	$100
Elgin W. Co., 15J, SW, LS, YGF, multicolor box	$300	$325	$500
Elgin W. Co., 15J, SW, LS, OF, silveroid	$50	$60	$75
Elgin W. Co., 15J, SW, LS, HC	$75	$100	$150

Photo 290 (left). Repeater watch. CREDIT: COOKSEY SHUGART. *Photo 291 (right). B. W. Raymond watch.* CREDIT: COOKSEY SHUGART *(See pp. 595, 598)*

Photo 292. Hamilton watch.
CREDIT: COOKSEY SHUGART
(See p. 600)

GRADE OR NAME, DESCRIPTION	AVERAGE	EXTRA-FINE	MINT
Elgin W. Co., 17J, SW, multicolor, 14K, HC	$1500	$1800	$2200
Elgin W. Co., 21J, SW, LS, silveroid	$60	$70	$90
Elgin W. Co., 21J, SW, LS, HC	$125	$150	$175
B. W. Raymond, 15J, gilded, KW, FULL, HC *(See photo 291)*	$125	$150	$175
B. W. Raymond, 15J, SW, HC	$75	$100	$125
B. W. Raymond, 17J, NI, FULL, OF	$50	$75	$100
B. W. Raymond, 17J, silveroid	$40	$60	$80
B. W. Raymond, 17J, NI, FULL, HC	$100	$125	$175
B. W. Raymond, 15J, box case, 14K	$700	$800	$1200
B. W. Raymond, 19J, NI, ¾, SW, OF, GJS, wind indicator, DMK	$500	$600	$850
B. W. Raymond, 19J, ¾, GJS, GT, diamond end stone	$75	$100	$125
B. W. Raymond, 19J, ¾, GJS, GT, diamond end stone, OF	$125	$150	$175
B.W. Raymond, 21J, NI, ¾, SW, GJS, DMK, GT	$100	$125	$175
Veritas, 21J, ¾, NI, GJS, OF, DMK, GT	$100	$125	$175
Veritas, 21J, ¾, GJS, GT, diamond end stones	$100	$125	$175
Veritas, 21J, ¾, GJS, GT, diamond end stones, HC	$175	$200	$250
Veritas, 21J, ¾, NI, GJS, OF, wind indicator, DMK	$1000	$1100	$1300
Veritas, 23J, ¾, NI, GJS, OF, DMK, GT, diamond end stone	$200	$225	$300
Veritas, 23J, ¾, NI, GHS, OF, DMK, GT	$175	$225	$300
Veritas, 23J, ¾, wind indicator, GJS, OF, DMK, GT, 14K	$1400	$1600	$2000
Veritas, 23J, G#214, ¾, NI, GJS, OF, wind indicator, DMK	$800	$1000	$1300
Veritas, 23J, G#214, SW, OF	$125	$150	$200
Veritas, 23J, SW, OF, 14K	$550	$575	$650

16 Size

GRADE OR NAME, DESCRIPTION	AVERAGE	EXTRA-FINE	MINT
Elgin W. Co., 9J, OF	$50	$75	$125
Elgin W. Co., 11J, HC	$75	$100	$150
Elgin W. Co., 13J, OF	$50	$100	$125
Elgin W. Co., 13J, OF, silveroid	$40	$50	$70
Elgin W. Co., 13J, HC	$75	$100	$150

GRADE OR NAME, DESCRIPTION	AVERAGE	EXTRA-FINE	MINT
Elgin W. Co., 15J, OF, silveroid	$40	$50	$70
Elgin W. Co., 15J, OF	$50	$75	$125
Elgin W. Co., 15J, HC, 14K	$400	$450	$550
Elgin W. Co., 17J, OF	$50	$75	$125
Elgin W. Co., 17J, HC	$100	$125	$175
Elgin W. Co., 21J, HC	$150	$175	$225
Convertible Model, 15J, silveroid	$50	$60	$90
Convertible Model, 21J, 3F BRG	$900	$1100	$1450
Convertible Model, 21J, G#91, 3F BRG, 14K	$1600	$1800	$2000
3F Bridge Model, 21J, Adj.5P, NI, DMK, GJS, GT	$200	$250	$325
Father Time, 17J, ¾, NI, OF, GJS, DR, DMK	$100	$125	$175
Father Time, 21J, ¾, NI, HC, DR,DMK	$175	$200	$275
Father Time, 21J, silveroid	$60	$70	$80
Father Time, 21J, NI, GJS, DR, OF	$100	$125	$175
Lord Elgin, 21J, GJS, DR, Adj.5P, 3F BRG, 14K★ ★	$1200	$1500	$2000
Lord Elgin, 23J, GJS, DR, Adj.5P, ¾, 14K, OF★ ★	$1000	$1200	$1400
B. W. Raymond, 17J, ¾, GJS, 14K, OF	$475	$525	$650
B. W. Raymond, 17J, 3F BRG★ ★	$400	$500	$650
B. W. Raymond, 17J, GJS, SW, OF	$150	$200	$250
B. W. Raymond, 19J, ¾, GJS, DR, Adj.5p, DMK, OF	$75	$100	$150
B. W. Raymond, 19J, OF, 14K, 30 DWT	$400	$450	$500
B. W. Raymond, 19J, M#8, G#240, OF, Adj.5P	$75	$100	$150
B. W. Raymond, 19J, GJS, Adj.5P, HC	$150	$175	$225
B. W. Raymond, 21J, 14K, OF	$425	$475	$525
B. W. Raymond, 21J, G#389, OF	$125	$150	$185
B. W. Raymond, 21J, ¾, GJS, DR, Adj.5P, HC	$175	$225	$275
B. W. Raymond, 21J, ¾, GJS, DR. Adj.5P, DMK, OF	$125	$150	$185
B. W. Raymond, 22J, WWII Model, sweep second hand	$125	$150	$175
B. W. Raymond, 23J, ¾, GJS, DR. Adj.5P, DMK, wind indicator, military-style	$425	$475	$550
Repeater, Terstegen, 5 min., 21J, 2 gongs★ ★	$2000	$3000	$4500
Veritas, 21J, GJS, DR, Adj.5P, DMK, ¾, HC	$250	$300	$375

HAMILTON
18 Size

GRADE OR NAME, DESCRIPTION	AVERAGE	EXTRA-FINE	MINT
922, 15J, OF ★	$450	$550	$700
923, 15J, HC ★	$500	$600	$750
926, 17J, NI, OF, DMK, ADJ	$50	$75	$100
927, 17J, NI, HC, DMK, ADJ	$100	$125	$175
928, 17J, NI, HC, DMK, ADJ	$125	$150	$200
929, 15J, NI, HC, 14K	$600	$700	$800
933, 16J, NI, HC ★ ★	$500	$550	$625
934, 17J, NI, OF, DMK, DR, Adj.5P	$100	$125	$175
935, 17J, NI, HC, DMK, DR, Adj.5P	$250	$300	$375
947, 23J, NI, HC, DMK, DR, Adj.5P, GJS, 14K, HC, not marked "947" (See photo 292)	$3500	$4000	$5000

16 Size

GRADE OR NAME, DESCRIPTION	AVERAGE	EXTRA-FINE	MINT
954, 17J, LS or PS, OF, ¾, DR, Adj.5P	$75	$100	$150
960, 21J, PS, OF, BRG, GJS, GT, DR, Adj.5P ★	$300	$325	$400
960, 21J, LS, OF, BRG, GJS, GT, DR, Adj.5P ★	$325	$350	$425
962, 17J, PS, OF, BRG ★ ★	$500	$600	$650
964, 17J, PS, OF, BRG ★ ★	$650	$700	$800
966, 17J, PS, OF, ¾ ★ ★	$600	$650	$750
968, 17J, PS, OF, ¾ ★	$325	$375	$475
972, 17J, PS & LS, OF, ¾, NI, GJS, DR, Adj.5P, DMK	$100	$125	$175
974, 17J, OF, PS, Adj.3P	$50	$75	$100
974, 17J, OF, 2-T	$125	$150	$200
978, 17J, LS, OF, NI, DMK	$50	$75	$100
990, 21J, LS, OF, GJS, DR, Adj.5P, DMK, NI, ¾, GT	$150	$175	$225
991, 21J, LS, HC, ¾, GJS, Adj.5P, DMK, NI, GT	$175	$200	$250
992, 21J, Extra, OF, ¾, PS & LS, GJS, Adj.5P, DR, NI, DMK	$150	$175	$225

12 Size

GRADE OR NAME, DESCRIPTION	AVERAGE	EXTRA-FINE	MINT
902, 19J, BRG, DR, Adj.5P, GJS, 14K	$300	$325	$375
904, 21J, BRG, DR, Adj.5P, GJS, GT	$100	$125	$175

GRADE OR NAME, DESCRIPTION	AVERAGE	EXTRA-FINE	MINT
910, 17J, ¾, DR, ADJ	$40	$50	$70
912, 17J, digital model, rotating seconds, OF	$80	$110	$150
916, 17J, Adj.3P, silver case	$30	$40	$60
918, 19J, Adj.3P, WGF	$75	$100	$150
920, 23J, BRG, Dr, Adj.5P, GJS, GT, OF	$200	$250	$325
922, 23J, BRG, DR, Adj.5p, GJS, GT, 14K	$400	$450	$525
922 MP, 18K case	$800	$900	$1100
922 MP, GF, Hamilton case	$300	$400	$550

ILLINOIS WATCH CO.

18 Size

GRADE OR NAME, DESCRIPTION	AVERAGE	EXTRA-FINE	MINT
Benjamin Franklin U.S.A., 21J, GJS, Adj.6P, NI★	$900	$1000	$1150
Benjamin Franklin U.S.A., 24J, GJS, Adj.6P, FULL, NI, DMK★	$2000	$2400	$3000
Benjamin Franklin U.S.A., 26J, GJS, Adj.6P, FULL, DR, NI, DMK★★★	$5000	$5500	$7000
Bunn, 15J, M#1, KW, KS, FULL, OF	$500	$600	$775
Bunn, 15J, KW/SW transition	$425	$500	$650
Bunn, 15J, M#1, KW, Coin	$500	$600	$775
Bunn, 17J, M#2, SW, NI, FULL, HC	$150	$200	$275
Bunn, 17J, SW, NI, Coin	$125	$150	$200
Bunn, 17J, SW, M#3, 5th pinion, gilded, OF	$350	$400	$475
Bunn, 17J, M#6, SW, NI, FULL, OF	$125	$150	$200
Bunn, 19J, SW, NI, FULL, OF, DR, LS, GJS, Adj.5P, J. barrel	$250	$300	$325
Bunn Special, 21J, SW, Coin	$150	$175	$225
Illinois Watch Co., 11J, M#1-2, KW, FULL	$75	$100	$125
Illinois Watch Co., 11J, M#3	$50	$75	$100
Illinois Watch Co., 13J, M#1-2, KW, FULL	$100	$125	$175
Illinois Watch Co., 17J, M#3, 5th pinion	$200	$225	$275
Illinois Watch Co., 15J, SW, ADJ, DMK, NI	$75	$100	$125
Illinois Watch Co., 15J, transition	$50	$75	$100
Illinois Watch Co., 15J, SW, silveroid	$60	$75	$100

GRADE OR NAME, DESCRIPTION	AVERAGE	EXTRA-FINE	MINT
Illinois Watch Co., 17J, SW, silveroid	$50	$60	$75
Illinois Watch Co., 17J, transition	$75	$100	$125
Illinois Watch Co., 21J, OF	$150	$175	$225
Interior, 7J, KW, FULL	$100	$125	$175
Interior, 7J, M#3	$75	$100	$150
Interstate Chronometer, 17J, OF	$300	$400	$550
Interstate Chronometer, 23J, Adj.5P, GJS, NI, OF	$850	$950	$1150
Iowa W. Co., 7J, M#1–2, KW, FULL	$175	$200	$250
King of the Road, 16 & 17J, NI, OF & HC, LS, FULL, ADJ★	$400	$500	$625
Lafayette, 24J, GJS, Adj.6P, NI, SW, OF	$950	$1050	$1250
Lakeshore, 17J, OF, LS, NI, FULL, SW	$100	$125	$175
Landis W. Co., 7–11J	$75	$100	$150
Liberty Bell, 17J, NI, SW, FULL	$100	$125	$175
Liberty Bell, 17J, silveroid	$75	$100	$150
A. Lincoln, 21J, silveroid	$75	$100	$150
A. Lincoln, 21J, Adj.5P, NI, DR, GJS, HC	$250	$300	$375
Maiden Lane, 17J, 5th pinion	$400	$475	$600
Manhattan, 11J, HC, NI, FULL, KW, LS	$125	$150	$200
Miller, 15J, silveroid	$75	$100	$125
Miller, 15J, M#1, HC, KW, FULL	$150	$175	$225
Miller, 15J, KW, FULL, OF	$125	$150	$200

16 Size

GRADE OR NAME, DESCRIPTION	AVERAGE	EXTRA-FINE	MINT
Bunn, 19J, LS, NI, ¾, Adj.5P, HC★★★	$800	$1000	$1500
Bunn, 19J, marked jeweled barrel	$175	$200	$250
Bunn Special, 19J, LS, OF, NI, ¾, Adj.6P, GT	$125	$150	$200
Bunn Special, 21J, NI, GJS, HC★	$400	$450	$525
Bunn Special, 21J, LS, OF, NI, ¾, GJS, Adj.6P, GT	$125	$150	$175
Bunn Special, 21J, 60-hour, 14K, OF, Bunn Special case★	$675	$725	$800
Bunn Special, 23J, LS, OF, NI, ¾, GJS, Adj.6P, GT, 60-hour	$350	$425	$475
Bunn Special, 23J, LS, NI, GJS, HC★	$1200	$1500	$1800
161 Bunn Special, 21J, ¾, Adj.6P, 60-hour	$250	$300	$375
163 Bunn Special, 23J, GJS, Adj.6P, ¾, 60-hour	$400	$475	$575

GRADE OR NAME, DESCRIPTION	AVERAGE	EXTRA-FINE	MINT
Great Northern Special, 17J, BRG, ADJ	$250	$275	$325
Great Northern Special, 19J, BRD, ADJ	$275	$300	$350
Illinois Central, 17J, 2-T, GT	$100	$125	$175
Illinois Watch Co., 7J, M#1–2–3	$50	$75	$125
Illinois Watch Co., 11J, ¾, OF	$50	$75	$125
Illinois Watch Co., 15J, M#1, HC	$100	$125	$175
Illinois Watch Co., 15J, M#3, OF	$50	$75	$125
Illinois Watch Co., 15J, 3F BRG, GJS	$50	$75	$125
Illinois Watch Co., 17J, 14K, HC	$400	$450	$525
Illinois Watch Co., 17J, M#7, OF	$75	$100	$150
Illinois Watch Co., 17J, M#5, ¾, ADJ, HC	$100	$125	$175
Illinois Watch Co., 19J, M#1, ¾, GJS, Adj.5P	$75	$100	$150
Illinois Watch Co., 21J, GJS, HC	$150	$175	$225
Illinois Watch Co., 21J, 3F BRG, GJS, Adj.5P	$125	$150	$200
Illinois Watch Co., 25J, 3F BRG, GJS, Adj.5P ★ ★	$3000	$3500	$4000
Imperial Sp, 17J, SW, LS, Adj.4P, OF	$75	$100	$150
Interstate Chronometer, 17J, GCW, Adj.5P, HC	$275	$300	$325
Interstate Chronometer, 23J, 1F BRG, ADJ, OF	$600	$700	$850
Interstate Chronometer, 23J, 1F BRG, ADJ, HC	$900	$1000	$1150
Lafayette, 23J, 1F BRG, GJS, Adj.5P, GT	$750	$850	$1000
Lakeshore, 17J, OF	$75	$100	$150
Landis W. Co., 15J	$75	$100	$150
Liberty Bell, 17J	$100	$125	$175
A. Lincoln, 21J, ¾, GJS, Adj.5P	$125	$150	$200
Marine Special, 21J, ¾, Adj.3P	$250	$275	$325
Monroe, 17J, NI, ¾, OF (Washington W. Co.)	$100	$125	$175
Monroe, 15J, ¾, OF (Washington W. Co.)	$75	$100	$150
Our No. 1, 15J, HC, M#1	$150	$200	$275
Paillard Non-Magnetic Watch Co., 11J, ¾	$75	$100	$150
Paillard Non-Magnetic Watch Co., 21J, ¾, GJS, Adj.5P, DMK	$300	$325	$375
Pennsylvania Special, 23J, ¾, GJS, Adj.5P ★	$1200	$1400	$1600
Plymouth W. Co., 17J, OF (add $25 for HC)	$75	$100	$125
Precise, 21J, OF, LS, Adj.3P	$125	$150	$200
Quincy Street, 17J, ¾, NI, DMK, ADJ	$75	$100	$125

GRADE OR NAME, DESCRIPTION	AVERAGE	EXTRA-FINE	MINT
Railroad Dispatcher, 11J, HC	$150	$175	$225
Railroad King, 17J, HC	$200	$225	$275
Railroad Official, 23J, 3F BRG★★	$800	$900	$1050
Railway King, 17J, OF	$150	$175	$225
Sangamo, 21J, GJS, HC	$275	$300	$350
Sangamo, 21J, ¾, GJS, DR, Adj.6P, OF	$150	$175	$225
Sangamo, 23J, ¾, GJS, DR, Adj.6P, HC	$425	$475	$550
Sangamo, 25J, M#5, ¾, GJS, DR, Adj.6P★★★	$4000	$5000	$6500
Sangamo Extra, 21J, ¾, GJS, DR, Adj.6P, OF★	$500	$600	$750
Sangamo Special, 19J, BRG, GJS, GT, Adj.6P	$350	$375	$425
Sangamo Special, 21J, M#7, OF	$325	$375	$450
Sangamo Special, 21J, BRG, GJS, GT, diamond end cap	$350	$400	$475
Sangamo Special, 23J, M#9–10, BRG, GJS, GT, Adj.6P, Sangamo Special case	$400	$450	$525
Sangamo, Special, 23J, BRG, GJS, GT, Adj.6P, diamond end stone, screw back, Sangamo Special case	$400	$450	$525
Santa Fe Special, 17J, BRG, Adj.3P	$150	$175	$225
Santa Fe Special, 21J, ¾, Adj.5P, HC	$200	$250	$300
Sears, Roebuck & Co. Special, 17J, ADJ	$75	$100	$150
Senate, 17J, OF, NI, ¾	$75	$100	$150
Standard, 15J	$50	$75	$125
Sterling, 19J, SW, PS, Adj.3P, OF	$50	$75	$125
Stewart, 17J	$50	$75	$125

COMIC AND CHARACTER WATCHES

GRADE OR NAME, DESCRIPTION	AVERAGE	EXTRA-FINE	MINT	MINT + BOX
Alice in Wonderland, WW, c. 1951, by U.S. Time	$15	$25	$45	$350
WW, c. 1953, by Bradley	$20	$30	$55	$150
Babe Ruth, WW, c. 1948, by Exacta Time, box baseball pledge card★★	$150	$250	$375	$1200
Bambi, WW, c. 1949, by U.S. Time	$100	$175	$250	$450
Batman, WW, c. 1970, by Gilbert (band in shape of bat)	$75	$125	$200	$350

Photo 293. Buck Rogers watch.
CREDIT: COOKSEY SHUGART
(See below)

GRADE OR NAME, DESCRIPTION	AVERAGE	EXTRA-FINE	MINT	MINT + BOX
Batman, WW, c. 1978, by Timex	$35	$60	$75	$120
Betty Boop, PW, c. 1934, by Ingraham (with die-embossed back) ★ ★ ★	$350	$600	$900	$1600
Big Bad Wolf and 3 Pigs, PW, c. 1936, by Ingersoll	$300	$500	$700	$1200
Buck Rogers, PW, c. 1935, by Ingraham (lightning bolt hands) *(See photo 293)*	$300	$400	$650	$1000
Bugs Bunny, WW, c. 1951, by Ingersoll (carrot-shaped hands) Swiss	$75	$150	$250	$500
Buster Brown, PW, c. 1928, by Ingersoll (2 models)	$125	$175	$250	$450
Buzz Corey, WW, c. 1952, by U.S. Time	$75	$100	$200	$450
Captain Liberty, WW, c. 1950, by U.S. Time	$50	$75	$150	$450
Captain Marvel, PW, c. 1945, by New Haven	$100	$125	$200	$400
Mickey Mouse, PW, c. 1933, by Ingersoll, #1 & 2 (tall stem)	$285	$350	$450	$650
Popeye, WW, c. 1936, by New Haven (tonneau style, with friends on dial) ★	$250	$375	$650	$1200
Popeye, WW. c. 1966, by Bradley (round style)	$75	$100	$125	$200
Porky Pig, WW, c. 1948, by Ingraham (tonneau)	$100	$175	$250	$450

GRADE OR NAME, DESCRIPTION	AVERAGE	EXTRA-FINE	MINT	MINT + BOX
Puss-N-Boots, WW, c. 1959, by Bradley	$100	$175	$250	$400
Robin, WW, c. 1978, by Timex	$25	$35	$50	$75
Robin Hood, WW, c. 1955, by Bradley (tonneau style)	$75	$100	$150	$300
Rocky Jones Space Ranger, WW, c. 1955, by Ingraham	$100	$200	$300	$700
Roy Rogers, WW, c. 1954, by Ingraham (Roy and Trigger)	$50	$75	$100	$250
Skeezix, PW, c. 1936, by Ingraham	$225	$275	$350	$650
Smitty, WW, c. 1936, by New Haven	$150	$200	$300	$550
Smokey Stover, WW, c. 1968, by Timex	$75	$100	$150	$225
Snow White, WW, c. 1938, by Ingersoll (tonneau)	$100	$125	$200	$400
Snow White, WW, c. 1952, by U.S. Time (round)	$25	$35	$50	$350
Snow White, WW, c. 1956, by U.S. Time (statue in box)	$25	$35	$50	$250
Snow White, WW, c. 1962, by U.S. Time (plastic watch)	$25	$35	$50	$250
Superman, PW, c. 1956, by Bradley	$150	$250	$350	$600

WRISTWATCHES (PRICING AT RETAIL LEVEL—COMPLETE WATCHES ONLY)

AMERICAN WALTHAM WATCH CO.

U.S.A.—Man's Wristwatch

GRADE OR NAME, DESCRIPTION	AVERAGE	EXTRA-FINE	MINT
Barrel, Cromwell, 17J, GF	$65	$80	$150
Barrel, Oberlin, 17J, GJ	$65	$80	$150
Curvex, Curvex style, GF, 2+″ long, 14K	$400	$500	$700
Curvex style, 14K case	$150	$200	$275
Curvex style, GF case	$65	$70	$100
Cushion, 14K case	$175	$200	$225

GRADE OR NAME, DESCRIPTION	AVERAGE	EXTRA-FINE	MINT
Cushion, GF	$75	$100	$125
Cushion, Hilton, 17J, GF	$65	$90	$110
Rectangular, 17J, G#750, stainless	$50	$60	$70
Rectangular, 21J, G#750-B, sub. sec., gold border, 14K	$175	$200	$250

BULOVA

GRADE OR NAME, DESCRIPTION	AVERAGE	EXTRA-FINE	MINT
Accutron, "Astronaut," M-214, 24-hour dial, 14K	$500	$600	$700
Accutron, skeletonized model, GF, "Spaceview"	$125	$150	$185
Accutron, skeletonized model, stainless, "Spaceview"	$100	$125	$150
Rectangular, 17J, "Curvex," c. 1939, 14K	$200	$250	$350
Rectangular, 17J, GF	$75	$100	$125
Rectangular, 17J, curved, fancy lugs, 14K white gold	$175	$200	$250
Round, GF	$40	$50	$60
Round, gold plate	$30	$40	$50
Round, chronograph, c. 1945	$200	$250	$300
Round, 30J, "Ambassador," auto-wind, 18K case	$200	$250	$300
Round, 23J, waterproof, 14K	$125	$150	$200
Round, 23J, day, date, self-wind, GF case	$75	$85	$110
Square, 14K case	$125	$150	$175
Tank, 15J, "Athlete," GF	$100	$115	$125
Tonneau, quartz, waterproof, 1960, SS	$150	$175	$200
Tonneau, 17J, "Lone Eagle" (Lindbergh model), c. 1930, GF	$200	$250	$300
Tonneau, 15J, "Ambassador," GF	$60	$70	$80
Tonneau, "Light Emitting Diode," 14K and stainless	$75	$100	$135

ELGIN WATCH CO.

U.S.A.—Man's Wristwatch

GRADE OR NAME, DESCRIPTION	AVERAGE	EXTRA-FINE	MINT
B. W. Raymond, RRA, 23J, 14K case	$300	$350	$400
B. W. Raymond, RRA, 23J, GF	$150	$200	$250
B. W. Raymond, RRA, 23J, stainless	$125	$150	$175

GRADE OR NAME, DESCRIPTION	AVERAGE	EXTRA-FINE	MINT
Lord Elgin, 17J, rectangular case, 14K	$200	$225	$250
Lord Elgin, 17J, rectangular GF case	$70	$80	$95
Lord Elgin, 21J, round 14K case	$100	$125	$150
Lord Elgin, 21J, round GF case	$50	$60	$70
Official Boy Scout on case, c. 1934	$100	$125	$175
Doctor's Model, "duo dial," rectangular GF case	$450	$500	$600
Rectangular, 14K case, diamond dial	$300	$350	$450
Rectangular, GF case	$75	$100	$125

GRUEN

Swiss and U.S.A.—Man's Wristwatch

GRADE OR NAME, DESCRIPTION	AVERAGE	EXTRA-FINE	MINT
Chevrolet grill, 15J, c. 1920s, nickel case	$800	$900	$1000
Curvex, 14K case, 1.5″ long	$400	$500	$650
Rectangular, duo dial (doctor), GF	$600	$700	$800
Round, 17J, alarm, date, YGF	$100	$120	$140
Round, 17J, 24-hour jump dial, 1–12 A.M. 13–24 P.M., YGF	$100	$120	$150
Round, 17J, diver's watch, autowind, stainless	$60	$70	$80
Round, 17J, Adj.5P, YGF	$50	$60	$70
Square, 18J, heavy 14K case	$250	$300	$350
Square, 17J, "Curvex," fancy lugs, 14K	$350	$400	$500
Tank, 14K case	$250	$300	$350
Tank, GF	$70	$80	$100
Tonneau, Precision, flip top, hunter, 14K GF	$500	$600	$700

HAMILTON WATCH CO.

Man's Wristwatch

GRADE OR NAME, DESCRIPTION	AVERAGE	EXTRA-FINE	MINT
Cushion, 17J, GF case	$100	$125	$150
Cushion, 17J, G#987, engraved bezel, 14K, 1920	$300	$350	$400
Round, Sentinel, 17J, GF	$100	$120	$140
Round, Spur, 19J, G-989, "Swirl Design," 14K	$2000	$2500	$3200

GRADE OR NAME, DESCRIPTION	AVERAGE	EXTRA-FINE	MINT
Round, Steeldon, 17J, G-747, SS	$50	$60	$70
Round, selfwind, 25J, GF, case	$50	$60	$70
Round, selfwind, 17J, 14K case	$125	$150	$200
Round, time zone dial (P.M.C.E.), 14K case	$250	$300	$375
Round, 22J, small diamonds on bezel and dial, 14K	$300	$350	$400
Round, 17J, small diamonds on dial, 14K	$250	$300	$350
Round, 17J, stainless steel	$40	$50	$60
Square, 17J, 14K, diamond on dial	$250	$300	$350
Square, 17J, 14K case	$125	$225	$250
Square, 17J, GF case	$100	$125	$150
Square, 17J, 2-T dial, 14K	$200	$250	$325
Square, drivers' watch, stem at 12:00, GF	$400	$450	$500
Tonneau, Piping Rock, 19J, G#979, round dial, 14K white gold	$800	$900	$1000
M#979, 19J, GJS, GF Hamilton case	$125	$150	$175
M#982, GJS, Hamilton 14K gold case	$200	$250	$325
M#987, 17J, GF Hamilton case, sweep second	$100	$125	$150
Altair, second hand, GF case, electric	$700	$800	$900
Aquatel "B," second hand, 10K GF case, electric	$100	$125	$150
Converta II, second hand, 10K GF case, electric	$100	$125	$150
Everest, 10J, trapezoidal, second hand, polished case, GF, electric	$125	$150	$175
Flight II, second hand, GF case	$500	$600	$700
Gemini, cushion, second hand, 10K GF case	$100	$125	$150

PATEK, PHILIPPE & CO.

Swiss—Wristwatch

GRADE OR NAME, DESCRIPTION	AVERAGE	EXTRA-FINE	MINT
Round, 18J, watertight, 18K rotor, gyromax balance, 18K	$3000	$3200	$3600
Round, Nautilus, 36J, diamond dial, c. 1970s, 18K and steel case	$4000	$4500	$5000
Round, 36J, M#13, self-wind, diamond dial and bezel, 1970s, 18K	$4000	$4500	$5000
Round, 36J, M#13, self-wind, Adj.5P, 1970, 18K	$2500	$3200	$3500

GRADE OR NAME, DESCRIPTION	AVERAGE	EXTRA-FINE	MINT
Round, Nautilus, 36J, M#7, date, 18K case and bracelet	$10,000	$11,000	$12,000
Round, 36J, 52 diamonds on bezel, diamond hour markers on blue dial, gold mesh bracelet, all 18K	$4000	$4500	$5000
Round, thin movement, 18K case, friction back	$1500	$1800	$2400
Round, self-wind with 18K rotor, 18K case, waterproof (See photo 294)	$2000	$2200	$2500
Round, 30J, 18K rotor, 18K case, waterproof	$3400	$3600	$4000
Round, 30J, M#10, "Calatrava," 18K	$3200	$3400	$4000
Round, 36J, free-sprung, caliber 28–255, 18K case	$2200	$2500	$3000
Round, 36J, M#12 ½, Adj.5P, 1970s	$2000	$2200	$2500
Round, 12 diamonds on bezel, 18K bracelet and case	$3500	$3800	$4500
Round, ¼ repeater, 18K case, lady's	$50,000	$90,000	$100,000
Round, min. repeater, 18K case	$130,000	$160,000	$180,000
Round, skeletonized, gyromax balance, free-sprung, 18K	$10,000	$12,000	$15,000
Round, 37J, M#13, watertight, self-wind, 18K	$3500	$4000	$4500
Rectangular, 18J, M#7, 1970s, dark blue dial, applied gold indexes, 18K case	$3000	$3500	$4000
Rectangular, 18J, 18K rose gold case, c. 1940	$10,000	$11,000	$12,500
Rectangular, 18J, hidden lugs, 18K 2-color gold case	$8000	$9000	$11,000
Rectangular, 18J, curvex long style, 11 diamonds on dial, platinum case, c. 1930s ★ ★ ★	$14,000	$15,000	$17,500

Photo 294. *Patek, Philippe and Co. watch.*
CREDIT: COOKSEY SHUGART *(See above)*

GRADE OR NAME, DESCRIPTION	AVERAGE	EXTRA-FINE	MINT
Rectangular, 18J, 18K hinged case, c. 1930s	$7000	$9000	$10,000
Rectangular, 23J, "8 Jours," 18K, c. 1920s ★ ★ ★	$80,000	$90,000	$100,000
Rectangular, curvex style, offset lugs, 1940	$8000	$9000	$10,500
Round, 15J, M#12, spade hands, 1910s, 18K, enamel dial	$12,000	$14,000	$16,000
Round, 15J, early time only, Adj.5P, heavy 18K case, c. 1910, enamel dial	$6000	$7000	$8000
Round, 16J, "Gondolo," 18K, c. early 1920s ★ ★	$7000	$8000	$10,000
Round, 18J, M#12, Adj.5P, auxiliary sec. dial, 1930, 18K	$3000	$3200	$3500

ROLEX

Swiss—Wristwatch

GRADE OR NAME, DESCRIPTION	AVERAGE	EXTRA-FINE	MINT
GMT-Master, oyster, perpetual, date, 18K case	$4000	$5000	$6000
GMT-Master, oyster, perpetual, date, SS case	$600	$700	$850
Round, oyster, manual wind, 14K case	$800	$900	$1000
Round, oyster, manual wind, stainless	$250	$300	$350
Round, oyster, perpetual (bubble back), 18K case	$3000	$3300	$3800
Round, oyster, perpetual (bubble back), 10K case	$1500	$1800	$2000
Round, oyster, perpetual (bubble back), stainless and gold	$1000	$1100	$1200
Round, oyster, perpetual, date just. (date only), 10K case	$1000	$1200	$1400
Round, oyster, perpetual, date just. (date only), stainless and 18K gold, Q. Set Jubilee band	$1400	$1600	$2000
Round, oyster, perpetual, date just. (date only), stainless	$500	$600	$750
Round, oyster, perpetual, day, date, 18K bracelet, Jubilee clasp, 12-diamond dial	$4000	$4500	$5500
Round, oyster, perpetual, date, president, 18K bracelet with hidden clasp, 18K case, Q. set	$5500	$6000	$6500

GRADE OR NAME, DESCRIPTION	AVERAGE	EXTRA-FINE	MINT
Round, 18K oyster, day, date, 18K early president band, 1950, diamond dial	$3000	$3500	$4000
Round, oyster, perpetual, day and date, 12-diamond dial, president, 18K bracelet with hidden clasp, 18K case, Q. set	$6000	$6500	$7000
Round, oyster, perpetual, day and date, 44 diamonds on bezel and 10 on dial, president, 18K bracelet with hidden clasp, 18K	$7500	$8000	$8500
Round, oyster, Daytona, 3 registers, calibrated bezel, 14K	$8000	$9000	$10,000
Round, oyster, Daytona, 3 registers, calibrated bezel, SS	$1800	$2000	$2500
Round, oyster, Speedking, SS case	$250	$300	$350
Round, oyster, milgass, antimagnetic, perpetual, stainless	$1000	$1200	$1400
Round, oyster, perpetual, submariner, date, SS, Q. set	$900	$1000	$1100
18K	$7000	$8000	$9000
Round, oyster, perpetual, explorer, stainless	$500	$550	$600
Round, oyster, perpetual, "Superlative chronometer," SS	$400	$500	$600
Round, Tudor, Prince, oyster, date, chronograph, 3 registers, SS	$350	$400	$500
Round, Tudor, oyster, automatic	$155	$165	$185
Square, 17J, chronograph, 2 registers, tachometer, c. 1940s, 18K case	$15,000	$20,000	$25,000
Square, 17J, ex. flat, SW, 1950s, 18K	$2200	$2400	$2700
Square, 17J, precision, c. 1940s, 14K case	$1000	$1200	$1400
Square, chronometer, perpetual, 18K case	$2500	$3000	$3200

BIBLIOGRAPHY

Britten, F.J. *Old Clocks and Watches and Their Makers*, 9th ed. London: Methuen, 1982.

Cuss, T. P., and T. A. *Antique Watches*. Woodbridge, Suffolk, England: Antique Collectors Club, 1976.

Daniels, George. *English and American Watches*. London: Abelard Schuman, 1967.

World's Fair
Memorabilia

***Advisor:* RICHARD FRIZ**

Richard Friz is a nationally recognized author of many books and articles, including The Official Price Guide to World's Fair Memorabilia, The Official Price Guide to Political Memorabilia, The Official Price Guide to Toys, *and* The Official Identification and Price Guide to Toy Trains *(New York: House of Collectibles). Mr. Friz is a member of the New Hampshire Appraisers Association. He can be reached at RFD 2, Box 155, Peterborough, NH 03458; (603) 563-8155.*

The first ancient world's fair was held in Persia in the third year of the reign of Xerxes, 486 B.C. In modern times the world's fair that has kindled the keenest competition among collectors is the 1939 New York World's Fair, and just slightly behind it is the 1893 World's Columbian in Chicago. Other events to capture the collector's imagination and fancy are the St. Louis World's Fair, 1904; the Chicago World's Fair, 1933; and the U.S. Centennial in Philadelphia in 1876.

A few years ago a major auction house in New England turned down world's fair items, stating that they didn't know anybody who would collect "that kind of stuff." Recently, over two thousand devotees attended the World's Fair Collector's Society annual two-day show at the Queens Museum, which overlooks the site of the 1964 New York World's Fair. Major museums and institutions now mount impressive exhibitions recalling past expositions.

Based on extensive research, a number of safe assumptions regarding world's fair collectibles can be made:

• Memorabilia squirreled away in closets and attics are generally preserved because of sentimental value, and the majority of these items will never achieve rarefied status on the market.

• The more exquisite, the more ingenious the item, the more its value will appreciate, often in staggering increments over the years. This includes limited editions, special presentation pieces, or awards to famous personalities.

• According to *World's Fair* magazine editor Afred Heller, as well as

Michael Pender of *Fair News*, souvenirs designed to commemorate a fair's anniversary or to tie in thematically with the fair itself are far more collectible. For example, a beanie from the Knoxville Expo in 1982, with its solar-powered propeller, forms a perfect link with the "Energy Turns the World" theme and is therefore highly collectible.

Two major areas of world's fair memorabilia are those items made of glass—busts, statuettes, bottles, etc.—and pinbacks. Expo buttons, or pinbacks, largely an American phenomenon, have served as colorful reminders of our periodic efforts to gather the best of our world into one location. Beginning with the Trans-Mississippi Exposition in Omaha in 1898, they have flourished up to the present. In their heyday, around 1930, there were 200 manufacturers of pinbacks in the United States.

Though today the form is often reduced to graphic design or word play, historically the pinback was an ingenious way to capture the spirit of a campaign or events within the confines of a square inch. Just 15 years ago these tin and celluloid collectibles could be had by the handful for $2 or $3. Today the more exceptional beauties hover between $75 and $100.

Here are some potential trendsetters as we head into the 1990s. The following key has been used as a guide to measure the quality of the items listed in this section.

QUALITY KEY

Good Quality: items collectors seek to round out their collection, not up to the standards of the other two categories.

Very Good Quality: highly desirable item that rarely comes up on the market.

Superior Quality: acknowledged classics, done by a recognized artist or artisan.

If an item does not have a specific price and condition grade, remember, use the price range as a condition range. The following key gives you some basic guidelines to follow when determining the worth of an item based on condition.

CONDITION KEY

Fine Condition: clean and crisp with no noticeable defects interfering with content.

Good Condition: defects blend into item or don't materially affect appearance.

Average Condition: defects noticeable and detract from appearance.

Poor Condition: numerous defects; it is best to pass by specimens in this condition unless you desire merely to fill a void until you can upgrade.

Glassware 1876 United States
Liberty Bell-embossed bottle, designed by Samuel C. Upham; marked "Proclaim Liberty"; dates separated by crack in bell; clear.
Good Quality/Good Condition $85 (D) **$75-$100**

Glassware 4″ H 1876 United States
George Washington bust bottle; designed by Edw. Newman; bust on pedestal base marked "Washington"; crystal (also appeared in blue or dark amber).
Good Quality/Good Condition $35 (D) **$35-$50**

Glassware 10.25″ H 1876 United States
"Simons Centennial Bitters" bottle; George Washington embossed portrait; in amber, dark green, blue, or aqua.
Good Quality/Good Condition $125 (D) **$100-$150**

Glassware 4.5″ H 1876 United States
Biblical Ruth (Ruth the Gleaner) statuette; Gillinder, Philadelphia; clear glass with frosted finish.
Good Quality/Good Condition $175 (D) **$150-$175**

Glassware 5.5″ H 1876 United States
U.S. Grant bust figure statuette; Gillinder, Philadelphia; white opaque with frosted finish.
Fine Quality/Fine Condition $400 (D) **$350-$375**
Same as above, but clear glass with frosted finish. **$325-$350**

Glassware 6″ H 1876 United States
Abraham Lincoln bust figure statuette; Gillinder, Philadelphia; white opaque with frosted finish.
Fine Quality/Fine Condition $400 (A) **$350-$400**
Same as above but clear glass with frosted finish. **$250-$275**

Glassware 6.5″ H 1876 United States
Benjamin Franklin statuette, Gillinder, Philadelphia; full-face bust; opaque white with frosted finish.
Fine Quality/Fine Condition $450 (D) **$400-$425**

Glassware 1876 United States
Charles Sumner statuette; bust figural; Gillinder, Philadelphia; clear glass with frosted finish.
Fine Quality/Fine Condition $300 **$225-$250**

Glassware 7″ H 1893 United States
Columbus figural bust on long column bottle by Dewitz Etienne; crystal.
Fine Quality/Good Condition $250 (D) **$200-$225**

Glassware 5″ H 1893 United States
Columbus Monument bottle with stopper; patented by Julius Librowicz; milk glass monument with figure of Columbus in gilt white metal.
Good Quality/Good Condition $200 (A) **$160-$175**

Glassware 1895 United States
Figural liquor bottle in shape of bale of cotton for Cotton States & International; rectangular panel on front for label; patented 1890; dark amber glass.
Good Quality/Good Condition $175 (D) **$150-$200**

Glassware 8.5″ H 1933 United States
Hall of Science refrigerator bottle with embossed building; "Century of Progress" in raised letters.
Good Quality/Good Condition $20 (D)   **$20–$25**

Pinback 1876 United States
"Immortal 56 Signers, Decl. of Ind., Centennial 1776" brass charm pendant, pyramid shaped; brass.
Good Quality/Good Condition $25 (D)   **$20–$30**

Pinback 1876 United States
Centennial Bell charm; die-cut brass; free-swinging Liberty Bell in center of suspended loop between pair of tiny winged angels.
Good Quality/Good Condition $60 (D)   **$50–$60**

Pinback 1893 United States
"Columbia Expo. Woman's Aux. Comm." enameled seal of state of Pennsylvania; gold.
Good Quality/Fine Condition $175 (A)   **$150–$200**

Pinback 1893 United States
Columbian half-dollar inlay brooch; reverse with illustration of Santa Maria; sky blue background.
Good Quality/Good Condition $90 (D)   **$75–$100**

Pinback 1895 United States
Black female field worker with bale of cotton atop head; "U.S. & Int. Expo/Atl., 1895"; slightly convex cello with brass frame; attaches to ribbon and "Souvenir" cello clasp; blue, orange, tan.
Good Quality/Good Condition $95 (A)   **$85–$100**

Pinback 1898 United States
"Souvenir of Peace Jubilee"; Uncle Sam dancing with Miss Liberty pendant; multicolored; portrait of President McKinley on reverse; black and white.
Good Quality/Good Condition $75 (D)   **$50–$75**

Pinback 1898 United States
"Official Trans Mississippi" emblem of seated deity; 2-sided cello hanger; Nebraska building and state flag on reverse; multicolored.
Good Quality/Good Condition $175 (D)   **$150–$175**

Where the value range clearly exceeds the amount sold for, this reflects price increases during the last year.

BIBLIOGRAPHY

Applebaum, Stanley. *The New York World's Fair, 1939/40.* Photographs by Richard Wurts and others. New York: Dover, 1987 (155 photos; paperbound, 152 pp.).

Badger, R. Reid. *The Great American Fair: The World's Columbian Expo and American Culture.* Chicago: Nelson-Hall, 1987, (266 pp., hardbound).

Beaver, Patrick. *The Crystal Palace.* London: Phillimore & Co., 1986 (154 pp., hardbound). History of the first international fair with details of grand reconstruction and life of the Palace at Sydenham, leading up to its destruction by fire in 1936.

Benedict, Burton. *The Anthropology of World's Fairs: San Francisco's Panama-Pacific International Exposition of 1915,* with contributions by Marjorie M. Dobkin, Gray Brechin, Elizabeth N. Armstrong, and George Starr. Brookfield, VT: Gower, 1983.

Expo '85 Architecture. Architectural Institute of Japan, 1986 (212 pp.; 300 photos).

Hilton, Suzanne. *Here Today and Gone Tomorrow: The Story of World's Fairs and Expositions.* Philadelphia: Westminister Press, 1978 (181 pp.).

Witherspoon, Margaret Johanson. *Remembering the St. Louis World's Fair.* St. Louis, MO: Folkestone Press, 1973.

Appendixes

Appendix A:
Periods of Antiques

ENGLAND: PERIODS BY REIGN

1558–1603	Elizabethan
1603–1688	Jacobean
1689–1701	William and Mary
1702–1713	Queen Anne
1714–1726	George I
1727–1759	George II
1760–1819	George III
1810–1820 (approximately)	Regency
1820–1830	George IV
1830–1836	William IV
1837–1901	Victorian
1901–1909	Edwardian

ENGLAND: PERIODS BY DESIGNER NAME

Chippendale	1750–1780
Adam	1760–1790
Hepplewhite	1770–1800
Sheraton	1795–1815

UNITED STATES: PERIODS BY MOST COMMON NAME

Pilgrim	1630–1690
William and Mary	1690–1725
Queen Anne	1725–1750
Chippendale	1750–1780
Federal	1780–1820
Empire	1815–1840
Victorian Revival Styles, esp. Louis XV and Renaissance Revival	1840–1880

Eastlake	1870–1890
Anglo-Japanese	1880–1910
Art Nouveau	1895–1910
Centennial	1885–1900
Colonial Revival	1900–1940
Arts and Crafts (Mission)	1895–1920
Golden Oak	1890–1930
Modern	1925–1950

FRANCE: PERIODS BY REIGN

1610–1643	Louis XIII
1643–1715	Louis XIV
1715–1774	Louis XV
1774–1792	Louis XVI
1795–1800	Directoire
1800–1815	Empire
1814–1830	Louis XVIII and Charles X (most commonly known for Charles X)
1830–1850	Louis-Philippe
1850–1870	Second Empire
1870–1930	Various revivals, especially Louis XV and Louis XVI

CHINA: PERIODS AND MARKS BY REIGN

MING DYNASTY, 1368–1644

Hung Wu
1368–1398

洪武
年製

永樂
年製

Yung Lo
1403–1424

德年製 大明宣

Hsüan Te
1426–1435

化年製 大明成

Ch'eng Hua
1465–1487

治年製 大明弘

Hung Chih
1488–1505

德年製 大明正

Ch'eng Te
1506–1521

靖年製 大明嘉

Chia Ching
1522–1566

慶年製 大明隆

Lung Ch'ing
1567–1572

曆年製 大明萬

Wan Li
1573–1619

T'ien Ch'i
1621–1627

大明天
啟年製

Ch'ung Cheng
1628–1643

年崇
製禎

CH'ING DYNASTY, 1644–1912

Shun Chih
1644–1661

大清順
治年製

K'ang Hsi
1662–1722

大清康
熙年製

Yung Cheng
1723–1735

大清雍
正年製

Ch'ien Lung
1736–1795

大清乾
隆年製

Chia Ch'ing
1796–1820

嘉慶
年製

Tao Kuang
1821–1850

大清道光年製

Hsien Feng
1851–1861

大清咸豐年製

T'ung Chih
1862–1874

大清同治年製

Kuang Hsü
1875–1908

大清光緒年製

Hsüan T'ung
1909–1912

大清宣統年製

REPUBLIC OF CHINA, 1912–

THE PEOPLE'S REPUBLIC OF CHINA, 1949–

JAPAN: PERIODS AND MARKS

Edo Period
1615–1868

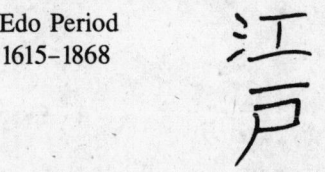

江戸

Meiji Period
1868–1912

明
治

Taishō Period
1912–1926

大
正

Shōwa Period
1926

昭
和

KOREA: PERIODS BY REIGN

1392–1910	Yi Dynasty
1910–1945	Japanese rule
1945–	Republic

Appendix B:
Appraisal Societies

Only two societies test and certify their members, thus only two are recommended.

American Society of Appraisers
International Headquarters
PO Box 17265
Washington, DC 20041

A.S.A. is a multidisciplinary organization established over 50 years ago. It tests and certifies members on two levels—Member and Senior Member—and recertifies every five years. Brochures and directories are available to the public at no cost from the above address.

International Society of
Appraisers
PO Box 726
Hoffman Estates, IL 60195

Established about ten years ago, I.S.A. is an organization of personal property appraisers. They offer a vast range of educational courses through their association with Indiana University—all of which are available to the general public—at a fee, of course. Some members have completed a set of required courses and others have advanced designations. Consult the I.S.A. administration at the above address.

Appendix C:
Dealer Organizations

In the United States, there is only one large, national organization. There are, however, several small organizations with members scattered throughout the country; there are several regional organizations, many state organizations, and a staggering number of local organizations. Most exist only to lobby and advertise and to provide an occasional social or educational event.

Only the National Association of Dealers in Antiques, Inc., is truly national in scope; thus, it is the only organization listed here.

National Association of Dealers in
Antiques, Inc.
PO Box 421
Barrington, IL 60011
(312) 381-7096

An organization established in 1961, its roster and Code of Ethics are available from the above address. Members are investigated by a committee and sign an agreement to abide by the Code of Ethics. National seminars held jointly with Kent State University are offered twice a year. The organization offers annual $3000 scholarships to the Cooper-Hewitt Museum Graduate Program in the History of the Decorative Arts.

Membership is open to show and shop dealers, educators in the antiques field, auction houses, show managers, and publishers in the antiques field.

Appendix D:
Periodicals of Interest

A. B. Bookman's Weekly, PO Box AB, Clifton, NJ 07015.

American Philatelist, PO Box 8000, State College, PA 16803.

American Rifleman, c/o National Rifle Association, 600 Rhode Island Avenue, NW, Washington, DC 20036.

Americana Magazine, 205 W. Center Street, Marion, OH 43302.

Antique & Collecting Hobbies, c/o Lightner Publishing Co., 1006 S. Michigan Avenue, Chicago, IL 60605.

Antique Collecting, PO Box 327, Ephrata, PA 17522.

Antique Market Report, PO Box 12830, Wichita, KS 67277.

Antique Monthly, 2100 Powers Ferry Road, Atlanta, GA 30339.

Antique Press, 12403 N. Florida Avenue, Tampa, FL 33612.

Antique Toy World, 3941 Belle Plaine, Chicago, IL 60618.

Antique Trader Weekly, PO Box 1050, Dubuque, IA 52001.

Antique Week, PO Box 90, Knightstown, IN 46148

Antiques, The Magazine, 551 Fifth Avenue, New York, NY 10017.

Antiques & Auction News, Joel Slater's, PO Box 500, Mount Joy, PA 17552.

Antiques and the Arts Weekly, c/o *The Newtown Bee,* Newtown, CT 06470.

Antiques & Collectible News, PO Box 171713, Arlington, TX 76003.

Antiques & Collectibles, PO Box 268, Greenvale, NY 11548.

Antiques Dealer, The, PO Box 2147, Clifton, NJ 07015.

Antiques Journal, PO Box 1046, Dubuque, IA 52001.

Art & Antiques, 89 Fifth Avenue, New York, NY 10003.

Art & Auction, 250 W. 57th Street, New York, NY 10019.

Beckett's Baseball Card Monthly, 3410 Midcourt Road, Suite 100, Carrollton, TX 75006.

Buckeye Marketeer, The, 2256½ E. Main Street, Columbus, OH 43209.

Carnival Glass News & Views, PO Box 5421, Kansas City, MO 64131.

Carolina Antique News, PO Box 241114, Charlotte, NC 28224.

Clarion, The, 49 W. 53rd Street, New York, NY 10019.

Coin Age, 16001 Ventura Boulevard, Encino, CA 91316.

Coin World, PO Box 150, Sydney, OH 45367.

Collector, 467 North Main Street, Pomona, CA 91768.

Collectors Journal, PO Box 601, Vinton, IA 52349-0601.

Collector's Showcase, PO Box 27948, San Diego, CA 92128.

Comics Buyer's Guide, The, 700 E. State Street, Iola, WI 54990.

Country Living Magazine, 224 W. 57th Street, New York, NY 10019.

Daze, The, PO Box 57, Otisville, MI 48463 (Depression glass).

Doll Reader, c/o Hobby House Press, Inc., 900 Frederick Street, Cumberland, MD 21502.

Dolls—The Collector Magazine, c/o Collector Communications, 170 Fifth Avenue, New York, NY 10010.

Glass Collector, The, PO Box 27037, Columbus, OH 43227.

Glass Review, PO Box 542, Marietta, OH 45750.

Goldmine, 700 E. State Street, Iola, WI 54990 (records).

Heisey Glass Newscaster, PO Box 102, Plymouth, OH 44865.

Heisey News, PO Box 27, Newark, OH 43055.

Hemmings Motor News, PO Box 380, Route 9W, Bennington, VT 05201.

Jersey Devil, The, PO Box 202, Lambertville, NJ 08530.

Jukebox Trader, PO Box 1081, Des Moines, IA 50311.

Knife World, PO Box 3395, Knoxville, TN 37927.

Linn's Stamp News, PO Box 29, Sidney, OH 45365.

Loose Change, c/o Mead Publishing Co., 21176 S. Alameda Street, Long Beach, CA 90810 (coin-operated machines).

Maine Antiques Digest, PO Box 645, Waldoboro, ME 04572.

Mass Bay Antiques, PO Box 293, Danvers, MA 01923.

Mid-Atlantic Antiques Magazine, PO Box 908, Henderson, NC 27536.

New England Antiques Journal, 4 Church Street, Ware, MA 01082 (formerly *New England Country Antiques*).

New York Antique Almanac, PO Box 335, Lawrence, NY 11559.

New York—Pennsylvania Collector, The, PO Drawer C, Fishers, NY 14453.

Numismatic News, 700 E. State Street, Iola, WI 54990.

Ohio Antique Review, 72 North Street, Worthington, OH 43085.

Old Bottles Magazine, PO Box 243, Bend, OR 97701.

Old Cars Weekly, 700 E. State Street, Iola, WI 54990.

Orientalia Journal, PO Box 94, Dept. T, Little Neck, NY 11363.

Paden City Partyline, 13325 Danvers Way, Westminster, CA 92683.

Paper & Advertising Collector, PO Box 500, Mount Joy, PA 17552.

Paper Collectors' Marketplace, 700 E. State Street, Iola, WI 54990.

Political Collector, 503 Madison Avenue, York, PA 17404.

Postcard Collector, 700 E. State Street, Iola, WI 54990.

Prints Magazine, PO Box 1468, Alton, IL 62002.

Renninger's Antique Guide, PO Box 495, Lafayette Hill, PA 19444.

Scott's Stamp Monthly, PO Box 828, Sidney, OH 45365.

Shotgun News, PO Box 669, Hastings, NE 68901.

Silver Magazine, PO Box 1243, Whittier, CA 90609.

Smithsonian Magazine, 900 Jefferson Drive, NW, Washington, DC 20560.

Tri-State Trader, 27 N. Jefferson, PO Box 90, Knightstown, IN 46158.

Vintage Collectibles, PO Box 5072, Chattanooga, TN 37406.

West Coast Peddler, PO Box 5134, Whittier, CA 90607.

Yesteryear, PO Box 2, Princeton, WI 54968.

Appendix E: Board of Advisors

In addition to editorial work throughout the book, any section that does not have a listed contributor or advisor was researched and compiled by me and my staff.

As author, I accept full responsibility for every error you discover (I hope a very limited number—we've tried hard). Credit goes to the people I asked to submit data and to the auction houses for their cooperation in gathering data. I asked these people for their assistance because of their proven abilities. Some of the individuals are nationally recognized authorities in their specific area. Many are gifted authors in their own right. Most are successful dealers known to sell large quantities of antiques and collectibles in an honest manner at shops, shows, and markets throughout the United States.

Because this is a national guide, I have particularly sought dealers with extensive show schedules, thus helping to factor out regionalism whenever possible. Those people have selflessly gathered data, taken photographs, and provided chapter material because they love this business and because they believe that the more the public knows, the healthier this antiques business will be for all of us. When you need assistance in their field of expertise, feel free to contact them—that's why we have provided their names, addresses, and telephone numbers.

A. Contributors list by subject order
B. Auction houses alphabetically

A. CONTRIBUTORS

AMERICAN INDIAN ART
Dawn E. Reno
3280 Shingler Terrace
Deltona, FL 32738
(904) 532-5451

ARTS AND CRAFTS MOVEMENT
Bruce E. Johnson
150 Cherokee Road
Asheville, NC 28801
(704) 254-1912

BAROMETERS
Charles E. and Jill Probst
Charles Edwin Antiques
PO Box 1340
Louisa, VA 23093
(703) 967-0416

CANDY CONTAINERS
Camille T. Zagaroli
128 Longshore Avenue
Yardley, PA 19067
(215) 493-8734

CERAMICS
Al and Susan Bagdade
The Country Peasants
3136 Elder Court
Northbrook, IL 60062
(708) 498-1468

CHARACTER COLLECTIBLES
Harry L. Rinker
5093 Vera Cruz Road
Emmaus, PA 18049
(215) 965-1122

CLOCKS
Robert O. Stuart
Box 104, Jo Joy Road
Limington, ME 04049
(207) 793-4522

Jonathan Snellenberg
Christie's
502 Park Avenue
New York, NY 10022
(212) 546-1012

COMIC BOOKS
Robert Overstreet
Overstreet Publications
780 Hunt Cliff Drive, N. W.
Cleveland, TN 37311
(615) 472-4135

DOLLS
Camille T. Zagaroli
128 Longshore Avenue
Yardley, PA 19067
(215) 493-8734

EPHEMERA
Harry L. Rinker
5093 Vera Cruz Road
Emmaus, PA 18049
(215) 965-1122

FURNITURE—AMERICAN
George Daniel
Elizabeth R. Daniel Antiques
2 Gooseneck Road
Chapel Hill, NC 27514
(919) 968-3041

*FURNITURE—AMERICAN—
WICKER*
Lee and Bill Stewart
The Collected Works
1405 Lake Avenue
Wilmette, IL 60091
(708) 251-6897

*FURNITURE—ARTS AND
CRAFTS*
Bruce E. Johnson
150 Cherokee Road
Asheville, NC 28801
(704) 254-1912

FURNITURE—CONTINENTAL
David P. Lindquist
Whitehall at the Villa Antiques
and Fine Art
1213 East Franklin Street
Chapel Hill, NC 27514
(919) 942-3179

GARDEN ACCESSORIES
Maggie Lindquist
Whitehall at the Villa Antiques
and Fine Art
1213 East Franklin Street
Chapel Hill, NC 27514
(919) 942-3179

GLASS
Alda Leake Horner
Whitehall at the Villa Antiques
and Fine Art
1213 East Franklin Street
Chapel Hill, NC 27514
(919) 942-3179

Jean L. Sloan
The Glass House
PO Box 5342
Madison, WI 53705
(608) 233-9493

JEWELRY
Arthur Guy Kaplan
Antique Jewelry—Fine
Collectibles
PO Box 1942
Baltimore, MD 21203
(301) 752-2090

KNIVES
C. Houston Price
Knife World
PO Box 3395
Knoxville, TN 37927
(615) 523-3339

METALWARE
Garland Pass
Fine Antique Metalware
98 Paper Chase Trail
Avon, CT 06001
(203) 673-0787

MOVIES
Richard De Thuin
Crouch International Ltd.
1156 Sixth Avenue
Suite 710
New York, NY 10036
(212) 944-2113

NUTTING, WALLACE
Michael Ivankovich
Michael Ivankovich Antiques
PO Box 2458
Doylestown, PA 18901
(215) 345-6094

ORIENTAL FINE AND DECORATIVE ARTS—JAPANESE PRINTS
Mitzie and Michael Verne
The Mitzie Verne Collection, Inc.
3326 Lansmere Road
Shaker Heights, OH 44122
(216) 397-4551

PAINTINGS—MINIATURE
Lester E. Sender
3482 Lee Road
Shaker Heights, OH 44120
(216) 752-2435

PEANUTS COLLECTIBLES
Freddi Margolin
12 Lawrence Lane
Bay Shore, NY 11706
(516) 666-6861

Andrea Podley
539 Sudden Valley
Bellingham, WA 98226
(206) 733-5209

POLITICAL MEMORABILIA
Richard Friz
RFD 2, Box 155
Peterborough, NH 03458
(603) 563-8155

POSTCARDS
Diane Allmen
PO Box 2648
Elkhart, IN 46514
(219) 262-9681

SILHOUETTES
Alda Leake Horner
Whitehall at the Villa Antiques
and Fine Art
1213 East Franklin Street
Chapel Hill, NC 27514
(919) 942-3179

SILVER
William Pillsbury and Robin
Michel
Pillsbury-Michel and Associates,
Inc.
2620 S. Shepherd #174
Houston, TX 77098
(713) 522-4790

STONEWARE—AMERICAN
George Sullivan
(no address)

TEDDY BEARS
Kim Brewer
Bruins, Inc.
PO Box 152
West Simsbury, CT 06092-0152
(203) 658-2054

Carol-Lynn Rössel Waugh
5 Morrill Street
Winthrop, ME 04364
(207) 377-6769

TEXTILES
Alda Leake Horner
Whitehall at the Villa Antiques
and Fine Art
1213 East Franklin Street
Chapel Hill, NC 27514
(919) 942-3179

TOYS AND TOY TRAINS
Richard Friz
RFD 2, Box 155
Peterborough, NH 03458
(603) 563-8155

VINTAGE CLOTHING
Cynthia Giles
1106 Cain Court
Cedarhill, TX 75104
(214) 291-8628

WATCHES
Cooksey Shugart and Richard E.
Gilbert
Cooksey Shugart Publications
PO Box 3147
Cleveland, TN 37320-3147
(615) 479-4813

WORLD'S FAIR COLLECTIBLES
Richard Friz
RFD 2, Box 155
Peterborough, NH 03458
(603) 563-8155

B. AUCTION HOUSES

The following auction houses cooperated by providing catalogs of their auctions, price lists, and in some instances, photographs. Their effort is greatly appreciated.

Alford Auction Company
4139 Magazine Street
New Orleans, LA 70115

Frank H. Boos Gallery
420 Enterprise Court
Bloomfield Hills, MI 48013

Butterfield and Butterfield
220 San Bruno Avenue
San Francisco, CA 94103

Butterfield and Butterfield
7601 Sunset Boulevard
Los Angeles, CA 90046

Christie's, New York
502 Park Avenue
New York, NY 10022

Christie's East
219 East 67th Street
New York, NY 10021

William Doyle Galleries
175 East 87th Street
New York, NY 10128

Dunning's
755 Church Road
Elgin, IL 60123

Freeman/Fine Arts Co. of Philadelphia, Inc.
1808–1810 Chestnut Street
Philadelphia, PA 19103

Garth's Auctions, Inc.
2690 Stratford Road
PO Box 369
Delaware, OH 43015

Grogan & Company
Fine Art Auctioneers and Appraisers
890 Commonwealth Avenue
Boston, MA 02215

Leslie Hindman, Inc.
215 West Ohio Street
Chicago, IL 60610

Litchfield Auction Gallery
PO Box 1337
Route 202
Litchfield, CT 06759

Oliver's Auction Gallery
Route 1, Plaza 1
PO Box 337
Kennebunk, ME 04043

Rafael Osona
PO Box 2607
Nantucket, MA 02584

Pettigrew Auction Gallery
1645 S. Tejon Street
Colorado Springs, CO 80906

Skinner, Inc.
Auctioneers and Appraisers of Antiques and Fine Art
Bolton Gallery
357 Main Street
Bolton, MA 01740

C. G. Sloan & Company, Inc.
4920 Wyaconda Road
North Bethesda, MD 20852

Sotheby's
1334 York Avenue
New York, NY 10021

Weschler's
909 E. Street, NW
Washington, DC 20004

Wolf's Fine Arts Auctioneers
1239 West 6th Street
Cleveland, OH 44113

Woody Auction Co.
PO Box 618
Douglass, KS 67039

Index

ABOUT THE AUTHOR

David Lindquist is a nationally recognized antiques dealer, educator, lecturer, appraiser, and author. He is a member of the National Association of Dealers in Antiques, Inc., and served as its president from 1983 to 1985. He is a senior member of the American Society of Appraisers and associate member of the International Society of Appraisers.

Mr. Lindquist travels and lectures extensively, participates in the major antiques shows in America, and has also written numerous articles; among the most notable are those that have appeared in *The Bulletin*, the publication of the National Association of Dealers in Antiques, Inc. "Lindquist on Antiques," a monthly column, is featured in many antiques newspapers across the country.

The author lives in Chapel Hill, North Carolina. He owns and operates Whitehall at the Villa Antiques and Fine Art.